Lecture Notes in Computer Science 693

Edited by G. Goos and J. Hartmanis

Advisory Board: W. Brauer   D. Gries   J. Stoer

Peter E. Lauer (Ed.)

Functional Programming, Concurrency, Simulation and Automated Reasoning

International Lecture Series 1991-1992
McMaster University, Hamilton, Ontario, Canada

Springer-Verlag
Berlin Heidelberg NewYork
London Paris Tokyo
Hong Kong Barcelona
Budapest

Series Editors

Gerhard Goos
Universität Karlsruhe
Postfach 69 80
Vincenz-Priessnitz-Straße 1
D-76131 Karlsruhe, FRG

Juris Hartmanis
Cornell University
Department of Computer Science
4130 Upson Hall
Ithaca, NY 14853, USA

Volume Editor

Peter E. Lauer
Department of Computer Science and Systems, McMaster University
1280 Main Street West, Hamilton, Ontario L8S 4K1, Canada

CR Subject Classification (1991): D.1-3, F.3

ISBN 3-540-56883-2 Springer-Verlag Berlin Heidelberg New York
ISBN 0-387-56883-2 Springer-Verlag New York Berlin Heidelberg

© Springer-Verlag Berlin Heidelberg 1993
Printed in Germany

Typesetting: Camera ready by author
Printing and binding: Druckhaus Beltz, Hemsbach/Bergstr.
45/3140-543210 - Printed on acid-free paper

Preface

This collection of papers arose from a series of lectures, given in the Department of Computer Science and Systems, McMaster University, Hamilton, Ontario, Canada, during 1991-92, at the invitation of Peter Lauer. The series was co-ordinated by Peter Lauer, Jeffery Zucker and Ryszard Janicki. The lectures were intended to familiarize workers in Computer Science and other disciplines with some of the most exciting advanced computer based systems for the conceptualization, design, implementation, simulation, and logical analysis of applications in these disciplines. The papers are mostly the work of individuals who were among the originators of the systems presented.

We hope that this volume will make it easier for colleagues at other universities and research establishments to evaluate the utility of these systems for their application areas. We also hope that this volume will be of paramount utility to graduate students in the various disciplines.

The collection of papers presents some strong motivational points for the use of theory based systems in the areas of functional programming, concurrency, simulation, and automated reasoning, highlighting some of their advantages and disadvantages relative to conventional systems.

At the editors invitation, the authors kindly agreed to furnish newly written papers on theory based systems which provide a guide into some of the major operational systems and which might form a useful basis for assessing knowledge and skills required for their informed use.

The four topic areas were selected for various related reasons.

Functional programming rather than procedural programming was chosen because it provides a good level of abstraction from the standpoints of the user, the tractability of full formalization of semantics, and providing good practical implementations, allowing for computer supported experimentation with concepts expressed in this basically declarative style.

Concurrency rather than sequentiality was chosen as basic because we feel that this is closer to real-world systems and human thought processes, and avoids the artificial introduction of sequentiality constraints due to one's sequential model and not due to the nature of the system modelled.

Simulation is used here as a synonym for modelling or prototyping and was chosen since it is a means to enhance understanding of complex situations and dynamically changing systems, and a basis for experimental study of such systems. Furthermore, simulation may be used to validate whether a computer implementation of some real-world situation is adequate for the purpose for which it was designed.

Automated reasoning, which we take to include not only fully automated theorem provers but especially interactive definition debuggers and proof checkers, was chosen because it relieves the user from tedious, time consuming and error prone activities involved in checking whether chains of inferences and logical conclusions about the system are justified. We feel that a similar advantage to that obtained by the presence of syntax checking in compilers, for developing error free programs, can be obtained by the presence of proof checkers for developing error free system models, and ultimately trustworthy computer systems implementing them.

The issue is how to make existing theory based systems more accessible to users of various kinds and at different levels.

Theory based systems have the advantages of precision, trustworthiness, and generality. They can be used effectively to enhance learning. However, they have the disadvantage of relative inefficiency in operation, and a greater learning gap to be closed by the user.

Conventional systems have the advantages of efficiency and a reputedly smaller learning gap, and they can also be used effectively to enhance learning, are more familiar to users, and have extensive application development.

However, familiarity with conventional computer systems may not be as much of an advantage as might appear at first sight. There is a more basic kind of familiarity which users have with theory based systems which is often overlooked and which, if exploited, has a much greater payoff than the exploitation of familiarity with conventional computer concepts. For example, familiarity with high school algebra, which can be relatively safely presupposed in all adults who have graduated from high school, makes for an easy road to computer systems based on the algebraic approach and its concomitant equational style of reasoning. The simple realisation that the objects of the algebra need not just be numbers, but can essentially come from any inductive domain, allows users to transfer the same algebraic understanding from the domain of numbers to domains such as programs, data, machines, and even systems as a whole. The same style of equational reasoning remains valid throughout. This permits frequent transfer of knowledge from one domain to another by a mathematical equivalent of analogical thinking.

Furthermore, conventional computer oriented concepts are rather far removed from human ways of thinking about real world systems, except in the case of the object oriented paradigm, whereas the algebraic approach has many aspects in common with the object oriented approach and hence can make similar claims to real world closeness. On the whole, theory based systems could be considered closer to real world situations, since they are descriptive and try to introduce the least amount of model specific formalism possible, whereas conventional systems force upon the user all the details of computer oriented models, including particularly the need to express concepts algorithmically and usually sequentially.

So it seems far from obvious that conventional systems are closer to real world situations, and hence to the non-computer specialist user, than theory based systems.

Even if the gaps for both were the same, there would still be the greater payoff from investing time in learning to understand and use theory based systems, since one obtains ability for very general knowledge transfer from domain to domain. One only needs to compare the general applicability of the results of one year's study of C++, which is the least amount of time required to become proficient in that complex language, with the general applicability of the results of one year's study of general algebraic topics.

Mind-set for this Series of Lectures and Papers.

At the outset of the lecture series, I formulated some general thoughts about the current intellectual environment of advanced system theory as it relates to computer science. Authors of papers were aware of this mind-set and have taken it into account in orienting their papers for inclusion in this volume. Since this original mind-set may be of interest to the general readership it is included here.

1. **Convergence of theoretical computer science and mathematics.** Formal and theoretical systems developed in computer science and mathematics are increasingly converging, as are the interests of researchers in both areas. This is witnessed by the regular occurrence of such conferences as the Annual IEEE Symposium on Logic in Computer Science, the International Workshops on Mathematical Foundations of Programming Semantics, and the special section on Logic, Mathematics and Computer Science of the International Congress of Logic, Methodology and Philosophy of Science. In addition four new journals have appeared in the past year, *Mathematical Structures in Computer Science* (Cambridge University Press), the *Journal of Logic and Computing* (Oxford University Press), the *International Journal of Foundations of Computer Science* (IOS Press), and *Category Theory for Computer Science* (Prentice Hall).

2. **Theory based environments are transforming system development.** Practical computer based realizations of such theory based systems are rapidly appearing, and promise radically to transform the entire process of software development, from conceptualization to implementation, permitting rigorous formulation and verification of most aspects of the process (see the paper by Peter Lauer in this volume).

3. **Environments must be efficient and semantically sound.** A practical environment for the rigorous development of software must be based on an efficiently executable programming notation which enjoys as clear and sound a semantics as the more abstract, and usually more mathematical and often non-executable notations used to express requirements, specifications, designs, etc.

4. **Functional languages best achieve efficiency and semantic clarity.** To date, functional programming languages (see the papers by David MacQueen on SML, and by R. Frost and S. Karamatos, in this volume) are the most successful in achieving efficiency comparable to the most efficient procedural languages such as C, while at the same time permitting the formulation of a clear mathematical semantics, which sometimes, for example, in the case of OBJ3 (see the paper by Tim Winkler in this volume), coincides with the actual operational (run time) semantics of the language, which is based on the notion of rewriting (see the paper by Nachum Dershowitz, in this volume).

5. **Domains of interest conceived analogously in mathematics and computing.** Mathematicians and logicians tend to characterize domains of interest by giving a structure consisting of some domains, and a number of operations or functions, and possibly relations, on these domains. The meanings of the functions and relations are then stated axiomatically, for instance as equations or inequalities.

   Increasingly, computer scientists tend to characterize executable representations by defining concrete or abstract data types, which essentially correspond to the mathematician's notion of (algebraic) structure, except that the meanings of the functions and relations are defined operationally in terms of language primitives which directly translate to executable machine code.

   This similarity of characterization of domains of interest inspired the proponents of the algebraic specification methods to work towards a new style of software development which would be pervaded by sound mathematical principles and supported by powerful mathematical tools (see the papers by Tim Winkler on

OBJ3, and by Stephen Garland, John Guttag and James Horning on LARCH in this volume).

6. **Type theory fits the general needs of domain independent systems.** Adequate support for reasoning about arbitrary formal systems (including executable notation) requires more than the ability to express domain specific information. It requires powerful logical systems in which to formulate, develop, analyze and compare different domain specific formalisms. Modern type theory has proved to be extremely fruitful when applied for this purpose. In fact, solutions of problems in computer science using type theoretical notions have greatly stimulated research into the lambda calculus and type theory by mathematicians and logicians, and have even contributed new developments in these areas. (See the papers by Douglas Howe on Nuprl, by K. van Hee, P. Rambags and P. Verkoulen on ExSpect, and by Sentot Kromodimoeljo, Bill Pase, Mark Saaltink, Dan Craigen and Irwin Meisels on EVES, in this volume.)

7. **Other disciplines have need of advanced theory based systems.** There exist a number of very interesting prototypical computer based systems which support rigorous and systematic development of executable software from specifications (e.g., OBJ3, LARCH, ExSpect, EVES, and IDEF/CPN, which are all presented in papers in this volume). Graduate students in computer science and other disciplines such as engineering, business, linguistics, philosophy, etc., need to gain experience with such systems so that they can usefully employ them in the process of producing dependable (verified) application oriented software. But this presupposes, especially in the case of non-mathematicians, that much of the theoretical underpinning of the system is hidden from the user, and that the remaining theory is taught in an appropriate manner and at the right time.

8. **SML is widely used to implement such advanced systems.** Standard ML and its extensions are proving to be the functional programming languages of preference for implementing many of the most advanced systems of the kind we have been discussing (see the papers by David MacQueen and John Ophel on SML, in this volume). This is in part due to the fact that they can be made to produce quite efficient code, while at the same time having a very well defined mathematical semantics. In fact, most of the systems covered during the series of talks are implemented in SML or in LISP, or use SML as part of their programming interface.

9. **Concurrency gives efficiency and conciseness.** Concurrency is of importance for efficiency reasons, but also due to the fact that decomposition into relatively independent concurrent subsystems often leads to much shorter code and increased clarity. Standard ML has been extended to support concurrency in a number of ways, which ensure that the advantages of functional programming are preserved (see the paper on Concurrent ML by John Reppy, and the general paper by David MacQueen on SML in this volume). On the other hand, concurrency introduces additional complexity into the problem of correctly conceptualizing the possible behaviours of the system and proving the correctness of the algorithms involved. To manage this complexity, the need for rigour and formality in proving properties of the system is even greater than in the case of sequential and centralized systems. Systems such as the Concurrency Workbench (see the paper by Rance Cleaveland, and the preparatory papers by Jeffery

Zucker in this volume), the IDEF/CPN system from Metasoft Corporation (see the paper by Jawahar Malhotra and Robert Shapiro, as well as the paper by Robert Shapiro, Valerio Pinci and Roberto Mameli in this volume), give much support to this endeavor. The effective implementation of concurrent systems is also difficult, as is the effective exploitation of parallel architectures by programmers. Mathematically well founded mechanical schemes for synthesising concurrent programs from programs that do not specify concurrency or communication also promise to reduce the complexity inherent in developing concurrent systems (see the paper by Michael Barnett and Christian Lengauer in this volume).

10. **Graphical representation of knowledge is important.** Graphical representation of knowledge is increasingly recognized as an important technique for visualizing complex relationships. Thus, in mathematics, category theory generalizes the conventional arrow representation of functional relationships, to obtain powerful and general ways of conceptualizing complex (functional) domains, and replacing specific combinatorial arguments by graph manipulation (arrow chasing).

11. **Level of performance of students rises when courses stress theory based approach and use of theory based systems.** Limited experiments with students indicates that use of rigorous specification techniques, particularly following the algebraic approach, enhances the student's ability for independent, verified , and complete program development, and allows for the ready transferral of knowledge from high school elementary algebra to the business of specifying and designing sofware. Using the algebraic approach also reinforces their knowledge of the algebraic techniques they learned in high school.

    This seems to indicate that this approach may well be the best for requirement specification, because it is to be assumed that any potential customer requesting a software system will have completed high school algebra.

    Theory based systems which are based on logic require more training and sophistication than can be expected from high school graduates. But as more programming takes place in languages like Prolog even at the high school level, this may change soon.

12. **Theory based systems should be human and problem oriented.**

    (a) In computer science, graphical representations have extended application in software engineering environments and particularly in the representation of concurrent systems. The IDEF/CPN system from MetaSoftware Corporation (see the paper by Robert Shapiro, Valerio Pinci and Roberto Mameli in this volume), is one of the most developed, integrated , and theoretically sound systems elegantly supporting graphical interaction.

    In IDEF/CPN it is possible to input an (inscribed) graph from which the system automatically generates a correct program. The ExSpect system is a similar system which at present has more system analysis support than IDEF/CPN (see the paper by K.van Hee, P. Rambags and P. Verkoulen in this volume).

    (b) In Nuprl (see the paper by Douglas Howe in this volume) it is possible to input a proof (a reasoned logical specification) from which the system automatically extracts a correct program.

    (c) Pattern matching is a natural human activity and the use of pattern matching in explaining the application of functions to their arguments in SML, OBJ, and W/AGE enhances readability greatly (see the papers by David MacQueen and John Ophel on SML, by Tim Winkler on OBJ3, and by R. Frost and S. Karamatos on W/AGE, in this volume).

(d) The dictum that system code be as high-level as possible and the same throughout, which is one of the aspects of parametric programming as introduced by J. Goguen, leads to ease of comprehension of the whole system in the case of all of the systems described in this volume.

Intended readers of this volume

This volume is meant as a modest contribution to narrowing the learning gap facing conventional computer users when they wish to use advanced theory based systems. The papers in this volume are meant for a wide audience and should not require great mathematical sophistication for their comprehension, in fact a high school knowledge of algebra, and perhaps a little set theory and formal logic should suffice. The papers contain numerous references for those wishing to pursue any of these topics to greater depth. These references may require more mathematical accumen from the reader, but the appropriate utilization of the available computer implementations of the mathematical theories, during the learning stages, should enhance the process of self-instruction required to acquire the necessary mathematical knowledge and skills for an informed use of these systems.

The collection of papers could also be used in advanced courses by students and researchers as an introduction and guide to advanced theory based systems, all of which are operational at McMaster and are readily available to other educational and research institutions.

Acknowledgements

Financial support for the series was given by the Department of Computer Science and Systems at McMaster University, supplemented with some support from Dr. H. A. Elmaraghy at the Flexible Manufacturing Research and Development Centre and the Department of Mechanical Engineering at McMaster, and Dr. W. Elmaraghy at the Design Automation and Manufacturing Research Laboratory and the Faculty of Engineering at the University of Western Ontario.

It is due to Ryszard Janicki's prompting that Peter Lauer undertook to produce this volume of papers which gives these lectures a more permanent form of use to a much wider audience.

Thanks are due to Alfred Hofmann and Hans Wössner, both of Springer-Verlag, for their continuing support and excellent advice during the production of this volume.

Last, but most important, we would like to thank the authors of the papers for taking the time in their busy schedules to produce such excellent papers in such a short time.

March 1993

Peter E. Lauer (Editor)
McMaster University

Contents

On the use of Theory Based Systems to Traverse Educational Gaps in Computer System Related Activities.

Peter E. Lauer

Department of Computer Science and Systems
McMaster University
Hamilton, Ontario L8S 4K1
CANADA

Abstract. Within the general setting of engineering trustworthy computer implementations of real-world systems, the paper delineates some of the gaps between theory and practice, and between system developers and users at various levels, and suggests how existing theory based systems could be used to help bridge these gaps more effectively than is the case at present.

Focus is on the gaps between conventional computer systems and theory based systems, and the gaps between knowledge and skill required for various levels of usage of the two types of system. Furthermore, identification of opportunities and tools supporting the transformation of systems and knowledge required to use them from the conventional to the theory based side will be of paramount interest.

Conventional Systems are considered to be based on *doctrine*, a *rigorous* body of knowledge and methods, for implementing real-world systems by computer systems.

Theory Based Systems are considered to be entirely based on *theory*, a *formal* body of knowledge and methodologies (calculi), for implementing real-world systems by trustworthy computer systems. Trustworthiness requires that all computer system components are theory based and have been verified relative the theory.

The distinction between method and methodology is made to indicate that a *method* is a collection of rules for achieving some goal, whereas a *methodology* is a systematized collection of formal rules for achieving some goal supported by sound theory.

Hence, to summarize, the paper is concerned with the controlled and systematic evolution from doctrine based system development to theory based system development, and the evolution of users from a doctrinal view of systems to a theory based view of systems. It tries to identify some concepts and computer based tools from both types of system which promote such evolution.

1 Introduction

The aim of this paper is not to add to the existing controversy about some of the issues discussed but to suggest a systematic approach to clarifying the issues, and to encourage others with similar concerns to help resolve some of the issues in the future.

The main intent of the paper is to initiate an attempt to systematically close existing "gaps" between theory and practice which have hampered the mutual appreciation of and benefiting from important contributions in these separate areas by theoreticians and practitioners. We want to provide "hooks" in some organized scheme from which theoreticians and practitioners can "attach" the points they want to make and which will make it possible to systematically analyze and resolve recognized problems. We feel that systems which include the right components to permit orderly and well-reasoned evolution of systems as well as similar evolution of knowledge about the system and evolution of users from one degree of usage to the next, can only be achieved through careful incorporation of the ideas and experience of the many researchers in the area of computer related activities, and over an extended period of time. What is required are systems which allow various groups of researchers to collaborate to formulate, study and experiment with new ideas and tools, and to co-operatively control the evolution of the systems towards the envisaged goals. This should be possible by extending existing systems rather than constructing new systems from scratch whenever possible, and it should be possible to "upgrade" existing conventional systems by providing entry points in the evolutionary process for arbirary existing (conventional or theory based) software components from which they could evolve by the same means as components generated within the evolutionary system to start with. In other words, our evolutionary systems should not be closed worlds, but allow for introduction and upgrading of independently existing components into the evolutionary systems.

In the general area of computer system develoment there is a perceivable gap between developers of conventional systems (so called "real programmers") and developers of theory based systems (so called "programmers of toys"). The former group insists that too much stress on theory and trustworthiness of resulting systems, and the fact that formalization is always in the wake of real practice and tends to make simplifying assumptions for the sake of theoretical tractability rendering the resulting theory unrealistic, make most of the formal theory based approaches to system development irrelevant to real practice.

This general gap is very reminiscent of the gap traditionally existing between conventional mathematicians and foundational workers in mathematics who are engaged in formally axiomatizing the basis of mathematical knowledge and reasoning. The conventional mathematician is also convinced that real new mathematical discoveries are based on informal but rigorous mathematical methods, indeed they might claim that even new results in foundational studies are based on informal but rigorous reasoning carried out in the meta-theory which is itself not formalized. Hence it is often stated that foundational studies are of a more philosophical nature and largely irrelevant to the progress of real mathematics. It is probably true that most mathematicians would be very formal in their definition and use of syntax (formulas) but conventional mathematicians would be less concerned to formalize their definitions of semantics and methodology.

Admittedly, both conventional mathematicians and computer system developers are correct in recognizing that practice will always precede theoretical comprehension, but trustworthy practice requires that it be based on theory as far as practical and methodologically fruitful, and practice can only make significant new advances when its theoretical basis, such as it is, makes significant advances as well.

There is a similar gap between conventional mathematicians and proponents of constructive mathematics and logic. Again the conventional mathematician feels that the constraint of constructiveness is too confining for many of the traditional areas of mathematics and most of the new areas emerging in ever greater proliferation.

Although one might accept this as a valid position for a mathematician to take one can still insist that constructive mathematics is eminently important and relevant for the development of computer systems, since feasible implementation of mathematical and logical concepts presupposes at least constructiveness, but additionally requires that they be implementable within reasonable time and space requirements.

Trustworthy engineering practices are certainly based on sound theoretical foundations but effective engineering practices must go beyond areas which are completely understood theoretically.

Unfortunately, conventional engineering is concerned with engineering non-linguistic physical structures for which required bodies of knowledge, or theories, have been developed and are used with great success. Computer system engineering is largely concerned with engineering linguistic structures and algorithms, both of which are non-physical, and for which less theory is established, and the theory which has been developed is little known to engineers developing conventional computer systems by conventional means.

Experienced conventional computer system engineers do have an accepted body of loosely related theory as can be seen from looking at the table of contents of recent books on Foundations of Computer Science [1], or Handbooks of Theoretical Computer Science [2].

The theoretical components most valued by conventional computer system engineers are those concerned with the syntactic aspects of linguistic structures. Hence, formal language theory and automata theory are valued for their support in the construction of parsers and type checkers for programming languages, development of pattern matching features of operating system shell languages, report generators (e.g. grep, egrep, Awk, Perl in UNIX), and editor generators.

The theoretical components most undervalued by conventional computer system engineers are those concerned with semantic aspects of liguistic structures. Hence, formal semantical theories and models are little known, appreciated and used.

On the pragmatic side conventional computer system engineers are also less appreciative of areas such as analysis of algorithms, and complexity and feasibility theories. They still keep writing reasonably efficient programs for problems which are considered infeasible in a complexity theoretic sense, but which will work well enough in most practical cases.

Theory based systems have the advantage of precision, trustworthiness and generality (e.g. can be used to transfer knowledge of semantic aspects of one programming language to another more easily). They can be used effectively to enhance learning (e.g. to close the gap between usage of conventional and usage of theory based systems). They have the disadvantages of relative inefficiency in operation, and a greater learning gap to be closed by the user.

Conventional systems have the advantage of efficiency, reputedly smaller learning gap, can also be used effectively to enhance learning, are more familiar to users, and have extensive application development.

However, familiarity with conventional computer systems may not be as much of an advantage as might appear at first sight. There is a more basic kind of familiarity which users have with theory based systems which is often overlooked and which if exploited has a much greater payoff than the expoitation of familiarity with conventional computer concepts. For example, familiarity with high school algebra, which can be relatively safely presupposed in all adults who have graduated from high school, makes for an easy road to computer systems based on the algebraic approach and its concomitant equational style of reasoning. The simple realisation that the objects of the algebra need not just be numbers, but can essentially come from any inductive domain, allows users to transfer the same algebraic understanding from the domain of numbers to domains such as programs, data, machines, and even systems as a whole. The same style of equational reasoning remains valid throughout. This permits frequent transfer of knowledge from one domain to another by a mathematical equivalent of analogical or lateral thinking.

Furthermore, conventional computer oriented concepts are rather far removed from human ways of thinking about real world systems, except in the case of the object oriented paradigm, whereas the algebraic approach has many aspects in common with the object oriented approach and hence can make similar claims to real world closeness. On the whole, theory based systems could be considered closer to real world situations, since they are descriptive and try to introduce the least amount of model specific formalism as possible, whereas conventional systems force upon the user all the details of computer oriented models, including particularly the need to express concepts algorithmically and usually sequentially. We feel the ability to model concurrency will result in specifications and systems which are closer to real-world systems and human thought processes, and avoids the artificial introduction of sequentiality due to the sequential nature of one's model, and not due to the nature of the system modelled.

So it seems far from obvious whether theory based systems or conventional systems are closer to real world situations and hence to the non-computer specialist user.

Even if the gaps for both were the same there would still be the greater payoff from investing time in learning to understand and use theory based systems since one obtains ability for very general knowledge transfer from domain to domain. One only needs to compare the general applicability of the results of one year of study of C++, which is the least amount of time required to become proficient in that complex language, with the general applicability of the results of one year study of general algebraic topics.

2   Context for Engineering Trustworthy Computer Implementations of Real-world Systems

The general context for the development of computer systems consists of three major components, first, the real-world system or situation (RWS) to be implemented, which is expressed by requirements (Req); second, the specification (Spec) of an appropriate abstraction of the real-world system which will be used to develop the computer model and relative to which the model will be verified; and third, the computer system (CS) itself. In Figure 1 these three components can be found at the three corners of the triangular arrangement.

There are three gaps located between these three components: the *Specification-Validation Gap* between RWS and Spec, the *Implementation-Verification Gap* between Spec and CS, and the *Validation-Realization Gap* between CS and RWS (see Figure 1).

However, requirements, specifications and computer systems constitute a spectrum from the conventional to the theory based, hence we get two new types of gap, a *Formalization Gap* between Conventional Requirements (CReq) and Theory-based Requirements (TBReq), and another *Formalization Gap* between Conventional Specifications (CSpec)and Theory-based Specifications (TBSpec), and a *System Gap* between Conventional Computer Systems (CCS) and Theory-based Computer Systems (TBCS).

The distinction between requirements and specifications is made because in software engineering parlance requirement analysis and specification are two different but interrelated activities which have a different focus and orientation. Requirement analysis is human oriented and is concerned with the economic, organizational and societal context of the real-world system to be (partially) "computerized", and its proper performance requires domain specific knowledge and analysis techniques. This area has given rise to so-called Information Systems and is concerned to maximize the ultimate *relevance* and *utility* of the proposed computer system.

In the specification stage it is assumed that the requirements are given and that the task is to apply sound engineering practice, technical (more or less computation and computer oriented) but application domain independent knowhow, to characterize precisely what is ultimately to be correctly realized in a computer system.

Recently, it has been suggested that IS development could not only benefit from some of the application domain independent concepts and techniques developed in software engineering, but that introducing more formality into the process would have additional beneficial effects [3]. Except for the broader and domain specific orientation of IS based requirement descriptions it is not clear what would differentiate formal requirement descriptions from formal specifications, but we will have to omit further comparison in this paper and concentrate on the specification and system gaps.

Conventional Computer Systems are considered to be based on *doctrine*, a *rigorous* body of knowledge and methods, for implementing real-world systems by computer systems.

Theory Based Computer Systems are considered to be entirely based on *theory*, a *formal* body of knowledge and methodologies (calculi), for implementing real-world systems by trustworthy computer systems. Trustworthiness requires that all computer system components are theory based and have been verified relative the theory.

The distinction between method and methodology is made to indicate that a *method* is a collection of rules for achieving some goal, whereas a *methodology* is a systematized collection of rules for achieving some goal supported by sound theory.

We will be concerned with the evolution from doctrine based system development to theory based system development and the evolution of users from a doctrinal view of systems to a theory based view of systems, and try to identify some concepts and

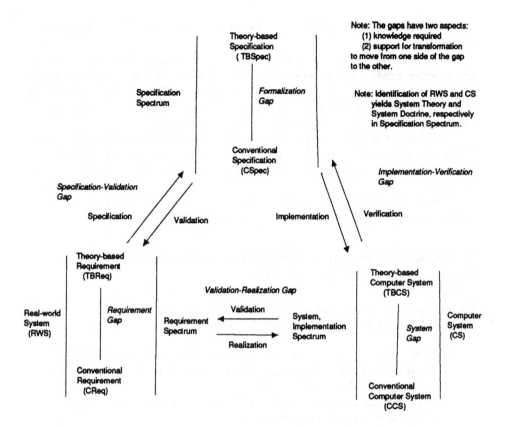

Figure 1: Context for Engineering Trustworthy Computer Implementations of Real-world Systems.

computer based tools from both types of system which promote such evolution (see Figure 2).

Focus on users gives rise to a final type of gap which we will call *Educational Gaps*, one of which exists between users of TBCSs and users of CCSs, and others which exist between average High-school Graduates and users of the two kinds mentioned above. It may sometimes also be advantageous to focus on the type of gap existing between knowledge required by developers and users of systems.

Note that the identification of RWS with CS would identify the two lower corners of the triangular arrangement in Figure 1. This specializes our contextual characterization to the area of computer science proper, which will be the main concern in the rest of the paper.

Finally, there is a gap between currently used systems and trustworthy systems about which we will also make a few remarks in what follows.

3 Requirement, Specification and Implementation Gaps between RWS, CSpec and CCS

We may set the scene by quoting from an abstract for a lecture on "Formal Specification of Information Systems" by Paul A. Swatman:

> " The specification problem may be approached from two perspectives:
> - ensuring that the specification reflects a system which meets the real needs of the users in an appropriate way;
> - ensuring that the specification is sufficiently precise to form the basis for design and construction of the system.
>
> During the last few years, the information systems community has concentrated on attacking the problem from the first of these perspectives. The most successful insights have led to increased user participation (and, indeed, user led development) and to a holistic approach to information analysis which recognizes the existence of multiple, often conflicting, perceptions of the problem context.
>
> Over roughly the same period, the software engineering community has attacked the specification problem from the other perspective, and has developed means of specifying functional requirements precisely."

During the lecture Swatman introduced both these bodies of work and discussed so-called Soft System Methodology and the specification language Object-Z [3]. He went on to suggest how the two approaches could, in principle, be combined through the medium of object oriented modelling.

So, in a sense, Swatman is concerned with obtaining a more realistic approach to obtaining formal specifications by ensuring that the starting point reflects the real-world needs and expectations of prospective users of the computer system to be realized. So he stresses the need for system developers to operate with realistic information about the real-world situation which can only be ascertained in close collaboration with domain specific experts. This is very reminiscent of our concern that formal specifications of computer systems should ultimately be directly based on

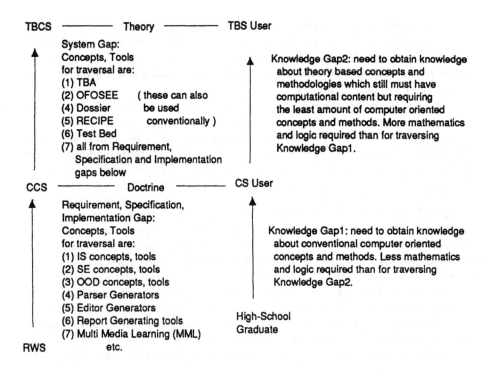

```
TBCS ———————— Theory ———————— TBS User
        System Gap:
      ↑ Concepts, Tools
      │ for traversal are:              ↑ Knowledge Gap2: need to obtain knowledge
      │ (1) TBA                         │   about theory based concepts and
      │ (2) OFOSEE      ( these can also │   methodologies which still must have
      │ (4) Dossier       be used       │   computational content but requiring
      │ (5) RECIPE        conventionally)│   the least amount of computer oriented
      │ (6) Test Bed                    │   concepts and methods. More mathematics
      │ (7) all from Requirement,       │   and logic required than for traversing
      │     Specification and Implementation│ Knowledge Gap1.
      │     gaps below
CCS ———————— Doctrine ———————— CS User
      ↑ Requirement, Specification,
      │ Implementation Gap:
      │ Concepts, Tools                 ↑ Knowledge Gap1: need to obtain knowledge
      │ for traversal are:              │   about conventional computer oriented
      │ (1) IS concepts, tools          │   concepts and methods. Less mathematics
      │ (2) SE concepts, tools          │   and logic required than for traversing
      │ (3) OOD concepts, tools         │   Knowledge Gap2.
      │ (4) Parser Generators           │
      │ (5) Editor Generators
      │ (6) Report Generating tools     High-School
      │ (7) Multi Media Learning (MML)  Graduate
RWS         etc.
```

Multi Media Learning (MML): allows effective learning in general and learning of
    mathematics, logic and computer science in particular.

Theory Based Abstraction (TBA) and On the Fly Operational Semantics based on
    Environment Enquiry (OFOSEE) are system ingredients which allow transformation
    of knowledge and systems from Doctrine to Theory based.

Dossier is a feature allowing integration of heterogeneous doctrines, theories and systems,
    and also allow control of evolution from conventional to theory based systems, as well
    as reflecting evolving knowledge which is user generated throughout the lifetime of
    the system. RECIPE is a collection of concepts and principles characterizing systems
    capable of such well-reasoned and controlled evolution.

Test Bed is a systematic combination of system ingredients allowing the transformation of
    paper and pencil use of theory into computer-based use of theory, and supporting the
    embedding of theory in the computer system such that more trustworthy systems result.

Figure 2: Knowledge-, Specification- or Implementation-, and System Gaps together with
    concepts, methods, methodologies and tools for traversing these gaps.

the information a computer system keeps about itself, a point we will discuss further in the context of on the fly operational semantics of systems based on environment enquiry (OFOSEE). It seems to us that such a basis is essential if we are ever to attain trustworthy systems with concomitant relevant and perpetually up-to-date formal and informal descriptions.

From Swatman's lecture it became evident that his efforts in the IS community are very similar to our efforts in the software engineering community, namely, to increase appreciation of the many excellent contributions of theoretical workers in the field of computer science, which now deserve more practical embodiments so as to attain a more systematic and enlightened process of system development, which promises to result from these more scientific foundations. Perhaps we place more importance on the use of theory based tools than Swatman, but this may be due to his Soft System orientation, which needs to work with inconsistent information which would be hard to accomodate in a fully formalized system. But as can be seen from the paper on LARCH [4] in this volume, there are other ways of allowing contradictions and incompletenesses in specifications which sacrifice less formality than seems to be the necessary in Swatman's view. Thus he stresses formal specification but informal development. On the other hand, he reports that he has had similar impressive results in closing educational gaps and furthering student learning and self reliance by using formal specifications even in second and third year undergraduate classes. We both feel that similar benefits can be found by using more formality of the right kind in commercial contexts. Successes in the use of formal specification techniques in industry, e.g. in the case of VDM and Z, seem to be acknowledged in Europe.

Concerning concepts and methods for closing the gap between real-world systems and conventional specifications, we will not go into a detailed discussion, since the topic of this volume is theory based concepts, systems and tools. We will only enumerate some activities and tools that promise to be of some value even in theory based approaches.

First of all, I feel that increased use of multi-media technology in all areas and stages of the conceptualization and development process will greatly enhance the perpetually needed learning processes required of system developers and users. For example, in the case of requirement analysis, in addition to documentation and data about the real-world system one might make video films about the system, organization, etc. specifically to obtain an additional starting point for the specification process as compared to the more conventional data.

In general, it should be possible to access (on-line) lectures and courses by experts in any area just as we access books in a library now, whenever we have need to learn more in order to obtain the knowledge necessary to close any knowledge gap that denies us the comprehension required for progressing to the next stage in system development or use. Furthermore, if we for the moment assume that all books, journals, reports are on-line, then it should be possible to consult and quote this material immediately when needed without requiring one to physically go to a library to obtain the material. Due to conferencing capabilities and electronic mail it is of course also possible to consult with expert individuals as a last resort. These kind of capabilities can be integrated in self-descriptive systems of the kind characterized by the RECIPE [17] approach using some of the ideas involved in the Dossier [16] facility, both of which will be discussed later.

To illustrate how multi media learning together with parser generating systems such as the Cornell Synthesizer Generator could be used to enhance the learning process consider the following scenario:

Assume you are reading a paper by Alan Turing (on-line) and you want a computer supported version of the paper which you can use as a platform for working on some problem with the help of some formalism defined in the paper. You could proceed as indicated in the following script:

⟶ Synthesizer Generator consumes grammar of the formalism in the paper producing a dynamic computer based platform for concept development, study, etc.

⟶ ? mathematics not understood

⟶ obtain an on-line course in the appropriate mathematics and iterate through course moving from level understood to level of mathematics necessary to proceed with Turing paper

⟶ continue reading and using computer based platform

⟶ etc.

⟶ ? ordinary language not understood

⟶ on-line Dictionary, Encyclopedia, is consulted

⟶ ? there is still information lacking for full comprehension, use further Monographs, Video, Film, Visual-Telephone, Conferencing, etc. to obtain information lacking.

The Dossier [16] facility allows the flexible combination of the various types of facility utilized during the above trace to produce systematically evolving documentation on some topic or about some system component or the system as a whole. We will discuss this further later.

3.1 Specification-Validation Gaps between RWS and Req or Spec

In general the specification-validation gaps between a RWS and Req or Spec is traversed by means of the axiomatic method. This method consists roughly of:

(1) Concept Abstraction and Enumeration which begins by identifying important concepts used to describe the RWS and its context, and enumerates them as the fundamental vocabulary for system characterization. This constitutes an abstraction since concepts deemed not to be important are left out of the vocabulary, and hence it will be impossible to express properties of the system in the resulting model which require these concepts, unless they can be defined in terms of the concepts included in the vocabulary, in which case their meanings will be contained in some logical combination of concepts in the vocabulary. Concepts which cannot be expressed in terms of the basic vocabulary are abstracted from when the vocabulary is formed.

(2) Concept Reduction to a minimum basic set of independent concepts in terms of which all other concepts in the original vocabulary can be defined. Intuitively, a concept $c2$ is logically independent of another concept $c1$ if it is possible to give two models, such that $c1$ has the same meaning in the two models, but $c2$ has

different meanings in the two models. Then c2 could not have been defined by logical means in terms of the meaning of c1.

(3) Fact or Law Enumeration which enumerates all important statements which can be expressed using the vocabulary and which are considered to be true or valid of the real world system.

(4) Fact and Law Reduction to a minimum basic set of independent statements (axioms) from which all other statements enumerated in the previous step follow logically. Mutual independence of a set of statements means that none logically follows from the others.

If the whole activity is conducted in ordinary language it is called *informal axiomatics*. If the concepts are expressed symbolically or mathematically, i.e. if the concepts are symbolized, and if the the logical dependence is expressed by means of a logical calculus it is called *formal axiomatics*. We will find that the basic distinction between conventional and theory-based approaches is that the former use informal axiomatics and the latter use formal axiomatics. We continue our enumeration by listing the steps necessary to obtain formal axiomatizations, or in other words to traverse the formalization gap from conventional to theory based specification (or requirement):

(5) Symbolize Concepts such that you obtain a formal language powerful enough to express all concepts in the primitive base.

(6) Express all the Facts and Laws in the primitive base of Facts and Laws in this formal language.

(7) Formalize the definitional facilities and logical rules in a logical calculus, or construct a mathematical model of the formal system of Facts and Laws, if a complete and consistent calculus can not be found.

Later, when we focus on the computer system spectrum, additional notions of formalization (programs, compilers, makefiles, etc.) will arise, and in addition to facts and laws we will have to consider algorithms, information representations, programs, simulations, etc., when characterizing systems.

It should be mentioned that in the RWS to Requirement gap the axiomatic method must give rise to a *Predictive Theory* which can be used for systematic experimentation to ensure the adequacy of the formal abstractions for the purpose of representing the RWS in a relevant way. Such an experimental approach which is characteristic of the natural sciences is also appropriate and necessary in the specific area of computer system development, since the complexity of systems we construct exceeds our ability to analyze their behaviours fully, although we have constructed these systems from components which we can completely analyze. Hence analytical reasoning must be augmented by the experimental method. Of course simulation can also be used to advantage to increase knowledge about system requirements, however, simulation is not enough to ensure adequacy of the formal concepts with respect to the RWS since it itself rests on the same abstractions that may make the formalization irrelevant to the RWS. So for the sake of completeness we can add the following to our enumeration:

(8) Reformulate the formalization into a Predictive Theory allowing the formulation of criteria for decisive and systematic experimentation.

3.2 Conventional Means to traverse Specification-Validation Gaps

Some conventional means to get from a RWS to CReq or CSpec which we consider important to the kind of computer system development we are envisaging are:

(1) The concepts and techniques developed in Information Systems (IS).
(2) The concepts and techniques developed in Software Engineering (SE) in general, and the concepts and techniques of Object Oriented Design (OOD) in particular.

If computer support is employed then the following tools can be used effectively in this gap, particularly in combination with computer based multi media learning facilities as illustrated earlier, to produce "dyna-book" style requirement and specification documents:

(3) Parser Generators, Language Sensitive Editor Generators, Report Generating Tools, Dyna-book Generators, etc.

If we identify the RWS side with CCS, then conventional requirements and specifications become specialized to the area of computer systems, i.e. we get something like CReq-of-CCS or CSpec-of-CCS etc. Important tools in this gap would include everything from (1)-(3) above and additionally for instance:

(4) Environment enquiry capabilities which characterize the system behaviour on the fly, e.g. the many commands of the various UNIX shells such as ps, who, df, pwd, etc.. But in addition, we will consider even compilers, or any arbitrary system component which is capable of giving information about the system or itself. For example, if we have a piece of program text which is written in a programming language which is represented by at least one compiler in our system, we should be able to ask the compiler what the meaning of the program is. In general, if there is a piece of text (a command, enquiry, output from some system component, etc.) for which there exists some component which would interpret it, then one should be able to use environment enquiry to obtain information about this piece of text by directly appealing to that component, rather than e.g. consulting some documentation. We will say more about this when we discuss on the fly operational semantics based on environment enquiry.
(5) Pattern Matching controlled text editing and report generating tools, e.g. AWK, Perl, sed, grep, etc. in UNIX. These are used to great advantage by experienced UNIX programmers to construct their own views of system states or behaviours for particular purposes and which usually constitute an appropriate level of abstraction of the total information the system keeps about itself, or which can be obtained on the fly by environment enquiry.
(6) Trace or Scripting facilities which can be used to generate semantic information on the fly which is based on environment enquiries and therefore always up to date.
(7) Prototyping facilities. Executable specifications.

Conventional computer-based environments are often constructed from independent components that provide facilities such as graphics, text processing, data-bases, message passing, mail processing, computing, resource management, conferencing, reasoning, etc.

Careful design and consideration of interfaces between such facilities permit them to be used cooperatively in synthesized components appropriate for user applications, e.g. standardized and redirectable input and output facilities of the UNIX operating system are advantageous for application development. UNIX also permits much metaprogramming due to its script facility and environment enquiry. We discuss this further later.

Unless care is taken in documenting it is unlikely that synthesized components become integrated into the user environment. Hence it is relatively easy to document a new component and its composition from subcomponents, but it is often more difficult to document the relationship between the primitive components and the ones they are used to construct. For instance minor operating system alterations have ramifications on user program operation beyond that expected from inspection of system documentation.

Components introduced to reflect user activity are invariably *independent* and operate within a *closed environment*. E.g. software development systems may not permit the incorporation of existing software into the development process.

We will now sketch how the various components of the enumerations above can be integrated in terms of *four notions of semantics* of systems; the concepts, requirements and principles characterizing evolutionary systems in the RECIPE approach [17]; the concepts, principles and tools of the on-the-fly operational semantics based on environment enquiry (OFOSEE) approach; and the notion of System Dossier [16].

3.3 Four Kinds of Behavioural Sematics

Our informal notion of system is basically modular or object oriented. A system consists of an evolving community of self-descriptive, self-managing (particularly regarding their evolution) objects as well as evolving relationships between these.

Our Standard Semantics of such systems is behaviour based and often described using such idioms as histories or conversations.

Systems will however permit overall heterogeneity, and be "open" in the sense of allowing extension of the system by introduction of new objects as a result of behaviours of existing objects. Our systems will always be "well-defined" relative the existing objects since implementation is presupposed, and any linguistic expression which can give rise to system behaviour must be understood by some group of existing objects. Introduction of new objects adds the possibility of further conversations, but these are well-defined as soon as the object has been introduced due to the required self-descriptive nature of objects. Furthermore, these systems will involve techniques or components supporting a *self-adaptive, reasoned* and *well-managed* evolution. They will be designed to support the integration of the separate approaches of *formal mathematics and logic, computer science, experimental science* and *engineering*.

Useful distinctions of *types of semantics of objects* (modules, sub-systems) for our purposes are:

1. **System Relative Semantics:** (Black Box Semantics).

   (a) **Generation Semantics:** The behaviour of the system which generated the object. It consists of some combination of the use semantics of pre-existing objects. The behaviours (conversations) of the existing objects which gave rise to the object.

   (b) **Use Semantics:** The possible behaviours of the system when the object is used. The behaviours of (conversations with) the object possible once it has been generated.

2. **Programming Language Relative Semantics:** (White Box Semantics). The possible behaviours of the system as determined by the semantics of the programming language(s) used to implement the object. The behaviour as defined by the programs of the language without interpretation in some extra linguistic domain. (Note: Notion of traces fundamental here and they are uninterpreted.)

3. **Application (Problem) Relative Semantics:** (Real World Interpretation of Black or White Box Semantics). The interpretation of behaviours of the system in terms of real world (usually extra linguistic) domains being modelled by the object. The interpretation of system behaviours as representing some real world situation or process, modelling some application domain.

3.4 Requirements for Evolutionary Environments (RECIPE)

RECIPE stands for "Requirements for an Evolutionary Computer-based Information Processing Environment" [17]. Some of the important attributes of evolutionary objects and systems composed of them as defined in the RECIPE approach are:

1. **Uniformity and Locality:**
   Principle of Uniformity: All the requirements we propose are recursively applied to all components of the system.
   Principle of Locality: Locality of activity, facilities and knowledge is preserved within the system structure.

2. **Self-adaption and Interaction:** The system and user community must be able to modify, maintain and develop the system to reflect their evolving goals and ambitions. The system may alter how users progress towards goals and users may alter the functions supplied by the system. The system adapts to needs of the users.

3. **Forum for Discussion and Decisison Making:** Evolutionary systems must be designed to support dialogue among users and between users and system components. Mechanisms to support decision making must be integrated into the environment and are subject to evolutionary forces.

4. **Self-containment:** Components and interrelationships must be self-contained. That is, each component has attributes which represent the knowledge that the system and users need to correctly apply the component for the purpose for which it was created. E.g. objects must contain facilities to:
   - learn about the object,
   - retrieve knowledge about the object,
   - manage the evolution of the object, etc.

Synthesized components satisfying the self-containment criterion require a formal definition of dependencies and interfaces through which the components interact.

All necessary information to understand a component, use it and trace its history should be stored attributes of the component:

- integrated hierarchical **help**, **learn** and **information retrieval** facility,
- integrated **directory of** and **cross reference table for** the knowledge and facilities available for each component.

5. **Object Oriented View**: Evolutionary systems are composed of objects which represent definitions of facilities, knowledge about activities, and declarations of activities. A *facility* is a set of measures and necessary mechanisms used to support the development process. *Knowledge* is an abstraction of information stored by developers and users. *Activities* may create, transform or destroy facilities and knowledge. E.g. A user source program is a definition within a software development environment. It can be compiled by declaring a translation activity parameterized by the user source program, object binary, and debugging information. The resulting declaration of object binary has documentation attributes that denote the source program and the activity which may be expected from declaring an activation of that program. The result of parameterizing activations of the program by definitions of test data may lead to modification of the program. This constitutes a declaration of a modification activity and may introduce a new program source with attributes which reflect that it is a different version of the old source and was created as a result of studying the execution of that program with particular test data. This sort of example is illustrated in the session record in Section 3.5 below.

A self-contained object includes many more attributes to support:

- **document** in text format the reasons for modifications,
- **display** the program text,
- **relate** the program to specifications,
- **verify** the program as a refinement of a specification,
- **validate** the appropriateness of tests with respect to a specification, etc.

6. **Historical perspective**: An evolving system must record its history for analysis and to aid future decision making. A history is a complete trace of all significant activities within the system. This trace consists of interleaved occurrences of events generated by the various activities within the system as it evolves. This historical record exists from the perspective of each system component as well as from the perspective of the system. Perspectives are represented as projections from the system trace.

This historical perspective is supported by:

- integrated facilities to **archive and retrieve histories**,
- integrated facilities to **analyze and summarize histories, create projections**, etc.

7. **Uniform nomenclature**: All objects can be characterized by the sequence of events that led to their construction. This method of characterization is independent of both the implementation and the meaning of the object. It provides a precise scheme for distinguishing an object from other objects and determining

upon which other objects this object depends. We require a uniform nomenclature that reflects the meaning of objects within their histories. The symbolic name of an object is the concatenation of the names of the histories in which they are introduced in the order of the process hierarchy, similar to the way a complete path name in the UNIX file system indicates the context of a file or directory which determines many of the attributes of the file or directory. In fact, we envisage our self-descriptive systems to include facilities for *syntax-directed file management* based on this uniform and semantically significant nomenclature.

For example, in dialogue 3 of session 1 in Section 3.5, the name

   "program1.trace1,trace2.fact1"

indicates that fact1 has been shown to hold in the context of trace1 and trace2 of program1.

3.5 Attributes of Objects, System Dossiers and Dialogues

Since notations for objects (modules) in existing programming languages and specification languages usually accomodate only a small number of conventional attributes such as values, types and operations (functions or procedures), we use the System Dossier concept and facility to permit the definition of new types of attributes to obtain richer notions of objects, and to support the integration of these into the original system as well as the evolution of poorer preexisting objects to become richer objects.

During our earlier discussion of multi-media learning we gave an example of a script producing a computer based platform for a paper by Turing. Subsequently, we mentioned that the Dossier facility is intended to support the integration of the various facilities utilized during the production of the script, as well as the organization and further evolution of the system or knowledge about the system.

This facility is intended to be particularly helpful if one has several complementary but differing viewpoints supported by possibly different formalisms and automated procedures, with the help of which one is gathering and analyzing information and managing the development of the system.

In the process of developing the dossier notion it became evident that it is presumptuous to fix the number of possible viewpoints once and for all, and that it should be possible to introduce new viewpoints provided each viewpoint is adequately defined with respect to its interface with other viewpoints which are already defined and implemented.

We mention some of the more unconventional aspects of the Dossier facility. Once a particular dossier about some system components has been defined and compiled, the following would be established in the system:

- certain communication paths would automatically arise between, for example, the users, maintainers, analysers, or designers of the components.
- interconnections between support software for the various viewpoints involved in the dossier would arise which, for example, allow:
  - output of one viewpoint to become input to another;

- system descriptions produced from a combination of different viewpoints, and hence expressed in different notations and supported by different formalisms, to be interpreted using the semantic facilities of the appropriate viewpoint. For example, it should be possible to compile and run a program written partly in ALGOL 68 and partly in Concurrent Pascal by linking the respective compilers in appropriate ways as a result of the compilation of a dossier definition.

Briefly, a *dossier* [16] is a finite collection of viewpoints which may even be parameterized. Each viewpoint must be implemented in the sense that there is some system component which is capable of interpreting or producing descriptions according to that viewpoint. Because of the self-description requirement on objects two basic viewpoints must always be present. These are a **syntax** and a **semantics**. For example, a dossier of a very conventional component such as a programming language system, might merely contain a viewpoint which is supported by a compiler for the language. In that case any syntactic question about any program written in the language will be resolved by submitting it to the compiler for parsing. Semantic questions can be answered by running the object code resulting from compilation, or alternatively from reading the source code of the compiler or reading intermediate code or even the object code of the compiler itself. But this is a very minimal set of viewpoints as compared to those corresponding to the richer attributes we mentioned earlier, so we would soon want to evolve the dossier to incorporate on-line documentation, tutorial systems, program anayzers, program animators, simulation systems, formal definitions of semantics, verification tools, etc.

A typical collection of viewpoints we have used in the past include: **Descriptions** which are intuitive descriptions of the component and its use, and may be generated by means of information retrieval systems, text editors, conferencing systems, etc., and additionally supported by on line dictionaries and other reference documents on the usage of ordinary language, e.g. English grammar and style, etc. **Syntax, semantics, specifications, programs, definitions, verifications, validations, models, relationships, intermediaries, nested (sub) dossiers.** We refer the interested reader to [16] for further information. Here we conclude with an outline of a typical more complete dossier about some programming component:

- **syntax** Syntax diagrams, BNF, etc.
- **semantics1** Structural Operational Semantics.
- **semantics2** Hoare Logic.
- **semantics3** Denotational Semantics.
- **semantics4** Algebraic Semantics.
- $\cdots$
- **semanticsi** compiler1.
- $\cdots$
- **semanticsi+k** compilerk.
- $\cdots$
- **description** Natural Language technically extended.
- **instruction** Tutorial facilities, example collections, etc.
- **system analysis** Execution profilers, dependency analyzers, etc.

- **program development - evolution management** Makefiles, version control, etc.
- **requirements analysis and specifications**
- **facts or theorems** about the component together with their proof in some formalism or evidence of their experimental confirmation.
- **nested dossier** Dossiers are also object oriented and use inheritance from other dossiers, etc.
- **etc.**

To summarize, dossiers organize system components and knowledge about these components generated by means of them and other components. In particular, dossiers manage translations between languages of the various components. The definition of viewpoints makes components available for use, which means that they enable dialogues among existing components (which include registered human users) which might generate semantic descriptions, analyses, etc. of existing components, or which might even generate new components or new versions of existing components, which would enable further extended dialogues, etc.

Note that our semantic approach to evolutionary systems based on the notions of dialogue and trace supports "open" systems due to the self-descriptive nature of components and the overall capability of environment enquiry, which allow the system to "learn new languages". When a new component is generated it must be self-descriptive, i.e. it must be possible to ask it by environment enquiry what its language (syntax and semantics) is. This immediately permits dialogues between the new component and the rest of the system.

Dialogues constitute a very rich semantic basis, and environment enquiry ensures a very relevant semantical basis. Furthermore, they are a source of "meta-programs" as well as a basis for analysis, generalization, development, translation, etc. A meta-program results from projecting away all system responses from some dialogue, after which it may be resubmitted to the system to reestablish the system situation that it led to in the first case. But a metaprogram obtained by projection from a given dialogue is often modified in a systematic manner to obtain a more adequate process of reaching the same system situation as that reached by the original metaprogram.

The notion of dialogue implies that for every syntactic unit of the dialogue there must exist at least one system component which is either capable of recognizing and interpreting the unit, or producing the unit. This gives rise to a natural notion of projection onto conversational partners.

The notions of trace used in other approaches are much narrower; e.g. in the Communicating Sequential Processes (CSP) approach of Hoare [19] the only means of communication is via channels, using only one message language, and decomposition of conversations is awkward due to limitations on the number of participants in information exchange. Our general notion of trace involves interleaving (non-arbitrarily) parts of (possibly more than two) conversations. Our notion of operational semantics, traces and dossiers, arose in the context of developing computer support for the COSY formalism, which we developed to formally design and analyze concurrent and distributed systems [20].

The following is a sketch of a session generating a number of dialogues representing a number of activities using an imaginary evolutionary system developed according to RECIPE. The session represents the following scenario: In dialogue1 a user develops a program using a program editor. In dialogue2 the user generates two semantic objects each of which is a trace of program execution. In dialogue3 the user uses a verifier to show that neither trace is a prefix of the other. In dialogue4 the user summarizes the fact that the two traces are in the set of traces of the program. In dialogue5 the user transforms program1 into program2 (say to optimize it) using the program editor, while at the same time obtaining a script of the user editor interaction (a potential metaprogram). In dialogue6 the user uses the meta-semantic software to project away the editor responses from the script, thus obtaining a metaprogram which, when applied by the editor to the program, yields another program. This metaprogram could also be generalized in further dialogues to apply to a whole class of similar programs. In dialogue7 the user shows that the set of all traces of the new program is the same as the set of traces of the old program, i.e. they have the same semantics in terms of traces. In dialogue8 the user shows that for any program the editor transformation obtained from dialoge5 will produce another program with the same behavioural semantics. Finally, in dialogue9 the user just summarizes some information which follows from the above, namely that trace1 and trace2 are also in the set of traces of the new program. The session is discussed in detail in [16].

> **session:** session1:
>> **dialogue:** dialogue1:
>>> *user and program-editor interaction*
>>> **syntactic object:**
>>>> program1: · · ·
>>>>> sub-program1: · · ·
>> **dialogue:** dialogue2:
>>> *user and semantic software (simulator) interaction*
>>> **semantic object:**
>>>> program1.trace1: · · ·
>>>>> sub-program1.subtrace1: · · ·
>>> **semantic object:**
>>>> program1.trace2: · · ·
>>>>> sub-program1.subtrace1: · · ·
>> **dialogue:** dialogue3:
>>> *user and verifier interaction*
>>> **assertion:**
>>>> program1.trace1,trace2.fact1:
>>>>> trace1 $\not\leq$ trace2 & trace2 $\not\leq$ trace1
>> **dialogue:** dialogue4:
>>> *user and reasoning (summarizing, reformulating) facility interaction*
>>> **assertion:**
>>>> program1.trace1,trace2.fact2:
>>>>> trace1,trace2 $\in$ Traces(program1)
>> **dialogue:** dialogue5:
>>> *user and program-editor and dialogue1 interaction*
>>> **syntactic object:**

      program2: $\cdots$
       sub-program1: $\cdots$

dialogue: dialogue6:

  user and meta-semantic software interaction
  meta-assertion:
    program1,program2.meta-fact1:
     (projection1(dialogue5))(program1) = program2

dialogue: dialogue7:

  user and meta-semantic software interaction
  meta-assertion:
    program1,program2.meta-fact2:
     Traces(program1) = Traces(program2)

dialogue: dialogue8:

  user and meta-semantic software interaction
  meta-assertion:
   meta-fact2:
  ($\forall$ program) Traces((projection1(dialogue5))(program)) = Traces(program)

dialogue: dialogue9:

  user and meta-reasoning software interaction
  assertion:
    program2.trace1,trace2.meta-fact2.fact3:
     trace1,trace2 $\in$ Traces(program2)

3.6   On the Fly Operational Semantics based on Environment Enquiry (OFOSEE)

The basic idea here is to use the environment enquiry facilities of the system to make snapshots before and after the execution of (system) commands and to use such utilities as UNIX "diff" and "cmp" to determine the *variant* and *invariant* parts of the successive snapshots, respectively. We have built a number of GRIPE and more general semantics facilities in UNIX based on this idea. They are programs which allow a user to enter and examine complaints, suggestions and comments on a variety of topics in an orderly fashion [18].

  Essentially, the gripe facility allows one to point to a command in the current trace of the system and request that the command and the relevant snapshots before and after the command be placed in a gripe file under the (primary) name of the command which is a copy of itself precisely as invoked.

PrimaryName : chmod go-rw file-name
SecondaryNames : ⋯

---

snapshot1   ⟵ produced by environment enquiry
                                       e.g. using "ls -lg file-name"
chmod go − rw file − name

snapshot2   ⟵ produced by environment enquiry

The advantage of using the verbatim quote of the command being griped about as the primary name of the gripe is that one can use the full power of UNIX commands and syntactic facilities to retrieve information from the gripe files as desired. E.g.

Get all commands using a certain file: * **file-name** .

Get all uses of a command regardless of options or files: **chmod * .**

Get precisely one use of command: **chmod go-rw file-name** , etc.

The use of the awk, perl, vi, etc. Unix tools to search and manipulate and even execute "chmod" with selected parameters, gives systematic access to the information in the gripe files and allows further production of needed information.

The idea of on the fly semantics extends the application of this notion from complaining to describing meanings. It is intended to use a similar mechanism for producing statements about the effect of any command in terms of pre- and post-conditions directly obtained from environment enquiry.

These concrete snapshots can then be systematically abstracted from, to obtain e.g. pre- and post-condition semantics in the style of Hoare or Dijkstra etc., using theory based abstraction tools (TBAT), as we shall describe later.

Teaching facilities can be built by specifying specific paths through the semantic facility, which are appropriate to the subject matter being taught. But since the semantics is based on environment enquiry about the actual current system, the teaching facility always remains up to date. More on this later.

An efficient and lucid implementation of these ideas, as well as the discovery of the fundamental utilities that systems should have in order to allow this type of development and semantic analysis of the system, are the subjects of ongoing research.

To reiterate, "on the fly" indicates that the semantic definition of a system is entirely based on **environment enquiries** about the actual current system. The semantic definition changes instantaneously as the system evolves, and the definition, help, teaching, verification, etc., facilities based on it are always "up to date". Conventional documentation and facilities based on them tend to become obsolete as the system evolves. We are seeking to identify the notions and system primitives so as to make such adaptive semantics a practical reality.

3.7 Theory Based Means to traverse Specification-Validation Gaps

One of the major distinguishing characteristic of all the conventional concepts and tools discussed above is that they usually depend on a formalization of syntactic matters, otherwise it would be impossible to implement recognizers for the notation used, but leave semantical matters informal, or at least non-mathematical and highly operational. Of course, as we indicated in the previous section, in the case of UNIX the various tools can be used very effectively to gather and display semantic information. This is because all text files have the same standardized relatively unstructured form, and any textual response from any system component can be input to any other, and analyzed and transformed using the pattern matching editing capabilities of UNIX.

The theory based means for traversing the specification-validation gaps extend all the useful concepts and tools from the conventional approach to include capabilities for formalizing the semantical aspects of systems as well formalizing the logics appropriate for formal reasoning within or about this semantics.

For example, SML [5] which has a formal semantics, is capable of inferring the type correctness of all SML programs, which can be considered to be a formalization and computerization of part of the semantics. But SML cannot express other semantical properties such as, for instance, that some operation (function) distributes over some other. Extended ML [24] [25] allows the formulation of the full semantics of SML programs but it is as yet not implemented, and must be used in an off-line paper and pencil mode. But OBJ3 [6] allows the expression of such semantics and is implemented so that it could be used systematically to formalize the informal information a system keeps about itself, as we will discuss further later. Of course LARCH [4], Nuprl [7] and EVES [8], which are presented in separate papers in this volume, and a number of other theory based systems which we have not been able to include in this volume, could be similarly applied in principle. But we believe that all of them would need more convenient access to the information a conventional system keeps about itself, than is the case today.

For the moment we will assume that real world systems will be characterized by requirements resulting from the theory based Information System (IS) approach of Swatman which we briefly mentioned above. In this approach Object-Z is used to formalize semantics of real world systems, but the formal semantics is used as a component of an otherwise informal system development process. Of course, any of the formalisms involved in the theory based systems presented in this volume such as Coloured Petri Nets [9], [10], Nuprl [7], OBJ3 [6], ExSpect [11], LARCH [4] and EVES [8] could be used instead of Object-Z in such a theory based IS approach.

Since our main concern here is with implemented theory based systems and their utility in computer system development and use, we will say no more about the specification-validation gap at this time.

4   System Gap between CCS and TBCS

The basic distinction between CCS and TBCS includes the general distinction between informal and formal axiomatics, but in addition involves the distinction between systems which do not contain computer components and tools which implement the formal axiomatics, and those which do. The latter give formal and computer supported reasoning capability, whereas the former only allow informal off-line paper and pencil reasoning about either the CS itself, or the RWS modelled by the CS.

To achieve maximal relevance of formal descriptions of computer systems, theory based systems should have access to all information which a system keeps about itself, or which could be generated by environment enquiry. The notion of OFOSEE is our initial characterization of this capability.

To achieve maximal expressiveness, flexibility, sophistication of computer support, reuse and trustworthiness, theory based systems should provide means to integrate different existing system components without much modification or needless duplication of function. Current systems involve much duplication, e.g. although there exist syntactic facilities for recognizing some program text as part of a compiler, programmers usually write their own "recognizers" for such text in their programs if they need to work with it, rather than borrowing the compiler facilities in some way when needed. Our notions of RECIPE and Dossier are initial attempts to achieve such integration and non-duplication.

To illustrate these two points, suppose we want to use a theory based system in environment enquiry mode. First, it must be possible to request information about the environment in the format defined by the environment. Second, it must be possible to obtain the formal syntax and possibly the accompanying syntactic facilities (parsers, analyzers, etc.) from the environment. Third, it must be possible to enquire about the semantics of the textual information.

To be more specific, when a theory based system obtains a syntactic unit, e.g. output from the "ps" (process status) command in UNIX, it should be possible for the theory based system to obtain the formal definition of the syntax from UNIX, so that it can translate the syntactic unit into the structures it uses to represent the information contained in the output. Of course to achieve the translation semantical information may also be required which can be obtained by environment enquiry.

Recently, we have been trying to use OBJ3 to obtain formal equivalents of output from UNIX commands in just this way, and this demonstrated the need to enhance the capabilities of OBJ3 to interface to the UNIX environment. Tim Winkler has privately communicated to us some preliminary ideas to achieve the necessary capabilities by means of user-defined built-in sorts, but we have not been able to pursue these ideas further at present.

5 Knowledge Gaps between Users and Developers of CCS and TBCS

One of our main contentions is that theory based systems have one of their most fruitful applications in the education of users. It is only recently that others have increasingly stressed the advantages of such use. Even many who feel that the impact of theory based systems on software development practice is negligible would agree that they could be very useful as educational tools, particularly since they allow the learners to practice on their own and to progress at their own pace without relinquishing the checking function performed by a human teacher. Inapplicability of these systems to complex real world situations due to inability to scale up is also less detrimental in the instructional context, since concepts can usually be adequately characterized by descriptions which are small enough so that their full exploration is possible using the theory based system. As more architecturally adequate evolutionary systems of the kind we envisage are developed, particularly those which improve the state of the art of modularization of systems and their descriptions, we should eventually be able to overcome the problem of scaling up to permit the application of these systems to complex real world systems.

6 Towards more Trustworthy Computer Systems

A system will be trustworthy to the degree its components have been verified with regard to some formal theory, and even to the degree its components are self-verifying at initiation time or during the entire run time. For example, the HOL [23] system verifies itself when it is invoked, the SML [22] system verifies its type correctness when it is invoked, at least with regard to the pervasives and its libraries. This is often possible because all system code is kept at as high a level as possible, which is also the case for most declarative programming systems.

What follows will illustrate how one might support the production of more trustworthy computer systems.

We will sketch the notion of "test-bed" in the context of the problem of developing an industrially relevant software documentation system based on the tabular formalism for relational or functional specification due to David Parnas in [26]. One of the major goals of the testbed system is the integration of a number of existing and reasonably trustworthy theory based software systems in such a way that it will become possible to characterize and analyse the semantics of systems using their underlying theories.

In the context of such a formal software documentation project, the idea is that the user will usually only see the tabular notation, but it will be possible to connect different semantical systems to this notation in such a way that properties of systems defined in the tabular notation can be studied by users with sufficient expertise using various semantical formalisms, each suitable for certain kinds of analysis, but none capable of all such analyses.

Furthermore, the integration of these systems would aim at the development of components facilitating the education of users concerning the various formalisms in the testbed. This way we hope to improve the process of technology transfer of theoretical results to practice.

Initially the test-bed might involve the following theory based sub-systems:

(1) The Cornell Synthesizer Generator [29] which will be used to develop:
An X-windows based, syntax-directed document production and syntactic transformation tool to support specification and production activities, which would interact with the user in such a way that:
- a specification successfully entered will be syntactically correct, including context dependencies;
- a specification transformed via the tool will preserve the meaning of the original specification.

Use of the Synthesizer Generator permits rapid, flexible and automatic production of full-screen window-based editors from given grammars and logical transformation rules, removing the need to write these editors by hand.

A number of such editors already exist for formal systems, which will play an important role in the development of the other experimental prototypes to be constructed, allowing us to extend the editors to new situations without additional programming of screen and window oriented aspects of our tools [31], [30].

(2) A Trustworthy Programming Language, which means that it must have a formal semantics and acceptable execution speed and storage requirements. Furthermore, there should be theory based semantic tools available as far as possible.

Since the tabular notation is used to express functional specifications, it seems natural to implement it in a functional programming language, which due to its closeness to the tabular specifications should quickly give rise to executable specifications, thus permitting almost immediate simulation of the specified system.

Since SML has a formal semantics, and a number of formal systems have been developed and implemented to reason about SML programs [32], [33], [24], [25], we should be able to extend computer based verification all the way from specification to implementation. Furthermore, since some of the most advanced theory based systems either are implemented in SML or use SML as a metalanguage for manipulating proofs and formulating proof strategies, the choice of this language would seem to give much of a common factor among theory based systems, which would augur well for the type of integration we seek.

Since we are also concerned to model concurrency, it would be advantageous for the programming language to countenance concurrency. This is the case for SML, which has several extensions to support concurrency [12], [34].

(3) A Graphical Concurrency Model integrated with the functional programming language and the algebraic approach. The extension of our specification techniques to permit design of parallel systems require use of an appropriate formal theory of concurrency. The most developed such formal theory is Petri net theory [40], and SML has been combined with high-level nets in a powerful graphics and windows based system, including tools for design, analysis, simulation and verification [9], [10]. This system also supports hierarchic decomposition of concurrent systems, which is not true of many other systems for specifying and analyzing concurrency.

This, and the fact that the COSY theory of concurrency we have developed over the past ten years is directly related to Petri nets [20], would permit us to conduct extensive experiments with specifications of parallel systems.

Furthermore, the Concurrency Workbench [13] is implemented in SML which should facilitate integration of the formalisms [14], [15] and techniques implemented there into the test-bed.

- **External Logic and Greater Expressiveness.** In the approach sketched above, the logic to reason about specifications is external to the specifications, which are written in a functional programming language, giving immediate efficient executability and allowing greater expressiveness in the logic used to reason about specifications, this being necessary to obtain high level and readable characterizations of systems.

- **Internal Logic and Computations as Proofs.** An alternative approach is to use algebraic specification languages which have internal equational or Horn

Relationships among test-beds and main prototype, compilers, operating systems and machines.

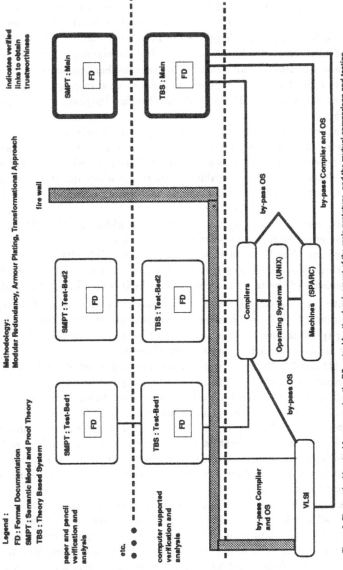

Figure 3: The test-bed is a tool for expressing the DC, a tool for the development of the main prototype, and the mutual comparison and testing of all prototypes.

clause logic, which is less expressive than the external logics considered above, but which can be interpreted as rewrite rules allowing direct (symbolic) execution, where every computation is simultaneously a proof. Furthermore, the most advanced formal results about the modular construction of large specifications from smaller ones have been obtained using the algebraic approach.

Our choice of SML again proves advantageous here, since some of the formal semantics and formal development techniques used in conjunction with ML are based on extensions of ML to a full specification language in the algebraic style [24] [25].

This suggests a third direction for developing exploratory tools.

(4) Algebraic Specification Systems. We have in mind an implementation of the tabular specification notation in an algebraic style based on rewrite logics [36] to obtain declarative but executable specifications which denote algebras, together with powerful combinators for composing specifications to obtain larger ones [41].

Initially, there are three systems of this type which involve different aspects of tools we envisage in the test-bed system. We hope to be able to readily express many of our ideas in all three without too much difficulty, but we need to look at all three, since each goes further than the other two with regard to different requirements of the tools and concepts to be included in the test-bed.

(4.1) Act2 [41] is a system which is based on early ideas of modularity of David Parnas [27], [28], and has the most extensive set of combinators for developing specifications of large systems, which have been precisely characterized by means of numerous mathematical theorems.

(4.2) OBJ3 and 2OBJ, [6] are systems based on order sorted algebras which permit elegant treatment of errors. They also support development of large specifications, and considerable work has been done towards parallel rewriting and the development of concurrent rewrite hardware [43].

The language Maude [6], [42] is an extension of Obj3 to permit concurrent object oriented specification and programming on a firm logical framework, which goes beyond the confines of algebraic semantics, and yields a semantics which incorporates Petri net semantics of concurrency, and hence our COSY concurrency semantics.

(4.3) Extended ML [24] which is one of the alternative formal systems for expressing SML semantics, is defined in terms of the algebraic specification language ASL [36] and implemented via the rapid prototyping system RAP [37].

Furthermore, ASL and RAP are used in an advanced tool supporting a theory of software testing based on formal (algebraic) specifications [39], [38].

Experimentation with these systems would provide insight into problems arising while attempting to integrate theory based systems into a test-bed of the kind we envisage.

Figure 3 depicts the relationship among various component test-beds, the main prototype test-bed, and other system components such as compilers, operating systems, machines, etc., all of which provide a framework for ultimately obtaining trustworthy implementations of our tools.

Briefly, the use of the framework can be characterized as:

- **if** TBS not considersed fully trustworthy
- **then** move its functionality into the formal documentation FD side in a verified manner
- **elseif** Compiler not trustworthy
- **then** bypass Compiler and/or OS to Machine or VLSI
- **elseif** OS not trustworthy
- **then** bypass OS to Machine or VLSI
- **else** prune TBS (and its formalism) to obtain greater trustworthiness (e.g. SML without some features and its direct implementation bypassing OS, Compiler, Machine, as appropriate).

7 Conclusion

Evolutionary systems and their components must be self-descriptive and self-managing. Conventional system management techniques (e.g. UNIX "make" facility and the Source Code Control System SCCS, etc.) must be integrated within the system and its components in new ways to make self-management a reality. To facilitate integration, management techniques must become syntax directed and must be supported by tools for generating syntax directed system interfaces (e.g. editor, compiler and environment generators). Such syntax directed tools will also prove useful (or even necessary) for integrating new subsystems into existing systems by generating interfaces to the new subsystems based on their syntactic and semantic attributes, which subsystems must contain to qualify as self-descriptive. Although interfaces will be generated in a uniform manner and with general tools, they will differ depending on their intended user classes (involving such spectra as novice to expert, application oriented to computer system oriented) and usage modes (learning mode, application development mode and system development mode).

Theory based systems and their components must additionally support formal self-description, system analysis and self-management, based on implemented (mathematical, logical) calculi, and for such systems to be realistic, the formal techniques must be integrated with the rest of the conventional tools for system description and development. It must be possible to use the system bottom-up starting from conventional self-descriptions and moving successively to abstract and formalized theory based self-descriptions. This bottom-up approach could be called "abstractive" and contrasted with the top-down or "transformational" approach which is more common in the development of trustworthy systems, where one typically begins with verified but readily comprehensible components and proceeds to efficient and less understandable components.

Trustworthy systems will additionally ensure that they are verified (in part or to various degrees) with respect to some formal semantics. This will usually mean using the system top down starting from verified levels and extending the verification throughout the system all the way to the hardware. Of course, if one begins with verified hardware one should also be able to work bottom-up. Finally, one may need to work inside out to spread the verification over more and more components laterally.

Systems of these various kinds will only be utilized effectively and widely if they include well designed, integrated, on-line and up-to-date facilities for learning the descriptive theories and doctrines implemented in the systems.

The development of such advanced and extensive systems is a very ambitious and long term undertaking, but one we feel is a necessary prerequisite for the realization of the full potential of the advent of the computer for the future of humanity. Both current computer systems and their consequences for human affairs far outstrip our ability to fully comprehend at present. To improve this situation, we must transform these systems so that they themselves offer maximum support for arriving at an adequate understanding of these systems and the complex consequences of their ubiquitous use to model and control real world systems.

To achieve ultimate success in our endeavour, we must not only identify the gaps which need to be bridged, but also appropriately locate these gaps in the overall context for developing computer models of the real world. The locations within this context must be appropriate in the sense that we can achieve maximal use of the general conventional and theory based concepts and tools throughout the system, and at the same time achieve maximal integration of these tools in the resulting system.

Hence, we do not suppose that our identification and location of gaps in this paper are in any sense definitive and final, but we offer them as an initial focus for further discussion and development in collaboration with the rest of the computer science and computer engineering communities, over an extended period of time.

8 Acknowledgements

I would like to thank Jeffery Zucker for his careful reading of this paper and for suggesting many improvements to enhace readability of the paper. The author has been supported by grants from the National Science and Engineering Research Council of Canada.

References

1. Aho A.V., Ullman J.D. *Foundations of Computer Science*. W.H. Freeman and Company, 1992.
2. Van Leeuwen J. (Ed.) *Handbook of Theoretical Computer Science*. Volume A: Algorithms and Complexity. Volume B: Formal Models and Semantics. Elsevier, 1990.
3. Swatman P.A., Swatman P.M.C. Formal Specification: An Analytic tool for (Management) Information Systems. *Journal of Information Systems*, Vol. 2, No.2, April 1992, 121-160.
4. Garland S.J., Guttag J.V., Horning J.J. An Overview of LARCH. In this volume.
5. Ophel John An Introduction to the High-Level Language Standard ML. In this volume.
6. Winkler Tim Programming in OBJ and Maude. In this volume.
7. Howe D.J. Reasoning About Functional Programs in Nuprl. In this volume.
8. Kromodimoeljo S., Pase Bill, Saaltink M., Craigen D., Meisels I. The EVES System. In this volume.
9. Malhotra J., Shapiro R.M. Generating an Algorithm for Executing Graphical Models. In this volume.

10. Shapiro R.M., Pinci V.O., Mameli R. Modeling a NORAD Command Post Using SADT and Colored Petri Nets. In this volume.
11. van Hee K.M., Rambags P.M.P, Verkoulen P.A.C. Specification and Simulation in ExSpect. In this volume.
12. MacQueen D.B. Reflections on Standard ML. In this volume.
13. Cleaveland R. Analyzing Concurrent Systems Using the Concurrency Workbench. In this volume.
14. Zucker J. Propositional Temporal Logics and their Use in Model Checking. In this volume.
15. Zucker J. The Propositional μ-Calculus and its Use in Model Checking. In this volume.
16. Lauer P.E. Computer System Dossiers. In *Distributed Computing Systems*, Academic Press, 1983, 109-147.
17. Lauer P.E., Campbell R.H. RECIPE: Requirements for an Evolutionary Computer-based Information Processing Environment. In *Software Process Workshop*, Egham U.K., 1984
18. Whiteside Fred GRIPE: A User Complaint and Maintainer Response System. Report on a Software Engineering Project, Dept. of Computer Science and Systems, McMaster University, Hamilton, Ontario, Canada, 1985.
19. Hoare C.A.R. *Communicating Sequential Processes.* Prentice-Hall, 1985.
20. Janicki R., Lauer P.E. *Specification and Analysis of Concurrent Systems: The COSY Approach.* Springer-Verlag, 1992.
21. Milner R., Tofte M., and Harper R. *The Definition of Standard ML.* The MIT Press, Cambridge, 1990.
22. Appel A. and MacQueen D. A standard ML compiler. In *Functional Programming Languages and Computer Architecture*, pages 301–324. Springer-Verlag Lecture Notes In Computer Science 274, 1987.
23. Gordon M.J.C. HOL: A Proof Generating System for Higher-Order Logic. In *VLSI Specification, Verification and Synthesis*, edited by G. Birtwistle and P.A. Subramanyam, Kluwer, 1988, 73-128.
24. Sannella D., Tarlecki A. Extended ML: an institution-independent framework for formal program development. Technical report, Report ECS-LFCS-86-16, Laboratory for Foundations of Computer Science, Computer Science Department, Edinburgh University, 1986.
25. Sannella D. Formal program development in Extended ML for the working programmer. Technical report, Report ECS-LFCS-89-102, Laboratory for Foundations of Computer Science, Computer Science Department, Edinburgh University, 1989.
26. Parnas D.L. Tabular Representation of Relations. Technical report, CRL Report No.260, Communications Research Laboratory, McMaster University, October 1992.
27. Parnas D.L. A technique for software module specification with examples. *CACM 15*, 5(1972), 330-336.
28. Parnas D.L. On the Criteria to be Used in Decomposing Systems into Modules. *CACM 15*, 12(1972), 1053-1058.
29. Reps T.W., Teitelbaum T. *The Synthesizer Generator: A system for constructing language-based editors.* Springer-Verlag, 1988.
30. Reps T.W., Teitelbaum T. *The Synthesizer Generator: Reference Manual.* Springer-Verlag, 1989.
31. Custeau R., Shelley C. Development of an Editor for Proving Theorems of First-order Logic. Senior Undergraduate Project, Department of Computer Science and Systems, McMaster University, 1990.
32. Pollack R. The Theory of LEGO. Manuscript, Laboratory for Foundations of Computer Science, Computer Science Department, Edinburgh University, 1988.

33. Luo Z., Pollack R., Taylor P. How to use LEGO. Preliminary User's Manual, Laboratory for Foundations of Computer Science, Computer Science Department, Edinburgh University, 1989.
34. Reppy J.H. Concurrent ML: Design, Application and Semantics. In this volume.
35. Reppy J.H. CML: A higher-order concurrent language. In *SIGPLAN'91 Conference on Programming Language Design and Implementation*, pages 293–305. SIGPLAN Notices 26(6), 1991.
36. Sanella D. A Survey of Formal Software Development Methods. Technical report, Report ECS-LFCS-88-56, Laboratory for Foundations of Computer Science, Computer Science Department, Edinburgh University, 1988.
37. Broy M., Geser A., Hussmann H. Towards Programming Environments Based on Algebraic Concepts. MIP-8826, Faculty of Mathematics and Informatik, University of Passau, 1988.
38. Dauchy P., Marre B. Test Data Selection from the Algebraic Specification of a Module of an Automatic Subway. Rapp. de Recherche no. 638, L.R.I. Universite de Paris Sud, 1991.
39. Bernot G., Gaudel M.C., Marre B. Software Testing Based on Formal Specifications: A Theory and a Tool. Rapp. de Recherche no. 581, L.R.I. Universite de Paris Sud, 1990.
40. Reisig W. *Petri Nets: An Introduction*. Springer-Verlag, 1985.
41. Ehrig H., Mahr B. *Fundamentals of Algebraic Specification 2: Module Specifications and Constraints*. Springer-Verlag, 1990.
42. Messeguer J. A Logical Theory of Concurrent Objects. SRI-CS-90-07, SRI International, Computer Science Laboratory, 1990.
43. Messeguer J. Conditional Rewriting Logic as a Unified Model of Concurrency. SRI-CS-91-05, SRI International, Computer Science Laboratory, 1991.
44. Paulson L.C. *ML for the Working Programmer*. Cambridge University Press, Cambridge, 1992.
45. Reade C. *Elements of Functional Programming*. Addison-Wesley, Reading, MA, 1989.
46. Hughes J. Why functional programming matters. *The Computer Journal*, 32(2):98–107, 1989.

Reflections on Standard ML

David B. MacQueen

AT&T Bell Laboratories
Murray Hill NJ 07974

Abstract. Standard ML is one of a number of new programming languages developed in the 1980s that are seen as suitable vehicles for serious systems and applications programming. It offers an excellent ratio of expressiveness to language complexity, and provides competitive efficiency. Because of its type and module system, Standard ML manages to combine safety, security, and robustness with much of the flexibility of dynamically typed languages like Lisp. It is also has the most well-developed scientific foundation of any major language. Here I review the strengths and weaknesses of Standard ML and describe some of what we have learned through the design, implementation, and use of the language.

1 Introduction

The goal of programming language design is to maximize expressiveness while minimizing conceptual complexity, within the constraint that the language must have an efficient implementation. If a language is to be suitable for large-scale, serious programming (*i.e.*, implementing software that will have users and will therefore have to be robust and maintainable), then it must provide security and facilities for organizing large programs. These are some of the desiderata that guided the design of Standard ML.

This paper presents my personal views about language design and the lessons we have learned from the design and implementation of Standard ML. As the field of programming language design matures, it is essential that a more scientific approach should come into play. The history of ML provides an example of how theoretical insights and practical programming requirements can be successfully synthesized.

The first section summarizes some of the strengths of Standard ML. We then proceed to some remarks on the process of language design in general and on the design of Standard ML in particular. Next comes a review of some particular lessons learned from the experience of implementing and using Standard ML. Section 5 illustrates the continuing language research activity associated with ML by describing a number of experimental language extensions. These efforts can be seen as exploring options for the next generation of ML-like languages. Finally I discuss the relation between ML and object-oriented programming and finish with some projections about the future development of Standard ML and its successors.

I will not review the history of ML here, since that topic is well covered in Appendix E of the *Definition of Standard ML* ([35]) and in Robin Milner's Turing award interview ([17]). I will also assume some familiarity with ML and refer the reader to John Ophel's paper in this volume ([37]) for an overview of the language, and to Larry Paulson's book ([38]) for a more extensive introduction. I will often use the shorter name "ML," which may refer either to Standard ML in particular or to the generic family of ML languages according to the context.

2 Why Standard ML Works

Here is an enumeration of some of the major strengths of Standard ML from the view of a user of the language. Not surprisingly, many of these points parallel those mentioned in Appel's critique ([3]).

A high-level programming model. A high-level model makes programming more efficient and more reliable by automating and suppressing many low level details such as memory management and data formating. Standard ML's programming model is based on the functional programming paradigm, which derives from the lambda calculus.

Safety. ML's type system, memory management system, and exception facilities combine to guarantee that even buggy ML programs do not "crash" (*i.e.*, fail catastrophically due to some corruption of the computational state or inappropriate manipulation of data). It *is* possible for a program to fail because an ML exception is raised and never handled. In the interactive system this returns one to top-level, but in a stand-alone program it terminates the program abnormally. It is, of course, also possible for an ML program to produce the wrong result because of a bug, or to fail to terminate.

Security and robustness. Static type checking detects many errors at compile time. Error detection is enhanced by the use of pattern matching, which helps ensure coverage of all cases because the compiler can statically detect and report incomplete matches, and by the exception mechanism, which provides a type-secure, disciplined way to deal with potential runtime exceptions. The result is that unexpected runtime errors can be largely avoided or dealt with appropriately.

Expressiveness and conciseness. The ability to treat functions as first-class values, the use of higher-order functions to express a wide range of control structures, the use of pattern matching for concise analysis of data, and the availability of imperative constructs provide great expressive power within a simple and uniform conceptual framework. The combination of state and higher-order functions is very powerful, but can cause difficulties in specifying and reasoning about programs (as in object-oriented programming).

Flexible strong typing. The ML type system is simple, uniform,[1] flexible, and sound. The flexibility is achieved through the use of parametric polymorphism. New types can be defined to match precisely the requirements of a problem, and data abstraction (*i.e.*, hiding of data representations) is well supported. Automatic inference of most general type schemes streamlines interactive programming. Type checking provides security by detecting statically a large fraction of common mistakes. But perhaps the most valuable aspect of the type system is that it provides a language for designing and expressing data representations and program interfaces and then automatically enforces their proper use through type checking.

---

[1] Any type constructor can be applied to any types without restriction – all types are treated equally. Also, user-defined types are treated the same as primitive types.

Modularity. The ML module system is an organic extension of the underlying polymorphic type system ([31, 36]). It provides for separation of interface specification and implementation and supports abstraction and parameterization. These facilities are very effective in structuring large programs and defining generic, reusable software components.

Efficiency. Highly optimizing compilers ([4]) have been developed for ML that, for many applications, produce code whose speed is competitive with those for corresponding programs written in much lower-level languages such as C. However, space efficiency tends to be significantly worse than for low level languages like C. The cost of automatic memory management and a uniform, simple type system is more intensive use of memory, though advancing compiler technology is reducing this overhead.

Multiple modes of usage. In its original incarnation as the metalanguage of the LCF system ([19]), ML played two roles. It was used to program proof tactics and tacticals to automate theorem proving, and it was used as the command language of the interactive LCF system. In several more recent systems such as HOL ([42]), ML also serves as the underlying implementation language for the whole system (LCF itself was implemented in Lisp). These roles can be separated; in particular, it is possible to use an ML compiler in a traditional batch style to generate binary object files that are later linked to create a stand-alone application. Such stand-alone applications must incorporate the runtime system, but they are independent of the compiler and the interactive system. ML has attributes that support all these modes of usage: type inference simplifies use as an interactive command language, many characteristics mentioned above suit it to the role of a symbolic metalanguage, and the module and type systems support large-scale systems implementation.

3 Comments on Language Design Methodology

A principled and scientific language design should be guided by parallel efforts and insights coming from three perspectives: *semantics*, *implementation*, and last but not least, *pragmatics*, or how the language is to be used in practice. Ideally, the design of a language should consist of several iterations, each involving development of semantics, experimental implementation, and application experiments. Each iteration should use feedback from all three perspectives to adjust design decisions from the previous iteration.

Writing a formal semantic definition clearly provides a strong discipline and encourages simplicity and clarity in the language design. Ideally the development of a formal definition should be backed up by investigation of the metatheory of the language (*e.g.*, type soundness theorems, principal typing theorems), and of how to formally specify and reason about programs in the language (*i.e.*, the *logic* of the language). Unfortunately, the state of program logics is currently rather weak, so designing a language to have a tractable logic seems to be an impractically severe constraint (advocates of pure functional and logic languages may disagree with this point, but such languages have had limited practical impact so far).

Developing a prototype implementation of the language forces one to consider the cost of language features and their interactions in terms of implementation complexity, and this also favors simplification. The implementation perspective also makes designers consider the consequences of their decisions on execution speed. A new language design may require new compilation technology, which is risky, but progress would be hindered if new languages were overly constrained by known compilation techniques.

How the language is to be used is obviously a central consideration in its design, but when novel features are included it is not easy to fully understand their utility. One excellent way of gaining experience with the use of a new language as it is being designed is to implement the language in itself. This works for general purpose languages, but may be impractical for special purpose languages that are not suitable for language implementations (e.g., implementing Awk in Awk [1]).

The pragmatic perspective tends to lead designers to add features to the language to enhance its perceived expressive power or convenience, and hence there is a danger of excessive complexity and featurism, especially if the interaction of different features is not carefully considered. One of the hardest tasks in language design is judging what should be left out of the language, because every feature has its constituency. Another difficult and critical problem is to judge the expressiveness/complexity tradeoff for a given feature. This is especially tricky because the use of a particular feature in programming may involve a high mental overhead for programmers even though the feature's semantic description is relatively straightforward (e.g., first-class continuations).

In the case of Standard ML, Robin Milner's leadership guaranteed that the semantic perspective would be emphasized, especially in the earlier stages of the language design. As is often the case, Standard ML was a new member of an existing family of languages (LCF/ML, Cardelli ML, Hope), which meant that there was already a body of pragmatic and implementation experience on which to draw. However, the design of Standard ML could have benefited from further iterations to feed back early implementation and usage experience, since a number of minor design problems surfaced fairly early in the implementation efforts, but after the relevant parts of the design had been frozen (e.g., the syntactic ambiguity of nested matches).

A final piece of advice about concrete syntax design: do it last! Though it would be quite difficult to carry out a language design without using a concrete syntax, at least for testing the implementation and pragmatic aspects of the design in progress, it should be remembered that the abstract syntax is the primary embodiment of the structure of the language, and endless time and effort can be wasted on premature arguments about concrete syntax. During the course of the design a simple, provisional version of the concrete syntax should be used. Only when the language design has entered its final stages of refinement and the abstract syntax has stabilized should serious concrete syntax design begin, ensuring that the concrete syntax will faithfully represent the semantics of the language. The provisional concrete syntax should be discarded and an expert in grammars and parsing with proven good taste should be assigned the task of designing the final syntax. Syntax design is like architecture: a blend of engineering and artistry best not left to a committee.

In syntax design, beware the temptation to make a language more "palatable" to potential users by having it masquerade in the inappropriate syntax of a more familiar language (e.g., by giving a functional language a Fortran-like syntax). On the other hand, it is quite appropriate to borrow from the linguistic tradition behind a language design (*e.g.*, most Pascal family languages have similar, Pascal-style, syntax properly reflecting their semantic similarities).

4 Experience with SML

Implementations of Standard ML have now been available for about six years and have been steadily improving their capabilities. The *Definition of Standard ML* was published three years ago, followed by the *Commentary on Standard ML* ([34]), and there is now a substantial body of research publications relating to the Standard ML type and module systems and to implementation and optimization techniques. We have also accumulated considerable application experience, including the implementation of several compilers and interpreters (*e.g.*, [4]), and a large number of systems designed to support theorem proving, verification, and specification of software and hardware (*e.g.*, HOL, Isabelle ([39]), Lego ([8]), ALF (Chalmers), Jape (Oxford), Lambda Prolog (CMU and Bell Labs), Concurrency Workbench ([12, 11])). It has been used to implement a large computer-aided design system (at Abstract Hardware, Ltd.) and CASE specification tools (Design ML at Meta Software, Inc.). Standard ML has also been widely used for teaching programming at various levels and as a tool in teaching and research in programming language theory, applied logic, and formal methods.

This accumulated experience has generally validated the design of the language. The type and module system provide an extremely valuable organizational discipline and safety net that makes systems implemented in ML particularly easy to modify and maintain. The language supports the implementation of large systems very well, though the facilities to support separate compilation are still evolving.

Our experience also suggests that Standard ML is about the right size. A language should be as simple as possible, but no simpler, to paraphrase Einstein. One way of judging this is to see whether a typical programmer who is conversant with the language uses all its facilities in a typical (nontrivial) application. Standard ML meets this test. Nevertheless, we can see a number of ways in which the language could be further simplified without loss of expressiveness.

ML is also a very good prototyping language. There is a general but fallacious impression that dynamically typed languages like Lisp are more appropriate for prototyping because it is "easy" to modify Lisp programs. The reason this impression is false is that serious prototypes can be large and complex programs, and if one changes the representation of data in one part of the prototype it can be a long, error-prone, and labor intensive process to trace all the consequences of such changes when using a dynamically typed language. In contrast, our experience with the Standard ML of New Jersey compiler (about 60,000 lines of ML code) is that we can make radical changes in fundamental data representations and interfaces that affect dozens of modules and still have the compiler working again within a day. Based on personal experience, these kinds of changes in a correspondingly large Lisp program might lead to weeks of debugging, even with a careful and disciplined style of programming.

Syntax is always a contentious subject, because of the subjective, aesthetic aspect of syntax design. The concrete syntax of Standard ML has received its share of criticism, and I shall add some of my own below, but I would claim that it is reasonably successful and no one has proposed a substantially better style of syntax. The rationale behind the Standard ML syntax is that ML is a language based on the lambda calculus, but the conventional lambda calculus notation is not well-engineered for large-scale programming, so some substantial amount of "syntactic sugar" is required. Landin proposed a sugared version of the lambda calculus called ISWIM ([26]), and this formed the basis of the original LCF/ML dialect. The ISWIM syntax was fairly light-weight, and was suited to small-scale and interactive programming. However, we felt that for large-scale programming readability becomes more important relative to convenience of writing code, so Standard ML was given a somewhat heavier syntax partly inspired by the Algol/Pascal syntactic tradition. This moved the language further from the underlying lambda calculus, and this compromise between lambda-calculus and Algol-style notation is workable though not entirely comfortable. The syntax was also influenced by the local POP-2 tradition ([7]) in Edinburgh, which in turn had ISWIM and CPL ([5]) in its linguistic heritage. The syntax is still reasonably light, as indicated very roughly by comparing the total number of keywords and special signs in ML with the corresponding numbers for other languages:

Standard ML	52
Scheme	33
Haskell	39
Pascal	59
Modula 2	68
C	76
Ada	88
C++	99
Common Lisp	100+

There were also a few features of the Standard ML syntax that could be viewed as mistakes. Here is my list (most of these problems are discussed at greater length in [3]).

- The parsing of nested matches (*i.e.*, nested **case** expressions, **fn** expressions, and exception handlers) is ambiguous. This ambiguity is similar to the nested **if** statement ambiguity in Pascal and is a common source of errors, especially for novice programmers; experienced SML programmers learn to parenthesize all nested matches. This could be easily be fixed by adding a terminator (probably **end**) to these expressions.
- The infix **handle** keyword used to attach an exception handler to an expression makes it difficult to determine the textual scope of the handler when it is a large expression. This could be corrected by having an initial keyword (say **try** as in Modula 3) delineating the scope of the handler, yielding an expression of the form "**try** *expression* **handle** *match* **end**."
- There is a danger of confusing variable and constructor identifiers. It is a common form of bug to misspell a constructor name, which is then interpreted as a variable in a pattern match, silently matching anything. The obvious solution is to lexically distinguish constructors, as is done in Haskell. This solution would

force us to discard the dubious capability to implicitly coerce constructors to values.

- Lexically-scoped infix directives were an ill-advised legacy from Pop-2. They complicate parsing and they do not work well with the module system because infix directives cannot be exported by structures or specified in signatures (and it would *not* be a good idea to add such a feature). One solution would be to assign a single precedence to all members of a lexically distinguished set of infix symbols, except for a fixed set of distinguished infix operators like "+" with special precedences and associativities.
- The syntax of parameter patterns in clausal function declarations is more complex than necessary and could be simplified.

Correcting these problems would eliminate most of the substantive complaints about the syntax of Standard ML, while leaving the "look and feel" of the language essentially unchanged.

A fairly common question from programmers coming to ML from a Lisp background is whether ML should support some form of macros. The CAML dialect of ML ([9]) has actually provided a form of macros, so it can be done, but there are many well-founded objections to macros, especially in a statically typed language. Macros are an admission that the syntax of the language is incomplete or inadequate, but they are not a principled or disciplined approach to enriching a language because they have no semantics or logic of their own. The semantics of macros is normally defined in terms of their expansion into the base syntax, so all static analysis, such as type checking, would be insensitive to the existence of macros in the original program and would generate messages (*e.g.*, type error messages) that could be difficult to relate to the code as it was written.[2]

There are a number of other "features" of Standard ML that can cause difficulties or make the language less elegant than it might be. Solutions for these problems are the subject of continuing research.

- Equality types add complexity, especially in their interaction with modules, that does not appear to justified by their utility. The treatment of equality properties (equality kinds) could be generalized and made more sophisticated ([20]), but it would probably be better to simplify the language by eliminating them. See also the comments on the problems that equality types cause for library design in [6].
- Overloading has some inconvenient interactions with polymorphism, as noted in [3], because both of them dilute the type information available in different ways. Another problem with overloading is that it is treated in an *ad hoc* manner in Standard ML. There are a few special identifiers (mainly arithmetic and relational operators like "+" and "<") that are overloaded in the conventional manner in the base environment (or "basis" as it is called in the Definition of Standard ML), but user-defined overloading is not supported. But on the other hand, it would not be a good idea to permit user-defined overloading because of

---

[2] Actually, in Standard ML of New Jersey the "derived" syntax forms like while-expressions and if-expressions are essentially macros, and indeed they are not accurately presented in type error messages.

the complexities of interaction between overloading and the module system. One principle that is violated by the current treatment of overloading is that the base environment should not be special or privileged and should be constructed using the same declaration facilities available to the Standard ML programmer (except for its incorporation of certain primitive types and operators like "int" and "+). Once again the language could be simplified at the cost of slight inconvenience by eliminating overloading.

- The "open" declaration has various drawbacks. It complicates certain kinds of static analysis of ML programs, such as determining the dependency graph over a set of modules without knowing *a priori* in what order the modules are defined, a task that is relevant to an ML "make" utility such as that provided by the SourceGroup separate compilation system ([41]). The open declaration also adds considerable complexity to the implementation of the module system, especially in its most recent versions supporting higher-order modules. It would be tempting to eliminate the open declaration from the language, but it is currently the only way to import a datatype and make it a component of another module.

- The interaction between polymorphism and imperative features is handled by the less than elegant device of weak or imperative type variables (see [3, Section 3]). The main problem with this treatment is that weak types tend to propagate excessively and "infect" the types of functions that should in principle have normal polymorphic types. Further refinement of the type checking algorithm may reduce this inconvenient effect, but at the cost of making type checking more mysterious than it ought to be. A truly satisfactory solution to this problem may not possible within the framework of the current Standard ML type system and may have to await the design of a successor language, but much useful theoretical progress is being made ([29, 23, 24, 45]).

- The Definition of Standard ML specifies an *initial basis* or standard environment, but this initial basis is rather parsimonious and has been significantly extended in all implementations. Unfortunately, these extensions were not coordinated, so different ML implementations have incompatible standard environments (*e.g.*, Standard ML of New Jersey, Poly ML, and Poplog ML all provide a substring function, but they are all different!). A library devised by Dave Berry at Edinburgh can be used to provide some commonality between implementations but the ML community still faces a difficult process of convergence to a common definition of a standard environment as a basis for portability among ML compilers. Designing a good standard environment is a time-consuming and difficult job, and it depends even more than the core language design on programming experience. In retrospect, the failure to provide an adequate standard environment was a major problem with the definition.

These design flaws are all fairly minor and do not materially degrade the utility of the language. The main limitations of Standard ML have to do with its automatic memory management and the uniform, high-level view of data that automatic memory management and polymorphism entail. The memory management system involves space overheads (*e.g.*, multiple heap spaces in a copy garbage collector), and the data representation is often less efficient than in a low-level language where the programmer has detailed control over the formating of data representations.

Garbage collectors also involve latency – pauses in computation that are inconvenient for interactive applications and may be unacceptable in applications with real-time constraints.

ML shares these limitations with other garbage collected languages like Lisp and Scheme, but as compiler technology improves ML's type system will provide better opportunities for optimizing data representations ([28]). The fact that most ML values are immutable also can be exploited in various ways in memory management. With regard to latency, low-latency concurrent garbage collectors have been implemented ([25]), showing that this problem can be overcome.

5   Experiments and Extensions

The Definition of Standard ML provides a solid, stable foundation for the language, but a number of significant experimental extensions to ML have been studied, designed, and implemented. It is a testament to the flexibility of the basic language that most of these extensions can be implemented essentially as library modules, without adding new syntactic constructs to the language. These library modules may require some "magic" in the form of new implementation primitives, but the magic is not externally visible. On the other hand, some of these extensions, such as first-class continuations and the concurrency features built on them, have a profound affect on the semantics of the language and would require considerable work to incorporate into the formal definition. The discussion below is biased toward Standard ML of New Jersey, which has been the basis for most experimentation because of its open nature.

5.1   Control Constructs

The basic control constructs of ML consist of function application, recursion, case analysis, and exception transmission. Another very powerful control construct that has been extensively studied and exploited in the context of (call-by-value) functional languages is that of first-class continuations. It turned out to be possible to define a typed version of first class continuations ([16, 23]), and an efficient dynamic representation of continuations was already available in the SML of New Jersey compiler, which is based on a continuation-passing-style (CPS) representation of ML code. The only visible change required to support first-class continuations was the addition of one type constructor, `'a cont`, and two associated functions: `callcc` (call-with-current-continuation) for capturing a continuation, and `throw` for "invoking" a continuation.

First-class continuations are a very powerful, but very dangerous construct. They represent a functional version of the "go to" statement of imperative languages, and can be misused to produce higher-order versions of spaghetti code that are extremely difficult to understand. Their main benefit is their use as a wizard's tool for implementing higher-level and more disciplined control constructs. In the case of Standard ML of New Jersey, they have been used to implement several concurrency libraries, notably Concurrent ML (described in this volume, [40]) and ML Threads ([13]). These libraries also depend on a signal handling module for the implementation of preemptive scheduling, and the interface of this signal handling module is also effectively expressed in terms of continuations.

These concurrency libraries support multiple threads running within a single address space, either on single or multiple processors. The work on distributed computing with Standard ML being pursued at Cornell ([14]), the Facile group at ECRC ([18]), and Edinburgh ([33]) represents a further step, dealing with the difficult problems of asynchronous communication and transmission of ML values between address spaces in a multicomputer.

5.2 Modules

The basic module system described in the Definition was strictly first-order. One could form functors by abstracting a structure expression with respect to other structures that it depended on, but not with respect to functors that it used. But a long-term goal of the design was to provide a truly higher-order module system in which structures and functors would be treated similarly. The semantic problems involved in such a generalization have been largely solved now ([43]), and a higher-order version of the module system has been implemented ([15]) and is part of the current release of Standard ML of New Jersey. Opportunities to exploit higher-order functors arise frequently, and the new facilities increase both the symmetry and expressive power of the module system.

The implementation of higher-order functors required that some new techniques and representations be developed, but it also opened up additional possibilities to exploit the generalized mechanisms that are the subject of ongoing research. This work is aiming toward a new level of polymorphism in the higher-order module system allowing one to parameterize with respect to an unknown signature.

Another extension of the module system that is under investigation is support for type abbreviations in signatures. Many ML programmers have noted the usefulness of such abbreviations, but the interaction between type abbreviations and sharing constraints has been problematical. Dealing with sharing constraints in the presence of type abbreviations with complete generality involves solving a special form of second-order unification problem. The general problem of second-order unification is undecidable, and it may also be the case that this specialized form is also undecidable. However, it is clear that in cases of practical interest, the unification problem is almost always trivial, so it should suffice to restrict the problem to a very limited form of second-order unification that would be tractable.

5.3 Metaprogramming and separate compilation

One concept we have been exploring recently is "turning the compiler inside-out." By this I mean externalizing various internal compiler representations and processes to make them available to ML applications. The facilities that have been externalized so far include symbols, environments (static and dynamic), syntax trees, object code, and a set of compilation functions (parsing, elaborating, translating to the lambda intermediate representation, code generation, and execution). These interfaces support separate compilation, the interactive system, and other applications that need to manipulate and then execute ML code.

One currently missing element in these externalized interfaces is type **dynamic** ([30]), which we expect to add in future versions. Type dynamic has applications in metaprogramming and also in distributed programming and in supporting persistence of data.

One amusing possibility opened up by these metaprogramming facilities is that those who are unhappy with the current concrete syntax can easily define their own syntax and provide an alternate parser to support it.

ML's interfaces and static environments are rich and highly structured. Because of generative declarations and the resulting sharing relations, separate compilation for ML has to be fairly sophisticated. The SourceGroup library developed by Gene Rollins at CMU ([41]) is able to determine dependencies among a set of ML source files and minimize recompilation when changes are made. The SourceGroup system is implemented using the metaprogramming interfaces (particularly environments and the compilation interface) made available by the compiler.

5.4 Miscellaneous experiments

Other features that have been investigated and experimentally implemented are "or" patterns and vector literals and patterns. "Or" patterns allow several alternative patterns in a single match, as in `fn ((nil,x::y) | (x::y,nil)) => (x,y)`. Vector literals and patterns make it easier to construct and destruct vectors, putting them more on a par with lists. A more elaborate extension of pattern matching has been investigated by Aitken and Reppy ([2]). At the simplest level this extension supports symbolic names for constants that can be used in place of those constants in patterns. Beyond this, it supports a kind of pattern macro that could be defined in structures and specified in signatures (and therefore abstracted over by functors). This proposal has been implemented and the semantics have been fully developed.

A couple of intriguing and potentially useful variations on datatype definitions have been suggested. One is a notion of existential datatypes, described in [27]), and the other is the idea of *extensible* datatypes, which generalizes the existing type **exn**. Laufer and Odersky have implemented their version of existential datatypes, and implementing extensible datatypes is mainly a matter of adding appropriate declaration syntax.

The idea of an extensible datatype is that one declares the datatype separately from its data constructors, and an unlimited number of constructors can be introduced by constructor declarations. This is analogous to the way that exception constructors are declared. An example would be

```
datatype any;    (* data constructors to be declared separately *)
...
con (any) Int of int;
...
con (any) Real of real;
...
datatype foo = ...;
con (any) Foo of foo;
fun f(Int i) = ...
  | f(Real r) = ...
  | f(Foo x) = ...;
```

As in the case of exception constructors, all constructors that are in scope may appear in a pattern match over type **any**. Extensible datatypes are unboundedly extensible tagged unions, while type **dynamic** is an infinite tagged union using types as tags. Extensible datatypes can perform some of the functions that type dynamic might be used for.

6 ML and Object Oriented Programming

A common question these days is "Is ML an object-oriented language?" or "Can you do object-oriented programming in ML?" As usual, the answer depends on what the questioner means by "object-oriented." In any higher-order language with state, such as ML, a function closure is a rudimentary form of object. To model more sophisticated objects one can use records of functions sharing common elements of their closure environments (corresponding to *instance variables*). There is also a useful analogy viewing structures as objects and functors as classes.

If by "object-oriented programming" one means encapsulization, data abstraction, and information hiding, it can be argued that ML supports these goals more straightforwardly and more elegantly than conventional object-oriented languages, and in addition provides better mechanisms for parameterization via higher-order functions, parametric polymorphism, and functors.

What about inheritance? Many uses of inheritance are covered by the simpler notion of subtyping. Subtyping in Standard ML can often be approximated by classical variant record techniques,[3] and signature matching provides another version of subtyping at the level of modules. Consequently, many algorithms involving simple uses of subtyping can be naturally expressed in Standard ML as it is. There have been many investigations of extensions to the ML type system based on record subtyping ([10]) or polymorphism over "row variables"([44, 22]), and it is reasonable to assume that future versions of ML or its successors will provide some such extension.[4] But really serious applications of inheritance involving method specialization or delegation are not so easy to approximate directly in ML (but see [32]). However, these more "advanced" features of object-oriented programming languages have proven to be semantically very complex, and there is a good deal of evidence that programmers also have difficulty coping with them. My claim is that even without enhancements like record subtyping or row variables, Standard ML provides structuring and abstraction mechanisms that are at least as expressive as inheritance and considerably less complex from both the semantic and pragmatic perspective. Substantiating such claims regarding relative expressiveness is difficult, and will require extensive empirical investigations through comparative programming case studies.

---

[3] The use of record variants as an approximation to subtyping would be strengthened by adding extensible datatypes.

[4] See [21] for extensive coverage of the semantics and type theory of object-oriented programming languages.

7 The Future of ML

Experimentation with extensions of Standard ML as described in Section 5 above will probably taper off in the next year or so. Considerable progress is still being made in the base technologies of code generation and optimization, garbage collection and the runtime system. Active topics of investigation include representation specialization, dataflow analysis, low-level and architecture-dependent optimizations, and floating point performance. A continuing task is the development of generic libraries and tools to support ML programming. The existing set of tools for Standard ML of New Jersey is fairly extensive, including a profiler, debugger, ml-yacc and ml-lex, the SourceGroup separate compilation system, Concurrent ML, and the eXene X-window interface library, but more tools are needed. Facilities are required to enable implementations to mix ML and foreign code (*e.g.*, C), and ML application development tools must interact gracefully with conventional software tools.

New text books will be published to support the teaching of ML, and the documentation of ML implementations and programming tools must increase in quality and quantity.

In the longer term, discussions have begun on a research program leading to the design of a successor to Standard ML. This hypothetical language, known as "ML 2000" or "Millenium," [5] would be a completely new design, not upward compatible with Standard ML, but representing the next step in the evolution of the family and remaining faithful to the "essence" of ML. This language should be based on the call-by-value lambda calculus augmented with imperative features and providing a more uniform static type system (probably stratified and predicative like that of Standard ML). The type system should gracefully accommodate polymorphism and mutable references, and it may well include either a form of subtyping or "record polymorphism" based on row variables.

8 Conclusions

How well has Standard ML met its design goals? It provides safety, security, and good structuring tools for large-scale programming. It has a relatively high expressiveness to complexity ratio and seems to be the right "size" in that programmers tend to use the whole language. It has proven to be implementable, and it is possible to generate competitive code for ML programs. On the negative side there are the relatively minor design problems noted above and in [3], and the language probably shows its history more than necessary (*e.g.*, in the distinction between Core ML and the module system). ML has been and continues to be the subject of intensive research and the future promises further advances leading to new (and, one hopes, improved) languages in the ML family.

References

1. Alfred V. Aho, Brian W. Kernighan, and Peter J. Weinberger. *The AWK Programming Language*. Addison-Wesley, Reading, Massachusetts, 1988.

---

[5] As suggested by Dana Scott.

2. William E. Aitken and John H. Reppy. Abstract value constructors: symbolic constants for Standard ML. Technical Report TR 92-1290, Dept. of Computer Science, Cornell Univ., June 1992.
3. Andrew W. Appel. A critique of Standard ML. *Journal of Functional Programming*, 1993. In press.
4. Andrew W. Appel and David B. MacQueen. Standard ML of New Jersey. In Martin Wirsing, editor, *Third Int'l Symp. on Prog. Lang. Implementation and Logic Programming*, pages 1–13, New York, August 1991. Springer-Verlag.
5. D. W. Barron, J. N. Buxton, D. F. Hartley, F. Nixon, and C. S. Strachey. The main features of CPL. *Computer Journal*, 6:134–143, 1963.
6. Dave Berry. Lessons from the design of a Standard ML library. *Journal of Functional Programming*, 1993. In press.
7. R. M. Burstall, J. S. Collins, and R. J. Popplestone. *Programming in POP-2*. Edinburgh University Press, 1977.
8. Rod Burstall. Computer assisted proof for mathematics: an introduction, using the LEGO proof system. In *Proc. of the Institute of Applied Math. Conf. on the Revolution in Mathematics caused by Computing*, 1989.
9. The CAML Reference Manual (Version 2.6). Projet Formel, INRIA-ENS, March 1989.
10. Luca Cardelli. A semantics of multiple inheritance. *Information and Computation*, 76:138–164, 1988.
11. Rance Cleaveland. The concurrency workbench, 1993. In this volume.
12. Rance Cleaveland, Joachim Parrow, and Bernhard Steffen. The concurrency workbench: a semantics-based tool for the verification of concurrent systems. *ACM TOPLAS*, 15(1):36–72, January 1993.
13. Eric C. Cooper and J. Gregory Morrisett. Adding threads to Standard ML. Technical Report CMU-CS-90-186, School of Computer Science, Carnegie Mellon University, Pittsburgh, PA, December 1990.
14. Robert Cooper and Clifford Krumvieda. Distributed programming with asynchronous ordered channels in Distributed ML. In Peter Lee, editor, *Proc. of ACM SIGPLAN Workshop on ML and its Applications*, pages 134–148, June 1992.
15. Pierre Crégut. Extensions to the SML module system. Rapport de Stage d'Ingenieur Eleve des Telecommunications, November 1992.
16. Bruce Duba, Robert Harper, and David MacQueen. Typing first-class continuations in ML. *Journal of Functional Programming*, 1993. In press.
17. Karen Frenkel. An interview with Robin Milner. *Comm. of the ACM*, 36(1):90–97, January 1993.
18. Alessandro Giacalone, Prateek Mishra, and Sanjiva Prasad. FACILE: A symmetric integration of concurrent and functional programming. *International Journal of Parallel Programming*, 18(2):121–160, April 1989.
19. M. J. C. Gordon, A. J. R. G. Milner, L. Morris, M. C. Newey, and C. P. Wadsworth. A metalanguage for interactive proof in LCF. In *Proc. 5th ACM Symp. on Principles of Programming Languages*, New York, 1978. ACM Press.
20. C. A. Gunter, E. L. Gunter, and D. B. MacQueen. Using abstract interpretation to compute ML equality kinds. *Information and Computation*, 1993. In press.
21. C. A. Gunter and J. C. Mitchell. *Theoretical Aspects of Object-Oriented Programming: Types, Semantics, and Language Design*. The MIT Press, 1993.
22. C. A. Gunter and R. Rémy. A proof-theoretic assessment of runtime type errors. unpublished, 1992.
23. Robert Harper and Mark Lillibridge. Explicit polymorphism and CPS conversion. In *Proc. 13th ACM Symp. on Principles of Programming Languages*, 1993.

24. My Hoang, John Mitchell, and Ramesh Viswanathan. Standard ML weak polymorphism and imperative constructs. Ftp: ftp/pub/jcm/weak-poly.dvi on theory.stanford.edu, 1993.

25. Lorenz Huelsbergen and James R. Larus. A concurrent copying garbage collector for languages that distinguish (im)mutable data. In *ACM Symp. on Principles and Practice of Parallel Programming*, 1993.

26. P. J. Landin. The next 700 programming languages. *Communications of the ACM*, 9(3):157–66, 1966.

27. Konstantin Laufer and Martin Odersky. An extension of ML with first-class abstract types. In Peter Lee, editor, *Proc. of ACM SIGPLAN Workshop on ML and its Applications*, pages 78–91, June 1992.

28. Xavier Leroy. Unboxed objects and polymorphic typing. In *Nineteenth Annual ACM Symp. on Principles of Prog. Languages*, pages 177–188, New York, January 1992. ACM Press.

29. Xavier Leroy. Polymorphism by name for references and continuations. In *Proc. 13th ACM Symp. on Principles of Programming Languages*, 1993.

30. Xavier Leroy and Michel Mauny. Dynamics in ML. In J. Hughes, editor, *Functional Programming Languages and Computer Architecture: 5th ACM Conference (LNCS 523)*, pages 406–426. Springer-Verlag, 1991. To appear in Journal of Functional Programming, 1993.

31. David B. MacQueen. Using dependent types to express modular structure. In *Proc. 13th ACM Symp. on Principles of Programming Languages*, pages 277–286, 1986.

32. Luigi V. Mancini. A technique for subclassing and its implementation exploiting polymorphic procedures. *Software—Practice and Experience*, 18(4):287–300, April 1988.

33. David C. J. Matthews. A distributed concurrent implementation of Standard ML. Technical Report ECS-LFCS-91-174, Laboratory for Foundations of Computer Science, Edinburgh University, August 1991.

34. Robin Milner and Mads Tofte. *Commentary on Standard ML*. MIT Press, Cambridge, Massachusetts, 1991.

35. Robin Milner, Mads Tofte, and Robert Harper. *The Definition of Standard ML*. MIT Press, Cambridge, MA, 1989.

36. John C. Mitchell and Robert Harper. The essence of ML. In *Proc. 15th ACM Symp. on Principles of Prog. Languages*, pages 28–46, New York, 1988. ACM Press.

37. John Ophel. An introduction to the high-level language Standard ML. In this volume.

38. Laurence C. Paulson. *ML for the Working Programmer*. Cambridge University Press, Cambridge, 1992.

39. Lawrence C. Paulson and Tobias Nipkow. Isabelle tutorial and user's manual. Technical Report Technical Report No. 19, University of Cambridge Computer Laboratory, January 1990.

40. John H. Reppy. Concurrent ML: design, application, and semantics, 1993. In this volume.

41. Eugene J. Rollins. SourceGroup: a selective-recompilation system. In Robert Harper, editor, *Third International Workshop on Standard ML*, September 1991.

42. Konrad Slind. HOL90: not just an ugly rumor! In *Proc. of the 1991 Int'l. Workshop on the HOL Theorem Proving System and its Applications*, 1991.

43. Mads Tofte. Principle signatures for higher-order program modules. In *Proc. 19th ACM Symp. on Principles of Programming Languages*, pages 189–199, 1992.

44. Mitchell Wand. Type inference for record concatenations and multiple inheritance. In *Proc. of the Symp. on Logic in Computer Science*, pages 92–97. IEEE, June 1989.

45. Andrew K. Wright. Polymorphism for imperative languages without imperative types. Ftp: public/languages/tr93-200.[dvi,ps].Z on titan.cs.rice.edu, 1993.

An Introduction to the High-Level Language Standard ML

John Ophel

Department of Computer Science
University of Waterloo
Waterloo, Ontario N2L 3G1
CANADA

Abstract. Standard ML is a modern high-level programming language. This paper presents an introduction to the language, concentrating on the high-level features of ML that assist in managing the complex process of developing software. The features of ML examined are its type system, the functional nature of ML, and its modularization and encapsulation facilities that include abstract data types, exceptions, and modules.

1 Introduction

Developing software is a difficult, error-prone, and expensive process. Standard ML [1] is a high-level general-purpose programming language with many interesting language features that assist the programmer in managing the complexity of software development. This paper gives an overview of Standard ML, providing a background to the language and an explanation of why it has been chosen for the projects described later in the McMaster series. Hopefully, it may convince some programmers to use ML, but even for programmers that may never use ML, the high-level aspects of the language are worth examining as they explore significant and wide-ranging issues in programming and software development.

The problems associated with developing software are not new - the term "software crisis" was coined in the 1960's. Some of the major techniques for improving the production, quality, and maintenance of software are:

Modularization and Encapsulation When dealing with a complex problem, a common approach is to reduce the problem into simpler and more manageable sub-problems – the process of "dividing and conquering". Software development benefits from the same approach. Modularization is the process of dividing a large software problem into largely independent components that can be individually developed and later combined to solve the problem. Encapsulation separates the specification of a modular component from its implementation, allowing users to concentrate on *what* a component does instead of *how* it does this.

As a simple example, most programming languages provide functions that encapsulate a sequence of actions. A program can then be modularized using functions. A well-written function can be used in terms of what it does without knowing how this is done.

Component Combination Given a set of modular components it is necessary to combine these components to solve problems. There are two aspects of combination: first, there must exist mechanisms to combine or "glue" the components together, and second, there must be some mechanism that ensures that components are combined in a sensible manner.

Higher-order functions and static type systems are examples of these two aspects of combination. Higher-order functions (see Sect 4.4) are functions that take other functions as arguments and therefore glue functions together to produce new components. A static type system ensures that components are correctly combined; for example, at the function level to ensure that the arguments supplied to a function match its expected arguments.

Software Re-use If software development is difficult and error prone, then re-using existing software is an obvious technique for increasing productivity. One method of increasing re-use is to use abstraction, the process of generalizing an existing component so that it can be used in different (but similar) situations. A familiar example of abstraction is having arguments to a function.

Unfortunately many factors work against software re-use. One example is inflexible type systems that ensure components are correctly combined but prevent components being re-used in different (but safe) type domains.

Reasonable Behaviour A complex piece of software needs to be reasoned about formally (or at least informally) to argue about its behaviour, and to demonstrate that it correctly implements its required specification. To do this, the language must have a well-defined semantics and have constructs that can be reasoned about.

For a language to have a well-defined semantics, it cannot have language constructs with undefined or ambiguous behaviour. The standard definition of C[2] contains language constructs that have ambiguous behaviour; for example, the value assigned to `result` in the statement `result = i + i++;` is undefined as the order of sub-expression evaluation is not well-defined.

To have a well-defined semantics, a language must also be *safe*. In a safe language, a program cannot corrupt the run-time system so that further execution of the program is inconsistent with the language semantics[3]. In the language C an out of bounds array reference (an error) can change an arbitrary part of the run-time system so that an unrelated part of the program may not behave as expected.

It is difficult to reason about a program in a language without a well-defined semantics. If a component may behave in an arbitrary manner, a program containing such a component may behave unpredictably.

Some programming language constructs enable programs to be reasoned about more easily than others. The use of aliases, for example, complicates the understanding of a program as changing the value of a variable may also change the value of another variable. Programs written in a declarative style, i.e., in terms of what the program must do instead of how the program must achieve this, are easier to reason about than non-declarative programs. One form of declarative programming, purely functional programming, is discussed in Sect 4.6.

The preceding techniques have been used in many software projects. Unless the programming language supports these methodologies, a software project must rely on programmers correctly obeying conventions. For example, a strong type system is not necessary if components are correctly combined. A strong type system, however, prevents accidental and deliberate attempts to use an operation incorrectly. Experience has shown that programmers do make mistakes and do cut corners; without programming language support, the positive impact of these techniques is severely compromised.

ML has many high-level language features that support the techniques above. Section 2 gives a brief overview of these features of ML. The following three sections of the paper then examine important highlights of ML: its type system, its functional nature, and its mechanisms for modularization and encapsulation.

This paper does not attempt to be a comprehensive introduction to ML, many parts of the language are mentioned only briefly or not at all; the interested reader is directed to other articles described in Sect. 7.

2 Overview of Standard ML

ML is a general-purpose programming language; some of its distinctive features are listed below.

Well-defined Semantics The language ML has a well-defined semantics. The formal definition of ML gives a complete operational semantics for the language, there are no ambiguous or undefined constructs in the language and ML is safe. It is then possible to demonstrate desirable properties of the language (e.g., that invalid programs can be detected by the type system). Many other languages such as Pascal, C, and Lisp are unsafe and contain semantic ambiguities where the behaviour of a program may not be defined by the language.

Strong, Static Type System ML has a *strong, static* type system. Strong typing means that every program that is executed must be correctly typed. Static typing means that type checking can be done at compile time, all type errors are therefore detected before execution. ML's type system ensures that components are correctly combined.

Polymorphic Types The type system has *polymorphic* types. For example, it is possible to write a single routine that reverses the elements in a list, no matter what the type of the elements in the list. (In contrast, in Pascal it would be necessary to write a separate routine for each element type, even though the same operations would be performed in each routine. In C it would be possible to write one routine by circumventing the type system, losing the security of strong typing.) ML's polymorphic type system makes it possible to abstract over types and re-use existing routines over new type domains, while maintaining the security of strong, static type checking.

Inferred Type System The type system of ML is *inferred*, the user does not have to provide explicit type declarations in a program.[1] The ML system infers the most general type (or "most polymorphic" type) of a program. The absence of redundant type declarations removes unnecessary verbiage from ML programs.

---

[1] See Sect. 3.5 for one exception to this general statement.

Functional Language ML is a *functional*[2] language. Functions are first-class objects, they can be passed as arguments to functions, returned as the result of functions, and stored in data structures. Functions can be used as the "glue" that combines different components together in a system. In a purely functional style of programming (with no side-effects) it is much easier to reason about the behaviour of a program.

Abstract Data Types *Abstract data types* in ML permit a user to separate the specification of what operations may be performed on a user-defined type, and the implementation of the type. Encapsulation is supported as users of the abstract data type cannot manipulate the implementation of the type, all actions performed on the type must be done by the operations provided.

Module System The sophisticated *module* system in ML has facilities for grouping components together (structures), for typing structures (signatures), and for defining generic structures that take other structures as arguments and produce new structures (functors). ML has strong type checking across all structures and their signatures. The module system therefore supports modularization and encapsulation, and functors provide a mechanism for component combination.

Exception Mechanism ML's type-safe *exception* facility permits users to define, raise, and to handle exceptions that indicate run-time error conditions. Exceptions are necessary for the robust handling of run-time errors.

Automatic Storage Management ML includes an automatic storage management system (sometimes known as a *garbage collector*). The storage of components that are no longer used can be re-used for new components. The user is freed from the low-level concerns of managing the allocation and de-allocation of memory for objects and can instead concentrate on the problem being solved.

ML has been used successfully in many projects, for example, in the Mu-calculus and Concurrency Workbench projects that are both topics of later papers in this series.

3 The ML Type System

The ML type system contains several distinctive and interesting ideas. Aspects of the type system are described in turn; Sect. 3.6 summarizes the type system.

ML typically works in an interactive session[3] where a user enters a phrase, the phrase is evaluated, and the result is displayed.[4] All examples in this introduction use the Standard ML of New Jersey compiler [4], the system prompt is "-" and all system responses are shown in italics in this paper.

```
- val a = 1 + 2;
val a = 3 : int
```

---

[2] The term *functional* is sometimes taken to mean having no side-effects. In this paper, a language with no side-effects is called *purely functional*.

[3] Batch ML compilers are available.

[4] To read phrases from a file the function **use** takes a string (the name of a file) and reads in phrases from this file.

The user has entered the definition **val a = 1 + 2;**. The system binds the identifier **a** to the value **3** and reports that **a** has the type *int* (integer).

3.1 Primitive Values and Their Types

Integers are sequences of digits, possibly proceeded by ⁻ to indicate negative values. Integers can be added, subtracted, multiplied, divided by **div** (integer division), and compared.

Floating point numbers are represented by elements of type *real*; two real numbers are **21.3** and **⁻3.4E7**. Reals can be added, subtracted, multiplied, divided, and compared.

Type *bool* represents boolean values **true** and **false**. Boolean values can be negated by the **not** function, the **andalso** and **orelse** syntactic forms take two boolean values and return the non-strict[5] conjunction or disjunction respectively. For example,

- **(21 > 3) orelse ((1 div 0) = 0);**
val it[6] = *true : bool*

Character sequences are of type *string*. Function **size** returns the number of characters in a string, the infix operator ⁻ concatenates two strings.

- **"hello " ^ "world";**
val it = "hello world" : string

3.2 Composite Types

A composite type has values built from other types. ML has four primitive composite types: functions, records, tuples, and lists. A *function* takes a value of its argument type and returns a value of its result type. The function type operator, →, reflects this mapping. As a function value does not have a printable representation, it is shown as *fn*.

- **size;**
val it = fn : string → int

Section 4 describes how functions are defined and used.

The *record* data structure is a collection of fields, each with a label. As the fields have labels, the order of the fields is unimportant. The type of a record includes the label and type of each field.

- **{age=21,name="mary"}**
val it = {age=21,name="mary"} : {age:int,name:string}

---

[5] For example, a non-strict disjunction does not evaluate its second boolean expression if the first is true.

[6] Top-level expressions *E* are converted to definitions **val it = *E*;**. The identifier **it** can then be used like any other identifier.

A *tuple* is the Cartesian product of its components. The type of a tuple is the product of its component types. In the following example, the type of the tuple has four fields: an integer, a boolean, a tuple consisting of a real and a string, and a function from string to integer.

```
- (3,true,(3.5,"hi"),size);
val it = (3,true,(3.5, "hi"),fn) : int * bool * (real * string) * (string → int)
```

It is possible to make more than one binding in one declaration by *pattern matching*, for example, a tuple of variables to a tuple of values.

```
- val (a,b) = (not true, "hello");
val a = false : bool
val b = "hello" : string
```

A *list* is a sequence of elements. A list is *homogeneous*, i.e., all elements in the list must have the same type.

```
- [8,2,4,7];
val it = [8,2,4,7] : int list
- 8 :: (2 :: (4 :: (7 :: nil)));
val it = [8,2,4,7] : int list
```

Lists have two textual representations. The first is a sequence of elements within square brackets, the second is elements "cons-ed" (:: is the ML infix cons operator) onto the empty list, nil (or []).

The function hd returns the first element in a list,[7] tl returns the "rest" of the list with the first element removed, null returns true if its argument is the empty list, false otherwise, and finally the infix operator ◑ appends two lists together.[8]

3.3 User-defined Types

ML permits the user to define new data types. The simple form of the *datatype* definition is similar to enumerated types in C and Pascal.

```
- datatype colours = Red | Green | Blue;
datatype colours
con Blue : colours
con Green : colours
con Red : colours
```

The ML compiler reports that the *type constructor* colours is now defined, and three *datatype constructors*, Blue, Green, and Red, of type colours exist. The two uses of the word *constructor* may be confusing at first; a *type* constructor, however, builds a type, while a *datatype* constructor builds a value of the type. In the above example, colours is a constant type constructor and builds the type colours, while Blue is a constant datatype constructor and builds a value of type colours.

---

[7] The behaviour when hd is applied to an empty list is discussed in Sect. 5.3
[8] [1,2,3] ◑ [4,5,6] evaluates to [1,2,3,4,5,6]

Datatype constructors can also take an argument, they can then be thought of as a "tag" that combines with a value to make an element of the type. An example is to use a datatype definition to define a list of integers and reals.

```
- datatype intOrReal = IntTag of int | RealTag of real;
datatype intOrReal
con IntTag : int → intOrReal
con RealTag : real → intOrReal
```

```
- [IntTag 2, RealTag 3.5, RealTag 0.0, IntTag 4];
val it = [IntTag 2, RealTag 3.5, RealTag 0.0, IntTag 4] : intOrReal list
```

As lists are homogeneous in ML, it is not possible to define a list with integer and real values. This limitation is easily handled as above, by defining a list of intOrReals where the datatype constructor IntTag takes an integer argument and builds a value of type intOrReal, and RealTag does the same for a real argument. See Sect. 4.1 for a function that totals the elements in a list of intOrReal's.

Recursive datatypes can also be defined. Consider a binary tree of integers with leaf nodes representing null, and internal nodes that contain an integer and two sub-trees. A datatype modelling this representation has the definition

```
datatype bTree = Leaf | Internal of (int * bTree * bTree);
```

The expression below represents a tree with an internal node with the value 3, with a left sub-tree containing 2 and a right sub-tree containing 5.

```
Internal (3,Internal (2,Leaf,Leaf),Internal (5,Leaf,Leaf))
```

The combination of datatype constructors and pattern-matching in functions is discussed in Sect. 4.1.

3.4 Type Constructors With Arguments

In the introduction it was argued that software re-use is essential to deal with the complexity of software development. The data type definition of integer binary trees in the previous section permits a user to write applications using integer binary trees, but in many cases, certain operations apply to the tree and not to the elements in the tree. It is desirable to abstract over the type of the element of the binary tree so that the tree operations developed for integer binary trees can be re-used for different element types, say for string binary trees.

ML provides this abstraction via parametric polymorphism. Type variables, written 'a, 'b, etc, (pronounced alpha, beta, etc.) represent any type. The generalized binary tree type definition would be

```
- datatype 'a binaryTree =
      Leaf | Internal of ('a * 'a binaryTree * 'a binaryTree);
```

The type constructor binaryTree takes a type as its argument and builds a type. Different arguments to BinaryTree will therefore build different types; for example, to build an integer binary tree type and a string binary tree type.

```
- val intTree =
      Internal (3,Internal (2,Leaf,Leaf),Internal (5,Leaf,Leaf));
val intTree =
      Internal (3,Internal (2,Leaf,Leaf),Internal (5,Leaf,Leaf)) : int binaryTree
- val stringTree =
      Internal ("june",Internal ("april",Leaf,Leaf),Leaf);
val stringTree =
      Internal ("june",Internal ("april",Leaf,Leaf),Leaf) : string binaryTree
```

Section 4.4 defines a function that uses type constructor **binaryTree** to define polymorphic routines.

3.5 Overloading

ML defines a small set of overloaded operators: +, -, *, <, >, <=, and >=. An overloaded operator is an identifier that represents two or more functions; for example + represents both integer and real addition.

An overloaded identifier can be *resolved* when the context in which it is used supplies enough information to decide the particular function it represents. For example,

```
- 4 + 5;
val it = 9 : int
```

In the above expression, the overloaded + identifier is resolved to its integer instance. It is an error if an overloaded identifier cannot be resolved within its context. It may therefore be necessary for a user to add a type specification to resolve potentially ambiguous overloaded identifiers. (See Sect. 4.2 for such an example in a function definition.)

The identifiers = and <> are also overloaded. Both of these identifiers have polymorphic equality types or *eqtypes* represented as a type variable with a double quote (such as ''a). Only data types that admit equality can be compared; for example, functions cannot be tested for equality and it is a static type error to attempt to do so. The function **member** that takes an element and a list and returns true if the element is in the list, false otherwise, has the following type:

$$member : (''a * ''a\ list) \rightarrow bool$$

As function **member** uses equality to determine if the element is in the list, the type of **member** restricts arguments to be an element and a list of a type that has equality defined. It would be a type error to apply **member** to a function and a list of functions as equality is not defined over functions.

3.6 Summary

ML has a strong, static, parametrically polymorphic type system. The strong type system means all components of a construct must have the correct type. For example, the **orelse** construct works only on boolean components. The static type system means that the type of all components is known at compile time (i.e., before the program is executed) and therefore all type errors are detected at compile time. For example,

```
- size 3;
std_in:4.1-4.6 Error: operator and operand don't agree (tycon mismatch)
operator domain: string
operand: int
in expression: size 3
```

The function **size** can only be applied to strings, the application of **size** above to the integer 3 is invalid and detected at compile time.

A strong, static type system is essential when combining modular components in any programming language to ensure that components are used in a meaningful manner.

In many other programming languages, a strong type system restricts the ability to re-use software. ML's polymorphic type system means that components can be re-used. In Sect. 3.4 a polymorphic binary tree was defined. This type can be instantiated to any binary tree (such as integer binary trees, string binary trees, employee record binary trees), and, as explained in the next section, any routines that manipulate only the tree can be used on the particular instances. It is therefore possible to develop general components (such as a binary tree with operations) that can be used for many different element types in a type safe manner.

ML has an *inferred* type system. The type system will automatically infer the most general (most polymorphic) type of a phrase. It is not necessary for the user to declare the types of components, except in the case of unresolved overloaded identifiers. Although type specifications are unnecessary, many ML programmers include them with their definitions as useful documentation.

Although the polymorphic type system is essential to developing good re-usable software, there are still issues that must be addressed. Given an arbitrary binary tree, how can arbitrary routines be applied to each node? How can the implementation of the binary tree be hidden from users? These issues are examined in the following sections.

4 Functions

ML is a *functional* programming language as functions are first-class objects. Functions can be used as any other data object in ML. Just as integers can be passed as arguments to functions, returned as the results of functions, and stored in data structures, so can functions.

In a *purely functional language*, a program consists of functions and basic data types. A purely functional program has no notion of state with side-effects (such as assignment statements). Although ML has reference objects that permit side-effects, it is possible to minimize the use of side-effects so that many components in an ML system are purely functional. The absence of side-effects makes it considerably easier to reason about the behaviour of components and therefore argue that a component fulfils its specification.

4.1   Basic Function Definitions

A function in ML takes an argument and returns a result. Functions can be defined using the **fun** syntactic construct.

```
- fun odd x = (x mod 2) <> 0;
val odd = fn : int → bool
- odd 33;
val it = true : bool
```

Function **odd** takes an integer argument and returns true if it is not divisible by two, false otherwise. The system responds that a binding is made to identifier **odd**. The type of the function indicates a mapping from an integer argument to a boolean result.

Functions bound by the **fun** construct can be recursive, for example the factorial function.

```
- fun fact n = if (n=0) then 1 else n * fact (n-1);
val fact = fn : int → int
```

It is possible to build anonymous functions in ML using the **fn** construct.[9] In the following example, the lambda expression **fn .. => ..** has an argument **x** and its body is the expression **(x mod 2) <> 0**. On application, the formal argument **x** is bound to the actual argument **444** and the body evaluated.

```
- (fn x => (x mod 2) <> 0) 444;
val it = false: bool
```

The **fun** construct is syntactic sugar for a recursive **val** binding to a **fn** form.

ML provides a convenient syntactic form called *pattern matching* for functions. A function can be defined with patterns in the argument positions, an actual argument to the function is matched against the patterns and the body of the first matching pattern is evaluated. The factorial function can be re-written as

```
fun fact 0 = 1
  | fact n = n * fact (n-1);
```

The first clause (line) of function **fact** matches the case where the argument is 0, returning the the result 1. The second clause matches all other (non-zero) arguments, binds n to the argument, and then evaluates the right-hand side of the clause. Each clause in a function definition must have the same function name and the same number of arguments.

A function to sum a list of the datatype *intOrReals* has the form

```
fun total [] = 0.0
  | total ((IntTag i)::xs) = (real i) + (total xs)
  | total ((RealTag r)::xs) = r + (total xs);
```

The first clause of function **total** defines the total of an empty list to be zero. The next clause pattern matches a non-empty list that has an **IntTag** element cons-ed

---

[9] **fn** is pronounced "lambda" in ML for historical reasons.

onto the rest of the list. The pattern matching binds i to the integer value of the first element in the list, and xs is bound to the rest of the list. The right-hand side of the clause converts the integer i to a real and adds it to the total of the rest of the list. The final clause adds the value of a RealTag element that is the head of the list to the total of the rest of the list.

The pattern-matched form of function definition is often more readable and easier to understand then a complicated series of if-then-else statements.

4.2 Curried Functions

Functions in ML take only one argument. To pass two arguments to a function it is necessary to pass them as the two fields of a tuple.

```
- fun plus (x:int,y) = x + y;¹⁰
val plus = fn : (int * int) → int ¹¹
```

It is, however, possible to define *curried* functions where a function takes one argument and returns a function, itself taking another argument.

```
- fun plusC x = fn (y:int) => x + y;
val plusC = fn : int → (int → int) ¹²
```

The type of function plucC can be read as, plusC is a function that takes an integer argument and returns a function that takes an integer argument and returns an integer. Curried functions permit functions to be specialized by being partially applied.

```
- val incByOne = plusC 1;
val incByOne = fn : int → int
- (incByOne 5,incByOne 36);
val it = (6,37) : int * int
```

The function plusC could have been equivalently defined using the convenient fun form:

```
- fun plusC x (y:int) = x + y;
val plusC = fn : int → (int → int)
```

In the following sections, many functions are defined in curried form and can then be partially applied.

---

¹⁰ The type specification is necessary to resolve the overloaded identifier + to integer addition.

¹¹ As * has higher precedence than →, brackets are not necessary, they are shown here to emphasize that plus takes a tuple as its first argument.

¹² As → is right associative, the brackets are not required; again, they are shown for emphasis.

4.3 Polymorphic Functions

Section 3.4 discussed the notion of polymorphic types. A polymorphic function is one that has a polymorphic type, i.e., a type with polymorphic type variables. What is the type of the function hd that returns the first element in a list? For example,

```
hd [1,2,3,4] returns 1
hd [true,false] returns true
hd [(3,true),(7,false),(0,true)] returns (3,true)
```

hd can work over lists of any type - integer lists, or boolean lists, or lists of integer and boolean tuples. In ML the type of hd is *'a list* → *'a*, i.e., hd takes a list of arbitrary type and returns an element of that type.

Polymorphic functions can be defined as any other ML function, the type system infers the most general type possible. For example, consider a function that counts the number of elements in a list,

```
- fun length [] = 0
  | length (x::xs) = 1 + length xs;
```
val length = fn : 'a list → int

Function length is defined by the recursive equations that the length of an empty list is 0, and the length of a non-empty list is 1 (for the first element) plus the length of the rest of the list. As the definition of length makes no assumptions about the type of the elements of its argument list, the type of the elements can be any type.

Polymorphic functions can similarly be defined over user-defined types (see mapBinaryTree in the next section).

4.4 First-Class Functions

Functions in ML are first-class objects, in other words they can be treated like any other data object in ML. Currying is an example of a function being returned as the result of a function. First-class functions permit many interesting, flexible and convenient programming constructs to be defined.

A function that takes a function as an argument is known as a *higher-order* function. Higher-order functions are very useful for combining other functions in interesting forms.

A common operation when programming is to create a new list by performing an operation to each element of an existing list; for example, producing a new list built from elements of the original list with each element squared.

```
- fun map f [] = []
    | map f (x::xs) = (f x) :: (map f xs);
```
val map = fn: ('a → 'b) → 'a list → 'b list
```
- map sq [1,2,3,4];
```
val it = [1,4,9,16] : int list
```
- map (fn x => x=0) [1,0,44,34,0];
```
val it = [false,true,false,false,true] : bool list

Function **map** takes a function and a list. If the list is empty it returns the empty list, otherwise it applies the function to the first element in the list and cons-es this onto the function mapped over the rest of the list. In the first use of **map**, its functional argument **sq** has type *int → int*. The type variables **'a** and **'b** in **map** are both instantiated to *int* and the final result is a list of integers. In the second use of **map**, the functional argument has type *int → bool*, and therefore the type variable **'a** of **map** is instantiated to integer and the type variable **'b** is instantiated to boolean.

A similar function mapBinaryTree constructs a new tree where each node in the new tree is the result of applying a function to the corresponding node in a polymorphic binary tree (defined in Sect. 3.4).

```
- fun mapBinaryTree f Leaf = Leaf
  | mapBinaryTree f (Internal (v,left,right)) =
    Internal (f v, mapBinaryTree f left, mapBinaryTree f right);
  val mapBinaryTree = fn : ('a → 'b) → 'a binaryTree → 'b binaryTree
```

In a language without polymorphism, it would be necessary to define a different routine for each type of binary tree used in the program. Similarly, in a language without higher-order functions, it would be necessary to define a different routine for each operation that is applied to all nodes of the binary tree. Both polymorphism and higher-order functions therefore encourage code re-use, as demonstrated in the routines **map** and **mapBinaryTree**.

4.5 List Comprehensions

Higher-order functions are a powerful method of combining existing functions. An interesting use of higher-order functions is programming with list comprehensions. A list comprehension generates a list of possible solutions and then applies a predicate to the possible solutions to produce the actual list of solutions. The use of higher-order functions allows the predicate and the list of possible solutions to be separately developed, and then combined to solve the required problem.

As a simple example, consider the problem of generating a list of all the odd numbers between one and ten. The list comprehension model generates a list of the integers between one and ten and applies a predicate testing for oddness to produce the solution set.

A predicate **odd** is defined to test if an integer is odd. The infix function **--** is used to generate the list of possible solutions. This function takes two integer values and produces a list of all integers between these values. Declaring function **--** as an infix identifier is syntactic sugaring that improves the readability of the program.[13]

```
- fun odd x = (x div 2 <> 0);
  val odd = fn : int → bool
- fun -- (low,high) =
            if (low>high) then [] else low::(-- (low+1,high));
  val -- = fn : int * int → int list
- infix --;
```

---

[13] Any function that takes a tuple with two fields can be declared as infix. The function call **f(x,y)** is then written **x f y**.

```
- 1 -- 10;
```
val it = [1,2,3,4,5,6,7,8,9,10] : int list

Function `filter` is the mechanism that combines the predicate and the list of possible solutions, and returns a new list containing all the elements in the argument list that satisfy the predicate.

```
- fun filter p [] = []
  | filter p (x::xs) =
        if (p x) then x::(filter p xs) else (filter p xs);
```
val filter = fn: ('a → bool) → 'a list → 'a list

A list containing the odd integers between one and ten can then be generated:

```
- filter odd (1 -- 10);
```
val it = [1,3,5,7,9] : int list

4.6 Programming In A Purely Functional Style

Interesting examples of programming in ML have been presented in the previous sections. None of the examples used operations that rely on a notion of the program state (such as assignment). The purely functional programming style is based on the notion of functions and evaluation that depends only on the arguments to the function.

The purely functional style of programming has the advantage that it is possible to reason about programs as mathematical objects. A given expression will always evaluate to the same value. In comparison, in the *imperative* programming style, the evaluation of an expression depends on the state. This leads to much greater complexity in reasoning about evaluation.

Consider the definition of `length` in Sect. 4.3. Does this definition of `length` correctly implement the *length* function? The specification of *length* is that the length of an empty list is 0, and the length of an element cons-ed onto a list L is one more than the length of L. It is no accident that this is very similar to the definition of `length` - purely functional languages are high-level in that the user programs at the specification level, not at the implementation level. As functions are mathematical objects, it is simple to make an inductive argument that `length` is correctly defined. For the base case, prove that the empty list ([]) returns 0 for the length. For the induction, assume that list L has length n, and prove that $(x::L)$ has length $1+n$.

4.7 Reference Objects in ML

In the previous section, the pure functional fragment of ML was discussed. ML does have non-functional operations that rely on changes to the program state. In some situations the use of side-effects are a natural and efficient abstraction; as argued in the previous section there are many cases where they are unnecessary and not required.

Reference objects in ML have type *ref* and "point" to a value that can be changed by the assignment operator :=. The value of a reference object can be accessed by the de-reference operator !.

```
- val x = ref 0;
val x = ref 0 : int ref
- x := 4;
val it = () : unit
- !x;
val it = 4 : int
- (x := (!x) + 1; !x);
val it = 5 : int
```

In the above example, x is a reference to an integer value. The value is changed by the assignment operation. The result of an assignment operation is () of type *unit*, the ML void type. In the final phrase, a sequence of expressions is executed, the first performing a side-effect and the second returning a value. The result of the phrase is the final expression in the sequence.

Standard ML includes an array data structure where the individual array elements can be updated by side-effects.

5 Modularization and Encapsulation Mechanisms in ML

This section examines four mechanisms that support modularization and encapsulation in ML. These include a mechanism for hiding local definitions in expressions and declarations, an abstract data type construct that permits the implementation of a type to be "hidden" from users of the type, and a sophisticated module system for programming in the large. As well, an exception facility provides a robust mechanism for controlling deviant run-time conditions across modularized components.

5.1 Local Definitions

It is often necessary to define temporary definitions within an expression or a declaration. These temporary definitions are local to the current phrase and should not be visible outside the phrase. The let construct binds local definitions within an expression, the local construct binds local definitions within a declaration.

```
- let val a = 2 + 3 in a * a end;
val it = 25 : int
- local val a = 2 + 3 in val b = a * a end;
val b = 25 : int
```

In both of the examples above, the local binding to a is not visible outside the let or local construct.

5.2 Abstract Data Types

Encapsulation provides the ability to concentrate on the specification of a component and to hide implementation details. Abstract data types define a new type while hiding the details of how the type is actually implemented.

Consider the type *set* implemented as a list. The empty set is represented by the empty list. Adding an element to a list is done by "cons-ing" it onto the list, the set operations member and union can be defined as operations on lists. Although this representation encourages users to think in terms of sets, it is possible to manipulate sets via their list implementation.

If a decision is made to change the implementation of sets, perhaps to binary trees for improved access costs, any applications using the set type through its defined interface (the empty set, add, union, member) will continue to work. Any applications using the set type that manipulate the list implementation directly will no longer work. It is therefore desirable for the programming language to provide a mechanism that enforces encapsulation and requires applications to use only the defined interface.

An abstract data type prevents direct manipulation of the implementation by defining a type and a set of operations on the type where the implementation of the type is hidden from the user. The user must manipulate the abstract data type through the operations defined (emptySet, add, member, and union).

```
- abstype 'a set = Rep of 'a list
  with
    val emptySet = Rep []
    local
      fun mem e [] = false
        | mem e (a::b) = (e=a) orelse mem e b;
    in
      fun add e (Rep s) =
              if mem e s then (Rep s) else (Rep (e::s))
      fun member e (Rep s) = mem e s
      fun union (Rep s1) (Rep s2) =
        let val newElements =
              maplist (fn x => if (mem x s1) then [] else [x]) s2
        in
          Rep (s1 @ newElements)
        end
    end
  end;
  type 'a set
  val emptySet = - : 'a set
  val add = fn : ''a → ''a set → ''a set
  val member = fn : ''a → ''a set → bool
  val union = fn : ''a set → ''a set → ''a set
```

The above definition of the abstract data type set uses lists to implement the sets. The bindings reported by the ML compiler, however, hide this implementation information. The binding to emptySet, for example, is shown as - to indicate that its representation is hidden. Recall from Sect. 3.5 that as add, member and union use equality, they are restricted to types that admit equality, hence the ''a type variable.

The implementations of the functions are fairly straightforward. In each case the set representation (using Rep) must be "untagged" to access the list implementation that is manipulated before being re-tagged. The maplist function used in union is similar to function **map** except it appends rather than cons-es the application of the functional argument to elements in the list.

Any changes to the implementation of the abstract data type are transparent to the user. All code that uses abstract data type *set* will still work if the implementation is changed but the specification is maintained (e.g., to change the implementation to a binary tree for efficiency reasons).

It would be possible to use a programming convention for "abstract data types" without programming language support. All users would be required to respect and adhere to the operations provided by the data type. Without programming language support, however, there is no way to enforce the correct interface.

The use of abstract data types encourages projects to write simple, correct implementations of data types that can be easily improved later (e.g., for better time or space efficiency) as required.

5.3 Exceptions

What does it mean to apply **hd** to an empty list? To divide by zero? In ML, these run-time errors cause an exception to be raised. An exception propagates back through the dynamic calling sequence until either it is caught or it reaches the top-level where it is reported as an uncaught exception.

```
- hd [];
uncaught exception Hd
- 1 div 0;
uncaught exception Div
```

Exceptions may be caught (handled) within an ML **handle** construct. The handle construct consists of an expression and an exception matching pattern. The expression is evaluated as normal in ML. If it successfully evaluates, its result is returned as the result of the handle construct. If it raises an exception, the patterns are matched (left to right) to find a matching pattern. If one is found, the body of the pattern is evaluated and returned as the result of the handle construct. If no matching exception is found, the exception continues through the dynamic calling sequence.

```
- (1 div 0) handle Div => 0 | Hd => 1;
val it = 0 : int
- (1 div 0) handle Hd => 1;
uncaught exception Div
```

Exceptions can be defined and raised by the user.

```
- exception NotFound
- fun find x [] = raise NotFound
    | find x (y::ys) = if (x=y) then y else (find x ys);
val find = fn : ''a → ''a list → ''a
- find 4 [1,2,3];
uncaught exception NotFound
```

Exceptions can also be defined to have arguments. Pattern matching can then be performed on the exception and the value of its argument.

Exceptions provide a robust mechanism that assist in delegating the responsibility of different components in a system. For example, the function **find** above fulfils the following contract, given an element and a list containing the element, the element is returned. What should the behaviour of **find** be if it is called incorrectly where the element does not appear in the list? In this case, **find** raises an exception to indicate that it did not adhere to its contract as the pre-conditions of the contract were not fulfilled by its caller.

Systems without exceptions usually rely on routines returning an error code to indicate success or failure. The caller of the routine should then check to ensure that the called routine did in fact succeed. Unfortunately there is no programming language mechanism to enforce this convention and prevent programs behaving incorrectly due to unchecked error codes.

5.4 The ML Module System

ML has a sophisticated module system for "programming in the large". When programming in the large, software development is concerned with managing large and complex projects. In these projects there may be many programmers working at one time, it may be that no one programmer understands all of the system, and the project may be evolving as project specifications change over time. The techniques of modularization and encapsulation are necessary to partition the project into manageable modules that communicate through well-defined interfaces.

The ML module system has three components. *Structures* group types, values, exceptions, and other structures into a single collection (or module). The components C_i of a structure S are not directly visible outside the structure and are accessed by the "dot" notation, i.e., $S.C_i$. Structures therefore provide a mechanism for controlling name spaces, developers of different structures do not have concern themselves with possible name clashes caused by conflicting names outside the structure.

```
- structure S = struct val x = 10; val y = (x,x) end;
structure S : sig val x : int val y : int * int end
- S.x;
val it = 10 : int
```

On defining the structure S, the system reports that structure S is defined and the "type" of S is a *signature* with the data type and value bindings of the type shown.

Signatures, the second component of the ML module system, can be thought of as the interfaces of modules. Signatures can be bound to identifiers, as in the following example.

```
- signature SSIG = sig val x : int end;
signature SSIG : sig val x : int end
```

A signature indicates the components that a structure must have. A signature can be used to constrain a structure (e.g., **structure S: SSIG = ..**). Any components in a constrained structure that are not specified by the signature are removed from the structure by a process known as *thinning*. For example, in the following phrases, structure **NewS** is defined as a thinned version of structure **S** and an attempt to access component **y** is therefore an error.

```
- structure NewS: SSIG = S;
structure NewS : SSIG
- NewS.x;
val it = 10 : int
- NewS.y;
std_in:3.1-3.6 Error: unbound variable or constructor y in path NewS.y
```

The third component of the module system are *functors* which can be loosely thought of as functions over structures. Functors are the mechanism provided by ML to combine module-level components into new modules. A functor takes a structure matching its formal parameter signature and produces another structure.[14] ML does not allow functors that take two or more structures as arguments, this minor syntactic restriction can be avoided by grouping the desired argument structures into one structure and using this structure as the argument.[15] ML also has a *sharing* mechanism that permits a signature for a structure containing two (or more) sub-structures to require a type appearing in two (or more) of its sub-structures to be the same. See Tofte [5] for an example of using sharing constraints.

The module system is best demonstrated on a "real" example. Consider a matrix package that lets matrices be created and multiplied. The functor **Matrix** takes a structure **Field** of signature **FieldSig** and produces a structure adapted for the particular argument. A **Field** must contain a type **element** (the type of elements in matrix), operations **times** and **plus** as well as a value **zero**.

The definition of signature **FieldSig** reflects the requirements of functor **Matrix**.

```
signature FieldSig=
sig
  type element
  val times : element * element -> element
  val plus : element * element -> element
  val zero : element
end;
```

The functor **Matrix** produces a structure with an abstract data type **matrix** that has an exception **MatrixError** and two associated routines **mkMatrix** and **multiply**. Notice that the components of the argument **Field** are used in various routines, for example in function **total**, **Field.zero** is used.

Matrices are represented as a tuple of three fields: an integer that is the number of rows, an integer that is the number of columns, and a function that given a row and column returns the corresponding entry. (ML arrays would have been a more efficient solution but a far less interesting programming exercise.) Note that the function **nth** takes a list and an integer i and returns the $(i-1)^{th}$ element in the

---

[14] In Ada terms, a structure is similar to a package body, a signature to a package specification, and a functor to a generic package.

[15] The New Jersey ML compiler has a non-standard extension permitting multiple arguments to a functor.

list. The function mkMatrix assumes that its argument is well-defined; a list of rows (represented as lists) where each row has the same number of elements.

```
functor Matrix(Field: FieldSig) =
struct
  abstype matrix = M of int * int * (int -> int -> Field.element)
  with
    local
      fun row (M (r,c,m)) i = fn j => m i j;
      fun col (M (r,c,m)) j = fn i => m i j;
      fun vectorMultiply (v1,v2,n) =
        let
          fun total 0 = Field.zero
            | total k = Field.plus(total(k-1),Field.times(v1 k,v2 k))
        in
          total n
        end

    in
      exception MatrixError
      fun mkMatrix l =
        M (length l,
           length (hd l),
           fn i => fn j => nth (nth (l,i-1),j-1))
      fun multiply (m1 as M(r1,c1,_),m2 as M(r2,c2,_)) =
        if (r2<>c1) then raise MatrixError
        else M(r1,
               c2,
               fn i => fn j => vectorMultiply(row m1 i,col m2 j,c1))
    end (* local *)
  end (* abstype/with *)
end (* Matrix *);
```

Functor Matrix can then be used to create particular matrix structures for different fields. For example, a matrix of integers,

```
structure IntegerField =
struct
  type element = int
  val times = (op *)[16] : int * int -> int
  val plus = (op +) : int * int -> int
  val zero = 0
end;
structure IntegerMatrix = Matrix(IntegerField);
```

Booleans also define a field where times corresponds to conjunction and plus corresponds to disjunction. A matrix of booleans can then be defined using functor

---

[16] An infix operator can be used in normal (non-infix) mode by using the op operator

Matrix.

```
structure BooleanField =
struct
  type element = bool
  fun times x y = x andalso y
  fun plus x y = x orelse y
  val zero = false
end;
```

```
structure BoolMatrix = Matrix(BooleanField);
```

The above matrix package example is clearly deficient as the elements of matrices cannot be displayed. A routine displayMatrix could be included in functor Matrix, a Field would then be required to contain a function display for printing elements.

Although the ML module system has been presented a tool for handling the complexity of "programming in the large", the module system provides a useful and practical framework for ML programs of any size.

6 Extensions to ML

The next two sections describe some current work investigating extensions to ML.

6.1 Overloading and Implicit Parameters

As described in Sect 3.5, the overloading mechanism in ML is fairly limited. A user cannot define new overloaded identifiers, and overloaded identifiers must be fully resolved in the context in which they appear. For example, the definition

```
- fun double x = x + x;
```
std_in:2.18 Error: overloaded variable "+" cannot be resolved

is invalid in ML as the overloaded identifier + cannot be resolved to either integer or real addition.

A user could define a more general version of double passing the addition operation as a parameter:

```
- fun double plus x = plus(x,x);
```
*val double = fn : ('a * 'a → 'b) → 'a → 'b*
```
- double (op +) 3;
```
val it = 6 : int

This more general version of double requires the explicit declaration of the abstraction over +, and each call to double must explicitly provide an addition operation. The disadvantage of this scheme is that the more a function is abstracted (promoting code re-use) the more work a user of the function must do to provide all the arguments correctly. This dissuades the use of general functions; users either demand simple specific functions or are encouraged to write their own specialized versions, contrary to the idea of code re-use.

A more flexible overloading scheme implemented as part of the watML system[6] makes implicit the explicit requirements at the definition and call sites in the example above. The system automatically converts unresolved overloaded identifiers into *implicit* parameters of the function, and these implicit parameters are inferred and automatically provided at call site.

Implicit parameters are denoted [?<identifier>:<type>] in watML type expressions. For example, in watML the user can define and use **double**:

```
- fun double x = x + x;
val double = fn : [?+: 'a * 'a → 'a] 'a → 'a
- (double 3, double 3.4);
val it = (6,6.8) : int * real
```

One advantage to this more general overloading scheme is that equality can be treated as an overloaded operation and there is therefore no need for the ML type system to include the special-purpose feature of eqtypes to handle equality.

Although the watML experiment has proved very promising, there remain technical details to be clarified. The main issue is balancing the desire to resolve overloaded identifiers versus abstracting over them. Abstracting produces more general types, but at some point the implicit parameters must be resolved. Various schemes are being examined to find one that is intuitive, well-defined, and expressive. General decidable resolution algorithms are currently being developed for the various schemes.

The language Haskell [7] has also explored overloading in a language with parametric polymorphism.

What is the relation between overloading using implicit parameters and ML's current type system? ML's parametric polymorphism permits abstraction over types where both declaration and instantiation are performed implicitly by the system. ML's module system permits functors to abstract over types, operations and exceptions but requires explicit declaration of the type of arguments to functors and the explicit instantiation of functors. Overloading provides the implicit instantiation of types and overloaded operations. Overloading therefore extends the expressiveness of parametric polymorphism, and is more convenient but less expressive than the module system.

6.2 Concurrency

Two recent concurrent extensions to the New Jersey Standard ML compiler have exploited the underlying architecture of this implementation. Using the *continuation* based implementation, the two extensions have examined alternative forms of concurrency.

Message-Passing

Concurrent ML[8] (CML) views concurrency as a useful programming paradigm, independent of any speed-ups due to parallel implementation. CML is based on the message-passing model of concurrency where processes interact via synchronized communication on typed channels.

CML is the topic of a later paper in the McMaster series.

Threads

A thread system for ML has been designed and implemented[9]. Threads are light-weight processes that communicate via shared memory. The low-level abstraction of threads can be used to implement other concurrency mechanisms; for example, implementing channels for a message-passing system.

The ML implementation includes **fork** that takes a function as an argument and commences evaluation of this function in a new thread. Mutual exclusion locks provide a mechanism to co-ordinate shared resources. Condition variables enable one thread to wait until another thread signals that some event has occurred.

The thread system has been implemented using both co-routines and preemption scheduling on a uni-processor and in a multi-processor version based on the Mach[10] operating system.

Although the thread system demonstrates that threads can be added to ML, the semantics of thread systems invalidate the formal semantics of ML. Current work is exploring various formal semantics for ML that incorporate threads.

7 Conclusions

ML provides mechanisms that assist in managing the complexity of developing software. Functions, abstract data types, exceptions, and modules assist in the process of modularization and encapsulation. Higher-order functions and functors provide mechanisms for combining these modular components; ML's strong, static type system checks that components are correctly combined. ML's polymorphic type system, along with higher-order functions and its module facility, encourage and allow reusable software components to be implemented and used. Finally, its well-defined semantics and functional nature permit the user to reason about the behaviour of ML programs.

This introduction has been far from comprehensive, many parts of the ML language have only been briefly covered, if at all. There are two excellent technical reports that describe ML. Harper [11] is a thorough and very readable introduction to ML (an up-to-date version of this report is available by anonymous ftp from `princeton.edu` in `/pub/ml`). A very lucid tutorial on the module system is contained in Tofte[5]. Both of these sources are highly recommended to anyone wishing to learn more about ML.

Two books covering ML are available: Wikstrom [12] is an introduction to programming using ML, Paulson [13] is intended for programmers wishing to learn about ML.

The strengths and weaknesses of ML are discussed by Appel [3].

See also Reade [14] for a discussion of pure functional programming and type systems such as ML's. Hughes [15] argues convincingly that pure functional programming is an important concern. Finally, Meyer [16] contains a good introduction to the difficulties of developing software and possible programming language solutions.

References

1. R. Milner, M. Tofte, and R. Harper. *The Definition of Standard ML*. The MIT Press, Cambridge, 1990.

2. ANSI. *American National Standard for Information Systems - Programming Language - C (ANSI Document ANSI X3.159-1989)*. American National Standards Institute, New York, 1990.

3. A. Appel. A critique of Standard ML. Technical report, CS-TR-364-92, Princeton University, February 1992.

4. A. Appel and D. MacQueen. A Standard ML compiler. In *Functional Programming Languages and Computer Architecture*, pages 301–324. Springer-Verlag Lecture Notes In Computer Science 274, 1987.

5. M. Tofte. Four lectures on Standard ML. Technical report, Report ECS-LFCS-89-73, Laboratory for Foundations of Computer Science, Computer Science Department, Edinburgh University, 1989.

6. J. Ophel, G. Cormack, and D. Duggan. Combining overloading and parametric polymorphism in ML. Technical report, CS-92-04, Department of Computer Science, University of Waterloo, 1992.

7. P. Hudak, S. Peyton Jones, and P. Wadler (eds). Report on the programming language Haskell. Technical report, March 1992. version 1.2.

8. J. Reppy. CML: A higher-order concurrent language. In *SIGPLAN'91 Conference on Programming Language Design and Implementation*, pages 293–305. SIGPLAN Notices 26(6), 1991.

9. E. Cooper and G. Morrisett. Adding threads to Standard ML. Technical report, CMU-CS-90-186, School of Computer Science, Carnegie Mellon University, 1990.

10. M. Accetta, R. Baron, W. Bolosky, D. Golub, R. Rashid, A. Tevanian, and M. Young. Mach: A new kernel foundation for UNIX development. In *USENIX Association Summer Conference Proceedings*, pages 93–112, 1986.

11. R. Harper. Introduction to Standard ML. Technical report, Report ECS-LFCS-86-14, Laboratory for Foundations of Computer Science, Computer Science Department, Edinburgh University, 1986.

12. A. Wikström. *Functional Programming Using Standard ML*. Prentice-Hall, Hertfordshire, 1987.

13. L.C. Paulson. *ML for the Working Programmer*. Cambridge University Press, Cambridge, 1992.

14. C. Reade. *Elements of Functional Programming*. Addison-Wesley, Reading, MA, 1989.

15. J. Hughes. Why functional programming matters. *The Computer Journal*, 32(2):98–107, 1989.

16. B. Meyer. *Object-oriented Software Construction*. Prentice-Hall, Hertfordshire, 1988.

Generating an Algorithm for Executing Graphical Models

Jawahar Malhotra and Robert M. Shapiro

Meta Software Corporation
125 CambridgePark Drive
Cambridge, MA 02140
USA

Abstract. Executable graphical models based on an underlying mathematical framework are very useful in the specification and design of complex systems. The major contribution of this paper is to show how such a general graphical modeling language can be "compiled" and executed. The paper takes a pragmatic approach by presenting, in reasonable detail, how such a model can be translated into a series of functions and then describes the execution as a sequence of function applications. The ideas are then extented to work for hierarchical graphical models.

1 Introduction

Graphical methods are being used more and more frequently in the specification and design of complex systems. The resulting models provide a basis for validating the design *concepts* because they can be understood by the original customer and scrutinized to determine whether the customer's requirements have been satisfied.

The model can then serve as a guide to the implementation of the real system. In current practice models are not *executable* and therefore do not address details of behavior. Validation of behavior occurs only after implementation. As a corollary, performance issues are addressed only after debugging the implementation. Serious bugs or performance limitations discovered at this stage often necessitate redesign and can be very expensive to correct.

Executable models are now being introduced into practice. In general they may be classified roughly into two categories:

1. models based on an underlying mathematical framework
2. models based on an ad hoc graphical representation tied to conventional programming languages.

Models in both categories can be executed. In that sense they can be thought of as a new mode of programming. Models in category 1, those based on an underlying mathematical framework, offer the possibility of formal analysis. By this we mean the ability to *analyze* the model, and discover from the analysis, behavioral properties. These properties include: deadlock, safety and various forms of invariance. They extend in some cases to performance evaluation as in Markovian analysis.

This paper focuses on the issue of deducing, from a graphical model based on an underlying mathematical framework, an algorithm for executing the model.

2 Flat Model

We first present a method for generating an algorithm for executing a flat (e.g. nonhierarchical) model. In the sequel we will generalize this approach to hierarchical models.

Intuitively, a *flat model* (figure 1) is a dataflow representation of a computational process. More formally, it is a bipartite directed graph with the vertex set partitioned into two sets. The two sets are referred to as *transitions* and *places* represented by rectangles and ellipses respectively (as in Petri Nets) [1]. The transitions denote elements of action; the places denote local states which may be viewed as the inputs and outputs of the transitions to which they are directly connected. The orientation of the connecting arc determines whether a place is an input or output. We continue with our discussion using this terminology although it should be clear that our method is independent of these representational details. In addition, graph models with only one vertex type (marked graphs, SADT models and data flow diagrams) [2, 3] can be trivially mapped into this bipartite framework [4].

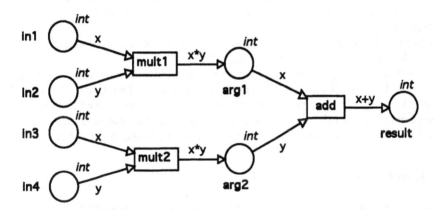

Fig. 1. A Simple Example of a Flat Model

A place is analogous to a variable in programming languages in that it contains structured values. It is different in that it can hold from 0 to any number of values, each of which is separately accessible. New values are put in the place by the occurrence of transitions that have the place as an output. Values are removed (read) by the occurrence of transitions that have the place as an input. Thus the values can be perceived as tokens that flow in the model. A place has two primary attributes:

1. *Color set.* A color set is analogous to a type in programming languages and specifies the set of legal contents for the place.
2. *Marking.* A marking is analogous to a value in programming languages. It is a *multi-set* which specifies symbolically the set of *tokens* that reside on the place. The *state* of a flat model is a function mapping each place to its marking.

In the example above we have added a third attribute: the *name* of the place. This plays no formal role in the model. Note also that the marking has been left out of the example.

A transition is analogous to a set of assignment statements in a conventional programming language; to a function in functional programming languages and to a rule in PROLOG. It can be viewed as a function which maps places values to places values. A transition has associated with it a number of attributes:

1. *Input Places.* The arcs from the input places to the transition are called the input-arcs of the transition and the inscriptions on the arcs the input arc-expressions of the transition.
2. *Output Places.* The arcs from the transition to its output places are called the output-arcs of the transition and the inscriptions on the arcs the output arc-expressions of the transition.
3. *Variables.* The set of all variables associated with a transition T, also written as $V(T)$, is the set of variables which appear in its input and/or output arc-expressions. The set of all input variables, $IV(T)$ is the set of variables which appear on the input arcs; analogously for $OV(T)$. Hence $V(T) = IV(T) \cup OV(T)$. All variables x in $V(T)$ such that x not in $IV(T)$ are known as free variables. It is important to note that the scope of all variables in $V(T)$ is local to the transition T.
4. *Guard.* A list of boolean expressions which constrain the possible combination of values assumed by the variables in $V(T)$.
5. *Code Segment.* A program fragment to be executed each time the transition T occurs. The variables in $IV(T)$ may be used as inputs. The variables in $OV(T)$ may be assigned values as outputs. Reference variables mentioned in other code segments but not otherwise in the model may be used as values or assigned new values. For brevity sake, we do not discuss code segments in the sequel.

3 Simulating a Flat Model

Given a flat model in state S_1, let us examine how it changes to state S_2. Recall that the state is a mapping from each place to its corresponding marking. The model can change from state S_1 to state S_2 by the occurrence of one or more of its transitions. In order for a transition to occur, we must first determine a binding for it.

3.1 Binding

A binding for a transition T simply binds each of the transition's variables to a concrete value. A transition is said to be enabled if there exists a binding such that the input places contain sufficient tokens to satisfy the binding. Before we illustrate how a binding is determined, let us examine how, given a binding BT for a transition T, the occurrence of T changes the state of the model.

Consider the simple example presented in Figure 2. In this example we have depicted the marking at each place by an inscription contained within the place. Note that places **arg1** and **arg2** each contain a single token of type *int*. In general

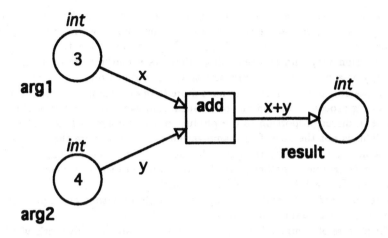

Fig. 2. Illustrating bindings

the marking at each place is a multi-set which we will represent in the sequel as a list of values.

Assume we are given the possible binding B_{add} such that $B_{add}(x) = 3$ and $B_{add}(y) = 4$. Let B'_{add} be the extension of B_{add} to arc expressions. As a result of the occurrence of transition **add**, the model changes state from S_1 to S_2 where $S_2 = S_1$ at all places except for the following:

1. *Input Places of* **add**. For each input place **p**, apply B'_{add} to the corresponding input arc-expression and evaluate the resulting expression to yield a multi-set value mv_p. Now $S_2(p) = S_1(p) \ominus mv_p$. (Note the use of $\oplus$ and $\ominus$ to represent multi-set addition and subtraction respectively). This is commonly known as "removing token(s) with value mv_p from place **p**".

   The transition **add** has two input places, **arg1** and **arg2** with arc-expressions x and y respectively. Applying B'_{add} to x yields 3; Applying B'_{add} to y yields 4. Hence $S_2(arg1) = \{\}$ and $S_2(arg2) = \{\}$. Note that we have so far placed no restrictions on the number of tokens in a multiset. In particular, a place may contain more than one token and an arc expression may evaluate to a multi-set with zero to an arbitrary number of tokens.

2. *Output Places of* **add**. For each output place **p**, apply B'_{add} to the corresponding output arc-expression and evaluate the resulting expression to yield a multi-set value mv_p. Now $S_2(p) = S_1(p) \oplus mv_p$. This is commonly known as "adding token(s) with value mv_p to place **p**".

   The transition **add** has only one output place **result** with output arc-expression $x+y$. Applying B'_{add} to $x+y$ yields the result 7. Thus $S_2(result) = S_1(result) \oplus 7 = \{\} \oplus 7 = \{7\}$. Note that if $S_1(result)$ was non-empty, e.g. 12, then $S_2(result) = \{7, 12\}$.

In the above example there is only one enabled binding possible. Had the input places contained more tokens, many bindings would be possible.

Let us now examine how a binding can be determined. For the moment we ignore *guards*. Let us assume that there is only one arc between an input place and a transition. The only requirement of a binding function B_T is that for every input arc-expression *iexp* and corresponding input place marking *im* of **T**, the value of $B'_T(iexp)$ be a multi-set value *mv* such that *im* contains *mv*.

It is possible for a transition to have more than one enabled binding. The goal of the binding process is to find one or all such bindings. The number of bindings can increase in direct proportion to the product of the number of tokens at each input place. This is not the case if the same variable is used in more than one input arc-expression or also occurs in the guard. In case more than one binding is legal, it still has to be determined whether more than one can be executed concurrently, i.e. in a single step. This will be discussed in the sequel.

Note also that some variables may appear only in output arc-expressions. Such a free variable can assume any value from its color set.

The process of finding a binding is a computationally intensive task as it involves traversing potentially large search trees and performing unification at each node.

3.2 Compiling Transitions

In this section, our goal is to translate each transition in the model into a single function. We will call this function the *occurrence-function*. Conceptually, each transition **T** is characterized as a function mapping a labeled record of multi-sets with a component for each input place into a labeled record of multi-sets with a component for each surrounding place . For example, the transition add can be represented by an occurrence function with the following type:

$$\mathbf{add} : \{arg1 : int\ ms, arg2 : int\ ms\}$$
$$\rightarrow \{arg1 : int\ ms, arg2 : int\ ms, result : int\ ms\}$$

Let us examine how the **add** function can be used to determine if the **add** transition can occur, and if so, to calculate the new markings of its adjacent places as a result of the occurrence. Assume that the current markings of arg1, arg2 and result are $a1m1$, $a2m1$ and $rm1$ respectively. If the **add** transition cannot occur, the application of **add** will fail. However, if the transition can occur, then the application will succeed and calculate the multiset of tokens $a1d$ to be removed from arg1, the multiset of tokens $a2d$ to be removed from arg2 and the multiset of tokens rd to be added to result. Now, as a consequence of the occurrence of the **add** transition, the new markings of arg1, arg2 and result will be: $a1m1 \ominus a1d$, $a2m1 \ominus a2d$ and $rm1 \oplus rd$ respectively.

This conceptual view emphasizes the localized nature of transitions. The only thing a transition depends on is the marking of all its input-places and the only thing it affects is the marking of all its input and output places. Pragmatically, such an occurrence function must encode all of the transition's arc-expressions and is, as a result, quite complex. Hence, we take a "layered approach" in order to build such an occurrence function. For each transition, we define:

1. A binding type

2. For each input place associated with the transition, we define an input arc-function. Analogously, for each output place we define an output arc-function.
3. A function to calculate bindings for the transition

Defining the Transition's Binding Type. Conceptually, a binding function for transition T is a function on $V(T)$. In practice, representing the binding itself as a labeled record is efficient. For example, bindings for the add transition are values of the following type:

```
type add'BT = {x:int,y:int}
```

where `add'BT` should be read as "add Binding Type".
We describe the process for generating binding functions in the sequel.

Defining the Transition's Arc-Functions. Given a binding, the arc-expressions are used to calculate the tokens to be removed from the input places and the tokens to be added to the output places. This calculation can be performed as a function application if each arc expression is cast as a function on the binding type of the transition.

```
fun arg1_add_AF   ( {x,y}:add'BT) : int ms = x      (*= 1'x *)
fun arg2_add_AF   ( {x,y}:add'BT) : int ms = y      (*= 1'y *)
fun add_result_AF ( {x,y}:add'BT) : int ms = (x+y)  (*= 1'(x+y) *)
```

The prefix `1'` exposes the multi-set aspect of a marking. In more detail, the syntax for input arc-expressions requires that an arc-expression evaluate to a multiset of the same type as is declared for the input place. We explicitly allow the prefix `<int>'` and the operation of multi-set addition. The former permits:

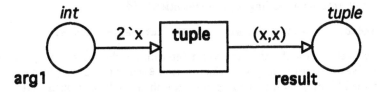

to express the removal of two identical tokens of color x from the input place. (Note that `2'x` is the same as `1'x ⊕ 1'x`.) The latter permits:

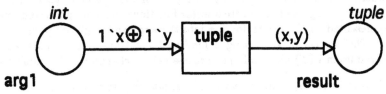

to express the removal of two tokens, one of color x and one of color y.

In the sequel, to simplify the definition of the binding process we will decompose input arc-expressions with explicit multi-set addition (or multiple identical tokens) by generating additional input arcs; e.g.:

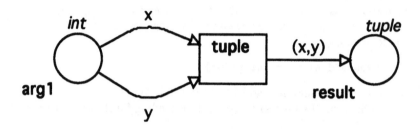

However, when we refer to an input arc function, we mean the unique (for each input place) function which evaluates to the appropriate multi-set.

Defining the Occurrence-Function. Assuming we can calculate the binding for a transition at a marking, we can then define the occurrence function in terms of its associated arc functions. The occurrence function applies each of the arc functions to the "value" generated by the binding function to determine the multi-sets to be subtracted from each input place and added to each output place.

3.3 Calculating Bindings

The only missing link in the definition of the occurrence function **add** is the binding function for **add** i.e. **Bindadd** which, given a marking for the place arg1 and the place arg2, returns a binding for the transition **add**.

    Bindadd : {arg1 : int ms, arg2 : int ms} -> add'BT

In the sequel we describe the process for determining the functionality of **Bindadd** in terms of search trees. The goal of the function **Bindadd** is to transform a completely unspecified binding b0 into a completely specified binding bn such that

    arg1_add_AF(bn) <= #arg1(ipm) and
    arg2_add_AF(bn) <= #arg2(ipm)

where **<=** denotes the subset operation for multi-sets and **ipm** is the argument of **Bindadd**. **#arg1** and **#arg2** are selector functions which map the compound marking represented by the record for **ipm** into the **arg1** and **arg2** components.

The process of generating a binding for a transition T starts with all of the variables in $V(T)$ unbound. The process can be characterized recursively as follows:

1. Are there any unbound variables? If not, skip to step 7.
2. Select an unprocessed input arc and the corresponding input arc-expression. If there are no more input arcs, skip to step 5.

3. Substitute for all bound variables occurring in the arc-expression the values to which they are bound. Perform any function applications that may now be carried out.

4. The arc-expression may now serve as a pattern for pattern matching against each of the tokens in the current marking of the input place associated with the input arc. There are three cases to consider:

   (a) Pattern match fails because constants and/or already bound variables in the arc-expression are incompatible with the current marking. The currently proposed partial binding cannot be completed and we have arrived at a failure node in the tree. Return a failure.

   (b) Pattern match succeeds: newly bound variables are added to the proposed binding. Each such match corresponds to a branch and hence the number of child nodes is equal to the number of different matchable values in the marking. Make a recursive call of the process for each child. If any child succeeds, return success; otherwise return failure.

   (c) The arc expression cannot be used as a pattern because it contains function applications (we include here infix operators) which cannot yet be evaluated due to the presence of unbound variables. Mark and ignore the arc-expression and proceed to step 2.

5. There are unbound variables. See if there are any arc-expressions marked by step 4c that are now evaluable. If so, repeat steps 1 – 4 until there are no more unbound variables or no more evaluable arc expressions.

6. There may be remaining unbound variables. This can occur for one of two reasons. Such a variable either a) only occurs in output arc expressions, in which case it can be assigned freely any value from the appropriate color set; or b) the variable occurs in input arc expressions that are marked by step 4c and remain unevaluable. If so we have two possibilities:

   (a) An unbound variable is declared to be of a color set (i.e. type) with only a small number of values. In this case we can generate branches for each such value as if we had a match (i.e. step 4b).

   (b) The color set is large. In this case we can generate a possible value by a random draw (possibly a number of attempts).

7. We can now evaluate the arc functions to determine whether the input places contain the appropriate tokens. At this stage multiple instances of the same token color, and multiple arcs from the same input place express themselves in the multisets resulting from the evaluation. Additionally, variable bindings made by random choice will be tested against what is actually possible. If the containment is satisfied, return success; otherwise failure.

An implementation of the binding process can traverse the tree in a depth-first or breadth-first manner in order to obtain a binding. (The depth-first approach works well for finding the first 'n' bindings fast.) A variant of this function could also return a list of all possible bindings instead of just one binding. Other factors affect the efficiency of this whole process. We discuss some of these factors in the sequel.

3.4 Simulating the Model

Assume we are given occurrence functions for each transition in the flat model. Also assume the system is in some state S_1. Let us now see how the process of performing a simulation step can be described as a sequence of function evaluations. We will focus on the **add** transition.

The first thing we need to determine is if the **add** transition is enabled in state S_1. Let us apply the occurrence function for **add** to the current markings on the input places of **add**. If the **add** transition is not enabled the evaluation will fail and we must then proceed to check the enabling of other transitions. Let us assume that **add** is enabled. Then the function will calculate multi-sets using the input arc functions and the output arc function. Let these be $a1d$, $a2d$ and rd respectively. Now, we can define the state S_2 – the state arrived at as a result of an occurrence of the **add** transition in state S_1 – as follows:

$$S_2(arg1) = S_1(arg1) \ominus a1d,$$
$$S_2(arg2) = S_1(arg2) \ominus a2d,$$
$$S_2(result) = S_1(result) \oplus rd;$$

with the rest of the elements in S_2 equal to the corresponding elements in S_1.

If we wanted to allow **add** to occur concurrently with itself or any other transition in the model, we would do the following:

$$S_1'(arg1) = S_1(arg1) \ominus a1d,$$
$$S_1'(arg2) = S_1(arg2) \ominus a2d,$$
$$S_1'(result) = S_1(result);$$

and then attempt to see if **add** or any other transition was enabled in state S_1'. If so the state S_2 would be:

$$S_2(arg1) = S_1(arg1) \ominus (a1d \oplus a1d'),$$
$$S_2(arg2) = S_1(arg2) \ominus (a2d \oplus a2d'),$$
$$S_2(result) = S_1(result) \oplus (rd + rd');$$

3.5 Extension of the Binding Function to Include Guards

The inclusion of *guard* functions associated with transitions places a further constraint on the binding function. First of all, we insist that all variables in the guard must be included in $V(T)$. Secondly, for any proposed binding, the guard must evaluate to *true*. (Recall that the guard is a boolean list. Each element of the list must evaluate to true). An easy way of incorporating the guard is simply to add it as a test on the proposed binding. In practice it is more efficient to use the guard in the process of determining the binding because it reduces the fan-out in the tree. This can be done in the following way:

1. Before processing any input arcs, and after the processing of each useful input arc, examine each unused element of the Guard that has the form:

    pattern = expression

    or

      expression = pattern.

2. For any such element, determine if, given the current partial binding, the expression is evaluable. If so, evaluate it and use the result to bind the variable(s) occurring in the pattern. If the binding fails (e.g. because already bound variables are in conflict with the equality), the current partial binding cannot be completed. Otherwise, add the new binding information to the current partial binding.

3.6 Efficiency of the Binding Process

The efficiency of the binding process can be greatly affected by the order in which arc expressions are used to bind variables. Consider the simple example, excised from a larger model, in figure 3. Suppose that the place **arg1** tends to have very few tokens

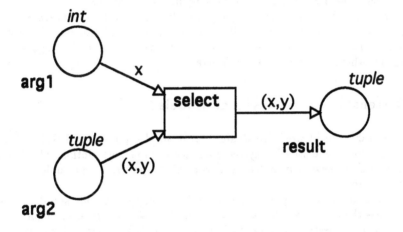

Fig. 3. An example to illustrate the efficiency of the binding process

on it, perhaps at most one at a time. Suppose further that place **arg2** typically has many tokens each with a unique value for **x**. Under these assumptions it is much better to use the arc expression from **arg1** first in the binding process.

If the occurrence function is generated dynamically during the simulation of the model, the actual token count can be used to make the occurrence function more efficient. On the other hand, repeatedly redefining occurrence functions during the simulation is in itself very expensive.

3.7 Precompiling the Binding Function

In the description of the binding process (Section 3.3), notice that the pattern matches are not precompiled. This is because both the patterns and the values used in the matches depend on values computed at binding time (i.e. on the partial binding; e.g. step 4). The idea of precompiling is to create a function definition such that all pattern matches are precompiled. As such the pattern matches cannot depend upon a particular value to which a variable is bound.

The advantage of precompiling all the pattern matches is simply that, having done this once, the model can be simulated for many steps, potentially executing the same transitions (and hence the same occurrence functions) many times without having to compile the pattern matches each time. This obviously imples a slow-down in the process of generating the binding function, but a great speedup in the execution.

To do this we have to sacrifice some subtlety in the binding process or generate a number of different subfunctions for the same transition, in effect choosing which one to use as a function of the current marking. To mention just a few points:

1. the occurrence of any function applications within an arc expression rules out its use in a pattern match, even if the binding process assigns values to variables such that the arc expression can be simplified to a pattern.

2. pattern matching on more than one variable can not take advantage of a previously bound variable. Consider the example in figure 3. Here, even if the process binds **x** first, because we are precompiling the pattern match for **arg2** would be (_,**y**), where '_' stands for don't care.

4 Extension to Hierarchical Models

Flat executable models are of little value in real-world applications. This is so because complexity forces the use of a layered approach to model description. The details of a hierarchical framework lie outside the scope of this paper. For a complete approach please refer to [5].

In the context of this paper, hierarchical models can be understood as a set of flat models that are fused together according to a set of formal principles. It will suffice for us to describe one type of fusion: place fusion. Here, places in two flat models typically have been fused by establishing the hierarchical relationship. In a simple case where one model uses another model as a submodel to further refine the detailed behavior of a transition, the set of places adjacent to the transition in the higher level model are fused with a set of places that are the input and output boundaries (ports) of the lower level model.

Figure 4 presents **level one** while Figure 5 presents **level two** of a two-level model based on the simple example of a flat model used earlier.

In this situation simulation proceeds concurrently across both flat models, constrained in the following way: the fused places are treated as if they are a single place. Thus the marking on each of two fused places is always regarded as identical; there is in effect only one marking shared by both places. Further, no occurrence function is generated for the refined transition. Thus the arc-inscriptions associated with the arcs between the higher level places and the refined transition are all ignored in favor of the arc-expressions on the arcs between the lower level places and their adjacent lower level transitions. The rules we have given for generating an algorithm for executing a flat model can in this way be directly carried over to the hierarchical model.

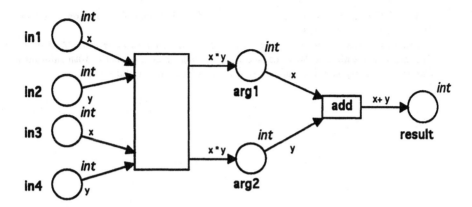

Fig. 4. Level One

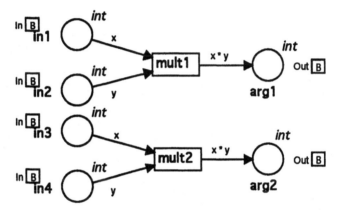

Fig. 5. Level Two

[5] provides a variety of fusion techniques which include both place fusion and transition fusion. Scoping rules allow hierarchical constructions based on both transition and place refinement, as well as resource sharing on a global, flat model or model instance basis. The execution algorithm is basically unaffected by these hierarchical enhancements.

References

1. K. Jensen. *Coloured Petri Nets.* In *Petri Nets: Central Models and Their Properties,* Advances in Petri Nets 1986-Part I, W. Brauer, W. Reisig and G. Rozenberg (eds.), Lecture Notes in Computer Science, vol. 254, 248–299, Springer Verlag, 1987.
2. F. Commoner, A. W. Holt, S. Even, and A. Pnueli. *Marked Directed Graphs.* Computer and System Sc. 5, 511–523, 1971.
3. D. A. Marca and C. L. McGowan. *SADT.* McGraw-Hill, New York, 1988.

4. *Design/IDEF User's Manual, Version 1.5.* Meta Software Corporation, Cambridge, Massachusetts, USA, 1989.
5. P. Huber, K. Jensen, and R. Shapiro. *Hierarchies in Coloured Petri Nets.* Meta Software Corporation, Cambridge Massachusetts, USA, 1989. Presented at the 10th International Conference on Application and Theory of Petri Nets, Bonn, June 1989.

Modeling a NORAD Command Post Using SADT and Colored Petri Nets

Robert M. Shapiro
Valerio O. Pinci
Roberto Mameli

Meta Software Corporation, 125 CambridgePark Drive, Cambridge, MA 02140 USA

Abstract

In this paper we focus on the task of modeling a NORAD Command Post, using SADT (Structured Analysis and Design Technique) and hierarchical Colored Petri Nets (CPN or CP-nets). The paper contains:
• a description of IDEF/CPN - an extension of SADT that incorporates behavioral information in SADT models.
• a discussion of the computer support for creating and editing IDEF/CPN models, their automatic translation into CPN models and their subsequent execution and analysis
• a detailed IDEF/CPN model of a NORAD command post.

1. Introduction and Overview

In a command post, the crew works together, interacting with displays, communication links and other equipment to recommend actions based on the changing status of surveillance networks, defensive weapons and air traffic information. The proper design of a command post, including procedures, equipment and staffing is an ongoing problem typical of the Command and Control area.

This class of problems has been described in the literature as *situation assessment* [1]: "Situation assessment relies on unique human capacities to merge and interpret information from many different sources." In the above-mentioned report, IDEF diagrams are used to capture the information flows and inter- dependencies among functions supporting situation assessment decision making in an SDI command center.

This paper represents an integrated approach to modeling this class of problems using IDEF/CPN: an extension of SADT that allows behavioral information to be incorporated directly in IDEF models. These models can then be translated **automatically** into hierarchical Colored Petri Nets. The net models may then be analysed using simulation and formal analysis tools.

Introduction to IDEF and CPN

IDEF is a diagramming method used to describe systems. It is based on SADT (Structured Analysis and Design Technique [3]), which was developed by SofTech Corporation in the 1970's. "Systems" may include manufacturing operations (such as an airplane or automotive assembly plant), computer systems (such as those which automate factories), and databases which keep track of and update information such as orders, sales and inventory. The functional components in a system may include people, hardware and software. A NORAD Command Post is an example of such a system.

IDEF was originally a 'pencil and paper' tool. The advent of relatively inexpensive graphical workstations has led to interactive computer support for the construction and editing of IDEF diagrams [4]. IDEF nowadays refers to several different diagramming methods. IDEF0 is used for functional or activity modeling. IDEF1 and IDEF1X are used for data modeling. People occasionally refer to IDEF2, conceived for behavioral modeling but it has never been fully implemented. For the rest of the paper we concern ourselves with IDEF0 and its extensions for behavioral modeling.

Colored Petri Nets [5] are executable models with a well-established formal basis that allows simulation and various types of formal analysis. Computer tools for working with CPN already exist [6]. We have developed an extension to IDEF0 that allows to incorporate, directly in the IDEF model, CPN inscriptions describing the dynamic behavior of the system being modeled. This, in conjunction with some minor syntactic restrictions on the IDEF connectivity (*arrow structure*) makes the translation process from IDEF to CPN trivial. IDEF/CPN is the outcome of this effort.

The remainder of this paper is organized in the following way:
* Section 2 discusses IDEF models for those readers who are not familiar with the method. Even if the reader is familiar, it is advisable to pay attention to the subsection on activation rules.
* Section 3 discusses the relationship between IDEF and CPN.
* Section 4 discusses existing computer support for creating IDEF/CPN Models.
* Section 5 presents an overview of the NORAD Command Post IDEF/CPN model.
* Section 6 discusses performance issues and timed simulation.

2. IDEF Models

A system is represented in an IDEF diagram by boxes and arrows. The boxes represent the activities or functions of the system. For example, a function in a NORAD Command Post is "monitor network status". The information or parts necessary to carry out the activities of a system and the information or products produced by the activity are represented in an IDEF diagram by arrows.

A top-down diagramming method goes from the general to the specific, from a single diagram that represents an entire system to more detailed diagrams that explain how the subsections of the system work. The collection of such diagrams is called an IDEF model.

The IDEF diagramming method enforces strict rules for the representation of information and activities and for establishing a hierarchy of diagrams. An IDEF model may contain hundreds of pages, from the top level single box description of, for example, the very general requirements for evaluating the air environment to a detailed diagram six pages down the model hierarchy explaining, for example, the identification of changes in the status of the surveillance network.

The paradigm for an IDEF diagram is a single activity box with its associated arrows:

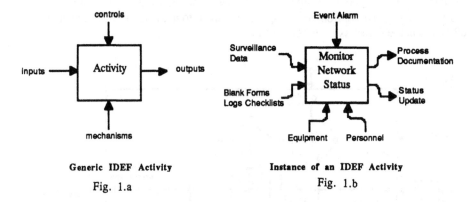

Generic IDEF Activity

Fig. 1.a

Instance of an IDEF Activity

Fig. 1.b

The text in the box is the name of the activity for which it stands, typically a verb or verb phrase. Each side of an activity box has a specific meaning. The left side is reserved for *inputs*, the top side is reserved for *controls*, the right side is reserved for *outputs* and the bottom side is reserved for *mechanisms* (Fig. 1.a).

This reflects system principles: inputs are transformed to outputs, controls constrain or dictate under which conditions transformations occur and mechanisms describe how the function is accomplished. See [3] for a detailed exposition of these concepts.

An arrow represents a collection of "things" (e.g., plans, computer data, machines, information, current status, available personnel). An arrow is typically labeled with a noun or noun phrase. Arrows interconnect boxes. An arrow may connect the output side of an activity with the input, control or mechanism side of another activity. No other interconnections are allowed.

Arrows may branch. A branch represents fan-out (multiple identical copies) or splitting (different parts of the things on different branches). Arrows may join. A join represents fan-in or merging. The relatively unrestricted branch and join structure of arrows combined with their ambiguous interpretation lead to the major obstacle in using IDEF to describe the behavior of a system.

An IDEF diagram (Fig. 2) consists, typically, of three to six activity boxes with arrow interconnections. Each activity may be described in greater detail in another diagram one level lower in the diagram hierarchy. The lower level diagram may be thought of as a set of activities contained within the higher level activity. The lower level shows the insides of the parent. The process of creating detail diagrams is called decomposing.

Decomposition forms boundaries. A box and the arrows that touch it define the precise boundary of the diagram which decomposes that box. Thus a diagram has external arrows that come and go from the edge of the diagram. These arrows are the interface between the diagram and the rest of the model. A diagram must be "plug-to-plug" compatible with its parent.

The boundary nodes (ports) in the decomposition diagram are coded according to where each arrow touches the decomposed activity box. The first character of the code indicates the edge, i.e., Input, Control, Output or Mechanism. The rest of the code is an integer which indicates position, from left to right or top to bottom, along an edge. The code is referred to in the sequel as the *ICOM code*.

Fig. 2

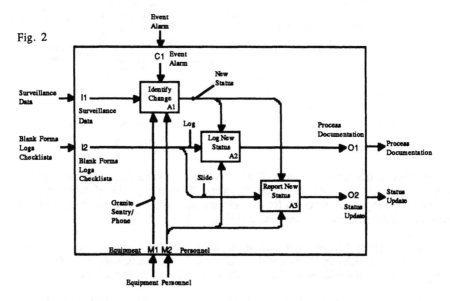

IDEF Activation Rules

The technique for specifying activation rules, as described in the literature [3], is as follows. To each activity associate a table. Each line of the table specifies a set of preconditions and postconditions. A precondition expresses the required presence (or absence) of any of the objects associated with the inputs, controls, outputs or mechanisms involved in the activity. A postcondition indicates presence (or absence) after the activity has occurred. For an activity to take place at least one line of the associated table needs to have all of its preconditions satisfied. Activation results in the objects being present (or absent) as specified in the postconditions.

It is not our intent to explore this schema in detail. We make the following observations:

1. This description is incomplete in that it does not fully explain issues concerning concurrency and choice.

2. Formal methods have not been developed for studying the behavioral and structural properties of models described this way, unlike for Colored Petri Nets.

3. The tabular approach to the specification of functionality is too low level. It suffers from the same practical difficulties encountered when trying to apply conventional Petri nets (i.e., condition/event or place/transition nets) to real world problems. The models and/or the tables specifying the activation rules become too large to be useful.

It is our intention to show how the objective of activation rules can be achieved by viewing the IDEF model as a hierarchical Colored Petri Net model and using the formal inscriptions of CPN to specify the behavior. In so doing, we will bypass the aforementioned difficulties.

3. Relationship Between IDEF and CPN

Arrows, Channels and Places

We start by reviewing a seminal idea of C.A. Petri described in [7]. Here Petri outlines an interpretation of nets known as Channel/Agency nets. The transforming elements (the events or transitions) are thought of as *agencies* (which perform some possibly complex activity). Agencies communicate with each other via *channels*.

Following this interpretation, it is natural to think of IDEF activity boxes as agencies. The difficult part is how to interpret the arrow structure in terms of channels. Let us ignore the classification of the arrows in Input, Control, Output and Mechanism introduced in SADT and focus solely on inputs and outputs, since this is the only distinction holding in Petri Net theory.

Consider the simplest case (fig.3.a). Activity A1 produces an output which is then used as an input by activity A2.

Fig. 3.a   Fig. 3. b

We observe that IDEF diagrams are not bipartite graphs. There is only a single vertex type, the activity box. On the other hand, a channel/agency net has two vertex types: channels represented by circles and agencies represented by boxes (fig. 3.b). Now, from what has been said so far, it is clear that activities A1 and A2 will be represented as agencies. The arrow between them will have to correspond to a channel plus the arcs associated with it that represent the *flow* relationship.

This is the trivial case. Let us now extend it. Next we see activity A1 communicating with A2 and A3 via separate channels (fig. 4.b).

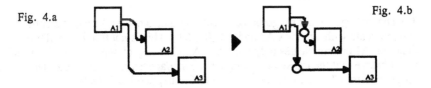

Fig. 4.a   Fig. 4.b

Next we show A1 communicating with A2 and A3 via the same channel (fig. 5.b).

Fig. 5.a   Fig. 5.b

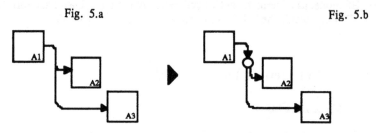

It is important to note that these two diagrams (fig. 5.a-5.b) **do not represent** concurrency and choice (in respect to the activities A2 and A3). The SADT arrow structure is not generally used in that way. The equivalent Petri nets would imply concurrency or choice only if they were low level Petri nets, e.g., Condition/Event nets. In high level nets the inscriptions must be analyzed in order to determine whether A2 and A3 can be concurrent in fig. 4.b and whether A2 and A3 are alternatives in fig. 5.b.

Now consider the following problematic situation (fig. 6.a).

Fig. 6.a   Fig. 6.b

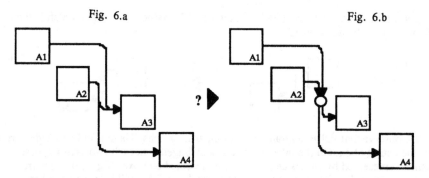

Here we can observe several difficulties:

1. It is easy to formalize a rule which deduces from the IDEF diagram (fig. 6.a) the existence of a single channel used by activities A1 and A2 to communicate with activities A3 and A4. We give such a rule in the sequel. However, the location of the channel and the routing of the arcs has become problematic. We now have potentially serious layout problems.

2. The channel/agency net suggests the possibility that agencies A1 and A2 both communicate with agencies A3 and A4 (fig. 6.b). This is not true in the IDEF diagram: A1 communicates only with A3 . Another way of appreciating this problem is to observe that the translation from the channel/agency net back to the IDEF is no longer possible. Some information in the IDEF diagram has been lost.

There are several possible approaches to these difficulties. To discuss them concretely we continue our discussion in terms of high-level nets, specifically Colored Petri Nets. Our agencies or activities are in this context *transitions*. The channels are *places*. Inscriptions on the connecting arcs are *arc expressions*. Inscriptions within the transitions are *guards*. We assume a rudimentary understanding of Colored Nets in the sequel. Refer to [5] for a detailed presentation of these concepts.

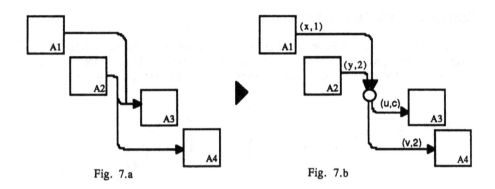

Fig. 7.a   Fig. 7.b

Here (fig. 7.b) we have introduced inscriptions (arc expressions) and used a component of the tuples on the arcs to carry some of the information represented graphically in the IDEF arrow structure. This use of inscriptions is similar to the role inscriptions play in allowing a conventional Petri net to be folded into a high level net [8].

Suitably generalized, this allows the information in the IDEF arrow structure to be captured in the CPN model. We do not pursue this approach for several reasons:

1. The graphic layout problem remains.
2. Automatic introduction of the additional tuple component and guards is sometimes rather complex.
3. The behavioral rules are difficult to specify and understand because the graphics is carrying less of the behavioral information.

Instead we propose a modest restriction on the arrow structure which allows the direct generation of equivalent CPN models.

First we give an operative definition of an *arrow bundle*.

Starting with any arrow, compute the set of all the arrows branching and joining it. For each new arrow added in the set, perform the same computation until no more arrows may be added. The set obtained after the last step is called an arrow bundle.

Now examine the arrow bundle. Does there exist a **common segment** before which all joins (if any) occur and after which all branches (if any) occur? If all arrow bundles in the IDEF model pass this restriction, we can proceed to generate the equivalent CPN graphic structure. Each common segment locates a channel (one per arrow bundle) which corresponds to a CPN place. The arrow structure before the common segment is represented by output arcs from all the appropriate transitions to the CPN place. The arrow structure after the common segment represents input arcs from the place to all the appropriate transitions.

Reconsidering the previous IDEF diagram, we can observe that there is a single arrow bundle without a common segment.

IDEF with CPN Inscriptions

Having imposed a restriction on the arrow structure, we can transform an IDEF diagram into an equivalent CPN diagram, preserving the graphical layout in the process. We now need to associate with the IDEF diagram the inscriptions required by CPN.

Fig. 8.a   Fig. 8.b

In this simplest case (fig. 8.b) we observe that the CPN model requires two arc expressions, one on the output from A1 and one on the input to A2. To do this in the IDEF diagram we have simply to associate arc expressions with each end of the arrow. In general, an arrow bundle has a number of output arrows joining together and then branching. The sources and destinations each require a single arc expression.

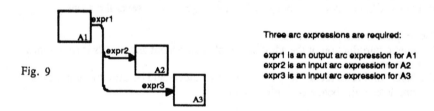

Fig. 9

Three arc expressions are required:

expr1 is an output arc expression for A1
expr2 is an input arc expression for A2
expr3 is an input arc expression for A3

Guards are associated with transitions. Hence their equivalent in the IDEF model will be asociated with activities.

CPN places require specification of a *color set*. Places correspond to the common segment of each arrow bundle. An IDEF label attached to the common segment of an arrow bundle serves perfectly as the designator of the color set for the corresponding place.

Hierarchies in IDEF and CPN

IDEF0, based on the principle of functional decomposition, makes extensive use of hierarchical models. We must now show how to map these hierarchical concepts into CPN. For a complete exposition of the treatment of hierarchies in CPN we refer the reader to [9]. Here we briefly review those concepts which pertain also to IDEF0.

A hierarchical CP-net contains a number of *interrelated subnets* — called *pages*. There are three different ways to relate these pages to each other:

1) *Substitution.* A place or transition is *replaced* by a page — which often gives a more detailed description of the corresponding state/activity. This works in a way similar to hardware plug-ins.

2) *Invocation.* The occurrence of a transition may *trigger* the creation and execution of a new *pageinstance* which can also be invocated recursively This works in a way similar to subroutines.

3) *Fusion.* A set of places (or a set of transitions) may be *unified* — i.e., folded into a single conceptual node. The nodes may reside on the same page or on different pages.

For substitution and invocation, we call the related node a *supernode* and its page a *superpage*. The related page is called a *subpage*. In the sequel we restrict ourselves to the use of transition substitution.

Components are *reusable* — in the sense that several nodes can be related to the *same* page. This means that a page — during execution — may have several *instances*, each with its own marking and related to a single node.

There is a well-defined *interface* between each subpage and the corresponding superpage. This interface relates *socket nodes* (surrounding the supernode) to *port nodes* (at the subpage). This is similar to the wiring of hardware plug-ins. The interface tells how the superpage *interacts* with the subpage.

Substitution of transitions works in a similar way as the refinement primitives found in many system description languages — e.g., IDEF or data flow diagrams.

The semantics of a substitution transition can be understood by replacing it with the corresponding subpage. Each socket place is merged into its assigned port. The substitution transition and its arcs are ignored (e.g., the guard and arc expressions).

Summary of Relationship Between IDEF/CPN and CPN

We now have completed our exposition of the relationship between IDEF0 models and CPN models. We review the details briefly.

IDEF/CPN model	Colored Petri Net model
node, diagram (i.e., page)	submodel (page)
activity (undecomposed)	transition
activity (decomposed)	substitution transition
channel (arrow bundle)	place plus surrounding arcs
label (of common segment of bundle)	color set for place
activation rule (arc expressions + guard)	arc expressions + guard
ICOM label	port place (boundary)
initial marking (of common segment)	initial marking (of place)

The CPN software allows CPN models to contain some additional functionality. We refer here to *code segments* and *fusion* which are currently supported by IDEF/CPN.

A code segment is an expression, written in Standard ML [10] and associated with a transition. It is executed whenever the transition occurs. A detailed description of code segments is not within the scope of this paper. We refer the reader to [6]. Code segments are useful in a variety of CPN models. We have included this functionality in IDEF/CPN as an extension to the activation rule. In addition to binding variables used in output arc expressions, the code segment can perform input/output, network communication and graphical display during simulation.

Fusion allows different CPN objects (either transitions or places) to be *fused* together. A detailed description is provided in [9]. Here we concern ourselves only with *global* place fusion. Two or more places declared to be in the same fusion set always share the identical marking. We allow the common segments of arrow bundles to be fused together. A fusion set can be used to model a shared resource.

Finally, CPN requires color (i.e., type) declarations for all of the color sets associated with places and all of the variables used in arc expressions, guards and code segments. Additionally, function declarations must be supplied for all functions used in the CPN model. In Design/CPN these declarations are contained within global and local declaration nodes. The global declarations apply to the whole model. The local declarations apply only to the specific submodel on whose page the local declaration occurs.

Switching from IDEF to CPN

To create, edit, execute and analyse IDEF/CPN models, the modeler uses two software products, Design/IDEF and Design/CPN. First the modeler creates and edits an IDEF0 model using Design/IDEF. Then the modeler adds IDEF/CPN inscriptions using the same software. When the model is complete and the CPN syntax requirements satisfied, the model is exported via 'Output CPN model' as a text file. The user then imports this file using the 'Load IDEF' command in Design/CPN. A complete hierarchical Colored Petri Net is constructed automatically by the software.

Each IDEF diagram corresponds precisely to a CPN page. An activity that has not been decomposed corresponds to a CPN transition. A decomposed activity corresponds to a substitution transition. In the IDEF model all arrows touching the decomposed activity define the boundary of the diagram which is the activity's decomposition. These boundary points correspond to the port nodes of the CPN subpage. The CPN places (on the superpage) associated with the arrows that touch the decomposed box are the socket nodes referred to above.

The interface relating socket nodes to port nodes is specified by the ICOM labelling scheme in IDEF.

The user may continue using Design/CPN to edit, simulate and analyze the model. Any changes made in the model during this phase are changes only to the CPN model. Such modifications may need to be made also to the original IDEF model and this is currently a manual task.

5. NORAD Command Post IDEF/CPN Model

Overview of the Project

A team of modelers working for Armstrong Aerospace Medical Research Laboratory (AAMRL) created the initial IDEF model. This was done by interviewing the crew of the command post and using the information so gathered to construct an eight-level model consisting of 21 diagrams. The model was subsequently reviewed by the command post crew.

A modeler at Meta Software Corporation added to the model those inscriptions required to define its behavior. The model was exported as a text file and then imported into the CPN simulator. The behavior of the model was studied using the simulator. Simple timing information was generated by the simulator to provide some idea of the performance of the model. Subsequently, AAMRL working with subcontractors, have constructed other models. They are currently extending this area of work.

Overview of the Command Post Model

At the highest level of the model, the function of the command post is to **evaluate the air environment**. The principal **inputs** to the evaluation include **data** needed to update current status information. **Resources** (mechanisms) needed to support the evaluation include **personnel** and **equip- ment**. The evaluation is **controlled** (triggered) by various **event alarms**. The **results** generated by the evaluation include **resource allocation recommendations** and updated **situation awareness**.

A detailed exposition of the entire model lies outside the scope of this paper. Instead we present a guided walkthrough of a selected subset (see diagrams of Appendix II):

A0: Evaluate Air Environment
   A1: Process Air Status
       A11: Process Surveillance Network
       A111: Monitor Network Status
   A2: Advise CMC and External Agencies

In the discussion that follows we will focus on behavioral issues.

We proceed to examine the decomposition sequence A0 - A1 - A11 - A111, roughly summarizing the behavior until we arrive at the lowest level detail where the inscriptions provide a precise description of the circumstances under which the undecomposed activities may take place and the effects these activities have.

Color Sets and other Global Declarations

A complete understanding of the inscriptions involves the color set definitions (data descriptions) of the objects represented by the arrows. Color sets can be interpreted as equivalent to data types in ordinary programming languages. They define the set of values and the type of operations which are allowed for each token [5].

A color set can be a primitive Standard ML type or an enumerative, a product, a record, a list, an indexed set and any combination of these. Moreover, a color set can be an Abstract Data Type.

For example, in the case of the NORAD model, *Time* and *Info*, used to construct other color sets, are primitive color sets defined as integer and string, respectively. *ESource*, describing the type of equipment used in the transmission of an event alarm, is an enumerative color set defined by listing all its elements (i.e., Granite and Tele). *NTEvent_Alarm*, describing the type of alarms handled by the Command Post, is a color set defined as a record of data where each component is referenced by a label, namely: *iD*, *etypE* and *estypE*. *Event_Alarm*, used to describe timed alarms, is the cartesian product of two previously defined color sets: *Time* and *NTEvent_Alarm*. In the IDEF/CPN model all these definitions, together with the declarations of all variables and constants used in the net inscriptions, are contained in a global definition box. We list here some of the pertinent definitions with each activity.

```
color Bool bool;
color Id = int;
color Info = String;
colore InfResource = unit;
color Time = int;
color ESource = with Granite I Tele;
color EType = with Surv I Force I Track
color ESType = with Ground I Airbom I New I Soviet I Deviate I Special I Unknown I Fade I Identified I Final;
color NTEvent_Alarm = record iD.Id * esourcE:Esource * etypE * estypE:ESType;
color Event_Alarm = product Time * NTEvent_Alarm;
...
var b: Bool;
var t1,t2,t: Time;
var evalarm : NTEvent_Alarm;
var esource : ESource;
...
val Sec = 1
val Min = 60 * Sec;
...
```

Fig. 10

Evaluate Air Environment

The evaluation is split into two main stages:

1: processing the air status (A1)
2: performing a set of briefings (A2)

The briefings needed are triggered by outputs from the first stage. In the model the contents of **process documentation** determine whether and which briefings are required. More about this in what follows.

Execute Assets (A3) and Maintain ADOC Operations (A4) are ongoing periodic activities not directly related to the two main stages. We ignore them in the sequel.

Since the first two stages are represented by decomposed activities we proceed to look at the lower level details. As a general rule, behavioral information need be provided only for the lowest level activities.

Independent of whether briefings are required, the air status processing generates **process documentation**, updated **situation awareness** and **resource allocation recommendations**.

Process Air Status

The processing is split into three parallel activities:

1: process surveillance network (A11)
2: process force assets (A12)
3: process aircraft tracks (A13)

Each of these update **situation awareness** which is dispersed internally and externally by activity A14. In addition, each generates **process documentation** which will eventually be an output of the command post, but which also triggers briefings when necessary. We proceed to investigate the details of the surveillance network.

Process Surveillance Network

The processing is split into two groups of activities:

1: monitor network status (A111)
2: collect data (A112)
   evaluate event data (A113)
   generate options (A114)
   recommend surveillance network changes (A115)

The monitoring activity preceeds the second group and determines under which circumstances the second group is required. Once it is determined that more data need be collected, the second group takes over and repeats until no more data is requested.

Both groups generate **process documentation** and update **situation awareness**. The second group also generates **initial recommendations** (activity A115)

We now examine the details of the Monitor Network Status activity.

Monitor Network Status

The processing is split into two groups of activities:

1: identify change (A1111)
2: log new status (A1112)
    report new status (A1113)

First the type of change must be identified. Once this has happened the logging and reporting of the new status may proceed concurrently. The logging activity generates **process documentation** and the reporting activity generates **status update**.

The activities at this level have no further decompositions and the behavior is characterized by the inscriptions associated with the arrows and activities. We proceed to discuss in detail the inscriptions associated with each activity.

A1111: Identify Change

The control (trigger) of this activity is an Event Alarm. The associated arc inscription breaks up the alarm into its two components: a time (t1) and an untimed event alarm record (evalarm). The guard requires the event alarm type to be surveillance (#etypE evalarm = Surv).

If we were to return to the topmost level of the model and trace the decomposition of the Event Alarm arrow to all its terminal undecomposed activities we would discover that the arc expression and guard at each of these activities results in exactly one activity being enabled (activated) for each possible event alarm.

Different equipment may be used in the transmission of an event alarm to the Command Post. Here we show two possibilities: the Granite Sentry monitor or Telephone. The equipment must be available. Thus, we require that the source of the alarm match the available equipment (#esourcE evalarm = esource). The source of the event alarm may also affect subsequent actions and we could further elaborate the behavior to handle this.

The data for this activity is Surveillance Data. The associated arc inscription breaks up the Data into its two components: a time (t2) and an untimed data record (data). The guard requires the identifier of the data record to be equal to the identifier of the event alarm record (#iD data = #iD evalarm). Thus, we are matching the event alarm with its associated data.

We have allowed for the possibility of handling Ground and Airborn surveillance alarms in different ways (e.g., using different personnel) but have not added the behavioral detail.

The output from this activity consists of two messages. One of these messages triggers the logging activity (A1112:Log New Status). The other message triggers the preparation of a slide (A1113:Report New Status).

The behavior here has been modeled in such a way that each of these subsequent activities can proceed concurrently. That is why two messages are generated. Each message contains two components:

1: a time calculated by taking the maximum of the time tags associated with the event alarm and the surveillance data and adding to it the processing time for this activity (t=max[t1,t2]+45*Sec).

2: newdata, whose first component designates its subsequent purpose (purposE=Log or purposE=Slide) and whose second component is a record (d1) whose field values are calculated from the contents of the event alarm and Surveillance data (d1 ={iD=#iD data, etypE=Surv; estype=#estypE evalarm, infO=#infO data}).

A1112: Log New Status

The arc inscription associated with the control of this activity breaks up the New Status message into its two components: a time (t1) and a record with a purpose (newdata). The guard requires the purpose be logging (#purposE newdata = Log).

We provide for the possibility that the lack of available Logs may influence when this activity takes place, but do not elaborate on this.

A code segment is used to calculate two variables used in the output arc expression for this activity. The time is calculated by adding to the incoming time tag a processing delay (t = t1 + 10*Sec). A random number generator is used to determine the value of a boolean variable, which, when TRUE will cause the generation of Process Documentation that will subsequently trigger a briefing. The random number generator can be replaced by an algorithm that examines the information content of the data and determines from it whether a briefing is required.

The output from this activity always includes one piece of process documentation which contains the time-tagged incoming newdata with a Nobriefing flag attached (t, #datA newdata, Nobrief).

If the calculated value of the boolean variable b is TRUE, then a second piece of process documentation is generated with an NCPbriefing flag attached. Subsequent handling of Process Documentation (See A2:Advise CMC and External Agencies) selectively triggers the appropriate briefings.

A1113: Report New Status

The arc inscription associated with the control of this activity breaks up the New Status message into its two components: a time (t1) and a record with a purpose (newdata). The guard requires the purpose be reporting (#purposE newdata = Slide). We provide for the possibility that the lack of available Slides may influence when this activity takes place, but do not elaborate on this.

A code segment is used to calculate two variables used in the output arc expression for this activity. The time is calculated by adding to the incoming time tag a processing delay (t = t1 + 3*Sec). A random number generator is used to determine the value of a boolean variable, which, when FALSE will cause the Status Update Message to trigger more data collection (see the second group of activities in Node A11:Process Surveillance Network, discussed above). The random number generator can be replaced by an algorithm that examines the information content of the data and determines from it if more data need be collected. The output from this activity is a **Status Update** message that consists of two components: the first component is a boolean flag that indicates whether sufficient data is present or more data must be collected. The second component is time-tagged new data. Subsequent handling of **Status Update** (See A11) selectively triggers the collection and analysis of new data.

Advise CMC and External Agencies

Process Documentation that is tagged with an **NCPbrief** flag is handled by this group of activities.   The processing is split into two groups of activities:

1:   BRIEF NCP(A21)
2:   BRIEF SPACC(A22)
     BRIEF RAPIER(A23)
     BRIEF Operations Center(A24)

First the NCP briefing must take place. As a consequence of this, any subset of the other three briefings may be triggered. These subsequent activities have been modeled in such a way that they may proceed concurrently if the other resources they require are available. Each briefing updates **situation awareness** and generates **resource allocation recommendations**.

A21: BRIEF NCP

The input to this activity is generated by the Air Status Processing activity which determines whether the briefing must take place and, if so, provides the information to be briefed: namely the **Process Documentation**.

The arc inscription associated with the process documentation input splits the incoming data into its two components, a time (t1) and a data record (d), and checks the presence of the NCPbrief flag to trigger the activity. The possibility of involving different personnel and different kind of equipment has been taken into account, but the behavioral detail has not been modeled.

The output from this activity includes time tagged data together with a string field containing the instance of the actual recommendation generated by the agency. The time tag t and three boolean values, bound to the variables, a, b, c in the output arc expression, are calculated by the code segment associated with this box. The time t is calculated by

adding to the incoming time tag a processing delay. The processing delay and the boolean variables are generated randomly, though more suitable algorithms may be used in the future. The *brfunc* function is used to raise the flags enabling the remaining briefing activities depending on the boolean value of a, b and c.

A22: BRIEF SPACC

This activity is triggered only if there is an input token carrying the SPACC flag. The arc inscription associated with the control to this activity is in charge of checking whether this condition is satisfied.

A guard is used to calculate the variable t present in the output arc expression. The time t is calculated by adding to the incoming time tag a processing delay of one minute.

As in the case of the previous activity, the output is a piece of resource allocation recommendation, which contains time tagged data with attached recommendation, and time tagged data updating the situation awareness.

The same personnel is involved in all of the four briefing activities, while different equipment may be used.

Activities A23 and A24 are analogous to A22.

6. Performance Issues and Time

In the NORAD command post model, timing properties have been represented explicitly. Appropriate color sets have included a 'time' component, arc expressions have included time variables and guards have calculated new time values on output arc expressions. Usually, the new time values are the maximum of the input times plus the delay representing the time taken to perform the activity.

Representation of time properties can be further improved with an extension to the IDEF/CPN and Design/CPN, which support all these functionalities and allow timed simulation [11].

In a timed simulation, each system state exists at a given *model time* and model time is monotonically increased throughout the simulation.

A *duration time* is associated to each activity (CPN transition) and *time delays* are associated to each channel (CPN arcs and place). In this way it is possible to describe and analyse automatically the time performance of the modelled system throughout the simulation.

Two kinds of tokens are used in timed simulation: those that carry a time stamp and those that do not. Each color set declaration determines whether time stamps are present or not.

During a timed simulation the system inspects not only the presence of the appropriate tokens but also their time stamp in order to determine whether a transition is allowed to occur or not.

Whenever a simulation step has been executed, the time stamps of the tokens involved in the step are updated automatically by the system according to the duration time and the time delays inscribed in the net.

Bibliography

[1] Jean MacMillan, Joseph G. Wohl: **TR-363, Human Roles in an SDI System: Situation Assessment Durig Peacetime and Transition,** Armstrong Aerospace Medical Research Laboratory, Wright Patterson Air Force Base, October 1987.

[2] M. Ajmone Marsan, G. Conte, and G. Balbo, **A Class of Generalized Petri Nets for the Performance Evaluation of MultiProcessor Systems.** In: ACM Trans. Comput. Sys., Vol. 2, No. 2, pp. 93-122, May 1984.

[3] D. A. Marca and C. L. McGowan: **SADT**, McGraw-Hill, New York, 1988.

[4] **Design/IDEF User's Manual,** Version 1.5. Meta Software Corporation, Cambridge, MA, 1989.

[5] K. Jensen: **Coloured Petri Nets** In: W. Brauer, W. Reisig and G. Rozenberg (eds.): Petri Nets: Central Models and their Properties, Advances in Petri Nets 1986 - Part I, Lecture Notes in Computer Science, vol. 254, Springer-Verlag 1987, 248-299.

[6] **Design/CPN User's Manual,** V. 1.21: Meta Software Corporation,Cambridge, MA, Oct. 1989.

[7] C. A. Petri: **Introduction to General Net Theory.** In: W. Brauer, (ed.): Net Theory and Applications: Proceedings of the Advanced Course on General Net Theory of Processes and Systems, Hamburg, 1979, Lecture Notes in Computer Science, Vol. 84, Springer-Verlag 1980, 1-19.

[8] H.J. Genrich: **Equivalence Transformation of Prt-Nets.** In G. Rozenberg (ed.), Advances in Petri Nets 1989, Lecture Notes in Computer Science, Springer-Verlag, to appear.

[9] P. Huber, K. Jensen, R. Shapiro: **Hierarchies in Colored Petri Nets.** Meta Software Corporation, Cambridge, Massachusetts, USA, 1989. Presented at the 10th International Conference on Application and Theory of Petri Nets, Bonn, June 1989.

[10] Robert Harper, Robin Milner, and Mads Tofte: **The Definition of Standard ML, Version 2.** Technical Report ECS-LFCS-88-62, University of Edinburgh, LFCS, Department of Computer Science, University of Edinburgh, The King's Buidings, Edinburgh EH9 3JZ, August 1988.

[11] K. Jensen: **Design/CPN Extension: Timed Simulation, Color Set Restrictions and Reporting Facilities.** Meta Software Corporation, Cambridge, MA. V. II - February, 1990.

[12] H. Genrich, K. Lautenbach, P.S. Thiagarajan: **Elements of General Net Theory.** In: W. Brauer, G. Goos and J. Hartmanis (eds.): Net Theory and Applications: Proceedings of the Advanced Course on General Net Theory of Processes and Systems, Hamburg, 1979, Lecture Notes in Computer Science, Vol. 84, Springer-Verlag 1980

[13] M. Jantzen, R. Valk: **Formal Properties of Place/Transition Nets.** In: W. Brauer (ed.): Net Theory and Applications: Proceedings of the Advanced Course on General Net Theory of Processes and Systems, Lecture Notes in Computer Science, Vol. 84, Springer-Verlag 1980

[14] W. Reisig: **Petri Nets: An Introduction.** EATCS Monographs on Theoretical Computer Science, Vol. 4, New York, Springer-Verlag, 1985.

[15] Tadao Murata: **Petri Nets: Properties, Analysis, and Applications.** Proceedings of the IEEE, Vol. 77, No. 4, pp. 541-580, April 1989.

[16] K.M. van Hee, L.J. Somers, M. Voorhoeve: **Executable Specifications for Distributed Information Systems.** In: E.D.Falkenberg and P. Lindgreen (eds.): Information System Concepts: An In-depth Analysis, North Holland, 1989, 139-156

Appendix I.
An IDEF Page and the Corresponding CPN SubPage

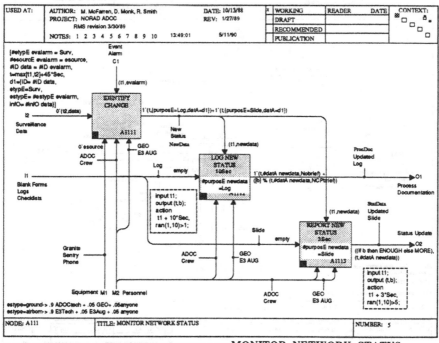

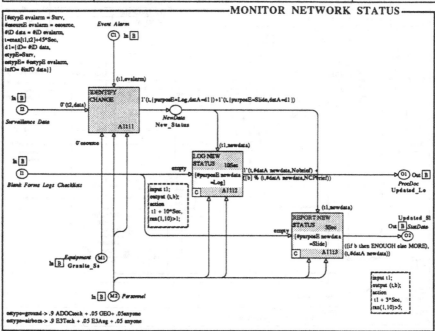

105

Appendix II.

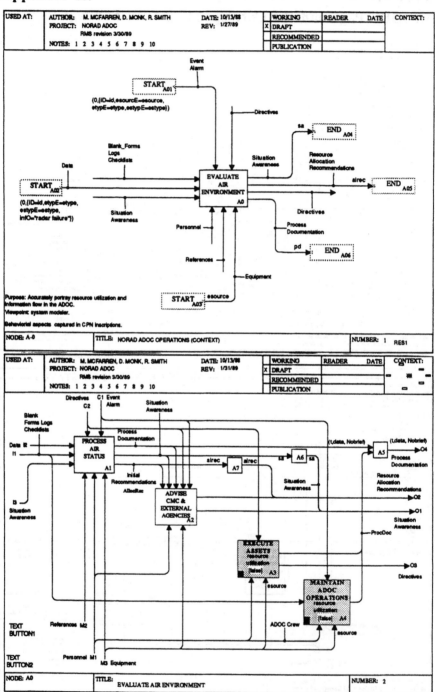

USED AT: AUTHOR: M. MCFARREN, D. MONK, R. SMITH   DATE: 10/13/88

PROJECT: NORAD ADOC   REV: 1/27/89

RMS revision 3/30/89

NOTES: 1 2 3 4 5 6 7 8 9 10

WORKING	READER	DATE	CONTEXT:
X DRAFT			
RECOMMENDED			
PUBLICATION			

Event Alarm

START A01

(0,{ID=id,esourcE=esource, etypE=etype,estypE=estype})

Directives

sa   END A04

Blank_Forms Logs Checklists

Situation Awareness

Resource Allocation Recommendations

Data

START A02

(0,{ID=id,etypE=etype, estypE=estype, infO="radar failure"})

Situation Awareness

EVALUATE AIR ENVIRONMENT A0

airec   END A05

Directives

Personnel

Process Documentation

References

pd   END A06

Equipment

START A03 esource

Purpose: Accurately portray resource utilization and information flow in the ADOC.

Viewpoint: system modeler.

Behavioral aspects captured in CPN inscriptions.

NODE: A-0	TITLE: NORAD ADOC OPERATIONS (CONTEXT)	NUMBER: 1	RES1

USED AT: AUTHOR: M. MCFARREN, D. MONK, R. SMITH   DATE: 10/13/88

PROJECT: NORAD ADOC   REV: 1/31/89

RMS revision 3/30/89

NOTES: 1 2 3 4 5 6 7 8 9 10

WORKING	READER	DATE	CONTEXT:
X DRAFT			
RECOMMENDED			
PUBLICATION			

Directives C1 Event

C2 Alarm

Situation Awareness

Blank Forms Logs Checklists

Process Documentation

Data I2

I1

PROCESS AIR STATUS A1

(t,data, Nobrief)   (t,data, Nobrief)

A5 O4

Process Documentation

airec   airec

A7   sa A6 sa

Initial Recommendations

AllocRec

I3

Situation Awareness

ADVISE CMC & EXTERNAL AGENCIES A2

Situation Awareness

Resource Allocation Recommendations

O2

O1

Situation Awareness

ProcDoc

EXECUTE ASSETS resource utilization [false] A3

esource

O3

Directives

MAINTAIN ADOC OPERATIONS resource utilization [false] A4

TEXT BUTTON1

References M2

ADOC Crew

esource

TEXT BUTTON2

Personnel M1

M3 Equipment

NODE: A0	TITLE: EVALUATE AIR ENVIRONMENT	NUMBER: 2

106

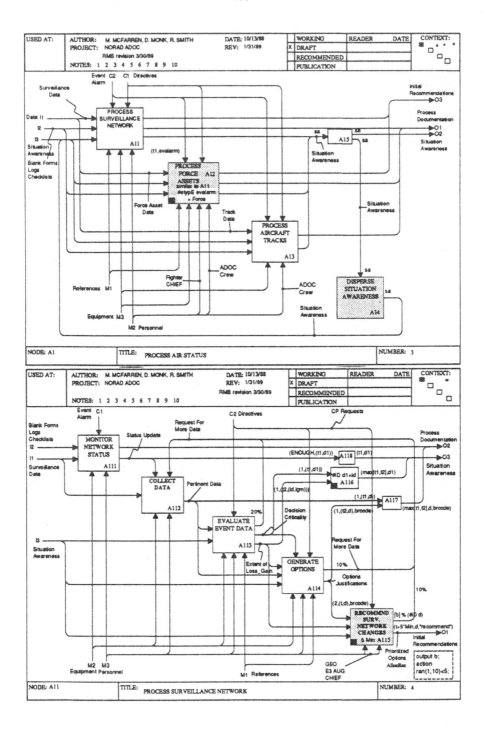

107

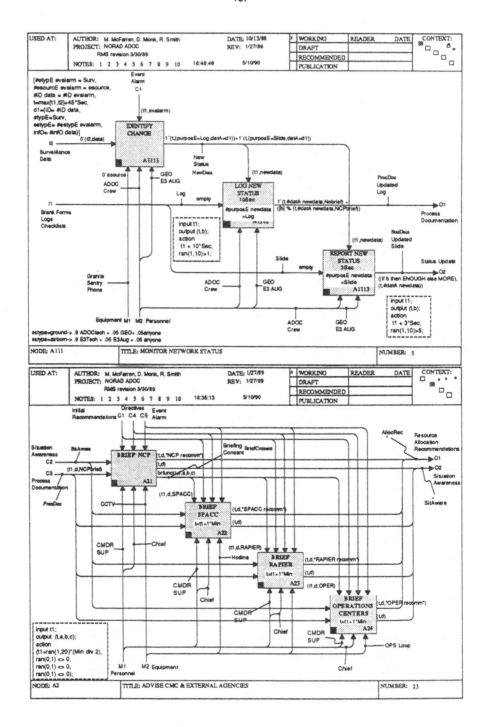

Propositional Temporal Logics and their Use in Model Checking

Jeffery Zucker[1]

Department of Computer Science and Systems, McMaster University, Hamilton,
Ontario L8S 4K1, Canada

Abstract. For the sake of proving correctness of programs with respect to
their specifications, a number of formalisms exist. A traditional one has been
proof systems involving Floyd-Hoare correctness formulae. More recently, especially with regard to concurrent programs such as air traffic control systems
or operating systems, which are nonterminating and concurrent, and in connection with the desire for automatic verification, other formalisms have been
found to be more useful. This paper, and the following one, survey two such
types of formalism which have proved to be particularly successful for efficient automatic verification, or "model checking". In this paper we consider
branching time propositional temporal logics, which serves as a good introduction for the more general formalism of the *propositional μ-calculus*, which
is considered in the next paper. The emphasis is on a broad understanding
rather than on technical details.

0 Introduction

Traditionally, *Floyd-Hoare formulae*, and associated proof systems, have been used
for program specification and proofs of correctness. However for concurrent programs
such as operating systems and air traffic control systems, which are *nondeterministic*
and *nonterminating*, Floyd-Hoare systems have limited applicability.

The behaviour of such systems can be described by a family of *infinite execution
traces*, i.e., *infinite branches of a computation tree*. A good formalism for investigating such structures is *propositional temporal logic*. This approach was already
proposed in Pnueli (1977).

Temporal logic is a type of *modal logic*. It has *temporal modalities*, which permit
the expression of properties such as *invariances*, *eventualities* and *precedences* (as
we will see). This makes it suitable for parallel, nonterminating programs.

There are many versions of propositional temporal logic. We will consider, in
particular, *branching time temporal logics*. Such logics describe partial ordered sets
of *discrete instants*. At each instant, several *alternative futures* are possible.

So the models of this logic are *labelled directed graphs*, resembling Kripke structures for modal logics. The nodes represent *states* or *time instants* ("possible worlds"
in Kripke semantics!), *labelled* with the set of *atomic propositions* true at that state.

---

[1]Research supported by a grant from the Natural Sciences and Engineering Research Council
of Canada.

A *directed edge* from node *s* to node *t* means that it is possible to pass from *s* to *t*, or that *t* is a possible future from *s*.

Note that the truth of a formula at a state will depend, in general, on the truth of subformulas at *other states*. This contrasts with classical propositional logic, where the truth of a formula in a particular state depends only on the truth of subformulas at that state.

Details of the syntax and semantics of this logic will be given in the following sections. We give a brief sketch here.

Suppose that we have a concurrent system consisting of an *n*-tuple of *processes* $P_1, \ldots \ldots, P_n$, with some synchronization mechanism between them.

First, each process P_i is represented by a graph as above (a "flow graph", usually finite) as follows. The process is divided into a number of *blocks* or *regions*, so as to suppress details irrelevant to its synchronization behaviour with the other processes. Each such region is then represented by a node, and a *transition* between two such regions by an edge.

In this way, we construct a *synchronization skeleton* of the system.

Next, the concurrency behaviour of the system as a whole is represented by all *nondeterministic interleavings* of these transitions. In this way, we get an infinite *computation tree*, with infinite *computation paths*.

This formalism is useful for a large class of common problems, and, in addition, serves as a good introduction for the more general formalism of the *propositional μ-calculus*, which is considered in the following paper (Zucker 1992).

This and the following paper do not contain new results, nor are they intended as complete surveys of the field. Rather they are intended as introductions to the field for non-specialists. The references should be consulted for further reading.

This paper has benefitted enormously from the papers Clarke and Emerson (1981), Clarke, Emerson and Sistla (1983, 1986) and Emerson and Srinivasan (1988).

Thanks also to Allen Emerson, Ryszard Janicki and Peter Lauer for comments on earlier versions of this and the following paper.

1   The system CTL^*

The strongest system of temporal logic we will consider is CTL^*, which we investigate in this section. Historically, CTL^* was a development of a weaker system CTL (for "Computation Tree Logic"), to which we will turn in §5.

We now give the syntax of CTL^*.

There are two classes of formulae: *state formulae* (true or false of states), and *path formulae* (true or false of paths).

Formulae are built up using the primitive *modalities* E*p* ("*p* holds for *some* path from the present state)", X*p* ("*p* holds from the *next* state on the current path)", and *p*U*q* ("at some state on the path *q* will hold, and *until* then, *p* holds").

The inductive definition of the class of formulae follows.

First, there is a class $PropAt$ of *propositional atoms* $P, \ldots.$

The classes $StateForm$ of state formulae and $PathForm$ of path formulae are then defined by mutual induction:

S1. *PropAt* ⊂ *StateForm*.

S2. $p, q \in$ *StateForm* $\Longrightarrow p \wedge q, \neg p \in$ *StateForm*.

S3. $p \in$ *PathForm* $\Longrightarrow$ E$p \in$ *StateForm*.

P1. *StateForm* ⊂ *PathForm*.

P2. $p, q \in$ *PathForm* $\Longrightarrow p \wedge q, \neg p \in$ *PathForm*.

P3. $p, q \in$ *PathForm* $\Longrightarrow$ Xp, pU$q \in$ *PathForm*.

We can now define other useful modalities (with their informal meanings).

Ap ≡ ¬E¬p "p holds for *all* paths from present state"

Fp ≡ true Up "p holds at *some* future state on current path"

Gp ≡ ¬F¬p "p holds at *all* future states on current path"

F$^\infty p$ ≡ GFp "p holds at *infinitely many* future states on current path"

G$^\infty p$ ≡ FGp "p holds at *almost all* future states on current path"

We can also define a "weak until" operator:

$$p\mathsf{W}q \equiv p\mathsf{U}q \vee \mathsf{G}p \qquad \text{"}p \text{ holds (at least) until } q \text{ holds"}$$

Note. For expository purposes, it will sometimes be convenient to (temporarily) add certain predicate constants, with specified meanings, to the language. (See, *e.g.*, §4.)

2 Formal semantics of *CTL**

The semantics is defined relative to a *model* $\mathcal{M} = (S, R, L)$ where S is a set of *states* $s, s', \ldots$, R is a binary relation on S such that

$$\forall s \exists s'(sRs'), \tag{1}$$

(s' is a "successor" state to s), and L is a *labelling* which assigns to each state a set of propositional atoms, *i.e.*, $L : S \to \mathcal{P}(\textbf{PropAt})$ (where $\mathcal{P}$ is the power set , so that $L(s)$ is the set of propositional atoms taken to be *true* at state s. A *full path* is an infinite sequence

$$x = s_0, s_1, s_2, \ldots$$

such that for all i, $s_i R s_{i+1}$. Note that R represents the "successor" relation in the computation tree of some program.

Remark 1. The elements of R are called *state transitions*. The condition (1) on R is not required by all authors. In its absence we would define a *full path* as a maximal (not necessarily infinite) R-related path. The resulting theory would not be significantly different.

Now we will define the *satisfaction predicates* for state and path formulae, *i.e.*, the two notions

$$\mathcal{M}, s \models p, \quad p \text{ a state formula}$$

$$\mathcal{M}, x \models p, \quad p \text{ a path formula}$$

by mutual recursion on the complexity of p. We let x be the full path $s_0, s_1, \ldots$, and for any i, x^i denotes the suffix full path $s_i, s_{i+1}, \ldots$. (And we drop the '$\mathcal{M}$' where it is understood.)

S1. $s \models P \iff P \in L(s)$ for P atomic.

S2. $s \models p \wedge q \iff s \models p$ and $s \models q$.

  $s \models \neg p \iff$ not $s \models p$.

S3. $s \models Ep \iff$ for some full path y starting from s, $y \models p$.

P1. $x \models p \iff s_0 \models p$ for p a state formula.

P2. $x \models p \wedge q \iff x \models p$ and $x \models q$.

  $x \models \neg p \iff$ not $x \models p$.

P3. $x \models Xp \iff x^i \models p$.

  $x \models pUq \iff \exists i \left[x^i \models q \text{ and } \forall j < i (x^j \models p) \right]$.

Definitions. Let p be a state formula.

(1) p is *satisfiable in* $\mathcal{M}$ iff $\mathcal{M}, s \models p$ for some state s in $\mathcal{M}$.

(2) p is *satisfiable* iff it is satisfiable in some model.

(3) $\models p$ (p is *valid*) iff $\mathcal{M}, s \models p$ for every model $\mathcal{M}$ and state s in $\mathcal{M}$.

Remark 2. To correlate this semantic definition with the one in the following paper, we can use the notation

$$[p] =_{df} \{ s \mid s \models p \}.$$

(See Remark 1 in §3, *loc. cit.*)

Remark 3. The temporal operators of CTL^* (E, X and U) are all *future temporal operators*, which means that the truth at some state s of a formula p defined with these operators depends only on the truth of subformulae of p at s or later states.

3 Fixed point characterizations

We first define some notation. For two formulas p and q, '$p = q$' means that p and q are *semantically equivalent*, i.e., for all models M and states s: $\mathcal{M}, s \models p \iff \mathcal{M}, s \models q$.

We will now display a series of semantic equivalences, some of which will be used later in the model checking section, and all of which are instances of the general theory of fixed points to be presented in the following paper.

These equivalences should be intuitively clear form the meanings of the modal operators given in §1.2. (Note that below by "future", we mean "present or future".)

$$EGp = p \wedge EXEGp. \tag{1}$$

The l.h.s. here says that for *some* path from the present state, p holds *everywhere* on that path. The r.h.s. says that p holds at the present state, *and also*, at *some* successor state ("EX"), for *some* path from that state, p holds *everywhere* on that path. So EGp is a solution of the equation (in the propositional variable Z) $Z = p \wedge EXZ$, or a *fixed point* of the functional $\lambda Z[p \wedge EXZ]$. (We have used underlining to clarify this.)

$$AGp = p \wedge AXAGp \tag{2}$$

The l.h.s. says that for *every* path from the present state, p holds *everywhere* on that path. (In other words, p holds at *all* future states.) The r.h.s. says that p holds at the present state, *and also*, at *every* successor state ("AX"), p holds at *all* states future to it. So AGp is a fixed point of $\lambda Z[p \wedge AXZ]$.

In the following 4 cases, the reader should similarly be able to provide the functional for which the expression on the l.h.s. is a fixed point.

$$EFp = p \vee EXEFp \tag{3}$$

The l.h.s. says that for *some* path from the present state, p holds *somewhere* on that path. (In other words, p holds at *some* future state.) The r.h.s. says that *either* p holds at the present state, *or* at *some* successor state ("EX"), p holds at *some* state future to it.

$$AFp = p \vee AXAFp \tag{4}$$

The l.h.s. says that for *every* path from the present state, p holds *somewhere* on that path. (In other words, p *must hold* at some future point.) The r.h.s. says that *either* p holds at the present state, *or* at *every* successor state ("AX"), p *must hold* at some point future to it.

The reader should be able to give informal meanings for the last two examples:

$$E(pUq) = q \vee (p \wedge EXE(pUq)) \tag{5}$$

$$A(pUq) = q \vee (p \wedge AXA(pUq)) \tag{6}$$

In the following paper, we will return to the topic of fixed points, and also distinguish between least and greatest fixed points.

4 Safety, Liveness and Fairness Properties

With the operators of CTL^*, we can express some important properties of programs.
1. *Safety:* This means that the system will never reach an undesirable state. This is typically an *invariance* assertion AGp for some property p. An example is *mutual exclusion*, which can be expressed by $AG(\neg cs_1 \vee \neg cs_2)$, where cs_i expresses that process number i is in its critical state ($i = 1, 2$).
2. *Liveness:* This means that the system will always reach a desirable state. This is typically an *inevitability* assertion AFp for some property p. An example is *absence of starvation* of process 1: $try_1 \Rightarrow cs_1$, where try_1 expresses that process 1 is in its "trying region".
3. *Fairness properties:* Consider the two path assertions: 'enabled$_i$' and 'executed$_i$', which say, respectively, that process i is enabled, and process i is executed (for $i = 1, \ldots, m$). We can then express the following properties of a computation path:

(a) The path is *impartial* or *unconditionally fair*: $\bigwedge_{i=1}^{m} F^{\infty} \text{executed}_i$.

(b) The path is *just* or *weakly fair*: $\bigwedge_{i=1}^{m} (G^{\infty} \text{enabled}_i \implies F^{\infty} \text{executed}_i)$.

(c) The path is *strongly fair*: $\bigwedge_{i=1}^{m} (F^{\infty} \text{enabled}_i \implies F^{\infty} \text{executed}_i)$.

5   The subsystem CTL of CTL^*

For many purposes, it is found convenient to work with a subsystem of the language CTL^*. This subsystem, presented, *e.g.*, in Clarke and Emerson (1981), has only *state formulae*, which use the temporal modalities only in certain combinations:

$$p ::= P \mid \text{true} \mid p \wedge q \mid \neg p \mid EXp \mid AXp \mid E(pUq) \mid A(pUq). \tag{1}$$

From these we can define:

$$\begin{aligned} AFp &\equiv A(\text{true} \cup p) \\ EFp &\equiv E(\text{true} \cup p) \\ EGp &\equiv \neg AF\neg p \\ AGp &\equiv \neg EF\neg p \end{aligned}$$

– and hence *safety* and *liveness* properties (see §1.2). We can also define, *e.g.*,

$$\begin{aligned} E(pWq) &\equiv E(pUq \vee Gp) \\ &\equiv E(pUq) \vee EGp \end{aligned}$$

However, we cannot, in general, express *fairness* properties (*loc. cit.*) in CTL.

In the rest of the paper, we will concentrate on CTL. It is simpler than CTL^*, but sufficiently expressive so that the model checking property for it is interesting, as we will see.

Remark. A mild modification of CTL is presented in Clarke and Emerson (1981) There the concurrent processes $P_1, \ldots, P_n$ are represented explicitly in the syntax (compare with (1)):

$$p ::= \ldots \mid EX_i p \mid AX_i p$$

($i = 1, \ldots, n$), where X_i refers to a state following a step by process P_i, and the edges of the flow graph are labelled with the process numbers. The semantics are modified in an obvious way.

6   The model checking algorithm for CTL

The model checking problem for a temporal logic may be stated as follows. *Given a formula p_0 and a model M, is p satisfiable in M?* Or, more specifically: *Given also a state s in M, does $M, s \models p_0$?*

We will show how to solve this problem for CTL, using essentially the algorithm in Clarke, Emerson and Sistla (1986).

Finiteness Assumption. *We assume that $\mathcal{M}$ is finite.* (This just means that S is finite.)

This assumption is reasonable, since: (*i*) it is often the case in practice; and (*ii*) many modal systems have the *Finite Model Property*: If p is satisfiable, then p is satisfiable by a finite model. (See Stirling 1992.)

Notation. For any formula p, $state_{\mathcal{M}}(p)$ is the set of states in $\mathcal{M}$ which satisfy p. (We will generally drop the subscript '$\mathcal{M}$'.)

Note that $state(p) = [p]$, in the notation of §2, Remark 2.

Suppose, then, we are give a finite model $\mathcal{M} = (S, R, L)$, and a formula p_0 of *CTL*. We want to test whether p_0 is satisfied in $\mathcal{M}$, or, more specifically, which states are in $state(p_0)$. In fact our algorithm will label each state s of $\mathcal{M}$ with those subformulas of p_0 which hold at s.

We will show how to compute $state(p)$ for all *subformulae* p of p_0 (including p_0 itself), by structural induction on p. (Compare the satisfaction definition in §2.)

Case 1. $p \in PropAt$. Then $state(p) = \{s \in S \mid p \in L(s)\}$.

Case 2. $p \equiv q_1 \wedge q_2$. Then $state(p) = state(q_1) \cap state(q_2)$.

Case 3. $p \equiv \neg q$. Then $state(p) = S \setminus state(q)$.

Case 4. $p \equiv \mathsf{EX}q$. Then $state(p) = \{s \in S \mid \exists t : sRt : t \in state(q)\}$.

Case 5. $p \equiv \mathsf{AX}q$. Then $state(p) = \{s \in S \mid \forall t : sRt : t \in state(q)\}$.

Case 6. $p \equiv \mathsf{E}(q_1\mathsf{U}q_2)$. This case and the next are the most interesting. Recall equation (5) in §1.3:

$$\mathsf{E}(q_1\mathsf{U}q_2) = q_2 \vee (q_1 \wedge \mathsf{EX}\underline{\mathsf{E}(q_1\mathsf{U}q_2)}). \qquad (1)$$

So p is a fixed point—in fact, the least fixed point—of $\lambda Z[q_2 \vee (q_1 \wedge \mathsf{EX}Z)]$. Hence we will construct $state(p)$ by "approximating from below", *i.e.*, as the union of an increasing sequence of sets

$$state_0(p) \subseteq state_1(p) \subseteq state_2(p) \subseteq \ldots$$

where the sets $state_k(p)$ are constructed in stages. At Stage k, $state_k(p)$ is constructed as follows.

Stage 0:

$$state_0(p) =_{df} state(q_2).$$

Stage $k+1$:

$$state_{k+1}(p) =_{df} state_k(p) \cup (state(q_1) \cap \{s \mid \exists t : sRt : t \in state_k(p)\}). \qquad (2)$$

Since S is finite (by the Finiteness Assumption), for some $k \leq \|S\|$ (the cardinality of S),

$$state_k(p) = state_{k+1}(p) = \ldots = state(p).$$

So we continue constructing these approximations $state_k(p)$ to $state(p)$ until $k = \|S\|$, or until we notice that the approximations are not growing any more.

Case 7. $p \equiv A(q_1 U q_2)$. This is like case 6, except that in equation (1) 'E' is replaced by 'A', and in equation (2) '∃' is replaced by '∀'.

In order to have a better intuitive understanding of these last two cases, let us consider important special cases of them:

Case 6'. $p \equiv EFq \equiv E(\text{true } Uq)$. This just says that p will hold at *some* future state on the current path. Now (1) becomes

$$\underline{EFq} = q \vee EX\underline{EFq}. \tag{1'}$$

So p is now the least fixed point of $\lambda Z[q \vee EXZ]$. So we construct *state*(p) as the union of approximations

$$state_0(p) \subseteq state_1(p) \subseteq state_2(p) \subseteq \ldots$$

constructed in stages as follows.

Stage 0:

$$state_0(p) =_{df} state(q).$$

Stage $k + 1$:

$$state_{k+1}(p) =_{df} state_k(p) \cup \{s \mid \exists t : sRt : t \in state_k(p)\}. \tag{2'}$$

Again, $state(p) = state_k(p)$ for some $k \leq \|S\|$.

Note that in this case, *state*(p) consists of those states s such that *for some path x from s, p holds at some state on x at most k steps away from s.*

Case 7'. $p \equiv AFq \equiv A(\text{true } Uq)$. This just says that p will hold at *all* future states on the current path. This is like Case 6', with 'A' replacing 'E' in (1') and '∀' replacing '∃' in (2').

Note that in this case, *state*(p) consists of those states s such that *for all paths x from s, p holds at some state on x at most k steps away from s.*

7 Time complexity of the algorithm

The algorithm is remarkably efficient, with time complexity $O(|p_0| \times |\mathcal{M}|)$ (in the notation of the previous section), where $|p_0|$ is the length of the formula p_0 and $|\mathcal{M}|$ is the *size* of the model $\mathcal{M} = (S, R, L)$, defined as $|\mathcal{M}| = \|S\| + \|L\|$. The factor $|p_0|$ comes in because of the structural induction on (subformulas of) p_0, and the factor $|\mathcal{M}|$ comes in with cases 6 and 7 of the algorithm, which involves up to $\|S\|$ stages, and (over all stages) an examination of up to $\|R\|$ possible successor states t of s (see equation (2)).

8 Conclusion

We have observed *regularities* in the languages CTL^* and CTL, leading to *fixed point characterizations* (see §1.3). In fact, the model checking algorithm (§3) was based on this.

In the following paper, the notion of fixed point will become central; in fact it will be basic to the syntax and semantics of the language!

References

Clarke, E.M., Emerson, E.A. (1981): Design and synthesis of synchronisation skeletons using branching time temporal logic. Proc. Workshop on Logics of Programs, Yorktown Heights, NY. Lecture Notes in Computer Science, 131, Springer-Verlag

Clarke, E.M., Emerson, E.A., Sistla, A.P. (1983): Automatic verification of finite state concurrent systems using temporal specifications: A practical approach. Proc. 10th Annual ACM Symp. on Principles of Programming Languages, Austin, TX, 117–126.

Clarke, E.M., Emerson, E.A., Sistla, A.P. (1986): Automatic verification of finite state concurrent programs using temporal logic. ACM TOPLAS 8, 244–263.

Emerson, E.A. (1990): Temporal and modal logic. In: Handbook of Theoretical Computer Science, Vol. B: Formal Models and Semantics (ed. J. van Leeuwen), Elsevier, 995–1072.

Emerson, E.A., Srinivasan, A.J. (1988): Branching time temporal logic. In: Linear Time, Branching Time and Partial Order in Logics and Models for Concurrency: School/Workshop, Noorwijkerhout, The Netherlands, May/June 1988 (ed. J.W. de Bakker, W.P. de Roever, G. Rosenberg). Lecture Notes in Computer Science, 354, Springer-Verlag.

Pnueli, A. (1977): The temporal logic of programs. 18th Annual Symp. on the Foundations of Computer Science, Providence, RI, 46–57.

Stirling, C. (1992): modal and temporal logics. In: Handbook of Logic in Computer Science (ed. S. Abramsky, D. Gabbay, T. Maibaum), Oxford University Press, to appear.

Zucker, J. (1992): The propositional μ-calculus and its use in model checking. In this volume.

Added in proof. A good survey of this topic is given in Emerson (1990), which unfortunately we only became aware of after completing this paper.

The Propositional μ-Calculus and its Use in Model Checking

Jeffery Zucker[1]

Department of Computer Science and Systems, McMaster University, Hamilton, Ontario L8S 4K1, Canada

Abstract. This paper, and the preceding one, survey two types of formalism which has proved to be particularly successful for efficient automatic verification, or "model checking", of concurrent systems. In the previous paper we considered *branching time propositional temporal logics*, and now we turn to a more general formalism, the *propositional μ-calculus*. The emphasis, as before, is on a broad understanding rather than on technical details.

0 Introduction

We saw in the previous paper (Zucker 1992, §2) that many of the temporal operators of CTL turned out to be *fixed points* of certain functionals. In this paper we adopt this approach systematically. We will define a language $\mathcal{L}_\mu$ of temporal propositional logic which incorporates least and greatest fixed points.

Thus, although this paper is self-contained, the previous paper may form a useful introduction to it.

We repeat the *caveat* given in the introduction to the last paper. These two papers are intended mainly as introductions to the field for non-specialists, and the references should be consulted for further reading. The many worked examples in the following sections may be useful.

The present paper should also provide useful background material for the paper (Cleaveland 1992) on the Concurrency Workbench in this volume.

This paper has benefited particularly from Emerson and Lei (1986).

1 Least and greatest fixed points

We first give a lightning introduction to the mathematical theory of fixed points of functionals.

Let A be any set, $\mathcal{P}A$ the set of subsets of A, and $\Phi : \mathcal{P}A \to \mathcal{P}A$ a functional which is

- *monotonic, i.e.,* $\quad B_1 \subseteq B_2 \implies \Phi(B_1) \subseteq \Phi(B_2)$;
- *continuous, i.e.,*
  if $\quad B_0 \subseteq B_1 \subseteq B_2 \subseteq \ldots \quad$ then $\quad \Phi(\bigcup_n B_n) = \bigcup_n \Phi(B_n)$, and
  if $\quad C_0 \supseteq C_1 \supseteq C_2 \supseteq \ldots \quad$ then $\quad \Phi(\bigcap_n C_n) = \bigcap_n \Phi(C_n)$.

[1]Research supported by a grant from the Natural Sciences and Engineering Research Council of Canada.

Then by the *Tarski-Knaster Theorem*, Φ has a *least fixed point*, i.e., a least $B \subseteq A$ such that $\Phi(B) = B$. This l.f.p. can be obtained by *approximations from below*, i.e.,

$$\mu\Phi = \bigcup_{n=0}^{\infty} B_n$$

where $\emptyset = B_0 \subseteq B_1 \subseteq B_2 \subseteq \ldots$, and for all n, $B_{n+1} = \Phi(B_n)$.

Similarly, Φ has a *greatest fixed point*, which can be obtained by *approximations from above*:

$$\nu\Phi = \bigcap_{n=0}^{\infty} C_n$$

where $A = C_0 \supseteq C_1 \supseteq C_2 \supseteq \ldots$, and for all n, $C_{n+1} = \Phi(C_n)$.

2 Syntax

We present the syntax of our propositional μ-calculus $\mathcal{L}_\mu$. The propositional atoms may now be either constants or variables. We therefore have the following syntactic classes:

PropCon, the class of *propositional constants* $P, Q, \ldots$,

PropVar, the class of *propositional variables* $X, Y, \ldots$,

ProgAt, the class of *program atoms* or *basic actions* $a, b, \ldots$,

Form, the class of *formulae* $p, q, \ldots$, defined by

$$p ::= P \mid X \mid p \wedge q \mid \neg p \mid \mu X.p \mid \langle a \rangle p$$

where (in $\mu X.p$) X occurs *positively* in p i.e., within the scope of an even number of negations. In other words, p is "syntactically monotonic in X". This guarantees the existence of a least (and) greatest fixed point.

We can then define $p \vee q$, etc., in the usual way, and also

$$\nu X.p \equiv \neg\mu X.\neg p[X/\neg X]$$
$$[a]p \equiv \neg\langle a\rangle\neg p$$

where, in the first equation, X occurs positively in p, and hence also in $\neg p[X/\neg X]$. (Here '$p[X/\neg X]$' is the result of substituting $\neg X$ for all free occurrences of X in p.)

These operators have the informal meanings:

$\mu X.p(X)$ is the *least fixed point* of '$\lambda X.p(X)$',

$\nu X.p(X)$ is the *greatest fixed point* of '$\lambda X.p(X)$',

$\langle a \rangle p$ says that p holds at *some* next state reachable by a,

$[a]p$ says that p holds at *all* next states reachable by a.

We will give their formal semantics in the next section.

3   Semantics

A *model* is a triple $\mathcal{M} = (S, \mathcal{R}, L)$ (compare §2 in previous paper) where (as before) S is a finite set of states and $L : S \to \mathcal{P}(PropCon)$ is a labelling of states with propositional atoms, but now $\mathcal{R} : ProgAt \to \mathcal{P}(S^2)$ is a mapping from program atoms a to sets of state transitions involving a.

Finiteness Assumption. We assume again that $\mathcal{M}$ is finite. (This means that S and $ProgAt$ are finite.)

The *size* of $\mathcal{M}$ is now defined (*cf.* previous paper, §7) as

$$|\mathcal{M}| \;=\; \|S\| + \sum_{a \in ProgAt} \|\mathcal{R}(a)\|$$
$$= \text{ no. of states } + \text{ total no. of transitions.}$$

Remark on König's Lemma. König's Lemma states that any finitely branching tree which is infinite has an infinite path. A consequence of the Finiteness Assumption is that König's Lemma applies to any subtree of the computation tree of $\mathcal{M}$. This has an effect on the semantics, and will be used with some of the semantic equivalences given in the examples in the following sections.

We will define the meanings of formulae relative to *valuations*, *i.e.*, functions

$$\rho : PropVar \longrightarrow \mathcal{P}(S).$$

In fact, we define $[\![p]\!]\rho \in \mathcal{P}(S)$ for all formulae p and valuations ρ, by structural induction on p. The various cases follow.

$$[\![P]\!]\rho \;=\; \{s \mid P \in L(s)\}$$
$$[\![X]\!]\rho \;=\; \rho(X)$$
$$[\![p \wedge q]\!]\rho \;=\; [\![p]\!]\rho \wedge [\![q]\!]\rho$$
$$[\![\neg p]\!]\rho \;=\; S \backslash [\![p]\!]\rho$$
$$[\![\langle a \rangle p]\!]\rho \;=\; \{s \mid \exists t : (s,t) \in \mathcal{R}(a) : t \in [\![p]\!]\rho\}$$

Note that, according to these definitions,

$$[\![[a]p]\!]\rho \;=\; \{s \mid \forall t : (s,t) \in \mathcal{R}(a) : t \in [\![p]\!]\rho\}$$

Finally, for the case $[\![\mu X.p]\!]$, we define the functional

$$\Phi_p^\rho : \mathcal{P}(S) \longrightarrow \mathcal{P}(S)$$

by

$$\Phi_p^\rho(T) = [\![p]\!]\rho\{X/T\}$$

where the *variant valuation* $\rho\{X/T\}$ is defined, for all $Y \in PropVar$, by

$$\rho\{X/T\}(Y) = \begin{cases} T & \text{if } Y \equiv X \\ \rho(Y) & \text{otherwise.} \end{cases}$$

Note that Φ_p^ρ is *monotonic* (since X occurs positively in p), and *continuous*. Hence, by the Tarski-Knaster Theorem (§2), Φ_p^ρ has *least* and *greatest fixed points*, $\mu\Phi_p^\rho$ and $\nu\Phi_p^\rho$ respectively. So define

$$[\mu X.p] = \mu\Phi_p^\rho.$$

Note that, according to these definitions,

$$[\nu X.p] = \nu\Phi_p^\rho.$$

Remarks. (1) To correlate this semantic definition with the one in the previous paper, we can use the notation

$$s,\rho \models p \iff s \in [p]\rho.$$

(Compare Remark 2 in §2, *loc. cit.*) Note that the valuation ρ is a new feature of our definition (not present in the previous paper) because of the presence of propositional variables.

(2) Let $\mathbf{PropVar}(p)$ be the set of propositional variables contained in p. If $\rho_1(X) = \rho_2(X)$ for all $X \in \mathbf{PropVar}(p)$, then $[p]\rho_1 = [p]\rho_2$. In particular, if p is a *sentence* (*i.e.*, $\mathbf{PropVar}(p) = \emptyset$), then $[p]\rho$ is *independent* of ρ.

(3) We have

$$[\mu X.p]\rho = \mu\Phi_p^\rho$$
$$= \bigcup_{n=0}^{\infty} T_n$$

where $\emptyset = T_0 \subseteq T_1 \subseteq T_2 \subseteq \ldots$, and for all n, $T_{n+1} = \Phi_p^\rho(T_n)$. But since S (and hence $\mathcal{P}(S)$) is *finite*, for some n $T_n = T_{n+1} = \cdots = \mu\Phi$.

Similarly,

$$[\nu X.p]\rho = \nu\Phi_p^\rho$$
$$= \bigcup_{n=0}^{\infty} T_n$$

where $S = T_0 \supseteq T_1 \supseteq T_2 \supseteq \ldots$, and for all n, $T_{n+1} = \Phi_p^\rho(T_n)$, and, again, for some n $T_n = T_{n+1} = \cdots = \nu\Phi$.

4 Worked examples

The 'μ' and 'ν' operators can be represented by infinite disjunctions and conjunctions respectively — informally, since these infinite operators are not part of the syntax of $\mathcal{L}_\mu$:

$$\mu X.p = \bigvee_{n=0}^{\infty} p_n, \qquad \text{where} \quad \begin{cases} p_0 = \text{false} \\ p_{n+1} = p[X/p_n] \end{cases}$$

$$\nu X.q = \bigwedge_{n=0}^{\infty} q_n, \qquad \text{where} \quad \begin{cases} q_0 = \text{true} \\ q_{n+1} = q[X/q_n]. \end{cases}$$

It is instructive to work through the (informal) meanings of some $\mathcal{L}_\mu$-expressions, via these infinite disjunctions and conjunctions. We will consider $\mu X.p$ and $\nu X.p$ for a number of formulae p.

Example 1. $p \equiv \langle a \rangle X$.

(a) $\mu X.p = \bigvee_n p_n$, where

$$
\begin{aligned}
p_0 &= \text{false} \\
p_1 &= \langle a \rangle p_0 = \langle a \rangle \text{false} = \text{false} \\
p_2 &= \langle a \rangle p_1 = \langle a \rangle \text{false} = \text{false}
\end{aligned}
$$

$$\vdots$$

So $\quad \mu X.\langle a \rangle X = \text{false}$.

(b) $\nu X.p = \bigwedge_n q_n$, where

$$
\begin{aligned}
q_0 &= \text{true} \\
q_1 &= \langle a \rangle q_0 = \langle a \rangle \text{true} \\
q_2 &= \langle a \rangle q_1 = \langle a \rangle \langle a \rangle \text{true}
\end{aligned}
$$

$$\vdots$$

$$q_n = \langle a \rangle^n \text{true} = \text{``there is a run of } a\text{'s of length } n\text{''}$$

$$\vdots$$

So $\qquad \nu X.\langle a \rangle X = \text{``there are arbitrarily long runs of } a\text{'s''}$

$\qquad\qquad\qquad\quad\; = \text{``there is an infinite run of } a\text{'s''}.$

This last equivalence is by König's Lemma, which holds in the computation tree by our Finiteness Assumption.

Example 2. $p \equiv [a]X$.

(a) $\mu X.p = \bigvee_n p_n$, where

$$
\begin{aligned}
p_0 &= \text{false} \\
p_1 &= [a]p_0 = [a]\text{false} \\
p_2 &= [a]p_1 = [a][a]\text{false}
\end{aligned}
$$

$$\vdots$$

$$p_n = [a]^n \text{false} = \text{``no run of } a\text{'s of length } n\text{''}$$

$$\vdots$$

So $\quad \mu X.[a]X = \text{``no infinite run of } a\text{'s''}$.

(Alternatively: $\mu X.[a]X = \neg \nu X.\neg[a]\neg X = \neg \nu X.\langle a \rangle X$, and use Example 1(b).)

(b) $\nu X.p = \bigwedge_n q_n$, where

$$q_0 = \text{true}$$
$$q_1 = [a]q_0 = [a]\text{true} = \text{true}$$
$$\vdots$$
$$q_n = \text{true}$$
$$\vdots$$

So $\quad \nu X.[a]X = \text{true}$.

(Alternatively: $\nu X.[a]X = \neg\mu X.\neg[a]\neg X = \neg\mu X.\langle a\rangle X$, and use Example 1(a).)

Example 3. $p \equiv P \wedge \langle a\rangle X$

(a) $\mu X.p = \text{false}$ (as in Example 1(a)).

(b) $\nu X.p = \bigwedge_n q_n$, where

$$q_0 = \text{true}$$
$$q_1 = P \wedge \langle a\rangle q_0 = P \wedge \langle a\rangle\text{true}$$
$$q_2 = P \wedge \langle a\rangle q_1 = P \wedge \langle a\rangle\big(P \wedge \langle a\rangle\text{true}\big)$$
$$\vdots$$
$$q_n = \text{"there is a run of } a\text{'s of length } n\text{, with } P \text{ holding throughout"}$$
$$\vdots$$

So $\quad \nu X.\big[P \wedge \langle a\rangle X\big] = $ "can perform a forever, with P holding throughout".

Example 4. $p \equiv P \vee \langle a\rangle X$

(a) $\mu X.p = \bigvee_n p_n$, where

$$p_0 = \text{false}$$
$$p_1 = P \vee \langle a\rangle p_0 = P \vee \langle a\rangle\text{false} = P$$
$$p_2 = P \vee \langle a\rangle p_1 = P \vee \langle a\rangle P$$
$$p_3 = P \vee \langle a\rangle p_2 = P \vee \langle a\rangle\big(P \vee \langle a\rangle P\big) = P \vee \langle a\rangle P \vee \langle a\rangle^2 P$$
$$\vdots$$
$$p_n = P \vee \langle a\rangle P \vee \langle a\rangle^2 P \vee \ldots \vee \langle a\rangle^{n-1} P$$
$$\vdots$$

So $\quad \mu X.\big[P \vee \langle a\rangle X\big] = $ "can perform (finite) run of a's until P holds".

(b) $\nu X.p = \bigwedge_n q_n,$ where

$$q_0 = \text{true}$$
$$q_1 = P \vee \langle a \rangle q_0 = P \vee \langle a \rangle \, \text{true}$$
$$q_2 = P \vee \langle a \rangle q_1 = P \vee \langle a \rangle \big(P \vee \langle a \rangle \, \text{true} \big) = P \vee \langle a \rangle P \vee \langle a \rangle^2 \, \text{true}$$

$$\vdots$$

$$q_n = P \vee \langle a \rangle P \vee \langle a \rangle^2 P \vee \ldots \vee \langle a \rangle^{n-1} P \vee \langle a \rangle^n \, \text{true}$$

$$\vdots$$

So $\quad \nu X.\big[P \vee \langle a \rangle X \big]$ = "can perform run of a's until P holds, or forever!".

5 Interpreting CTL in the μ-Calculus: More examples

Recall (§5 of the previous paper) the definition of the "state formulae" of CTL:

$$p ::= P \mid \text{true} \mid p \wedge q \mid \neg p \mid \mathsf{EX}p \mid \mathsf{AX}p \mid \mathsf{E}(p\mathsf{U}q) \mid \mathsf{A}(p\mathsf{U}q).$$

We will see how to interpret these as $\mathcal{L}_\mu$-formulae. First, we can define

$$\mathsf{EX}p \equiv \bigvee_a \langle a \rangle p, \quad \text{which we write as} \quad \langle - \rangle p$$
$$\mathsf{AX}p \equiv \bigwedge_a \langle a \rangle p, \quad \text{which we write as} \quad [-]p.$$

Note that the disjunction and conjunction over program atoms a shown above are *finite*, by our Finiteness Assumption, and hence '$\langle - \rangle p$' and '$[-]p$' are $\mathcal{L}_\mu$-formulae.

What about $\mathsf{E}(p\mathsf{U}q)$ and $\mathsf{A}(p\mathsf{U}q)$? To help us, let us first try some more examples.

Example 5. $\mu X.\big[p \vee \langle - \rangle X \big] = \bigvee_n p_n,$ where (as in Example 4(a))

$$p_n = p \vee \langle - \rangle p \vee \langle - \rangle^2 p \vee \ldots \vee \langle - \rangle^{n-1} p$$
$$= \text{"along } some \text{ path, } p \text{ holds in at most } n-1 \text{ steps"}.$$

So $\quad \mu X.\big[p \vee \langle - \rangle X \big]$ = "along *some* path, p eventually holds"
$$= \mathsf{EF}p$$
$$= \mathsf{E}(\text{true} \, \mathsf{U} \, p) \quad \text{(as in §5 of previous paper)}$$

Example 6. $\mu X.[p \vee [-]X] = \bigvee_n p_n,$ where

$$p_0 = \text{false}$$
$$p_1 = p \vee [-]p_0 = p \vee [-]\text{false} = p$$
$$p_2 = p \vee [-]p_1 = p \vee [-]p$$
$$p_3 = p \vee [-]p_2 = p \vee [-](p \vee [-]p)$$
$$\vdots$$
$$p_n = \text{``along } every \text{ path, } p \text{ holds in at most } n-1 \text{ steps''}$$
$$\vdots$$

So
$$\mu X.[p \vee [-]X] = \text{``along } every \text{ path, } p \text{ eventually holds''} \quad \text{(by König's Lemma)}$$
$$= \mathsf{AF}p$$
$$= \mathsf{A}(\text{true}\,\mathsf{U}\,p) \quad \text{(as in §5 of previous paper)}$$

Example 7.
$$\nu X.[p \wedge \langle - \rangle X] = \neg \mu X.\neg[p \wedge \langle - \rangle \neg X]$$
$$= \neg \mu X.[\neg p \vee \neg\langle - \rangle \neg X]$$
$$= \neg \mu X.[\neg p \vee [-]X]$$
$$= \neg \mathsf{AF}\neg p \quad \text{(by Example 6)}$$
$$= \mathsf{EG}p$$

Example 8. $\nu X.[p \wedge [-]X] = \mathsf{AG}p$
(similarly, by working with duals from Example 5).

Example 9. $\mu X.[q \vee (p \wedge \langle - \rangle X)] = \bigvee_n p_n,$ where (*cf.* Example 5)

$$p_0 = \text{false}$$
$$p_1 = q \vee (p \wedge \langle - \rangle p_0) = q \vee (p \wedge \langle - \rangle \text{false}) = q$$
$$p_2 = q \vee (p \wedge \langle - \rangle p_1) = q \vee (p \wedge \langle - \rangle q)$$
$$p_3 = q \vee (p \wedge \langle - \rangle p_2) = q \vee (p \wedge \langle - \rangle(q \vee (p \wedge \langle - \rangle q)))$$
$$\vdots$$
$$p_n = \text{``along } some \text{ path, } q \text{ holds in at most } n-1 \text{ steps, and } p \text{ holds until then''}$$
$$\vdots$$

So $\mu X.[q \vee (p \wedge \langle - \rangle X)]$

$$= \text{``along } some \text{ path, } q \text{ eventually holds, and } p \text{ holds until then''}$$
$$= \mathsf{E}(p\mathsf{U}q).$$

Example 10. $\mu X.[q \vee (p \wedge [-]X)] = \bigvee_n p_n$, where
(working as in Example 9, but with '$\langle - \rangle$' replaced by '$[-]$' throughout)

p_n = "along *every* path, q holds in at most $n-1$ steps, and p holds until then"

So $\mu X.[q \vee (p \wedge [-]X)]$

$\qquad$ = "along *every* path, q eventually holds, and p holds until then"
$\qquad\quad$ (by König's Lemma)
$\qquad$ = $A(p U q)$.

Hence we have, from Examples 9 and 10, a translation of CTL into $\mathcal{L}_\mu$.

6 Expressing safety, liveness and fairness properties

Remember (see previous paper, §4) that
(1) a *safety property* means that something bad never happens; it is typically associated with the prefix AG or with ν (see Example 8);
(2) a *liveness property* means that something good eventually happens; it is typically associated with the prefix AF or with μ (see Example 6).
$\qquad$ We give two final examples, involving an alternation of μ and ν, which are associated with fairness.

Example 11. $\nu X.\mu Y.\langle - \rangle [(p \wedge X) \vee Y]$
$\qquad$ To work out the meaning of this, first consider the subformula

$$p(X) \equiv \mu Y.\langle - \rangle [p \wedge X) \vee Y].$$

By the technique of Example 5, it is easy to see that

$$p(X) = \text{"along some path, } p \wedge X \text{ eventually holds".}$$

Then the given formula is $\mu X.p(X) = \bigwedge_n q_n$, where

$\qquad q_0$ = true
$\qquad q_1$ = "along some path, p eventually holds (at least) once"
$\qquad q_2$ = "along some path, p eventually holds (at least) twice"

$\qquad\quad \vdots$

$\qquad q_n$ = "along some path, p eventually holds (at least) n times"

$\qquad\quad \vdots$

Then by König's Lemma, $\mu X.p(X) =$

$\qquad$ "along *some* path, p holds *infinitely often*" = $EF^\infty p$.

(See previous paper, §1, for the notation.)

Example 12. $\nu X.\mu Y.[-]\big[(p \vee X) \wedge Y\big]$

This is the dual of Example 11, so its meaning is

$$\text{"along } every \text{ path, } p \text{ holds } almost \; always\text{"} \; = \; \text{AG}^{\infty} p.$$

7 The model checking algorithm for the μ-Calculus

We adapt the algorithm of the previous paper (§6) to $\mathcal{L}_{\mu}$, following the method of Emerson and Lei (1986).

First, for convenience, we extend the syntax of $\mathcal{L}_{\mu}$ given in §2, to include '$\vee$', 'ν' and '$[\cdot]$'. Each sentence of $\mathcal{L}_{\mu}$ is then equivalent to one in *pnf* (positive normal form), *i.e.*, having at most single negations immediately before the propositional constants.

A sentence can be put into pnf by:
- giving all the bound propositional variables distinct names;
- driving all negations inward, by the rules:

$$\neg\neg p \; = \; p$$
$$\neg(p \wedge q) \; = \; \neg p \vee \neg q$$
$$\neg(p \vee q) \; = \; \neg p \wedge \neg q$$
$$\neg\langle a\rangle p \; = \; [a]\neg p$$
$$\neg[a]p \; = \; \langle a\rangle\neg p$$
$$\neg\mu X.p \; = \; \nu X.\neg p[X/\neg X]$$
$$\neg\nu X.p \; = \; \mu X.\neg p[X/\neg X]$$

Notation. Given a finite model $\mathcal{M} = (S, \mathcal{R}, L)$, let us write $state(p) = state_{\mathcal{M}}(p)$ for the set of states in $\mathcal{M}$ which satisfy a sentence p.

Note that for a sentence p, $state(p) = [\![p]\!]\rho$ (in the notation of §3), for *any* valuation ρ (see Remark 2 in §3).

Suppose now that we are given a sentence p_0 in pnf. We want to find $state(p_0)$.

Suppose that the propositional variables contained in p_0 are among $\{X_1, \ldots, X_n\}$. Note that these are all bound in p_0, since p_0 is a sentence, but they may be free in subformulae of p_0! Hence for subformulae p of p_0, $[\![p]\!]\rho$ is, in general, *not* independent of ρ.

We will compute $state(p_0)$ by computing $state(p)$ for subformulae p of p_0, where $state(p) = [\![p]\!]\rho$, for successive "approximate" valuations ρ, defined by

$$X_1 \mapsto T_1, \ldots, X_n \mapsto T_n \tag{1}$$

for suitable $T_1, \ldots, T_n \subseteq S$.

To begin with, *initialize* $T_1, \ldots, T_n$ to $\emptyset$.

Now compute *state(p)* for subformulae p of p_0, by structural induction on p:

- $p \equiv P$. Then *state(p)* $= \{s \in S \mid P \in L(s)\}$.
- $p \equiv \neg P$. Then *state(p)* $= \{s \in S \mid P \notin L(s)\}$.
- $p \equiv X_j$ $(j = 1, \ldots, n)$. Then *state(p)* $= T_j$.
- $p \equiv q_1 \wedge q_2$. Then *state(p)* $=$ *state(q_1)* $\cap$ *state(q_2)*.
- $p \equiv q_1 \vee q_2$. Then *state(p)* $=$ *state(q_1)* $\cup$ *state(q_2)*.
- $p \equiv \langle a \rangle q$. Then *state(p)* $= \{s \in S \mid \exists t : (s,t) \in \mathcal{R}(a) : t \in state(q)\}$.
- $p \equiv [a]q$. Then *state(p)* $= \{s \in S \mid \forall t : (s,t) \in \mathcal{R}(a) : t \in state(q)\}$.
- $p \equiv \mu X_j q$. This case and the next are the most interesting. We construct *state(p)* ($= T_j$), by approximating from below (*cf.* Case 6 in §6 of the previous paper), starting with $T_j = \emptyset$. We execute the following loop, which uses the auxiliary variable T for a subset of S:

$$
\begin{aligned}
&T_j \leftarrow \emptyset; \\
&\text{repeat } T \leftarrow T_j; \\
&\qquad T_j \leftarrow state(q) \\
&\text{until } T_j = T; \\
&state(p) \leftarrow T_j.
\end{aligned}
$$

Note that this loop terminates, *i.e.*, T_j attains a constant size after finitely many iterations, since S is finite by the Finiteness Assumption.

- $p \equiv \mu X_j q$. Exactly as the previous case, except that at the start of the loop, T_j is initialized to S instead of $\emptyset$:

$$
T_j \leftarrow S;
$$

$$
\vdots
$$

8 Time complexity of the algorithm

The *alternation depth* of a formula p means the maximum depth of alternating nestings of 'μ' and 'ν' in p. The idea is clear, but the exact definition is complicated. It can be found in Emerson and Lei (1986).

We then define $\mathcal{L}_{\mu_k}$ to be the fragment of $\mathcal{L}_\mu$ restricted to formulae of alternation depth $\leq k$.

Note that *CTL* (and many other interesting formalisms) can be interpreted in $\mathcal{L}_{\mu_1}$ (see §5). Also fairness properties such as 'EF$^\infty p$' and 'AG$^\infty p$' can be interpreted in $\mathcal{L}_{\mu_2}$.

Now it is not hard to see (compare §7 of previous paper) that the complexity for $\mathcal{L}_{\mu_k}$ is a *polynomial of degree k* in $|\mathcal{M}|$ and $|p_0|$ (where $|\mathcal{M}|$ was defined in §3 and $|p_0|$ is the length of the $\mathcal{L}_{\mu_k}$ sentence p_0).

9 Further developments

9.1 "Local" algorithms

A drawback with the algorithm outline above (§7) is that one has to compute the *whole fixed point set* $[\mu X.q]$ (or $[\nu X.q]$) to determine whether $s, \rho \models \mu X.q$ (or $s, \rho \models \nu X.q$), for a given s. More "local" (and hence efficient) approaches which avoid this problem have been given in Stirling and Walker (1991), Winskel (1989) and Cleaveland (1990), all of which use *proof systems* in *tableau form* to derive inferences of the form (something like) $s \models q$. These systems use "syntax-directed" proof rules. For example, for 'ν', there is a *fixed point induction rule* of the form

from $s \models \nu X.q \implies s \models q[X/\nu X.q]$

infer $s \models \nu X.q$.

It is shown in these papers that the corresponding systems are *sound* and *complete*. For details, see the papers.

9.2 Dropping the Finiteness Assumption

Finally we point out that Bradfield and Stirling (1990) have succeeded in dropping the Finiteness Assumption. They extend the syntax to formulae of the form '$\langle K \rangle p$' and '$[K]P$' for arbitrary subsets K of a (possibly infinite) set S of states. Again, we refer the reader to the paper for details.

References

Bradfield, J. Stirling, C. (1990): Local model checking for infinite state spaces. Report no. ECS-LFCS-90-115, Laboratory for Foundations of Computer Science, University of Edinburgh.

Cleaveland, R. (1990): Tableau-based model checking in the propositional mu-calculus. Acta Informatica **27**, 725–747

Cleaveland, R. (1992): The Concurrency Workbench. In this volume.

Emerson, E.A., Lei, C.-L. (1986): Efficient model checking in fragments of the propositional mu-calculus (Extended abstract). In: Proc. IEEE Symp. on Logic in Computer Science, June 1986, Cambridge, MA, pp. 267–278

Stirling, C., Walker, D. (1991): Local model checking in the modal mu-calculus. Theoretical Computer Science **89**, 161–177.

Winskel, G. (1989): A note on model checking the modal ν-calculus. In: 16th International Colloq. on Automata, Languages and Programming, Stresa, Italy, July 1989 (ed. G. Ausiello, M. Desani-Ciancaglini, S. Ronchi della Rocca). Lecture Notes in Conputer Science, vol. 372, Springer-Verlag, pp. 761–772

J.I. Zucker (1992): Propositional temporal logics and their use in model checking. In this volume.

Analyzing Concurrent Systems Using the Concurrency Workbench*

Rance Cleaveland

Department of Computer Science
North Carolina State University
Raleigh, North Carolina 27695-8206
USA
e-mail: rance@csc.ncsu.edu

Abstract. This paper presents a case study illustrating the different analytical facilities provided by the Concurency Workbench, an automatic verification tool for finite-state systems. The system we consider is the Alternating Bit Protocol, a communications protocol designed to ensure error-free data transfer over lossy media. Using the Workbench we investigate several features of the protocol, and we isolate a crucial property (the assumption of which is unstated in the protocol definition) that media must have in order for the protocol to be deadlock-free.

1 Introduction

In recent years researchers have begun investigating the practicality of automating the process of reasoning about finite-state systems. Several tools have been developed [19, 22] to provide support for various approaches to analyzing the correctness such systems, with some tools based on temporal logic model checking [7, 30] and others built around the determination of different behavioral relations between systems [9, 10, 11, 15, 17, 25, 31]. Typically, the tools give users one verification methodology with which to work; the Concurrency Workbench [9, 10, 11] is noteworthy in that it gives users a spectrum of techniques for establishing the correctness of systems. It does so by providing implementations of three "low-level" algorithms that may then be specialized in order to yield routines for checking different correctness criteria. As a result of this philosophy, the tool is flexible and easy to extend.

This paper describes the application of the Concurrency Workbench to the Alternating Bit Protocol [2]. The goal of this exercise is to illustrate how the Workbench in particular, and the verification techniques that it supports in general, may be used to analyze finite-state communicating systems. The remainder of the paper is structured as follows. The next section provides an overview of the Workbench and describes the Alternating Bit Protocol. Section 3 then shows

* Research supported by NSF/DARPA research grant CCR-9014775, NSF research grant CCR-9120995, ONR Young Investigator Award, N00014-92-J-1582, and a NSF Young Investigator Award.

how the protocol may be formalized in the system, while Section 4 describes the results of the different analyses performed on the protocol. The final section concludes with a discussion of work that is underway on the Workbench.

2 Background

This section gives a brief overview of the Concurrency Workbench and introduces the Alternating Bit Protocol. The level of detail provided here is necessarily sketchy, and the interested reader is referred to [2, 9, 10, 11] for more in-depth discussion.

2.1 The Concurrency Workbench

The Concurrency Workbench supports the automated analysis of finite-state systems expressed in Milner's CCS [26]. The tool implements a number of commands for defining networks of processes and analyzing their behavior; it also provides support for three major approaches to verification, which we now describe.

The first such approach is grounded in the theory of process algebra and relies on the use of a *behavioral equivalence* to relate specifications, formulated as finite-state machines, and implementations, also formulated as finite-state machines. The intention is that the specification details the high-level behavior that the system is supposed to exhibit, with the implementation describing the ways in which the behavior is to be realized. In the Workbench, one uses CCS to specify both implementations and specifications in this approach; the CWB then applies the operational semantics of CCS to the systems entered by the user to generate the associated finite-state machines. Verification, then, consists in showing that the implementation and the specification are behaviorally indistinguishable. Different equivalences have been proposed in the literature to capture an appropriate notion of "same behavior" [4, 14, 16, 20, 21, 26], and the Workbench includes algorithms for deciding a number of them. It does so by providing a generic equivalence checker based on the bisimulation equivalence of Milner [26] and Park [28] that can be specialized in various ways to compute other equivalences.

The second major verification technique provided by the Workbench also has roots in process algebra; in this approach, one uses a *behavioral* preorder to relate specifications and implementations. In one preorder-based verification methodology, the specification is viewed as providing the maximum allowable behavior, and an implementation is correct if it is "less" than the specification in the preorder (i.e. if it provides no more behavior than that allowed by the specification). In another approach, specifications are interpreted as providing the minimum allowable behavior, and an implementation is deemed correct if it is larger in the preorder. Different preorders have been proposed as suitable for relating implementations and specifications in this fashion [4, 14, 20, 24, 28, 32].

131

The third approach to verification that the Workbench caters for relies on the use of a modal (temporal) logic as a language for writing specifications. Intuitively, formulas in the logic permit one to make statements about the behavior of a system as it evolves over time; to verify a system, then, one establishes that it satisfies the formulas constituting the specification. In the case of finite-state systems, algorithms that make this determination automatically are called *model checkers*; the Workbench includes a model checker for the *propositional mu-calculus*, which is described in some detail in the paper by Zucker in this volume.

The Workbench also provides other commands for analyzing the operational behavior of agents. One command, for instance, returns all the reachable deadlocked states contained in a system, while others permit users to explore the sequences of transitions available to an agent. The most recent version of the system also includes an interactive simulator for CCS [27].

The Concurrency Workbench consists of approximately 15,000 lines of Standard ML of New Jersey code and is available via anonymous ftp from several sites around the world.

2.2 The Alternating Bit Protocol

The Alternating Bit Protocol [2] was proposed as a method for "achieving reliable full-duplex transmission over half-duplex lines." The protocol is in fact an instance of what today would be called a sliding-window protocol [3], where the send and receive windows are of size one.

Figure 1 contains finite-state machines describing the actions to be taken by the sender and receiver in the protocol as described in the original paper. In essence, these work as follows. Both protocol entities maintain single bits, initially 0, that record the "sequence number" of the next message the sender will send and the receiver expects to receive, respectively. When the sender is given a message to transmit to the receiver, it appends the value of its bit, sends this augmented message, and awaits an acknowledgement containing the same bit value from the receiver. If it receives such a response from the receiver, then it increments its bit (mod 2), and the process is repeated for the next message. If the acknowledgement contains the wrong bit value, then the sender retransmits its message and awaits another response from the receiver.

When a message arrives, the receiver compares the "sequence bit" of the message with its bit value. If they match, then the receiver delivers the message, sends an acknowledgement containing the sequence bit of the message, and increments its bit (mod 2). If they do not match, then the receiver sends an acknowledgement containing the erroneous sequence bit and awaits the next message from the sender.

In addition, new versions of the protocol include a time-out facility (to handle lossy media): while waiting for an acknowledgement (message), the sender (receiver) may time-out, in which case it resends the message (acknowledgement) it most recently sent.

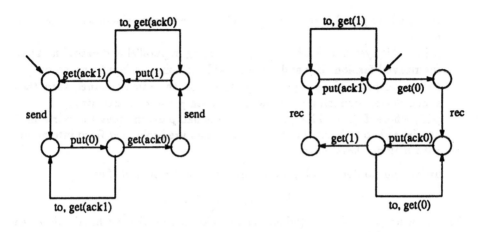

Sender   Receiver

"get" and "put" actions correspond to interactions between the protocol entities and the medium. "to" actions represent time-outs.

Fig. 1. The Alternating Bit Protocol.

3 Formalizing the Protocol in the Workbench

In this section we show how the sender and receiver in the Alternating Bit Protocol may be entered into the Workbench, and we also address the question of formalizing the media over which the protocol entities communicate.

3.1 The Sender and Receiver in CCS

The Workbench provides a version of Milner's Calculus of Communicating Systems (CCS) as the language in which users render their systems. CCS is an example of a process algebra; it provides operators that permit users to build larger systems out of a designated set of atomic actions and other systems.

The atomic actions in CCS correspond intuitively to "communication actions" that systems may engage in. Formally, let Λ be a set of port names; in the Workbench, Λ contains all strings of printing characters beginning with something other than an upper-case letter. Then an action is either:

- an input on port a, written as just a in the Workbench; or
- an output on port a, written as 'a in the Workbench; or
- an internal action τ, written as t in the Workbench.

Given these atomic actions, the following lists the CCS process constructors provided by the Workbench that we will use in this paper.

- a.p, where a is an action and p is a process. This process first engages in a and then behaves like p.

- $p + q$, where p and q are processes. This process may behave like either p or q.
- $p \mid q$. This system consists of p and q running in parallel and executing in an interleaved fashion. If p and q are capable of doing an input and an output (or an output and an input) respectively on the same channel, then they synchronize, producing a τ action, and both p and q change state.
- $p \backslash L$, where $L \subseteq \Lambda$. This process behaves like p except that the ports in L are defined to be local. Thus, other processes are prohibited from interacting with p along these ports.

Recursive and nonterminating processes may also be defined. Let

$$X_1 = p_1, \ldots, X_n = p_n$$

be a sequence of equations (where, in the Workbench, the left-hand side of an equation may be any sequence of printing characters beginning with an upper-case letter). Then in the process

$$p \text{ where } X_1 = p_1 \text{ and } \cdots \text{ and } X_n = p_n \text{ end}$$

p may contain references to the X_i; these references are resolved by replacing X_i by p_i whenever the former is encountered as p executes.

The formal semantics of these operators may be found in [26]; they are given in terms of a relation $p \xrightarrow{a} q$, which may be read as "p performs action a and then behaves like q." Using the semantics, transition graphs may be generated for any CCS term.

```
bi Sender S0 \
    where S0  = send.S0' \
    and   S0' = 'put0.(get_ack0.S1 + get_ack1.S0' + t.S0') \
    and   S1  = send.S1' \
    and   S1' = 'put1.(get_ack1.S0 + get_ack0.S1' + t.S1') \
    end

bi Receiver R0 \
    where R0  = get0.'rec.'put_ack0.R1 \
              + get1.'put_ack1.R0 \
              + t.'put_ack1.R0 \
    and   R1  = get1.'rec.'put_ack1.R0 \
              + get0.'put_ack0.R1 \
              + t.'put_ack0.R1 \
    end
```

Fig. 2. Workbench Definitions for the Sender and Receiver.

We now turn to specifying the sender and receiver of the Alternating Bit Protocol in CCS. Figure 2 contains two Workbench-style definitions for these protocol entities. The **bi** keyword indicates that the identifier to follow is to be bound to the CCS expression that appears next. The \ at the end of some of the lines is a continuation marker indicating that the CCS expression continues on the next line. So the identifier Sender is bound to the CCS process

```
SO \
where SO  = send.SO' \
and   SO' = 'put0.(get_ack0.S1 + get_ack1.SO' + t.SO') \
and   S1  = send.S1' \
and   S1' = 'put1.(get_ack1.SO + get_ack0.S1' + t.S1') \
end
```

and similarly for **Receiver**. The reader should compare these definitions with those given in Figure 1. Note that time-out transitions here are modeled using internal **t** actions.

3.2 Modeling the Medium

The original definition of the Alternating Bit Protocol places no requirements on the media over which the sender and receiver communicate other than they are to be "half-duplex" lines. In order to analyze the protocol using the Workbench, however, it is necessary to develop a model of the medium in CCS. In this section we in fact present several models of lossy and safe media, since as we will see in the next section the correctness of the protocol in fact depends on the specific model of the medium adopted.

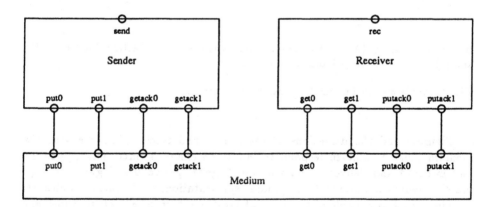

Fig. 3. The Architecture of the Alternating Bit Protocol.

In order to define these media models we must first understand how they are to be used by the protocol entities. We begin by looking at the network architecture of the Alternating Bit Protocol, which appears in Figure 3. The system consists of three components: a sender, a receiver and a *medium*. The first two were described in the previous section; here we concentrate on the medium, for which we give five models that differ in subtle yet important ways.

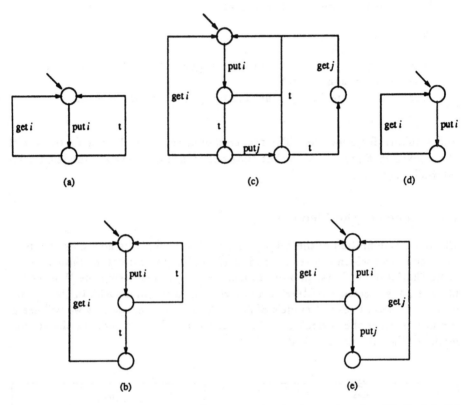

In the above, $i, j \in \{0, 1, ack0, ack1\}$. Action t is the internal action. Media (a), (b) and (c) are lossy, while (d) and (e) are safe.

Fig. 4. Media models for the Alternating Bit Protocol.

Figure 3 and the definitions of the sender and receiver indicate that the medium must be able to respond to inputs on channels put0, put1, putack0 and putack1 and deliver outputs on get0, get1, getack0 and getack1. Figure 4 presents the finite-state automata representations of the media models we consider. Each is capable of buffering at most one "message", where a message may either be 0, 1, ack0 or ack1. The first three are also *faulty*, meaning that as a result of an internal move on the part of the medium, any buffered message may be lost. The first two differ only in the way in which the medium may lose the message; the first may lose a message at any time until the message is retrieved by the receiver, while the second, after deciding that the message is to be delivered, remains in a state in which the delivery cannot be pre-empted. The third faulty medium, and the second safe medium, also permit *overwriting*;

if the medium is full (i.e. buffering one message), and another message arrives, then the buffered message is discarded and the new message takes its place. The Workbench account of each of these media appears in Figure 5.

4 Analyzing the Protocol Using the Workbench

We now turn to an analysis of the Alternating Bit Protocol using the Concurrency Workbench. We focus on using the equivalence checking facility provided by the tool; accordingly, we begin by formalizing the specification of the protocol as a process, and then we compare the protocol (in the context of the different media models discussed in the last section) with the specification to see if they provide the same behavior. We show that with respect to certain media models, the protocol is incorrect, and we use the model-checking and other features of the Workbench to locate the source of the error.

4.1 Specifying the Protocol

Intuitively, the "service" that the Alternating Bit Protocol is to provide is that of a reliable communications channel in which at most one message is outstanding at any given time. This suggests the simple two-state specification given in Figure 6, which requires that the protocol alternately provide send and 'rec actions, with send enabled initially.

4.2 Verifying the Protocol

We now illustrate how the Workbench may be used to analyze the correctness of the Alternating Bit Protocol. To begin with, we must show how the three pieces of the protocol—the sender, receiver and medium—are to be "glued together". Figure 7 indicates how this is done for each of the five media. The declaration beginning bsi defines a set of ports named LocalPorts; intuitively, this set contains all ports that are to be local to the protocol. In this case, all ports used by the media are local. Then five different systems are defined; each consists of the sender and receiver running in parallel with one of the five media, with the media ports declared to be local using the \ operator.

The remainder of this section describes an actual session with the Concurrency Workbench during which the five different "versions" of the Alternating Bit Protocol are analyzed. The Workbench is based on a command loop; the user enters a command, awaits the system's response, and then enters his next command. When the tool is first invoked, the user sees the following.

The Edinburgh Concurrency Workbench
(Version 6.0, August 15, 1991)

Command:

```
bi Lossy-Medium1 LM1 \
    where LM1 = put0.(t.LM1 + 'get0.LM1) \
                + put1.(t.LM1 + 'get1.LM1) \
                + put_ack0.(t.LM1 + 'get_ack0.LM1) \
                + put_ack1.(t.LM1 + 'get_ack1.LM1) \
    end


bi Lossy-Medium2 LM2 \
    where LM2 = put0.(t.LM2 + t.'get0.LM2) \
                + put1.(t.LM2 + t.'get1.LM2) \
                + put_ack0.(t.LM2 + t.'get_ack0.LM2) \
                + put_ack1.(t.LM2 + t.'get_ack1.LM2) \
    end


bi Lossy-Medium3 LM3 \
    where LM3 = put0.LM3p0 \
                + put1.LM3p1 \
                + put_ack0.LM3a0 \
                + put_ack1.LM3a1 \
    and LM3p0 = 'get0.LM3 + t.LM3 + LM3 \
    and LM3p1 = 'get1.LM3 + t.LM3 + LM3 \
    and LM3a0 = 'get_ack0.LM3 + t.LM3 + LM3 \
    and LM3a1 = 'get_ack1.LM3 + t.LM3 + LM3 \
    end


bi Safe-Medium1 SM1 \
    where SM1 = put0.'get0.SM1 \
                + put1.'get1.SM1 \
                + put_ack0.'get_ack0.SM1 \
                + put_ack1.'get_ack1.SM1 \
    end


bi Safe-Medium2 SM2 \
    where SM2 = put0.SM2p0 \
                + put1.SM2p1 \
                + put_ack0.SM2a0 \
                + put_ack1.SM2a1 \
    and SM2p0 = 'get0.SM2 + SM2 \
    and SM2p1 = 'get1.SM2 + SM2 \
    and SM2a0 = 'get_ack0.SM2 + SM2 \
    and SM2a1 = 'get_ack1.SM2 + SM2 \
    end
```

Fig. 5. Workbench Accounts of the Media in Figure 4.

```
bi SERVICE send.'rec.SERVICE
```

Fig. 6. The Service Specification of the Alternating Bit Protocol.

```
bsi LocalPorts put0,put1,get0,get1,put_ack0,put_ack1,get_ack0,get_ack1

bi ABP-LOSSY1
(Sender | Lossy-Medium1 | Receiver)\LocalPorts

bi ABP-LOSSY2
(Sender | Lossy-Medium2 | Receiver)\LocalPorts

bi ABP-LOSSY3
(Sender | Lossy-Medium3 | Receiver)\LocalPorts

bi ABP-SAFE1
(Sender | Safe-Medium1 | Receiver)\LocalPorts

bi ABP-SAFE2
(Sender | Safe-Medium2 | Receiver)\LocalPorts
```

Fig. 7. The Alternating Bit Protocol in CCS.

Our first task is to read in CCS definitions of the processes that have been presented up to this point. We could enter them one at a time at the command line; however, it is also possible to store definitions in files that may then be loaded into the Workbench, and this is what we do here. The file containing the relevant CCS is called "abp." To load it into the the Workbench, we execute the command if abp, where if is short for "input file".

```
Command: if abp
done.
Command:
```

The Workbench responds with done when it has finished processing the file; to see what declarations the tool knows about as a result, we can execute the pe command (for "print environment"). The system responds by printing out a list of all sets, processes, etc. that have been defined in the current session.

```
Command: pe

  ABP-LOSSY1 = (Sender | Lossy-Medium1 | Receiver)\LocalPorts
  ABP-LOSSY2 = (Sender | Lossy-Medium2 | Receiver)\LocalPorts
  ABP-LOSSY3 = (Sender | Lossy-Medium3 | Receiver)\LocalPorts
  ABP-SAFE1 = (Sender | Safe-Medium1 | Receiver)\LocalPorts
  ABP-SAFE2 = (Sender | Safe-Medium2 | Receiver)\LocalPorts
  ...
```

We have elided the output of this command in the interest of saving space.

The Workbench provides commands for computing several different equivalences. In this paper we concentrate on *observational equivalence* [26], which is designed to be sensitive to the visible actions a system can perform as well as its deadlock behavior while abstracting away from the internal action a system might engage in. Intuitively, for two systems to be observationally equivalent it must be the case that whenever one can engage in a visible action (with some internal computation possibly preceding and following it) and evolve to a particular process, then the other system must also be able to perform this action and evolve to an equivalent process. The interested reader is referred to [26] for a more formal treatment of this equivalence.

In the Workbench the command for computing bisimulation equivalence is eq. The result of invoking this command on SERVICE and each of the versions of the Alternating Bit Protocol is as follows.

```
Command: eq
Agent: SERVICE
Agent: ABP-LOSSY1
true
```

```
Command: eq
Agent: SERVICE
Agent: ABP-LOSSY2
false
```

```
Command: eq
Agent: SERVICE
Agent: ABP-LOSSY3
true
```

```
Command: eq
Agent: SERVICE
Agent: ABP-SAFE1
false
```

```
Command: eq
Agent: SERVICE
Agent: ABP-SAFE2
true
```

So for three media—the first and third lossy media and the second safe medium—the Alternating Bit Protocol is correct, but for the second lossy medium and the first safe medium, it is incorrect! The question that immediately arises concerns the source of this incorrectness. It should be noted that future versions of the Workbench will generate diagnostic information automatically to explain why equivalence checking (and preorder checking) fails [5, 6, 8]; here, however, to determine the source of the error in ABP-LOSSY2, we use the method outlined in [11]. We first use the sort command to determine which visible actions ABP-LOSSY2 and SERVICE are capable of, since a discrepancy would indicate a reason for inequivalence.

```
Command: sort
Agent: SERVICE
{send,'rec}
```

```
Command: sort
Agent: ABP-LOSSY2
{send,'rec}
```

Both systems have the same sort, so this is not the source of the inequivalence. The next check is to determine if the systems are capable of the same sequences of visible actions. If they are not, then this is an explanation of why they are observationally inequivalent. The Workbench command for this is mayeq.

```
Command: mayeq
Agent: SERVICE
Agent: ABP-LOSSY2
true
```

The result indicates that SERVICE and ABP-LOSSY2 are in fact capable of the same sequences of visible actions, so this is not the source of the problem.

The next potential source of inequivalence is deadlock; if one of the systems is capable of deadlocking and the other is not, then they would fail to be equivalent. We use a two-step procedure to check this. First, we use the model checker to determine if the systems are capable of deadlocking, and if one is and the other is not, then we invoke a special command provided by the Workbench that prints out all deadlocked states. We use this procedure rather than just invoking the deadlock-finding command directly because the special command is computationally expensive, whereas the detection of the possibility of deadlock using the model checker is very efficient.

In order to use the model checker to determine whether deadlocks exist in a system, we must first devise a formula that is true of processes if and only if they are deadlock-free. Intuitively, a process is *live* if it is capable of some further computation, and it is deadlock-free if every reachable state is live. The property Live may be defined as follows, where the command bpi enables identifiers to be bound to propositions.

```
Command: bpi Live <->T
```

The proposition <->T is a modal one; the modality <-> indicates that in order for a process to satisfy a formula having it as the outermost constructor, the process must have some transition, labeled by any action, that satisfies the remainder of the formula. In this case, what follows the modality is the formula T, or "true"; so a process satisfies Live if it is capable of some step of computation.

To define DeadlockFree, we first introduce a new proposition constructor using the macro definition facility of the Workbench. The constructor is AG, for "always", and its translation into the Workbench's logic is discussed in the papers of Zucker in this volume. The command bmi introduces new macros.

Command: bmi AG P
Body: max(X. P & [-]X)

Here AG is the name of the macro, P is its parameter, and the body, which the system prompts for, is as indicated. Intuitively, a process satisfies AG P if any reachable process satisfies P. We can now formulate our deadlock-freedom formula as follows.

Command: bpi DeadlockFree (AG Live)

We now check whether SERVICE and ABP-LOSSY are deadlock-free using the command cp, for "check proposition."

Command: cp
Agent: SERVICE
Proposition: DeadlockFree
true

Command: cp
Agent: ABP-LOSSY2
Proposition: DeadlockFree
false

So ABP-LOSSY2 is capable of deadlock! To determine why, we invoke the command fd, for "find deadlocks".

```
Command: fd
Agent: ABP-LOSSY2
--- send t t t 'rec t t t send t t t t 'rec t t t ---> ((S1'  \
     where S0 = send.S0'  \
        and S0' = 'put0.(get_ack0.S1 + get_ack1.S0' + t.S0')  \
        and S1 = send.S1'  \
        and S1' = 'put1.(get_ack1.S0 + get_ack0.S1' + t.S1')  \
     end
) | ('get_ack1.LM2  \
     where LM2 = put0.(t.LM2 + t.'get0.LM2)  \
                + put1.(t.LM2 + t.'get1.LM2)  \
                + put_ack0.(t.LM2 + t.'get_ack0.LM2)  \
                + put_ack1.(t.LM2 + t.'get_ack1.LM2)  \
     end
) | ('put_ack1.R0  \
     where R0 = get0.'rec.'put_ack0.R1  \
              + get1.'put_ack1.R0 + t.'put_ack1.R0  \
        and R1 = get1.'rec.'put_ack1.R0  \
              + get0.'put_ack0.R1 + t.'put_ack0.R1  \
     end
))\LocalPorts
```

...

142

There turn out to be numerous deadlocked states; here we look at one that indicates what the general problem is. In this state, which is reachable via the given sequence of actions, the sender, which is in state S1', wishes to execute 'put1; the medium, on the other hand, is only willing to execute 'get_ack1. In other words, we have a collision on the medium; the sender wishes to give something to the medium, which is trying to give something to the sender. The same problem occurs in ABP-SAFE1; notice that it cannot occur with any of the other media because they permit contents of the media to be overwritten.

The Alternating Bit Protocol may be altered to "flush" (i.e. receive any outstanding messages) the medium before it sends a message; the resulting altered protocol may be shown correct for all of the five media. The interested reader may find the altered protocol in [11].

5 Conclusions

In this paper we have illustrated some of the analytical capabilities of the Concurrency Workbench, a tool supporting the automatic analysis of finite-state systems, by conducting a case study involving the Alternating Bit Protocol. We showed that the correctness of the protocol in fact hinges on an assumption, unstated in the definition of the protocol, involving the nature of the underlying medium, and we briefly mentioned how the protocol may be changed to remove dependence on this assumption. All the analysis described in the paper was carried out using the Workbench.

The Workbench is being extended in a number of ways, and we briefly mention some of them here. First, some of the analysis routines are being altered to include the automatic generation of diagnostic information when a process fails to meet its specification [5, 6, 8]. Secondly, more efficient verification algorithms have been developed [12, 13], and these are in the process of being implemented in the system. Also, work is underway on a "front-end generator" that will permit users to define the process algebra that they wish to use and then generate a Workbench that supports this process algebra. Finally, we are developing a front end to the system that will enable users to describe their systems, and simulate them, graphically.

Related Work

Other researchers have used the Concurrency Workbench to analyze various communications protocols; here we mention some of them. Parrow [29] used the tool to analyze a simplified version of the Carrier Sense Multiple Access with Collision Detection (CSMA/CD) protocol. Goyer [18] employed the tool to debug the design of the interprocessor communications protocols used in the BHIVE multiprocessor. Finally, Bruns and Anderson [1] studied the Multiprocessor Shared Memory Information Exchange protocol, which is used in control applications in the nuclear power plants; they located a livelock in the protocol (whose existence was already known) and showed how it could be fixed.

References

1. Bartlett, K.A., Scantlebury, R.A., and Wilkinson, P.T. "A Note on Reliable Full-Duplex Transmission over Half-Duplex Links." *Communications of the ACM* 12, n. 5, pp. 260–261, May 1969.

2. Bertsekas, D. and Gallager, R. *Data Networks.* Prentice-Hall, Englewood Cliffs, 1987.

3. Brookes, S.D., Hoare, C.A.R., and Roscoe, A.W. "A Theory of Communicating Sequential Processes." *Journal of the ACM*, v. 31, n. 3, July 1984, pp. 560–599.

4. Bruns, G. and Anderson, S. "The Formalization and Analysis of a Communications Protocol." Submitted for publication.

5. Celikkan, U. and Cleaveland, R. "On Computing Diagnostic Information for Preorder Checking." To appear in *Proceedings of the 1992 Workshop on Computer-Aided Verification. Lecture Notes in Computer Science.* Springer-Verlag, Berlin, 1993.

6. Celikkan, U. and Cleaveland, R. "Computing Diagnostic Tests for Incorrect Processes." With U. Celikkan. To appear in *Proceedings of the Twelfth International Symposium on Protocol Specification, Testing and Verification.*

7. Clarke, E.M., Emerson, E., and Sistla, A.P. "Automatic Verification of Finite State Concurrent Systems Using Temporal Logic Specifications." *ACM Transactions on Programming Languages and Systems*, v. 8, n. 2, pp. 244–263, 1986.

8. Cleaveland, R. "On Automatically Distinguishing Inequivalent Processes." In *Computer-Aided Verification '90*, pp. 463–477. American Mathematical Society, Providence, 1991. Also Lecture Notes in Computer Science 531, Springer-Verlag, Berlin, 1991.

9. Cleaveland, R., Parrow, J. and Steffen, B. "A Semantics-Based Tool for the Verification of Finite-State Systems." In *Proceedings of the Ninth IFIP Symposium on Protocol Specification, Testing and Verification,* June 1989, pp. 287–302. North-Holland, Amsterdam, 1990.

10. Cleaveland, R., Parrow, J. and Steffen, B. "The Concurrency Workbench." In *Proceedings of the Workshop on Automatic Verification Methods for Finite-State Systems*, pp. 24–37. Lecture Notes in Computer Science 407, Springer-Verlag, Berlin, 1989.

11. Cleaveland, R., Parrow, J. and Steffen, B. "The Concurrency Workbench: A Semantics-Based Tool for the Verification of Finite-State Systems." Technical Report 91-26, North Carolina State University, 1991. To appear in *ACM TOPLAS.*

12. Cleaveland, R. and Steffen, B. "Computing Behavioural Relations, Logically." In *Proceedings International Colloquium on Automata, Languages and Programming.* Lecture Notes in Computer Science 510, Springer-Verlag, Berlin, 1991.

13. Cleaveland, R. and Steffen, B. "A Linear-Time Model-Checking Algorithm for the Alternation-Free Modal Mu-Calculus." In *Proceedings of Computer-Aided Verification '91*, Lecture Notes in Computer Science 575. Springer-Verlag, Berlin, 1992.

14. DeNicola, R. and Hennessy, M.C.B. "Testing Equivalences for Processes." *Theoretical Computer Science*, v. 34, pp. 83–133, 1983.

15. Fernandes, J.-C. *Aldébaran: Une Système de Vérification par Réduction de Processus Communicants.* Ph.D. Thesis, Université de Grenoble, 1988.

16. van Glabbeek, R. and Weijland, P. "Branching Time and Abstraction in Bisimulation Semantics." In *Information Processing 89*, pp. 613–618. North-Holland, Amsterdam, 1989.

17. Godskesen, J.C., Larsen, K.G., and Zeeberg, M. "TAV—Tools for Automatic Verification." Technical Report R89-19, Aalborg University, 1989.

18. Goyer, J.H. *Communications Protocols for the B-HIVE Multicomputer.* Master's Thesis, North Carolina State University, 1991.

19. Har'el, Z. and Kurshan, R.P. "Software for Analytical Development of Communications Protocols." *AT&T Technical Journal*, v. 69, n. 1, pp. 45–59. February, 1990.

20. Hennessy, M.C.B. *Algebraic Theory of Processes.* MIT Press, Boston, 1988.

21. Hoare, C.A.R. *Communicating Sequential Processes.* Prentice-Hall, London, 1985.

22. Holzmann, G. *Design and Validation of Computer Protocols.* Prentice-Hall, Englewood Cliffs, 1991.

23. Larsen, K.G. "Proof Systems for Hennessy-Milner Logic with Recursion." In *Proceedings of CAAP*, Lecture Notes in Computer Science 299, Springer-Verlag, Berlin, 1988.

24. Larsen, K.G. and Thomsen, B. "Compositional Proofs by Partial Specification of Processes." Report R 87-20, University of Aalborg, July 1987.

25. Malhotra, J., Smolka, S.A., Giacalone, A. and Shapiro, R. "Winston: A Tool for Hierarchical Design and Simulation of Concurrent Systems." In *Proceedings of the Workshop on Specification and Verification of Concurrent Systems*, University of Stirling, Scotland, 1988.

26. Milner, R. *Communication and Concurrency.* Prentice Hall 1989.

27. Moller, F. "The Edinburgh Concurrency Workbench (Version 6.0)." Technical Note LFCS-TN-34, University of Edinburgh, 1991.

28. Park, D.M.R. "Concurrency and Automata on Infinite Sequences." In *Proceedings of the 5th GI Conference*, Lecture Notes in Computer Science 104. Springer-Verlag, Berlin, 1981.

29. Parrow, J. "Verifying a CSMA/CD-Protocol with CCS." In *Proceeding of the Eighth IFIP Symposium on Protocol Specification, Testing, and Verification*, pp. 373–387. North-Holland, Amsterdam, 1988.

30. Richier, J., Rodriguez, C., Sifakis, J., and Voiron, J.. "Verification in XESAR of the Sliding Window Protocol." In *Proceedings of the Seventh IFIP Symposium on Protocol Specification, Testing, and Verification.* North-Holland, Amsterdam, 1987.

31. Roy, V. and de Simone, R. "Auto/Autograph." In *Computer-Aided Verification '90*, pp. 477–491. American Mathematical Society, Providence, 1991.

32. Walker, D.J. "Bisimulation Equivalence and Divergence in CCS." In *Proceedings of the Third Annual Symposium on Logic in Computer Science*, 1988, pp. 186–192. Computer Society Press, Los Alamitos, 1988.

Reasoning About Functional Programs in Nuprl

Douglas J. Howe

Department of Computer Science, Cornell University
Ithaca, NY 14853, USA

Abstract. There are two ways of reasoning about functional programs in
the constructive type theory of the Nuprl proof development system. Nuprl
can be used in a conventional program-verification mode, in which functional
programs are written in a familiar style and then proven to be correct. It can
also be used in an *extraction* mode, where programs are not written explicitly,
but instead are extracted from mathematical proofs. Nuprl is the only constructive type theory to support both of these approaches. These approaches
are illustrated by applying Nuprl to Boyer and Moore's "majority" algorithm.

1 Introduction

A type system for a functional programming language can be *syntactic* or *semantic*.
In a syntactically typed language, such as SML[1] [25], typing is a property of the syntax of expressions. Only certain combinations of language constructs are designated
"well-typed", and only well-typed expressions are given a meaning. Each well-typed
expression has a type which can be derived from its syntax, and evaluation of the
program results in a value which is "in" the type. It is usually taken to be a requirement of syntactic typing that there be an algorithm deciding whether an expression
is well-typed and has a certain type; we adopt this convention here.

In a semantically typed language, such as Lisp, typing is a property of the *meaning* of programs. Evaluation is defined for essentially any combination of constructs.
A program has a type exactly if the value of the program (if it exists) is in the type.
This kind of typing is usually undecidable. For example, there is no algorithm which
decides whether an arbitrary Lisp program produces an integer.

Consider the expression *head([1,2,true])* which takes the head of a list consisting
of two integers and a boolean. In SML, list elements must all have the same type,
so this would not be a well-typed program. Even though the evaluation semantics
of SML make sense for the expression, it need not be accounted for by a compiler or
mathematical semantics for the language. On the other hand, the analogous program
in Lisp has type integer simply because it evaluates to an integer.

Existing syntactically type functional languages are clearly more restrictive than
semantically typed ones. There are useful programs that can be written in Lisp, for
example, that have no analog in SML. However, syntactic type systems currently in
use are in fact quite flexible and usually do not hinder natural styles of coding.

In a *constructive type theory*, which we here define to be a functional programming language with a type system that is sufficiently rich to serve as a logic for

---

[1] When referring to a language as functional, we mean the functional portion of the
language.

specifying and reasoning about programs, the cost of having a syntactic type system is that strong restrictions are made on the kinds of programs that can be written. Consider the type

$$T \equiv x{:}N \rightarrow \{\, y{:}N \mid y^2 \leq x < (y+1)^2 \,\}.$$

This is a *dependent* version of the ordinary function type. T has as members functions which map each natural number x to a member of the type of all natural numbers y such that $y^2 \leq x < (y+1)^2$. We can consider this type to be a specification of a square-root program. A program satisfies this specification if it has T as its type. With semantic typing, in order to show a program e has type T, we need to argue that for every x of type N, evaluating the application $e(x)$ results in a number y such that $y^2 \leq x < (y+1)^2$. With syntactic typing, there must be an algorithm deciding whether e has type T. This is a strong requirement, and essentially means that e must somehow encode its own correctness proof.

Two of the most well-known constructive type theories are Martin-Löf's theory [23], which we will refer to here as CMCP, and the Calculus of Constructions [13]. The Calculus of Constructions is syntactically typed, and CMCP, although semantic in conception, places restrictions on programs similar to those of its syntactically typed descendents (such as in [27]).

Neither of these theories permits the definition of a well-typed function by ordinary recursion. For example, encoding the function

```
exp(x,n) = if n=0 then 1
           else if even(n) then square(exp(x,n/2))
           else x*exp(x,n-1)
```

in CMCP requires the use of *primitive recursion* over the natural numbers, as in

```
exp'(x,n) =
  letrec f(m) = if m=0 then λn.0
                else λn. if n=0 then 1
                         else if even(n) then square(f(m-1)(n/2))
                         else x*(f(m-1)(n-1))
  in f(n+1)(n).
```

Here we use lambda-abstraction to form functions (so $\lambda n.0$ is the function mapping n to 0). We also use some syntactic sugar for CMCP's rather unconventional syntax. The *letrec* form, although it looks like a normal recursive definition, is being used here as notation for CMCP's unfamiliar construct for primitive recursion. It locally defines a primitive recursive function $f(m)$ whose recursive calls are only on $m-1$. For each m, $f(m)$ returns a *function* which computes $exp(x,n)$ for any $n<m$. Thus in $f(n+1)(n)$ the $n+1$ only serves to bound the number of recursive calls. A version of exp in the Calculus of Constructions would be quite different from exp', but would be at least as far-removed from the original definition. In addition to having an unconventional form, the programs in the Calculus of Constructions, and in syntactically typed versions of CMCP (in [27] for example), would be annotated with type information.

One of the main attractions of most constructive type theories is that one need not write programs explicitly as above. Instead, one can *extract* a program from a mathematical proof. This is possible because of the *propositions-as-types* correspondence, whereby logical statements are encoded as types. For example, using this encoding, the type given above for square root programs corresponds to

$$\forall x \colon N. \, \exists y \colon N. \, y^2 \le x < (y+1)^2.$$

A proof of this statement, using only constructive rules of inference, will implicitly give a program that belongs to the corresponding type. Thus, instead of writing a program and then showing that it satisfies a specification (that is, belongs to some type), one can treat the specification as a logical statement, prove it, and have the program automatically constructed.

This paper has two main purposes. The first is to give an introduction to the Nuprl proof development system from a functional programming perspective. The second is to illustrate an important feature of the type theory of Nuprl that has neither been described in previous publications nor been exploited in past applications of the system. In particular, although it is a descendent of CMCP and supports a similar propositions-as-types principle, it is a "fully" semantic type system and supports explicit programming in a conventional style.

One way of viewing Nuprl's type theory is that it is CMCP with Martin-Löf's informal semantics taken seriously. The informal semantics he gives in [23] starts with a fairly simple untyped programming language, and the meaning of the judgment $e \in T$, for a program e and a type expression T, is that e has a *canonical form*, or, in other words, a value under evaluation, that has the appropriate form. However, this informal semantics is not fully reflected in the inference rules. Removing this discrepancy requires some substantial changes to the semantics and rules, as we will explain.

We will not give a detailed description of Nuprl in this paper. Nuprl is a system supporting formal proofs in its constructive type theory. The features that distinguish Nuprl from other interactive theorem proving systems are its approach to display and editing of mathematical text, its type theory, and its mechanism for automating formal reasoning, which is based on the *tactic* mechanism of the LCF system [15]. The reader is referred to the Nuprl book [12] for a roughly complete account of the implemented system. Modifications made to the system since the book was published are documented in a reference manual distributed with the system. Information on how to obtain the system can be obtained from the author. A number of research papers related to Nuprl have been published. Some extensions to the type theory are described in [1, 2, 3, 6, 10, 19, 20, 24, 26]. Numerous applications of Nuprl have been made; these include [5, 8, 9, 11, 16, 17, 18, 21, 22].

In order to illustrate explicit and implicit programming in Nuprl, and to show how the system works, we focus on a simple case study in which we verify Boyer and Moore's "majority" algorithm. We first take a conventional approach, writing the program and then proving that the output is appropriately related to the input. We then show how the algorithm (or, rather, something close to it) can be extracted from a proof. We explain the features of the type theory that make these two approaches possible, and in particular point out some semantic subtleties on which the first approach depends. Finally, we make some concluding remarks.

2 The Majority Algorithm

A *poll* is an array $p[0..i-1]$ of "candidates" ($i \geq 0$). The *vote count* for a candidate c is the number k of distinct j, $0 \leq j < i$, such that $p[j] = c$. c has a *majority* if $2k > i$. The problem is to find the majority candidate if one exists. Boyer and Moore's solution [7] is a very simple algorithm: step through the poll from start to end, keeping track of a single "leading" candidate c, arbitrary initially, and the size l of his "lead", 0 initially. At each step, if the next candidate a in the poll is c, increase l by one. If $a \neq c$, decrease l by one, unless $l = 0$, in which case take a as the new c and set $l = 1$. Although the algorithm is simply described, it is not so obvious why it works. A key point is that the algorithm is allowed to return an arbitrary candidate in the case where there is no majority candidate.

Nuprl's type theory has built-in types for integers and character strings. We use the latter for the type Cand of candidates. We represent a poll as a function mapping integers to candidates.

We define two recursive functions: m computes the majority candidate together with its "lead" over the other candidates, and count (later displayed as #) computes vote counts.

```
letrec m(p,i)=
  if 0<i then
    let <c,l> = m(p,i-1) in
    if p(i-1)=c then <c,l+1>
    else if 0<l then <c,l-1>
    else <p(i-1),1>
  else <"noname",0>

letrec count(p,c,i)=
  if 0<i then
    if p(i-1)=c then 1+count(p,c,i-1)
                else count(p,c,i-1)
  else 0
```

The above programs make use of Nuprl's definition mechanism. Objects such as programs and types are entered into Nuprl using a structure editor. Instead of typing text which is then parsed, a user builds an object by calling up templates with slots to be filled in. This provides a great deal of liberty in defining new notations, since there is no need for them to be parsed. The syntax of Nuprl's base language is quite primitive. The programs above are written directly in the base language, but new notations, such as let, letrec and if, have been introduced for readability. The letrec form uses ordinary recursion, and should not be confused with the primitive-recursion form used in the definition of *exp'*.

The first task is to show that these functions return values of the right kind. m should return a candidate-integer pair whenever it is applied to a poll and an integer in the correct range. We can formalize this statement in Nuprl directly.

$\forall$p:$\mathbb{N}$->Cand. $\forall$i:$\mathbb{N}$. m(p,i) in Cand#$\mathbb{N}$

Here -> and # are Nuprl's type constructors for function space and Cartesian product. The type **N** of natural numbers is formed from the primitive integer type by using a subtype constructor. The proof of this is given in Figs. 1 and 2 as a pair of "windows" on a tree structured proof.

```
* top
>> ∀p:N->Cand. ∀i:N. m(p,i) in Cand#N

BY (Id ...) THEN
   (On 'i' Induction...) THEN
   (Unwind1 ''mjrty'' 0 ...)

1* 1. p: N->Cand
   2. j6: int
   3. 0<j6
   4. m(p,j6-1) in Cand#N
   5. 0<j6
   6. p(j6-1)=fst(m(p,j6-1))
   7. snd(m(p,j6-1))+1 < 0
   >> False
```

Fig. 1. First step of the proof that **m** is well-typed.

```
* top 1
1. p: N->Cand
2. j6: int
3. 0<j6
4. m(p,j6-1) in Cand#N
5. 0<j6
6. p(j6-1)=fst(m(p,j6-1))
7. snd(m(p,j6-1))+1 < 0
>> False

BY (Properties ['snd(m(p,j6-1))'] ...)
```

Fig. 2. Second step.

Each window shows a part of the tree. What is displayed here is identical to what the system actually shows, except for some white space adjustment and removal of a few redundant parentheses. In the second line of a Nuprl window begins the *goal* statement. >> is Nuprl's turnstile (⊢), which is used to separate hypotheses from conclusions. In Fig. 1, the goal is the statement of the theorem we are proving. In Fig. 2, the goal is to prove **False** (the contradictory proposition, equivalent to $0 = 1$), under the hypotheses 1 to 7 listed above the turnstile. A hypothesis list together with a conclusion is called a *sequent*.

The text following **BY** is entered by the user and is a *tactic*, which is an ML program that reduces the goal to some (hopefully) simpler subgoals. The tactic applied in the first step of the proof (Fig. 1) is

```
(Id ...) THEN
(On 'i' Induction...) THEN
(Unwind1 ''mjrty'' 0 ...).
```

It executes the informal reasoning step of "do induction on i, then unwind the definition of majority function". By "unwind", we mean replace an application of a recursively defined function by its definition.

The text of the tactic used in Fig. 1 corresponds quite closely to this informal step. **Unwind** unwinds an application of a recursive function. **Unwind1** applies only to the specified hypothesis, with 0 indicating the conclusion of the goal. The argument **mjrty** to **Unwind1** is the full name of the definition of m. The "..." in the tactic text signals a hidden use (hidden by Nuprl's text editor) of the *autotactic*, a tactic that attempts to clean up nasty formal details. **Id** does nothing, so the tactic (**Id** ...) simply has the effect of invoking the autotactic, which in this case just moves assumptions, such as the assumption that p has type **N->Cand**, into the hypothesis list. Another autotactic notation of this kind is "...+". This means that a stronger, but slower, version of the autotactic is used. Finally, **THEN** is used to sequentially apply two tactics.

The execution of the tactic in Fig. 1 produces a single subgoal, which is displayed in the window just below the tactic. Note that this subgoal is the goal in the window in Fig. 2. The subgoal is a detail that the autotactic was unable to take care of. It corresponds to the first branch of the inner **if** expression in the definition of m, and requires showing the the second component of the returned result in this case is non-negative. This follows easily from the induction hypothesis (4): we just need to note that $snd(m(p,j6-1))$ is non-negative since it is in **N**. This is accomplished in Fig. 2 by using the tactic **Properties**, which adds as new hypotheses all the properties of the given term that follow directly from its type.

As this example shows, a Nuprl proof is tree-structured and built in a top-down manner. The theorem being proved is at the root of the tree. The proof editor displays a node of the proof tree through a window which shows a sequent, the tactic applied to it, and the subgoals produced by the tactic. The first character of the first line of a window gives the *status* of the subproof rooted at the displayed node. The * in Figs. 1 and 2 indicate that subproofs are *complete*, so that the goals at each node have been proven. The remainder of the first line gives an address of the node within the entire proof tree.

The statement that **count** is well-typed,

$$\forall p: N\text{->}Cand. \ \forall c: Cand. \ \forall i: N. \ \#(p,c,i) \text{ in } Int,$$

is proved in exactly the same way as for **m**, except that only the first step is required.

151

We prove m correct by first proving an "invariant" lemma. The formulation of the lemma, as well as the exact form of the program m, is due to N. Shankar, who proved the program correct in the PVS system currently under development at SRI. We prove by induction on i that if m(p,i) returns a pair <c,l>, then an upper bound for twice the vote count in p[0..i-1] of each candidate a is i+1 if a=c and i-1 if ¬a=c. The formalization of this statement is the goal in Fig. 3.

```
* top
>> ∀p:N->Cand. ∀i:N.
        let <c,l> = m(p,i) in
        ∀a:Cand. 2 * ( #(p,a,i) + (if a=c then 0 else 1) ) < i+1+1

BY (New ''p j'' (On 'i' Induction ...) ...)

1* 1. p: N->Cand
   >> let <c,l> = m(p,0) in
      ∀a:Cand. 2*(#(p,a,0)+(if a=c then 0 else 1)) < (0+1)+1

2* 1. p: N->Cand
   2. j: int
   3. 0<j
   4. let <c,l> = m(p,j-1) in
      ∀a:Cand. 2*(#(p,a,j-1)+(if a=c then 0 else 1)) < ((j-1)+1)+1
   >> let <c,l> = m(p,j) in
      ∀a:Cand. 2*(#(p,a,j)+(if a=c then 0 else 1)) < (j+1)+1
```

Fig. 3. The main lemma.

The first step simply applies induction. The tactic New just picks some nice variable names to be used in the subproofs. The first subgoal is knocked off in one step, shown in Fig. 4.

```
* top 1
1. p: N->Cand
>> let <c,l> = m(p,0) in
   ∀a:Cand. 2*(#(p,a,0)+(if a=c then 0 else 1)) < (0+1)+1

BY (Unwind ''count mjrty'' ...+)
```

Fig. 4. Base case of induction.

The induction step is shown in Fig. 5. An obvious approach to proving this goal is to unwind m, replacing m(p,j) with the body of m, and then do the case analysis suggested by the if expression in the definition of m. The tactic UnwindTerm accomplishes the first task, and Cases the second. The purpose of ETerm is as follows. When we unwind m, we get an expression containing

```
let <c,l> = m(p,j-1)
```

ETerm 'm(p,j-1)' generalizes m(p,j-1) to a variable, and then, since the variable has a type which is a product, splits the variable into a pair of variables (so it "eliminates" the term). This enables the simplifier (in the autotactic) to remove the let expression.

Each of the three subgoals generated by the case analysis in Fig 5 is proved in one step. Rather than show the entire step, which would include redisplaying the subgoal, we just show the tactics used. The first subgoal is proven by

```
(InstHyp ['a'] 7 ...)
THEN UnwindTerm '#(p,a,j)'
THEN (Cases ['a=c'] THEN Cases ['a=p(j-1)'] ...+)
```

The step here is to use the induction hypothesis on a and do the case analysis suggested by the if expressions in the instantiated induction hypothesis and in the conclusion of the goal. InstHyp instantiates the universally quantified formula in hypothesis 7 on the term a.

The proof of the second subgoal of Fig. 5 is identical to that of the first, except that 7 becomes 8, and the proof of the third is the same as that of the second, except that we need to give a hint to the simplifier by using the tactic

```
(Assert 'l = 0' ...)
```

This simply notes as a new hypothesis the obvious fact that 1=0; the simplifier will use this to simplify 1 to 0 wherever it occurs.

The final statement of correctness of m is the goal in Fig. 6. It says that if a is a majority candidate, then m computes it. The theorem is proved by instantiating the lemma we just proved, and breaking m(p,i) into a pair <c,l>. The autotactic is not smart enough to complete the proof. We help it in Fig. 7 by pointing out the case analysis suggested by the if expression in hypothesis 7 and then proving the resulting subgoal by doing some low-level reasoning about the monotonicity properties of integer inequalities, using the tactic

```
(Mono 7 '-' 8 THEN OnLast λi. MonoWithR i '-' 'l = 1' ...)
THEN (Assert '0≤1' ...)
```

It would be straightforward to encapsulate in a tactic the operation of performing case analyses suggested by if expressions, and the low-level inequality reasoning can be dealt with automatically by a procedure such as Shostak's [28], (a Nuprl implementation of which has just been completed).

```
* top 2
1. p: N->Cand
2. j: int
3. 0<j
4. let <c,l> = m(p,j-1) in
   ∀a:Cand. 2*(#(p,a,j-1)+(if a=c then 0 else 1)) < ((j-1)+1)+1
>> let <c,l> = m(p,j) in
   ∀a:Cand. 2*(#(p,a,j)+(if a=c then 0 else 1)) < (j+1)+1

BY (New ''c l'' (UnwindTerm 'm(p,j)' THEN ETerm 'm(p,j-1)' ...) ...)
   THEN (Cases ['p(j-1)=c'; '0<l'] ...+)
        % suggested by the definition of mjrty %

1* 1. p: N->Cand
   2. j: int
   3. c: Cand
   4. l: N
   5. a: Cand
   6. p(-1+j)=c
   7. ∀a1:atom. 2*#(p,a1,-1+j)+2*(if a1=c then 0 else 1) < j+1
   8. 0<j
   >> 2*#(p,a,j)+2*(if a=p(-1+j) then 0 else 1+1) < 2+(j+1)

2* 1. p: N->Cand
   2. j: int
   3. c: Cand
   4. l: N
   5. a: Cand
   6. 0<l
   7. ¬(p(-1+j)=c)
   8. ∀a1:atom. 2*#(p,a1,-1+j)+2*(if a1=c then 0 else 1) < j+1
   9. 0<j
   >> 2*#(p,a,j)+2*(if a=c then 0 else -1+1) < j+1

3* 1. p: N->Cand
   2. j: int
   3. c: Cand
   4. l: N
   5. a: Cand
   6. ¬(0<l)
   7. ¬(p(-1+j)=c)
   8. ∀a1:atom. 2*#(p,a1,-1+j)+2*(if a1=c then 0 else 1) < j+1
   >> 2*#(p,a,j)+2*(if a=p(-1+j) then 0 else 1) < 2+j
```

Fig. 5. Induction step.

```
* top
>> ∀p:N->Cand. ∀i:N. ∀a:Cand.
   i < 2 * #(p,a,i)  =>  a = fst(m(p,i))

BY (Id ...)
   THEN (InstLemma 'invariant' ['p';'i';'a'] ...)
   THEN ((New ''c l'' ((ETerm 'm(p,i)') ...) ...+) ...+)

1* 1. p: N->Cand
   2. i: N
   3. a: Cand
   4. c: Cand
   5. l: N
   6. i < 2*#(p,a,i)
   7. 2*#(p,a,i)+2*(if a=c then 0 else 1) < 1+(i+1)
   >> a=c
```

Fig. 6. Correctness of m.

```
* top 1
1. p: N->Cand
2. i: N
3. a: Cand
4. c: Cand
5. l: N
6. i < 2*#(p,a,i)
7. 2*#(p,a,i)+2*(if a=c then 0 else 1) < 1+(i+1)
>> a=c

BY (Cases ['a=c'] ...+)

1* 1. p: N->Cand
   2. i: N
   3. a: Cand
   4. c: Cand
   5. l: N
   6. ¬(a=c)
   7. 2*1+2*#(p,a,i) < 1+(i+1)
```

Fig. 7. An obvious case analysis.

3 Extracting a Majority Algorithm

The proof presented in the previous section can easily be modified so that a majority vote algorithm can be extracted from it. Before we explain the features of Nuprl's type theory that make this extraction possible, we will show the modified proof and point out the steps which implicitly introduce parts of the program.

We modify the statement of the correctness theorem by replacing the statement that m produces appropriate output with a statement that just says that an appropriate output value exists. So, instead of

```
∀p:N->Cand. ∀i:N.
    ∀a:Cand. i < 2 * #(p,a,i)  =>  a = fst(m(p,i)),
```

we have

```
∀p:N->Cand. ∀i:N. ∃c:Cand.
    ∀a:Cand. i < 2 * #(p,a,i) => a=c.
```

To prove this, we first prove an analogous modification of the invariant lemma. The prove is again by induction. The first step is shown in Fig. 8. Although this step is the same as before, it now has the additional effect of introducing part of a program. In particular, its contribution to the program extracted from the proof of this theorem is a construct for primitive recursion over the integers; this will play the role of the ordinary recursion in the definition of m.

```
* top
>> ∀p:N->Cand. ∀i:N. ∃c:Cand. ∃l:N.
      ∀a:Cand. 2 * ( #(p,a,i) + (if a=c then 0 else 1) ) < i+1+1

BY (New ``p j`` (On `i` Induction ...) ...)

1* 1. p: N->Cand
   >> ∃c:Cand. ∃l:N. ∀a:Cand.
         2*(#(p,a,0)+(if a=c then else 1)) < (0+1)+1
2* 1. p: N->Cand
   2. j: int
   3. 0<j
   4. a19: Cand
   5. a21: N
   6. ∀a:Cand. 2*(#(p,a,j-1)+(if a=a19 then 0 else a21))
            < ((j-1)+a21)+1
   >> ∃c:Cand. ∃l:N. ∀a:Cand.
         2*(#(p,a,j)+(if a=c then 0 else 1)) < (j+1)+1
```

Fig. 8. First step in modified lemma.

The first subgoal is proved as before, except that we additionally need to provide witnesses for the existential quantifiers. The goal is proved by the tactic

```
(ITerms ['"noname"';'0'] ...) THEN (Unwind ''count'' ...+)
```

where ITerms provides the values to be used for c and l. This step introduces the "base case" value into the program, which corresponds to last line of the definition of m (the i=0 case).

The proof of the second subgoal proceeds as before, except that we first use a tactic that repairs the unfortunate choice the tactic made of a19 and a21 as names for the witnesses in the induction hypothesis. Fig. 9 shows the step following the repair. We do the same case analysis as before, but we additionally provide the existential witnesses for each of the three cases. The bulk of the extracted program is built in this step. The case analysis contributes a conditional expression corresponding to the inner if in the definition of m, and supplying the witnesses contributes the pairs to be returned in the branches of the conditional. We do not show the subgoals in Fig. 9 because they are almost identical to those in Fig. 5, and are proved exactly the same way.

```
* top 2 1
1. p: N->Cand
2. j: int
3. 0<j
4. c: Cand
5. l: N
6. Va:Cand. 2*(#(p,a,j-1)+(if a=c then 0 else 1))<((j-1)+1)+1
>> Ec:Cand. El:N. Va:Cand.
      2*(#(p,a,j)+(if a=c then 0 else 1))<(j+1)+1

BY (Cases ['p(j-1)=c'; '0<l'] ...) THENL
   [(ITerms ['c';'l+1'] ...+);
    (ITerms ['c';'l-1'] ...+);
    (ITerms ['p(j-1)';'1'] ...+)
   ]
```

Fig. 9. Induction step in modified lemma.

The first step of the proof of the modified correctness theorem is shown in Fig. 10. The step is the same as before, except that we use a tactic to explicitly point out that the candidate satisfying the theorem is the one give by the lemma. The contribution of this step to the final extracted program is to apply the program from the lemma to the arguments p and i, and to project out the first component (c) of the returned result.

Fig. 11 shows the program, syntactically beautified for readability, that was extracted from this theorem. The program refers to the extraction of the lemma (which

```
* top
>> ∀p:N->Cand. ∀i:N.
      ∃c:Cand. ∀a:Cand. i < 2 * #(p,a,i) => a=c

BY (Id ...) THEN
   (New ''c 1'' (InstLemma 'invariant_ext' ['p';'i'] ...) ...) THEN
   (ITerm 'c' ...)

1* 1. p: N->Cand
   2. i: N
   3. c: Cand
   4. l: N
   5. ∀a:Cand. 2*(#(p,a,i)+(if a=c then 0 else 1))<(i+1)+1
   6. a: Cand
   7. i<2*#(p,a,i)
   >> a=c
```

Fig. 10. Modified correctness theorem: first step.

is named **invariant_ext**); this program is also shown in the figure. Although one can recognize the elements of **m** in these programs, some parts could be simplified, and there is a large amount of what seems to be junk. The **letrec** here is notation for primitive recursion, not general recursion as in the definition of **m**. The **case** statements do a case analysis on the form of their first argument. The value of

```
case e of
inl(x) -> a
inr(x) -> b,
```

if **e** has a value of the form **inl(u)**, is **a**, where **x** takes on the value **u**, and analogously if **e** is **inr(u)**. Note that the **case** statements in the extracted program could be eliminated. The program also contains "junk", most of which involves λ-abstraction or the constant **axiom**. For example, instead of the expected pair **<"noname",0>** in the base case, we have

```
<"noname",<0,λa.axiom>>.
```

There are two sources for this clutter. First of all, the form of an extracted program is very sensitive to the structure of the relevant proofs, and also to the exact way in which relevant lemmas are stated. Developers of tactics and libraries of theorems for Nuprl have focused on the mathematics. Little attention has been paid to whether the design of the tactics or the statements of theorems yields the best programs. A more fundamental reason for the clutter is due to the nature of the program extraction feature. We will return to this point after we discuss the propositions-as-types correspondence in the next section.

An important point to keep in mind is that we can deal with an extracted program abstractly. When writing other programs, we can use it simply by referring to

```
λp λi. let <c,x>=term_of(invariant_ext)(p)(i) in
       let <y,z>=x in
       <c, λu λv. axiom>

λp λi.
   letrec f(n) =
     if n=0 then λx.<"noname",<0,λa.axiom>>;
     else
       λx.
          (let <c,x> = f(n-1)(axiom) in
           let <l,x> = x in
           case (if p(j-1)=c then inl(axiom) else inr(λx.x)) of
           inl(x) -> <c,<l+1,λa.axiom>>
           inr(x) -> case (if 0=l then inl(axiom) else inr(axiom)) of
                      inl(x) -> <c,<l-1,λa.axiom>>
                      inr(x) -> <p(j-1),<l,λa.axiom>>
          )(axiom)
   in f(i)
```

Fig. 11. Extraction from the lemma.

the name of the theorem from which it was extracted. When reasoning about the extracted program, we do not look at its implementation, but rather just use the fact that it satisfies the specification which is the statement of the theorem. Typically, we do not explicitly refer the extracted program at all. Instead, we build further programs by extraction, and it is uses of the rule to invoke previous lemmas that implicitly add previously extracted programs.

4 The Nuprl Type Theory

4.1 Propositions-as-Types

It is the propositions-as-types correspondence that is responsible for the ability to extract programs from proofs. The idea is that for each way of forming a logical statement, there is a corresponding type constructor. Thus logical statements are encoded as types. The members of the types correspond to "computational evidence" for the corresponding propositions. The truth of a logical statement is identified with the corresponding type having a member. "Truth" here is truth in a constructive sense. One way to think of constructive truth is as a refinement of ordinary (i.e. classical) truth: a statement is constructively true if it is true and in addition there is a program, or construction, that "witnesses" the truth. This characterization is philosophically incorrect, but accurate enough for a practical understanding. Table 1 shows the basic correspondence. Each element of the second column uses a built-in type constructor of Nuprl. The third column shows typical elements of the types.

The type $x: A \rightarrow B$ is the *dependent function type*, so-called because the type of a value of the function can depend on the argument. Values in this type have the

Table 1. The propositions-as-types correspondence.

False	void	
$A \Rightarrow B$	$A \rightarrow B$	$\lambda x. b$
$A \,\&\, B$	$A \# B$	$\langle a, b \rangle$
$A \vee B$	$A \mid B$	$inl(a),\ inr(b)$
$\forall x{:}A.\ B$	$x{:}A \rightarrow B$	$\lambda x. b$
$\exists x{:}A.\ B$	$x{:}A \# B$	$\langle a, b \rangle$

form $\lambda x. b$ and have the property that for every $a \in A$, $b[a/x] \in B[a/x]$. The type $x{:}A \# B$ is a dependent version of the usual Cartesian product. Values in it have the form $\langle a, b \rangle$ where $a \in A$ and $b \in B[a/x]$. $A \mid B$ is a disjoint union type, and *void* is the empty type.

How do we represent the proposition that two objects are equal? In ordinary mathematics, which takes place in set theory, there is one single notion of equality: two objects are equal if and only if they are the same set. The situation is different in type theory because the objects are not sets but programs from an untyped programming language. Consider the programs

$$f \equiv \lambda n.\ 0$$
$$f' \equiv \lambda n.\ if\ n{<}0\ then\ 1\ else\ 0$$

Let N be the type of natural numbers, and let *Int* be the type of all integers. Both f and f' are members of both $N \rightarrow N$ and $Int \rightarrow N$. However, they are equal when considered as members of the first type, since they both output 0 on any $n \in N$, but they are unequal when considered as members of the second type, since they differ on -1. Hence the notion of equality depends on types.

The type theory has a special type constructor to reflect this notion of equality. In particular, for any type A and members a, b of A there is a type denoted

$$a = b \in A$$

which has a single value *axiom* as a member when a and b are equal as members of A, and which is empty otherwise. The formulas of the form a **in** A, used in the theorems that m and count are well-typed, are actually defined in terms of the equality type: a **in** A stands for $a = a \in A$.

For convenience, Nuprl also has a type that reflects integer inequality: if a and b are integers (that is, they are programs that evaluate to integers), then $a < b$ is a type which has *axiom* as a member if (the value of) a is less than (the value of) b.

The description given above of the dependent function type is incomplete because it does not take equality into account. There is an additional restriction that a member of $x{:}A \rightarrow B$ must respect equality, mapping equal members a, a' of A to equal members of $B[a/x]$. Note that for this to make sense, we must also require that $B[a/x]$ and $B[a'/x]$ have the same members and same equality relation.

To illustrate the propositions-as-types correspondence, consider the statement of the main theorem of the previous section. When we change the logical connectives to the type constructors they stand for, the statement is as follows.

$$p: (N \to Cand) \to i: N \to c: Cand \,\#\, (a: Cand \to i < 2 * \#(p, a, i) \to a = c \in Cand).$$

A member of this type is a function f that takes p and i as arguments and returns a pair whose first component is a member of $Cand$ and whose second component is a member of the type

$$a: Cand \to i < 2 * \#(p, a, i) \to a = c \in Cand$$

The only possible member of this type (up to equality) is $\lambda a. \lambda v.\ axiom$, and it is a member if and only if for every $a \in Cand$, if $i < 2 * \#(p, a, i)$ then a and c are equal. Thus f applied to p and i returns a pair $< c, u >$ where c is a candidate and u is "evidence" that c is a majority candidate if there is a majority candidate. It is this latter kind of uninteresting evidence which clutters up the program in Fig. 11. It seems to be unavoidable if one sticks to the subset of Nuprl similar to CMCP. For example, it is present in Backhouse's hand-crafted version of the majority algorithm in [4]. One way in which the uninteresting evidence can be eliminated is to use Nuprl's subtype constructor in place of the dependent Cartesian product. See the Nuprl book [12] for more on this approach.

The rules of Nuprl are designed so that whenever a sequent $\gg T$ has a proof, then T is a type and we can compute from the proof a member $t \in T$, called the *extraction* of the proof. A sequent with hypotheses also has an extraction, which may mention the variables declared in the hypothesis list. The extraction of a proof can be computed bottom-up since each rule of Nuprl specifies how to compute the extraction for its conclusion given extractions for its premises.

To give an idea of how the rules are designed, we look at two simplified rules for the function type. We show the rules upside-down, with the premises of the rule listed below the conclusion of the rule, in order to parallel the goal/subgoal view taken in the previous sections. We also annotate the rule with a specification of how the extraction is to be computed. The first rule is as follows.

$$\gg x: A \to B \quad \textbf{ext } \lambda x.\, b$$
$$x: A \gg B \quad \textbf{ext } b.$$

In terms of the corresponding logical statements, this rule says that to prove $\forall x: A.\ B$ it suffices to prove B under the assumption that x is in A. The parts following **ext** in the rule say that if b (which may refer to x) is the extraction for a proof of the subgoal, then the extraction for the goal is $\lambda x.\, b$.

The second rule is

$$\gg B \quad \textbf{ext } f(a)$$
$$\gg A \to B \quad \textbf{ext } f$$
$$\gg A \quad \textbf{ext } a.$$

In logical terms, this is modus ponens: to prove B, it suffices to prove A and $A \Rightarrow B$ for some A. If the extraction for the first subgoal is f (so $f \in A \to B$), and the extraction for the second subgoal is a (so $a \in A$) then the extraction for the goal is $f(a)$ $(f(a) \in B)$.

Each of these two rules introduces a single programming-language construct into an extraction. The first introduces λ-abstraction, and the second introduces application. Every construct in Nuprl's programming language has a corresponding rule that introduces it. As another example, the primitive-recursion form, which appears in the extracted majority program, is introduced by the rule for integer induction.

4.2 Reasoning About Explicit Programs

The ability to reason about explicit programs as we did in the proof that m is correct relies on some rather subtle points of Nuprl's type theory. These points are related to the induction rule(s) and the "direct computation" rules. Before discussing these, we need to say more about the relationship of equality to the inference rules.

Consider the following "explicit" version of the first rule above for function types.

$$\gg \lambda x. b \in A \rightarrow B$$
$$x : A \gg b \in B.$$

This essentially says that $\lambda x. b$ is a member of $A \rightarrow B$ if for every argument it produces a value of the right type. This is a stronger rule than it might at first appear, since a member of $A \rightarrow B$ must also preserve equality. Thus we need to give a semantics to sequents such that if

$$x : A \gg b \in B.$$

is true, then it follows that if a and a' are equal members of A then $b[a/x]$ and $b[a'/x]$ are equal members of B. The basic idea for such a semantics is due to Martin-Löf [23], and is one of the most important innovations in the design of his type theory. The idea involves incorporating a *functionality* requirement in the semantics of sequents (our sequents correspond to the *hypothetical judgements* of [23]). Part of the meaning of a sequent is that the conclusion is functional in the hypotheses, in the sense that equal members of the hypothesis types give equal conclusions, and also that each hypothesis is functional in previous hypotheses.

To see how Nuprl's rules are used to reason about explicit programs, let us consider a simple example. Define g by

$$\textit{letrec } g(n) = \textit{if } n{=}0 \textit{ then } 1 \textit{ else } n * g(n-1).$$

To prove

$$n : N \gg g(n) \in N$$

we use the rule for induction on the natural numbers.[2] The subgoals are

$$\gg g(0) \in N$$

and

---

[2] Actually, Nuprl has a built-in induction rule for the integers, and the restriction to natural numbers is a derived rule.

$$n : N, \ n > 0, \ g(n-1) \in N \ \gg \ g(n) \in N.$$

Proving both of these subgoals involves using Nuprl's *direct computation* rules, which allow one to perform symbolic computation steps on parts of a sequent. For the first subgoal, we can replace $g(0)$ by the result, 1, of evaluating it. For the second subgoal, by performing some symbolic computation steps, we reduce the sequent to

$$n : N, \ n > 0, \ g(n-1) \in N \ \gg \ (if \ n{=}0 \ then \ 1 \ else \ n * g(n-1)) \in N.$$

This is easily proved using the induction hypothesis.

The direct computation rules are justified because of Nuprl's semantic typing. The soundness proof for these rules is based on results in [19]. The induction rule is surprisingly difficult to justify, and is in fact false if straightforward adaptations of Martin-Löf's definition of functionality are used. A version of functionality under which the rule is valid was discovered by Allen [2]. This version, called *pointwise functionality*, is fairly complicated, but does capture an intuitively appealing notion of functionality.

Direct computation and the induction rule can be used to derive a new induction rule which does not introduce an **ind** form into extractions, but, instead, introduces a scheme for ordinary recursion of the kind used in **m**. To illustrate this, we consider a simple example. Suppose N_k is the type of all integers $0 \le i < k$. N_k is definable in Nuprl as a subtype of the integers. A derived induction rule, in the form of a lemma, is

$$\forall P{:}\,N \rightarrow U. \ [\forall k{:}\,N. \ (\forall n{:}\,N_k. \ P(n)) \Rightarrow P(k)] \ \Rightarrow \ \forall n{:}\,N. \ P(n).$$

where U is the type of all "small" types (U itself is not "small"). We can prove the lemma in such a way that the extracted program is a scheme for general recursion. To do this, we simply supply the desired scheme in the first step of the proof. The resulting subgoal is to show that the scheme is a member of the above type.

The scheme is

$$\lambda P. \ \lambda F. \ \mu(F),$$

where

$$\mu(F) \ \equiv \ letrec \ f(x){=}F(x)(f).$$

We need to prove

1. $P{:} \ N \rightarrow U$
2. $F{:} \ \forall k{:}\,N. \ (\forall n{:}\,N_k. \ P(n)) \Rightarrow P(k)$
3. $n{:} \ N$
$\gg \mu(F)(n) \in P(n)$

The proof of this uses induction on n and is similar to the proof for g above. It uses the fact that $\mu(F)(n)$ can be rewritten to $F(n)(\mu(F))$ with some symbolic computation steps. The induction step uses hypothesis 2, which implies that if $\mu(F)(n) \in P(n)$ for all $n < k$, then $F(k)(\mu(F)) \in P(k)$.

5   Conclusion

It was Stuart Allen who first noticed that Nuprl's induction rule permitted reasoning about programs defined by general recursion. In this paper we have pursued this insight a bit further, and have provided some evidence that there is no practical reason to include cumbersome constructs like primitive recursion in the underlying programming language of Nuprl's type theory. As with Feferman's theories [14], there is a large degree of flexibility to reason about the computational behaviour of programs, and it seems clear that a Nuprl-like type theory could be based on just about any untyped functional programming language. In fact, it should be possible to use the functional portion of Standard ML [25] (discarding ML's types).

References

1. S. F. Allen. A non-type theoretic definition of Martin-Löf's types. In *Proceedings of the Second Annual Symposium on Logic in Computer Science*, pages 215–221. IEEE Computer Society, 1987.

2. S. F. Allen. *A Non-Type-Theoretic Semantics for Type-Theoretic Language.* PhD thesis, Cornell University, 1987.

3. S. F. Allen, R. L. Constable, D. J. Howe, and W. B. Aitken. The semantics of reflected proof. In *Proceedings of the Fifth Annual Symposium on Logic and Computer Science*, pages 95–107. IEEE Computer Society, June 1990.

4. R. Backhouse. Algorithm development in Martin-Löf's type theory. Technical report, University of Essex, 1984.

5. D. A. Basin and P. Delvecchio. Verification of combinational logic in Nuprl. In *Hardware Specification, Verification and Synthesis: Mathematical Aspects*, Ithaca, New York, 1989.

6. D. A. Basin and D. J. Howe. Some normalization properties of Martin-Löf's type theory, and applications. In T. Ito and A. Meyer, editors, *Theoretical Aspects of Computer Software*, Lecture Notes in Computer Science, pages 475–494. Springer-Verlag, 1991.

7. R. Boyer and J. Moore. MJRTY, a fast majority vote algorithm. Technical report, University of Texas at Austin, 1981.

8. J. Chirimar and D. J. Howe. Implementing constructive real analysis: a preliminary report. In *Symposium on Constructivity in Computer Science*, Lecture Notes in Computer Science. Springer-Verlag, 1991. To appear.

9. R. Constable and D. Howe. Nuprl as a general logic. In P. Odifreddi, editor, *Logic in Computer Science*, pages 77–90. Academic Press, 1990.

10. R. Constable and S. Smith. Partial objects in constructive type theory. *Proceedings of the Second Annual Symposium on Logic in Computer Science*, pages 183–193, March 1987. (Cornell TR 87-822).

11. R. L. Constable and D. J. Howe. Implementing metamathematics as an approach to automatic theorem proving. In R. Banerji, editor, *Formal Techniques in Artificial Intelligence: A Source Book*, pages 45–76. Elsevier Science Publishers (North-Holland), 1990.

12. R. L. Constable, et al. *Implementing Mathematics with the Nuprl Proof Development System.* Prentice-Hall, Englewood Cliffs, New Jersey, 1986.

13. T. Coquand and G. Huet. The Calculus of Constructions. *Information and Computation*, 76:95–120, 1988.

14. S. Feferman. A language and axioms for explicit mathematics. In Dold, A. and B. Eckmann, editor, *Algebra and Logic*, volume 450 of *Lecture Notes in Mathematics*, pages 87–139. Springer-Verlag, 1975.

15. M. J. Gordon, R. Milner, and C. P. Wadsworth. *Edinburgh LCF: A Mechanized Logic of Computation*, volume 78 of *Lecture Notes in Computer Science*. Springer-Verlag, 1979.

16. D. Howe. The computational behaviour of Girard's paradox. *Proc. of Second Symp. on Logic in Comp. Sci., IEEE*, pages 205–214, June 1987.

17. D. J. Howe. *Automating Reasoning in an Implementation of Constructive Type Theory*. PhD thesis, Cornell University, 1988.

18. D. J. Howe. Computational metatheory in Nuprl. *Ninth Conference on Automated Deduction*, pages 238–257, May 1988.

19. D. J. Howe. Equality in lazy computation systems. In *Proceedings of the Fourth Annual Symposium on Logic in Computer Science*, pages 198–203. IEEE Computer Society, June 1989.

20. D. J. Howe. On computational open-endedness in Martin-Löf's type theory. In *Proceedings of the Sixth Annual Symposium on Logic in Computer Science*. IEEE Computer Society, 1991.

21. P. B. Jackson. Developing a toolkit for floating-point hardware in the Nuprl proof development system. In *Proceedings of the Advanced Research Workshop on Correct Hardware Design Methodologies*. Elsevier, 1991.

22. P. B. Jackson. Nuprl and its use in circuit design. In V. Stavridou, T. Melham, and R. Boute, editors, *Theorem Provers in Circuit Design*, pages 311–336. North-Holland, 1992.

23. P. Martin-Löf. Constructive mathematics and computer programming. In *Sixth International Congress for Logic, Methodology, and Philosophy of Science*, pages 153–175, Amsterdam, 1982. North Holland.

24. P. Mendler. *Inductive Definition on Type Theory*. PhD thesis, Cornell University, Ithaca, NY, 1988.

25. R. Milner, M. Tofte, and R. Harper. *The Definition of Standard ML*. MIT Press, 1990.

26. C. Murthy. An evaluation semantics for classical proofs. In *Proceedings of the Sixth Annual Symposium on Logic in Computer Science*, pages 96–107. IEEE Computer society, 1991.

27. B. Nördstrom, K. Petersson, and J. M. Smith. *Programming in Martin-Löf's Type Theory*, volume 7 of *International Series of Monographs on Computer Science*. Oxford Science Publications, 1990.

28. R. E. Shostak. On the SUP-INF method for proving Presburger formulas. *J. ACM*, 24(4):529–543, October 1977.

Concurrent ML:
Design, Application and Semantics

John H. Reppy

Department of Computer Science
Cornell University *

1 Introduction

Concurrent ML (**CML**) is a high-level, high-performance language for concurrent programming. It is an extension of Standard ML (**SML**) [MTH90], and is implemented on top of Standard ML of New Jersey (**SML/NJ**) [AM87]. **CML** is a practical language and is being used to build real systems. It demonstrates that we need not sacrifice high-level notation in order to have good performance. **CML** is also a well-defined language. In the tradition of **SML**, it has a formal semantics and its type-soundness has been proven.

Although most research in the area of concurrent language design has been motivated by the desire to improve performance by exploiting multiprocessors, I believe that concurrency is also a useful programming paradigm for certain application domains. For example, interactive systems often have a naturally concurrent structure [CP85, RG86, Pik89, Haa90, GR92]. Another example is distributed systems: most systems for distributed programming provide multi-threading at the node level (e.g., Isis [BCJ+90] and **Argus** [LCJS87]). Sequential programs in these application domains often must use complex and artificial control structures to schedule and interleave activities (e.g., event-loops in graphics libraries). They are, in effect, simulating concurrency. These application domains need a high-level concurrent language that provides both efficient sequential execution and efficient concurrent execution: **CML** satisfies this need.

1.1 An Overview of CML

CML is based on the sequential language **SML** [MTH90] and inherits the useful features of **SML**: functions as first-class values, strong static typing, polymorphism, datatypes and pattern matching, lexical scoping, exception handling and a state-of-the-art module facility. An introduction to **SML** can be found elsewhere in this volume [Oph92]; also see [Pau91] or [Har86]. The sequential performance of **CML** benefits from the quality of the **SML/NJ** compiler [AM87]. In addition **CML** has the following properties:

---

* Author's current affiliation: AT&T Bell Laboratories, Murray Hill NJ 07974, `jhr@research.att.com`.

- CML provides a high-level model of concurrency with dynamic creation of threads and typed channels, and *rendezvous* communication. This distributed-memory model fits well with the mostly applicative style of SML.

- CML is a higher-order concurrent language. Just as SML supports functions as first-class values, CML supports synchronous operations as first-class values [Rep88, Rep91a, Rep92]. These values, called *events*, provide the tools for building new synchronization abstractions. This is the most significant characteristic of CML.

- CML provides integrated I/O support. Potentially blocking I/O operations, such as reading from an input stream, are full-fledged synchronous operations. Low-level support is also provided, from which distributed communication abstractions can be constructed.

- CML provides automatic reclamation of threads and channels, once they become inaccessible. This permits a technique of speculative communication, which is not possible in other threads packages.

- CML uses preemptive scheduling. To guarantee interactive responsiveness, a single thread cannot be allowed to monopolize the processor. Pre-emption insures that a context switch will occur at regular intervals, which allows "off-the-shelf" code to be incorporated in a concurrent thread without destroying interactive responsiveness.

- CML is efficient. Thread creation, thread switching and message passing are very efficient (benchmarks results are reported in [Rep92]). Experience with CML has shown that it is a viable language for implementing usable interactive systems [GR91].

- CML is portable. It is written in SML and runs on essentially every system supported by SML/NJ (currently four different architectures and many different operating systems).

- CML has a formal foundation. Following the tradition of SML [MTH90, MT91], a formal semantics has been developed for the concurrency primitives of CML.

1.2 Organization of this Paper

This paper is organized into three main parts. The first, consisting of Sections 2 and 3, describes the design and rationale of CML. The second part focuses on the practical aspects: Section 4 describes the use of CML in real applications, and Section 5 briefly discusses the implementation of CML. The third part presents the formal underpinnings of CML: Section 6 gives the dynamic semantics a small concurrent language that supports the core CML concurrency mechanisms, and then Section 7 gives a static semantics (i.e., a type system) for this language and presents type-soundness results. The paper concludes with a discussion of related work and a summary.

2   Basic Concurrency Primitives

We start with a discussion of the basic concurrency operations provided by **CML**.
A running **CML** program consists of a collection of *threads*, which use synchronous
message passing on typed channels to communicate and synchronize. In keeping with
the flavor of **SML**, both threads and channels are created dynamically (initially, a
program consists of a single thread). The signature of the basic thread and channel
operations is given in Figure 1. The function **spawn** takes a function as an argument

```
val spawn : (unit -> unit) -> thread_id

val channel : unit -> '1a chan

val accept  : 'a chan -> 'a
val send    : ('a chan * 'a) -> unit
```

Fig. 1. Basic concurrency primitives

and creates a new thread to evaluate the application of the function to the unit value.
Channels are also created dynamically using the function **channel**, which is weakly
polymorphic.[2] The functions **accept** and **send** are the synchronous communication
operations. When a thread wants to communicate on a channel, it must *rendezvous*
with another thread that wants to do a complementary communication on the same
channel. **SML**'s lexical scoping is used to share channels between threads, and to
hide channels from other threads (note, however, that channels can be passed as
messages).

Most **CSP**-style languages (e.g., **occam** [Bur88] and **amber** [Car86]) provide
similar rendezvous-style communication. In addition, they provide a mechanism for
selective communication, which is necessary for threads to communicate with multiple partners. It is possible to use polling to implement selective communication, but
to do so is awkward and requires busy waiting. Usually selective communication is
provided as a multiplexed I/O operation. This can be a multiplexed input operation,
such as **occam**'s **ALT** construct [Bur88]; or a generalized (or symmetric) select operation that multiplexes both input and output communications, such as **Pascal-m**'s
select construct [AB86]. Implementing generalized select on a multi-processor can
be difficult [Bor86], but there are situations in which generalized selective communication is necessary (an example of this is given in Section 3.1).

Unfortunately, there is a fundamental conflict between the desire for abstraction
and the need for selective communication. For example, consider a server thread

---

[2] The "1" in the type variable of **channel**'s result type is the *strength* of the variable. This
   is a technical mechanism used to allow polymorphic use of updatable objects without
   creating type loopholes.

that provides a service via a *request-reply* (or *remote procedure call* (RPC) style) protocol. The server side of this protocol is something like:

```
fun serverLoop () = if serviceAvailable()
    then let
      val request = accept reqCh
    in
        send (replyCh, doit request);
        serverLoop ()
    end
    else doSomethingElse()
```

where the function `doit` actually implements the service. Note that the service is not always available. This protocol requires that clients obey the following two rules:

1. A client must send a request before trying to read a reply.
2. Following a request the client must read exactly one reply before issuing another request.

If all clients obey these rules, then we can guarantee that each request is answered with the correct reply, but if a client breaks one of these rules, then the requests and replies will be out of sync. An obvious way to improve the reliability of programs that use this service is to bundle the client-side protocol into a function that hides the details, thus ensuring that the rules are followed. The following code implements this abstraction:

```
fun clientCall x = (send(reqCh, x); accept replyCh)
```

While this insures that clients obey the protocol, it hides too much. If a client blocks on a call to `clientCall` (e.g., if the server is not available), then it cannot respond to other communications. Avoiding this situation requires using selective communication, but the client cannot do this because the function abstraction hides the synchronous aspect of the protocol. This is the fundamental conflict between selective communication and the existing forms of abstraction. If we make the operation abstract, we lose the flexibility of selective communication; but if we expose the protocol to allow selective communication, we lose the safety and ease of maintenance provided by abstraction. The next section describes our solution to this dilemma.

3 First-class Synchronous Operations

To resolve the conflict between abstraction and selective communication requires introducing a new abstraction mechanism that preserves the synchronous nature of the abstraction. First-class synchronous operations provide this abstraction mechanism [Rep88, Rep89, Rep91a].

The traditional **select** construct has four facets: the individual I/O operations, the actions associated with each operation, the nondeterministic choice, and the synchronization. In **CML**, we unbundle these facets by introducing a new type of values, called *events*, that represent synchronous operations. By starting with *base-event* values to represent the communication operations, and providing combinators to associate actions with events and to build nondeterministic choices of events, a flexible mechanism for building new synchronization and communication abstractions is realized. Event values provide a mechanism for building an abstract representation of a protocol without obscuring its synchronous aspect.

To make this concrete, consider the following loop (using an **Amber** style **select** construct [Car86]), which implements the body of an accumulator that accepts either addition or subtraction input commands and offers its contents:

```
fun accum sum = (
        select addCh?x => accum(sum+x)
            or subCh?x => accum(sum-x)
            or readCh!sum => accum sum)
```

The **select** construct consists of three I/O operations: addCh?x, subCh?x, and readCh!sum. For each of these operations there is an associated action on the right hand side of the =>. Taken together, each I/O operation and associated action define a clause in a nondeterministic synchronous choice. It is also worth noting that the input clauses define a scope: the input operation binds an identifier to the incoming message, which has the action as its scope.

Figure 2 gives the signature of the event operations corresponding to the four facets of generalized selective communication. The functions **receive** and **transmit**

```
    val receive  : 'a chan -> 'a event
    val transmit : ('a chan * 'a) -> unit event

    val choose   : 'a event list -> 'a event
    val wrap     : ('a event * ('a -> 'b)) -> 'b event

    val sync     : 'a event -> 'a
```

Fig. 2. Basic event operations

build base-event values that represent channel I/O operations. The **wrap** combinator binds an action, represented by a function, to an event value. And the **choose** combinator composes event values into a nondeterministic choice. The last operation is **sync**, which forces synchronization on an event value. I call this set of operations "PML events," since they constitute the mechanism that I originally developed in **PML** [Rep88].

The simplest example of events is the implementation of the synchronous channel I/O operations that were described in the previous section. These are defined using function composition, **sync** and the channel I/O event-value constructors:

```
val accept = sync o receive
val send   = sync o transmit
```

A more substantial example is the accumulator loop from above, which is implemented as:

```
fun accum sum = sync (
    choose [
        wrap (receive addCh, fn x => accum (sum+x)),
        wrap (receive subCh, fn x => accum (sum-x)),
        wrap (transmit (readCh, sum), fn () => accum sum)
    ])
```

Notice how wrap is used to associate actions with communications.

The great benefit of this approach to concurrency is that it allows the programmer to create new first-class synchronization and communication abstractions. For example, we can define an event-valued function that implements the client-side of the RPC protocol given in the previous section as follows:

```
fun clientCallEvt x = wrap (transmit(reqCh, x), fn () => accept replyCh)
```

Applying clientCallEvt to a value v does not actually send a request to the server, rather it returns an event value that can be used to send v to the server and then accept the server's reply. This event value can be used in a choose expression with other communications; in which case the transmit base-event value is used in selecting the event. This example shows that we can use first-class synchronous operations to abstract away from the details of the client-server protocol, without hiding the synchronous nature of the protocol.

This approach to synchronization and communication leads to a new programming paradigm, which I call *higher-order concurrent programming*. To understand this the higher-order nature of this mechanism, it is helpful to draw an analogy with first-class function values. Table 1 compares these two higher-order mechanisms.

Table 1. Relating first-class functions and events

Property	Function values	Event values
Type constructor	->	event
Introduction	λ-abstraction	receive transmit etc.
Elimination	application	sync
Combinators	composition map etc.	choose wrap etc.

3.1 An Example

An example that illustrates a number of key points is an implementation of a *buffered channel* abstraction. Buffered channels provide a mechanism for asynchronous communication, which is similar to the actor mailbox [Agh86]. The source code for this abstraction is given in Figure 3. The function buffer creates a new buffered

```
abstype 'a buffer_chan = BC of {
    inch : 'a chan,
    outch : 'a chan
  }
with
  fun buffer () = let
        val inCh = channel() and outCh = channel()
        fun loop ([], []) = loop([accept inCh], [])
          | loop (front as (x::r), rear) = sync (
              choose [
                  wrap (receive inCh, fn y => loop(front, y::rear)),
                  wrap (transmit(outCh, x), fn () => loop(r, rear))
                ])
          | loop ([], rear) = loop(rev rear, [])
        in
          spawn (fn () => loop([], []));
          BC{inch=inCh, outch=outCh}
        end
  fun bufferSend (BC{inch, ...}, x) = send(inch, x)
  fun bufferReceive (BC{outch, ...}) = receive outch
end (* abstype *)
```

Fig. 3. Buffered channels

channel, which consists of a buffer thread, an input channel and an output channel; the function bufferSend is an asynchronous send operation; and the function bufferReceive is an event-valued receive operation. The buffer is represented as a queue of messages, which is implemented as a pair of stacks (lists). This example illustrates several key points:

- Buffered channels are a new communication abstraction, which have first-class citizenship. A thread can use the bufferReceive function in any context that it could use the built-in function receive, such as selective communication.
- The buffer loop uses both input and output operations in its selective communication. This is an example of the necessity of generalized selective communication. If we have only a multiplexed input construct (e.g., occam's ALT), then we must to use a request/reply protocol to implement the server side of the bufferReceive operation (see pp. 37-41 of [Bur88], for example). But if a re-

quest/reply protocol is used, then the bufferReceive operation cannot be used in a selective communication by the client.

- The buffer thread is a good example of a common **CML** programming idiom: using threads to encapsulate state. This style has the additional benefit of hiding the state of the system in the concurrency operations, which makes the sequential code cleaner. These threads serve the same role that *monitors* do in some shared-memory concurrent languages.

- This implementation exploits the fact that unreachable blocked threads are garbage collected. If the clients of this buffer discard it, then the buffer thread and channels will be reclaimed by the garbage collector. This improves the modularity of the abstraction, since clients do not have to worry about explicit termination of the buffer thread.

3.2 Other Synchronous Operations

The event type provides a natural framework for accommodating other primitive synchronous operations.[3] There are three examples of this in **CML**: synchronization on thread termination (sometimes called *process join*), low-level I/O support and time-outs. Figure 4 gives the signature of the **CML** base-event constructors for these other synchronous operations. The function wait produces an event for syn-

```
val wait : thread_id -> unit event

val syncOnInput  : int -> unit event
val syncOnOutput : int -> unit event

val waitUntil : time -> unit event
val timeout   : time -> unit event
```

Fig. 4. Other primitive synchronous operations

chronizing on the termination of another thread. This is often used by servers that need to release resources allocated to a client in the case that the client terminates unexpectedly. Support for low-level I/O is provided by the functions syncOnInput and syncOnOutput, which allow threads to synchronize on the status of file descriptors [UNI86]. These operations are used in **CML** to implement a multi-threaded I/O stream library. There are two functions for synchronizing with the clock: waitUntil and timeout. The function waitUntil returns an event that synchronizes on an absolute time, while timeout implements a relative delay. The function timeout can be used to implement a timeout in a choice. The following code, for example, defines an event that waits for up to a second for a message on a channel:

---

[3] This is the reason that the I use the term "event" to refer to first-class synchronous operations instead of using "communication."

```
choose [
    wrap (receive ch, SOME),
    wrap (timeout(TIME{sec=1, usec=0}), fn () => NONE)
]
```

By having a uniform mechanism for combining synchronous operations, **CML** provides a great deal of flexibility with a fairly terse mechanism. As a comparison, **Ada** has two different timeout mechanisms: a time entry call for clients and delay statement that servers can include in a select.

CML also provides a polling mechanism. The operation

```
val poll : 'a event -> 'a option
```

is a non-blocking form of the `sync` operator. It returns **NONE** is the case where `sync` would block.

3.3   Extending PML events

Thus far, I have described the **PML** subset of first-class synchronous operations. In this section, I motivate and describe two significant extensions to **PML** events that are provided in **CML**.

Consider a protocol consisting of a sequence of communications: $c_1; c_2; \cdots; c_n$. When this protocol is packaged up in an event value, one of the c_i is designated as the *commit point*, the communication by which this event is chosen in a selective communication (e.g., the message send operation in the `clientCallEvt` abstraction above). In **PML** events, the only possible commit point is c_1. The `wrap` construct allows one to tack on $c_2; \cdots; c_n$ after c_1 is chosen, but there is no way to make any of the other c_i the commit point. This asymmetry is a serious limitation.

A good illustration of this problem is a server that implements an input-stream abstraction. Since this abstraction should be smoothly integrated into the concurrency model, the input operations should be event-valued. For example, the function

```
val input : instream -> string event
```

is used to read a single character. In addition, there are other input operations such as `input_line`. Let us assume that the implementation of these operations uses a request-reply protocol; thus, a successful `input` operation involves the communication sequence

$$\text{send} (ch_{req}, \text{REQ\_INPUT}); \quad \text{accept} (ch_{reply})$$

Packaging this up as an event (as we did in Section 3) will make the `send` communication be the commit point, which is the wrong semantics. To illustrate the problem with this, consider the case where a client thread wants to synchronize on the choice of reading a character and a five second timeout:

```
sync (choose [
    wrap (timeout(TIME{sec=5, usec=0}), fn () => raise Timeout),
    input instream
])
```

The server might accept the request within the five second limit, even though the wait for input might be indefinite. The right semantics for the input operation requires making the accept be the commit point, which is not possible using only the **PML** subset of events. To address this limitation, **CML** provides the guard combinator.

Guards. The guard combinator is the dual of wrap; it bundles code to be executed *before* the commit point; this code can include communications. It has the type

```
val guard : (unit -> 'a event) -> 'a event
```

A guard event is essentially a suspension that is forced when sync is applied to it. As a simple example of the use of guard, the timeout function, described in Section 3.2, is actually implemented using waitUntil and a guard:

```
fun timeout t = guard (fn () => waitUntil (add_time (t, currentTime())))
```

where currentTime returns the current time.

Some languages support guarded clauses in selective communication, where the guards are boolean expressions that must evaluate to true in order that the communication be enabled. **CML** guards can be used for this purpose too, as illustrated by the following code skeleton:

```
sync (choose [
    ...
    guard (fn () => if pred then evt else choose[])
    ...
])
```

Here *evt* is part of the choice only if *pred* evaluates to true. Note that the evaluation of *pred* occurs each time the guard function is evaluated (i.e., each time the sync is applied).

Returning to the RPC example from above, we can now build an abstract RPC operation with the reply as the commit point. The two different versions are:

```
fun clientCallEvt1 x = wrap (transmit(reqCh, x), fn () => accept replyCh)

fun clientCallEvt2 x = guard (fn () => (send(reqCh, x); receive replyCh)
```

where the clientCallEvt1 version commits on the server's acceptance of the request, while the clientCallEvt2 version commits on the server's reply to the request. Note the duality of guard and wrap with respect to the commit point. Using guards to generate requests in this way raises a couple of other problems. First of all, if the server cannot guarantee that requests will be accepted promptly, then evaluating the guard may cause delays. The solution to this is to spawn a new thread to issue the request asynchronously:

```
fun clientCallEvt3 x = guard (fn () => (
      spawn(fn () => send(reqCh, x));
      receive replyCh)
```

Another alternative is for the server to be a clearing-house for requests; spawning a new thread to handle each new request.

The other problem is more serious: what if this RPC event is used in a selective communication and some other event is chosen? How does the server avoid blocking forever on sending a reply? For idempotent services, this can be handled by having the client create a dedicated channel for the reply and having the server spawn a new thread to send the reply. The client side of this protocol is

```
fun clientCallEvt4 x = guard (fn () => let
      val replyCh = channel()
      in
        spawn(fn () => send(reqCh, (replyCh, x)));
        receive replyCh
      end)
```

When the server sends the reply it evaluates

```
spawn (fn () => send(replyCh, reply))
```

If the client has already chosen a different event, then this thread blocks and will be garbage collected. For services that are not idempotent, this scheme is not sufficient; the server needs a way to *abort* the transaction. The wrapAbort combinator provides this mechanism.

Abort actions. The wrapAbort combinator associates an *abort action* with an event value. The semantics are that if the event is *not* chosen in a sync operation, then a new thread is spawned to evaluate the abort action. The type of this combinator is:

```
val wrapAbort : ('a event * (unit -> unit)) -> unit
```

where the second argument is the abort action. This combinator is the complement of wrap in the sense that if you view every base event in a choice as having both a wrapper and an abort action, then, when sync is applied, the wrapper of the chosen event is called and threads are spawned for each of the abort actions of the other base events.

Using wrapAbort, we can now implement the RPC protocol for non-idempotent services. The client code for the RPC using abort must allocate two channels; one for the reply and one for the abort message:

```
fun clientCallEvt5 x = guard (fn () => let
    val replyCh = channel()
    val abortCh = channel()
    fun abortFn () = send (abortCh, ())
    in
      spawn(fn () => send (reqCh, (replyCh, abortCh, x)));
      wrapAbort (receive replyCh, abortFn)
    end)
```

When the server is ready to reply (i.e., commit the transaction), it synchronizes on
the following event value:

```
choose[
    wrap (receive abortCh, fn () => abort the transaction),
    wrap (transmit (replyCh, reply), fn () => commit the transaction)
  ]
```

This mechanism can be used to implement the input-stream abstraction discussed at
the beginning of this section, and in fact, the concurrent stream I/O library provided
by **CML** is implemented in this way.

3.4 Stream I/O

CML provides a concurrent version of the **SML** stream I/O primitives. Input operations in this version are event valued, which allows them to be used in selective
communication. For example, a program might want to give a user 60 seconds to
supply a password. This can be programmed as:

```
fun getpasswd () = sync (choose [
        wrap (timeout{sec=60, usec=0}, fn () => NONE),
        wrap (input_line std_in, SOME)
      ])
```

This will return **NONE**, if the user fails to respond within 60 seconds, otherwise it
wraps **SOME** around the user's response. Streams are implemented as threads which
handle buffering. The input operations are actually request/reply/abort protocols,
similar to the one discussed above.

4 Applications

CML is more than an exercise in language design; it is intended to be a useful
tool for building large systems. I have implemented **CML** on top of **SML/NJ**.
This implementation has been used by a number of people, including myself, for
various different applications. This practical experience demonstrates the validity
and usefulness of the design as well as the efficiency of the implementation. In this
section, I describe two applications of **CML**, and how they use the features of **CML**.

4.1 Interactive Systems

Providing a better foundation for programming interactive systems, such as programming environments, was the original motivation for this line of research [RG86]. Because of their naturally concurrent structure, interactive systems are one of the most important application areas for **CML**. Concurrency arises in several ways in interactive systems:

User interaction. Handling user input is the most complex aspect of an interactive program. Most interactive systems use an *event-loop* and *call-back* functions. The event-loop receives input events (e.g., mouse clicks) and passes them to the appropriate *event-handler*. This structure is a poor-man's concurrency: the event-handlers are coroutines and the event-loop is the scheduler.

Multiple services. For example, consider a document preparation system that provides both editing and formatting. These two services are independent and can be naturally organized as two separate threads. Multiple views are implemented by replicating the threads.

Interleaving computation. A user of a document preparation system may want to edit one part of a document while another part is being formatted. Since formatting may take a significant amount of time, providing a responsive interface requires interleaving formatting and editing. If the editor and formatter are separate threads, then interleaving comes for free.

Output driven applications. Most windowing toolkits, for example **Xlib** [Nye90], provide an *input oriented* model, in which the application code is occasionally called in response to some external event. But many applications are *output* oriented. Consider, for example, a computationally intensive simulation with a graphical display of the current state of the simulation. This application must monitor window events, such as refresh and resize notifications, so that it can redraw itself when necessary. In a sequential implementation, the handling of these events must be postponed until the simulation is ready to update the displayed information. By separating the display code and simulation code into separate threads, the handling of asynchronous redrawing is easy.

The root cause of these forms of concurrency is computer-human interaction: humans are asynchronous and slow.

CML has been used to build a multi-threaded interface to the **X** protocol [SG86], called **eXene** [GR91]. This system provides a substantially different, and we think better, model of user interaction than the traditional **Xlib** model [Nye90]. Windows in **eXene** have an *environment*, consisting of three streams of input from the window's parent (mouse, keyboard and control), and one output stream for requesting services from the window's parent. For each child of the window, there will be corresponding output streams and an input stream. The input streams are represented by event values and the output streams by event valued functions. A window is responsible for routing messages to its children, but this can almost always be done using a generic router function provided by eXene. Typically, each window has a separate thread for each input stream as well as a thread, or two, for managing state and coordinating the other threads. By breaking the code up this way, each individual thread is quite simple. This model is similar to those of [Pik89] and [Haa90]).

This structure allows us to use *delegation* techniques to define new behavior from existing implementations. Delegation is an object-oriented technique that originated in concurrent actor systems [Lie86]. As an example, consider the case of adding a menu to an existing text window. We can do this in a general way by defining a wrapper that takes a window's environment and returns a new, wrapped, environment. The wrapped environment has a thread monitoring the mouse stream of the old environment. Normally, this thread just passes messages along to the wrapped window, but when a mouse "button down" message comes along, the thread pops up the menu and consumes mouse messages until an item is chosen. Emden Gansner, of AT&T Bell Laboratories, has developed a "widget" toolkit on top of eXene, which uses these delegation techniques heavily.

The implementation of eXene, which is currently about 8,500 lines of CML code, uses threads heavily. At the lowest level, threads are used to buffer communication with the X server. There are threads to manage shared state, such as graphics contexts, fonts and keycode translation tables. Because the internal threads are fairly specialized and tightly integrated, there is not much use of events as an abstraction mechanism.

The use of events as an abstraction mechanism is common at the application programmer's level. In addition to the event-valued interface of the window environments, there are higher-level objects that have abstract synchronous interfaces. One example is a *virtual terminal* window (vtty). This provides a synchronous stream interface to its clients, which is compatible with the signature of CML's concurrent I/O library. If the client-code is implemented as a *functor* [Mac84] (parameterized module), then it can be used with either the concurrent I/O library or the vtty abstraction.

The vtty abstraction is a good example of where user-defined abstract synchronous operations are necessary for program modularity. At any time, the vtty thread must be ready to receive input from the user and output from the application; thus it needs selective communication. The underlying window toolkit (eXene) provides an abstract interface to the input stream, but, since it is event-valued, it can be used in the selective communication.

Another example of the use of new communication abstractions is a *buffered multicast* channel (a simple version is described in [Rep90b]). This abstraction has proven quite useful in supporting multiple views of an object. When the viewed object is updated, the thread managing its state sends a notification on the multicast channel. The multicast channel basically serves the role of a call-back function, while freeing the viewed object from the details on managing multiple views. All of the details of creating/destroying views and distributing messages are taken care of by the multicast abstraction.

4.2 Distributed systems programming

Many distributed programming languages have concurrent languages at their core (e.g., **SR** [AOCE88]), and distributed programming toolkits often include thread packages (e.g., **Isis** [BCJ+90]). This is because threads provide a needed flexibility for dealing with the asynchronous nature of distributed systems. The flexibility provided by **CML** is a good base for distributed programming. Its support for low-level I/O is sufficient to build a structured synchronous interface to network communication (as was done in **eXene**). Higher-level linguistic support for distributed programming, such as the promise mechanism described in [LS88], can be built using events to define the new abstractions.[4]

Another example is Chet Murthy's reimplementation of the **Nuprl** environment [Con86] using **CML**. His implementation is structured as a collection of "proof servers" running on different workstations. When an expensive operation on a proof tree is required, it can be decomposed and run in parallel on several different workstations. This system uses **CML** to manage the interactions between the different workstations.

Another project involving **CML** is the development of a distributed programming toolkit for **ML** that is being developed at Cornell University [Kru91, CK92, Kru92]. This work builds on the mechanisms prototyped in Murthy's distributed **Nuprl** and on the protocols developed for **Isis** [BCJ+90]. A new abstraction, called a *port group* has been developed to model distributed communication. The communication operations provided by port groups are represented by event-value constructors (for details see [Kru91]).

4.3 Other applications of CML

CML has been used by various people for a number of other purposes. Andrew Appel has used it to teach concurrent programming to undergraduates at Princeton University (Appel, personal communication, January 1991). Gary Lindstrom and Lal George have used it to experiment with functional control of imperative programs for parallel programming [GL91]. And Clément Pellerin has implemented a compiler from a concurrent constraint language to **CML** [Pel92].

5 Implementation

CML is written entirely in **SML**, using a couple of non-standard extensions provided by **SML/NJ**: *first-class continuations* [DHM91] and *asynchronous signals* [Rep90a]. We added one minor primitive operation to the compiler (a ten line change in a 30,000 line compiler), which was necessary to guarantee that tail-recursion is preserved by sync. Threads are implemented using *first-class continuations* (a technique owed to

---

[4] See [GR91] or [Rep92] for a description of the implementation of promises in **CML**.

Wand [Wan80]), and the **SML/NJ** asynchronous signal facility is used to implement preemptive scheduling.

Unlike other continuation-passing style compilers, such as **Rabbit** [Ste78] and **Orbit** [KKR+86], the code generated by the **SML/NJ** compiler does not use a run-time stack [App92]. This means that callcc and throw are constant-time operations. While this is possible using a stack [HDB90]; heap-based implementations are better suited for implementing light-weight threads (Haahr's experience bears this out [Haa90]).

Event values have a natural implementation in terms of first-class continuations. Without the choose operator, an event value could be represented as

```
type 'a event = 'a cont -> 'a
```

with sync being directly implemented by callcc. This representation captures the intuition that an event is just a synchronous operation with its synchronization point continuation as a free variable. The choose operator requires polling, since we need to see which (if any) base events are immediately available for synchronization. Thus, the implementation of an event value is a list of base events, with each base event represented by a polling function, a function to call for immediate synchronization and a function for blocking. The implementation of **CML** is described in detail, including detailed performance measurements, in the author's dissertation [Rep92].

6 Dynamic Semantics

In this section, I present the dynamic semantics of λ_{cv}, a concurrent extension of Plotkin's λ_v calculus [Plo75]. Although λ_{cv} lacks many of the features of **CML**, it contains the core of the concurrency primitives, including first-class synchronous operations, and the various event-value combinators. A discussion of how λ_{cv} can be extended to include many of the missing features of **CML** can be found in [Rep92].

The dynamic semantics of λ_{cv} is defined by two evaluation relations: a sequential evaluation relation "$\longmapsto$," and a concurrent evaluation relation "$\Longrightarrow$," where concurrent evaluation is an extension of sequential evaluation to finite sets of processes.

6.1 The Syntax of λ_{cv}

We start with disjoint sets of *variables, function constants, base constants* and *channel names*, which comprise the ground terms of λ_{cv}:

$x \in \text{VAR}$	variables
$b \in \text{CONST} = \text{BCONST} \cup \text{FCONST}$	constants
$\text{BCONST} = \{(), \text{true}, \text{false}, 0, 1, \ldots\}$	base constants
$\text{FCONST} = \{+, -, \text{fst}, \text{snd}, \ldots\}$	function constants
$\kappa \in \text{CH}$	channel names

The set FConst includes the following event-valued combinators and constructors:

> choose, guard, never, receive, transmit, wrap, wrapAbort

There are three syntactic classes of terms in λ_{cv}:

$$\begin{aligned}
e &\in \text{Exp} &&\text{expressions} \\
v &\in \text{Val} \subset \text{Exp} &&\text{values} \\
ev &\in \text{Event} \subset \text{Val} &&\text{event values}
\end{aligned}$$

where values are the irreducible terms in the dynamic semantics. The terms of λ_{cv} are defined by the grammar in Figure 5. Pairs have been included to make the handling

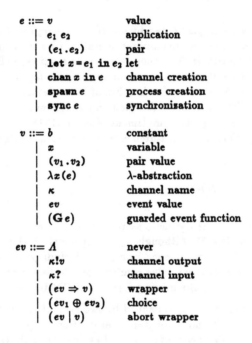

$$\begin{aligned}
e ::= \;& v &&\text{value} \\
| \;& e_1\, e_2 &&\text{application} \\
| \;& (e_1 . e_2) &&\text{pair} \\
| \;& \text{let } x = e_1 \text{ in } e_2 &&\text{let} \\
| \;& \text{chan } x \text{ in } e &&\text{channel creation} \\
| \;& \text{spawn } e &&\text{process creation} \\
| \;& \text{sync } e &&\text{synchronization} \\[4pt]
v ::= \;& b &&\text{constant} \\
| \;& x &&\text{variable} \\
| \;& (v_1 . v_2) &&\text{pair value} \\
| \;& \lambda x (e) &&\lambda\text{-abstraction} \\
| \;& \kappa &&\text{channel name} \\
| \;& ev &&\text{event value} \\
| \;& (G\, e) &&\text{guarded event function} \\[4pt]
ev ::= \;& \Lambda &&\text{never} \\
| \;& \kappa ! v &&\text{channel output} \\
| \;& \kappa ? &&\text{channel input} \\
| \;& (ev \Rightarrow v) &&\text{wrapper} \\
| \;& (ev_1 \oplus ev_2) &&\text{choice} \\
| \;& (ev \mid v) &&\text{abort wrapper}
\end{aligned}$$

Fig. 5. Grammar for λ_{cv}

of two-argument functions easier. Note that the syntactic class of the term $(v_1 . v_2)$ is either Exp or Val; this ambiguity is resolved in favor of Val. The value Λ is a base event value that is never matched (equivalent to choose[] in CML). There are three binding forms in this term language: let binding, λ-abstraction and channel creation. Unlike CML, new channels are introduced by the special binding form for channel creation. This is done to simplify the presentation of the next chapter, and the channel function of CML can be easily defined in terms of λ_{cv}. The set Val° is the set of *closed* value terms (i.e., those without free variables); note, however, that closed values may contain free channel names. The free channel names of an expression e are denoted by $\text{FCN}(e)$. Note that, since there are no channel name binding forms, $\text{FCN}(e)$ is exactly the set of channel names that appear in e. There is no term for sequencing, but we write "$(e_1 ; e_2)$" for "snd $(e_1 . e_2)$," which, since the language is call-by-value, has the desired semantics.

Channel names and event values are not part of the concrete syntax of the language; rather, they appear as the intermediate results of evaluation. A *program* is a closed term, which does not contain any guarded event functions (i.e., $(\mathbf{G}\, e)$ terms), or any subterms in the syntactic classes EVENT or CH. In other words, programs do not contain intermediate values.

6.2 Sequential Evaluation

There are a number of different ways to specify the dynamic semantics of programming languages. I use the style of *operational semantics* developed by Felleisen and Friedman [FF86], because it provides a good framework for proving type soundness results [WF91]. In this approach, the objects of the dynamic semantics are the syntactic terms in EXP.

The meaning of the function constants is given by the partial function

$$\delta : \text{FCONST} \times \text{VAL}^\circ \rightarrow \text{VAL}^\circ$$

Since a closed value $v \in \text{VAL}^\circ$ can have free channel names in it, we require, that if $b \in \text{FCONST}$ and $\delta(b, v)$ is defined, then

$$\text{FCN}(\delta(b, v)) \subseteq \text{FCN}(v)$$

In other words, δ is not allowed to introduce new channel names. For the standard built-in function constants, the meaning of δ is the expected one. For example:

$$\delta(+, (0.1)) = 1$$
$$\delta(+, (1.1)) = 2$$
$$\delta(\texttt{fst}, (v_1 . v_2)) = v_1$$
$$\delta(\texttt{snd}, (v_1 . v_2)) = v_2$$

The meaning of δ is straightforward for most of the event-valued combinators and constructors:

$$\delta(\texttt{never}, ()) = \Lambda$$
$$\delta(\texttt{transmit}, (\kappa . v)) = \kappa ! v$$
$$\delta(\texttt{receive}, \kappa) = \kappa ?$$
$$\delta(\texttt{wrap}, (ev . v)) = (ev \Rightarrow v)$$
$$\delta(\texttt{choose}, (ev_1 . ev_2)) = (ev_1 \oplus ev_2)$$
$$\delta(\texttt{wrapAbort}, (ev . v)) = (ev \mid v)$$

The only complication arises in the case of guarded-event values:

$$\delta(\texttt{guard}, v) = (\mathbf{G}\, (v\, ()))$$
$$\delta(\texttt{wrap}, ((\mathbf{G}\, e) . v)) = (\mathbf{G}\, (\texttt{wrap}\, (e . v)))$$
$$\delta(\texttt{choose}, ((\mathbf{G}\, e_1) . (\mathbf{G}\, e_2))) = (\mathbf{G}\, (\texttt{choose}\, (e_1 . e_2)))$$
$$\delta(\texttt{choose}, ((\mathbf{G}\, e_1) . ev_2)) = (\mathbf{G}\, (\texttt{choose}\, (e_1 . ev_2)))$$
$$\delta(\texttt{choose}, (ev_1 . (\mathbf{G}\, e_2))) = (\mathbf{G}\, (\texttt{choose}\, (ev_1 . e_2)))$$
$$\delta(\texttt{wrapAbort}, ((\mathbf{G}\, e) . v)) = (\mathbf{G}\, (\texttt{wrapAbort}\, (e . v)))$$

These rules reflect guard's role as a delay operator; when another event constructor is applied to a guarded event value, then the guard operator (**G**) is pulled out to delay the event construction.

An *evaluation context* is a single-hole context where the hole marks the next redex (or is at the top if the term is irreducible) The evaluation of λ_{cv} is call-by-value and left-to-right, which leads to the following grammar for the evaluation contexts of λ_{cv}:

$$E ::= [\,] \mid E\,e \mid v\,E \mid (E.e) \mid (v.E)$$
$$\mid \text{let } x = E \text{ in } e \mid \text{spawn } E \mid \text{sync } E$$

The sequential evaluation relation is defined in terms of these contexts:

Definition 1 ($\longmapsto$). The *sequential evaluation relation*, written "$\longmapsto$," is the smallest relation satisfying the following four rules:

$$
\begin{array}{lll}
E[b\,v] & \longmapsto E[\delta(b,v)] & (\lambda_{cv}\text{-}\delta) \\
E[\lambda x(e)\,v] & \longmapsto E[e[x \mapsto v]] & (\lambda_{cv}\text{-}\beta) \\
E[\text{let } x = v \text{ in } e] \longmapsto E[e[x \mapsto v]] & & (\lambda_{cv}\text{-let}) \\
E[\text{sync } (\text{G}\,e)] & \longmapsto E[\text{sync } e] & (\lambda_{cv}\text{-guard})
\end{array}
$$

Note that the rule (λ_{cv}-guard) forces the expression delayed by guard. As usual, $\longmapsto^*$ is the transitive closure of $\longmapsto$. The evaluation of the other new forms (e.g., spawn) is defined as part of the concurrent evaluation relation in Section 6.4.

6.3 Event Matching

The key concept in the semantics of concurrent evaluation is the notion of *event matching*, which captures the semantics of rendezvous and communication. Informally, if two processes synchronize on matching events, then they can exchange values and continue evaluation. Before we can make this more formal, we need an auxiliary definition

Definition 2. The *abort action* of an event value ev is an expression, which, when evaluated, spawns the abort wrappers of ev. The map

$$\text{AbortAct} : \text{EVENT} \to \text{EXP}$$

maps an event value to its abort action, and is defined inductively as follows:

$$
\begin{array}{l}
\text{AbortAct}(\Lambda) = (\,) \\
\text{AbortAct}(\kappa?) = (\,) \\
\text{AbortAct}(\kappa!v) = (\,) \\
\text{AbortAct}(ev \Rightarrow e) = \text{AbortAct}(ev) \\
\text{AbortAct}(ev_1 \oplus ev_2) = (\text{AbortAct}(ev_1);\ \text{AbortAct}(ev_2)) \\
\text{AbortAct}(ev \mid v) = (\text{AbortAct}(ev);\ \text{spawn } v)
\end{array}
$$

With this definition we can define the matching of event values formally:

Definition 3 (Event matching). The matching of event values is defined as a family of binary symmetric relations (indexed by C_H). For $\kappa \in C_H$, define

$$ev_1 \overset{\kappa}{\subset} ev_2 \text{ with } (e_1, e_2)$$

(pronounced "ev_1 *matches* ev_2 *on channel* κ *with respective results* e_1 *and* e_2") as the smallest relation satisfying the six inference rules given in Figure 6. This relation is abbreviated to $ev_1 \overset{\kappa}{\subset} ev_2$ when the results are unimportant.

$$\frac{}{\kappa!v \overset{\kappa}{\subset} \kappa? \text{ with } ((), v)}$$

$$\frac{ev_1 \overset{\kappa}{\subset} ev_2 \text{ with } (e_1, e_2)}{ev_2 \overset{\kappa}{\subset} ev_1 \text{ with } (e_2, e_1)}$$

$$\frac{ev_1 \overset{\kappa}{\subset} ev_2 \text{ with } (e_1, e_2)}{ev_1 \overset{\kappa}{\subset} (ev_2 \Rightarrow v) \text{ with } (e_1, v\, e_2)}$$

$$\frac{ev_1 \overset{\kappa}{\subset} ev_2 \text{ with } (e_1, e_2)}{ev_1 \overset{\kappa}{\subset} (ev_2 \oplus ev_3) \text{ with } (e_1, (\text{AbortAct}(ev_3); e_2))}$$

$$\frac{ev_1 \overset{\kappa}{\subset} ev_2 \text{ with } (e_1, e_2)}{ev_1 \overset{\kappa}{\subset} (ev_3 \oplus ev_2) \text{ with } (e_1, (\text{AbortAct}(ev_3); e_2))}$$

$$\frac{ev_1 \overset{\kappa}{\subset} ev_2 \text{ with } (e_1, e_2)}{ev_1 \overset{\kappa}{\subset} (ev_2 \mid v) \text{ with } (e_1, e_2)}$$

Fig. 6. Rules for event matching

An example of event matching is:

$$(\kappa? \Rightarrow \lambda x((x.x))) \overset{\kappa}{\subset} (\kappa!17 \oplus (\kappa? \Rightarrow \lambda x())) \text{ with } (\lambda x((x.x))\, 17, ())$$

Informally, if two processes attempt to synchronize on matching event values, then we can replace the applications of sync with the respective results. This is made more precise in the next section where the concurrent evaluation relation is defined.

Note that event matching is nondeterministic; for example, both

$$\kappa? \overset{\kappa}{\subset} (\kappa!17 \oplus \kappa!29) \text{ with } (17, ())$$

and

$$\kappa? \overset{\kappa}{\mathbin{\mathrm{C}}} (\kappa!17 \oplus \kappa!29) \text{ with } (29, ())$$

It is also worth noting that even if one of the wrappers of an event value is non-terminating, the necessary abort actions for that event will be executed (assuming fair evaluation). This property is important because a common **CML** idiom is to have tail-recursive calls in wrappers (e.g., the buffered channel abstraction in Figure 3).

6.4 Concurrent Evaluation

Concurrent evaluation is defined as a transition system between finite sets of process states. This is similar to the style of the "Chemical Abstract Machine" [BB90], except that there are no "cooling" and "heating" transitions (the process sets of this semantics can be thought of as perpetually "hot" solutions). The concurrent evaluation relation extends "$\longmapsto$" to finite sets of terms (i.e., processes) and adds additional rules for process creation, channel creation, and communication. We assume a set of *process identifiers*, and define the set of *processes* and *process sets* as:

$$\begin{array}{ll} \pi \in \textsc{ProcId} & \text{process IDs} \\ p = \langle \pi; e \rangle \in \textsc{Proc} = (\textsc{ProcId} \times \textsc{Exp}) & \text{processes} \\ \mathcal{P} \in \mathrm{Fin}(\textsc{Proc}) & \text{process sets} \end{array}$$

We often write a process as $\langle \pi; E[e] \rangle$, where the evaluation context serves the role of the program counter, marking the current state of evaluation.

Definition 4. A process set $\mathcal{P}$ is *well-formed* if for all $\langle \pi; e \rangle \in \mathcal{P}$ the following hold:

- $\mathrm{FV}(e) = \emptyset$ (e is *closed*), and
- there is no $e' \neq e$, such that $\langle \pi; e' \rangle \in \mathcal{P}$.

It is occasionally useful to view well-formed process sets as finite maps from ProcId to Exp. If $\mathcal{P}$ is a finite set of process states and $\mathcal{K}$ is a finite set of channel names, then $\mathcal{K}, \mathcal{P}$ is a *configuration*.

Definition 5. A configuration $\mathcal{K}, \mathcal{P}$ is *well-formed*, if $\mathrm{FCN}(\mathcal{P}) \subseteq \mathcal{K}$ and $\mathcal{P}$ is well-formed.

The concurrent evaluation relation "$\Longrightarrow$" extends "$\longmapsto$" to configurations, with additional rules for the concurrency operations. It is defined by four inference rules that define single step evaluations. Each concurrent evaluation step affects one or two processes, called the *selected* processes. I first describe each of these rules independently, and then state the formal definition. In stating these rules, we use the notation $S + x$ for $S \cup \{x\}$.

The first rule extends the sequential evaluation relation ($\longmapsto$) to configurations:

$$\frac{e \longmapsto e'}{\mathcal{K}, \mathcal{P} + \langle \pi; e \rangle \Longrightarrow \mathcal{K}, \mathcal{P} + \langle \pi; e' \rangle} \qquad (\lambda_{cv}\text{-}\longmapsto)$$

The selected process is π.

The creation of channels requires picking a new channel name and substituting for the variable bound to it:

$$\frac{\kappa \notin \mathcal{K}}{\mathcal{K}, \mathcal{P}+\langle\pi;\ E[\text{chan } x \text{ in } e]\rangle \Longrightarrow \mathcal{K}+\kappa, \mathcal{P}+\langle\pi;\ E[e[x \mapsto \kappa]]\rangle} \qquad (\lambda_{cv}\text{-chan})$$

Again, π is the selected process.

Process creation requires picking a new process identifier:

$$\frac{\pi' \notin \text{dom}(\mathcal{P})+\pi}{\mathcal{K}, \mathcal{P}+\langle\pi;\ E[\text{spawn } v]\rangle \Longrightarrow \mathcal{K}, \mathcal{P}+\langle\pi;\ E[()]\rangle+\langle\pi';\ v\ ()\rangle} \qquad (\lambda_{cv}\text{-spawn})$$

This rule has two selected processes: π and π'.

The most interesting rule describes communication and synchronization. If two processes are attempting synchronization on matching events, then they may rendezvous — i.e., exchange a message and continue evaluation:

$$\frac{ev_1 \overset{\kappa}{\backsim} ev_2 \text{ with } (e_1, e_2)}{\begin{array}{c}\mathcal{K}, \mathcal{P}+\langle\pi_1;\ E_1[\text{sync } ev_1]\rangle+\langle\pi_2;\ E_2[\text{sync } ev_2]\rangle \\ \Longrightarrow \mathcal{K}, \mathcal{P}+\langle\pi_1;\ E_1[e_1]\rangle+\langle\pi_2;\ E_2[e_2]\rangle\end{array}} \qquad (\lambda_{cv}\text{-sync})$$

The selected processes for this rule are π_1 and π_2. We say that κ is *used* in this transition.

More formally, concurrent evaluation is defined as follows:

Definition 6 $(\Longrightarrow)$. The *concurrent evaluation relation*, written "$\Longrightarrow$," is the smallest relation satisfying the rules: $(\lambda_{cv}\text{-}\mapsto)$, $(\lambda_{cv}\text{-chan})$, $(\lambda_{cv}\text{-spawn})$, and $(\lambda_{cv}\text{-sync})$.

Under these rules, processes live forever; i.e., if a process evaluates to a value, it will never again be selected, but it remains in the process set. We could add the following rule, which is similar to the *evaporation* rule of [BB90]:

$$\mathcal{K}, \mathcal{P}+\langle\pi;\ [v]\rangle \Longrightarrow \mathcal{K}, \mathcal{P}$$

This rule is not included because certain results are easier to state and prove if the process set is monotonically increasing.

The following evaluation illustrates the concurrent evaluation relation:

$$\{\}, \{\langle\pi_0;\ [\text{chan } k \text{ in } (\text{spawn } \lambda x(\text{sync } (\text{transmit } (k.5))); \text{ sync } (\text{receive } k))]\rangle\}$$
$$\Longrightarrow \{\kappa_0\}, \{\langle\pi_0;\ ([\text{spawn } \lambda x(\text{sync } (\text{transmit } (\kappa_0.5)))]; \text{ sync } (\text{receive } \kappa_0))\rangle\}$$
$$\Longrightarrow \{\kappa_0\}, \{\langle\pi_0;\ (();\ \text{sync } ([\text{receive } \kappa_0])), $$
$$\qquad\qquad \langle\pi_1;\ [\lambda x(\text{sync } (\text{transmit } (\kappa_0.5)))\ ()]\rangle\}$$
$$\Longrightarrow \{\kappa_0\}, \{\langle\pi_0;\ (();\ \text{sync } ([\text{receive } \kappa_0])), \langle\pi_1;\ \text{sync } ([\text{transmit } (\kappa_0.5)])\rangle\}$$
$$\Longrightarrow^* \{\kappa_0\}, \{\langle\pi_0;\ (();\ [\text{sync } (\kappa_0?)])), \langle\pi_1;\ [\text{sync } (\kappa_0!5)]\rangle\}$$
$$\Longrightarrow \{\kappa_0\}, \{\langle\pi_0;\ [((); 5)]\rangle, \langle\pi_1;\ [()]\rangle\}$$
$$\Longrightarrow \{\kappa_0\}, \{\langle\pi_0;\ [5]\rangle, \langle\pi_1;\ [()]\rangle\}$$

Note that this is only one of several possible evaluation sequences, although, in this example, all evaluation sequences produce the same result.

6.5 Traces

Because of the non-deterministic semantics of $\Longrightarrow$, a λ_{cv} program can have many (often infinitely many) different evaluations. Furthermore, there are many interesting programs that do not terminate. Thus some new terminology and notation for describing evaluation sequences is required. This is used to state type soundness results for λ_{cv} in the next section.

First we note the following properties of $\Longrightarrow$:

Lemma 7. *If $\mathcal{K}, \mathcal{P}$ is well-formed and $\mathcal{K}, \mathcal{P} \Longrightarrow \mathcal{K}', \mathcal{P}'$ then the following hold:*

1. $\mathcal{K}', \mathcal{P}'$ *is well-formed*

2. $\mathcal{K} \subseteq \mathcal{K}'$

3. $\operatorname{dom}(\mathcal{P}) \subseteq \operatorname{dom}(\mathcal{P}')$

Proof. By examination of the rules for $\Longrightarrow$.

Corollary 8. *The properties of Lemma 7 hold for $\Longrightarrow^*$.*

Proof. By induction on the length of the evaluation sequence.

Note that property (1) implies that evaluation preserves closed terms.

Definition 9. A *trace* T is a (possibly infinite) sequence of well-formed configurations
$$T = \langle\!\langle \mathcal{K}_0, \mathcal{P}_0; \mathcal{K}_1, \mathcal{P}_1; \ldots \rangle\!\rangle$$
such that $\mathcal{K}_i, \mathcal{P}_i \Longrightarrow \mathcal{K}_{i+1}, \mathcal{P}_{i+1}$ (for $i < n$, if T is finite with length n). The *head* of T is $\mathcal{K}_0, \mathcal{P}_0$.

Note that if a configuration $\mathcal{K}_0, \mathcal{P}_0$ is well-formed, then any sequence of evaluation steps starting with $\mathcal{K}_0, \mathcal{P}_0$ is a trace (by Corollary 8).

The possible states of a process with respect to a configuration are given by the following definition.

Definition 10. Let $\mathcal{P}$ be a well-formed process set and let $p \in \mathcal{P}$, with $p = \langle \pi; e \rangle$. The *state* of π in $\mathcal{P}$ is either *zombie*, *blocked*, or *ready*, depending on the form of e:

- if $e = [v]$, then p is a *zombie*,
- if $e = E[\text{sync } ev]$ and there does not exist a $\langle \pi'; E'[\text{sync } ev'] \rangle \in (\mathcal{P} \setminus \{p\})$, such that $ev \overset{\kappa}{\supset} ev'$, then π is *blocked* in $\mathcal{P}$.

– otherwise, π is *ready* in $\mathcal{P}$.

We define the set of ready processes in $\mathcal{P}$ by

$$\text{Rdy}(\mathcal{P}) = \{\pi \mid \pi \text{ is ready in } \mathcal{P}\}$$

A configuration $\mathcal{K}, \mathcal{P}$ is *terminal* if $\text{Rdy}(\mathcal{P}) = \emptyset$. A terminal configuration with blocked processes is said to be *deadlocked*.

Definition 11. A trace is a *computation* if it is maximal; i.e., if it is infinite or if it is finite and ends in a terminal configuration. If e is a program, then we define the computations of e to be

$$\text{Comp}(e) = \{T \mid T \text{ is a computation with head } \langle \pi_0; e \rangle\}$$

Note, I follow the convention of using π_0 as the process identifier of the initial process in a computation of a program.

Definition 12. The *set of processes of a trace* T is defined as

$$\text{Procs}(T) = \{\pi \mid \exists \mathcal{K}_i, \mathcal{P}_i \in T \text{ with } \pi \in \text{dom}(\mathcal{P}_i)\}$$

Since a given program can evaluate in different ways, the sequential notions of convergence and divergence are inadequate. Instead, we define convergence and divergence relative to a particular computation of a program.

Definition 13. A process $\pi \in \text{Procs}(T)$ *converges* to a value v in T, written $\pi \Downarrow_T v$, if $\mathcal{K}, \mathcal{P} + \langle \pi; v \rangle \in T$. We say that π *diverges* in T, written $\pi \Uparrow_T$, if for every $\mathcal{K}, \mathcal{P} \in T$, with $\pi \in \text{dom}(\mathcal{P})$, π is ready or blocked in $\mathcal{P}$.

Divergence includes deadlocked processes and terminating processes that are not evaluated often enough to reach termination, as well as those with infinite loops. It does not include processes with run-time type errors, which are called *stuck* (see Section 7.3).

7 Static Semantics

It is well known that references (i.e., updatable memory cells) can be coded using channels and processes [GMP89, Rep91b, BMT92]. This fact makes it apparent that polymorphic channels incur the same typing problems as polymorphic references (see [Tof90] for a good description of these problems). It is possible, however, to give a sound typing to λ_{cv} programs using the imperative type scheme of **SML** [MTH90, Tof90]. In this section, I present a type system for λ_{cv} programs, and state soundness results about the system. The sound typing of λ_{cv} is discussed in greater detail (including a proof of the soundness of the type system) in [Rep92].

The presentation uses standard notation (e.g., see [Tof90] or [WF91]). Let $\iota \in$ TyCon $= \{\text{int}, \text{bool}, \ldots\}$ designate the *type constants*. Type variables are partitioned into two sets:

$$u \in \text{ImpTyVar} \qquad\qquad \text{imperative type variables}$$
$$t \in \text{AppTyVar} \qquad\qquad \text{applicative type variables}$$
$$\alpha, \beta \in \text{TyVar} = \text{ImpTyVar} \cup \text{AppTyVar} \;\; \text{type variables}$$

The set of types, $\tau \in \text{Ty}$, is defined by

$$
\begin{aligned}
\tau ::= {}& \iota && \text{type constants} \\
\mid {}& \alpha && \text{type variables} \\
\mid {}& (\tau_1 \to \tau_2) && \text{function types} \\
\mid {}& (\tau_1 \times \tau_2) && \text{pair types} \\
\mid {}& \tau \text{ chan} && \text{channel types} \\
\mid {}& \tau \text{ event} && \text{event types}
\end{aligned}
$$

and the set of type schemes, $\sigma \in \text{TyScheme}$, are defined by

$$
\begin{aligned}
\sigma ::= {}& \tau \\
\mid {}& \forall \alpha.\sigma
\end{aligned}
$$

We write $\forall \alpha_1 \cdots \alpha_n.\tau$ for the type scheme $\sigma = \forall \alpha_1 \cdots \forall \alpha_n.\tau$, and write $\text{FTV}(\sigma)$ for the free type variables of σ. We define the set of *imperative types* by

$$\theta \in \text{ImpTy} = \{\tau \mid \text{FTV}(\tau) \subset \text{ImpTyVar}\}$$

Note that all of the free type variables in an imperative type are imperative.

Type environments assign type schemes to variables in terms. Since we are interested in assigning types to intermediate stages of evaluation, channel names also need to be assigned types. Therefore, a *typing environment* is a pair of finite maps: a *variable typing* and a *channel typing*:

$$\text{VT} \in \text{VarTy} = \text{Var} \xrightarrow{\text{fin}} \text{TyScheme}$$
$$\text{CT} \in \text{ChanTy} = \text{Ch} \xrightarrow{\text{fin}} \text{ImpTy}$$
$$\text{TE} = (\text{VT}, \text{CT}) \in \text{TyEnv} = (\text{VarTy} \times \text{ChanTy})$$

We use $\text{FTV}(\text{VT})$ and $\text{FTV}(\text{CT})$ to denote the sets of free type variables of variable and channel typings, and

$$\text{FTV}(\text{TE}) = \text{FTV}(\text{VT}) \cup \text{FTV}(\text{CT})$$

where $\text{TE} = (\text{VT}, \text{CT})$. Note that there are no bound type variables in a channel typing, and that $\text{FTV}(\text{CT}) \subset \text{ImpTyVar}$. The following shorthand is useful for type environment modification:

$$\text{TE} \pm \{x \mapsto \sigma\} \equiv_{def} (\text{VT} \pm \{x \mapsto \sigma\}, \text{CT})$$
$$\text{TE} \pm \{\kappa \mapsto \theta\} \equiv_{def} (\text{VT}, \text{CT} \pm \{\kappa \mapsto \theta\})$$

where $x \in \text{Var}$, $\kappa \in \text{Ch}$, and $\text{TE} = (\text{VT}, \text{CT})$.

Because of the need to preserve imperative types, we require that substitutions map imperative type variables to imperative types. As before, we allow substitutions to be applied to types and type environments.

Definition 14. A type τ' is an *instance* of a type scheme $\sigma = \forall \alpha_1 \cdots \alpha_n.\tau$, written $\sigma \succ \tau'$, if there exists a finite substitution, S, with $\text{dom}(S) = \{\alpha_1, \ldots, \alpha_n\}$ and $S\tau = \tau'$. If $\sigma \succ \tau'$, then we say that σ is a *generalization* of τ'. We say that $\sigma \succ \sigma'$ if whenever $\sigma' \succ \tau$, then $\sigma \succ \tau$.

Definition 15. The *closure* of a type τ with respect to a type environment TE is defined as: $\text{CLOS}_{\text{TE}}(\tau) = \forall \alpha_1 \cdots \alpha_n.\tau$, where

$$\{\alpha_1, \ldots, \alpha_n\} = \text{FTV}(\tau) \setminus \text{FTV}(\text{TE})$$

And the *applicative closure* of τ is defined as: $\text{APPCLOS}_{\text{TE}}(\tau) = \forall \alpha_1 \cdots \alpha_n.\tau$, where

$$\{\alpha_1, \ldots, \alpha_n\} = (\text{FTV}(\tau) \setminus \text{FTV}(\text{TE})) \cap \text{APPTYVAR}$$

7.1 Expression Typing Rules

To associate types with the constants, we assume the existence of a function

$$\text{TypeOf} : \text{CONST} \to \text{TYSCHEME}$$

For the concurrency related constants, it assigns the following type schemes:

never	: $\forall \alpha.(\text{unit} \to \alpha \text{ event})$
receive	: $\forall \alpha.(\alpha \text{ chan} \to \alpha \text{ event})$
transmit	: $\forall \alpha.((\alpha \text{ chan} \times \alpha) \to \text{unit event})$
wrap	: $\forall \alpha\beta.((\alpha \text{ event} \times (\alpha \to \beta)) \to \beta \text{ event})$
choose	: $\forall \alpha.((\alpha \text{ event} \times \alpha \text{ event}) \to \alpha \text{ event})$
guard	: $\forall \alpha.((\text{unit} \to \alpha \text{ event}) \to \alpha \text{ event})$
wrapAbort	: $\forall \alpha.((\alpha \text{ event} \times (\text{unit} \to \text{unit})) \to \alpha \text{ event})$

We also assume that there are no event-valued constants. More formally, we require that there does not exist any b such that $\text{TypeOf}(b) = \tau$ event, for some type τ.

The typing rules for λ_{cv} are divided into two groups. The core rules are given in Figure 7. There are two rules for let: the rule (τ-app-let) applies in the non-expansive case (in the syntax of λ_{cv}, this is when the bound expression is in VAL); the rule (τ-imp-let) applies when the expression is expansive (not a value). There are also rules for typing channel names, and pair expressions. The rule (τ-chan) restricts the type of the introduced channel to be imperative. In addition to these core typing rules, there are rules for the other syntactic forms (see Figure 8). Given the appropriate environment, these rules can be derived from rule (τ-app) (rule (τ-const) in the case of Λ). It is useful, however, to include them explicitly. As before, it is worth noting that the syntactic form of a term uniquely determines which typing rule applies.

In order that the typing of constants be sensible, we impose a typability restriction on the definitions of δ and TypeOf. If $\text{TypeOf}(b) \succ (\tau' \to \tau)$ and $\text{TE} \vdash v : \tau'$, then $\delta(b, v)$ is defined and $\text{TE} \vdash \delta(b, v) : \tau$. It is worth noting that the δ rules we defined for the concurrency constants respect this restriction.

$$\frac{\text{TypeOf}(b) \succ \tau}{\text{TE} \vdash b : \tau} \qquad\qquad (\tau\text{-const})$$

$$\frac{x \in \text{dom}(\text{VT}) \quad \text{VT}(x) \succ \tau}{(\text{VT}, \text{CT}) \vdash x : \tau} \qquad\qquad (\tau\text{-var})$$

$$\frac{\text{CT}(\kappa) = \theta}{(\text{VT}, \text{CT}) \vdash \kappa : \theta} \qquad\qquad (\tau\text{-chvar})$$

$$\frac{\text{TE} \vdash e_1 : (\tau' \to \tau) \quad \text{TE} \vdash e_2 : \tau'}{\text{TE} \vdash e_1\, e_2 : \tau} \qquad\qquad (\tau\text{-app})$$

$$\frac{\text{TE} \pm \{x \mapsto \tau\} \vdash e : \tau'}{\text{TE} \vdash \lambda x(e) : (\tau \to \tau')} \qquad\qquad (\tau\text{-abs})$$

$$\frac{\text{TE} \vdash e_1 : \tau_1 \quad \text{TE} \vdash e_2 : \tau_2}{\text{TE} \vdash (e_1 . e_2) : (\tau_1 \times \tau_2)} \qquad\qquad (\tau\text{-pair})$$

$$\frac{\text{TE} \vdash v : \tau' \quad \text{TE} \pm \{x \mapsto \text{Clos}_{\text{TE}}(\tau')\} \vdash e : \tau}{\text{TE} \vdash \text{let } x = v \text{ in } e : \tau} \qquad\qquad (\tau\text{-app-let})$$

$$\frac{\text{TE} \vdash e_1 : \tau' \quad \text{TE} \pm \{x \mapsto \text{AppClos}_{\text{TE}}(\tau')\} \vdash e_2 : \tau}{\text{TE} \vdash \text{let } x = e_1 \text{ in } e_2 : \tau} \qquad\qquad (\tau\text{-imp-let})$$

$$\frac{\text{TE} \pm \{x \mapsto \theta \text{ chan}\} \vdash e : \tau}{\text{TE} \vdash \text{chan } x \text{ in } e : \tau} \qquad\qquad (\tau\text{-chan})$$

Fig. 7. Core type inference rules for λ_{cv}

7.2 Process Typings

A *process typing* is a finite map from process identifiers to types:

$$\text{PT} \in \text{ProcTy} = \text{ProcId} \xrightarrow{\text{fin}} \text{Ty}$$

Typing judgements are extended to process configurations by the following definition.

Definition 16. A well-formed configuration $\mathcal{K}, \mathcal{P}$ has type PT under a channel typing CT, written

$$\text{CT} \vdash \mathcal{K}, \mathcal{P} : \text{PT}$$

if the following hold:

- $\mathcal{K} \subseteq \text{dom}(\text{CT})$,
- $\text{dom}(\mathcal{P}) \subseteq \text{dom}(\text{PT})$, and
- for every $\langle \pi; e \rangle \in \mathcal{P}$, $(\{\}, \text{CT}) \vdash e : \text{PT}(\pi)$.

$$\frac{TE \vdash e : (\text{unit} \to \tau)}{TE \vdash \text{spawn } e : \text{unit}} \qquad (\tau\text{-spawn})$$

$$\frac{TE \vdash e : \tau \text{ event}}{TE \vdash \text{sync } e : \tau} \qquad (\tau\text{-sync})$$

$$\frac{TE \vdash e : \tau \text{ event}}{TE \vdash (G e) : \tau \text{ event}} \qquad (\tau\text{-guard})$$

$$\frac{\forall \alpha. \alpha \text{ event} \succ \tau}{TE \vdash \Lambda : \tau} \qquad (\tau\text{-never})$$

$$\frac{TE \vdash \kappa : \tau \text{ chan} \quad TE \vdash v : \tau}{TE \vdash \kappa!v : \text{unit event}} \qquad (\tau\text{-output})$$

$$\frac{TE \vdash \kappa : \tau \text{ chan}}{TE \vdash \kappa? : \tau \text{ event}} \qquad (\tau\text{-input})$$

$$\frac{TE \vdash ev : \tau' \text{ event} \quad TE \vdash e : (\tau' \to \tau)}{TE \vdash (ev \Rightarrow e) : \tau \text{ event}} \qquad (\tau\text{-wrap})$$

$$\frac{TE \vdash ev_1 : \tau \text{ event} \quad TE \vdash ev_2 : \tau \text{ event}}{TE \vdash (ev_1 \oplus ev_2) : \tau \text{ event}} \qquad (\tau\text{-choice})$$

$$\frac{TE \vdash ev : \tau \text{ event} \quad TE \vdash v : (\text{unit} \to \text{unit})}{TE \vdash (ev \mid v) : \tau \text{ event}} \qquad (\tau\text{-abort})$$

Fig. 8. Other type inference rules for λ_{cv}

For **CML**, where spawn requires a (unit $\to$ unit) argument, the process typing is $PT(\pi) = \text{unit}$ for all $\pi \in \text{dom}(\mathcal{P})$.

7.3 Type Soundness

This section presents a statement of the soundness of the above type system with respect to the dynamic semantics of Section 6. To prove these results, I use the "syntactic" approach of Wright and Felleisen [WF91] (see [Rep92] for the proofs). The basic idea is to show that evaluation preserves types (also called *subject reduction*); then characterize run-time type errors (called *"stuck states"*) and show that stuck states are untypable. This allows us to conclude that well-typed programs cannot go wrong.

The first step in this process is to show that the sequential evaluation relation preserves the types of expressions:

Theorem 17 Sequential type preservation. *For any type environment* TE, *expression e_1 and type τ, such that* $TE \vdash e_1 : \tau$, *if $e_1 \longmapsto e_2$ then* $TE \vdash e_2 : \tau$.

This result is then extended to concurrent evaluation and process typings.

Theorem 18 (Concurrent type preservation). *If a configuration* $\mathcal{K}, \mathcal{P}$ *is well-formed with*

$$\mathcal{K}, \mathcal{P} \Longrightarrow \mathcal{K}', \mathcal{P}'$$

and, for some channel typing CT,

$$\mathrm{CT} \vdash \mathcal{K}, \mathcal{P} : \mathrm{PT}$$

Then there is a channel typing CT' *and a process typing* PT', *such that the following hold:*

- CT $\subseteq$ CT',
- PT $\subseteq$ PT', *and*
- CT' $\vdash \mathcal{K}', \mathcal{P}' : $ PT'.
- CT' $\vdash \mathcal{K}, \mathcal{P} : $ PT'.

With these results, it is fairly easy to show soundness results:

Theorem 19 (Syntactic soundness). *Let* e *be a program, with* $\vdash e : \tau$. *Then, for any* $T \in \mathrm{Comp}(e)$, $\pi \in \mathrm{Procs}(T)$, *with* $\mathcal{K}_i, \mathcal{P}_i$ *the first occurrence of* π *in* T, *there exists a* CT *and* PT, *such that*

$$\mathrm{CT} \vdash \mathcal{K}_i, \mathcal{P}_i : \mathrm{PT}$$

and $\mathrm{PT}(\pi_0) = \tau$. *And either*

- $\pi \Uparrow_\tau$, *or*
- $\pi \Downarrow_\tau v$ *and there exists an extension* CT' *of* CT *with* $(\{\}, \mathrm{CT}') \vdash v : \mathrm{PT}(\pi)$.

Theorem 20 (Soundness). *If* e *is a program with* $\vdash e : \tau$, *then for any computation* $T \in \mathrm{Comp}(e)$ *and any process ID* $\pi \in \mathrm{Procs}(T)$, *the following hold:*

(Strong soundness) *If* $\mathrm{eval}_\tau(\pi) = v$, *and* $\mathcal{K}_i, \mathcal{P}_i$ *is the first occurrence of* π *in* T, *then for any* CT *and* PT, *such that* $\mathrm{CT} \vdash \mathcal{K}_i, \mathcal{P}_i : \mathrm{PT}$ *and* $\mathrm{PT}(\pi_0) = \tau$, *there is an extension* CT' *of* CT, *such that* $(\{\}, \mathrm{CT}') \vdash v : \mathrm{PT}(\pi)$.

(Weak soundness) $\mathrm{eval}_\tau(\pi) \neq \mathrm{WRONG}$

8 Related Work

There are many approaches to concurrent language design (see either [AS83] or [And91] for an overview); our approach is an offshoot of the **CSP**-school of concurrent language design. **CML** began as a reimplementation of the concurrency primitives of **PML** [Rep88] in **SML/NJ**, but has evolved into a significantly more powerful language. **PML** in turn was heavily influenced by **amber** [Car86]. There have been other attempts at adding concurrency to various versions of **ML**. Most of these have been based on message passing ([Hol83], [Mat89], and [Ram90] for example), but there is at least one shared memory approach [CM90]. As we have shown in this paper, message passing fits very nicely into **SML**. It allows an applicative style of programming to be used most of the time; the state modifying operations are hidden in the thread and channel abstractions. **CML** extends the message passing paradigm by making synchronous operations first-class, which provides a mechanism for building user-defined synchronization abstractions.

Using concurrency to implement interactive systems has been proposed and implemented by several people. In [RG86], we made the argument that concurrency is vital for the construction of interactive programming environments. Pike (in [Pik89]) and Haahr (in [Haa90]) describe experimental window systems built out of threads and channels, but neither of these were fast enough for real use.

The semantics of **Facile** have been proposed as a model for **PML** in [PGM90], but no translation from **PML** to **Facile** is given. Independent work by Berry, Milner and Turner at the University of Edinburgh has resulted in an operational semantics for a small concurrent language, which includes the **PML** version of events [BMT92]. The semantics presented in this paper has some strong similarities with that of [BMT92], but λ_{cv} is a richer language; in particular, the language of [BMT92] does not include the **guard** and **wrapAbort** event value constructors found in **CML**. An earlier version of the semantics of first-class synchronous operations was presented in [Rep91b], and a more complete treatment of the version presented here can be found in [Rep92] (including extensions to cover features such as polling and exceptions).

9   Conclusions

We have described a higher-order concurrent language, **CML**, its use in real-world applications, and its formal semantics. **CML** supports first-class synchronous operations, which provide a powerful mechanism for communication and synchronization abstraction. Our experience with **CML** "in-the-field" and our measurements of the performance of the implementation show that **CML** is a practical tool for building real systems. We feel that **CML** is unique in that it combines a flexible high-level notation with good performance. In addition, it is well-defined, with a formal semantics.

CML is a stable system, and is freely available for distribution. The latest version of both **CML** and its manual are available via anonymous ftp in the /pub directory on ftp.cs.cornell.edu; for more information send electronic mail to cml-bugs@cs.cornell.edu. In addition, both **CML** and eXene will be included as part of the **SML/NJ** system (most likely in the fall of 1992).

Acknowledgements

Most of this work was done while the author was a graduate student at Cornell University, and was supported, in part, by the NSF and ONR under NSF grant CCR-85-14862, and by the NSF under NSF grant CCR-89-18233. Anne Rogers helped with proof reading this paper.

References

[AB86] Abramsky, S. and R. Bornat. Pascal-m: A language for loosely coupled distributed systems. In Y. Paker and J.-P. Verjus (eds.), *Distributed Computing Systems*, pp. 163–189. Academic Press, New York, N.Y., 1986.

[Agh86] Agha, G. *Actors: A Model of Concurrent Computation in Distributed Systems.* The MIT Press, Cambridge, Mass., 1986.

[AM87] Appel, A. W. and D. B. MacQueen. A Standard ML compiler. In *Functional Programming Languages and Computer Architecture*, vol. 274 of *Lecture Notes in Computer Science*. Springer-Verlag, September 1987, pp. 301–324.

[And91] Andrews, G. R. *Concurrent Programming: Principles and Practice.* Benjamin/Cummings, Redwood City, California, 1991.

[AOCE88] Andrews, G. R., R. A. Olsson, M. Coffin, and I. Elshoff. An overview of the SR language and implementation. *ACM Transactions on Programming Languages and Systems*, 10(7), January 1988, pp. 51–86.

[App92] Appel, A. W. *Compiling with Continuations.* Cambridge University Press, New York, N.Y., 1992.

[AS83] Andrews., G. R. and F. B. Schneider. Concepts and notations for concurrent programming. *ACM Computing Surveys*, 15(1), March 1983, pp. 3–43.

[BB90] Berry, G. and G. Boudol. The chemical abstract machine. In *Conference Record of the 17th Annual ACM Symposium on Principles of Programming Languages*, January 1990, pp. 81–94.

[BCJ+90] Birman, K., R. Cooper, T. A. Joseph, K. Marzullo, M. Makpangou, K. Kane, F. Schmuck, and M. Wood. *The ISIS system manual, version 2.0.* Department of Computer Science, Cornell University, Ithaca, N.Y., March 1990.

[BMT92] Berry, D., R. Milner, and D. N. Turner. A semantics for ML concurrency primitives. In *Conference Record of the 19th Annual ACM Symposium on Principles of Programming Languages*, January 1992, pp. 119–129.

[Bor86] Bornat, R. A protocol for generalised occam. *Software – Practice and Experience*, 16(9), September 1986, pp. 783–799.

[Bur88] Burns, A. *Programming in occam 2.* Addison-Wesley, Reading, Mass., 1988.

[Car86] Cardelli, L. Amber. In *Combinators and Functional Programming Languages*, vol. 242 of *Lecture Notes in Computer Science*. Springer-Verlag, July 1986, pp. 21–47.

[CK92] Cooper, R. and C. D. Krumvieda. Distributed programming with asynchronous ordered channels in Distributed ML. In *Proceedings of the 1992 ACM SIGPLAN Workshop on ML and its Applications*, June 1992, pp. 134–148.

[CM90] Cooper, E. C. and J. G. Morrisett. Adding threads to Standard ML. *Technical Report CMU-CS-90-186*, School of Computer Science, Carnegie Mellon University, December 1990.

[Con86] Constable, R. et al. *Implementing Mathematics with The Nuprl Development System.* Prentice-Hall, Englewood Cliffs, N.J., 1986.

[CP85]   Cardelli, L. and R. Pike. Squeak: A language for communicating with mice. In
           SIGGRAPH '85, July 1985, pp. 199–204.

[DHM91]   Duba, B., R. Harper, and D. MacQueen. Type-checking first-class continua-
           tions. In *Conference Record of the 18th Annual ACM Symposium on Principles
           of Programming Languages*, January 1991, pp. 163–173.

[FF86]   Felleisen, M. and D. P. Friedman. Control operators, the SECD-machine, and
           the λ-calculus. In M. Wirsing (ed.), *Formal Description of Programming Con-
           cepts – III*, pp. 193–219. North-Holland, New York, N.Y., 1986.

[GL91]   George, L. and G. Lindstrom. Using a functional language and graph reduction
           to program multiprocessor machines. *Technical Report UUCS-91-020*, Depart-
           ment of Computer Science, University of Utah, October 1991.

[GMP89]   Giacalone, A., P. Mishra, and S. Prasad. Facile: A symemetric integration of
           concurrent and functional programming. In *TAPSOFT'89 (vol. 2)*, vol. 352 of
           Lecture Notes in Computer Science. Springer-Verlag, March 1989, pp. 184–209.

[GR91]   Gansner, E. R. and J. H. Reppy. eXene. In *Proceedings of the 1991 CMU
           Workshop on Standard ML*, Carnegie Mellon University, September 1991.

[GR92]   Gansner, E. R. and J. H. Reppy. A foundation for user interface construction.
           In B. A. Myers (ed.), *Languages for Developing User Interfaces*, pp. 239–260.
           Jones & Bartlett, Boston, Mass., 1992.

[Haa90]   Haahr, D. Montage: Breaking windows into small pieces. In *USENIX Summer
           Conference*, June 1990, pp. 289–297.

[Har86]   Harper, R. Introduction to Standard ML. *Technical Report ECS-LFCS-86-14*,
           Laboratory for Foundations of Computer Science, Computer Science Depart-
           ment, Edinburgh University, August 1986.

[HDB90]   Hieb, R., R. K. Dybvig, and C. Bruggeman. Representing control in the presence
           of first-class continuations. In *Proceedings of the SIGPLAN'90 Conference on
           Programming Language Design and Implementation*, June 1990, pp. 66–77.

[Hol83]   Holmström, S. PFL: A functional language for parallel programming. In *Declar-
           ative programming workshop*, April 1983, pp. 114–139.

[KKR+86]   Krans, D., R. Kelsey, J. Rees, P. Hudak, J. Philbin, and N. Adams. Orbit: An
           optimising compiler for Scheme. In *Proceedings of the SIGPLAN'86 Symposium
           on Compiler Construction*, July 1986, pp. 219–233.

[Kru91]   Krumvieda, C. D. DML: Packaging high-level distributed abstractions in SML.
           In *Proceedings of the 1991 CMU Workshop on Standard ML*, September 1991.

[Kru92]   Krumvieda, C. D. Expressing fault-tolerant and consistency-preserving pro-
           grams in Distributed ML. In *Proceedings of the 1992 ACM SIGPLAN Workshop
           on ML and its Applications*, June 1992, pp. 157–162.

[LCJS87]   Liskov, B., D. Curtis, P. Johnson, and R. Scheifler. Implementation of Argus.
           In *Proceedings of the 11th ACM Symposium on Operating System Principles*,
           November 1987, pp. 111–122.

[Lie86]   Lieberman, H. Using prototypical objects to implement shared behavior in
           object oriented systems. In *OOPSLA'86 Proceedings*, September 1986, pp. 214–
           223.

[LS88]   Liskov, B. and L. Shrira. Promises: Linguistic support for efficient asynchronous
           procedure calls in distributed systems. In *Proceedings of the SIGPLAN'88 Con-
           ference on Programming Language Design and Implementation*, June 1988, pp.
           260–267.

[Mac84]   MacQueen, D. B. Modules for Standard ML. In *Conference record of the 1984
           ACM Conference on Lisp and Functional Programming*, July 1984, pp. 198–207.

[Mat89]   Matthews, D. C. J. Processes for Poly and ML. In *Papers on Poly/ML, Tech-
           nical Report 161*. University of Cambridge, February 1989.

197

[MT91]   Milner, R. and M. Tofte. *Commentary on Standard ML*. The MIT Press, Cambridge, Mass, 1991.

[MTH90]   Milner, R., M. Tofte, and R. Harper. *The Definition of Standard ML*. The MIT Press, Cambridge, Mass, 1990.

[Nye90]   Nye, A. *Xlib Programming Manual*, vol. 1. O'Reilly & Associates, Inc., 1990.

[Oph92]   Ophel, J. An introduction to the high-level language Standard ML, 1992. In this volume.

[Pau91]   Paulson, L. C. *ML for the Working Programmer*. Cambridge University Press, New York, N.Y., 1991.

[Pel92]   Pellerin, C. The concurrent constraint programming language taskell. Master's dissertation, School of Computer Science, McGill University, Montréal, Québec, Canada, January 1992.

[PGM90]   Prasad, S., A. Giacalone, and P. Mishra. Operational and algebraic semantics for Facile: A symemetric integration of concurrent and functional programming. In *Proceedings of the 17th International Colloquium on Automata, Languages and Programming*, vol. 443 of *Lecture Notes in Computer Science*. Springer-Verlag, July 1990, pp. 765–780.

[Pik89]   Pike, R. A concurrent window system. *Computing Systems*, 2(2), 1989, pp. 133–153.

[Plo75]   Plotkin, G. D. Call-by-name, call-by-value and the λ-calculus. *Theoretical Computer Science*, 1, 1975, pp. 125–159.

[Ram90]   Ramsey, N. Concurrent programming in ML. *Technical Report CS-TR-262-90*, Department of Computer Science, Princeton University, April 1990.

[Rep88]   Reppy, J. H. Synchronous operations as first-class values. In *Proceedings of the SIGPLAN'88 Conference on Programming Language Design and Implementation*, June 1988, pp. 250–259.

[Rep89]   Reppy, J. H. First-class synchronous operations in Standard ML. *Technical Report TR 89-1068*, Department of Computer Science, Cornell University, December 1989.

[Rep90a]   Reppy, J. H. Asynchronous signals in Standard ML. *Technical Report TR 90-1144*, Department of Computer Science, Cornell University, August 1990.

[Rep90b]   Reppy, J. H. *Concurrent programming with events – The Concurrent ML manual*. Department of Computer Science, Cornell University, Ithaca, N.Y., November 1990. (Last revised October 1991).

[Rep91a]   Reppy, J. H. CML: A higher-order concurrent language. In *Proceedings of the SIGPLAN'91 Conference on Programming Language Design and Implementation*, June 1991, pp. 293–305.

[Rep91b]   Reppy, J. H. An operational semantics of first-class synchronous operations. *Technical Report TR 91-1232*, Department of Computer Science, Cornell University, August 1991.

[Rep92]   Reppy, J. H. *Higher-order concurrency*. Ph.D. dissertation, Department of Computer Science, Cornell University, Ithaca, NY, January 1992. Available as Technical Report TR 92-1285.

[RG86]   Reppy, J. H. and E. R. Gansner. A foundation for programming environments. In *Proceedings of the ACM SIGSOFT/SIGPLAN Software Engineering Symposium on Practical Software Development Environments*, December 1986, pp. 218–227.

[SG86]   Scheifler, R. W. and J. Gettys. The X window system. *ACM Transactions on Graphics*, 5(2), April 1986, pp. 79–109.

[Ste78]   Steele Jr., G. L. Rabbit: A compiler for Scheme. Master's dissertation, MIT, May 1978.

[Tof90]   Tofte, M. Type inference for polymorphic references. *Information and Computation*, **89**, 1990, pp. 1–34.

[UNI86]   University of California, Berkeley. *UNIX Programmer's Reference Manual (4.3bsd)*, 1986.

[Wan80]   Wand, M. Continuation-based multiprocessing. In *Conference Record of the 1980 Lisp Conference*, August 1980, pp. 19–28.

[WF91]   Wright, A. and M. Felleisen. A syntactic approach to type soundness. *Technical Report TR91-160*, Department of Computer Science, Rice University, April 1991.

A Taste of Rewrite Systems

Nachum Dershowitz

Department of Computer Science, University of Illinois, Urbana IL 61801, USA

Abstract. This survey of the theory and applications of rewriting with equations discusses the existence and uniqueness of normal forms, the Knuth-Bendix completion procedure and its variations, as well as rewriting-based (functional and logic) programming and (equational, first-order, and inductive) theorem proving. Ordinary, associative-commutative, and conditional rewriting are covered. Current areas of research are summarized and an extensive bibliography is provided.

0 Menu

Equational reasoning is an important component in symbolic algebra, automated deduction, high-level programming languages, program verification, and artificial intelligence. Reasoning with equations involves deriving consequences of given equations and finding values for variables that satisfy a given equation.

Rewriting is a very powerful method for dealing with equations. Directed equations, called "rewrite rules", are used to replace equals by equals, but only in the indicated direction. The theory of rewriting centers around the concept of "normal form", an expression that cannot be rewritten any further. Computation consists of rewriting to a normal form; when the normal form is unique, it is taken as the value of the initial expression. When rewriting equal terms always leads to the same normal form, the set of rules is said to be "convergent" and rewriting can be used to check for equality.

This chapter gives a brief survey of the theory of rewriting and its applications to issues in programming languages and automated deduction. Section 1 offers a few motivating examples as appetizer. The "bread and butter" concepts come next: Sect. 2 addresses the question of existence of normal forms; Sect. 3 addresses their uniqueness. Section 4 describes a brew for constructing convergent systems. The main course is a choice of Sect. 5, a method for proving validity of equations, and, Sect. 6, a method for solving equations. As side dishes, Sections 7 and 8 consider extensions of rewriting to handle associative-commutative function symbols and conditional equations. Dessert is Sect. 9, which applies conditional and unconditional rewriting to programming, while, the *pièce de résistance*, Sect. 10, shows how rewriting is used to facilitate deductive and inductive proofs. Finally, over coffee, Sect. 11 mentions some current areas of research. An extensive bibliography for further reading (the "check") is attached.

1 Rewriting

We begin our rewriting feast with the following three puzzles:

Puzzle 1 (Hercules and Hydra). Hydra is a bush-like creature with multiple heads. Each time Hercules hacks off a head of hers, Hydra sprouts many new branches identical to—and adjacent to—the weakened branch that used to hold the severed head. But whenever he chops off a head coming straight out of the ground, no new branches result. Suppose Hydra starts off as a lone stalk ten branches tall. The question is: Does Hercules ever defeat Hydra? □

Puzzle 2 (Chamelion Island). The chamelions on this strange island come in three colors, red, yellow, and green, and wander about continuously. Whenever two chamelions of different colors meet, they both change to the third color. Suppose there are 15 red chamelions, 14 yellow, and 13 green. Can their haphazard meetings lead to a stable state, all sharing the same color? □

Puzzle 3 (Grecian Urn). An urn contains 150 black beans and 75 white. Two beans are removed at a time: if they're the same color, a black one is placed in the urn; if they're different, the white one is returned. The process is repeated as long as possible. Is the color of the last bean in the urn predetermined and, if so, what is it? □

All three puzzles give rules for going from one state to another. The first two concern the possibility of getting from some starting state to a final state; the last asks how the final state is related to the initial state.

In general, a *rewrite system* consists of a set of *rules* for transforming terms. Hercules and Hydra can be expressed pictorially as in Fig. 1.

Fig. 1. Hercules versus Hydra.

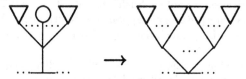

Chamelion Island can be expressed by three rules:

$$\begin{aligned} red\ yellow &\longrightarrow green\ green \\ green\ yellow &\longrightarrow red\ red \\ red\ green &\longrightarrow yellow\ yellow\ , \end{aligned}$$

with the added proviso that chamelions can rearrange themselves at will.

The Grecian Urn may be expressed as the following system of four rules, one per possible pair of beans:

$$\begin{aligned} black\ black &\longrightarrow black \\ white\ white &\longrightarrow black \\ black\ white &\longrightarrow white \\ white\ black &\longrightarrow white\ . \end{aligned}$$

In the sequel, we will solve these puzzles by applying techniques from the theory of rewriting. But, first, let's take a look at some more prosaic examples of rewrite systems.

Example 1 (Insertion Sort). The following is a program to arrange a list of numbers in non-increasing order by inserting elements one by one into position:

$$
\begin{aligned}
max(0, x) &\rightarrow x \\
max(x, 0) &\rightarrow x \\
max(s(x), s(y)) &\rightarrow s(max(x, y)) \\
min(0, x) &\rightarrow 0 \\
min(x, 0) &\rightarrow 0 \\
min(s(x), s(y)) &\rightarrow s(min(x, y)) \\
sort(nil) &\rightarrow nil \\
sort(cons(x, y)) &\rightarrow insert(x, sort(y)) \\
insert(x, nil) &\rightarrow cons(x, nil) \\
insert(x, cons(y, z)) &\rightarrow cons(max(x, y), insert(min(x, y), z)) \,.
\end{aligned}
$$

Lists are represented in "cons" notation and numbers in successor (unary) notation. We would like to ascertain that every term constructed from *sort*, *cons*, *nil*, *s*, and 0 leads to a unique term, not containing *sort*, nor the auxiliary symbols, *insert*, *max*, and *min*. □

As in the previous example, both sides of a rule $l \rightarrow r$ can contain variables which refer to arbitrary terms. A rule is used to *rewrite* any subterm that is an instance of the left-hand side l. That is, $u[l\sigma]$ rewrites to $u[r\sigma]$, where σ is a substitution of terms for variables of the rule (the same term substituted for each occurrence of the same variable), $u[\cdot]$ is the "context" in which the instance $l\sigma$ of l occurs as a subterm, and $u[r\sigma]$ is $u[l\sigma]$ with that subterm replaced by the right-hand side after its variables have had the same substitution σ applied. Such a rewrite step is written $u[l\sigma] \rightarrow u[r\sigma]$ or, backwards, as $u[r\sigma] \leftarrow u[l\sigma]$. Rules are applied nondeterministically, since, in general, more than one rule can be applied, and any one rule may apply at more than one position within a term.

Rewrite systems have long been used as decision procedures for validity in equational theories, that is, for truth of an equation in all models of the theory.

Example 2 (Loops). Consider the following system of a dozen rules:

$$
\begin{aligned}
x \backslash x &\rightarrow e & x \cdot (x \backslash y) &\rightarrow y \\
x / x &\rightarrow e & (y/x) \cdot x &\rightarrow y \\
e \cdot x &\rightarrow x & x \backslash (x \cdot y) &\rightarrow y \\
x \cdot e &\rightarrow x & x \cdot (x \backslash y) &\rightarrow y \\
e \backslash x &\rightarrow x & x / (y \backslash x) &\rightarrow y \\
x / e &\rightarrow x & (x/y) \backslash x &\rightarrow y \,.
\end{aligned}
$$

Each rule follows by algebraic manipulation from some combination of the following five axioms for algebraic structures called "loops":

$$x \cdot (x\backslash y) = y \qquad (y/x) \cdot x = y$$
$$x\backslash(x \cdot y) = y \qquad (x/y)\backslash x = y$$
$$y/y = x\backslash x .$$

To use the rewrite system to decide whether an arbitrary equation is a valid identity for all loops (in which case it can be proved by purely equational reasoning), we need to ascertain that *any* two terms equal in the theory have the same normal forms. □

Rewrite systems can also be used to "interpret" other programming languages.

Example 3 (Interpreter). The state of a machine with three integer-valued registers can be represented as a triple $\langle x, y, z \rangle$. The semantics of its instruction set can be defined by the rules for the interpreter shown in Fig. 2. The penultimate rule, for example, can clearly be applied *ad infinitum*. The question is what strategy of rule application, if any, will lead to a normal form whenever there is one. □

Fig. 2. Three-register machine interpreter.

$$
\begin{aligned}
eval(\text{set0 } n, \langle x, y, z \rangle) &\rightarrow \langle n, y, z \rangle \\
eval(\text{set1 } n, \langle x, y, z \rangle) &\rightarrow \langle x, n, z \rangle \\
eval(\text{set2 } n, \langle x, y, z \rangle) &\rightarrow \langle x, y, n \rangle \\
eval(\text{inc0}, \langle x, y, z \rangle) &\rightarrow \langle s(x), y, z \rangle \\
eval(\text{inc1}, \langle x, y, z \rangle) &\rightarrow \langle x, s(y), z \rangle \\
eval(\text{inc2}, \langle x, y, z \rangle) &\rightarrow \langle x, y, s(z) \rangle \\
eval(\text{dec0}, \langle s(x), y, z \rangle) &\rightarrow \langle x, y, z \rangle \\
eval(\text{dec1}, \langle x, s(y), z \rangle) &\rightarrow \langle x, y, z \rangle \\
eval(\text{dec2}, \langle x, y, s(z) \rangle) &\rightarrow \langle x, y, z \rangle \\
eval(\text{ifpos0 } p, \langle 0, y, z \rangle) &\rightarrow \langle 0, y, z \rangle \\
eval(\text{ifpos0 } p, \langle s(x), y, z \rangle) &\rightarrow eval(p, \langle s(x), y, z \rangle) \\
eval(\text{ifpos1 } p, \langle x, 0, z \rangle) &\rightarrow \langle x, 0, z \rangle \\
eval(\text{ifpos1 } p, \langle x, s(y), z \rangle) &\rightarrow eval(p, \langle x, s(y), z \rangle) \\
eval(\text{ifpos2 } p, \langle x, y, 0 \rangle) &\rightarrow \langle x, y, 0 \rangle \\
eval(\text{ifpos2 } p, \langle x, y, s(z) \rangle) &\rightarrow eval(p, \langle x, y, s(z) \rangle) \\
\text{whilepos0 } p &\rightarrow \text{ifpos0 } (p; \text{whilepos0 } p) \\
\text{whilepos1 } p &\rightarrow \text{ifpos1 } (p; \text{whilepos1 } p) \\
\text{whilepos2 } p &\rightarrow \text{ifpos2 } (p; \text{whilepos2 } p) \\
eval((p; q), u) &\rightarrow eval(q, eval(p, u)) .
\end{aligned}
$$

Two important properties a rewrite system may possess are termination and confluence. We address these in the following two sections.

2 Termination

Definition 1 (Termination). A rewrite system is *terminating* if there are no infinite derivations $t_1 \rightarrow t_2 \rightarrow \cdots$.

The rules for the Chamelion Puzzle are not terminating; to wit *red yellow yellow* → *green green yellow* → *green red red* → *yellow yellow red*, which rearranges to *red yellow yellow*, from which point the same three steps may be repeated over and over again. On the other hand, each step in the Grecian Urn Puzzle decreases the number of beans, so it always terminates. The Loop system also terminates, since it always shortens the length of the expression, but, as pointed out above, our Interpreter does not.

Termination is an undecidable property of rewrite systems. Nonetheless, the following general method is very often helpful in termination proofs:

Definition 2 (Termination Function). A *termination function* takes a term as argument and is of one of the following types:

- a function that returns the outermost function symbol of a term, with symbols ordered by some precedence (a "precedence" is a well-founded partial ordering of symbols);
- a function that extracts the immediate subterm at a specified position (which position, can depend on the outermost function symbol of the term);
- a function that extracts the immediate subterm of a specified rank (the kth largest in the path ordering defined recursively below);
- a homomorphism from terms to some well-founded set of values;
- a monotonic homomorphism, having the strict subterm property, from terms to some well-founded set (a homomorphism is *monotonic* with respect to the well-founded ordering if the value it assigns to a term $f(\ldots s \ldots)$ is greater than or equivalent to that of $f(\ldots t \ldots)$ whenever the value of s is greater than t; it has the *strict subterm property* if the value of $f(\ldots t \ldots)$ is always strictly greater than that of its subterm t);
- a strictly monotonic homomorphism, having the strict subterm property, from terms to some well-founded set (it is *strictly monotonic* if the value of $f(\ldots s \ldots)$ is strictly greater than that of $f(\ldots t \ldots)$ whenever s is of greater value than t); or
- a constant function.

Simple examples of homomorphisms from terms to the natural numbers are size (number of function symbols, including constants), depth (maximum nesting of function symbols), and weight (sum of integral weights of function symbols). Size and weight are strictly monotonic; depth is monotonic.

Definition 3 (Path Ordering). Let $\tau_0, \ldots, \tau_{i-1}$ ($i \geq 0$) be monotonic homomorphisms, all but possibly τ_{i-1} strict, and let $\tau_i, \ldots, \tau_k$ be any other kinds of termination functions. The induced *path ordering* $\succ$ is as follows:

$$s = f(s_1, \ldots, s_m) \succeq g(t_1, \ldots, t_n) = t$$

if either of the following hold:

(1) $s_i \succeq t$ for some s_i, $i = 1, \ldots, m$; or

(2) $s \succ t_1, \ldots, t_n$ and $\langle \tau_1(s), \ldots, \tau_k(s) \rangle$ is lexicographically greater than or equal to $\langle \tau_1(t), \ldots, \tau_k(t) \rangle$, where function symbols are compared according to their precedence, homomorphic images are compared in the corresponding well-founded ordering, and subterms are compared recursively in $\succ$.

A tuple $\langle x_1, \ldots, x_m \rangle$ is *lexicographically* greater than $\langle y_1, \ldots, y_n \rangle$ if (a) x_i is greater than y_i for some i $(1 \leq i \leq n)$ and x_j is equivalent to y_j for all j up to, but not including, i, or if (b) the x_i and y_i are equivalent for all i up to and including n and also $m > n$. We say that $s \succ t$ if $s \succeq t$, but $s \not\preceq t$.

This ordering mixes and matches syntactic considerations (the first three types of termination functions) with semantic considerations (the others).

Theorem 4 [20]. *A rewrite system terminates if $l\sigma \succ r\sigma$ in a path ordering $\succ$ for all rules $l \to r$ and substitutions σ, and also $\tau(l\sigma) = \tau(r\sigma)$ for each of the nonmonotonic homomorphisms among its termination functions.*

The proof of this theorem is based on Kruskal's Tree Theorem and the fact that $s \to t$ and $s \succ t$ imply $f(\ldots, s, \ldots) \succ f(\ldots, t, \ldots)$, for all terms s, t, $\ldots$ and function symbols f.

The path ordering encompasses many of the orderings described in the literature. The simplest, and perhaps most generally useful, version of this ordering, called the *lexicographic path ordering*, uses a precedence for τ_0 and the ith subterm for the remaining τ_i (or any other permutation of all the subterms). The precedence typically encapsulates the dependency of some function definitions on others. The resultant path ordering is "syntactic" in that it depends only on the relative order of the function symbols appearing in the terms being compared. Terms s and t are compared by first comparing their outermost function symbols: if they're equal, then subterms are compared recursively, in order; if the outermost symbol of s is larger, all that needs to be shown is that s is larger than t's subterms; otherwise, the only way s can be larger than t is if one of its subterms is.

To prove that Insertion Sort terminates, note that five of the rules show a decrease for $\succ$ by virtue of clause (1) of the definition of the path ordering, regardless of what we choose for the τ_i. For the recursive rules of *max* and *min*, we can use the precedence *max* and *min* greater than s as τ_0. For the base case of *insert*, we let *insert* > *cons* in the precedence. For the recursive rule of *sort*, we let *sort* > *insert*, and have τ_1 give the sole argument of *sort*. Finally, for the recursive rule of *insert*, we make *insert* > *max*, *min* in the precedence, and have τ_1 return the second argument of *insert*.

Another important class of orderings, the *polynomial path orderings*, uses a polynomial interpretation for τ_0. The interpretation associates a (multivariate) monotonic integer polynomial with each function symbol and constant, which is extended to a homomorphism to give meaning to terms. The remaining τ_i select subterms as before. For example, Loops may be shown terminating by letting each binary symbol take the sum of its arguments. This "semantic" ordering acts like the lexicographic path ordering when the polynomials are all of degree 0 (constants). The advantage of polynomials over other classes of interpretations is that tools are available to help compute inequalities.

To show that Hercules invariably defeats Hydra, we need to show that after each chop and regrowth, Hydra is smaller than before. To this end, we let nodes have variable arity. This *multiset path ordering*, in effect, uses a precedence for τ_0 and has τ_i give the ith largest subterm. The precedence for Hydra makes branching nodes larger than heads. Replacing a branch with any number of smaller branches is a decrease in this ordering.

3 Confluence

We will use $s \leftrightarrow t$ to mean $s \rightarrow t$ or $t \rightarrow s$. We say s *derives* t and write $s \rightarrow^* t$ if $s \rightarrow \cdots \rightarrow t$ in zero or more steps. We say that s and t are *convertible*, symbolized $s \leftrightarrow^* t$, if $s \leftrightarrow \cdots \leftrightarrow t$ in zero or more steps, and that s and t are *joinable*, or that $s = t$ has a *rewrite proof*, if s and t derive the same term.

The following two definitions are easily shown equivalent:

Definition 5 (Church-Rosser Property). A rewrite system is *Church-Rosser* if terms are joinable whenever they are convertible. (See Fig. 3(a).)

Definition 6 (Confluence). A rewrite system is *confluent* if terms are joinable whenever they are derivable from the same term. (See Fig. 3(b).)

Fig. 3. Confluence Properties.

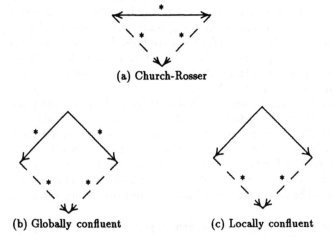

(a) Church-Rosser

(b) Globally confluent   (c) Locally confluent

Terminating confluent systems are called *convergent* or *complete*. Often, we are only interested in confluence for ground (variable-free) terms.

A weaker form of confluence is the following:

Definition 7 (Local Confluence). A rewrite system is *locally confluent* if two terms are joinable whenever they are both obtainable by rewriting (in one step) from the same term. (See Fig. 3(c).)

The following, sometimes referred to as the "Diamond Lemma", connects local and global confluence:

Theorem 8 [21]. *A terminating rewrite system is Church-Rosser if and only if it is locally confluent.*

A rewrite system is locally confluent if (but not only if) no left-hand side unifies with a non-variable subterm (except itself) of any left-hand side, taking into account that variables appearing in two rules (or in two instances of the same rule) are always treated as disjoint. To get confluence for nonterminating systems we have an additional requirement:

Definition 9 (Orthogonal System). A rewrite system is *orthogonal* if no left-hand side unifies with a renamed non-variable subterm of any other left-hand side or with a renamed proper subterm of itself, and no variable appears more than once on any left-hand side.

The importance of orthogonal systems stems from the following result:

Theorem 10 [23]. *Every orthogonal system is confluent.*

In particular, our erstwhile interpreter is confluent.

Example 4 (Combinatory Logic). Combinatory Logic is a prime example of a (non-terminating) orthogonal system (juxtaposition and $\langle \cdot, \cdot \rangle$ are binary operators):

$$
\begin{aligned}
Ix &\rightarrow x \\
(Kx)y &\rightarrow x \\
((Sx)y)z &\rightarrow (xz)(yz) \ .
\end{aligned}
$$

This system can be used to implement any recursive function. The combinators K and S were dubbed "kestrel" and "starling" by Smullyan; I is the identity combinator. □

Example 5 (Cartesian Closed Categories).
The following non-orthogonal, non-confluent system is used in the compilation of functional languages (juxtaposition represents the binary composition operator):

$$
\begin{aligned}
Ix &\rightarrow x & (xy)z &\rightarrow x(yz) \\
xI &\rightarrow x & \langle x, y \rangle z &\rightarrow \langle xz, yz \rangle \\
F\langle x, y \rangle &\rightarrow x & E\langle Cx, y \rangle &\rightarrow x\langle I, y \rangle \\
S\langle x, y \rangle &\rightarrow y & (Cx)y &\rightarrow C(x\langle yF, S \rangle) \ .
\end{aligned}
$$

The combinators E and C stand for "evaluation" and "Currying", respectively; I is the identity morphism; F and S project the components of pairs $\langle \cdot, \cdot \rangle$. □

For terminating confluent systems, any rewriting strategy will lead to the unique normal form of any given term; for nonterminating orthogonal systems, we defer to the discussion in Sect. 9. Also, for terminating systems, there is a stronger result, relating confluence to joinability in a finite number of cases:

Definition 11 (Critical Pair). If $l \to r$ and $s \to t$ are two rewrite rules (with variables made distinct) and μ is a most general unifier of l and a nonvariable subterm s' of s, then the equation $t\mu = s\mu[r\mu]$, where $r\mu$ has replaced $s'\mu$ $(= l\mu)$ in $s\mu$, is a *critical pair*.

A finite rewrite system has a finite number of critical pairs.

Theorem 12 [29][26]. *A rewrite system is locally confluent if and only if all its critical pairs are joinable. Therefore, a terminating system is confluent (hence, convergent) if and only if all its critical pairs are joinable.*

Insertion Sort has one trivially joinable critical pair, $0 = 0$, formed from either the first two rules, or the fourth and fifth.

Example 6 (Fragment of Group Theory). Each of the rules

$$
\begin{aligned}
0 + x &\to x & x + 0 &\to x \\
(-x) + x &\to 0 & x + (-x) &\to 0 \\
-0 &\to 0 & -(-x) &\to x \\
(-x) + (x + y) &\to y & x + ((-x) + y) &\to y
\end{aligned}
$$

follows from some combination of the following three axioms:

$$
\begin{aligned}
x + 0 &= x \\
0 + x &= x \\
(-x) + (x + y) &= y \,.
\end{aligned}
$$

This system has numerous critical pairs, all of which are joinable. For example, the rules $x + (-x) \to 0$ and $x + ((-x) + y) \to y$ form a critical pair $x + 0 = -(-x)$, both sides of which reduce, via other rules, to x.   □

Definition 13 (Encompassment). A term s *encompasses* a term t if a subterm of s is an instance of t. We write $s \rhd t$ if s encompasses t, but not vice-versa.

Definition 14 (Reduced System). A system R is *reduced* if, for each rule $l \to r$ in R, the right-hand side r is irreducible (unrewritable) and if $l \rhd l'$, for the left-hand side l, then l' is irreducible (proper subterms of l are in normal form, as is any term more general than l).

The above Fragment is reduced, but the Interpreter isn't.

Definition 15 (Canonical System). A rewrite system is *canonical* if it is confluent, terminating, and reduced.

The following interesting fact was observed by a number of people:

Theorem 16 [30]. *Suppose two canonical (not necessarily finite) rewrite systems have the same equational theory (that is, their convertibility relations are the same) and when combined are still terminating. Then the two must be identical up to renaming of variables.*

Two interesting results with practical repercussions are:

Theorem 17 [28]. *The union of two confluent rewrite systems sharing no function symbols (or constants) is also confluent.*

Theorem 18 [94]. *The union of two convergent rewrite systems sharing no function symbols (or constants), and in which no variable appears more than once on any left-hand side, is also convergent.*

4 Completion

To construct confluent systems, a method is used, called *completion*, which turns critical pairs into rewrite rules. Completion uses an ordering to orient equations and to allow use of unoriented equations to simplify. This ordering should be a *reduction ordering*, defined as follows:

Definition 19 (Reduction Ordering). A well-founded partial ordering $\succ$ on terms is a *reduction ordering* if $s \succ t$ implies $u[s\sigma] \succ u[t\sigma]$, for any context $u[\cdot]$ and substitution σ.

The path ordering is not necessarily a reduction ordering, but its major special cases, including the lexicographic and multiset path orderings, are.

The encompassment ordering also plays a role in most versions of completion. It is used to determine which of two rules is more general, and hence preferred.

In our version of completion, not only rules, but also equations, are used to rewrite with. A term $u[l\sigma]$ containing an instance of l of an equation $l = r$ or $r = l$ may be rewritten to $u[r\sigma]$ whenever $u[l\sigma]$ is greater than $u[r\sigma]$ in the given reduction ordering.

We require a broader notion of critical pair:

Definition 20 (Ordered Critical Pair). Given a reduction ordering $\succ$, if $l = r$ and $s = t$ are two (not necessarily distinct) equations (with variables distinct), μ is a most general unifier of l and a nonvariable subterm of s, and $s\mu$ is not necessarily smaller than either $t\mu$ or $s\mu[r\mu]$, then the equation $t\mu = s\mu[r\mu]$ is a *(ordered) critical pair* formed from those equations. (Term s is not necessarily smaller than term t if there is a substitution σ such that $s\sigma \succ t\sigma$.)

Completion maintains a set of unoriented equations E and a set of rules R oriented according to the given reduction ordering $\succ$. These sets are manipulated in the following six ways:

Deduce: Add a critical pair of R and/or E to E.

Simplify: Use a rule in R to rewrite either side of an equation $s = t$ in E. Or use an equation $l = r$ in E (or use $r = l$ in E) to rewrite s (or t), provided l strictly encompasses s (or t).

Delete: Remove an equation from E whose sides are identical.

Orient: Remove an equation $s = t$ (or $t = s$) from E such that $s \succ t$. Add the rule $s \rightarrow t$ to R.

Compose: Use R or E to rewrite the right-hand side of an existing rule.

Collapse: Use a rule $l \rightarrow r$ in R or equation $l = r$ in E to rewrite the left-hand side s of a rule in R, provided l strictly encompasses s. Remove the rewritten rule from R and place it as an equation in E.

One simple version of completion mixes the above inference steps according to the following strategy:

$$(((\mathbf{Simplify} \cup \mathbf{Delete})^*; (\mathbf{Orient}; \mathbf{Compose}^*; \mathbf{Collapse}^*))^*; \mathbf{Deduce})^* .$$

In words: simplify and delete equations as much as possible before orienting. Use the newly oriented equation to fully compose right-hand sides and collapse left-hand sides of all non-reduced existing rules; then, go back and simplify over again. When there are no equations left to orient, generate one new critical pair, and repeat the whole process.

Different versions of completion differ in which equations they orient first and in how they keep track of critical pairs that still need to be deduced. They, in fact, often skip some critical pairs. A version of completion is *fair* if it does not altogether avoid processing any relevant critical pair. Running completion with a fair strategy can have one of three outcomes: It might converge on a finite system that is a decision procedure for the initial set of equations; it might reach a point in which all (ordered) critical pairs have been considered and all have rewrite proofs—using rules *and* equations; or it might loop and generate an infinite number of rules and/or equations.

Theorem 21 [43][40]. *For any fair completion strategy, if at some point all critical pairs between persisting rules have been considered and no equation persists forever in E, then the (finite or infinite) set of rules persisting in R is convergent.*

This means that eventually both sides of any identity in the theory of the initial set of equations will become joinable.

Example 7 (Abelian Groups I). Completion, given

$$\begin{aligned} x \cdot 1 &= x & x \cdot y &= y \cdot x \\ x \cdot (y \cdot z) &= (x \cdot y) \cdot z & x \cdot x^- &= 1 \,, \end{aligned}$$

and a lexicographic path ordering (in which $^- > \cdot > 1$ and $\cdot$ looks at its left argument first) will generate the following decision procedure for free Abelian (commutative) groups:

$$\begin{aligned} 1^- &\rightarrow 1 & x \cdot y &\leftrightarrow y \cdot x \\ x \cdot 1 &\rightarrow x & x \cdot (y \cdot z) &\leftrightarrow y \cdot (x \cdot z) \\ 1 \cdot x &\rightarrow x & (x \cdot y) \cdot z &\rightarrow x \cdot (y \cdot z) \\ (x^-)^- &\rightarrow x & x \cdot (x^- \cdot z) &\rightarrow z \\ x \cdot x^- &\rightarrow 1 & (y \cdot x)^- &\rightarrow x^- \cdot y^- \,. \end{aligned}$$

Those equations used in both directions have a two-headed arrow. To decide validity of an equation $s = t$, the lexicographic path ordering is extended to a total ordering that includes any constants appearing in s or t. The double-headed rules are then used only in a direction that reduces in this ordering. The equation is valid if and only if both s and t have the same normal form. □

Definition 22 (Completable Simplification Ordering). A reduction ordering is a *completable simplification ordering* if it can be extended to a reduction ordering that is total on ground terms (in which any two distinct terms—made up of function symbols and constants occurring in the given equations—are comparable).

Such orderings have the property that every term is strictly greater than its proper subterms. Examples include the empty ordering, the lexicographic path ordering with a partial or total precedence, and the polynomial path ordering.

Theorem 23 [34][40]. *Suppose R is a finite convergent system for axioms E and $\succ$ is a completable simplification ordering for which all rules in R decrease. Any fair completion strategy will generate a finite convergent system for E (not necessarily identical to R).*

If R is canonical and the strategy performs all compositions and collapses, then, by Theorem 16, completion will actually produce R.

The efficiency of completion depends on the number of critical pairs deduced. In general, an equation $s = t$ is *redundant* if there exist proofs Q_i of equations $u_{i-1} = u_i$, $i = 1, \ldots, n$, such that $u_0 = s$, $u_{n+1} = t$, $u \succ u_0, \ldots, u_{n+1}$, and the proof $s \leftarrow u \rightarrow t$ from which the critical pair was formed is greater than each of the Q_i in some well-founded ordering $\gg$ on equational proofs. (The proof ordering $\gg$ must have the property that a proof decreases by replacing a subproof with one involving terms that are all smaller vis-a-vis the reduction ordering $\succ$ supplied to completion.)

The following can be shown by induction with respect to $\gg$:

Theorem 24 [40]. *For any fair completion strategy, if at some point all non-redundant critical pairs between persisting rules have been considered and no equation persists forever in E, then the (finite or infinite) set of rules persisting in R is convergent.*

For the Group Fragment, the critical pair $y = (-0) + y$, obtained by rewriting $(-0) + (0 + y)$ with $0 + x \rightarrow x$ and $(-x) + (x + y) \rightarrow y$, is redundant since $(-0) + (0 + y)$ is greater than each of the terms in the alternative proof $y \leftarrow 0 + y \leftarrow (-0) + y$.

Various techniques have been used in practice to check for redundancy. In particular, a critical pair can be ignored if the variable part of either of the rules involved becomes reducible. Experimental results that give some indication of the utility of such redundancy criteria have been reported, particularly in the associative-commutative case described in the next section.

5 Validity

In addition to its use for generating canonical systems to serve as decision procedures for the given axioms, completion may also be used as an equational theorem prover.

Classical forward reasoning systems work from the axioms, "expanding" the set of established formulæ by inferring new ones from old ones. Completion may be viewed as an inference engine that also "contracts" formulæ by constantly rewriting them, making forward reasoning practical. The potentially infinite set of rules and equations generated by completion are used to simplify the two sides of the equation in question. Rules are used in the indicated direction only, while equations are used in whichever direction reduces the term it is applied to in the given ordering. An identity is proved when both sides reduce via rules and equations to the identical term.

For completeness of this theorem-proving methodology, we require a completable ordering.

Theorem 25 [75][44][34]. *Suppose $s = t$ is a theorem of E. For any fair completion strategy starting with E and a completable simplification ordering, at some point s and t will rewrite to the identical term using the generated rules and equations.*

The word problem in arbitrary equational theories can always be semi-decided in this way. With an empty ordering, completion amounts to ordinary paramodulation of unit equations; with more of an ordering, completion can be more effective, by reducing the number of allowed inferences and increasing the amount of simplification that may be performed without loss of completeness.

Example 8 (Distributive Lattices). With axioms:

$$
\begin{aligned}
x \wedge x &= x & x \vee x &= x \\
x \wedge y &= y \wedge x & x \vee y &= y \vee x \\
(x \wedge y) \wedge z &= x \wedge (y \wedge z) & (x \vee y) \vee z &= x \vee (y \vee z) \\
(x \vee y) \wedge x &= x & (x \wedge y) \vee x &= x \\
x \vee (y \wedge z) &= (x \wedge y) \vee (x \wedge y) \, ,
\end{aligned}
$$

and a lexicographic path ordering that makes meet bigger than join, completion generates endless rules, including:

$$
x \wedge (y \vee z) \quad \rightarrow \quad (x \vee y) \wedge (x \vee y) \, .
$$

$\square$

The above method can be refined to ignore critical pairs that have different rewrite proofs, each depending on the relative ordering of terms substituted for variables.

6 Satisfiability

We turn now from questions of validity to satisfiability.

If ground terms are joinable whenever they are convertible, we say the system is *ground confluent*. If it is, in addition, terminating, then it's *ground convergent*:

Definition 26 (Ground Convergence). A system is *ground convergent* if every ground (variable-free) term always rewrites to a unique normal form.

Ground convergence is a reasonable property to expect from a rewrite system, like Insertion Sort, used as a program. Such programs compute the value of a ground term by rewriting it to its unique normal form.

Definition 27 (Narrowing). A term s *narrows* to a term t, symbolized $s \rightsquigarrow t$, if $t = s\mu[r\mu]$, for some non-variable subterm s' of s, renamed rule $l \rightarrow r$ in R, and most general unifier μ of s' and l.

By $\rightsquigarrow^*$ we denote the reflexive-transitive closure of this narrowing relation.

Theorem 28 [48]. *If R is a rewrite system, σ is an irreducible substitution (that is, $x\sigma$ is irreducible for all variables x), and $s\sigma \rightarrow^* t$, then there exists a term u such that $s \rightsquigarrow^* u$ and u is at least as general as t.*

A term u is at least as general as a term t if there is a substitution τ such that $t\tau = u$.

Thus, narrowing can be used with such systems to solve equational goals; a solution is a substitution σ for which $s\sigma$ has normal form t. Narrowing a goal $eval(p, \langle x, 0, 0 \rangle)$ with the Interpreter, where p is some fixed program, will find all inputs x that lead to various final triples. The unifiers of each step are composed to get the solution to the original goal.

Theorem 29 [8]. *If R is a ground convergent rewrite system and $s\sigma \rightarrow^* t$, then there exist terms u and v such that $s \rightsquigarrow^* u$, $t \rightarrow^* v$, and u is at least as general as v.*

Example 9 (List Append). With the program

$$
\begin{aligned}
append(nil, y) &\rightarrow y \\
append(cons(x, z), y) &\rightarrow cons(x, append(z, y))
\end{aligned}
$$

the goal $append(x, y)$ generates all lists x and the result of appending them to y. For example, $append(x, y) \rightsquigarrow y$ with $x \mapsto nil$. □

Without convergence, reducible solutions are lost. Variations on narrowing include: *normal narrowing* in which terms are rewritten to normal form before narrowing; *basic narrowing* in which the substitution part of prior narrowings is not subsequently narrowed; *top-down narrowing* in which terms are decomposed from top down to identify necessary narrowings; *left-to-right narrowing* in which the leftmost possible narrowing is performed at each step; other restrictions obtain all solutions only in special cases.

7 Associativity and Commutativity

Many axioms are difficult to handle by rewriting. We could not, for example, include the non-terminating rule $x + y \rightarrow y + x$ in a rewrite-system decision procedure. Instead, we can restrict application of the rule to commute only in the direction that decreases the term in some given ordering. For example, we might allow $2 + 1$ to be replaced by $1 + 2$, but not vice-versa, as done in Sect. 5. Another approach is to use commutativity only to enable the application of other rules. For example, we would apply a rule $x + 0 \rightarrow x$ to $0 + 1$, as well as to $1 + 0$. In the associative-commutative (AC) case, this means that $u[s] \rightarrow u[r\sigma]$ whenever s is equal under AC to an instance $l\sigma$ of the left-hand side of some rule $l \rightarrow r$ (that is, s and $l\sigma$ may have arguments to AC symbols permuted). Thus, AC-matching must be used to detect applicability of rules in this case for AC-rewriting.

To better handle these problematic identities, reasonably efficient special-purpose completion procedures have been designed. For instance, the completion procedure given in the previous section may be modified in the following ways to handle AC symbols:

1. An equation $s = t$ is oriented only if $s' \succ t'$ for any AC variants s' of s and t' of t. This ensures that each AC-rewrite reduces the term it is applied to.
2. AC-unification is used to generate critical pairs instead of ordinary unification. This means that we look at the *set* of most general substitutions that allow a left-hand side to be AC-equal to a nonvariable subterm of another left-hand side, and get a critical pair for each such ambiguously rewritable term.
3. AC-rewriting is used for composition, collapsing, and simplification.
4. Any equation between AC-variants is deleted.
5. An additional expansion operation is needed: whenever a new equation $f(s,t) = r$ is formed, where f is an AC symbol and $f(s,t) \not\prec r$, an *extended* equation $f(s, f(t, z)) = f(r, z)$ is added, too, for some new variable z. This ensures that $f(s,t) = r$ can be used even when rearrangement is needed to get an instance of its left-hand side.

Recall that the Chamelions do not terminate. But if we turn any of the rules around, they do! Though the result is not confluent, AC completion can be used to generate a confluent system of rules and equations: Start off with the three rules as unoriented equations, and use an ordering with $red > yellow > green$. The oriented equations are:

$$
\begin{aligned}
red\ yellow\ &\rightarrow\ green\ green \\
red\ red\ &\rightarrow\ green\ yellow \\
red\ green\ &\rightarrow\ yellow\ yellow \ .
\end{aligned}
$$

Notice how the second rule acts contrary to the "real" chamelions. The extended rules are:

$$
\begin{aligned}
yellow\ (red\ z)\ &\rightarrow\ green\ (green\ z) \\
red\ (red\ z)\ &\rightarrow\ green\ (yellow\ z) \\
green\ (red\ z)\ &\rightarrow\ yellow\ (yellow\ z) \ ,
\end{aligned}
$$

and their commutative variants. The *green red* and extended *yellow red* rules produce an critical pair $yellow\ (yellow\ yellow) = green\ (green\ green)$, which gets oriented from left to right:

$$
yellow\ (yellow\ yellow)\ \rightarrow\ green\ (green\ green) \ .
$$

The complete system reduces the initial state and the monochrome states to distinct normal forms. (Which?) Since the system is Church-Rosser, there is no way to get from the initial arrangement of chamelions to one in which they are of uniform color, no matter which way any of the rules are used.

Example 10 (Abelian Groups II). The AC-completion procedure, given

$$x \cdot 1 = x$$
$$x \cdot x^- = 1 ,$$

where $\cdot$ is AC, and a polynomial ordering in which $\tau_0(x \cdot y) = \tau_0(x) + \tau_0(y) + 1$, $\tau_0(x^-) = 2\tau_0(x)$, and $\tau_0(1) = 1$, generates the following decision procedure for Abelian groups:

$$1^- \to 1 \qquad\qquad x \cdot 1 \to x$$
$$(x^-)^- \to x \qquad\qquad (y \cdot x)^- \to x^- \cdot y^-$$
$$x \cdot x^- \to 1 \qquad\qquad x \cdot (x^- \cdot z) \to z .$$

The last rule is a composed version of the extension $x \cdot (x^- \cdot z) \to 1 \cdot z$ of $x \cdot x^- \to 1$. This extended rule, together with with $(y_0 \cdot x_0)^- \to x_0^- \cdot y_0^-$, forms a critical pair

$$(x_2 \cdot z_1)^- (x_2 \cdot (x_1 \cdot x_2)^- \cdot z_2)^- = (z_1 \cdot z_2)^-$$

via AC-unifier $x \mapsto x_1 \cdot x_2$, $z \mapsto z_1 \cdot z_2$, $y_0 \mapsto x_1 \cdot z_1$, and $x_0 \mapsto x_2 \cdot x^- \cdot z_2$. Both sides reduce to $z_2^- \cdot z_1^-$.

With this system, both sides of any identity reduce by AC-rewriting to AC-equal terms. □

The Grecian Urn may also be viewed as an AC-rewriting system. Beans are rearranged until the pair to be removed are adjacent. Extended with rules $l\ z \to r\ z$ for each original bean rule $; \to r$, this is system is confluent. For instance, *black white* $\to$ *white* and the extended rule *white white z* $\to$ *black z*, rewrite a *black white white* bean arrangement to *white white* and *black black*, respectively, both of which rewrite to *black*. This means that the normal form is independent of the order in which rules are applied. If there are an even number of white beans, they can be paired and reduced to black, and then all the black beans reduce to one; if there are an odd number, the leftover white bean swallows all remaining blacks.

Example 11 (Ring Idempotents). The ring axioms

$$x + 0 = x \qquad\qquad x(y + z) = (xy) + (xz)$$
$$x + (-x) = 0 \qquad\qquad (y + z)x = (yx) + (zx)$$
$$x + y = y + x \qquad\qquad (x + y) + z = x + (y + z)$$
$$(xy)z = x(yz) ,$$

plus

$$aa = a \qquad\qquad bb = b \qquad\qquad cc = c$$
$$(a + b + c)(a + b + c) = a + b + c ,$$

can be completed, with an appropriate ordering, to a convergent AC system that includes the rules

$$ba \to -(ab) + -(bc) + -(cb) + -(ac) + -(ca)$$
$$bca \to abc + acb + cab + cac + cbc + ab + ab + ac + ac + cb + cb + bc + ca .$$

The normal forms of this system include (besides inverses and sums) all monomials (the order of factors matters) not containing aa, bb, cc, ba, or bca. □

8 Conditional Rewriting

A *conditional rewrite system* is a collection of rules of the form

$$u_1 = v_1 \wedge \cdots \wedge u_n = v_n \mid l \quad \to \quad r \,,$$

meaning that terms $u[l\sigma]$, containing an instance of left-hand side l, rewrite to $u[r\sigma]$ only when all the conditions $u_i\sigma = v_i\sigma$ hold. The most popular operational semantics for such a system require both sides of each condition to rewrite to the same normal form before an instance of l may be rewritten.

Example 12 (Conditional Append). To get the flavor of this expanded notion of rewriting, consider the system

$$
\begin{aligned}
null(nil) &\to true \\
null(cons(x, y)) &\to false \\
car(cons(x, y)) &\to x \\
cdr(cons(x, y)) &\to y \\
append(nil, y) &\to y \\
null(x) = false \mid \quad append(x, y) &\to cons(car(x), append(cdr(x), y))
\end{aligned}
$$

and its derivation

$$append(cons(a, cons(b, nil)), cons(c, nil)) \xrightarrow{*} cons(a, cons(b, cons(c, nil))) \,.$$

$\square$

Definition 30. A conditional rewrite system is *orthogonal* if each variable occurs at most once in a left-hand side of each rule, one side of each condition in each rule is a ground normal form, and no left-hand side unifies with a renamed non-variable subterm of any other left-hand side or with a proper subterm of itself.

Theorem 31 [56]. *Every orthogonal conditional rewrite system is confluent.*

This definition of orthogonality could be weakened to allow overlaps when the conjunction of the conditions of the overlapping rules cannot be satisfied by the rules of the system. This is the case with the Conditional Append example, since only the last two rules overlap, but $null(nil)$ can never be *false*.

For non-orthogonal systems, another approach is required. Under certain circumstances terminating systems are confluent if all their critical pairs are joinable, but we need a suitable notion of critical pair:

Definition 32 (Conditional Critical Pair). Let R be a conditional rewrite system. The conditional equation $c\mu \wedge p\mu \Rightarrow s\mu[r\mu] = t\mu$ is a *conditional critical pair* of R if $c \mid l \to r$ and $p \mid s \to t$ are conditional rules of R, l unifies via most general unifier μ with a nonvariable subterm of s and $c\mu \wedge p\mu$ is satisfiable in R.

Theorem 33 [59]. *If no left-hand side unifies with a nonvariable proper subterm of a left-hand side, and if every critical pair is joinable, then the system is confluent.*

A conditional critical pair $p \Rightarrow s = t$ is joinable if $s\sigma$ and $t\sigma$ are joinable for all σ satisfying p.

Definition 34 (Decreasing Systems). A conditional system is *decreasing* if there exists a well-founded ordering $\succ$ containing the rewrite relation $\rightarrow$ and which satisfies two additional requirements: (a) $\succ$ has the subterm property $f(\ldots, s, \ldots) \succ s$, and (b) $l\sigma \succ c\sigma$ for each rule $c \mid l \rightarrow r$ and substitution σ.

Decreasing systems exactly capture the finiteness of recursive evaluation of terms. The notion needs to be extended, however, to cover systems (important in logic programming) with variables in conditions that do not also appear in the left-hand side.

Theorem 35 [57][59]. *A decreasing system is confluent (hence, convergent) if and only if there is a rewrite proof of $s\sigma = t\sigma$ for each critical pair $c \Rightarrow s = t$ and substitution σ such that $c\sigma$ holds.*

Conditional Append is decreasing.

Example 13 (Stack). The following is a decreasing conditional rewrite system:

$$
\begin{aligned}
top(push(x, y)) &\rightarrow x \\
pop(push(x, y)) &\rightarrow y \\
empty?(empty) &\rightarrow true \\
empty?(push(x, y)) &\rightarrow false \\
empty?(x) = false \mid push(top(x), pop(x)) &\rightarrow x \ .
\end{aligned}
$$

□

Completion has been extended to conditional equations, with "ordered" conditional critical pairs turned into rules only if they are decreasing.

9 Programming

Rewrite systems are readily used as a programming language. If one requires of the programmer that all programs be terminating, then rewriting may be used as is to compute normal forms. With ground confluence, one is assured of their uniqueness.

Many programs (interpreters, for example) do not always terminate. Still, we would want to compute normal forms whenever they exist. Confluent systems have at most one normal form per input term. To find the unique normal form for orthogonal systems, we use the following strategy for choosing the point at which to apply a rule:

Definition 36 (Outermost Rewriting). A rewriting step $s \rightarrow t$ is *outermost* if no rule applies at a symbol closer to the root symbol (in the tree representation of terms).

Theorem 37 [64]. *For any orthogonal system, if no outermost step is perpetually ignored, the normal form—if there is one—will be reached.*

Outermost rewriting of expressions is used to compute normal forms in Combinatory Logic.

In this way, orthogonal systems provide a simple, pattern-directed (first-order) functional programming language, in which the orthogonal conditional operator

$$if(true, x, y) \;\rightarrow\; x$$
$$if(false, x, y) \;\rightarrow\; y$$

can also conveniently be incorporated. Various strategies have been developed for efficient computation in special cases. Moreover, orthogonal systems lend themselves easily to parallel evaluation schemes.

Conditional equations provide a natural bridge between functional programming, based on equational semantics, and logic-programming, based on Horn clauses. Interpreting definite Horn clauses $p \vee \neg q_1 \vee \ldots \vee \neg q_n$ as conditional rewrite rules, $q_1 = true \wedge \cdots \wedge q_n = true \mid p \rightarrow true$ gives a system satisfying the constraints of Theorem 33, because predicate symbols are never nested in the "head" (p) of a clause. Furthermore, all critical pairs are joinable, since all right-hand sides are the same ($true$).

Solving existential queries for conditional equations corresponds to the logic-programming capability of resolution-based languages like Prolog. Goals of the form $s \rightarrow^? t$ can be solved by a linear restriction of paramodulation akin to narrowing (for unconditional equations) and to the SLD-strategy in Horn-clause logic. If s and t are unifiable, then the goal is satisfied by any instance of their most general unifier. Alternatively, if there is a (renamed) conditional rule $c \mid l \rightarrow r$ such that l unifies with a nonvariable (selected) subterm of s via most general unifier μ, then the conditions in $c\mu$ are solved, say via substitution ρ, and the new goal becomes $s\mu\rho \rightarrow^? t\mu\rho$.

Suppose we wish to solve

$$append(x, y) \;\overset{?}{\rightarrow}\; x$$

using Conditional Append. To apply the conditional rule, we need first to solve $null(x) =^? false$ using the (renamed) rule $null(cons(u, v)) \rightarrow false$, thereby narrowing the original goal to

$$cons(car(cons(u, v)), append(cdr(cons(u, v)), y)) \;\overset{?}{\rightarrow}\; cons(u, v) \,.$$

Straightforward rewriting reduces this to

$$cons(u, append(v, y)) \;\overset{?}{\rightarrow}\; cons(u, v) \,,$$

to which the first rule for *append* applies (letting v be *nil*), giving a new goal $cons(u, y) \rightarrow^? cons(u, v)$. Since the two terms are now unifiable, this process has produced the solution $x \mapsto cons(u, nil)$ and $y, v \mapsto nil$.

For ground confluent conditional systems, any equationally satisfiable goal can be solved by the method outlined above. Some recent proposals for logic programming languages, incorporating equality, adopt such an operational mechanism.

Simplification via terminating rules is a very powerful feature, particularly when defined function symbols are allowed to be arbitrarily nested in left-hand sides (which is not permitted with orthogonal rules). Assuming ground convergence, any strategy can be used for simplification, and completeness of the goal-solving process is preserved. One way negation can be handled is by incorporating negative information in the form of rewrite rules which are then used to simplify subgoals to *false*. Combined with eager simplification, this approach has the advantage of allowing unsatisfiable goals to be pruned, thereby avoiding some potentially infinite paths. Various techniques are also available to help avoid some superfluous paths that cannot lead to solutions.

10 Theorem Proving

We have already seen how completion is used to prove validity of equations in equational theories (that is, truth in all models) and also how narrowing and related methods can be used to solve equational goals in conditional and unconditional theories. In this section we will see how to handle the non-equational case.

Completion can be used to prove validity of Horn clauses in Horn theories by writing each clause $\neg q \vee p$ as an equation $p \wedge q = q$, amd each unit clause p as $p = true$. The completeness of completion for equational reasoning means that an equational proof will be found for any atomic formula, the validity of which follows from a given set of clauses, all expressed as just indicated (plus the Boolean equation $true \wedge x = x$).

One approach to extending rewriting methods to the full first-order predicate calculus is to add inference rules for restricted forms of paramodulation to refutational theorem provers. An ordering of terms and formulæ is used to restrict inferences and to allow simplification.

Alternatively, one can apply completion to the full first-order case by employing Boolean algebra. The following AC system does the trick:

$$
\begin{array}{ll}
x \vee true \;\rightarrow\; true & x \equiv true \;\rightarrow\; x \\
x \vee false \;\rightarrow\; x & (x \equiv y) \vee z \;\rightarrow\; (x \vee z) \equiv (y \vee z) \\
x \vee y \;\leftrightarrow\; y \vee x & x \vee (y \vee z) \;\leftrightarrow\; (x \vee y) \vee z \\
x \equiv y \;\leftrightarrow\; y \equiv x & x \equiv (y \equiv z) \;\leftrightarrow\; (x \equiv y) \equiv z \\
x \vee x \;\rightarrow\; x & x \vee x \vee y \;\rightarrow\; x \vee y \\
x \equiv x \;\rightarrow\; true & x \equiv x \equiv y \;\rightarrow\; y \,,
\end{array}
$$

where $\vee$ is "or" and $\equiv$ is "equivalent". With this system, all propositional tautologies reduce to *true* and contradictions, to *false*. To prove validity of a formula, one Skolemizes its negation to obtain a universally quantified formula, and expresses it using the above connectives. Then, were the original formula true, there would be an equational proof of the contradiction $true = false$. Completion can be used to discover such a proof.

As a very simple example, consider the theorem

$$\exists x \, p(f(f(x))) \vee \neg \, [\exists x \, p(x) \wedge \forall x \, (\neg p(x) \vee p(f(x)))] \;.$$

Its Skolemized negation is equivalent to the following equations:

$$
\begin{aligned}
p(f(f(x))) &= false \\
p(a) &= true \\
p(x) \vee p(f(x)) &= p(f(x)) \,,
\end{aligned}
$$

where a is a Skolem constant. These equations entail the contradiction:

$$true = true \lor p(f(a)) \lor p(f(f(a))) = p(a) \lor p(f(a)) \lor p(f(f(a))) =$$
$$p(f(a)) \lor p(f(f(a))) \quad = \quad\quad p(f(f(a))) \quad\quad = false \ .$$

For program verification, one often needs to prove that an equation or formula holds in the standard (initial) model, rather than in all models. Such proofs typically require the use of induction. Rewriting techniques have been applied to inductive proofs of equations, establishing $s = t$ in the standard model of the axioms by proving that $s\sigma$ and $t\sigma$ are joinable for all substitutions σ of ground terms constructed from function symbols and constants appearing in the axioms.

The equation $append(x, nil) = x$ is true for all lists x, but is not true in all other models of the List Append axioms. The equation $black\ x = x$ is true for all strings of beans x, but does not follow equationally from AC and the Grecian Urn rules.

Definition 38 (Cover Set). Let R be a rewrite system and $\succ$, a reduction ordering containing its rewriting relation $\rightarrow$. A *cover set* S for conjecture c is a set of equations such that every ground instance $c\tau$ is equal (in the equational theory of R) to an instance $e\sigma$ of an equation e in S, such that $c\tau \succeq e\sigma$.

The set of critical pairs between R and c is always a cover set.

Definition 39 (Rewriting Induction). Let R be a rewrite system and $\succ$, a reduction ordering containing its rewriting relation $\rightarrow$. Let c be a conjecture and S, its cover set. *Rewriting induction* is the rule of inference which allows one to conclude that every ground instance of c is true for R by showing, for each case e in S, that e follows (equationally) from R and instances $c\sigma$ of the hypothesis that are smaller than e vis-à-vis $\succ$.

In practice, a conjecture $s = t$ is proved by expanding it into cases $s\sigma_1 = t\sigma_1$, $\ldots$, $s\sigma_n = t\sigma_n$, for some "covering" substitutions $\sigma_1, \ldots, \sigma_n$, rewriting each at least once using R, then attempting to construct rewrite proofs for them, freely using the inductive hypothesis $s = t$. The rewrite step guarantees that all instances of the hypothesis used are smaller than the case of the conjecture under consideration. Narrowing at a particular position in a term is often a convenient method of generating cover sets and taking the requisite step.

Theorem 40 [89]. *Rewriting induction is sound.*

Example 14 (Reversal of Lists). Consider the following canonical system for reversing lists:

$$
\begin{aligned}
reverse(nil) &\rightarrow nil \\
reverse(cons(x, y)) &\rightarrow append(reverse(y), cons(x, nil)) \\
append(nil, x) &\rightarrow x \\
append(x, nil) &\rightarrow x \\
append(cons(x, y), z) &\rightarrow cons(x, append(y, z)) \\
append(append(x, y), z) &\rightarrow append(x, append(y, z)) \ ,
\end{aligned}
$$

and suppose one wishes to prove that

$$reverse(append(x, y)) \quad = \quad append(reverse(y), reverse(x)) \ .$$

All cases are covered by $x \mapsto nil$ and $x \mapsto cons(x_1, x_2)$, since ground terms containing *reverse* or *append* reduce to lists built of *cons* and *nil*. The corresponding two instances of the conjecture form a cover set. For $x = nil$, we need $reverse(y) = reverse(y)$, which is trivially the case. For $x = cons(x_1, x_2)$, we need to show

$$append(reverse(append(x_2, y)), cons(x_1, nil)) \quad =$$
$$append(reverse(y), append(reverse(x_2), cons(x_1, nil))) \ .$$

The left side rewrites by hypothesis to

$$append(append(reverse(y), reverse(x_2)), cons(x_1, nil)) \ ,$$

which rewrites to the right-hand side. □

In more complicated cases, additional lemmata may need to be added to R along the way. Completion can help find them.

Unlike traditional inductive proof methods, rewriting induction is guaranteed to disprove a false conjecture. (Of course, no method can prove all true ones.)

Definition 41 (Ground Reducibility). A term s is *ground reducible* with respect to a rewrite system if all its ground instances $s\gamma$ are rewritable.

Theorem 42 [80][84]. *Ground reducibility is decidable for finite rewrite systems, but undecidable for AC systems.*

Theorem 43 [35][88][38]. *An equation $s = t$ is not an inductive theorem of a ground convergent rewrite system R if and only if deducing critical pairs by unifying left-hand sides of rules in R on the larger (rather, not necessarily smaller) side of conjectures derived in this way from $s = t$ produces an equation $u = v$ such that the larger of u and v is ground irreducible by R, or else u and v are distinct, but neither is ground reducible.*

Simplification by rules and lemmas may be incorporated into the proof procedure.

11 Future Research

Rewriting is an active field of theoretical and applied research. Current research topics include the following:

Typed Rewriting Under reasonable assumptions, virtually everything we have done extends to the multisorted case. Adding subsorts allows functions to be completely defined without having to introduce error elements for when they are applied outside their intended domains. But deduction in such "order-sorted" algebras presents some difficulties. The most popular approach is to insist that the sort of the right-hand side is always contained in that of the left.

AC termination The methods we have described for proving termination of ordinary rewriting are of only limited applicability when associativity and commutativity are built into the rewriting process. Special techniques have been devised to handle this case, which is of great practical importance.

Higher-order rewriting In the previous sections, we worked with first-order terms only. Since the typed lambda calculus is terminating and confluent, some researchers have been looking at ways of combining it with first-order rewriting in such a way as to preserve convergence, thereby endowing rewriting with higher-order capabilities.

Hierarchical systems From the point of view of software engineering, it is important that properties of rewrite programs, like termination and confluence, be modular. That is, we would like to be able to combine two terminating systems, or two convergent systems, and to have the same properties hold for the combined system. This is not true in general, not even when one system makes no reference to the function symbols and constants used in the other. Finding useful cases when systems may safely be combined is a current area of study.

Concurrency Confluent systems, in general, and orthogonal systems, in particular, are natural candidates for parallel processing, since rewrites at different positions are more or less independent of each other. Work is being undertaken on language and implementation issues raised by this possibility.

Infinite rewriting Rewriting can be extended to apply to structures other than the finite terms we have considered. Indeed, graph rewriting has important applications, since graphs allow one to represent structure-sharing, as well as infinite terms.

First-order theorem proving In Sect. 10, we saw how to simulate resolution-like inference equationally. A productive area of research is the application of ideas from rewriting to more traditional refutational theorem provers. Using orderings on terms and formulæ helps restrict deduction and increase the amount of simplification and redundancy elimination that can be incorporated without forfeiting completeness.

Acknowledgments

I thank Jieh Hsiang for his comments. This work was supported in part by the National Science Foundation under Grants CCR-90-07195 and CCR-90-24271 and by a Lady Davis fellowship at the Hebrew University of Jerusalem.

Selected Bibliography

The hundred items in this bibliography were chosen from among English language references on rewriting. They are divided into sections, corresponding to Sections 1–11 above, and are listed chronologically within section. (Beware that chronology oftentimes does not reflect the dependency of ideas, particularly as only the most polished versions are listed here.) Included are most books and surveys, plus many articles that were historically important, represent major stepping stones, or present the current state of research. Related topics, including the Lambda Calculus, Combinatory Logic, unification theory, and resolution theorem proving, have been omitted, as have most descriptions of implementations. Several new books and surveys are in the works.

1. Rewriting

1. Gorn, S.: Handling the growth by definition of mechanical languages. In: Spring Joint Computer Conference, Philadelphia, PA (1967) 213–224
2. Huet, G., Oppen, D. C.: Equations and rewrite rules: A survey. In: Book, R., ed., Formal Language Theory: Perspectives and Open Problems. Academic Press, New York (1980) 349–405
3. Musser, D. R., Kapur, D.: Rewrite rule theory and abstract data type analysis. In: Calmet, J., ed., Proc. of the European Computer Algebra Conference (Marseille, France), vol. 144 of Lect. Notes in Computer Sci. Springer-Verlag, Berlin (1982) 77–90
4. Jouannaud, J.-P., Lescanne, P.: Rewriting systems. Technology and Science of Informatics 6 (1987) 181–199
5. Benninghofen, B., Kemmerich, S., Richter, M. M.: Systems of Reductions, vol. 277 of Lect. Notes in Computer Sci. Springer-Verlag, Berlin (1987)
6. Jantzen, M.: Confluent String Rewriting, vol. 14 of EATCS Monographs on Theoretical Computer Science. Springer-Verlag, Berlin (1988)
7. Avenhaus, J., Madlener, K.: Term rewriting and equational reasoning. In: Banerji, R. B., ed., Formal Techniques in Artificial Intelligence: A Sourcebook. Elsevier, Amsterdam (1990) 1–41
8. Dershowitz, N., Jouannaud, J.-P.: Rewrite systems. In: van Leeuwen, J., ed., Handbook of Theoretical Computer Science, vol. B: Formal Methods and Semantics. North-Holland, Amsterdam (1990) 243–320
9. Wechler, W.: Reductions. In: Universal Algebra for Computer Scientists, vol. 25 of EATCS Monographs on Theoretical Computer Science. Springer-Verlag, Berlin (1991) 89–133
10. Klop, J. W.: Term rewriting systems. In: Abramsky, S., Gabbay, D. M., Maibaum, T. S. E., eds., Handbook of Logic in Computer Science, vol. 1. Oxford University Press, Oxford (1992) 1–117

223

2. Termination

11. Manna, Z., Ness, S.: On the termination of Markov algorithms. In: Proc. of the Third Hawaii International Conference on System Science, Honolulu, HI (1970) 789–792
12. Huet, G., Lankford, D. S.: On the uniform halting problem for term rewriting systems. Rapport laboria 283, Institut de Recherche en Informatique et en Automatique, Le Chesnay, France (1978)
13. Lankford, D. S.: On proving term rewriting systems are Noetherian. Memo MTP-3, Mathematics Department, Louisiana Tech. University, Ruston, LA (1979)
14. Dershowitz, N., Manna, Z.: Proving termination with multiset orderings. Commun. ACM **22** (1979) 465–476
15. Kamin, S., Lévy, J.-J.: Two generalizations of the recursive path ordering. Unpublished note, Department of Computer Science, University of Illinois, Urbana, IL (1980)
16. Dershowitz, N.: Orderings for term-rewriting systems. Theoretical Comput. Sci. **17** (1982) 279–301
17. Dershowitz, N.: Termination of rewriting. J. Symb. Comput. **3** (1987) 69–115. Corrigendum: 4, 3 (1987), 409–410
18. Comon, H.: Solving inequations in term algebras (Preliminary version). In: Proc. of the Fifth Annual IEEE Symposium on Logic in Computer Science, Philadelphia, PA (1990) 62–69
19. Jouannaud, J.-P., Okada, M.: Satisfiability of systems of ordinal notations with the subterm property is decidable. In: Albert, J. L., Monien, B., Artalejo, M. R., eds., Proc. of the Eighteenth EATCS Colloquium on Automata, Languages and Programming (Madrid, Spain), vol. 510 of Lect. Notes in Computer Sci. Springer-Verlag, Berlin (1991) 455–468
20. Dershowitz, N., Hoot, C.: Topics in termination. In: Kirchner, C., ed., Proc. of the Fifth International Conference on Rewriting Techniques and Applications (Montreal, Canada), Lect. Notes in Computer Sci. Springer-Verlag, Berlin (1993)

3. Confluence

21. Newman, M. H. A.: On theories with a combinatorial definition of 'equivalence'. Annals of Math. **43** (1942) 223–243
22. Selman, A.: Completeness of calculii for axiomatically defined classes of algebras. Algebra Universalis **2** (1972) 20–32
23. Rosen, B.: Tree-manipulating systems and Church-Rosser theorems. J. Assoc. Comput. Mach. **20** (1973) 160–187
24. Staples, J.: Church-Rosser theorem for replacement systems. In: Crossley, J., ed., Algebra and Logic, vol. 450 of Lect. Notes in Mathematics. Springer-Verlag, Berlin (1975) 291–307
25. Bergman, G. M.: The Diamond Lemma for ring theory. Advances in Mathematics **29** (1978) 178–218
26. Huet, G.: Confluent reductions: Abstract properties and applications to term rewriting systems. J. Assoc. Comput. Mach. **27** (1980) 797–821

27. Klop, J. W.: Combinatory Reduction Systems, vol. 127 of Mathematical Centre Tracts. Mathematisch Centrum, Amsterdam (1980)
28. Toyama, Y.: On the Church-Rosser property for the direct sum of term rewriting systems. J. Assoc. Comput. Mach. **34** (1987) 128–143

4. Completion

29. Knuth, D. E., Bendix, P. B.: Simple word problems in universal algebras. In: Leech, J., ed., Computational Problems in Abstract Algebra. Pergamon Press, Oxford, U. K. (1970) 263–297
30. Métivier, Y.: About the rewriting systems produced by the Knuth-Bendix completion algorithm. Inf. Process. Lett. **16** (1983) 31–34
31. Le Chenadec, P.: Canonical Forms in Finitely Presented Algebras. Pitman-Wiley, London (1985)
32. Buchberger, B.: History and basic features of the critical-pair/completion procedure. J. Symb. Comput. **3** (1987) 3–38
33. Kapur, D., Musser, D. R., Narendran, P.: Only prime superpositions need be considered for the Knuth-Bendix procedure. J. Symb. Comput. **4** (1988) 19–36
34. Bachmair, L., Dershowitz, N., Plaisted, D. A.: Completion without failure. In: Aït-Kaci, H., Nivat, M., eds., Resolution of Equations in Algebraic Structures, vol. 2: Rewriting Techniques. Academic Press, New York (1989) 1–30
35. Dershowitz, N.: Completion and its applications. In: Aït-Kaci, H., Nivat, M., eds., Resolution of Equations in Algebraic Structures, vol. 2: Rewriting Techniques. Academic Press, New York (1989) 31–86
36. Lescanne, P.: Completion procedures as transition rules + control. In: Diaz, M., Orejas, F., eds., Proc. of the Conference on Theory and Practice of Software Development, vol. 351 of Lect. Notes in Computer Science. Springer-Verlag, Berlin (1989) 28–41
37. Dick, A. J. J.: An introduction to Knuth-Bendix completion. Comput. J. **34** (1991) 2–15
38. Bachmair, L.: Canonical Equational Proofs. Birkhäuser, Boston (1991)
39. Duffy, D. A.: Knuth-Bendix Completion. In: Principles of Automated Theorem Proving. Wiley, Chichester (1991) 147–175
40. Bachmair, L., Dershowitz, N.: Equational inference, canonical proofs, and proof orderings. J. Assoc. Comput. Mach. (to appear)

5. Validity

41. Evans, T.: On multiplicative systems defined by generators and relations, I. Proc. of the Cambridge Philosophical Society **47** (1951) 637–649
42. Slagle, J. R.: Automated theorem-proving for theories with simplifiers, commutativity, and associativity. J. Assoc. Comput. Mach. **21** (1974) 622–642
43. Huet, G.: A complete proof of correctness of the Knuth-Bendix completion algorithm. J. Computer and System Sciences **23** (1981) 11–21
44. Hsiang, J., Rusinowitch, M.: On word problems in equational theories. In: Ottmann, T., ed., Proc. of the Fourteenth EATCS International Conference on

Automata, Languages and Programming (Karlsruhe, West Germany), vol. 267 of Lect. Notes in Computer Sci. Springer-Verlag, Berlin (1987) 54–71

45. Martin, U., Nipkow, T.: Ordered completion. In: Stickel, M., ed., Proc. of the Tenth International Conference on Automated Deduction (Kaiserslautern, West Germany), vol. 449 of Lect. Notes in Computer Sci. Springer-Verlag, Berlin (1990) 366–380

46. Peterson, G. E.: Solving term inequalities. In: Proc. of the Eighth National Conference on Artificial Intelligence, Boston, MA (1990) 258–263

6. Satisfiability

47. Fay, M.: First-order unification in an equational theory. In: Proc. of the Fourth Workshop on Automated Deduction, Austin, TX (1979) 161–167

48. Hullot, J.-M.: Canonical forms and unification. In: Kowalski, R., ed., Proc. of the Fifth International Conference on Automated Deduction (Les Arcs, France), vol. 87 of Lect. Notes in Computer Science. Springer-Verlag, Berlin (1980) 318–334

49. Dershowitz, N., Sivakumar, G.: Solving goals in equational languages. In: Kaplan, S., Jouannaud, J.-P., eds., Proc. of the First International Workshop on Conditional Term Rewriting Systems (Orsay, France), vol. 308 of Lect. Notes in Computer Sci. Springer-Verlag, Berlin (1987) 45–55

50. Nutt, W., Réty, P., Smolka, G.: Basic narrowing revisited. J. Symb. Comput. 7 (1989) 295–318

51. Bockmayr, A., Krischer, S., Werner, A.: An optimal narrowing strategy for general canonical systems. In: Rusinowitch, M., ed., Proc. of the Third International Workshop on Conditional Rewriting Systems (Pont-a-Mousson, France, July 1992), vol. 656 of Lect. Notes in Computer Sci. Springer-Verlag, Berlin (1993)

7. AC-Completion

52. Peterson, G. E., Stickel, M. E.: Complete sets of reductions for some equational theories. J. Assoc. Comput. Mach. 28 (1981) 233–264

53. Jouannaud, J.-P., Kirchner, H.: Completion of a set of rules modulo a set of equations. SIAM J. Comput. 15 (1986) 1155–1194

54. Bachmair, L., Dershowitz, N.: Completion for rewriting modulo a congruence. Theoretical Comput. Sci. 67 (1989)

55. Zhang, H., Kapur, D.: Unnecessary inferences in associative-commutative completion procedures. Mathematical Systems Theory 23 (1990) 175–206

8. Conditional Rewriting

56. Bergstra, J. A., Klop, J. W.: Conditional rewrite rules: Confluency and termination. J. Comput. System Sciences 32 (1986) 323–362

57. Kaplan, S.: Simplifying conditional term rewriting systems: Unification, termination and confluence. J. Symb. Comput. 4 (1987) 295–334

58. Padawitz, P.: Computing in Horn Clause Theories, vol. 16 of EATCS Monographs on Theoretical Computer Science. Springer-Verlag, Berlin (1988)

59. Dershowitz, N., Okada, M., Sivakumar, G.: Canonical conditional rewrite systems. In: Proc. of the Ninth Conference on Automated Deduction (Argonne, IL), vol. 310 of Lect. Notes in Computer Sci. Springer-Verlag, Berlin (1988) 538–549
60. Kaplan, S., Rémy, J.-L.: Completion algorithms for conditional rewriting systems. In: Aït-Kaci, H., Nivat, M., eds., Resolution of Equations in Algebraic Structures, vol. 2: Rewriting Techniques. Academic Press, Boston (1989) 141–170
61. Klop, J. W., de Vrijer, R. C.: Extended term rewriting systems. In: Kaplan, S., Okada, M., eds., Proc. of the Second International Workshop on Conditional and Typed Rewriting Systems (Montreal, Canada, June 1990), vol. 516 of Lect. Notes in Computer Sci. Springer-Verlag, Berlin (1991) 26–50
62. Padawitz, P.: Reduction and narrowing for Horn clause theories. Comput. J. **34** (1991) 42–51
63. Ganzinger, H.: A completion procedure for conditional equations. J. Symb. Comput. **11** (1991) 51–81

9. Programming

64. O'Donnell, M. J.: Computing in systems described by equations, vol. 58 of Lect. Notes in Computer Sci. Springer-Verlag, Berlin (1977)
65. Guttag, J. V., Horowitz, E., Musser, D. R.: Abstract data types and software validation. Commun. ACM **21** (1978) 1048–1064
66. Futatsugi, K., Goguen, J. A., Jouannaud, J.-P., Meseguer, J.: Principles of OBJ2. In: Reid, B., ed., Conference Record of the Twelfth Annual ACM Symposium on Principles of Programming Languages. Association for Computing Machinery, New Orleans, LA (1985) 52–66
67. Dershowitz, N.: Computing with rewrite systems. Information and Control **64** (1985) 122–157
68. O'Donnell, M. J.: Equational Logic as a Programming Language. MIT Press, Cambridge, MA (1985)
69. Reddy, U. S.: On the relationship between logic and functional languages. In: DeGroot, D., Lindstrom, G., eds., Logic Programming: Functions, Relations, and Equations. Prentice-Hall, Englewood Cliffs, NJ (1986) 3–36
70. Goguen, J. A., Meseguer, J.: EQLOG: Equality, types, and generic modules for logic programming. In: DeGroot, D., Lindstrom, G., eds., Logic Programming: Functions, Relations, and Equations. Prentice-Hall, Englewood Cliffs, NJ (1986) 295–363
71. Dershowitz, N., Plaisted, D. A.: Equational programming. In: Hayes, J. E., Michie, D., Richards, J., eds., Machine Intelligence 11: The logic and acquisition of knowledge. Oxford Press, Oxford (1988) 21–56
72. Hölldobler, S.: Foundations of Equational Logic Programming, vol. 353 of Lect. Notes in Artificial Intelligence. Springer-Verlag, Berlin (1989)
73. Dershowitz, N., Okada, M.: A rationale for conditional equational programming. Theoretical Comput. Sci. **75** (1990) 111–138
74. Huet, G., Lévy, J.-J.: Computations in orthogonal rewriting systems, I and II. In: Lassez, J.-L., Plotkin, G., eds., Computational Logic: Essays in Honor of Alan Robinson. MIT Press, Cambridge, MA (1991) 395–443

10. Theorem Proving

75. Lankford, D. S.: Canonical inference. Memo ATP-32, Automatic Theorem Proving Project, University of Texas, Austin, TX (1975)
76. Lankford, D. S., Ballantyne, A. M.: The refutation completeness of blocked permutative narrowing and resolution. In: Proc. of the Fourth Workshop on Automated Deduction, Austin, TX (1979) 53–59
77. Musser, D. R.: On proving inductive properties of abstract data types. In: Proc. of the Seventh ACM Symposium on Principles of Programming Languages, Las Vegas, NV (1980) 154–162
78. Huet, G., Hullot, J.-M.: Proofs by induction in equational theories with constructors. J. Comput. System Sciences 25 (1982) 239–266
79. Peterson, G. E.: A technique for establishing completeness results in theorem proving with equality. SIAM J. Comput. 12 (1983) 82–100
80. Plaisted, D. A.: Semantic confluence tests and completion methods. Information and Control 65 (1985) 182–215
81. Hsiang, J.: Refutational theorem proving using term-rewriting systems. Artif. Intell. 25 (1985) 255–300
82. Paul, E.: Equational methods in first order predicate calculus. J. Symb. Comput. 1 (1985) 7–29
83. Kapur, D., Musser, D. R.: Proof by consistency. Artif. Intell. 31 (1987) 125–157
84. Kapur, D., Narendran, P., Zhang, H.: On sufficient completeness and related properties of term rewriting systems. Acta Inf. 24 (1987) 395–415
85. Jouannaud, J.-P., Kounalis, E.: Automatic proofs by induction in equational theories without constructors. Info. and Comput. 81 (1989) 1–33
86. Küchlin, W.: Inductive completion by ground proof transformation. In: Aït-Kaci, H., Nivat, M., eds., Resolution of Equations in Algebraic Structures, vol. 2: Rewriting Techniques. Academic Press, New York (1989) 211–244
87. Comon, H., Lescanne, P.: Equational problems and disunification. J. Symb. Comput. 7 (1989) 371–425
88. Fribourg, L.: A strong restriction of the inductive completion procedure. J. Symb. Comput. 8 (1989) 253–276
89. Reddy, U. S.: Term rewriting induction. In: Stickel, M., ed., Proc. of the Tenth International Conference on Automated Deduction (Kaiserslautern, West Germany), vol. 449 of Lect. Notes in Computer Sci. Springer-Verlag, Berlin (1990)
90. Dershowitz, N., Pinchover, E.: Inductive synthesis of equational programs. In: Proc. of the Eighth National Conference on Artificial Intelligence. AAAI, Boston, MA (1990) 234–239
91. Dershowitz, N.: Ordering-based strategies for Horn clauses. In: Proc. of the Twelfth International Joint Conference on Artificial Intelligence, Sydney, Australia (1991) 118–124
92. Kapur, D., Narendran, P., Zhang, H.: Automating inductionless induction using test sets. J. Symb. Comput. 11 (1991) 83–112

11. Future Research

93. Goguen, J. A., Kirchner, C., Meseguer, J.: Concurrent term rewriting as a model of computation. In: Keller, R., Fasel, J., eds., Proc. of Graph Reduction Workshop (Santa Fe, NM), vol. 279 of Lect. Notes in Computer Sci. Springer-Verlag (1987) 53–93

94. Toyama, Y., Klop, J. W., Barendregt, H. P.: Termination for the direct sum of left-linear term rewriting systems. In: Dershowitz, N., ed., Proc. of the Third International Conference on Rewriting Techniques and Applications (Chapel Hill), vol. 355 of Lect. Notes in Computer Sci. Springer-Verlag, Berlin (1989) 477–491

95. Dick, A. J. J., Watson, P.: Order-sorted term rewriting. Comput. J. **34** (1991) 16–19

96. Dershowitz, N., Kaplan, S., Plaisted, D. A.: Rewrite, rewrite, rewrite, rewrite, rewrite,.... Theoretical Comput. Sci. **83** (1991) 71–96

97. Dershowitz, N., Jouannaud, J.-P., Klop, J. W.: Open problems in rewriting. In: Book, R., ed., Proc. of the Fourth International Conference on Rewriting Techniques and Applications (Como, Italy), vol. 488 of Lect. Notes in Computer Sci. Springer-Verlag, Berlin (1991) 445–456

98. Jouannaud, J.-P., Okada, M.: Executable higher-order algebraic specification languages. In: Proc. of the Sixth IEEE Symposium on Logic in Computer Science (1991)

99. Bachmair, L.: Associative-commutative reduction orderings. Inf. Process. Lett. **43** (1992) 21–27

100. Hsiang, J., Kirchner, H., Lescanne, P., Rusinowitch, M.: Automated theorem proving in the presence of equalities. J. Autom. Reas. **14** (1992) 71–100

Programming in OBJ and Maude

Tim Winkler*

SRI International, Menlo Park CA 94025, USA

Abstract: This is a introduction to the gentle art of programming in OBJ and Maude. The features of OBJ that are highlighted are its logic—order-sorted equational logic—connections of this logic with unsorted first-order equational logic, newer features of the language, and parameterized programming. The language Maude—which contains OBJ as its functional sublanguage and extends OBJ to include object-oriented programming and concurrent systems programming—is briefly introduced with a focus on its logic and some simple examples.

1 Introduction

This paper hopes to give a quick introduction to OBJ, to give basic examples of the use of OBJ, to present a simplified version of order-sorted equational reasoning, and to show some further connections between the semantic framework of OBJ, order-sorted algebra, and unsorted first-order logical systems. In addition, a very modest introduction to a newer language called Maude is given, a language that could play the role for programming in general that OBJ does for functional programming.

Languages like OBJ could be considered to relate to typed programming much as (pure) Lisp relates to untyped functional programming. There is a fair amount of convergence on something like OBJ (or like Haskell in the many-sorted case). One could consider this paper as an introduction to OBJ for Lisp programmers. Or, one could consider this paper as an introduction to OBJ for logicians. In either case, there is an attempt to connect and unify the typed and the untyped cases. Sometimes one starts with a clear notion of the sort structure and can naturally assign sorts to operators from the start. On the other hand, sometimes the structure of the operators may come first; one starts with a (somewhat) untyped description and works towards a more strongly typed version.

The papers [6, 15] provide the essential framework for the discussion of OBJ in this paper. This paper is complementary to [6, 15] and, inevitably, some familiarity with these is assumed. The attempt here will be to give an intuitive introduction to different aspects of the language through examples and to present some additional thoughts on the logical aspects of OBJ. Some of the examples have been chosen because they focus on newer features of OBJ3. The papers [29, 30, 28] provide the essential background for Maude. In fact, the semantic framework for Maude includes that of OBJ and the two languages are closely related.

Here is the outline of the remainder of the paper:

---
* Supported by Office of Naval Research Contract N00014-90-C-0086, and by the Information Technology Promotion Agency, Japan, as a part of the R & D of Basic Technology for Future Industries "New Models for Software Architecture" sponsored by NEDO (New Energy and Industrial Technology Development Organization).

2 A Brief Introduction to OBJ

OBJ is a functional programming language. Its central concept is that of functions that map given kinds of data to other kinds. It is also an equational programming language and one can make a rich use of pattern matching in writing programs.

As a recurrent example we will look at Peano arithmetic, i.e., the natural numbers as expressed in terms of the properties of the constant zero and the successor function. The principal kind of data is the natural number data type, which will be called Nat. This example is chosen not because it is the best, but because it is widely familiar.

Let us jump in and look at the NATS module as expressed in OBJ and discuss the elements of this description. Modules of this kind are called *objects*, and are introduced with the keyword obj and ended with the keyword endo.

```
obj NATS is
  sort Nat . --- Sorts (sets of values)
  sort NzNat .
  subsort NzNat < Nat . --- Subsort relations
  op 0 : -> Nat . --- Operators declarations
  op s_ : Nat -> NzNat .
  op _+_ : Nat Nat -> Nat .
  var X Y : Nat . --- Variable declarations
```

```
    eq X + 0 = X . --- Equations (rewrite rules)
    eq X + (s Y) = s (X + Y) .
endo
```

One fundamental rule in OBJ is that entities must be defined before they are used; this is fairly natural, and allows earlier and simpler detection of errors. The (names for the) kinds of data are called *sorts* and are introduced in sort declarations such as "sort Nat" (the terminal "." is just an end-marker). In this example another sort for non-zero natural numbers is introduced with the name "NzNat". It is possible to indicate that one sort is a subset of another using a subsort declaration such as "subsort NzNat < Nat". Operators can be introduced by operator declarations such as "op 0 : -> Nat", which defines a constant of sort Nat, i.e., a function with no arguments, and "op _+_ : Nat Nat -> Nat", which introduces the addition operator mapping two arguments of sort Nat to a Nat result. The sequence of sorts Nat Nat is the arity of the operator _+_ and Nat is the coarity of the operator. The name of the operator also specifies the syntax of the operator; the underline character, "_", is used to indicate argument positions in the syntax of the operator. The sorts and their subsort relations taken together with the operators are called the signature.

We can form ground terms using only the operators; non-ground terms can be formed similarly using sorted variables. For this module the ground terms are "0", "s 0", "s s 0", and so forth. Functions appearing in reduced terms for a sort will be called constructors for the sort (this usage does not entirely agree with the usual practice). Terms with variables, such as "X + 0", are used in equations. Variables are introduced in variable declarations such as "var X Y : Nat" which defines two variables "X" and "Y" both of sort Nat. Note that the sort of variables is not automatically inferred. The effect of unsorted variables can be obtained using the special sort Universal. The sort Universal has had an uncertain status in OBJ3, one of the goals of the current discussion is to clarify its role.

Equations are specified by giving two terms separated by the "=" sign. For example,

```
    eq X + 0 = X
```

Operationally equations are treated as left-to-right rewrite rules; rewriting with a rule means that an instance of the lefthand side (LHS) is replaced by a corresponding instance of the righthand side (RHS). The equation above indicates that 0 added to anything is just that thing. However, since the sort of the variable X is Nat, the equation only applies in those cases where X is chosen to be a Nat. In addition, it is possible to have *conditional equations* with syntax

```
    cq ⟨LHS⟩ = ⟨RHS⟩ if ⟨Condition⟩
```

The mathematical semantics selects from all possible models satisfying the assertions of the specification module that one which is inductive (has no junk), and furthermore is initial (has no confusion as well as no junk). Initiality of model M implies that an equation between ground terms holds in M if and only if it holds in all models satisfying the specification. Inductiveness allows the use of induction principles to prove properties of programs written in OBJ. There is an interesting discussion on the relation of induction and initiality (or freeness) for this example by Henkin [21]. In the broader context of general many-sorted algebraic data types, the notion of initiality was recognized as central by the ADJ group [17, 18]. A later paper giving a thorough discussion of initiality is [31]. Another semantics for a module is the collection of all models that satisfy the specification. In OBJ, this interpretation of a specification is associated with a slightly different kind of module called a theory.

The operational semantics of OBJ is based on treating equations as oriented rewrite rules and applying the rules using equational reasoning. In the case that the evaluation of terms always terminates, if the choice of rule to apply at each point does not affect the result, then the set of rules is called confluent. In general, confluence means that if u rewrites both to v and w, then there always exists an x such that both v and w rewrite to x. Confluence of the set of rules is assumed in OBJ.

Rules are applied until no more can be applied; the final result is called reduced and considered to be the value of the starting term. Another article by Henkin [22] discusses basic equational reasoning in an unsorted context. Many-sorted equational reasoning is discussed, for example, in [11]; order-sorted equational reasoning is discussed, for example, in [15] and later in this paper. In OBJ, computation is equational inference by rewriting. Specifically, the application of rewrite rules corresponds to equational deduction in order-sorted equational logic.

The basic operational request is:

```
red 〈Term〉 .
```

Within the context of a module, this request will result in the given term being reduced and the final result being printed out. (If a specification presented to OBJ is not confluent, then the notion of the "value" of a term is not well-defined, but the rewriting performed is still an equational proof, so that reduction results are always equal to the starting term.)

In OBJ, modules may be hierarchically structured so that one module may incorporate another, for example, "pr NATS". For example:

```
obj NATS-DBL is
  pr NATS .
  op dbl : Nat -> Nat .
  var N : Nat .
  eq dbl(N) = N + N .
endo
```

The keyword pr is short for protecting and indicates that the module structure is exactly preserved in the new context. Instead, one may incorporate a module extending it (where new terms, not provably equal to any old term, may be introduced into old sorts, but equality of old terms remains unchanged) or using it (where new equations identifying previously different terms may be introduced). This module also uses an operator with the default syntax, which is the usual functional notation.

Furthermore, modules may be parameterized with parameters that are described by theories (modules that describe classes of models, not just the initial model). A brief sketch of an example, a module that creates a list sort from a sort of elements provided as a parameter, is

```
obj LIST[X :: TRIV] is
  ...
endo
```

where TRIV is predefined as

```
th TRIV is
  sort Elt .
endth
```

and LIST may be instantiated as in LIST[NATS]. In this case the theory TRIV just requires some structure, a sort, of its corresponding actual parameter. A correspondence between the formal theory and the actual parameter, which is called a *view*, must be used in the instantiation. In LIST[NAT] a default view (automatically computed) is used. (It maps the principal sort Elt of TRIV to the principal sort Nat of NATS, thus this instantiation creates lists of Nats.) Renamings and sums of modules are expressed by additional module expressions. The parameterized programming paradigm is based on the use of parameterized modules and module expressions. It can be argued that this approach to programming compares favorably with inheritance, in the sense of object-oriented programming, as it relates to the construction of programs (see Section 14).

One important feature of the OBJ language is the sort constraint. The simplest form is

as ⟨Sort⟩ : ⟨Term⟩ if ⟨Condition⟩ .

However, in this paper we will instead pretend that the syntax is

as ⟨Term⟩ : ⟨Sort⟩ if ⟨Condition⟩ .

bowing to widespread convention. Furthermore, we will assume that sort assertions, i.e., terms of the form T : Sort, can be used in conditions (this can at least be partially implemented as will be discused later). A sort constraint asserts that the given term has the specified sort under a certain condition. An example would be

as X * Y : NzNat if X : NzNat and Y : NzNat

Unfortunately, sort constraints are not currently implemented in OBJ.

There are many additional features of OBJ that we will not go into here such as parsing options, pattern matching attributes, evaluation strategies, memoization, etc. For a thorough discussion of OBJ3 see [6].

OBJ nicely supports a number of different styles of programming: functional, equational, specificational, higher-order, interpreter-based, and parameterized.

3 Simple OBJ Examples

Let us now consider some small examples that are natural and familiar:

A definition of the computation of the n-th Fibonacci number:

```
obj FIBO is  *** [functional style]
  protecting INT .
  op fibo_ : Int -> Int .
  var x : Int .
  eq fibo x = if x < 2
        then x
        else (fibo (x - 1)) + (fibo (x - 2)) fi .
endo
```

This is an example in the classical functional programming style. One of the predefined modules, INT, which defines a built-in integer sort using Lisp representations,
is used for efficiency. One defining equation is provided for each defined function.

A sample reduction for this example is

```
OBJ> red fibo(10) .
reduce in FIBO : fibo 10
rewrites: 1147
result NzNat: 55
```

If one wants to compute larger Fibonacci numbers one might prefer the following
definition.

```
obj FIBOL is
  protecting 2TUPLE[INT,INT] * (sort 2Tuple to PairInt) .

  op prod : PairInt PairInt -> PairInt .
  op sqr : PairInt -> PairInt .
  op power : PairInt Int -> PairInt .
  op even : Int -> Bool .
  op fibo_ : Int -> Int .

  var p : PairInt .
  var a b c d n : Int .

  eq prod(<< a ; b >>, << c ; d >>) =
    << (a * c) + (b * d) ; ((a + b) * d) + (b * c) >> .
  eq sqr(p) = prod(p,p) .
  eq even(n) = ((n rem 2) == 0) .
  eq power(p,n) =
    if n == 0 then << 1 ; 0 >> else
    if even(n) then sqr(power(p, n quo 2))
    else prod(p,sqr(power(p, n quo 2))) fi fi .
  eq fibo(n) = 2* power(<< 0 ; 1 >>, n) .
endo
```

The parameterized module 2TUPLE introduces tuples with two elements, with syntax << _ ; _ >>, with sorts provided by the two parameters of the module, and selectors for the first and second elements of the tuple, with syntax 1*_ and 2*_.

The operator fibo of this module will compute the n-th Fibonacci number using a logarithmic number of arithmetic operations. It is based on the idea of computing powers of the matrix

$$\begin{pmatrix} 0 & 1 \\ 1 & 1 \end{pmatrix}$$

using repeated squaring. Adjacent elements in the resulting matrix will be consecutive Fibonacci numbers. Using this definition we can compute considerably larger Fibonacci numbers.

```
OBJ> red fibo(200) .
reduce in FIBOL : fibo 200
rewrites: 136
result NzNat: 280571172992510140037611932413038677189525
```

Different number systems such as the NAT, INT, RAT, etc., provide a rich source of order-sorted algebra examples. These examples were presented in Appendix A of [15], and built-in versions up to RAT are in the standard prelude of OBJ3. The rational numbers, in highly abridged form, are:

```
obj RAT is  *** [equational style]
  sorts Rat NzRat .
  protecting INT .
  subsort Int < Rat .
  subsorts NzInt < NzRat < Rat .
  op _/_ : Rat NzRat -> Rat .
  op _/_ : NzRat NzRat -> NzRat .
  .....
  vars I' J' : NzInt .   vars R S : Rat .
  vars R' S' : NzRat .
  *** [reduce fraction to lowest terms]
  cq J' / I' =
    quot(J',gcd(J',I')) / quot(I',gcd(J',I'))
    if gcd(J',I') =/= s 0 .
  eq R / s 0 = R .
  eq 0 / R' = 0 .
  .....
  eq R + (S / R') = ((R * R') + S) / R' .
  .....
endo
```

This is a much more equational-style programming example. Many equations are provided for the operator _/_. Furthermore, it shows that operators that are constructors for sorts, such as _/_, can have conditional equational relationships. Giving many equations to define a function is a very natural way of defining by cases. Here all ratios are reduced to those in lowest terms. Note that the key rule must be made conditional or else there would be termination problems.

4 Simplified Order-Sorted Equational Logic

This is a quick sketch of a simplified version of the complete formal presentation of order-sorted equational logic in [15].

An *order-sorted signature* is a triple $(S, \leq, \Sigma)$ consisting of the sort poset $(S, \leq)$ and a collection of ranks for operators, Σ. In general, an operator may have several different ranks. Here we will use the notation $f : w \to s$ for elements of Σ, where w, in general, is a sequence of sorts from S. We will restrict ourselves to the case in which the sets S and Σ are finite.

It is required that the signature be coherent, i.e., the sorts must be locally filtered and the set of operator ranks must be regular. *Locally filtered* is the condition that connected components of sorts—i.e., equivalence classes in the smallest equivalence relation generated by the sort ordering $\leq$—always have a maximal sort. *Regularity* is the condition that: if $f : w1 \to s1$ and $w0 \leq w1$, then there is a least rank $f : w \to s$ with $w0 \leq w$. ($\leq$ is extended componentwise to sequences of sorts in arities and ranks.) Given regularity, one can assign a least sort to a term, working bottom up with the operator ranks providing sort inference rules. A term is *strictly well-formed* if it can be assigned a sort this way. The main point of difference between the logic presented here and that in [15] is that ranks of operators at the tops of connected components are here implicitly assumed (this is discussed more in the next section).

The Σ-terms over a sorted set of variables X are denoted $\mathcal{T}_\Sigma(X)$. We will be using the notation $t : s$ to assert that the term t has sort s. Given a order-sorted signature $(S, \leq, \Sigma)$ and two sorted variable sets X and Y, a *substitution* is a sorted map $\theta: X \to \mathcal{T}_\Sigma(Y)$. The map is sorted if $x : s$ implies that $\theta(x) : s$.

Equations are assertions of the form $(\forall X)\ t = t'$, where X is a sorted set of variables. It is required that the sorts of t and t' be in the same connected component of the sort structure.

Given an order-sorted signature Σ, we have the following inference rules:

1. **Reflexivity.**

$$\overline{(\forall X)\ t = t}$$

2. **Symmetry.**

$$\frac{(\forall X)\ t_1 = t_2}{(\forall X)\ t_2 = t_1}$$

3. **Transitivity.**

$$\frac{(\forall X)\ t_1 = t_2 \qquad (\forall X)\ t_2 = t_3}{(\forall X)\ t_1 = t_2}$$

4. **Congruence.**

$$\frac{(\forall X)\ t_1 = t'_1 \quad \ldots \quad (\forall X)\ t_n = t'_n}{(\forall X)\ f(t_1, \ldots, t_n) = f(t'_1, \ldots, t'_n)}$$

where uses of this rule are restricted to the case in which arguments to f in the conclusion are in the same connected component as the sort required by the operator f. That is, if $f : s_1 \ldots s_n \to s$ then, for each i, t_i and t'_i must be in the same connected component as s_i.

5. **Replacement [or Substitutivity].** Let $\theta\colon X \to T_\Sigma(Y)$ be a (sorted) substitution.

$$\frac{(\forall X)\ t_1 = t_2\ \ if\ \ u_1 = v_1, \ldots, u_n = v_n \quad (\forall Y)\ \theta(u_i) = \theta(v_i), \text{for } i = 1, \ldots, n}{(\forall Y)\ \theta(t_1) = \theta(t_2)}$$

The operational semantics is given by rewriting. It is required that the set of rules be confluent. A term t is evaluated by rewriting it until a term t' is reached to which no rule can be applied, this term t' is considered the value of t and is called the *normal form* of t and will be called $NF(t)$. If t can be rewritten, using any number of steps, into t' we will write $t \longrightarrow t'$. It is also required that, if $NF(t)$ exists, then $\mathrm{NF}(t) : \mathrm{LS}(t)$, i.e., that the normal form of a term, should have the sort of the starting term. More generally, we want a confluence for sorts and terms, if $t : s$ and $t \longrightarrow t'$, then, for some t'', $t' \longrightarrow t''$ with $t'' : s$ (this condition is closely related to the notion of "reasonable rules" in [6]).

The replacement rule is basically a quantifier rule combined with detachment of conditions. It is also the key rule in which sort requirements appear. One may only use substitutions that respect the sorts of variables in this rule.

The comments in this paragraph should probably be skipped unless one has a copy of [15] at hand. The congruence rule as presented in [15] is more restrictive than that presented above, since there the conclusion is $(\forall Y)\ \theta(t) = \theta'(t)$, for a substitution θ, and uses of x in t, t' must be strictly well-typed. All the rules, except for the congruence rule, presented above are the same as in [15], although in all cases a slightly different notation is used in this presentation. The above liberalized version of the congruence rule is a derivable rule in the deductive system of [15] relative to an expansion of the given signature, as will be discussed below. The given congruence rule is more compatible with unsorted equational reasoning. The above rule can always be used to rewrite a well-formed term and will preserve the well-formedness of the term (as discussed below). The condition on the congruence rule is always satisfied in the context of the operational semantics of OBJ.

The goal is to treat the question of well-formedness of terms in a way that is invariant under equational reasoning. I.e., if $t = t'$ and t' is strictly well-formed, then t should not be considered ill-formed. A term will be clearly ill-formed if it is a normal form and cannot be properly typed.

The claim is that $\Gamma \vdash_{\mathrm{SimplOSA},\Sigma} t_1 = t_2$ iff $\Gamma \vdash_{\mathrm{OSA},\Sigma^+} t_1 = t_2$, where SimplOSA is the deductive system presented above, Σ is a coherent signature, OSA is the deductive system of [15], Γ is a set of assertions (conditional equations), and Σ^+ is Σ expanded by the addition of "top" ranks for operators as discussed in the next section.

5 Semantics from Order-sorted Algebra I

This discussion is inspired by the discussion in section 5.2 of [15].

An "interesting" feature of the formal rules for order-sorted deduction presented in [15] is that *the equational rules depend on context*. (An example is given below.) This very likely is undesirable. In fact, it creates significant problems for the treatment of the operational semantics by rewriting as implemented in OBJ3.

An example:

```
obj PROBLEM is
  sort A B .
  subsort A < B .
  op a : -> A .
  op b : -> A .
  op c : -> B .
  op f : A -> A .
  eq a = c .
  eq c = b .
end
```

Our task is to prove: $f(a) = f(b)$ (it is possible). But, one cannot apply $a = c$ to a in $f(a)$ since the congruence rule cannot be used because the sort of c, B, is incompatible with the argument sort of f (as is required by the rules of [15]). The essential problem is that the well-formedness of terms is not preserved by rewriting.

A key motivating example is the rule for the square modulus of a complex number with rational coefficients: $| x |^2 = x \times \text{conj}(x)$, where the sort of the operator $| \_ |^2$ is Rat, but the sort of the righthand side term is Complex. This example shows that it is natural for rules to rewrite up, and so this cannot simply be prohibited.

We want to select formal rules for equational deduction that are highly compatible with unsorted equational reasoning—the very familiar case—and furthermore retain all the desired algebraic properties, in particular, compatibility with many-sorted algebra. We want to improve the "referential transparency"; we want the meaning of an expression should be independent of its context.

Instead of the fully general system of [15], *we should focus on a special case*. We want to restrict ourselves to a case similar to $\mathbf{OSAlg}''_\Sigma$ (of Section 5.2 of [15]), but instead of the *global* uniformity of semantics in $\mathbf{OSAlg}''_\Sigma$ we instead provide semantics for each connected component of the sort structure. We provide a single function as the semantics of an operator for each connected component of the (arity) sorts and change the notion of homomorphism so that the notion of connected component is also central, one mapping per connected component. (Do not force a single universe "u" as in Theorem 5.6 of [15]. This is a more minor technical point, since logically coherence forces the many functions to be the same.) We can do this without losing expressiveness since we can implicitly (and automatically) expand a given (coherent) signature so that it satisfies the desired properties by adding operator ranks to the signature. We can interpret the user provided signature by the *implicit* expansion of it with operator declarations pushed up to the tops of connected components.

We require that the signature is coherent (or regular and locally filtered). Call the set of the tops of the connected components $TOPS$. Let *top* be the function from S to $TOPS$ that maps a sort to the top of its connected component (and extend this to sort sequences too). The key requirement for the compatibility of the above rule system with the system [15] is that we require ranks for all operators at tops of connected components. If $f : w \to s$ is given, then $f : top(w) \to top(s)$ is also required. This could easily be automatically ensured by creating these new ranks for operators at the tops of connected components.

Given that the ranks satisfy this requirement, the congruence rule as presented in Section 4 is, in fact, a restatement of that presented in [15] for the special case that we are focusing on. The term t of the congruence rule of [15] can be constructed entirely at the top of the components, specifically, the sorts of all variable in t can chosen to be tops of connected sort components. A (S-sorted) substitution will then allow anything in the appropriate component which is the condition imposed on the congruence rule in Section 4.

There are some different cases, if one has a Universal sort, then it is the top of everything and the extended signature at the top is particularly simple. If one has distinct connected components in the sort structure (we want this case for compatibility with many-sorted algebra), then the tops of the components must be considered to include "error values." If error sorts are automatically added at the tops of components, then there will be no problem, but if the user provides the complete sort structure, then the user is responsible for introducing error sorts as needed. For example, if one is using the rationals with sort Rat, this sort might be the top of the obviously required sorts, but a Top–Rat sort should be introduced above it. For example one needs to be able to assign a meaning to the term 1 / (1 - 1) and we don't want it to fall in Rat. In order to allow a more liberal congruence rule, one must be able to assign meanings to more terms, i.e. those that naturally arise in rewriting.

In this context, these are natural additional changes:

- Simplify the definition of homomorphism so that one function is given per connected component.
- In general, all restrictions reduce to "are in the same connected component".
  - well-formedness of terms
  - compatibility of the LHS and RHS of equations
  - substitutions in congruence rule (as formulated in [15]), but not the substitutivity rule.

  The first two are consistent, so well-formedness is closed under rewriting, which is one of the key desirable properties.
- Usually one wants, however, terms appearing in equations to be strictly well-formed with respect to the user supplied signature. A simple rule might be: terms are only well-defined if they are provably equivalent to a term in a sort that is not a top-of-component sort.

Given these choices, we don't need retracts [6, 15] to ensure that equations don't rewrite up (although this might be very desirable, optionally, as a evaluation-time error check). The approach presented here has been influenced by (discussions of) and is strongly related to the use of ?-sorts in the, as yet unpublished, sequel to [15], which provides these ?-sorts as an alternative to retracts. However, the ?-sort approach seems to be more complex than the approach presented here.

The resulting structure is very much like many-sorted algebra on the connected components of the sorts (and is compatible with this). The change to the notion of homomorphism is motivated by this and makes the connection between order-sorted algebra and many-sorted closer.

It seems preferable to assign meaning to all terms or as many as possible. This corresponds to having a Universal sort. (See Theorem 5.6 of [15].) We want broad semantics. This can be done without losing strong-typing, since the type-checking of terms should really be considered as a separate issue from the semantics. Terms are not ill-formed because you could not assign them a meaning, but instead, outlawed because you choose them to be so. In proper, strongly typed, specifications, the meaning of terms does not depend on extraneous sort structure above. Hence, adding extra sort structure above has no semantic affect.

It may be desirable to extend error handling with some new explicit choices. We want to try and unify the many-sorted and the unsorted views (Smolka, Goguen, Meseguer, et al. have pursued this goal in [33, 35], see also the discussion in Section 5.2 of [15]). The rule "only an error if meaningless" is not exactly the right conception, in part since meanings can always be consistently assigned to all terms. Instead, what is proposed is that type-checking should consider as an error a term that has a subterm that is not of an allowed sort, where the set of allowed sorts is an explicit choice. (This also appears to be an essential element of the notion of ?-sorts, which are considered disallowed sorts.) This is very consistent with what is done in the OBJ implementation since the sort Universal exists, but is carefully treated as disallowed. Instead, one could allow the user to specify at any point the allowed or the disallowed sorts, for the purposes of type checking. This would allow much more flexible and powerful type-checking. Just because the Universal sort exists in your program or specification, this does not mean that you always want to allow everything (e.g., in [15] to allow any pair of terms as a LHS and a RHS of an equation). As noted above, one could use the rule that top sorts are disallowed.

It might also be desirable to more systematically separate syntax and semantics, to separate the notions "name of" and "syntax of" for operators. Merging these two usages gives rise to conflicting impulses (syntax is often chosen to be very abbreviated and this choice tends to introduce gratuitous operator overloading). If these two notions are separated, it would also be easy and natural to have multiple syntactic notations for an operator (in OBJ operators do have more than one syntactic representation; there exists more explicit forms with module or sort qualifications).

The simpler special case for order-sorted algebra may also have advantages in that it allows a more natural evolution of specifications from less to greater detail. How can you prove $\_ + \_ : \text{Nat Nat} \longrightarrow \text{Nat}$ beginning with the (implicit) $\_ + \_ : \text{Universal Universal} \longrightarrow \text{Universal}$? (The implicitness is the point here. This example will be discussed later.)

In place of conditions such as "rewrite rules must rewrite down" [24] we have a new requirement: $\text{NF}(t) : \text{LS}(t)$ (provided $\text{NF}(t)$ is defined).

We could allow sorts, such as Universal, that are only unions of connected component sorts below. That is, one could specify the set $TOPS$, but allow sort structure above the sorts that are considered component tops. These sorts can easily be allowed in the arities of operators (this can be re-interpreted as a family of specializations of the operator to connected component tops). The simplest case would be when all operator coarities fall inside the sort components, but we could even allow broader cases provided that normal forms all fall in the sort components or (in case of non-termination) all terms can always be rewritten to a term with a sort in a component. The connected sort components could be used for sort checking, assignment of meanings to operators, and provide the basic structure for homomorphisms.

One of the motivations for the above formulation, specifically the change in the congruence rule, is that we should have

$$x = y \Rightarrow (x : A \Longleftrightarrow y : A)$$

or, in another form,

$$x = y \wedge x : A \Rightarrow y : A$$

This can be viewed as congruence on the sort predicate x : A. If we have this then we can always apply the congruence rule preserving the well-formedness of terms.

The rules presented above are derivable from those in [15]. The rules as presented in [15] are complete, since one can expose subterms in subproofs (do congruence last), but are awkward for rewriting operational semantics. The rules presented here are more flexible, and better suited to operational semantics provided by rewriting. The additional required structure for the operators can be considered to be added implicitly and automatically.

It appears that the approach presented here is very similar to that of [34]. Poigné indicates that order-sorted signatures fail to satisfy the condition (ii) of 1.2 of [34], but in the special case we are focusing on, with operators at the tops of components, this condition is satisfied because of regularity (actually, it follows even from just preregularity).

6 Relation to Conditional Equational Logic

There is a way of expressing in unsorted first-order logic with equality the structural features of order-sorted (and many-sorted) algebra that converts some of the implicit structure of the presentations of the algebras into explicit logical assertions. We can translate the structural features of algebras into assertions in a logic that *a priori* imposes less structure. The framework is (conditional) unsorted first-order equational logic with a sort assertion predicate. One goal is to explore the relationship of order-sorted equational reasoning with unsorted equational reasoning. Some compatibility is desirable here too, just as with many-sorted algebra.

Let's show translations for the original example:

```
sort Nat . — Allows uses of "X : Nat"
subsort NzNat < Nat . — NzNat ⊆ Nat; ∀ X [ X : NzNat ⇒ X : Nat ]
op 0 : -> Nat . — 0 : Nat
op s_ : Nat -> NzNat .
— ∀ X [ X : Nat ⇒ (s X) : NzNat ]
op _+_ : Nat Nat -> Nat .
— ∀ X Y [ X : Nat ∧ Y : Nat ⇒ X + Y : Nat]
— (Operators are part of the first-order logic signature.)
var X Y : Nat .
— Variable declarations affect the conditions on the equations.
eq X + 0 = X . — ∀ X [ X : Nat ⇒ X + 0 = X ]
eq X + (s Y) = s (X + Y) .
— ∀ X [ X : Nat ∧ Y : Nat ⇒ X + (s Y) = s (X + Y)]
```

242

A conditional equation cq $L = R$ if C translates to $(SA \wedge C) \Rightarrow L = R$, where SA is a conjunction of sort assertions for variables expressing the sorts of the variables. A sort constraint as $T : S$ if C translates to $(SA \wedge C) \Rightarrow T : S$, where SA, once again, expresses the sorts of the variables.

There are strong relationships between the formal systems in one case and the other. The relationship between an order-sorted specification Γ and its unsorted translation $\overline{\Gamma}$ is $\Gamma \vdash_{OSA} A$ iff $\overline{\Gamma}, M \vdash_{FOL=} \overline{A}$, where OSA is the order-sorted equational deduction system, $FOL =$ is a first-order logical system with equality, M is the logical content of the module (i.e., the conjunction of the translations of its elements into logical form), and $\overline{X}$ is the translation of the assertion or assertions X. This is true only for theories, in general. (We cannot expect to capture the meaning of initiality in a first-order fashion.) We can make similar statements about the truth of assertions for models in one case and the other.

A complete formal system would consist of: first-order logic with equality (propositional axioms; quantifier axioms; reflexive, transitive, symmetric, and congruence properties of equality), the sort assertions X : A, *modus ponens*, and induction axioms (when we consider the inductive, or initial, model). This will be sketched in more detail below.

Unfortunately induction schemas are complex, but they are the preferable form for initiality in this context. One can (incompletely) express initiality at this level, but it is even more complex and less intuitively clear than induction.

We can get semantics for order-sorted algebra by appeal to the semantics for first-order logic with equality. We get a complete deductive system by appeal to results for standard first-order logic.

For more operational semantics, inference of the sort of a term is considered part of the computation process. (One could implement sort assertions as annotations on term structures.) Abstractly, the state of the computation consists of an equality (the RHS is being rewritten, the LHS is the original term), and a conjunction of sort assertions (indicating what is known about subterms of the term being rewritten). In the framework of [15], the assignment of sorts is an algorithm that is defined outside the logic, whereas here it is just part of the logic, i.e., sort inference is just inference.

The resulting "signatures" will always be regular by Theorem 5.7 of [15] (assuming finiteness). We will naturally have both finite unions and intersections. We don't need to assume regularity for the declared ranks of operators. In addition to having a Universal sort we might have terms without a specified sort. We could, of course, take $\forall x[x : Universal]$ as axiomatic.

This can be viewed as taking Eqlog [13, 12, 10] as the basic system, without some of the logic programming ideas. In Eqlog, there already was the ambiguity of the assertion

```
nzrat(X / Y) :- nzint(X), nzint(Y)
```

versus the operator declaration

```
_/_ : nzint nzint -> nzrat
```

Instead of standard unsorted first-order logic, one can use a single-sorted order-sorted (or many-sorted) first-order logic. In this single-sorted context, this discussion is about how different expressions of algebraic structure are possible within that one language. There is also strong connection with quasivarieties as discussed in Chapter 25 of [32], and the work of Mal'cev. The equational type logic of Manca, Salibra, and Scollo [26] seems to be similar to the logical framework that is being briefly discussed here.

In specifications with sort constraints, it may be necessary to constrain the range of application of rules involving sort-constrained operators. This is not necessary in the context of [15], since there the sorts of terms appearing in equations are adequately constrained by the sorts of variables appearing in them. In this wider context, the sort of a term cannot be inferred just from the sorts of its arguments, sort inference is necessarily dynamic, and the range of applicability of equations may need to be restricted. For example, for a presentation of the rationals, one might give the operator declaration op `_/_` : Rat Rat -> Top-Rat, where Top-Rat is a top-of-component error sort, and the sort constraint as (X / Y) : Rat if Y =/= 0, where X Y : Rat. For the intended semantics, it may be necessary to restrict the range of applicability of an equation like 0 / X = 0 (it may, of course, be desired to apply the rule in complete generality). This could be done by either making the rules conditional with conditions derived from the sort constraint, as in 0 / X = 0 if X =/= 0, or by restricting the range of the rule directly, as in 0 / X = 0 if (0 / X) : Rat.

Possible instances of unsound equational reasoning do not arise—making the conditions explicit takes care of this. For example, in a signature where no ground term has sort a, from the order-sorted equations, $(\forall x : a) \neg f(x) = f(x)$, $(\forall x : a) f(x) = true$, and $\neg true = false$, we get the translations $(\forall x)[x : a \Rightarrow \neg f(x) = f(x)]$, $(\forall x)[x : a \Rightarrow f(x) = true]$, and $\neg true = false$, which have as a consequence $(\forall x)[x : a \Rightarrow true = false]$, but no contradiction results. One can prove $x : a \Rightarrow true = false$, but we don't get a contradiction (there is no ground instance of $x : a$ that is provable). There may often be undischarged sort predicate requirements: $x : Nat \Rightarrow x + 0 = x$ can be instantiated arbitrarily: $(Su) : Nat \Rightarrow (Su) + 0 = (Su)$; $abc : Nat \Rightarrow abc + 0 = abc$ (possibly). Free variables in assertions are considered to be universally quantified and can be instantiated with arbitrary terms, not just ground.

7 Sketch of a Simple Logical System

A first-order signature will be a set of functions (and possibly predicates) with numerical arities and the special (two-place) sort assertion predicate "$x : A$" along with a specification of the sort identifiers (in place of simple identifiers it is interesting to consider an algebra of sort names, in general).

A signature might be presented as a set of sort declarations and a set of operator ranks in the form $f : \_\_ \rightarrow \_$.

The formal system would consist of:

- **Propositional**
  (Axioms and inference rules for the propositional connectives, e.g., [36])
- **Quantifier**

(Axioms and inference rules for quantifiers, e.g., [36])

In particular, $\forall x A(x) \Rightarrow A(t)$, which replaces substitutivity or replacement.

– **Equality Axioms**

(Cf. [22])

Reflexivity. $(x = x)$

Symmetry. $(x = y \Rightarrow y = x)$

Transitivity. $(x = y \wedge y = z \Rightarrow x = z)$

Congruence. $(x_1 = y_1 \wedge ... \wedge x_n = y_n) \Rightarrow f(x_1, ..., x_n) = f(y_1, ..., y_n)$

$(x_1 = y_1 \wedge ... \wedge x_n = y_n) \Rightarrow (p(x_1, ..., x_n) \equiv p(y_1, ..., y_n))$ (Congruence of predicates)

[In particular, $x : A \wedge x = y \Rightarrow y : A$]

– **Induction Axiom Schemata**

These depend on the specific algebraic system.

Example: $(P(0) \wedge \forall X[X : \text{Nat} \wedge P(X) \Rightarrow P(s\,X)]) \Rightarrow \forall X[X : \text{Nat} \Rightarrow P(X)]$

(Induction rules are discussed in [31].)

Note that all variables are unsorted and $\equiv$ indicates logical equivalence.

Typical assertions: implications between two conjunctions of $L = R$ and $x : A$ assertions.

Goal: a simple formal system that is easy to use, flexible, and allows partially defined or partially worked out algebras. The claim is that the system sketched above is remarkably simple and clear.

In this context it is easy to consider extensions to the OBJ language. E.g. we could have algebraic structure on sort names, and we could have variables ranging over sorts.

8 Some Simple Logical Examples

Below we consider some simple examples of how the logical approach just described could be used.

8.1 Reconstruction of Lists

A typical definition of list is the following (this is one of the examples distributed with OBJ3):

```
obj LIST[X :: TRIV] is
  sorts List NeList .
  op nil : -> List .
  subsorts Elt < NeList < List .
  op __ : List List -> List [assoc id: nil] .
  op __ : NeList List -> NeList .
  op __ : NeList NeList -> NeList .
  protecting NAT .
  op |_| : List -> Nat .
  eq | nil | = 0 .
```

```
      var E : Elt .    var L : List .
      eq | E L | = 1 + | L | .
      op tail_ : NeList -> List .
      var E : Elt .    var L : List .
      eq tail (E L) = L .
   endo
```

Note: Elt coms from the parameter theory X. The unsorted logical form of this would be:

```
   obj LIST[X :: TRIV] is
     protecting NAT .

     sort List .
     sort NeList .

     op nil : -> _ .
     op _ _ : _ _ -> _ [assoc id: nil] .
     op |_| : _ -> _ .
     op tail_ : _ -> _ [prec 120] .

     var X Y N E L .

     X : Elt implies X : NeList .
     X : NeList implies X : List .

     nil : List .
     X : List and Y : List implies (X Y) : List .
     ((X : List and Y : List) and (X : NeList or Y : NeList))
         implies X Y : NeList .
     L : List implies | L | : Nat .
     N : NeList implies tail N : List .

     | nil | = 0 .
     E : Elt and L : List implies | E L | = 1 + | L | .
     E : Elt and L : List implies tail (E L) = L .
   endo
```

We are using implies for logical implication.
   We could also use a constructor for sort identifiers List(-) as sketched below.

```
     sort List
     sort NeList
     sort List(Elt)
     sort NeList(Elt)

     op nil : -> _ .
     op _ _ : _ _ -> _ .
```

```
op |_| : _ -> _ .
op tail_ : _ -> _ .

var X Y L N E .

X : Elt implies X : NeList(Elt) .
X : NeList(Elt) implies X : List(Elt) .

X : List(Elt) implies X : List .
X : NeList(Elt) implies X : NeList .

X : List(Elt) and X =/= nil implies X : NeList(Elt) .

nil : List(Elt) .
X : List and Y : List implies X Y : List .
X : List(Elt) and Y : List(Elt) implies X Y : List(Elt) .
(X : List(Elt) and Y : List(Elt))
 and (X : NeList(Elt) or Y : NeList(Elt))
    implies X Y : NeList(Elt) .

L : List implies | L | : Nat .
N : NeList(Elt) implies tail N : List(Elt) .

X : List implies nil X = X .
X : List implies X nil = X .

| nil | = 0 .
E : Elt and L : List implies | E L | = 1 + | L | .
E : Elt and L : List implies tail (E L) = L .
```

We would really like to consider Elt to be a sort variable in the rules above, but we would need to disallow Elt = List, i.e., we would like to have rules with conditions on the sorts, such as:

```
(S <sort S') implies (X : NeList(S) implies X : NeList(S'))
```

The simple treatment of sort descriptions like this would seem to have strong connections with typing in ML. It would also seem possible to treat Church's simple theory of types in this context, and incorporate first-order theories of higher-order functions in this context. It seems that this framework, the system of first-order logic with equality and a sort predicate (_:_), is a very expressive.

8.2 A Sample Proof

Suppose one is developing the natural number example, one might already have $0 : \text{Nat}$ and $X : \text{Nat} \Rightarrow (sX) : \text{Nat}$. Furthermore, one might have decided that these are the constructors of the sort Nat, i.e. that an induction principle holds for 0 and s in Nat.

In this context, one could introduce _+_ simply via

$$\_ + \_ : \_\_ \rightarrow \_$$

(We are just assuming that $+$ is a binary operator.)

Equations:

$$X : \text{Nat} \Rightarrow X + 0 = X$$
$$X, Y : \text{Nat} \Rightarrow X + (sY) = s\,(X + Y)$$

In this context we might want to prove: $\forall X, Y[X : \text{Nat} \wedge Y : \text{Nat} \Rightarrow (X+Y) : \text{Nat}]$. This is easily done using induction with $P(Y) \equiv \forall X[X : \text{Nat} \Rightarrow (X + Y) : \text{Nat}]$. The base case uses the first equation above, and inductive case uses the second (the only tricky part is dispatching the conditions).

Having shown that $\forall X, Y[X : \text{Nat} \wedge Y : \text{Nat} \Rightarrow (X + Y) : \text{Nat}]$, we have proved the correctness of the operator declaration $\_ + \_ : \text{Nat Nat} \rightarrow \text{Nat}$. We can now add this to the specification.

It seems better to have some implicit operator structure, the declarations at the top, rather than to have to introduce $\_ + \_ : \text{Universal Universal} \rightarrow \text{Universal}$ and then remove it. It is argued that "saying nothing" is sometimes better than "saying something not quite right."

9   Using Sort Predicates

Assertions of the form t : s are not supported in OBJ within terms. Below is a definition of a built-in module using the underlying Lisp (for more details on such modules see [6]) that (partially) provides the ability to use sort conditions in OBJ.

```
evq (progn
; definitions for Capitalized sort names as a built-in sort
(defun obj_SORT$is_token (token)
  (and (<= 2 (length token))
       (upper-case-p (char token 0))
       (every #'(lambda (c)
                   (or (lower-case-p c) (digit-char-p c)
                       (eql #\- c)))
               (subseq token 1))))
(defun obj_SORT$create (token) token)
(defun obj_SORT$print (x) (princ x))
(defun obj_SORT$is_a (x)
  (and (stringp x) (obj_SORT$is_token x)))
(defun is_sort (x s)
  (let ((srt (mod_eval$$find_sort (term$built_in_value s)))
        (so (module$sort_order *mod_eval$$current_module*)))
    (sort_order$is_included_in so (term$sort x) srt)))
)

obj SORT-PRED is
  bsort SortId (obj_SORT$is_token obj_SORT$create obj_SORT$print
      obj_SORT$is_a) .
  op (_/:_) : Universal SortId -> Bool [strat (2 0)] .
```

```
op (_:_) : Universal SortId -> Bool .
var X : Universal .
var S : SortId .
beq (X /: S) = (obj_BOOL$coerce_to_Bool (is_sort X S)) .
eq X : S = X /: S .
endo
```

Unfortunately this only works for simple-named sorts and furthermore is not robust. However it does allow one to experiment with the use of sort predicates. It does allow the following, for example:

```
red (1 + 2) : Nat . *** => true
red (1 + 2) : Bool . *** => false
```

10   Logic in OBJ

The Hsiang decision procedure for propositional logic [23] can easily be described in OBJ. (This example is borrowed from [6].)

```
obj PROPC is sort Prop .
  protecting TRUTH + QID .
  subsorts Id Bool < Prop .

  op _and_ : Prop Prop -> Prop [assoc comm prec 2] .
  op _xor_ : Prop Prop -> Prop [assoc comm prec 3] .
  vars p q r : Prop .
  eq p and false = false .
  eq p and true = p .
  eq p and p = p .
  eq p xor false = p .
  eq p xor p = false .
  eq p and (q xor r) = (p and q) xor (p and r) .

  op _or_ : Prop Prop -> Prop [assoc comm prec 7] .
  op not_ : Prop -> Prop [prec 1] .
  op _implies_ : Prop Prop -> Prop [prec 9] .
  op _iff_ : Prop Prop -> Prop [assoc prec 11] .
  eq p or q = (p and q) xor p xor q .
  eq not p = p xor true .
  eq p implies q = (p and q) xor p xor true .
  eq p iff q = p xor q xor true .
endo
```

This provides normal forms for propositional formulas modulo associativity and commutativity (unfortunately with an exponential blow-up in the size of terms, in general). This definition makes critical use of OBJ's pattern matching facility. In particular, the matching of the rules p and p = p and p xor p = false requires associative-commutative pattern matching. This definition is quite useful in practice (see [8, 20]).

Here are some sample reductions:

```
OBJ> red 'a or (not 'a) .
reduce in PROPC : 'a or not 'a
rewrites: 9
result Bool: true
OBJ> red 'a implies ('b implies 'a) .
reduce in PROPC : 'a implies ('b implies 'a)
rewrites: 10
result Bool: true
OBJ> red 'a and ('a implies 'b) .
reduce in PROPC : 'a and ('a implies 'b)
rewrites: 8
result Prop: 'b and 'a
```

One can also do proof systems in OBJ. Here is a simple (and perhaps a little odd) example that will help us see the value of sort constraints, i.e., conditional sort assertions. We will try to do a proof system in OBJ where certain terms will be proofs and evaluation of them will be both check the proof and produce the conclusion of the proof. (It could be argued that the result should be a representation of the proof, which is why this is a bit odd.)

```
--- constructive propositional logic
obj PROPL is
  protecting QID .

  sort Term ErrTerm . sort Theorem .
  subsorts Id < Term < ErrTerm .
  subsorts Theorem < Term .

  op ff : -> Term .   --- contradiction
  op _=>_ : Term Term -> Term .

  op thm : Term -> Theorem . *** hidden ***
  op reveal : Theorem -> Term .
  op mp : Theorem Theorem -> ErrTerm .
  ops ax1 ax3 : Term Term -> Theorem .
  op ax2 : Term Term Term -> Theorem .

  var a b c : Term .  var th : Theorem .

  eq mp(thm(a), thm(a => c)) = thm(c) .
  eq thm(th) = th . *** N.B.
  eq reveal(thm(a)) = a .
  eq ax1(a, b) = thm(a => (b => a)) .
  eq ax2(a, b, c) =
```

```
    thm((a => (b => c)) => ((a => b) => (a => c))) .
  eq ax3(a, b) =
    thm(((b => ff) => (a => ff)) => (a => b)) .
endo
```

Our focus is the sort Theorem with constructor thm. The function mp is only partially defined.

Example reduction:

```
reduce in PROPL as Theorem :
  reveal(mp(ax1('p, 'q),
    mp(ax1('p, 'q => 'p),
      ax2('p, 'q => 'p, 'p)))) .
```

```
---> 'p => 'p
```

The fact that reveal produces 'p => 'p and that thm was not explicitly used in the starting term, means that final result is a theorem (although it has the sort Term).

Here is an alternative formulation of this example that makes use of sort constraints.

```
--- constructive propositional logic

obj PROPL is
  protecting QID .

  sort Term ErrTerm .    sort Theorem .
  subsorts Id < Term < ErrTerm
  subsorts Theorem < Term .

  op ff : -> Term .   --- contradiction
  op _=>_ : Term Term -> Term .
  op mp : Theorem Theorem -> ErrTerm .

  ops ax1 ax3 : Term Term -> Theorem .
  op ax2 : Term Term Term -> Theorem .

  var a b c : Term . var s t : Theorem .

  eq mp(a, a => c) = c [as: Theorem] .

  eq ax1(a, b) = a => (b => a) .
  eq ax2(a, b, c) =
    (a => (b => c)) => ((a => b) => (a => c)) .
  eq ax3(a, b) =
    ((b => ff) => (a => ff)) => (a => b) .
endo
```

The operators thm and reveal have been eliminated. The mp equation has been changed to include a sort constraint. This equation should be considered equivalent to:

```
eq mp(a, a => c) = c .
as c : Theorem if (a : Theorem) and (a => c) : Theorem .
```

Note that we want to use the equation and the sort constraint together, which is suggested by the formulation eq mp(a, a => c) = c [as: Theorem]. Computing the sort of the result is a central part of the computation in this example, and this sort constraint equation both tells about the structure of the result and its sort.

```
red mp(ax1('p, 'q),
       mp(ax1('p, 'q => 'p),
          ax2('p, 'q => 'p, 'p))) .
---> 'p => 'p
```

We would like to know that the result is a Theorem. This kind of example requires a different, more dynamic, treatment of the sorts of terms. Currently, in OBJ, the sort of the term is given, internally, by the disambiguated top operator. It is a bit awkward to use this approach for these more dynamic cases.

The logical content of the special rule eq mp(a, a => c) = c [as: Theorem] is:

$$a : \text{Theorem} \land (a => c) : \text{Theorem}$$
$$\Rightarrow \quad mp(a, (a => c)) = c \land c : \text{Theorem}$$

Part of this is a : Theorem $\land$ (a => c) : Theorem $\Rightarrow$ c : Theorem, which is just *modus ponens*.

Of course, for this example we want $(x : A) \land (x = y) \Rightarrow (y : A)$ (That is, we want substitutivity/congruence for x : A too.)

With these, and the logical interpretations of the structure of the module, we can get the desired result, i.e., we will be able to reduce the initial term to 'p => 'p and at the same time infer that it is a Theorem.

This kind of framework is good for "defining" or experimenting with logics, and in fact work (very broadly) along these lines is being carried out at Oxford [16].

11 A Proof Using "Apply"

Work has been done to incorporate controlled rewriting into OBJ3. Below is a very simple example of the use of these new features. (This example is related to one appearing in [20].)

```
th GROUP is
  sort Elt .
  op _*_ : Elt Elt -> Elt [assoc] .
  op e : -> Elt .
  op _-1 : Elt -> Elt [prec 2] .
```

```
   var A : Elt .
   [id] eq e * A = A .        *** [labeled rules]
   [inv] eq A -1 * A = e .
endth

*** Goal: show that a left inverse is also a right inverse

open .          *** [temporarily add structure]

op a : -> Elt . ***> Functions as a variable

*** [Use of controlled rewriting: apply]
start a * a -1 . ***> (a * a -1)
apply -.id at term . ***> (e * a * a -1)
apply -.inv with A = (a -1) within term .
    ***> ((a -1) -1 * a -1 * a * a -1)
apply .inv at [2 .. 3] of term .
    ***> ((a -1) -1 * e * a -1)
apply reduction at term . ***> e

[invr] eq (A * (A -1)) = e .
    ***> equation just demonstrated [generalized]

*** Goal: show that a left identity is also a right identity

start a * e .
apply -.inv with A = a within term .
    ***> a * a -1 * a
apply .invr at [1 .. 2] . ***> e * a
apply reduction at term . ***> a

[idr] eq A * e = A .
    ***> equation just demonstrated

. . . . . . . .
OBJ> show rules .
1: [invr] eq A * A -1 = e
2: [idr] eq A * e = A
3: [id] eq e * A = A
4: [inv] eq A -1 * A = e

close
```

12   LIST Example and Non-Coregularity

In release 1.0 of OBJ3, the property coregularity was required of the signature. Coregularity [19] is the condition that given an operation f and a sort s, if there is any rank for f with coarity $s' \leq s$, then there is a unique (pointwise) largest such rank. Here is an example that violates coregularity.

```
obj LIST-NAT is
  pr NAT .

  sorts NeList List .
  subsorts Nat < NeList < List .

  op nil : -> List .
  op __ : List List -> List [assoc id: nil] .
  op __ : NeList List -> NeList [assoc id: nil] .
  op __ : List NeList -> NeList [assoc id: nil] .
  op __ : NeList NeList -> NeList [assoc] .

  op first : NeList -> Nat .
  op last : NeList -> Nat .
  op rest : NeList -> List .

  var X : List .
  var N : Nat .

  eq first(N X) = N .
  eq last(X N) = N .
  eq rest(N X) = X .
endo
```

There would be trouble with parsing all of these equations without all of the operator declarations, but the collection of operator declarations is not coregular and would not have been acceptable in release 1.0 of OBJ3, but is with release 2.0.

13 Introduction to Parameterized Programming

OBJ has a powerful higher-level abstraction facility on program modules which gives rise to the parameterized programming paradigm. For more discussion of this technique see [9, 6, 7].

- Instantiations of parameterized modules create a new module incorporating the actual parameter modules.
- Formal module parameters are described by theories.
- A view (with defaults) indicates the mapping from formal parameter to actual. Many different views can exist indicating how a given module can function as a parameter to a given parameterized procedure in different ways.
- Instantiations are given by expressions of the form A[B,...].
- Other module expressions are A + B (union or sum of modules), and A * (op f to g, sort A to B) (renaming).

Parameterized programming greatly increases the expressiveness of the langauge.

- Parameterized programming gives a lot of the expressiveness of higher-order programming, but in a more disciplined way. The program is clearly distinguished from the way the program is created or described. This distinction is not clear in higher-order programming, in general, where, although one may program in the disciplined way described here, one may also define functions where the creation of functions is intrinsic to the execution of the program itself.
- Parameterized programming gives a lot of the expressiveness of inheritance of methods in object-oriented programming, but with much greater flexibility.

14 Parameterized Programming Examples

Here is a basic "higher-order" functional programming example.

```
--- Reduction functional: f: A x B -> B
--- creates a function that maps:
---      B x LIST[A] -> B

obj LIST[X :: TRIV] is  *** [A very simple LIST definition]
  subsorts Elt < List .
  op nil : -> List .
  op __ : List List -> List [assoc id: nil] .
endo

th TRIV is  *** [Actually part of standard prelude]
  sort Elt .
endth

th TH-REDUCE-ARG is
  sort A B .
  op reducer-fn : A B -> B .
endth

obj REDUCE[ARG :: TH-REDUCE-ARG] is
  protecting LIST[ARG] .
  op reduce : B.ARG List -> B.ARG .
  var b : B.ARG .
  var a : A.ARG .
  var la : List .
  eq reduce(b, nil) = b .
  eq reduce(b, a) = reducer-fn(a,b) .
  eq reduce(b, (a la)) =
    reducer-fn(a, reduce(b, la)) .
endo
```

This is a very explicit version.

```
obj SUM-OF is
```

```
  protecting
    REDUCE[
      view from TH-REDUCE-ARG to INT is
        sort A to Int .
        sort B to Int .
        var x : A .
        var y : B .
        op reducer-fn(x,y) to x + y .
      endv] .
  op sum-of : List -> Int .
  var x : List .
  eq sum-of(x) = reduce(0, x) .
endo

reduce in SUM-OF :
  (sum-of (1 2 3 4 5))

.
---> 15
```

Alternative choices for the mapping of **reducer-fn** in the view are

```
  op reducer-fn(x,y) to y
```

which would produce the first element of the list to reduce, an

```
  op reducer-fn(x,y) to x
```

which would produce the last.

An example of a parameterized "object-oriented method" is the following:

```
th LOCATED-THING is
  pr FLOAT .
  sort Thing .
  op x : Thing -> Float .
  op y : Thing -> Float .
endth

obj DISTANCE[THG :: LOCATED-THING] is
  var T : Thing .
  op sqr : Float -> Float .
  var X : Float .
  eq sqr(X) = X * X .
  op distance(T) = sqrt(sqr(x(T)) + sqr(y(T))) .
endo
```

This could be instantiated in many ways, e.g. as suggested by the following,

```
  pr DISTANCE[view to POINT is op x to x-of . op y to y-of . endv] .
  pr DISTANCE[view to FLOAT is var X : Float .
```

```
        op x(X) to ((X - (X rem 100)) / 100) .
        op y(X) to (X rem 100) . endv ] .
pr DISTANCE[view to 2TUPLE[FLOAT,FLOAT] is
        op x to 1*_ .   op y to 2*_ . endv] .
pr DISTANCE[view to 3TUPLE[QID,FLOAT,FLOAT] is
        op x to 2*_ .   op y to 3*_ . endv] .
```

A more complex example is given next. We could specify an n-body simulator but have the details of the underlying physics be a parameter.

```
obj NUMBER is
  pr FLOAT .
  op _^_ : Float Float -> Float .
  var X Y : Float .
  bq X ^ Y = (expt X (round y)) .
endo
```

```
th PHYSICS is
  pr NUMBER .
  sort Position Mass Velocity Acceleration .
  op g : -> Float .
  op _+_ : Acceleration Acceleration -> Acceleration .
  op _+_ : Velocity Velocity  -> Velocity .
  op _+_ : Position Position  -> Position .
  op _-_ : Position Position -> Position .
  op dist : Position Position -> Float .
  op _*_ : Float Acceleration -> Velocity .
  op _*_ : Float Velocity -> Position .
  op _*_ : Mass Mass -> Float .
  op accel : Float Position -> Acceleration .
  op null-accel : -> Acceleration .
endth
```

This theory will be mapped to specific underlying geometries.

```
th NUMERICAL-PARAMETER is
  pr NUMBER .
  op t : -> Float .
endth
```

This theory specifies the time-step parameter of the simulation.

```
obj N-BODY[PHYS :: PHYSICS, T :: NUMERICAL-PARAMETER] is
  sort System .
  sort Body .
  subsort Body < System .

  op (_ : _,_) : Mass Velocity Position -> Body .
```

```
  op _&_ : System System -> System .   *** possibly AC

  op sim-step : System -> System .
  op sim-distrib : System System -> System .
  op sim-sum-accel : Body System -> Acceleration .
  op sim-action : Body Acceleration -> Body .

  var S S1 S2 : System .
  var B : Body .
  var M M1 M2 : Mass .
  var P1 P2 : Position .
  var V1 V2 : Velocity .
  var A : Acceleration .

  eq sim-step(S) = sim-distrib(S,S) .

  eq sim-distrib((S1 & S2),S) =
    sim-distrib(S1,S) & sim-distrib(S2,S) .
  eq sim-distrib(B,S) =
    sim-action(B,sim-sum-accel(B,S)) .

  eq sim-sum-accel(B,(S1 & S2)) =
    sim-sum-accel(B,S1) + sim-sum-accel(B,S2) .
  eq sim-sum-accel(M1 : V1, P1, M2 : V2, P2) =
    if P1 == P2 then null-accel else
    accel((g * (M1 * M2)) / (dist(P1,P2) ^ 3),
          P2 - P1) fi .

  eq sim-action(M : V1, P1, A) =
    M : (V1 + (t * A)),
      (P1 + ((t * V1) + (t * ((t / 2) * A)))) .
endo
```

This parameterized module gives the simulation in terms of the abstract description of the physics.

```
  obj GEOMETRY is
    pr NUMBER .
    sort Point .
    op [_,_] : Float Float -> Point .
    ops (_+_) (_-_) : Point Point -> Point .
    op _*_ : Float Point -> Point .
    op dist : Point Point -> Float .
    var X Y X1 Y1 X2 Y2 D : Float .
    eq [X1,Y1] + [X2,Y2] = [X1 + X2, Y1 + Y2] .
    eq [X1,Y1] - [X2,Y2] = [X1 - X2, Y1 - Y2] .
```

```
  eq D * [X,Y] = [D * X, D * Y] .
  eq dist([X1,Y1],[X2,Y2]) =
    sqrt(((X1 - X2)^ 2) + ((Y1 - Y2)^ 2)) .
endo
```

This object provides basic two dimensional notions. This will used to instantiate N-BODY as shown next.

```
obj TIME-PARAMETER is
  pr NUMBER .
  op t : -> Float .
  eq t = .5 .
endo
```

```
obj TEST is pr N-BODY[
              view to GEOMETRY is
                  sort Position to Point .
                  sort Mass to Float .
                  sort Velocity to Point .
                  sort Acceleration to Point .
                  op g to 3.4 .
                  op null-accel to [0,0] .
                  var X : Float .  var P : Position .
                  op accel(X,P) to X * P .
              endv,
                TIME-PARAMETER] .
endo
```

The two dimensional GEOMETRY could be changed to a three dimensional one. Note that many of the sorts in the parameter theory are mapped to the same actual parameter sort; the distinctions made in the abstract version are being lost. The relation of theory to actual corresponds to the relation of abstract definition to implementation. In this way we can get the "code reuse" of object-oriented inheritance (and better). One of the main virtues of inheritance is the inheritance of structure and methods. This can be obtained instead by parameterization, which moreover gives a great deal more flexibility, since parameterized methods can be instantiated in many different ways.

15   Interpreters in OBJ

It is easy to write definitions of languages, giving interpreters of languages in OBJ. These examples also show how the syntactic facilities of OBJ allow one to choose a syntax that is fairly natural.

15.1   Combinators

The combinators are a familiar and not entirely trivial example of this type.

```
obj COMB-ALG-SIGN is
  sort Ca .
  op S : -> Ca .
  op K : -> Ca .
  op I : -> Ca .
  op __ : Ca Ca -> Ca [gather (E e)] .
endo

obj COMBIN-ALG is
  using COMB-ALG-SIGN .
  vars X Y Z : Ca .
  eq I X = X .
  eq K X Y = X .
  eq S X Y Z = X Z (Y Z) .
endo

obj ACOMBA is
  using COMBIN-ALG .
  protecting INT .
  subsorts Int < Ca .
endo
```

This example was developed in a particular stepwise fashion. First uninterpreted term structures were introduced, then the semantics, in COMBIN-ALG. Here is a sample reduction:

```
OBJ> red S K K 1 .
reduce in ACOMBA : ((S K) K) 1
rewrites: 2
result NzNat: 1
```

15.2 LUCID

It is possible to give a sketch of the LUCID programming language [4, 37]. The style of programming that this sketch supports is indexical. The treatment of expressions depends on context, i.e. on an index. For the sake of space some details have been omitted.

```
obj LUCID is
  pr INT . pr QID .

  sorts Val Expr Context .
  subsorts Bool Int < Val .
  .....
  op _@_ : Expr Context -> Val [memo] .
       ***[Indexical programming: Form @ Index; efficient]
  subsort Int < Context .
```

```
  op val : -> Context .

  subsort Id Int < Expr .
  op first _ : Expr -> Expr .
  op next _ : Expr -> Expr .
  op (_fby_) (_wvr_) (_asa_) (_upon_)
     (_QQ_) (_+_) (_*_) (_<_) : Expr Expr -> Expr .
  op odd_ : Expr -> Expr .
  op wvrf : Expr Expr Int Int -> Val .
  .....
  var E X Y P : Expr .  var C : Context .
  var I N M : Int .  var B : Bool .

  .....
  eq (first X) Q C = X Q 0 .
  eq (next X) Q I = X Q (I + 1) .
  eq (X fby Y) Q I =
    if I == 0 then X Q val else Y Q (I - 1) fi .

  eq (X wvr P) Q I = wvrf(X,P,0,I) .
  eq wvrf(X,P,N,I) =
    if the-bool(P Q N) == true then
      if 0 == I then (X Q N)
      else wvrf(X,P,N + 1,I - 1) fi
    else wvrf(X,P,N + 1,I) fi .

  eq 'Fibos Q C =
    (0 fby (1 fby ('Fibos + (next 'Fibos)))) Q C .
  .....
endo
```

Note: n Q c = n, for n : Int.

These definitions, with the memo attribute on _Q_, even have desirable computational properties. The n-th element of 'Fibo is computed in linear time.

15.3 An FP-like language

A simple FP-like language could be also easily be defined.

```
obj FNL is
  protecting BOOL .
  protecting INT .
  sort Fnl .
  subsorts Int < Fnl .
  subsorts Bool < Fnl .
  op (_:_) : Fnl Fnl -> Fnl .
  op <_,_> : Fnl Fnl -> Fnl .
```

```
ops Sel1 Sel2 Id Cons Cond1 Cond
    Comp Apply Const Atom Eq0 Succ
    Pred Fix : -> Fnl .
op Condi : Fnl Fnl Fnl Fnl -> Fnl [(1 0)] .
vars x y z u : Fnl .    var n : Int .
var b : Bool .
```

In interpreters, one tends to end up with one connect component, as in this case.

```
eq Sel1 : < x, y > = x .
eq Sel2 : < x, y > = y .
eq Id : x = x .
eq (Cons : < x, y >) : z = < x : z, y : z > .
eq Cond1 : < true, < x, y > > = x .
eq Cond1 : < false, < x, y > > = y .
eq (Const : x) : y = x .
eq Apply : < x, y > = x : y .
eq (Comp : < x, y >) : z = x : (y : z) .
eq Atom : < x, y > = false .
eq Atom : n = true .
eq Atom : b = true .
eq Eq0 : 0 = true .
ceq Eq0 : x = false if not (x == 0) .
eq Succ : n = n + 1 .
eq Pred : n = n - 1 .
eq (Fix : x) : y = (x : (Fix : x)) : y .
eq (Cond : < x, < y, z > > ) : u =
    Condi(x : u, y, z, u) .
eq Condi(true,y,z,u) = y : u .
eq Condi(false,y,z,u) = z : u .
endo
```

This is a relatively untyped treatment of functions. It is more of a challenge to handle typed functions in this fashion. This is an example where the natural sort structure, which creates a "universal" sort Fnl, significantly weakens the type checking. One can also do CAM and versions of type theory in the same way.

One might even be tempted to say that there is a programming paradigm lurking here. To express computational concepts, one invents the appropriate language and writes an interpreter for it, and then one uses this to describe structures and algorithms. OBJ provides a very nice environment for using this paradigm.

16   Introduction to Maude

Maude [29, 30, 28] is a new language based on (Order-sorted) rewriting logic that nicely models object-oriented programming as well as functional computation.

There are three kinds of modules in Maude, functional modules (with initial keyword fmod), system modules (keyword mod), and object-oriented modules (keyword omod). Functional modules are very much like obj modules in OBJ with fmod instead of obj and endfm instead of endo.

When we use system modules, defined with mod ... endm, we drop the expectation of confluence for the set of rules. In Maude, we don't have equations, instead we have oriented rewrite rules, even at the level of the logic. (In fact, this is very close to what is implemented in OBJ3.)

Variations in the syntax:

```
rl ⟨LHS⟩ => ⟨RHS⟩ .
rl ⟨Label⟩ : ⟨LHS⟩ => ⟨RHS⟩ .
crl ⟨Label⟩ : ⟨LHS⟩ => ⟨RHS⟩ if ⟨Condition⟩ .
ax ⟨Term⟩ = ⟨Term⟩ . *** "Structural" axioms
```

The first three are the notation for rules in system or object-oriented modules. The last is notation that could be used in specifications to give structural axioms for the terms. Rewriting should be considered to take place modulo these structural axioms.

We also have conditional rules. We can have "=>" in conditions too. We can also have new variables in conditions, i.e., ones that don't appear in the LHS of the rule.

The *Structural axioms* play a very important role (loosening the limitations of syntax).

The nature of the *modeling relationship* is this: to model (part of) a system, represent the (partial) state of the system by a term. The application of rewrite rules correspond to events causing state changes in the system. Intrinsic to the notion of a rewrite rule is that you only need to know about a limited part of the state to be able to decide whether an action is possible; and actions can only change a limited part of the state. (If there are structural axioms, then the state is described by the equivalence class of the term at a given point.)

We can, in fact, view OBJ3 as a partial implementation of a (limited) version of Maude. For non-confluent rules sets, the OBJ3 implementation will carry out some arbitrarily chosen rewriting sequence on the starting term. With controlled rewriting, one can systematically explore chosen rewriting sequences.

17 Elementary Maude Examples

Here are some basic Maude system module examples.

This first (borrowed from [28]) is very a simple example of non-confluence.

```
mod NAT-CHOICE is
  extending NAT .
  op _?_ : Nat Nat -> Nat .
  vars N M : Nat .
  rl N ? M => N .
  rl N ? M => M .
endm
```

This is not confluent. Since 3 ? 4 => 3 and 3 ? 4 => 4, we cannot think of => as equality, since 3 ≠ 4. (Perhaps with additional assumptions about the strategy used to apply the rules, we can view this as a description of a "random" operation.)

We could also define a choose operator, which selects a number less than or equal to its argument, like this:

```
op choose : Nat -> Nat .
rl choose(0) = 0 .
crl choose(N) = N ? choose(N - 1) if 0 < N .
```

The following system module is very basic to many of the system programming examples presented below.

```
mod SYSTEM is
  sorts System EId .
  op __ : System System -> System
  [assoc comm id: empty] .
  op _:_ : Eid Universal -> System.
endm
```

(This is related to the CONFIGURATION module of [28].) "A : x" will represent an entity called A with structure x. This is very similar to A = x. Thus EId is the sort of names of entities in the system. Entities can be active or passive objects, messages, or anonymous agents.

A locking protocol could be described this way

```
mod LOCKS is
  extending SYSTEM .
  ops lock locked unlock unlocked : EId EId -> System .
  var A B : EId .  var X : Universal .
  eq lock(A,B) (A : X) => locked(B,A) [A : X] .
  eq unlock(A,B) [A : X] => unlocked(B,A) (A : X) .
endo
```

Note that "[" must be distinguished from "(".

Digital circuits can nicely be described in system modules. Wires will be named, names have sort WireId, and their state represented as x : *val*, where val is 0 or 1. We can describe a NAND gate with inputs x and y and output z by the following rules:

```
rl (x : 0) (z : 0) => (x : 0) (z : 1) .
rl (y : 0) (z : 0) => (y : 0) (z : 1) .
rl (x : 1) (y : 1) (z : 1) => (x : 1) (y : 1) (z : 0) .
```

A variation on this with more explicit representation of the circuit structure allows the dynamic creation can be described by:

```
var U V W : WireId .
rl (U : 0) (W : 0) nand(U,V,W) =>
   (U : 0) (W : 1) nand(U,V,W) .
rl (V : 0) (W : 0) nand(U,V,W) =>
   (V : 0) (W : 1) nand(U,V,W) .
rl (U : 1) (V : 1) (W : 1) nand(U,V,W) =>
   (U : 1) (V : 1) (W : 0) nand(U,V,W) .
```

The rules in the previous example then correspond to having nand(x,y,z) as part of the system. This might also nicely allow the expression of circuit transformation by rules that rewrite the nand(x,y,z) expressions. This example was inspired by [27].

One may describe graph rewriting at this level. Nodes will be represented by a named collection of nodes that are connected to the given node. A typical rule might be:

```
var N1 N2 N3 : EId .
var NS1 NS2 : SetEId .
crl (N1 : {N2,NS1}) (N2 : {N3,NS2}) =>
    (N1 : {N2,N3,NS1}) (N2 : {N3,NS2})
    if not (N3 in {N2,NS1})
```

Where (N1 : NS1) represenets a node named N1 with outgoing edges to the nodes in the set NS1. This rule introduces a transitive link in the graph.

We can easily describe data-flow computations. We will have named ports, where the identifiers have sort PortId.

```
op m : EId Universal -> System .
var P1 P2 P3 : PortId .
var M N : Int .
rl m(P1,M) m(P2,N) add(P1,P2,P3) =>
   add(P1,P2,P3) m(P3,(M + N)) .
```

m(P,M) is a message to port P with content M. This is a curious case of data-flow, since out of order messages are allowed.

We could do sorting this way:

```
subsort Int < EId .
var M N X Y : Int .
crl (M : X) (N : Y) => (M : Y) (N : X)
    if M < N and Y < X .
```

Here is an explicit (fair) merge:

```
op m : EId Nat Data -> Msg .
var U X Y Z : EId .
var D : Data .
crl m(U,D) merge(X,Y,Z) => merge(X,Y,Z) m(Z,D)
    if U == X or U == Y .
```

If it is assumed (in practice, if the underlying mechanism provide) that messages are treated fairly, then this will be a fair merge.

It would not be hard to work out the details of other examples, such as semaphores and meeting scheduling, from [3]. Certain things, such as "merge" are "built into" the model. An entity automatically receives the merge of all messages addressed to it and this merge will be as fair as the underlying mechanisms.

18 Concurrent Rewriting

Rewriting is naturally concurrent in an implicit fashion. Here is a slightly modified version of a simple matrix multiply example from [38]:

```
fmod LIST[X :: TRIV] is
  sort List .
  op empty : -> List .
  op __ : Elt List -> List .
endfm

fmod ROW-INT is
  using LIST[INT] * (sort List to Row,
      op (empty) to (empty-row)) .
  eq 0 empty-row = empty-row .
endfm

fmod ARRAY-2D-INT is
  using LIST[ROW-INT]  * (sort List to Matrix,
  op (empty) to (empty-matrix)) .
  eq empty-row empty-matrix = empty-matrix .
endfm

fmod MM is
  pr ARRAY-2D-INT .

  op firsts_ : Matrix -> Row .
  op rests_ : Matrix -> Matrix .
  op tr_ : Matrix -> Matrix .

  op _ip_ : Row Row -> Int .

  op _*m_ : Matrix Matrix -> Matrix .
  op mmtr : Matrix Matrix -> Matrix .
  op rowxtr : Row Matrix -> Row .

  var x y i : Int .
  var M N : Matrix .
  var A B R : Row .

  eq firsts empty-matrix = empty-row .
  eq firsts (empty-row M) = 0 (firsts M) .
  eq firsts ((i R) M) = i (firsts M) .

  eq rests empty-matrix = empty-matrix .
  eq rests (empty-row M) = empty-row (rests M) .
  eq rests ((i R) M) = R (rests M) .
```

```
    eq tr empty-matrix = empty-matrix .
    ceq tr M = (firsts M) (tr (rests M)) if M =/= empty-matrix .

    eq empty-row ip A = 0 .
    eq A ip empty-row = 0 .
    eq (x A) ip (y B) = (x * y) + (A ip B) .

    eq M *m N = mmtr(M, tr N) .

    eq mmtr(empty-matrix,N) = empty-matrix .
    eq mmtr(A M, N) = rowxtr(A,N) mmtr(M,N) .

    eq rowxtr(A,empty-matrix) = empty-row .
    eq rowxtr(A,B N) = (A ip B) rowxtr(A,N) .
  endfm
```

The operator _*m_ is multiplication of matrices represented as a list of rows, ip is inner product, and tr is transpose. First of all, it is claimed that this is a very natural functional program for matrix multiply. However, even this very natural program, which uses only implicit parallelism, when executed by concurrent rewriting on matrices of size $n \times n$ might take only time n to perform the multiplication giving a speedup of n^2 over a simple n^3 sequential algorithm. It is very natural for computations that produce complex structured results to naturally take advantage of a great deal of concurrency. However, it should be said that one should not expect this speedup in practice, since communication costs, which are not counted in the abstract concurrent rewriting model, likely will dominate.

The Rewrite Rule Machine project [5, 2, 14, 25, 1] is constructing a massively parallel machine that uses concurrent rewriting as its basic model of computation.

19 Petri Nets

As another example of its generality, we can see that Petri nets can easily be expressed in terms of concurrent rewriting. (This example is taken from [28].)

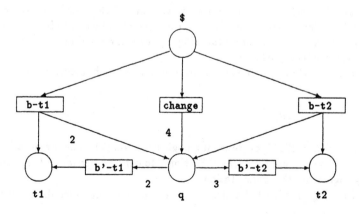

```
mod TICKET is
  subsorts Place < Marking .
  ops $,q,t1,t2 : -> Place .
  op _⊗_ : Marking Marking -> Marking
              [assoc comm id: λ] .
  rl b-t1 : $ => t1 ⊗ q ⊗ q .
  rl b-t2 : $ => t2 ⊗ q .
  rl change : $ => q ⊗ q ⊗ q ⊗ q .
  rl b'-t1 : q ⊗ q => t1 .
  rl b'-t2 : q ⊗ q ⊗ q => t2 .
endm
```

Note: labeled rules are being used here.

Example: $ $ ⟶ q q q q q t2 ⟶ t2 t1 t2.

20   Concurrent Rewriting as a Unifying Model

José Meseguer has shown that rewriting logic is a very general unifying model for concurrency [29, 30]. Many models can be seen as special cases of concurrent rewriting.

CR_{Ax} is rewriting modulo the structural axioms Ax; in particular, $\emptyset$, for no such axioms; AI, for associativity and identity; and ACI, for associativity, commutativity, and identity.

General concurrent rewriting includes $CR_\emptyset$, CR_{AI}, and CR_{ACI}. These, in turn, include many models:

- $CR_\emptyset$ includes Labeled transition systems, functional programming, including λ-calculus, Herbrand-Gödel-Kleene computability, and Algebraic ADTs.
- CR_{AI} includes Post systems which include phrase structure grammars which include Turing machines.
- CR_{ACI} includes Petri nets, Cham (and hence CCS), circuits, graph rewriting, and concurrent object-oriented programming including Actors, POP, and UNITY.

Herbrand-Gödel-Kleene computability was one of the very earliest notions of computability. The presentations vary, but the essential idea is to base computation on equational reasoning. So computation by equational reasoning is one of the earliest general models of computation.

It seems clear that concurrent rewriting is a very fundamental model.

21   Rewriting Logic

Here we give a brief sketch of Rewriting Logic based on [30]. The presentation here is unsorted, but we can use the ideas of Section 7 to derive a version of the order-sorted rewriting logic from this presentation.

Rewriting logic is a logic that generalizes equational logic (including it as a special case).

A *signature* is a pair (Σ, E) with Σ a ranked alphabet of function symbols and E a set of Σ-equations.

Rewriting will operate on equivalence classes of terms modulo a given set of equations E. (The E are the *structural axioms*.)

The *sentences* that we consider are sequents of the form $[t]_E \longrightarrow [t']_E$ with t, t' Σ-terms, where t and t' may possibly involve some variables. We will typically abbreviate $[t]_E$ to $[t]$ or even t.

We will write $t(\overline{w}/\overline{x})$ to indicate the parallel substitution of w_i for x_i, where $\overline{w}$ is short for $w_1 \dots$ and the range of i should be clear from the context.

Given a rewrite theory $\mathcal{R}$, we say that $\mathcal{R}$ *entails* a sequent $[t] \longrightarrow [t']$ and write

$$\mathcal{R} \ \vdash \ [t] \longrightarrow [t']$$

if and only if $[t] \longrightarrow [t']$ can be obtained by finite application of the following *rules of deduction*:

1. **Reflexivity.** For each $[t] \in T_{\Sigma,E}(X)$,

$$\overline{[t] \longrightarrow [t]}$$

2. **Congruence.** For each $f \in \Sigma_n$, $n \in \mathbb{N}$,

$$\frac{[t_1] \longrightarrow [t'_1] \quad \dots \quad [t_n] \longrightarrow [t'_n]}{[f(t_1, \dots, t_n)] \longrightarrow [f(t'_1, \dots, t'_n)]}$$

3. **Replacement.** [Substitutivity, see unconditional case] For each rewrite rule

$$r : [t(\overline{x})] \longrightarrow [t'(\overline{x})] \ \ if \ \ [u_1(\overline{x})] \longrightarrow [v_1(\overline{x})] \wedge \dots \wedge [u_k(\overline{x})] \longrightarrow [v_k(\overline{x})]$$

in R,

$$\frac{[w_1] \longrightarrow [w'_1] \quad \dots \quad [w_n] \longrightarrow [w'_n]}{[u_1(\overline{w}/\overline{x})] \longrightarrow [v_1(\overline{w}/\overline{x})] \quad \dots \quad [u_k(\overline{w}/\overline{x})] \longrightarrow [v_k(\overline{w}/\overline{x})]}$$
$$\overline{[t(\overline{w}/\overline{x})] \longrightarrow [t'(\overline{w'}/\overline{x})]}$$

That is, if for a substitution $x_i \mapsto w_i$, $1 \le i \le n$, we can deduce sequents

$$[u_j(\overline{w}/\overline{x})] \longrightarrow [v_j(\overline{w}/\overline{x})], \ 1 \le j \le k,$$

then, if in addition we can deduce $[w_i] \longrightarrow [w'_i]$, $1 \le i \le n$, we are then allowed to deduce

$$[t(\overline{w}/\overline{x})] \longrightarrow [t'(\overline{w'}/\overline{x})]$$

4. **Transitivity.**

$$\frac{[t_1] \longrightarrow [t_2] \quad [t_2] \longrightarrow [t_3]}{[t_1] \longrightarrow [t_3]}$$

Note that for unconditional rules the rule of replacement specializes to the simpler:

5. **Unconditional Replacement.** For each $r : [t(x_1, \ldots, x_n)] \longrightarrow [t'(x_1, \ldots, x_n)]$ in R,

$$\frac{[w_1] \longrightarrow [w_1'] \quad \ldots \quad [w_n] \longrightarrow [w_n']}{[t(\overline{w}/\overline{x})] \longrightarrow [t'(\overline{w'}/\overline{x})]}$$

The last is a combination of replacement (rule application) and congruence.

Equational logic (modulo a set of axioms E) is obtained from rewriting logic by adding the following rule:

7. **Symmetry.**

$$\frac{[t_1] \longrightarrow [t_2]}{[t_2] \longrightarrow [t_1]}$$

Rewriting logic very naturally has an operational interpretation. Rewriting logic is a logic of "becoming". Assertions of the form $[t_1] \longrightarrow [t_2]$ can be read "t_1 becomes t_2" or "t_1 possibly may become t_2".

22 Concurrent Objects in Maude

An *object* is represented as a term

$$\langle O : C \mid a_1 : v_1, \ldots, a_n : v_n \rangle$$

where O is the object's name or identifier, C is its class, the a_i's are the names of the object's *attributes*, and the v_i's are their corresponding *values*.

The distributed state of a concurrent object-oriented system is a multiset (associativity and commutativity as structural axioms) of objects and messages called a *configuration*. Modules in Maude that have a configuration operator (the key multiset operator) are called system modules.

22.1 Library Example

Object-oriented Maude is syntactic sugar and implicit structure for system modules. (This example is related to one in [28].)

```
omod LIBRARY is
    subsort OId < HolderId .
    op NONE : -> HolderId .
    class Book .
    att holder : Book -> HolderId .
    msgs check-out, return : OId OId -> Msg .
    msg held-by : OId OId OId -> Msg .
    msg transfer_from_to_ :
        OId OId OId -> Msg .
    vars X Y : OId .
    var B : OId .
    rl check-out(B,X) < B : Book | holder: NONE > =>
        < B : Book | holder: X > .
```

```
  rl check-out(B,X) < B : Book | holder: Y > =>
      held-by(Y,X)
      < B : Book | holder: Y > if Y =/= NONE .
  rl return(B,X) < B : Book | holder: X > =>
      < B : Book | holder: NONE > .
  rl transfer B from X to Y
      < B : Book | holder: X > =>
      < B : Book | holder: Y > .
endom
```

Both data and program are described in small pieces. This can be an advantage for implementations. Programmers can describe programs at a higher level by using parameterized programming.

This omod has an associated system module as its translation. This translation uses the following basic module.

```
mod CONFIGURATION is
  protecting ID . *** provides OId
  sorts Configuration Object Msg .
  subsorts Object Msg < Configuration .
  op __ : Configuration Configuration -> Configuration
                            [assoc comm id: Ø] .
endm
```

Here is the translation of LIBRARY.

```
omod LIBRARY# is
  extending CONFIGURATION .   ***[added]
  subsort Book < Object .
  sort HolderId .
  subsort OId < HolderId .
  op NONE : -> HolderId .
  sort Book . ***[modified]
  op < _ : Book | holder: _ > : OId OId -> Book .
  op check-out, return : OId HolderId -> Msg .
      ***[modified]
  op held-by : OId OId OId -> Msg . ***[modified]
  op transfer_from_to_ : OId OId OId -> Msg .
      ***[modified]
  op holder._replyto_ : OId OId -> Msg . ***[added]
  op to_holder._is_ : OId OId -> Msg . ***[added]
  vars X Y : HolderId .
  var B : OId .
  rl check-out(B,X) < B : Book | holder: NONE > =>
      < B : Book | holder: X > .
  rl check-out(B,X) < B : Book | holder: Y > =>
      held-by(Y,X)
      < B : Book | holder: Y > if Y =/= NONE .
```

```
  rl return(B,X) < B : Book | holder: X > =>
     < B : Book | holder: NONE > .
  rl transfer B from X to Y
     < B : Book | holder: X > =>
     < B : Book | holder: Y > .
  rl (holder. B replyto X)
     < B : Book | holder: Y) =>
     (to X holder. B is Y) < B : Book | holder: Y) .
     ***[added]
endom
```

Here is an illustration of concurrent rewriting in this library example. In one concurrent rewriting step

```
check-out(Topoi,Tim) < Topoi : Book | holder: NONE >
return(Beautiful-Maui,Mary)
< Beautiful-Maui : Book | holder: Mary >
check-out(Algebra,Jim) < Algebra : Book | holder: NONE >
check-out(Algebra,Bob)
```

  becomes

```
< Topoi : Book | holder: Tim >
< Beautiful-Maui : Book | holder: NONE >
< Algebra : Book | holder: Jim >
check-out(Algebra,Bob)
```

In the next step we might get held-by(Bob,Algebra,Jim). The nature of multiset rewriting guarantees that a book will be checked out to just one person at a time.

22.2   In-order Message Passing

Next we consider a somewhat more system-oriented example: the goal is to generate an in-order communication mechanism from one where ordering is not preserved. In fact, this is a very basic example for Maude, since the basic semantics of Maude allows out-of-order delivery of messages. It is assumed that execution of the rules is "fair." In fact, this will also guarantee the correct behavior when messages might be duplicated, but cannot deal with the case that messages are lost. (For a more sophisticated version that can handle the loss of messages see [28].)

```
oth CLASS is
  class Cl .
endoth
```

```
omod IN-ORDER-PROTOCOL[ELT :: TRIV, S :: CLASS, R :: CLASS] is
  protecting NAT .

  sort Contents .
```

```
     subsorts Elt < Contents .
     op empty : -> Contents .
     msg to:_[_]_ : OId Nat Elt -> Msg . *** data to receiver

     class Sender .
     subclass Sender < Cl.S .
     att rec : Sender -> OId . *** the receiver
     att sendnumber : Sender -> Nat . *** sender sequence number
     att sendmsg : Sender -> Contents . *** empty or current data

     vars S R : OId .
     var N : Nat .
     var E : Elt .
     var C : Contents .

     rl send :
         < S : Sender | rec: R, sendnumber: N, sendmsg: E > =>
         < S : Sender | rec: R, sendnumber: (N + 1), sendmsg: empty >
         (to: R [N] E) .
         *** Note that E cannot be empty

     class Receiver .
     subclass Receiver < Cl.R .
     att sender : Receiver -> OId . *** the sender
     att recnumber : Receiver -> Nat . *** receiver sequence number
     att recmsg : Receiver -> Contents . *** empty or current data

     rl receive :
        (to: R [N] E)
        < R : Receiver | sender: S, recnumber: N, recmsg: empty > =>
        < R : Receiver | sender: S, recnumber: (N + 1), recmsg: E > .
endom
```

We can in fact execute a transliteration of this example in OBJ, and this was done in order to test it.

Without actually using this module, but using the basic idea of sequence numbered streams of messages, we can easily do some additional system module examples (based on SYSTEM).

Boundedly unfair merge, with bound "bound":

```
op merger : EId Nat EId Nat EId Nat -> System .
op _,[_]_ : EId Nat Data -> System .
var A B C : EId .
var M N L : Nat .
crl (A,[M]D) merger(A,M,B,N,C,L) =>
    merger(A,(M + 1),B,N,C,(L + 1)) (C,[L]D)
    if M < N + bound .
crl (B,[N]D) merger(A,M,B,N,C,L) =>
```

```
merger(A,M,B,(N + 1),C,(L + 1)) (C,[L]D)
if N < M + bound .
```

Input messages come from A or B and are forwarded to C. The positions in the input messages sequences, M and N, are not allowed to get too far apart.

A prime number sieve can be described this way.

```
op sv : Nat -> EId .
op gen : EId Nat Nat -> System .
op sieve : EId Nat Nat EId Nat -> System .
op final : EId Nat EId -> System .
op _,[_]_ : EId Nat Nat -> System .
op prime : EId Nat Nat -> System .
var I J N P K : Nat .
var E F : EId .
rl gen(E,I,K) => gen(E,I + 1,K + 1) (E,[I]K) .
rl (sv(N),[I]P) final(sv(N),I,E) =>
   sieve(sv(N),I + 1,P,sv(N + 1),1)
   final(sv(N + 1),1,E) prime(E,N,P) .
rl (E,[I]K) sieve(E,I,P,F,J) =>
   if (K rem P) == 0 then
     sieve(E,I + 1,P,F,J)
   else
     sieve(E,I + 1,P,F,J + 1) (F,[J]K)
   fi .
```

The system component gen(E,I,K) generates a stream of messages consisting of the natural numbers from K upwards. The system component sieve(E,I,P,F,J) is a sieve element that receives a stream of natural numbers and forwards to F all that are not multiples of the prime P. The system component final(F,I,E) is the final element in the sieve. It simply forwards each input, which must be a prime, to E, creates a new sieve element using the new prime, and reconnects itself as the final element of the sieve.

From the starting configuration:

```
gen(sv(1),1,2) final(sv(1),1,T)
```

The above definitions will result in the creation of prime($T, i, prime_i$), where $prime_i$ is the i-th prime, for $1 \leq i$. One of the reachable configurations is:

```
prime(T,1,2) prime(T,2,3) prime(T,3,5) prime(T,4,7)
gen(sv(1),7,8)
sieve(sv(1),7,2,sv(2),4) sieve(sv(2),4,3,sv(3),3)
sieve(sv(3),3,5,sv(4),2) sieve(sv(4),2,7,sv(5),1)
final(sv(5),1,T)
```

The sequence of sieves are a dynamically created pipeline of processes. Note that gen(sv(1),1,2) is a process run amok; it will run forever and can always be busy.

It is easy to do many other examples in this style, e.g., the Hamming problem.

23 System Interfaces in Maude

It is relatively easy to define abstract interfaces to such system elements as file systems, devices, networks, and even special-purpose processors, at the system level of Maude. (One may, of course, be tempted to simplify things a bit.) Here is a sketch of very simple interface to a file system:

```
open(EID,TAG,SERVER,FILE) FS(...) =>
    handle(EID,TAG,HANDLE) FS(...)
close(EID,TAG,SERVER,HANDLE) FS(...) =>
    done(EID,TAG,HANDLE) FS(...)
read(EID,TAG,SERVER,HANDLE,START,END) FS(...) =>
    data(EID,TAG,HANDLE,DATA) FS(...)
write(EID,TAG,SERVER,HANDLE,START,DATA) FS(...) =>
    done(EID,TAG) FS(...)


Error response: error(EID,TAG)
```

The details of the file system, FS, are omitted. An EID is supposed to be unique to each active agent. The TAG allows an agent to identify the thread of control associated with a given result in the case that the agent is performing many file system operations at once. Thus, done(EID,TAG) will be unambiguous. Errors can, of course, take place and will be signaled with a different return message.

Interfaces, such as the one sketched above, can also be used to incorporate programs, processes, or servers written in other languages.

24 Summary

One of the key goals of this paper has been to present a simplified version of the order-sorted equational deductive system of [15]. In order to develop formal systems used for reasoning and operational semantics it seems desirable to explore connections between many-sorted or order-sorted algebra and (unsorted) logic. To fully explore the connections between the sorted and unsorted cases we can examine relations between reducts of an algebra, formed as restrictions of the algebra to a subsignature, and by the use of homomorphisms relative to a subsignature (given by set of sorts) of a given algebra. These kinds of relationships will assist in the process of going from unsorted algebras to sorted algebras. Understanding these relationships will clarify the connections between sorted and unsorted systems and support the refinement of unsorted descriptions into sorted descriptions. Order-sorted algebra provides an ideal framework in which to explore the relationships between the sorted and unsorted (or single-sorted) cases.

OBJ3 and Maude are languages that combine:

- A very clear and simple mathematical semantics.
- A very simple logical formalization.
- The expressiveness of order-sorted algebra.
- Powerful program composition facilities.

– Implicit concurrent rewriting.

Maude especially seems to cover a very wide range of program semantics, computational models, and programming styles.

Acknowledgements

I would like to gratefully thank Pat Lincoln and Narciso Martí-Oliet for very valuable discussions related to the content of this paper. I would like to thank Peter Thiemann for many valuable comments and suggestions on this paper. Kokichi Futatsugi has my greatest admiration and gratitude for his work on OBJ which, in fact, has inspired this work. I would especially like to thank José Meseguer for his invaluable advice, gracious assistance, and very valuable discussion.

References

1. Hitoshi Aida, Joseph Goguen, and José Meseguer. Compiling concurrent rewriting onto the rewrite rule machine. In S. Kaplan and M. Okada, editors, *Conditional and Typed Rewriting Systems, Montreal, Canada, June 1990*, pages 320–332. Springer LNCS 516, 1991.
2. Hitoshi Aida, Sany Leinwand, and José Meseguer. Architectural design of the rewrite rule machine ensemble. To appear in J. Delgado-Frias and W.R. More, editors, *Proc. Workshop on VLSI for Artificial Intelligence and Neural Networks*, Oxford, September 1990; also, Tech. Report SRI-CSL-90-17, December 1990.
3. K. Mani Chandy and Jayadev Misra. *Parallel Program Design: A Foundation.* Addison-Wesley, 1988.
4. A. A. Faustini and R. Jagannathan. Indexical lucid. In R. Jagannathan, editor, *Proceedings, 4th International Symposium on Lucid and Intensional Programming*, pages 19–34. SRI International, 1991.
5. J.A. Goguen, S. Leinwand, J. Meseguer, and T. Winkler. The rewrite rule machine, 1988. Technical Report PRG-76, Oxford University, Programming Research Group, 1989.
6. J.A. Goguen, T. Winkler, J. Meseguer, K. Futatsugi, and J.-P. Jouannaud. Introducing OBJ. Technical report, Computer Science Lab, SRI International, 1992. To appear in J.A. Goguen, D. Coleman and R. Gallimore, editors, *Applications of Algebraic Specification Using OBJ*, Cambridge University Press.
7. Joseph Goguen. Higher-order functions considered unnecessary for higher-order programming. In David Turner, editor, *Proc., University of Texas Year of Programming, Institute on Declarative Programming.* Addison-Wesley, 1988. Preliminary version as SRI Tech. Rep. SRI-CSL-88-1, January 1988.
8. Joseph Goguen. OBJ as a theorem prover with application to hardware verification. In P.S. Subramanyam and G. Birtwistle, editors, *Current Trends in Hardware Verification and Automated Theorem Proving*, pages 218–267. Springer-Verlag, 1989.
9. Joseph Goguen. Principles of parameterized programming. In Ted Biggerstaff and Alan Perlis, editors, *Software Reusability, Volume I: Concepts and Models*, pages 159–225. Addison-Wesley, 1989.
10. Joseph Goguen and José Meseguer. Equality, types, modules and generics for logic programming. In S.-A. Tärnlund, editor, *Proc. 2nd Intl. Logic Programming Conf., Uppsala, July 2-6, 1984*, pages 115–125. Uppsala University, 1984.

11. Joseph Goguen and José Meseguer. Completeness of many-sorted equational logic. *Houston Journal of Mathematics*, 11(3):307–334, 1985. Preliminary versions have appeared in: *SIGPLAN Notices*, July 1981, Volume 16, Number 7, pages 24-37; SRI Computer Science Lab Technical Report CSL-135, May 1982; and Report CSLI-84-15, Center for the Study of Language and Information, Stanford University, September 1984.

12. Joseph Goguen and José Meseguer. Eqlog: Equality, types, and generic modules for logic programming. In Douglas DeGroot and Gary Lindstrom, editors, *Logic Programming: Functions, Relations and Equations*, pages 295–363. Prentice-Hall, 1986. An earlier version appears in *Journal of Logic Programming*, Volume 1, Number 2, pages 179-210, September 1984.

13. Joseph Goguen and José Meseguer. Models and equality for logical programming. In Hartmut Ehrig, Giorgio Levi, Robert Kowalski, and Ugo Montanari, editors, *Proceedings, 1987 TAPSOFT*, pages 1–22. Springer-Verlag, 1987. Lecture Notes in Computer Science, Volume 250; extended version to appear in *J. Logic Programming*.

14. Joseph Goguen and José Meseguer. Software for the rewrite rule machine. In *Proceedings of the International Conference on Fifth Generation Computer Systems, Tokyo, Japan*, pages 628–637. ICOT, 1988.

15. Joseph Goguen and José Meseguer. Order-sorted algebra I: Equational deduction for multiple inheritance, overloading, exceptions and partial operations. Technical Report SRI-CSL-89-10, SRI International, Computer Science Lab, July 1989.

16. Joseph Goguen, Andrew Stevens, Keith Hobley, and Hendrik Hilberdink. 2OBJ, a meta-logical framework based on equational logic, 1991. To appear, *Philosophical Transactions of the Royal Society*.

17. Joseph Goguen, James Thatcher, and Eric Wagner. An initial algebra approach to the specification, correctness and implementation of abstract data types. Technical Report RC 6487, IBM T. J. Watson Research Center, October 1976. Appears in *Current Trends in Programming Methodology, IV*, Raymond Yeh, Ed., Prentice-Hall, 1978, pages 80-149.

18. Joseph Goguen, James Thatcher, Eric Wagner, and Jesse Wright. Initial algebra semantics and continuous algebras. *Journal of the Association for Computing Machinery*, 24(1):68–95, January 1977.

19. Joseph Goguen and Timothy Winkler. Introducing OBJ3. Technical Report SRI-CSL-88-9, SRI International, Computer Science Lab, August 1988. Revised version to appear with additional authors José Meseguer, Kokichi Futatsugi and Jean-Pierre Jouannaud, in *Applications of Algebraic Specification using OBJ*, edited by Joseph Goguen, Derek Coleman and Robin Gallimore, Cambridge, 1992.

20. Joseph A. Goguen. Proving and rewriting. In Proc. Conf. on Algebraic and Logic Programming, Nancy, Springer LNCS 463, 1990.

21. Leon Henkin. On mathematical induction. *American Mathematical Monthly*, 67:323–338, 1960.

22. Leon Henkin. The logic of equality. *American Mathematical Monthly*, 84:597–612, 1977.

23. Jieh Hsiang. *Refutational Theorem Proving using Term Rewriting Systems*. PhD thesis, Univeristy of Illinois at Champaign-Urbana, 1981.

24. Claude Kirchner, Hélène Kirchner, and José Meseguer. Operational semantics of OBJ3. In T. Lepistö and A. Salomaa, editors, *Proceedings, 15th Intl. Coll. on Automata, Languages and Programming, Tampere, Finland, July 11-15, 1988*, pages 287–301. Springer-Verlag, Lecture Notes in Computer Science No. 317, 1988.

25. S. Leinwand, J.A. Goguen, and T. Winkler. Cell and ensemble architecture for the rewrite rule machine. In *Proceedings of the International Conference on Fifth Genera-*

tion Computer Systems, Tokyo, Japan, pages 869–878. ICOT, 1988.

26. V. Manca, A. Salibra, and G. Scollo. Equational type logic. *Theoretical Computer Science*, 77:131–159, 1990.

27. Alain J. Martin. The limitations to delay-insensitivity in asynchronous circuits. In William J. Dally, editor, *Advanced research in VLSI: proceedings of the sixth MIT conference*, pages 263–278. MIT Press, 1990.

28. J. Meseguer and T. Winkler. Parallel Programming in Maude. In J.-P Banâtre and D. Le Mètayer, editors, *Research Directions in High-level Parallel Programming Languages*, pages 253–293. Springer-Verlag, 1992. Lecture Notes in Computer Science, Volume 574; also, SRI Technical Report SRI-CSL-91-08, November 1991.

29. José Meseguer. A logical theory of concurrent objects. In *ECOOP-OOPSLA'90 Conference on Object-Oriented Programming, Ottawa, Canada, October 1990*, pages 101–115. ACM, 1990.

30. José Meseguer. Conditional rewriting logic as a unified model of concurrency. *Theoretical Computer Science*, 96(1):73–155, 1992. also, SRI International, Computer Science Laboratory technical report SRI-CSL-91-05, February, 1991.

31. José Meseguer and Joseph Goguen. Initiality, induction and computability. In Maurice Nivat and John Reynolds, editors, *Algebraic Methods in Semantics*, pages 459–541. Cambridge University Press, 1985.

32. J. Donald Monk. *Mathematical Logic*. Springer-Verlag, 1976.

33. Werner Nutt, Pierre Réty, and Gert Smolka. Basic narrowing revisited. *J. Symbolic Computation*, 7:295–317, 1989.

34. Axel Poigné. Once more on order-sorted algebras. In A. Tarlecki, editor, *Proceedings, Mathematical Foundations of Computer Science*, pages 397–405. Springer-Verlag, 1991. Lecture Notes in Computer Science, Volume 520.

35. Gert Smolka, Werner Nutt, Joseph Goguen, and José Meseguer. Order-sorted equational computation. In Maurice Nivat and Hassan Aït-Kaci, editors, *Resolution of Equations in Algebraic Structures*, volume 2, pages 297–367. Academic Press, 1989.

36. Raymond M. Smullyan. *First-Order Logic*. Springer-Verlag, 1968. Ergebnisse der Mathematik und ihrer Grenzgebiete, Band 43.

37. W. W. Wadge and E. A. Ashcroft. *Lucid, the Dataflow Programming Language*. Academic Press, 1985.

38. Timothy Winkler, Sany Leinwand, and Joseph Goguen. Simulation of concurrent term rewriting. In Steven Kartashev and Svetlana Kartashev, editors, *Proceedings, Second International Supercomputing Conference, Volume I*, pages 199–208. International Supercomputing Institute, Inc., 1987.

Supporting the Attribute Grammar Programming Paradigm in a Lazy Functional Programming Language

R. A. Frost and S. Karamatos

School of Computer Science, University of Windsor, Ontario, Canada N9B 3P4

Abstract. Attribute grammars were introduced in the late 60's. In the 70's they found use in compiler work, a use that is continuing to grow. A more recent development is that of the 'attribute grammar programming paradigm'. A number of environments have been built to support this paradigm. W/AGE is one such environment. It consists of several functions that extend the standard environment of the pure lazy functional programming language Miranda. W/AGE has been used in the construction of various types of program including natural language interpreters, database front-ends, file-processors, theorem provers, and VLSI specification transformers.

1 Introduction

Over the last several years researchers at the University of Windsor have been involved in various projects involving the investigation of new theories and techniques in the areas of database management, VLSI design and natural language processing. These investigations have all required the construction of special purpose language processers. The design and construction of these processors required a good deal of effort. It became evident that substantial resources were being used for this purpose and that this was having a deleterious effect on our research. We decided, therefore, to construct a programming environment that would enable researchers to produce language processors with minimum effort. The environment that we have built is called the Windsor Attribute Grammar Programming Environment W/AGE. This environment allows language processors to be constructed as executable specifications of the syntax and semantics of the languages required.

W/AGE was initially used in the construction of natural language interpreters, database front-ends, and specification transformers. Subsequently, it was recognised that other types of program could be profitably constructed as language processors and W/AGE has since been used to build theorem provers, tree procesors and even file processors.

The purpose of this paper is twofold: firstly to introduce readers to W/AGE and secondly to illustrate the wide applicability of the technique of constructing programs as executable attribute grammars.

2 Attribute Grammars

Attribute grammars were introduced by Knuth in 1968[10] as a means for specifying the semantics of context free languages. Since then, attribute grammars have been used extensively in compiler work.

3.1 Notation Used in this Section

The following Miranda notation is used in this section:

    x == y introduces x as an acronym for the type name y.

    x :: y declares x to be of type y.

Where the set **type** is defined inductively as follows:

num, char, bool ∈ **type**.
If t ∈ **type**   then so is [t],
                    ie. the type of lists whose elements are of type t.
If t1..tn ∈ **type**   then so is (t1,..,tn),
                    ie. the type of tuples with elements of type t1 to tn.
If t1, t2 ∈ **type**   then so is t1 -> t2,
                    ie. the type of functions with arguments in t1 and results in t2.
If y and z ∈ **type** then so is x
                    where x ::= C1 y |..| Cn z and C1 to Cn are
                    user defined *constructors*.

3.2 The Type of Terminals

The type **terminal** is predefined in W/AGE as follows:

```
terminal ::= INT_TERM            [char]  | REAL_TERM            [char]
           | IDENTIFIER_TERM      [char]  | SPECIAL_SYMBOL_TERM [char]
           | RESERVED_WORD_TERM   [char]  | UNCATEGORISED_TERM  [char]
           | ANY_TERM             [char]
```

In addition to defining the type **terminal** this introduces seven new identifiers:
INT_TERM, REAL_TERM, etc. as constructors for terminals. Note that each of these
constructors is of type [char] -> **terminal**. We introduce an acronym for this
type:

```
terminal_constructor == [char] -> terminal
```

3.3 The Type of the Lexical Scanning Function tokenise

```
tokenise :: string_to_be_processed -> [terminal]
            where
            string_to_be_processed == [char]
```

3.4 The Type of Attributes

The type **attribute** is defined by W/AGE users according to the application. For
example:

```
attribute ::= LITERAL_VAL terminal | VAL num
            | OP num -> num -> num | PAIR num [char]
```

Note that constructors can have any number of fields. For example, the constructor
PAIR has two fields. A field may be any Miranda type as defined in 3.1. To analyse
an attribute, we use Miranda pattern matching as illustrated later.

With a little change in perspective, many other types of program can be constructed as executable attribute grammars. We refer to such programs as *passages*. This style of programming was first suggested by Knuth in 1971[12], and subsequently developed by Katayama[9], Hehner and Silverberg[7], Simon[16], Johnsson[8], Panayiotopoulos, Papakonstantinou, and Stamatopoulos[14], Forbig and Lammel[3], Frost[4][5] and others. Several environments have been built to support the attribute grammar programming paradigm, *eg.* PLASTIC [16], SAGE[15], AGILP[14], FLR[3], and W/AGE.

W/AGE consists of a several functions that extend the standard environment of the pure lazy programming language Miranda[17]. The resulting combination of programming paradigms facilitates software development in several ways:

1. Programs are completely declarative, extremely modular, and are largely variable free. This simplifies reasoning about them for the purpose of verification, complexity analysis, transformation, etc.
2. The inductive program structure that results from the combined paradigm lends itself well to the technique of deriving 'programs from proofs'.
3. The structure of a program that is built in this way is closely related to the structure of the data that it is to process. This results in code that is easier to maintain and easier to modify.

This paper will introduce readers to the attribute grammar programming paradigm, show how this paradigm can be readily supported in a pure functional programming language, and briefly discuss some of the advantages that derive from this approach.

3 An Overview of W/AGE

We use the notation of the Miranda[1] functional programming language throughout the paper. We give brief explanation of this notation where appropriate. Readers who are unfamiliar with functional notation are referred to Turner[17].

W/AGE currently consists of five components:

A lexical scanning function:	`tokenize`
A set of functions for applying interpreters:	`{apply_recogniser,` `apply_interpreter}`
A set of functions for building basic interpreters:	`{literal, interpreted,` `uninterpreted}`
A set of interpreter combinators:	`{$orelse, $excl_orelse,` `structure}`
A function for creating attribute lists:	`meaning_of`

---

[1] Miranda is a trademark of Research Software Ltd.

3.5 The Type of Interpreters

We have chosen to define the type **interpreter** as follows:

```
interpreter == [([attribute], [terminal])]  ->  [([attribute], [terminal])]
```

That is, an interpreter is a function that maps a list of pairs of type (**[attribute]**, **[terminal]**) to a list of pairs of the same type, such that:

1. Each pair **(as,ts)** that is in the list that is input to an interpreter is such that the list of attributes **as** may be regarded as a context in which the list of terminals **ts** is to be interpreted.
2. Each pair **(as',ts')** in the list that is output by an interpreter is related to exactly one pair **(as,ts)** in the input list such that: (i) **as'** is a subset of the union of **as** and the interpretation of some initial segment of **ts**, and (ii) **ts'** is the list of remaining uninterpreted terminals in **ts**.
3. Interpreters return lists of pairs because each pair in the input may have more than one interpretation.
4. Interpreters are regarded as accepting lists of pairs for a number of reasons, such as it simplifies composition.

3.6 The Type of Functions for Top-level Application of Interpreters

The types of the functions **apply_recognizer** and **apply_interpreter** are as follows:

```
apply_recognizer :: interpreter -> string_to_be_recognized -> message
                 where    string_to_be_recognized == [char]
                          message                  == [char]

apply_interpreter :: interpreter -> string_to_be_interpreted -> [attribute]
                  where  string_to_be_interpreted == [char]
```

Throughout the paper, we use the notation **x => y** to indicate that output **y** is returned by the Miranda interpreter when **x** is evaluated. For example:

```
apply_interpreter number "12"  =>  [VAL 12]
```

3.7 The Type of Functions for Building Basic Interpreters

There are three functions in W/AGE that may be used to build interpreters for single terminals:

```
literal       :: terminal_constructor    -> interpreter
uninterpreted :: terminal                 -> interpreter
interpreted   :: (terminal, [attribute]) -> interpreter
```

3.8   The Type of Interpreter Combinators

There are three functions in W/AGE that may be used to define new interpreters
in terms of other interpreters:

```
$orelse       :: interpreter -> interpreter -> interpreter
$excl_orelse :: interpreter -> interpreter -> interpreter
structure     :: list_of_tagged_interpreters -> list_of_attribute_rules
                     -> interpreter
  where
  list_of_tagged_interpreters == [(tag, interpreter)]
  list_of_attribute_rules     == [(rule_num, att_id, att_function, [att_id])]
                                  where
                                  att_id == ((tag, att_direction), att_type)
                                  att_function == [attribute] -> attribute
                                  att_type      == [char]
                                  att_direction ::= UP | DOWN
```

3.9   The Type of the meaning_of Function

The type of the function **meaning_of** is as follows:

```
meaning_of :: interpreter -> string_to_be_interpreted -> [attribute]
              where string_to_be_interpreted == [char]
```

In the next few sections, we give examples of various passages that have been built
using W/AGE. All of the passages are complete and can be executed as Miranda
programs just as they appear provided that the W/AGE script is available in the
Miranda 'local' directory.

4   Lexical Analysis

Passage #1 illustrates how the function **tokenise** can be tailored for particular
applications through definition of the reserved words and special symbols.

```
|| Passage #1:
%insert <local/header_for_WAGE_VERSION_1_RELEASE_0.m>
||--------------------------------------------------------------------------
attribute     :: type
||--------------------------------------------------------------------------
reserved_words = ["begin", "end", "one"]
special_symbols = ['(', ')', '-', '/', '+', '-']
||--------------------------------------------------------------------------
|| EXAMPLE APPLICATION
|| tokenise "123 begin sas ddd a234 b3.2 3.4 (ff%"  =>
|| [INT_TERM "123", RESERVED_WORD_TERM "begin",IDENTIFIER_TERM "sas",
|| IDENTIFIER_TERM "ddd",IDENTIFIER_TERM "a234", UNCATEGORISED_TERM "b3.2",
|| REAL_TERM  "3.4", SPECIAL_SYMBOL_TERM "(", UNCATEGORISED_TERM "ff%"]
```

5 Constructing Basic Recognisers and Interpreters

Passage #2 illustrates how the W/AGE functions **literal**, **interpreted**, and **un-interpreted** can be used to build basic recognisers and interpreters, *ie.* recognisers and interpreters for single terminals.

```
|| Passage #2:
%insert <local/header_for_WAGE_VERSION_1_RELEASE_0.m>

||-----------------------------------------------------------------------

attribute     ::= LITERAL_VAL terminal   | VAL    num
                | ENGLISH [char]          | GENDER char

||-----------------------------------------------------------------------

reserved_words = ["begin", "one"]

special_symbols = []

||-----------------------------------------------------------------------

int      = literal       INT_TERM
anything = literal       ANY_TERM
key      = uninterpreted (IDENTIFIER_TERM any)
begin    = uninterpreted (RESERVED_WORD_TERM "begin")
one      = interpreted   (RESERVED_WORD_TERM "one", [VAL 1])
salaire  = interpreted   (IDENTIFIER_TERM "salaire",[ENGLISH "wage",
                          GENDER 'm'])
||-----------------------------------------------------------------------
|| EXAMPLE APPLICATIONS
||
|| apply_recognizer  int        "64"    => input is recognized successfully
|| apply_interpreter int        "106"   => [LITERAL_VAL (INT_TERM "106")]
|| apply_interpreter anything    "3.21" => [LITERAL_VAL (REAL_TERM "3.21")]
|| apply_interpreter key         "sas"  => []
|| apply_interpreter begin       "begin" => []
|| apply_interpreter begin       "sas"  => input not recognized
|| apply_interpreter one         "one"  => [VAL 1]
|| apply_interpreter salaire "salaire"  => [ENGLISH "wage", GENDER 'm']
```

6 Constructing Non-Basic Recognizers

Passage #3 illustrates how non-basic recognizers can be built by 'gluing' other recognisers together using the combinators $orelse and $structure.

```
|| Passage #3: A recogniser of arithmetic expressions
%insert <local/header_for_WAGE_VERSION_1_RELEASE_0.m>
||-----------------------------------------------------------------------
attribute      ::= LITERAL_VAL terminal
||-----------------------------------------------------------------------
reserved_words = []
special_symbols = ['(', ')', '*', '/', '+', '-']
||-----------------------------------------------------------------------
op                      = uninterpreted  (SPECIAL_SYMBOL_TERM "+")
                          $orelse
                          uninterpreted  (SPECIAL_SYMBOL_TERM "*")
                          $orelse
                          uninterpreted  (SPECIAL_SYMBOL_TERM "/")

negate                  = uninterpreted  (SPECIAL_SYMBOL_TERM "-")
opbr                    = uninterpreted  (SPECIAL_SYMBOL_TERM "(")
clbr                    = uninterpreted  (SPECIAL_SYMBOL_TERM ")")
uninterpreted_number    = uninterpreted  (INT_TERM any)
                          $orelse
                          uninterpreted  (REAL_TERM any)
||-----------------------------------------------------------------------
rec_expr = structure (s1 uninterpreted_number)
           []
           $orelse
           structure (s1 opbr ++ s2 rec_expr ++ s3 op ++ s4 rec_expr ++ s5 clbr)
           []
           $orelse
           structure (s1 negate ++ s2 rec_expr)
           []
||-----------------------------------------------------------------------
|| EXAMPLE APPLICATIONS
|| apply_recognizer op    "+"              => input is recognized successfully
|| apply_recognizer rec_expr "(12 + 45)" => input is recognized successfully
|| apply_recognizer rec_expr "12 + 5"    => end of input not recognized
||                               ie [SPECIAL_SYMBOL_TERM "+",INT_TERM "5"]
|| apply_recognizer rec_expr "(12 + 45) + 3"
||                               => end of input not recognized
||                               ie [SPECIAL_SYMBOL_TERM "+",INT_TERM "3"]
|| apply_recognizer rec_expr "((one + 45) + 3)"=> input not recognized
```

Notice that the lists of attribute rules in the definition of **rec_expr** are empty. This is because **rec_expr** is a recognizer and not an interpreter, therefore no attributes are to be computed.

7   Constructing Non-Basic Interpreters

Passage #4 illustrates how non-basic interpreters can be built by 'gluing' other interpreters together using the combinators **orelse** and **structure**.

```
|| Passage #4: An arithmetic evaluator
%insert <local/header_for_WAGE_VERSION_1_RELEASE_0.m>
%insert <local/number_intepeter_for_WAGE_VERSION_1_RELEASE_0.m>
||-------------------------------------------------------------------------
attribute ::= LITERAL_VAL terminal | VAL num  | OP num -> num -> num
||-------------------------------------------------------------------------
reserved_words = []
special_symbols = ['(', ')', '*', '/', '+', '-']
||-------------------------------------------------------------------------

op    = interpreted   (SPECIAL_SYMBOL_TERM "+", [OP (+)])
          $orelse
          interpreted   (SPECIAL_SYMBOL_TERM "*", [OP (*)])
          $orelse
          interpreted   (SPECIAL_SYMBOL_TERM "/", [OP (/)])
negop = uninterpreted (SPECIAL_SYMBOL_TERM "-")
opbr  = uninterpreted (SPECIAL_SYMBOL_TERM "(")
clbr  = uninterpreted (SPECIAL_SYMBOL_TERM ")")

||-------------------------------------------------------------------------

expr = structure (s1 number)
       [c_rule 1 (VAL $u lhs) EQ            (VAL $u s1)]
       $orelse
       structure (s1 opbr ++ s2 expr ++ s3 op ++ s4 expr ++ s5 clbr)
       [a_rule 2 (VAL $u lhs) EQ  apply_op [VAL $u s2,OP $u s3,VAL $u s4]]
       $orelse
       structure (s1 negop ++ s2 expr)
       [a_rule 3 (VAL $u lhs) EQ    negate [VAL $u s2]]

apply_op       [VAL x, OP y, VAL z]       = VAL (y x z)
negate         [VAL x]                    = VAL (-x)

||-------------------------------------------------------------------------
|| EXAMPLE APPLICATIONS
||
|| apply_interpreter expr "(12 + 4.5)"              => [VAL 16.5]
|| apply_interpreter expr "((4 + (4 * 3))/-2)"      => [VAL (-8.0)]
```

The syntax used for the attribute rules is a variant of standard BNF notation. The following provides an informal semantics for our notation:

v $u s	stands for "the synthesized **v** attribute passed *up* by the structure **s**"
v $d s	stands for "the inherited **v** attribute passed *down* to the structure **s**"
c_rule n x EQ y	indicates that the attribute **x** is to be *copied* from the attribute **y**
a_rule n x EQ f l	indicates that the attribute **x** is obtained by *applying* the attribute function **f** to the list of attributes **l**
i_rule n x EQ y	indicates that the attribute **x** is to be *initialised* to the value **y**

8   Examples of Passages

8.1   A Simple Data Processing Example

Passage #5 calculates the average number of entries per record in a file in which each record consists of an integer key followed by one or more alphanumeric string entries. Records are separated by semicolons, fields by commas, and end-of-file is signified by a period.

```
|| Passage #5: Calculating average number of entries of records in a file
%insert <local/header_for_WAGE_VERSION_1_RELEASE_0.m>
||-----------------------------------------------------------------------
attribute ::= LITERAL_VAL terminal | NUM_RECS num | NUM_ENTS num
              | AV_ENTS num
||-----------------------------------------------------------------------
reserved_words = []
special_symbols = ['.', ';', ',']
||-----------------------------------------------------------------------
key       = uninterpreted (INT_TERM any)
entry     = uninterpreted (IDENTIFIER_TERM any)
period    = uninterpreted (SPECIAL_SYMBOL_TERM ".")
semicolon = uninterpreted (SPECIAL_SYMBOL_TERM ";")
comma     = uninterpreted (SPECIAL_SYMBOL_TERM ",")
||-----------------------------------------------------------------------
file   = structure (s1 records ++ s2 period)
         [c_rule 1 (NUM_ENTS $u lhs) EQ (NUM_ENTS $u s1),
          c_rule 2 (NUM_RECS $u lhs) EQ (NUM_RECS $u s1),
          a_rule 3 (AV_ENTS  $u lhs) EQ   calc_average[NUM_ENTS $u lhs,
                                                       NUM_RECS $u lhs]]

records = structure (s1 record ++ s2 semicolon ++ s3 records)
         [a_rule 4 (NUM_RECS $u lhs) EQ add_one_to_num_recs[NUM_RECS $u s3],
          a_rule 5 (NUM_ENTS $u lhs) EQ       add_num_ents [NUM_ENTS $u s1,
                                                           NUM_ENTS $u s3]]

         $excl_orelse
         structure (s1 record)
         [i_rule 6 (NUM_RECS $u lhs) EQ (NUM_RECS 1),
          c_rule 7 (NUM_ENTS $u lhs) EQ (NUM_ENTS $u s1)]
```

287

```
record  = structure (s1 key ++ s2 comma ++ s3 entries)
          [c_rule 8 (NUM_ENTS $u lhs) EQ  (NUM_ENTS $u s3)]

entries = structure (s1 entry ++ s2 comma ++ s3 entries)
          [a_rule 9 (NUM_ENTS $u lhs) EQ add_one_to_num_ents[NUM_ENTS $u s3]]
          $excl_orelse
          structure (s1 entry)
          [i_rule 10 (NUM_ENTS $u lhs)  TO (NUM_ENTS 1)]

calc_average        [NUM_ENTS x, NUM_RECS y] = AV_ENTS  (x/y)
add_one_to_num_recs [NUM_RECS x]             = NUM_RECS (1 + x)
add_num_ents        [NUM_ENTS x, NUM_ENTS y] = NUM_ENTS (x + y)
add_one_to_num_ents [NUM_ENTS x]             = NUM_ENTS (1 + x)
||-------------------------------------------------------------------
|| EXAMPLE APPLICATION
|| apply_interpreter  file "1234,hesselink,hensen,jones;2345,
||                            bauer,partsch,sharir,morgan;5678,heath,lin."
||              => [NUM_ENTS 9,NUM_RECS 3,AV_ENTS 3.0]
```

8.2 A Passage to Reverse a List

Passage #6 reverses its input. The combinator **$excl_orelse** avoids unnecessary backtracking and ensures that the list is parsed in only one way (*ie.* the parse should include all elements). Reverse here has $O(n^2)$ complexity, owing to the fact that the append operator ++ is $O(m)$ where m is the length of its left operand. It is relatively straightforward to transform this passage to one with $O(n)$ complexity.

```
|| Passage #6: Reversing a list
%insert <local/header_for_WAGE_VERSION_1_RELEASE_0.m>
||-------------------------------------------------------------------------
attribute   ::= LITERAL_VAL terminal | RES list_of_terminals
||-------------------------------------------------------------------------
reserved_words = []
special_symbols = []
||-------------------------------------------------------------------------
elem  = literal ANY_TERM

list = structure (s1 elem ++ s2 list)
        [a_rule 1 (RES $u lhs) EQ stick_on_end [LITERAL_VAL $u s1,
                                                RES $u s2]]
        $excl_orelse
        structure (s1 elem)
        [a_rule 2 (RES $u lhs) EQ make_list    [LITERAL_VAL $u s1]]

make_list    [LITERAL_VAL x]        = RES [x]
stick_on_end [LITERAL_VAL x, RES y] = RES (y ++ [x])
||-------------------------------------------------------------------------
|| EXAMPLE APPLICATION
|| apply_interpreter list "5 six 7 8"
||    => [RES [INT_TERM "8",INT_TERM "7",IDENTIFIER_TERM "six",
||              INT_TERM "5"]]
```

8.3 A Passage to Calculate Fibonacci Numbers

Passage #7 recognizes numbers and returns their Fibonacci values. It would appear that the attribute grammar paradigm is not appropriate for this problem. However, an alternative passage for calculating fibonacci numbers in linear time can be obtained by transforming this passage as discussed in Frost[5].

```
|| Passage #7: Calculating Fibonacci numbers
%insert <local/header_for_WAGE_VERSION_1_RELEASE_0.m>
%insert <local/number_interpreter_for_WAGE_VERSION_1_RELEASE_0.m>
||-------------------------------------------------------------------------
attribute   ::= LITERAL_VAL terminal | FIB num | VAL num
||-------------------------------------------------------------------------
reserved_words  = []
special_symbols = []
||-------------------------------------------------------------------------
fibnumb = structure (s1 number)
          [a_rule 1 (FIB $u lhs) EQ calc_fib [VAL $u s1]]

calc_fib [VAL  x] = FIB (fib  x)
                    where  fib n = 1                        , n <= 2
                           fib n = fib (n - 1) + fib (n - 2), otherwise
||-------------------------------------------------------------------------
|| EXAMPLE APPLICATION
||                    apply_interpreter fibnumb "5" => [FIB 5]
```

9 Use of the Function meaning_of

The function **meaning_of** allows lists of attributes to be defined in terms of the application of an interpreter to an expression. The following passage illustrates such use.

Notice that in this passage, the proper noun "john" does not denote an entity. Rather, it denotes a function defined in terms of the entity denoted by the number 1. This idea is loosely based on a notion from Richard Montague's approach to the interpretation of natural language.

```
|| Passage #8:
%insert <local/header_for_WAGE_VERSION_1_RELEASE_0.m>
||-------------------------------------------------------------------------
attribute ::= ANS bool             | DETVAL   ([entity] -> [entity] -> bool)
            | CNOUNVAL [entity] | T_PHRASEVAL ([entity] -> bool)
            | INTRVBVAL [entity] | LITERAL_VAL terminal
entity == num
||-------------------------------------------------------------------------
reserved_words   = []
special_symbols  = []
||-------------------------------------------------------------------------
cnoun  = interpreted          (IDENTIFIER_TERM "person",[CNOUNVAL [1..10]])
         $orelse interpreted  (IDENTIFIER_TERM "woman", [CNOUNVAL [6..10]])
intrvb = interpreted          (IDENTIFIER_TERM "runs",  [INTRVBVAL [2..7]])
```

```
det     = interpreted        (IDENTIFIER_TERM "every", [DETVAL    f_every])
          $orelse interpreted (IDENTIFIER_TERM "a",     [DETVAL    f_a])
pnoun   = interpreted        (IDENTIFIER_TERM "john",  [T_PHRASEVAL f_john])
          $orelse interpreted (IDENTIFIER_TERM "someone",
                                         meaning_of detphrase "a person")
||------------------------------------------------------------------------


sent       = structure (s1 termphrase ++ s2 intrvb)
               [a_rule 1 (ANS $u lhs) EQ   apply1[T_PHRASEVAL $u s1,
                                                  INTRVBVAL $u s2]]
termphrase = structure (s1  pnoun)
               [c_rule 2 (T_PHRASEVAL $u lhs) EQ (T_PHRASEVAL $u s1)]
               $orelse
               structure (s1 detphrase)
               [c_rule 3 (T_PHRASEVAL $u lhs) EQ (T_PHRASEVAL $u s1)]

detphrase = structure (s1 det ++ s2 cnoun)
               [a_rule 4 (T_PHRASEVAL $u lhs)  EQ   apply2[ DETVAL $u s1,
                                                           CNOUNVAL $u s2]]
apply1   [T_PHRASEVAL f, INTRVBVAL s] = ANS (f s)
apply2   [DETVAL f, CNOUNVAL s]       = T_PHRASEVAL (f s)

f_every x  y   = (x --- y) = []
f_a     x  y   = (intersect  x  y) ~= []
                 where intersect  x  y = (x --- (x --- y))

f_john   x      = member x  1
||------------------------------------------------------------------------
|| EXAMPLE APPLICATIONS
||
|| apply_interpreter sent "every woman runs" => [ANS False]
|| apply_interpreter sent "someone runs"     => [ANS True]
|| apply_interpreter sent "john runs"        => [ANS False]
```

10   Left Recursion

W/AGE has recently been extended to accommodate attribute grammars with left recursive productions. The technique that allows left recursive productions to co-exist with top down parsing is described in Frost [6].

11   Interpreting Ambiguous Input

In no example given so far, have we applied an interpreter directly to an input. We have always used the higher order function **apply_interpreter**. This approach is only appropriate when at most one parse of the input is anticipated. However, there are applications in which it is necessary to return multiple interpretations, one for each way in which the input can be parsed. Recall, from section 3.5, that the type **interpreter** is defined as follows:

```
interpreter == [(([attribute], [terminal]))] -> [(([attribute], [terminal]))]
```

This means that if an interpreter is applied directly to a 'suitably packaged' input string, several results may be returned. For example, suppose that the interpreter list of passage#6 had been defined using $orelse in place of $excl_orelse. Direct application of the modified interpreter to any input with more than one terminal, will give multiple results. For example:

```
list [([], tokenise "5 six 7 8")]
=>
  [(([RES [INT_TERM "8",INT_TERM "7",IDENTIFIER_TERM "six",INT_TERM "5"]],[]),
   ([RES [INT_TERM "7",IDENTIFIER_TERM "six",INT_TERM "5"]],[INT_TERM "8"]),
   ([RES [IDENTIFIER_TERM "six",INT_TERM "5"]],[INT_TERM "7",INT_TERM "8"]),
   ([RES [INT_TERM "5"]],[IDENTIFIER_TERM "six",INT_TERM "7",INT_TERM "8"])]
```

Each of these four results is related to a parse of the input as a list. The first result corresponds to a parse of the whole of the input as a list. The last result corresponds to a parse of the input as a singleton list followed by three uninterpreted terminals.

The ability to handle ambiguous input is useful in many applications including natural language processing. However, it is also a fundamental property of the W/AGE system. All interpreters are implemented as top down, fully backtracking, syntax directed, lazy evaluators. There is one major advantage of this: passages are modular. A different, but somewhat related, approach to lazy recursive descent parsing for modular language implementation is described in Koskimies[13]. Many of the arguments given there apply to the parsing strategy that we have adopted in W/AGE.

12 An Example of a Complex Passage

Passage #9 converts expressions of propositional logic to clausal form. If the expression is valid, the interpreter wff returns the empty clause set, and may therefore be regarded as a decision procedure for propositional logic.

```
|| Passage #9:
%insert <local/header_for_WAGE_VERSION_1_RELEASE_0.m>
||-------------------------------------------------------------------------
attribute  ::= LITERAL_VAL terminal | CCFSET [disjclause] | CONTEXT [char]
disjclause ::= DISJCL [[char]]
||-------------------------------------------------------------------------
reserved_words = ["and", "or", "implies"]
special_symbols = ['.', '(', ')', '-']
||-------------------------------------------------------------------------
|| opbr, clbr, period and negate as defined in earlier passages
orr      = uninterpreted (RESERVED_WORD_TERM "or")
aand     = uninterpreted (RESERVED_WORD_TERM "and")
implies  = uninterpreted (RESERVED_WORD_TERM "implies")
var      = literal IDENTIFIER_TERM
||-------------------------------------------------------------------------
wff      =  structure   (s1 expr   ++   s2 period)
              [c_rule 1 (CCFSET $u lhs)    EQ    (CCFSET $u s1),
               i_rule 2 (CONTEXT $d s1)    EQ    (CONTEXT "pos") ]
```

```
expr        =  structure (s1 var)
                [a_rule 3  (CCFSET $u lhs)   EQ  make_ccfset
                                                  [LITERAL_VAL $u s1,
                                                   CONTEXT $d lhs]]

            $orelse
            structure (s1 opbr ++ s2 (conjunction $orelse  disjunction
                                        $orelse  implication) ++ s3 clbr)
                [c_rule 4   (CCFSET $u lhs) EQ    (CCFSET $u s2),
                 c_rule 5   (CONTEXT $d s2) EQ    (CONTEXT $d lhs)]
            $orelse  structure   (s1 negate   ++   s2 expr)
                [c_rule 6   (CCFSET $u lhs) EQ    (CCFSET $u s2),
                 a_rule 7   (CONTEXT $d s2) EQ  opposite [CONTEXT $d lhs]]

conjunction =  structure (s1 expr    ++    s2 aand    ++    s3 conjunction)
                [a_rule 8   (CCFSET $u lhs) EQ  context_and
                                                  [CONTEXT $d lhs,
                                                   CCFSET $u s1,
                                                   CCFSET $u s3],
                 c_rule 9  (CONTEXT $d s1)  EQ    (CONTEXT $d lhs),
                 c_rule 10 (CONTEXT $d s3)  EQ    (CONTEXT $d lhs)]
            $orelse structure    (s1 expr)
                [c_rule 11 (CCFSET  $u lhs) EQ    (CCFSET  $u s1),
                 c_rule 12 (CONTEXT $d s1)  EQ    (CONTEXT $d lhs)]

disjunction =  structure (s1 expr    ++    s2 orr    ++    s3 disjunction)
                [a_rule 13 (CCFSET $u lhs) EQ  context_or
                                                  [CONTEXT $d lhs,
                                                   CCFSET  $u s1,
                                                   CCFSET  $u s3],
                 c_rule 14 (CONTEXT $d s1)  EQ    (CONTEXT $d lhs),
                 c_rule 15 (CONTEXT $d s3)  EQ    (CONTEXT $d lhs)]
            $orelse structure    (s1 expr)
                [c_rule 16 (CCFSET  $u lhs) EQ    (CCFSET  $u s1),
                 c_rule 17 (CONTEXT $d s1)  EQ    (CONTEXT $d lhs)]
```

The function **sort** is required in the definition of **unite_clauses** in order that **mkset** performs as required.

```
implication =  structure  (s1 expr    ++    s2 implies    ++    s3 expr)
                [a_rule 18 (CCFSET  $u lhs) EQ   context_or
                                                  [CONTEXT $d lhs,
                                                   CCFSET  $u s1,
                                                   CCFSET  $u s3],
                 a_rule 19 (CONTEXT $d s1)  EQ    opposite
                                                  [CONTEXT $d lhs],
                 c_rule 20 (CONTEXT $d s3)  EQ    (CONTEXT $d lhs)]
||------------------------------------------------------------------------
```

```
context_and [CONTEXT "pos", x, y] = ccf_and x y
context_and [CONTEXT "neg", x, y] = ccf_or  x y

context_or  [CONTEXT "pos", x, y] = ccf_or  x y
context_or  [CONTEXT "neg", x, y] = ccf_and x y

opposite    [CONTEXT "pos"]        = CONTEXT "neg"
opposite    [CONTEXT "neg"]        = CONTEXT "pos"

make_ccfset [LITERAL_VAL (IDENTIFIER_TERM v),CONTEXT "pos"]
                            = CCFSET[DISJCL [v]]
make_ccfset [LITERAL_VAL (IDENTIFIER_TERM v),CONTEXT "neg"]
                            = CCFSET[DISJCL [negate_lit v]]
||-------------------------------------------------------------------------
|| FUNCTIONS FROM CLAUSE FORM LOGIC
|| The function ccf_and forms the clausal conjunction of two conjunctive
|| clause sets

ccf_and (CCFSET dcs) (CCFSET dcs') = CCFSET (mkset (dcs ++ dcs'))

|| The function ccf_or forms the clausal disjunction of two clause sets
|| tautologous clauses are removed when produced. mkset makes a set
|| from a list

ccf_or (CCFSET dcs) (CCFSET dcs') =
    CCFSET (mkset [newclause | ( DISJCL c1 )- dcs; ( DISJCL c2 )- dcs';]
            newclause - [DISJCL (unite_clauses c1 c2)]; not_taut newclause])

not_taut (DISJCL c) =  [l1 | l1 - c; l2 - c; l1 = (negate_lit l2)] = []

negate_lit ('-' : x) = x
negate_lit      y     = ('-' : y)

unite_clauses c1 c2 = (sort . mkset) (c1 ++ c2)
||-------------------------------------------------------------------------
|| EXAMPLE APPLICATIONS
||
|| apply_interpreter wff "---((p implies q) implies (r implies (s and t)))."
||
||  => [[CCFSET [DISJCL ["-r","p","s"], DISJCL ["-r","p","t"],
||              DISJCL ["-q","-r","s"],DISJCL ["-q","-r","t"]]]]
||
|| apply_interpreter wff "((john_has_money and (john_has_money implies
||                          john_could_pay)) implies john_could_pay)."
||  => [CCFSET []]
|| The second example shows how a valid formula is converted to an empty
|| clause form set.Therefore, to see if a formula F is a theorem of a set of
|| formulas S, you simply apply convert to "(S implies F).". If an empty
|| clause set is returned, then F is a theorem of S, otherwise it is not.
```

13 Concluding Comments

13.1 Experimentation with W/AGE

During the last twelve months, W/AGE has been used extensively in a number of application areas. In particular, it has been used in the construction of a sophisticated experimental natural language interface to a database, in the transformation component of a VLSI designer's assistant, and as a teaching aid in a third year 'Grammars and Translators' course. The natural language interface that was constructed using W/AGE can handle both syntactic and semantic ambiguity and provides 'dialogue' answers to user's questions. The interpreter was built as part of an investigation into the feasibility of extending Montague's compositional semantics to accommodate semantic ambiguity. The VLSI project involved the construction of (i) programs to translate mathematical specifications of finite impulse response filters to executable specifications of systolic circuits based on a standard VLSI cell, and (ii) programs to translate the executable specifications to EDIF netlist representations suitable for input to a VLSI layout package. The viability of the approach was confirmed by testing the translators on a real FIR filter design comprising 3 moduli and 64 coefficients. A detailed description of this work is given in Master's theses available from the University of Windsor. W/AGE has also been used in the construction of various other programs in a separate study into the use of the attribute grammar paradigm in constructive (transformational) programming[4].

13.2 Findings

We have found that the integration of the lazy functional programming and attribute grammar paradigms is straightforward. Construction of a programming environment to support this combined paradigm was helped significantly by the declarative nature of the host language Miranda. Some of the more difficult aspects of the W/AGE were constructed using the method of 'programs from proofs' in which induction is used 'in reverse' to design a complex recursive function definition. We chose to implement the syntax analyzers as top-down fully backtracking parsers. It has been argued elsewhere[13] that such parsers are more modular than those built using other strategies. The lazy evaluation order allows attribute evaluation to be closely related to syntax analysis carried out by top-down fully backtracking parsers without incurring the redundant computation that would occur if a strict evaluation order were used.

Our experimentation with W/AGE has convinced us that application of the new combined programming paradigm results in extremely clear and modular executable specifications of language interpreters. However, the actual construction of the interpreters was hindered by the poor debugging facilities of both W/AGE and Miranda. In particular, the absence of trace facilities in W/AGE was a very noticeable shortcoming. Adding a trace facility to W/AGE is not a simple task. The fact that pure functional programming languages do not allow any kind of side effects requires one to adopt a completely different approach to the provision of de-bugging facilities. We hope to overcome this problem in the next few months.

During our investigation, we found that it would have been useful if W/AGE could have supported the construction of language transformers (*ie.* syntactic rewriters) as well as language interpreters. If these transformers are of the same type as interpreters, the two could be combined in various ways enabling wider experimentation in language processing. Such extension of both the programming paradigm and the environment to support it is the subject of our current work.

W/AGE is currently undergoing experimental use at a number of university sites. Potential users can obtain a copy of the W/AGE code through request to `richard@cs.uwindsor.ca`.

The authors acknowledge the assistance of N.S.E.R.C. of Canada, and of Subir Bandyopadhyay and Walid Saba of the School of Computer Science at the University of Windsor.

References

1. B. Edupuganty and B. R. Bryant, Two-level grammar as a functional programming language. The Computer Journal, 32 (1), 36 - 44 (1989).
2. M. S. Feather, A survey and Classification of some program transformation approaches and techniques. In L. G. L. T. Meertens (Editor) Program Specification and Transformation. IFIP 1987. Elsevier Science Publishers B. V. North-Holland.
3. P. Forbig, and U. Lammel, Knowledge based program generation using attribute grammars, in: Grabowski, J (ed), Proc. of the Berliner Informatik Tage bit '89. Akademie d. Wissenschaften der DDR, iir–Report, 114–123, (1989).
4. R. A. Frost, Constructing Programs in a Calculus of Interpreters, Proceedings of the 1990 ACM International Workshop on Formal Methods in Software Development, (1990).
5. R. A. Frost, Constructing programs as executable attribute grammars, The Computer Journal (to appear in the August 1992 issue).
6. R. A Frost, Guarded Attribute Grammars: Top Down Parsing and Left Recursive Productions, ACM SIGPLAN 27(6), 72-76, (1992).
7. E. C. R. Hehner and B. A. Silverberg, Programming with grammars: an exercise in methodology-directed language design. The Computer Journal 26 (3), 227 - 281 (1983).
8. T. Johnsson, Attribute grammars as a functional programming paradigm. Springer Lecture Notes 274, 155 - 173 (1987).
9. T. Katayama, HFP : A hierarchical and functional programming based on attribute grammars, Proceedings of 5th International Conf. on Software Engineering, 343–353, (1981).
10. D. E. Knuth, Semantics of context-free languages. Math. Syst. Theory. 2(2), 127–145, (1968).
11. D. E. Knuth, Semantics of context-free languages: correction. Math. Syst. Theory. 5, 95–96, (1971).
12. D. E. Knuth, Examples of Formal Semantics. Springer Lecture Notes in Computer Science Vol 188, 212–235 (1971).
13. K. Koskimies, Lazy recursive descent parsing for modular language implementation. Software Practice and Experience, 20 (8), 749–772 (1990).
14. T. Panayiotopoulos, G. Papakonstantinou, and G. Stamatopoulos, Attribute grammars and logic programming, Agnew. Inf. No 5 (1988) 227.
15. Y. Shinoda and T. Katayama, Attribute grammar based programming and its environment, Proceedings of 21st Hawaii International Conference on System Sciences, Kailu-Kona, Hawaii, 612–620, (1988).

16. E. Simon, A new programming methodology using attribute grammars, Acta Cybernetica, 7 (4), 425–436 (1986).
17. D. Turner, A non-strict functional language with polymorphic types. Proc. IFIP Int. Conf. on Functional Programming Languages and Computer Architecture, Nancy, France. Springer Lecture Notes in Computer Science 201. (1985).

Specification and Simulation with ExSpect[*]

K.M. van Hee[1,2], P.M.P. Rambags[1], P.A.C. Verkoulen[1]

[1] Department of Mathematics and Computing Science, Eindhoven University of
Technology, P.O. Box 513, NL-5600 MB Eindhoven, the Netherlands
e-mail: verkoulen@win.tue.nl
[2] Department of Mathematics and Computer Science, University of Waterloo, Canada

Abstract. In the ExSpect framework, a system is modelled as a network
consisting of two kinds of nodes, called places and processors, through which
objects move as in Petri nets. Processors are generalizations of transitions,
while the objects in the ExSpect model are generalizations of tokens in classical Petri nets. Objects may have a complex data structure: for instance an
object may represent a whole database. In addition to the data structure,
an object has a time-stamp. The time-stamp denotes the earliest possible
moment an object can be 'consumed' by a processor. The firing rules of processors (describing which processors may execute at what moment and with
which result) are based on both the values and the time-stamps of the objects. The processors do not have any memory, so their effect only depends
on the consumed objects. As we will see in this paper, the combination of
modelling facilities for describing both static and dynamic aspects of systems
makes that ExSpect is an integrated framework for modelling complex systems. Moreover, it has some strong simulation facilities.
The CASE tool of ExSpect allows to simulate the behaviour of specified systems. The CASE tool has been operational since 1989. It has been used by
several organizations for various applications such as modelling and analyzing logistic systems and distributed computer systems.
In the paper we sketch the foundations of the ExSpect framework: an object model and and a net model (which is in fact a high-level Petri Net
model). Further we give an overview of the language of ExSpect which is a
combination of graphical languages to define net and object structures and a
functional language to specify the behaviour of processors. Finally we give an
example to illustrate the preceding theoretical descriptions. In an appendix,
we give the formal definitions of our framework.

1 Introduction

In systems engineering and in software engineering in particular, the *analyst* or
designer needs a *framework* in which he can describe all the relevant *views* of a
system in a *coherent* way. Before we consider these views in more detail, we have
to tell what kind of systems we have in mind: computerized information systems.
These systems are *monitoring* and *controlling* some other system, often called the
target system. In order to fulfill their tasks, these computerized information systems

---

[*] This research is supported by a grant from NFI (Netherlands Facility for Informatics) as
part of project NF-74 'ISDF' (Information System Description Formalisms).

interact with human beings and devices belonging to the target system. In order to specify an information system, it is useful to consider the information system together with the target system as one *total system*, although we may describe only part of it in detail.

In the development process of such an information system, the analyst defines *requirements* based on a model of the target system. The requirements themselves are often formulated in terms of an abstract model of the information system. An abstract model of the system to be build together with a set of requirements form the *specification* of the computer system. The designer also makes models of the computer systems; however, his models are closer to the realization and therefore less abstract. His final model is used as a *blue print* for the information system. Note that in software engineering we only construct a software layer on top of hardware and some other software instead of developing a complete computer system from scratch.

From a *holistic* point of view, the target system and its information system can be considered as one *closed system*, i.e. a system that does not communicate with an environment (because the environment is already part of the system). Such a system can be modelled as a *transition system* (without labels). This means that the system has a *state space* and that there exists a binary relation over this state space, called the *transition relation*. The system is always in some state; at discrete points in time it makes a transition to a new state. Such a transition is *instantaneous* and is only allowed if the pair consisting of the old and new state belongs to the transition relation. The fact that there is a transition relation instead of a transition function, shows that we allow systems to be *non-deterministic*. Although holistic models of systems are attractive because of their simplicity, they have some drawbacks. First of all, the assumption that transitions are instantaneous (which allows more than one at a time), is not realistic. However, this can be considered as an approximation of reality in the sense that we assume a system is in its old state until the transition to a new state is completed. And since we consider systems only at discrete points in time, this assumption is not a limitation. Another drawback of holistic models is that, using these models, it is very difficult to specify complex systems in a easy and structured way. Instead of abandoning the holistic models of systems, which is a common way of describing systems in many disciplines, we introduce another view, called the *reductionistic* view and we integrate both views.

The reductionistic view adds new concepts to our framework: *objects* and *networks*, or *nets*. According to this view a system is modelled as a directed network with two kinds of nodes, called *places* and *processors*, 'through' which objects 'flow'. Places are only connected to processors and processors to places, so the networks are bipartite graphs. There may be several arcs going from one place to a processor or vice versa. The arcs are called *connectors*. Often, we call them input or output connectors depending on their roles. Objects always reside at some place. Processors may 'consume' objects from the places they are connected to by an input connector and 'produce' tokens for places to which they are connected by an output connector. There are rules according to which processors perform their consumption/production activity, which is called *firing*. These rules are called *firing rules*. Processors perform these activities instantaneously and several processors may fire at the same time. Objects have a unique *identity, (possibly) complex data structures* and a *time-stamp*.

Objects have a type and places may only contain objects of one type. In the next sections we elaborate the structure of objects and the firing rules further. Here, we will establish the link between reductionistic models and holistic ones.

A *distribution* of objects over places in a reductionistic model corresponds to a *state* in a holistic model. Each *firing* of one or more processors in a reductionistic model corresponds to a *transition* in the equivalent holistic model. So the distributions of objects determine the states and the network of places and processors determines the transition relation. We will use a reductionistic model to define the holistic one; we never define a holistic model of a system directly.

In the ExSpect model, time is based on the time-stamps of the objects. In fact, every state of a system, i.e. every distribution of objects over the places, determines a unique moment in time: the earliest moment at which some processor will be able to fire. This moment is called the *transition time* of the state. It is a property of our framework that all objects consumed by a processor have a time-stamp that is smaller than or equal to the transition time, which expresses that objects can only be consumed at a time greater than or equal to their time-stamp. Note that there is the notion of a *global time* in our framework, although there is no *clock*. Since every state has a unique transition time, all sequences of successive states that obey the law of the transition relation determine a sequence of transition times. It can be proven that these time sequences are non-decreasing which means that time is 'not going back'. In fact the holistic models are *timed* transition systems, i.e. there is a transition relation over the product space of time axis and state space.

The ExSpect framework allows for specifying systems in which the following views can be represented in a coherent way:

- *database view*: provided by the objects;
- *process view*: provided by the network of processors and places;
- *behavioural view*: provided by the timed transition system.

In ExSpect, it is possible to represent the process view in a *hierarchical* way similar to *data-flow diagrams*. In the ExSpect language, a sub-network may be aggregated to one node. Since these nodes do not have the same semantics as processors, we give them a different notation in the language. ExSpect uses *graphical* languages to specify the network structure and the structure of objects. Furthermore, there is a *typed functional language* that is used to define the firing rules of processors.
Expressive comfort is one of the main issues in the ongoing research of ExSpect. With expressive comfort of a framework we mean the facilities to express the details of a system in an easy, concise and understandable way. (There are no objective measures for expressive comfort). Another aspect of the ongoing research is methods for *analysis* of models. Since our models are generalizations of classical Petri nets, the *invariance analysis* methods of Petri nets (Jensen 1981) are applicable to models in our framework, after some modifications. These modifications essentially boil down to deleting the values and time-stamps of the objects of our models, which reduces them to 'valueless tokens'. Another kind of analysis concerns the *analysis of time*. Here we are interested in bounds on the time certain sets of states are reached. In (Aalst 1991), these methods are described. Both type of analysis methods are partial in the sense that they 'throw away' details of our models, in the first case value and time-stamps and in the second case only the values. Other analysis methods

are still under study. Since models in the ExSpect framework can always be considered as (timed) transition systems, many questions of a reductionistic model can be answered by analyzing the underlying holistic model.

Although there are many frameworks to make models for one of these views, frameworks that provide an integrated view are rare. ExSpect is one of the first (Hee et al. 1989). We do not give a survey of other frameworks here, but we will shortly mention some important ones. Our framework is closely related to the framework of Coloured Petri Nets, CPN for short (Jensen 1991). Note that CPN is in fact a generalization of *predicate-transition nets* (Genrich 1987). The main differences are the additional data modelling facilities in the ExSpect framework, the fact that CPN has only finite colour sets and the time concept, which does not (yet) occur in CPN. In the CPN framework, the functional language ML (Harper 1986) is used where we developed a typed functional language ourselves; this has the advantage that it is better integrated with the graphical languages to define object types and nets.

An example of another important framework is LOTOS (Brinksma 1988), which is based on process algebra (Bergstra and Klop 1986) and algebraic specifications (Ehrig and Mahr 1985,1990). This framework is based on totally different principles, however in some experiments we found that the expressive comfort is comparable. LOTOS is rather weak in its data modelling capabilities and (not yet) equipped for time analysis (Brinksma 1988). In (Aalst and Waltmans 1991, Hee et al. 1989, Hee and Verkoulen 1991, Verkoulen 1989, Broek and Verkoulen 1992), more details of the language, the tool and applications of ExSpect are given.

We conclude this introduction with an overview of the remainder of this paper. In the next section, we consider the object model of ExSpect in more detail and in Sect.3 we discuss the net model and its semantics in terms of timed transition systems. In Sect.4 we sketch the language. In Sect.5, an example is given and in Sect.6 we formulate some conclusions and indicate some future research.

2 The ExSpect Object Model

In many frameworks that can be compared to ExSpect, the description of the state space of the system is not very well supported. E.g., it is very difficult to describe real-time systems with a large and complex state space in formalisms like process algebra (Bergstra and Klop 1986), CCS (Milner 1980) or Petri Nets (Reisig 1985). In the Petri Net world, this has triggered the development of higher level net models like Coloured Petri Nets (Jensen 1991) and ExSpect (Hee et al. 1989). In such models, the state space of the net is modelled using a functional language with a type system. E.g., in CPN the functional language ML is used.

In the ExSpect framework, we have used also a typed functional language (cf. Sect.4) until now for defining the state space of a system under consideration. However, though data modelling with a textual type system has a great expressive power, there is a problem: it lacks overview and (graphical) support. So although you can specify anything you want, it can be difficult to make and understand your specification and explain it to other people.

For this reason, we have integrated an object model within our existing specification framework. In brief, this object model³ consists of a binary data model (Shipman 1981) with some object oriented concepts, like object identity and inheritance. We will deal with this model shortly in this section. We will give only informal explanations about the object model. Formal definitions are given in the appendix. More details can be found in (Hee and Verkoulen 1991, Houben and Verkoulen 1991).

2.1 Informal Description of the ExSpect Object Model

When we are modelling a system, one of the aspects we have to describe is its *state space*, i.e. the set of all possible states the system may "reach". Such a state is characterized by (the properties of) the *objects* the system contains. Some of these objects are concrete such as materials and patients, others are abstract such as orders, treatments and data. All objects belong to an *(object) type*, which is a set of objects with the same characteristics. In our model, we will distinguish two kinds of object types: *simple* types and *container* types, of which the "inhabitants" are called *simple objects* and *containers* respectively. Container objects are built of simple objects and so there are in fact two levels. We will first consider the simple level.

Each simple object represents one entity in the real world. The properties of a simple object can be divided into three parts: an *administrative* part, a *reference* part and a *value* part.

The administrative part records the identity of the object and the simple type to which it belongs.

The reference part registers the *relationships* of a simple object with other simple objects. Each of these relationships has a name (a label): the *reference name*. The reference part of a simple object contains for each reference name a set of object identities. References can be considered to represent the *knowledge* an entity has about other entities. Notice that this does not only represent the fact that entities have some knowledge about each other, but also which entity *"possesses this knowledge"*. We will come back to this aspect below. Finally, the value part is a tuple which has an arbitrarily structured value for each attribute of the type the object belongs to.

In a *simple schema* the types to which the simple objects in a system belong, and the relationships between those types are described. We define all this in a schema using a labeled directed graph. The *nodes* of the graph are the simple types and the attributes. Relationships between types are represented by *labeled directed arcs*. An arc from a type D to a type R denotes that to each object in D belongs a *set* of objects in R. So the functions are multi-valued, as in (Shipman 1981). Moreover, the model supports *structural inheritance*, as *is-a* edges between simple types are allowed. Finally, attributes are connected to the type they belong to by an unlabeled and undirected edge.

In our schemas, we will denote simple types by boxes and attributes by circles. References (relationships) between simple types are represented by labeled directed arcs. The arrow heads on the arcs denote which simple object "knows" and which simple object "is known".

---

³ We will refer to it by "the ExSpect object model" in this paper.

301

An *instance* of a type is a set of objects belonging to that type. We will provide facilities for formulating constraints which allow only certain instances of a type. Typical constraints for the library case we will study in this paper are: the amount of books lent by a member may not exceed the number of 10 at any moment in time. Also the due date (ddate) of a lending must fall after its lending date (ldate).

Now consider Fig.1 which shows a simple schema represented graphically. This schema represents the state space structure of a simple library system. The library possesses books, which have a title. Two books may have the same title. Furthermore, the members of the library are registered. They may lend books and they may reserve titles (when making a reservation, they are only interested in a title, not in one specific copy). Constraints are not taken into account in this example.

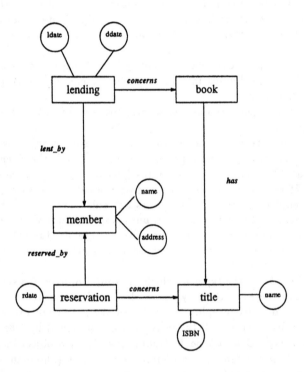

Fig. 1. Library simple schema.

We will now say something about *containers*. In conventional database theory, complex objects are often regarded as representations of *views* on the database. But when systems are to be modelled where the *flow* of entities and distribution aspects are important, complex objects play another role. Examples of such applications are distributed databases, message handling systems, logistic systems, etc. In this kind of applications, it is necessary to be able to describe that some piece of information is (only) available during a certain period of time at a certain spot in the system. For example, we want to be able to treat a reservation, the book which is reserved and the person reserving it as one (complex) object.

A *container type* consists of a set of simple types; one specific simple type in this set is called the *root type* or simply the *root*. We require that each container type is *connected*, i.e. every simple type in a container type can be reached from the root via a directed path of references to simple types that belong to the container type. Container types may overlap. Finally, container types may have names that occur also as names of simple types.

We will illustrate the definition of container types using the same library example in Fig.2. The container types are represented by curves around their composing simple types and a dashed line leading from this curve to the root; in the example the names of the "singleton" container types consisting of only one simple type have been omitted: we assume that they have the same name as their (only) simple type[4].

In Fig.2, we see a schema which contains three "singleton container types" containing only one simple type, and two non-atomic container types: request and lending. The figure speaks for itself.

The elements of a container type are called *container objects*. The properties of some container object c consist of three parts: an administrative part, the identity of its root simple object and a set of contained simple objects.

The administrative part contains the *unique identity* of the container, the *location* where the container resides, the *availability time* of the object at that location (the time the object becomes available) and the *type* to which the container belongs.

We will now extend our notion of a schema in order to account also for container types: an *object schema* defines both simple and container types. The simple types are defined as described before. The container types are defined by assigning a root simple type and a set of contained simple types to each container type. As we will see below, we impose some constraints upon a schema. One of them is the constraint that each simple type has to be part of at least one container type.

A container object must have a structure in accordance with the structure of the container type it belongs to. This means that a container object c can only contain simple objects that belong to the contained simple types of the container type of c. At each moment, a system is in a certain *state* (which is a set of containers satisfying some constraints). In such a state, all simple objects must be part of some container.

In our paradigm, the objects that move through a network will be container objects. So only containers can exist on their own, simple objects only exist within containers. Simple objects inherit the location and the time-stamp from the container they are part of.

We have seen that *schemas* and *instances* are distinguished. A schema describes the structure of objects belonging to types in the schema; an instance of a type is a set of objects belonging to that type. A set of instances of all types in a schema is called a *state*. All objects in a state have to have different identities. We have de-

---

[4] These graphical conventions are only used in paper presentations. In the tool, a graphical language will be used that slightly differs from these conventions (Broek and Verkoulen 1992).

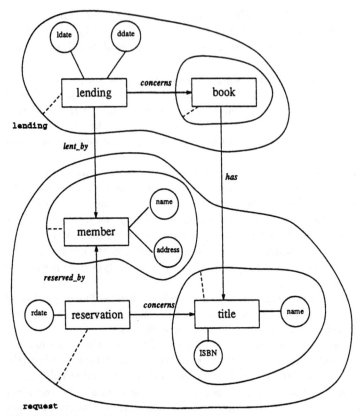

Fig. 2. Container object types.

scribed a method for assigning object identities in (Hee and Verkoulen 1991) which preserves this uniqueness property. This method does not destroy the local state change paradigm of Petri Net models, nor does it require extra memory cells in a specification (which would not be natural). A summary of this identification assignment scheme can be found in the appendix.

3 The ExSpect Net Model

In the previous section, we presented a method to *describe* data in a structured fashion. In this section, we build a network layer on top of the ExSpect object model in order to *manipulate* the data, too.

A network in the ExSpect Net model consists of two kinds of components, viz. *processors* and *places*, corresponding to *transitions* and *places* in Petri Net terminology. Processors are *active* components, interconnected via places. They communicate by sending *tokens* over the places. Tokens are *passive* objects which have a, possibly complex, *value* and a *time stamp*. The time stamp denotes the *availability time*, i.e. the token may not be consumed before that time.

Tokens will be container objects, so they have much structure, e.g., as compared to

CPNs. The structure will be described by the ExSpect object model. With container objects, object-oriented ideas have been incorporated, too.

A processor has at least one input place and zero or more output places. When a processor has enough tokens for each input place and no processor is able to perform an action at an earlier time, it may *execute (fire)* by removing the input tokens and producing tokens for its output places. Actually, the functionality of a processor is defined by a *mathematical function* and hence, inherent *deterministic*. The number of output tokens and their values depend only on the values of the consumed tokens. *Nondeterminism* is accounted for in two ways: cases of conflict, i.e. situations where different processors share the same input place, are resolved in a nondeterministic way and in case of more tokens in an input place than strictly necessary, input tokens are selected nondeterministically.

A distribution of tokens over channels is called a *state*. We use the ExSpect object model to model the state space of an ExSpect net. As a consequence, ExSpect nets will be considered in the context of some valid object universe $\mathcal{U}$ (cf. Def.5).

The ExSpect language allows for defining *processors, places, stores* and *systems*. A *store* is a special place which always contains exactly one token; if a processor consumes the store token and does not put another one into the place, the old one will automatically remain. A *system* is an aggregate of processors, places, stores and systems. A system may contain subsystems, which permits hierarchically structured specifications. Stores and systems are not part of the formal model, they are considered as *sugar* in the language. In (Verkoulen 1989) a formal semantics of ExSpect is given without introducing stores and systems.

It is not convenient to study the (mathematical) definition of the ExSpect object model and next, define the operations upon these objects in terms of this mathematical definition. We have developed an Algebra (SCA) (Houben and Verkoulen 1991) for manipulating simple and container objects in terms of the ExSpect object model. Within the ExSpect tool, the ExSpect object model with its algebra have been implemented on top of the functional language of ExSpect. This has several advantages: among others it keeps ExSpect upward compatible and it assures a natural integration of the algebra and the ExSpect functional language.

To indicate the processors and places and their input and output relations, we use a diagram technique where processors are represented by triangles and places by circles[5]. For input/output relations we use arrows and lines (lines represent bidirectional relations) and for multiple input relations between a processor and a place, we mention the multiplicity. Stores are denoted with a dot (•). See Fig.3 for an example.

A firing has a *firing time*, that is the maximum time stamp of all consumed tokens. Each processor can compute its firing time locally. Processors can fire in parallel only if their firing times are equal and as least as possible. A parallel firing results in the same state as if the involved processors would have fired after each other (Th.19). We call this the *serializability* property. Parallel firings are described by an *event*, i.e. an assignment of tokens to processors such that each processor has just the number of tokens needed to fire for each input place. An event has an *event time*, which is the maximum of all firing times in that event. The *transition time* of a certain state is the minimum event time of all possible events in that state.

---

[5] In the ExSpect CASE tool, these symbols are customizable.

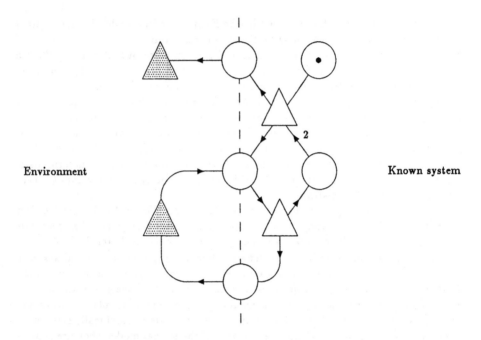

Fig. 3. Example of an ExSpect net.

It denotes the time the system will jump to another state. At that time, an event with event time equal to the transition time is selected and executed; the input tokens are removed from the state and instantaneously, new tokens are added to the state as determined by the processors. Consequently, processors cannot locally (i.e. independent of other ones) determine whether they can fire, the network has to take care for that.

We require the time stamps of all produced tokens to be at least as large as the firing time. This guarantees non-decreasing transition times (Th.18).

During the 'execution' of an ExSpect net, objects are generated and deleted. At any time, each object must have a unique identity. Name clashes are avoided by means of a so-called *identification structure*. If a net starts in a so-called *one-generation state* (Def.23), the object identities will always be different (Th.26). Definition 8 presents the formal ExSpect net model.

4 Language

To specify the net structure of a system, ExSpect has a graphical language that we used in examples in preceding sections. However, with this language we are neither able to specify the functionality of the processors, nor are we able to specify the attribute types of simple objects. To specify these missing elements, we could use for instance an imperative programming language. However, this does not give sufficient expressive comfort. Instead, we have used a typed functional language. This functional language is in fact a sugared typed λ-calculus. There are several good typed functional languages available of which ML seems to be the most succesfull one. We have chosen to develop a functional language ourselves, for the following reasons. First of all, we want to integrate the functional language with the language describing the net structure (the graphical net language has a textual equivalent for storage purposes); this allows us to extend *static type checking* over the net structure as well. Secondly, the objects flowing through our nets are always *finite* in the sense that they can be represented as finite sets. Since most interesting functions can be thought of as *infinite* sets, they are in fact *second class citizens*. Functions transform objects into objects and functions may not be applied to functions, nor may functions have other functions as result. This is not a serious restriction when modelling systems. It has the advantage that the semantics of our language can be expressed easily in naive set theory, which is important for users of our framework: system analysts.

A good alternative for our functional language would be Z (Spivey 1989), which is more powerful in that it allows also non-constructive specifications. This implies for instance, that using Z it is possible to specify a processor that computes the largest prime number, while such a specification in ExSpect is not possible. So Z can be used to specify systems that can not be specified using ExSpect, but it does not always give *executable* specifications. We prefer a framework that gives executable specifications because it allows analysts to communicate with laymen about complex models using a prototype or simulation model.

Now that the ExSpect object model has been integrated within the ExSpect framework (cf. Sect.3), this functional language has been extended with a mechanism for manipulating objects. We will not deal with this manipulation mechanism here; interested readers are referred to (Houben and Verkoulen 1991) and to forthcoming papers.

4.1 Values and Value Types

From some finite or countable sets called *basic types*, we define a *universe* of values. These basic types have to be disjoint. In practice we consider the following basic types: the boolean values, the numbers and the set of strings of ASCII characters. Note that we assume these sets to be disjoint! The next step is to introduce some *value constructors*. These constructors are defined syntactically using interpunction symbols like brackets and commas, and *labels* from some countable *label set* (disjoint with the basic types).

The value constructors have been defined as follows.

– Set constructor
  If $b_1, \ldots, b_n$ are values then $\{b_1, \ldots, b_n\}$ is also a value, called an *f-set*.
– Row constructor
  If $b_1, \ldots, b_n$ are values then $\langle b_1, \ldots, b_n \rangle$ is also a value, called a *row*.
– Tuple constructor
  If $b_1, \ldots, b_n$ are values then $[l_1 : b_1, \ldots, l_n : b_n]$ is also a value, called a *tuple*, where $l_1, \ldots, l_n$ are different labels.

The set of all values that can be constructed this way is called the *free universe of values*. Although we have used several kinds of brackets and labels, it is easy to verify that we can represent all these constructions using set notation only, in a way similar to representing the natural numbers with the symbol for the empty set, set brackets and commas only. Note that values like

$$\{2,'computer', \langle 5,'desk' \rangle\}$$

belong to the free universe. We certainly want to exclude such a value because it is a set of values of different structure! Therefore we introduce *type constructors* analogously to the value constructors. Type constructors will be used to restrict the free universe of values to a set of well-formed values. The type constructors are defined as follows. The semantics of a type is just a set of values from the free universe.

- Set type constructor
  If T is a type then $F(T)$ is also a type, namely the set of all finite subsets of T.
- Row type constructor
  If $T_1, \ldots, T_n$ are types then $T_1 \times \ldots \times T_n$ is also a type, namely the set of all rows $\langle t_1, \ldots, t_n \rangle$ such that for all i, t_i belongs to the type T_i.
- Tuple type constructor
  If $T_1, \ldots, T_n$ are types and $l_1, \ldots, l_n$ are distinct labels, then

$$[l_1 : T_1, \ldots, l_n : T_n]$$

  is also a type, namely the set of all tuples of the form $[l_1 : t_n, \ldots, l_n : t_n]$ such that for all i, t_i belongs to the type T_i.

The *type universe* is now defined as the smallest set TU, such that:

- All basic types belong to TU;
- TU is closed under the three type constructors.

It is clear that all values that belong to some type of TU are elements of the free universe of values. Now we are able to define the *value universe U* of *well-formed* values:

$$U = \bigcup_{T \in TU} T$$

We conclude this section with some examples of type definitions:

```
type Address is [street: Street, number: Natural, city: String]
type Date    is Natural >< Natural >< Natural
```

These type definitions have the following informal meaning: the type Address is a tuple type containing at least three fields, representing a street, number, and city, respectively[6]. A Date is a triple of natural numbers. The types that have not been defined are primitive.

---

[6] The semantics of the tuple type is such that all tuples that have more than these three fields, also belong to this type.

4.2 Functions

In order to define the set of all relevant functions, we define first the set $U_\perp$: it is the set U extended with a new element $\perp$, called *bottom* or *abort*. The functions we will consider will be elements of $U_\perp \to U_\perp$. This set contains all total functions from U to U as well as the partial ones, that are mapped to $\perp$ outside there domain. Furthermore, the application of a function onto $\perp$ will return $\perp$. This set of functions is not countable. We will consider only a countable subset that can be constructed from some set of given functions. Functions have a *name* and a *graph*, which is a set of pairs. The names do not need to be unique: overloading is allowed. We distinguish two kinds of functions: *monomorphic* functions and *polymorphic* ones. Each function has a so-called *signature*, that determines the subset of $U_\perp \to U_\perp$ to which the function belongs. Before being able to define the concept of a signature, we have to introduce *type variables* and *type expressions*. We have already seen type expressions without type variables, e.g. the basic types and the example in the previous subsection. If we also allow to replace a sub-expression in these expressions by a type variable, we get the full set of type expressions. A type expression can be interpreted as the set of all types that can be obtained by substituting for each type variable a type expression without type variables.

A *signature* is an expression of the form:

$$TE_1 \Rightarrow TE_2$$

where TE_1 and TE_2 are type expressions.

A *monomorphic* function is a function with a signature without type variables, while a *polymorphic function* has a signature with type variables. For example:

$$Natural \Rightarrow String \times Boolean$$

denotes the signature of a monomorphic function, while:

$$X \times Boolean \Rightarrow F(X \times Rational)$$

denotes the signature of a polymorphic function because of the type variable X. The meaning of this is that a function with the first signature has *Natural* as domain and *String* $\times$ *Boolean* as range. A function with the second signature is an element of the set of functions:

$$\bigcup_{X \in TU} (X \times Boolean \to F(X \times Rational))$$

Most *predefined* (or *primitive*) functions are polymorphic. For example the *selection* function *if-then-else* has signature $Boolean \times X \times X \Rightarrow X$ which means that *if-then-else* must be applied to triples with the first one of the Boolean type and the others of an equal, but arbitrary, type. Usually we write this function in infix notation, for instance

if y $\leq$ 17 **then** y $\times$ 2 **else** y $\times$ 3 **fi**,

where $\leq$ and $\times$ are functions in infix notation, too. Another example of a primitive function is the equality function, denoted by $=$ in infix notation. Its signature is

$$X \times Y \Rightarrow Boolean$$

This function evaluates to *true* iff the arguments evaluate to (semantically) identical values. So

$$[a : 2, b : 3] = [b : 3, a : 2]$$

evaluates to **true**.

There is only a small number of primitive functions (about 20). It is out of the scope of this article to give a complete list. The interested reader is referred to (Hee et al. 1988, Verkoulen 1989). All non-primitive functions can be constructed using these primitive functions. This will be illustrated at the end of this section. In order to be able to construct new functions we will introduce some syntax. The syntactic construct we introduce is a term which is an expression composed of values, function names and variables. A *term* is defined by[7]:

$$term ::= value \mid variable| \tag{1}$$

$$value\ construction \mid application| \tag{2}$$

$$map\ construction \tag{3}$$

$$terms ::= \epsilon \mid term \mid term, terms \tag{4}$$

A variable may be replaced by any term. A *value construction* is a construction using the set, row and tuple constructors, but now also variables are allowed. So $\{x, 2, 3, y\}$ is an example of a term. An *application* is defined by:

$$application ::= function\_name(terms)$$

An example is minus$(x,7)$, where minus is a primitive function.

The *map construction* is very useful to define values in an implicit way, i.e. without enumerating all (basic) values that compose that value. For instance

$$[x : S \mid 3 \times x + 5]$$

denotes the set of pairs (in the meta language):

$$\{(x,y) \mid x \in S \wedge\ y = 3 \times x + 5\}$$

where S is a set value. In fact the map construct is a finite λ-expression; it denotes a (multi-valued) function with finite domain (which is itself a value!). The syntax of mappings is:

$$mapping ::= [variable\ :\ f\_set \mid term]$$

New *functions* are defined by the following syntax:

$$function\_definition ::= function\_name[variable\_list] := term : signature$$

In the term only function names are allowed that have been defined before, or the name of the function that is defined by this statement. So we allow recursion in a restricted way. We give some examples:
dom[x] := if x= { } then { } else ins$(\pi_1(\text{pick}(x)),\text{dom}(\text{rest}(x)))$ fi:
$\quad$ F(T$\times$ S)$\Rightarrow$F(T)

---

[7] Here, ϵ will denote the empty row of terms.

Here we defined a function dom that assigns to an arbitrary set of pairs of types T and S respectively, the set of first elements, called the domain of the binary relation. We used ins, π_1, pick and rest as known functions. These functions are primitive: ins adds an element to a set and has signature: $T \times F(T) \Rightarrow F(T)$

π_1 takes the first element of a pair and has signature: $T \times S \Rightarrow T$

pick takes an element from a set (we do not specify which one, but it is a function, so pick takes always the same element of a set), its signature is: $F(T) \Rightarrow T$

rest is the complement of pick so it gives the set after pick took one element.

Analogously, we can define rng with signature $F(T \times S) \Rightarrow F(S)$, which determines the range of a finite binary relation. Using the rng function, we are able to define the logical universal quantor for finite binary relations with a boolean range, i.e. the function evaluates to true iff all range values of its argument are true:

$$\forall[x] := \neg(\texttt{false} \in \text{rng}(x)) : F(T \times \texttt{Boolean}) \Rightarrow \texttt{Boolean}$$

Here we used again some auxiliary functions: $\neg$ and $\in$, and the boolean value false. These are defined as follows:

```
¬[x]:=if x= true then false else true fi:Boolean ⇒ Boolean
∈[x,y]:=if y = { } then false else
            if x = pick(y) then true else ∈(x,rest(y)) fi fi:
        T×F(T) ⇒ Boolean
```

(note that we used $\in$ above in infix notation).

In this way, we are able to define a *mathematical toolkit*. Of course, the ExSpect CASE tool has such a toolkit, so analysts do not have to define these elementary functions themselves. In fact, we hope to be able to extend this toolkit such that analysts only have to define functions that are specific for there *application domain*.

It is beyond the scope of this article to discuss the *typing rules* according to which the typing of a list of type and function specifications can verified. Neither do we consider the *evaluation* of function applications. Both typing and evaluation are quite obvious. Besides the ExSpect literature, (Thompson 1991) is a good general reference.

4.3 Processors and Places

For the net structure we use a graphical language. To give a place a type we simply assign a type definition to a place name[8]. An example of a processor definition is:

```
counter[ in x: T× Natural, store y: F(T × Natural), out z: String]:=
if π₁(x) ∈ dom(y) then
      y <- ins(⟨π₁(x),π₂(x)+π₂(select(x,y))⟩ , del(select(x,y),y)),
      z <- 'updated' delay 3
else z <- 'out of domain' delay 2 fi
where
      select[x,y]:= if π₁(x)=π₁(pick(y)) then pick(y)
```

---

[8] When the ExSpect object model is integrated within the ExSpect framework (cf. Sections 2-3), this situation changes: then a so-called *container object type* determines which kinds of objects may occur in the places. However, for this example, it is sufficient to use only the functional language that we described in the previous subsection.

$$\text{else select}(x, \text{rest}(y)) \text{ fi:}$$
$$(S \times T) \times F(S \times T) \Rightarrow (S \times T)$$
end

Here **del** is a primitive function with signature $T \times F(T) \Rightarrow F(T)$, that takes the first argument out of the second (if it is in), and π_2 is defined similarly to π_1; it takes the second component of pair.

We see that we have defined in the definition of **counter** an auxiliary function **select**, that picks out an element of its second argument that has the same first component as its first argument. The processor **counter** maintains a store y which contains a mapping from some type **T** to **Natural**, and it counts the frequency of all **T** objects that were consumed by it. Note that this definition only makes sense if the mapping y is single-valued; however this can not be checked automatically. This is an *invariant* of the system to be verified by the analyst.

Furthermore, we see the keyword **delay** in this definition, which means that the produced objects (z) get a delay of 3 and 2 respectively, relative to the firing time of the processor (in this example, updating apparently takes more time than just checking).

Finally, we note that the <- denotes a *concurrent* assignment, so all occurrences of variables at the right-hand side of these arrows have the same value! If a variable occurs more than once on the left-hand side of such an arrow, the analyst should be sure that only one of them will be executed.

5 An Example

In this section, we will deal with a (simple) example in order to illustrate how the ExSpect framework can be used to model a system in an integrated way, i.e. to cover both static and dynamic aspects. Moreover, a way of working will be demonstrated, which will often be used to solve a specification problem by stepwise-refinement. The example partially specifies a library system. It has been kept simple (i.e., we do not elaborate the full case and we do not model all aspects of a 'real-life' library) because of space limitations in this paper. However, this does not mean that ExSpect has been used only to make toy examples! E.g., ExSpect is being used momentarily in the Esprit project PROOFS for modelling several 'real-life' applications.

The static aspects of our library case are described by the object schema of Fig.2 in Sect.2.1.

In this section, we will develop a model of a distributed library: a library that consists of several (more or less) autonomous departments and one central department. We will give an informal introduction in more detail below. In order to describe (some of) the dynamic aspects of the library we will develop an ExSpect net. The state space of this net is modelled by assigning a container type from the afore-mentioned object schema to each place in the net.

In Fig.4, we see the highest level of the net model describing the library case. There are four ExSpect systems, viz. **centre**, two **branches** and the system **lenders**. The latter one has been drawn with a dotted line to indicate that it belongs to the environment: we have to model the lenders in order to be able to simulate our specification, but we are not really interested in modelling their exact behaviour.

Globally, the library works according to the following procedures. A lender may visit one of the two branches[9] and request books (in fact, they are interested in titles, not in a specific copy of a book). If the title is available at that branch, the lender may take it home for a while. Otherwise, the branch sends a request for the book to the centre, which distributes the incoming requests among the other branches. After the requested book has become available, the 'owner' branch sends a message to the lender who has ordered the book. Finally, lenders will return books to the branch they have lent them from after a while.

We have used some of the graphical facilities of the ExSpect tool when making this specification. The first one we have seen already: the environment has been drawn with a dotted line. Furthermore, the flow of books (physical flow) has been drawn bold-faced, whereas the information flow (requests, messages) have been drawn in normal face.

In Fig.4, the typing of the places has not been given. In the tool, one can access this information by clicking on the place one is interested in. The following table shows the typing of the places, i.e. which type of container objects can be contained by each of the places.

Table 1. Typing of the places in Fig.4.

place	container type
req1	request
req2	request
inbook1	lending
inbook2	lending
outbook1	lending
outbook2	lending
branchrequest	request
branchorder	request
messages	request

In the next figure, we see the definition of a branch. It consists of a system handlerequest and a processor handlereturn. Moreover, there are three stores. The store availablebooks is of type book and contains all available books at a branch that have not been reserved. The store reservations is of type request and contains information about books (of that branch) that have been reserved. The store reservedbooks is of type book and contains all books of a branch that have been reserved, until the lender who has reserved them, comes to get them.

The handlerequest system deals with requests, both from lenders and from other branches. When a request arrives at the branch, handlerequest checks whether the requested title is available (in availablebooks). If not, a request is sent to the centre and the lender is informed that the requested title is not available (yet). Otherwise, the lender is given a copy of the requested title.

---

[9] In a real-life situation, there will be (far) more than two branches, but in order to keep the specification simple, we have chosen to model a library with two branches.

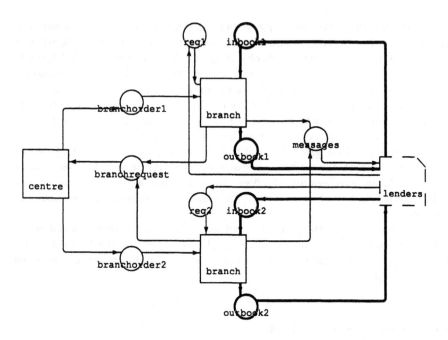

Fig. 4. Library net model: The highest level of abstraction

The processor **handlereturn** deals with returned **lendings** (consisting of a simple object of type **lending** and one or more simple objects of type **book**). Upon receiving a returned **lending**, **handlereturn** checks whether these contained book(s) have been reserved by another lender. If so, the reserved **books** are placed into **reservedbooks** and a message is sent to the lender(s) who have reserved them. The other ones are placed into **availablebooks**.

Finally, we will develop the **handlereturn** processor formally. The ExSpect definition of **handlereturn** looks as follows:

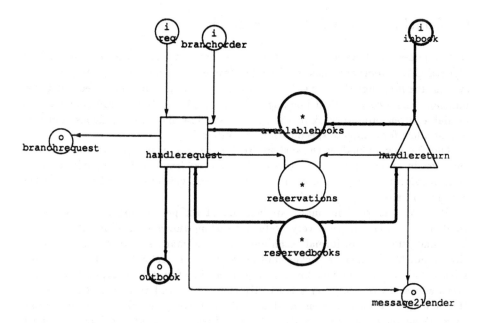

Fig. 5. A branch

```
proc handlereturn [in inbook: book, out message2lender: request,
                   store availablebooks: book,
                   store reservations: request,
                   store reservedbooks: book,
                   ] :=
   if check_reserved(inbook,reservation)
     then reservedbooks <- insert(inbook,reservedbooks),
          message2lender <- available(inbook)
     else availablebooks <- insert(inbook,availablebooks),
   fi;
```

We do not want to define the functions check_reserved, available and insert
here. However, their intuitive meaning will be clear to the reader.

6 Conclusion and Future Research

In this paper, we have given a survey of the ExSpect framework. It is one of the modern CASE tools that has facilities for developing a complete specification of a system; the language that is used for this purpose is a mixture of a typed functional language and two graphical languages. Many CASE tools that are commercially available, often support weak methods, e.g. data flow diagram techniques, and they do not allow for complete specifications of systems.

Our framework enables the systems analyst to specify systems from several perspectives in an integrated way. As a by-product our framework is capable to model distributed data base systems on a conceptual level, which is, to our best knowledge, very rare in any of today's data models.

We have learned from many applications of ExSpect in practice, that such a combination of languages is very useful for system analysts. However, it requires a good understanding of formal techniques, whereas many system analysts in practice do not have sufficient background in the more theoretical aspects of computer science. So, we aim in fact on a new generation of system analysts with a rigorous education in computer science. Hpwever, as it will take some time because this new generation of system analysts will be there (if ever), we are momentarily working on a more pragmatical layer defined *on top of* the ExSpect framework (Ramackers and Verkoulen 1992). Using this layer, also non-experts can use the ExSpect framework.

The framework of ExSpect can be defined formally in a few pages (cf. the appendix). However, it takes some time to understand it and even more time to be able to apply it. One could argue that the framework is too complex, and that a more simple framework will do. However, history has proven that e.g. classical Petri Nets (having tokens without colours), which are much simpler to understand than coloured nets, have far less expressive comfort. This makes their applicability very limited. So, there is always a trade-off between a complex but powerful formalism and a simple formalism which is hardly feasible to specify real-life systems. In our opinion, the expressive power of ExSpect justifies its complexity.

For the future, we plan to develop analysis techniques for ExSpect. At the moment, only analysis techniques for time behaviour and the classical Petri Net invariants are available. However, we are looking for techniques that enable us to verify whether constraints that are imposed on container or simple object types, are left invariant by the processors.

A Appendix

This appendix presents the formal ExSpect net model with its underlying ExSpect object model and as well as a survey of its properties. We will show that the definitions given here are sound with respect to time and identity aspects.

A.1 Formal ExSpect Object Model

This section gives a formal elaboration of the concepts described in Sect.2.

A *simple schema* has much resemblance with many structurally object oriented data models. Such a schema defines which simple types exist, their attributes, and their relationships with other simple types. Moreover, the inheritance relationships (also called *is-a* relationships) and the set of identities used to distinguish simple objects are defined.

Definition 1 Simple Schema.
A *simple schema* is a tuple $\langle ST, ID, AS, RF, IS \rangle$ where:

- ST is the set denoting the *simple types*.
- ID is the set of all possible *object identities*.
- $AS = \langle AN, AF, DD \rangle$: the *attribute* structure;
  Here AN is the set of *attribute names* and $AF \in ST \to (AN \hookrightarrow \mathcal{P}(DD))$ is a function[10] assigning to each simple type and each suitable attribute name the set of all possible attribute values, which is a subset of the *attribute domain* set DD. For $s \in ST$ and $a \in dom(AF.s)$[11], we call $AF.s.a$ the attribute domain of attribute a of type s.
- $RF = \langle RN, RF \rangle$: the *reference* structure;
  Here RN is the set of *reference names* and $RF \in ST \to (RN \hookrightarrow ST)$ assigns to each simple type and each suitable reference name a simple type.
- $IS \in ST \to \mathcal{P}(ST)$ defines the *inheritance structure*;
  For each simple type $t \in ST$ the set $IS.t$ denotes the simple types of which t is a specialisation. Note that this allows for multiple inheritance.
  A simple type is not allowed to inherit directly or indirectly from itself (a-cyclicity constraint):
  $$(\forall t \in ST : t \notin (\textstyle\bigcup_{n=1}^{\infty} IS^n.t))^{12} \quad . \qquad \qquad \Box$$

So, a simple schema defines which kinds of simple objects can occur in a system. The allowed simple objects are defined in a so-called *valid simple object universe*, as defined below.

Definition 2 Simple Object Universe.
Let Σ be a simple schema $\langle ST, ID, AS, RF, IS \rangle$. Then, a *simple object universe* S_Σ is a set of simple objects of the form $\langle id, st, av, rf \rangle$, where

---

[10] We denote the set of all partial functions from A to B by $A \hookrightarrow B$.

[11] Function application will be denoted by $f.x$ instead of $f(x)$.

[12] Here, IS is generalised in a straightforward way for sets:
$IS.\{x_1, \ldots, x_m\} = \{IS.x_1, \ldots, IS.x_m\}$.

- $id \in ID$, the *identity* of the simple object s;
- $st \in ST$, the *simple type* to which s belongs;
- $av \in (AN \hookrightarrow D)$, a function assigning to each *attribute name* an attribute value;
- $rf \in (RN \hookrightarrow \mathcal{P}(ID))$, a function assigning to each suitable reference r a set of object identities of simple objects which are *related* to s in the context of r. $\square$

We will only consider simple object universes that satisfy some conditions regarding the structure of references and attributes.

Definition 3 Valid Simple Object Universe.
A simple object universe $\mathcal{S}_\Sigma$ as described in Def.2 is called *valid* iff the following constraints are satisfied:

- $(\forall s \in \mathcal{S}_\Sigma : (\forall r \in dom(rf.s) : r \in dom(RF.(st.s))))$
  which means that s has only references of the simple type to which s belongs;
- $(\forall s \in \mathcal{S}_\Sigma : (\forall a \in dom(av.s) : a \in dom(AF.(st.s)) \wedge av.s.a \in AF.(st.s).a))$,
  which means that each simple object has an associated tuple of attribute values that fits into the attribute structure of its simple type. $\square$

We extend the simple schemas (Def.1) in order to have the container level in the ExSpect object model. We add a set of *container types* CT and a function CS that maps each container type to a set of "reference-connected" simple types. There is also a *root function* RT that assigns to each container type the simple type that is its root. Finally, there is a set TP of *time-stamps* and a set LN of *location names*. In the integrated model, this set LN will be the set of places of the underlying net.

Definition 4 Object Schema.
An *object schema* is a tuple $\langle CL, CT, SC, LN, TP \rangle$ where

- SS is a simple schema;
- CT is the set of container types;
- $SC = \langle RT, CS \rangle$ defines the *structure of the container types*:
  * $RT \in CT \to ST$ is called the *root function*. It assigns to each container type the simple type that is the root type of the container.
  * $CS \in CT \to \mathcal{P}(ST)$ assigns to each container type a set of *contained simple types*, such that
    $(\forall c \in CT : RT.c \in CS.c \wedge$
    $\quad (\forall s \in CS.c : (\exists n \in \mathbb{N} : (\exists s_0, \ldots, s_n \in CS.c : s_0 = RT.c \wedge s_n = s \wedge$
    $\quad\quad (\forall 0 \leq i < n : s_{i+1} \in rng(RF.s_i))))))$.
    This means that for any simple type s that is part of a container type c there must be a path of references within c from the root of c to s.
  It must hold that $(\bigcup_{c \in CT} CS.c) = ST$ (no "dangling" simple types).
- LN is the set of *location names* where (container) objects may reside;
- TP is the set of *time points*; it is a totally ordered set with an addition operator $+$. $\square$

The structure of container objects in the context of an object schema is described formally in the next definition.

Definition 5 Valid Object Universe.
Let Σ be an object schema and $\mathcal{S}_\Sigma$ the corresponding valid simple object universe.
The *container object universe* $\mathcal{C}_\Sigma$ is a set of container objects according to Σ. Such
a *container object* c is a tuple $\langle id, ct, rt, cs, loc, at \rangle$, where

- $id \in ID$: the object identity of c;
- $ct \in CT$: the container type to which c belongs;
- $rt \in \mathcal{S}_\Sigma$: the root simple object of c;
- $cs \in \mathcal{P}(\mathcal{S}_\Sigma)$: the set of contained simple objects of c;
- $loc \in LN$: the location of c;
- $at \in T$: the time-stamp of c.

We will only consider valid container object universes, which means that they
satisfy the following condition:
$$(\forall c \in \mathcal{C}_\Sigma : st.(rt.c) = RT.(ct.c) \wedge (\forall x \in cs.c : st.x \in CS.(ct.c))).$$
This means that the root of a container object c has to be an element of the root
type of the container type of c in the object schema, and that the simple types of
all contained simple objects have to be an element of the contained simple types of
the container type of c. □

A *state* of a net in the integrated model is a set of container objects. Not each
state is valid, because additional constraints have to be satisfied. We define a *state
space* of valid states as follows.

Definition 6 State Space.
Let Σ be an object schema, $\mathcal{S}_\Sigma$ the corresponding valid simple object universe and
$\mathcal{C}_\Sigma$ the corresponding valid container object universe. We then define the *state space*
$SS_\mathcal{U}$ to be a set, of which the elements are sets of container objects which satisfy
the following additional constraints: All containers and simple objects have to have
a unique identity. Furthermore, the simple objects within these containers have to
satisfy the reference structure of Σ:
$$SS_\mathcal{U} = \{\sigma \in \mathcal{P}(\mathcal{C}_\Sigma) \mid (\forall c_1, c_2 \in \sigma : c_1 \neq c_2 \Rightarrow id.c_1 \neq id.c_2 \wedge$$
$$(\forall s_1 \in cs.c_1, s_2 \in cs.c_2 : id.s_1 = id.s_2 \Rightarrow (c_1 = c_2 \wedge s_1 = s_2)) \wedge$$
$$(\forall s \in cs.c_1 : (\forall r \in dom(rf.s) : (\forall x \in cs.c_2 :$$
$$id(x) \in rf.s.r \Rightarrow st.x = RF.(st.s).r))))\}$$ □

Without proof we mention that subsets of valid states are valid states.

Corollary 7. $\qquad (\forall \sigma \in SS_\mathcal{U} : (\forall \sigma' \subseteq \sigma : \sigma' \in SS_\mathcal{U}))$. □

A.2 Formal ExSpect Net Model

In this section, we give the formal definition of the ExSpect net model.

Definition 8 ExSpect Net.
Let $\mathcal{U}$ be a valid object universe with state space $SS_\mathcal{U}$ and identification structure
ID with child function $\mathcal{F}$.
We define an ExSpect net to be a tuple $\langle R, V, Con, Match, \mathcal{U} \rangle$, where

- $PI = dom(R)$: the *processor* indices;
- $CI = \bigcup_{p \in PI}(dom(Match_p))$: the *connector* indices;
- $Con = \langle ConI, ConO \rangle$, where
    * $ConI : PI \to \mathcal{P}(CI)$: for $p \in PI$, $ConI_p$ is the set of *input-connectors* of p;
    * $ConO: PI \to \mathcal{P}(CI)$: for $p \in PI$, $ConO_p$ is the set of *output-connectors* of p.
  The following constraints have to be satisfied:
    * $(\forall p \in PI :: ConI_p \cap ConO_p = \emptyset)$: input- and output connector sets are disjoint;
    * $(\forall p \in PI :: ConI_p \neq \emptyset)$: each processor has at least one input connector.
- $Match$: $PI \to (CI \hookrightarrow LN)$: for each $p \in PI$, $Match_p$ is a function that assigns to each connector $c \in ConI_p \cup ConO_p$ a channel $x \in LN$ to which c is connected;
- $V \in LN \to CT$, assigning to each channel c the container type of containers in c.

  Container objects should reside in a channel with the proper container type. Formally:
  $$(\forall \sigma \in SS_{\mathcal{U}} :: (\forall \tau \in \sigma :: ct(\tau) \preceq V(loc(\tau))))$$
- For $x \in \mathcal{P}(C)$ and $p \in PI$, $R_p \in \mathcal{P}(C) \hookrightarrow \mathcal{P}(C)$ is such that
    * $dom(R_p) =$
      $$\{x \in \mathcal{P}(C) \mid (\forall c \in LN :: \#\{\tau \in x \mid loc(\tau) = c\} =$$
      $$\#\{x \in ConI_p \mid Match_p(x) = c\})\}$$
    Intuitively, this means that for each processor p and for each channel c, the number of tokens in x with channel identification c is equal to the number of input connectors of p to which c is connected. This is the so-called *firing condition*, which has to be satisfied for a processor to be enabled.
    * $(\forall \tau \in R_p(x) :: loc(\tau) \in \{Match_p(y) \mid y \in ConO_p\})$.
    Intuitively, this means that only tokens are generated for output channels to which p is connected.
    * $(\forall \tau \in x :: (\forall \tau' \in R_p(x) :: at(\tau') \geq at(\tau)))$
    This means that the time stamps of the generated tokens are equal to or larger than the firing time (the largest time stamp of all consumed tokens).
    * $(\bigcup_{\tau \in R_p(x)} id(\tau)) \subseteq (\bigcup_{\tau \in x} \mathcal{F}(id(\tau)))$
    This means that the way identities are assigned to generated containers satisfies the conditions of Def.20. A similar condition holds for the identities of simple objects.
    * $(\forall c \in R_p(x) :: (\forall s \in cs(c) :: (\forall r \in dom(s.rf) :: (\forall i \in I : i \doteq s.rf.r :$
      $$(\exists \sigma \in \bigcup_{\tau \in x} cs(\tau) :: id(\sigma) \doteq i \wedge st.\sigma \preceq RF.(st.s).r) \vee$$
      $$(\exists \sigma \in \bigcup_{\tau \in x} cs(\tau) :: i \in rf(\sigma) \wedge RF.(st.\sigma).r \preceq RF.(st.s).r) \vee$$
      $$(\exists \sigma \in \bigcup_{\tau \in R_p(x)} cs(\tau)))) :: id(\sigma) \doteq i \wedge st.\sigma \preceq RF.(st.s).r))))$$
    Intuitively, this means that each simple object s in a generated container c can only refer to some simple object b with identity i if b was involved in the production of c, if b is referred to by some other object involved in the production of c or if b is produced together with c. Moreover, the type of b has to fit the reference structure of the type to which s belongs.
    * The generated containers and the simple objects therein have to be elements of the valid (simple) object universe induced by $\mathcal{U}$, according to Defs.3 and 5.

$\square$

In the definition given above we have given a minimal set of constraints each ExSpect net should satisfy. We think the ExSpect process model is well-defined this way without having imposed constraints which are not strictly necessary for *each* system which will be specified.

It is easy to think of other constraints one may want to impose upon an ExSpect net and give necessary and sufficient conditions for an ExSpect net to satisfy these constraints. The way these constraints will be specified and validated in a specific case is a subject for further research.

A.3 Properties of ExSpect Nets

This section addresses several features of ExSpect nets. We distinguish time aspects and identity aspects. We start with the former.

Time Aspects.

Below we prove a lot of properties of ExSpect nets, most of them concerning time aspects. E.g., time in not going back in an ExSpect net. In the end, we give a non-interleaving semantics for the ExSpect net model and we prove the serializability property (Th.19).

First, we need some basic definitions. An event is a mapping of objects to a set of processors. The event set gives all events possible in a certain state, regardless of their time. The timed event set selects those elements from an event set that are the earliest ones.

Definition 9 Event Set, Event Time, Transition Time, Timed Event Set.
Let $\mathcal{O}$ be an ExSpect net with valid object universe $\mathcal{U}$ and $\sigma \in SS_{\mathcal{U}}$.
The *event set* $E(\sigma)$ of $\mathcal{O}$ in state σ is defined by:
$$E(\sigma) = \{e \in P \hookrightarrow \mathcal{P}(\mathcal{C}) \mid dom(e) \neq \emptyset, dom(e) \text{ finite } \wedge$$
$$(\forall p, p' \in dom(e) : e_p \in dom(R_p) \cap \sigma \wedge$$
$$(p \neq p' \Rightarrow e_p \cap e(p') = \emptyset))\}$$
The *event time* of an event $e \in E(\sigma)$ is defined by:
$$etime(e) = max(\{at(\tau) \mid \tau \in \cup rng(e)\})$$
The *transition time* of a state σ is defined by:
$$ttime(\sigma) = min(\{etime(e) \mid e \in E(\sigma)\})$$
The *timed event set* $TE(\sigma)$ gives the earliest events:
$$TE(\sigma) = \{e \in E(\sigma) \mid etime(e) = ttime(\sigma)\} \qquad \square$$

Our definition of timed event set allows for a non-interleaving semantics, as more processors are allowed to act simultaneously.

The following lemmas mainly deal with split events and time aspects. The first two are directly derivable from the event set definition.

Function E is monotonous:

Corollary 10. $\forall \sigma, \sigma' \in SS_{\mathcal{U}} : \sigma \subseteq \sigma' \Rightarrow E(\sigma) \subseteq E(\sigma')$. $\qquad \square$

An event restricted to some of the involved processors is again an event:

Corollary 11. Let $\sigma \in SS_U$. For $e \in E(\sigma)$ and $P \subseteq dom(e)$, $P \neq \emptyset : e \upharpoonright P \in E(\sigma)$.[13]

$\square$

When containers are added, time cannot increase:

Lemma 12. $\forall \sigma, \sigma' \in SS_U : \sigma \subseteq \sigma' \Rightarrow ttime(\sigma) \geq ttime(\sigma')$.

Proof. Corollary 10 gives $E(\sigma) \subseteq E(\sigma')$, hence $ttime(\sigma) = min(\{etime(e) \mid e \in E(\sigma)\}) \geq min(\{etime(e) \mid e \in E(\sigma')\}) = ttime(\sigma')$.

$\square$

An *earliest* event (that is, an event with event time equal to the transition time) restricted to some of the involved processors is again an earliest event.

Lemma 13. Let σ be a state and $e \in TE(\sigma)$. Then:
$$\forall P \subseteq dom(e), P \neq \emptyset : etime(e \upharpoonright P) = ttime(\sigma) .$$

Proof. Corollary 11 gives $e \upharpoonright P \in E(\sigma)$ and the definition of $ttime$ yields $etime(e \upharpoonright P) \geq ttime(\sigma)$. Let $dom(e) = \{p_1, ..., p_n\}$. By Defs. *timed event set* and *event time*, $ttime(\sigma) = etime(e) = max(\{etime(e \upharpoonright \{p_i\}) \mid i \in \{1, ..., n\}\}) \geq etime(e \upharpoonright P) \geq ttime(\sigma)$.

$\square$

Last lemma can be combined with Cor.11.
An earliest event being split is again an earliest event:

Corollary 14. Let σ be a state, $e \in TE(\sigma)$ and $P \subseteq dom(e)$ with $P \neq \emptyset$.
Then $e \upharpoonright P \in TE(\sigma)$.

$\square$

The transition time does not change if we add containers with availability times equal to or greater than the current transition time.

Lemma 15. Let $\sigma, \sigma' \in SS_U$ and assume $\sigma \subseteq \sigma'$.
If $(\forall \tau \in \cup(\sigma' \backslash \sigma) : at(\tau) \geq ttime(\sigma))$, then $ttime(\sigma) = ttime(\sigma')$.

Proof.
$$
\begin{aligned}
ttime(\sigma') &= min(\{etime(e) \mid e \in E(\sigma')\}) \\
&= \quad \{ \text{Cor.10: } E(\sigma) \subseteq E(\sigma') \, \} \text{[14]} \\
&\quad min(min(\{etime(e) \mid e \in E(\sigma') \backslash E(\sigma)\}), min(\{etime(e) \mid e \in E(\sigma)\})) \\
&= \quad \{ \text{For } e \in E(\sigma') \backslash E(\sigma), \exists \tau \in rng(e) : \tau \in \cup(\sigma' \backslash \sigma), \\
&\quad \text{ since } at(\tau) \geq ttime(\sigma), \text{ also } etime(e) \geq ttime(\sigma); \\
&\quad \text{Def.} ttime(\sigma) \, \} \\
&\quad ttime(\sigma) \ .
\end{aligned}
$$

$\square$

Now we give a formal definition of the *transition function* and the *transition relation* of an ExSpect net $\mathcal{O}$. The transition function of $\mathcal{O}$ gives, for a given state σ and an event $e \in TE(\sigma)$, a new state. The transition relation of $\mathcal{O}$ determines which states are reachable by $\mathcal{O}$ from a certain state.

---

[13] We denote function restriction by $\upharpoonright$.

[14] We use $\{ ... \}$ for comment.

Definition 16 Transition Function and Transition Relation.
Let $\mathcal{O}$ be an ExSpect net with valid object universe $\mathcal{U}$ and $\sigma \in SS_{\mathcal{U}}$.
   The *transition function* TF of $\mathcal{O}$ is defined by:
   $dom(TF) = \{\langle \sigma, e \rangle \mid \sigma \in SS_{\mathcal{U}} \wedge e \in TE(\sigma)\}$ and
   $TF(\sigma, e) = \sigma \backslash rng(e) \cup \bigcup_{p \in dom(e)} R_p(e_p)$

Remarks: Each created object has a unique identity, hence $\{R_p(e_p) \mid p \in dom(e)\}$
is pairwise disjoint. Even all containers in $TF(\sigma, e)$ are different.
The definition of R_p (see Def.8) is such that $TF(\sigma, e) \in SS_{\mathcal{U}}$.

   The *transition relation* TR is defined by:
   $TR = \{\langle \sigma, \sigma' \rangle \in SS_{\mathcal{U}} \times SS_{\mathcal{U}} \mid (\exists e \in TE(\sigma) : TF(\sigma, e) = \sigma')\}$ □

The behaviour of $\mathcal{O}$ is determined by its *process space*: a possibly infinite sequence
of states $\langle \sigma_0, \sigma_1, \ldots \rangle$ where $\langle \sigma_i, \sigma_{i+1} \rangle$ is an element of the transition relation of $\mathcal{O}$
for each $i \in \mathbb{N}$.

Definition 17 Semantics.
Let $\mathcal{O}$ be an ExSpect net with transition relation TR. The *semantics* or *process space*
of $\mathcal{O}$ is the set of all finite or infinite sequences $\langle \sigma_0, \sigma_1, \ldots \rangle$ with σ_0 a one-generation
state[15] and $(\forall n \in \mathbb{N} : \langle \sigma_n, \sigma_{n+1} \rangle \in TR)$. Such a σ_0 might be regarded as an *initial
state* of $\mathcal{O}$.   □

Definition 17 is correct because of Th.26, as this theorem guarantees that the
process space will only contain one-generation states provided that the initial state
is a one-generation state. Moreover, our semantics is a non-interleaving one because
a single event may involve several processors.
   Time is not going back in an ExSpect net:

Theorem 18 Ascending Transition Times.
   $\forall \langle \sigma, \sigma' \rangle \in TR : ttime(\sigma) \leq ttime(\sigma')$.

Proof. We abbreviate $\bigcup_{p \in dom(e)} R_p(e_p)$ with r. Let $\langle \sigma, \sigma' \rangle \in TR$, then it holds that
$\exists e \in TE(\sigma) : \sigma' = \sigma \backslash rng(e) \cup r$ and

$$ttime(\sigma)$$
$$= \quad \langle\!\langle \text{Lemma 15} \rangle\!\rangle$$
$$ttime(\sigma \cup r)$$
$$\leq \quad \langle\!\langle \text{Lemma 12} \rangle\!\rangle$$
$$ttime(\sigma \backslash rng(e) \cup r)$$
$$= ttime(\sigma') \ .$$
     □

An event in which more events are involved can always be split into smaller events
and their successive execution results in the same state as if the former compound
event were executed. We prove this for the case an event is split into two parts, but
repeated application of this result leads to the general case where an event is split
into arbitrarily many parts.

---

[15] See Def.23 for one-generation states.

Theorem 19 Serializability of Events.
Let $\sigma \in SS_U$, $e \in TE(\sigma)$, P_1 and $P_2 \subseteq dom(e)$ and suppose $dom(e) = P_1 \cup P_2$, $P_1 \cap P_2 = \emptyset$, $P_1 \neq \emptyset$ and $P_2 \neq \emptyset$.
Then $e \restriction P_1 \in TE(\sigma)$, $e \restriction P_2 \in TE(TF(\sigma, e \restriction P_1))$ and
$$TF(\sigma, e) = TF(TF(\sigma, e \restriction P_1), e \restriction P_2) \ .$$

Proof. By Cor.14, $e \restriction P_1 \in TE(\sigma)$ and $e \restriction P_2 \in TE(\sigma)$, hence $etime(e \restriction P_1) = etime(e \restriction P_2) = ttime(\sigma)$ and $ttime(\sigma \backslash rng(e \restriction P_1)) = ttime(\sigma)$.
$TF(\sigma, e \restriction P_1) = \sigma \backslash rng(e \restriction P_1) \cup \bigcup_{p \in P_1} R_p(e_p)$.
Since $rng(e \restriction P_2) \subseteq \sigma \backslash rng(e \restriction P_1)$, we have $e \restriction P_2 \in E(\sigma \backslash rng(e \restriction P_1))$, even $e \restriction P_2 \in TE(\sigma \backslash rng(e \restriction P_1))$. Corollary 10 gives $e \restriction P_2 \in E(TF(\sigma, e \restriction P_1))$ and because all produced tokens have an availability time of at least $ttime(\sigma)$, we have with Lemma 15, $ttime(\sigma \backslash rng(e \restriction P_1)) = ttime(TF(\sigma, e \restriction P_1))$. Hence $e \restriction P_2 \in TE(TF(\sigma, e \restriction P_1))$ and

$$
\begin{aligned}
&TF(TF(\sigma, e \restriction P_1), e \restriction P_2) \\
&= (\sigma \backslash rng(e \restriction P_1) \cup \bigcup_{p \in P_1} R_p(e_p)) \backslash rng(e \restriction P_2) \cup \bigcup_{p \in P_2} R_p(e_p) \\
&= \sigma \backslash rng(e) \cup \bigcup_{p \in P_1 \cup P_2} R_p(e_p) \\
&= TF(\sigma, e) \ .
\end{aligned}
$$

$\square$

Identity Aspects.

This subsection addresses identities (names) of objects. All identities in an Ex-Spect net should always be different, especially upon creation of new objects. Main theorem is Th.26 which guarantees identity uniqueness.

All objects that are induced by an instance of our object model will have a unique identification. This gives us, among others, the possibility to formulate statements about referential integrity, inconsistency, etc. We choose a way of assigning new object identities that does not require a central daemon and/or extra memory cells in the specification of a system. For this would be very unnatural, because it would not reflect the system as it is in the real world. The formal vehicle that we need to make this local assignment of identities possible, is introduced in this section. In Sect.A.3 it is demonstrated that this definition is sound. There it can also be seen how other properties like referential integrity could be proved.

Part of a ExSpect object schema is a so-called *identification structure*. Such an identification structure consists of a countable set I (an *identification set*), a set $A \subseteq I$ (the *atomic* or *initial identities*) and the functions $\mathcal{F}$ and $\mathcal{G}$ which are defined upon I. The $\mathcal{F}$ function assigns to each identity i a set $\mathcal{F}(i) \in \mathcal{P}(I)$ of identities which are "children" of i. For different i and j, the sets of children $\mathcal{F}(i)$ and $\mathcal{F}(j)$ must be disjoint. This implies that no identity can "survive": an identity i cannot be an element of $\mathcal{F}(i)$ as this would violate the aforementioned disjointness constraint (cf. Lemma 21). This might seem contradictory to the idea of a never-changing unique identification. We solve this as will be described below. It is possible (and sometimes necessary) to consider one child of a parent as the *continuation* of its parent. In an identification structure, this is done by defining the continuation function $\mathcal{G}$. In that case, i and $\mathcal{G}(i)$ refer to the same real-world entity, but in different states of the system under consideration. Actually, one could say that i and $\mathcal{G}(i)$ are elements of one and the same *equivalence type*, viz. the set of all object identities referring to one and the same real-world object, but at different points in time. That is why in an auxiliary definition we will introduce the predicates $\doteq$ (*equality modulo $\mathcal{G}$*) and $\dot{\in}$ (*membership modulo $\mathcal{G}$*). Intuitively, two identities are equal modulo $\mathcal{G}$ if one of them is the transitive $\mathcal{G}$-continuation of the other.

Definition 20 Identification structure.
An *identification structure* is a tuple $\langle I, \mathcal{F}, \mathcal{G}, A \rangle$ where I is a countable set called the *identification set*, $\mathcal{F}$ is called the *child function*, $\mathcal{G}$ is called the *continuation function* and $A \subseteq I$ is called the *initial set*. It has to satisfy the following conditions:[16]

1. $\mathcal{F} \in I \rightarrow \mathcal{P}(I \setminus A)$
2. $(\forall i, j \in I :: i \neq j \Rightarrow \mathcal{F}(i) \cap \mathcal{F}(j) = \emptyset)$
3. $(\forall i \in I :: (\exists j \in A :: (\exists n \in \mathbb{N} :: i \in \mathcal{F}^n(\{j\}))))$[17]
4. $\mathcal{G} \in I \hookrightarrow I$ such that $(\forall i \in dom(\mathcal{G}) :: \mathcal{G}(i) \in \mathcal{F}(i))$ $\qquad \square$

Hence if ID is an identification structure with identification set I, initial set A and child function $\mathcal{F}$, then the elements of A do not occur as $\mathcal{F}$-children, all other elements of I are $\mathcal{F}$-descendants of some element in A and two elements of I have different $\mathcal{F}$-children.

It is obvious that the following transitivity property holds for $\mathcal{F}$:
$$(\forall x, y, z \in I :: (\forall m, n \in \mathbb{N} :: x \in \mathcal{F}^m(y) \wedge y \in \mathcal{F}^n(z) \Rightarrow x \in \mathcal{F}^{m+n}(z)))$$
It is easy to prove the following lemma, which states that an identity can never be an $\mathcal{F}$-descendant of itself.

Lemma 21. Given an identification structure ID with identification set I as in Def.20, it holds that $(\forall i \in I :: (\forall n \in \mathbb{N} : n > 0 : i \notin \mathcal{F}^n(i)))$. $\qquad \square$

In the definition below we will introduce the notion of "equality modulo $\mathcal{G}$". This is necessary because of the following: we will see that no identity can "survive" a state transition. We have introduced the $\mathcal{G}$ function to account for this. However, this would mean that we would have to update all references to an object when the identity i of that object would become $\mathcal{G}(i)$. This would mean a global check of all objects in the system, destroying our local state transition paradigm. Therefore, we define the notion of equality modulo $\mathcal{G}$. Intuitively, this means that the object identities i and $\mathcal{G}(i)$ can be considered the same.

Definition 22 $\doteq$ (equality modulo $\mathcal{G}$).
Let ID be an identification structure with identification set I and continuation function $\mathcal{G}$.
Then the predicates $\doteq$ and $\dot{\in}$ are defined as follows:

1. For $i, j \in I$, we define $(i \doteq j) \overset{\text{def}}{=} (\exists n \in \mathbb{N} :: i = \mathcal{G}^n(j) \vee j = \mathcal{G}^n(i))$;
2. For $i \in I$ and $X \subseteq I$, we define $i \dot{\in} X \overset{\text{def}}{=} (\exists j \in X :: i \doteq j)$. $\qquad \square$

---

[16] For a function f and $S \subseteq dom(f)$, $f(S) = \{f(s) \mid s \in S\}$.
[17] We define $\mathcal{F}^n$ for $n \in \mathbb{N}$ as follows:
    For all $n \in \mathbb{N}, \mathcal{F}^n \in \mathcal{P}(I) \rightarrow \mathcal{P}(I)$ is such that
    $\quad (\forall B \in \mathcal{P}(I) :: \mathcal{F}^0(B) = B \wedge$
    $\quad\quad\quad (\forall k \in \mathbb{N} :: \mathcal{F}^{k+1}(B) = \{j \in I \mid (\exists i \in \mathcal{F}^k(B) :: j \in \mathcal{F}(i))\}))$.
    We will write $\mathcal{F}^n(x)$ instead of $\mathcal{F}^n(\{x\})$.

We conclude this section with an example of an identification structure. It can be verified easily that this construction satisfies the constraints of Def.20.

Example Construction Identification Structure.
We propose the following construction of an identification structure *ID*.

- $I = \mathbb{N}^+$, the finite (non-empty) sequences of natural numbers.
- $A = \mathbb{N}$.
- For $i \in I$, $\mathcal{F}(i) \subseteq \{j \cdot i \mid j \in \mathbb{N}\}$, so new identities are created from old ones by adding a natural number in front of the old identity.
- For $i \in I$, it holds that $\mathcal{G}(i) = 0 \cdot i$.
- For $i, j \in I$ it holds that $i \doteq j$ iff:
  $$(\exists n \in \mathbb{N} :: i = 0^n \cdot j \vee 0^n \cdot i = j).$$
  Informally, this means that all identities which are equal after deleting (some) leading zeros refer to the same real-world entity. □

Definition 23 One-generation state.
Let $\mathcal{O}$ be an ExSpect net as in Def.8. Then a state $\sigma \in SS_\mathcal{U}$ is called a *one-generation state* iff

$$(\forall \tau, \tau' \in \sigma ::$$
$$(\forall x \in \tau, x' \in \tau' :: x \neq x' \Rightarrow \neg(\exists m \in \mathbb{N} :: id(x) \in \mathcal{F}^m(id(x')))) \wedge$$
$$\tau \neq \tau' \Rightarrow \neg(\exists n \in \mathbb{N} :: id(\tau) \in \mathcal{F}^n(id(\tau')))))$$ □

This means that in a one-generation state the identity of a container cannot be the descendant of the identity of another container in the same state, and analogously for simple objects. As a consequence, all containers generated from containers in a one-generation state will have different identities from the remaining containers in the state, because *ID* is an identification structure. If a state would contain containers x and y and x is a descendant of y, then in a state transition y could generate another descendant with the same identity as x. In a one-generation state, such an "identification clash" cannot occur.

In particular, a one-generation state cannot contain two different containers c_1 and c_2 with the same identifications, because this would mean $c_1 \neq c_2 \wedge id(c_1) = \mathcal{F}^0(id(c_2))$.

In order to prove Lemma 25, we need one auxiliary lemma. It is in fact a reformulation of the requirement that for different identities i and j the sets of their $\mathcal{F}$-descendants ($\mathcal{F}(i)$ and $\mathcal{F}(j)$) are disjoint.

Lemma 24. Given an identification structure *ID* with identification set I as in Def.20, it holds that

$$(\forall i, j \in I :: (\forall X \subseteq I :: (j \in \mathcal{F}(i) \wedge j \in \mathcal{F}(X)) \Rightarrow (i \in X \wedge \mathcal{F}(i) \subseteq \mathcal{F}(X)))).$$
□

Lemma 25 states that if an ExSpect net is in a one-generation state, it will remain in a one-generation state if *ID* is an identification structure as in Def.20. This implies that all identities in the state will remain different.

Lemma 25 Invariance of Unicity. Let $\mathcal{O}$ be an ExSpect net and σ a one-generation state of $\mathcal{O}$. Then the following holds:

$(\forall p \in PI :: (\forall e \in SS_u ::$
$\quad e \in dom(R_p) \cap \sigma \Rightarrow \sigma' = (\sigma \setminus e) \cup R_p(e)$ is a one-generation state$))$

Proof. Let $\mathcal{O}$ be an ExSpect net according to Def.8. Let $p \in PI$ and assume that $\mathcal{O}$ makes a state transition from a one-generation state $\sigma \in SS_u$ to another state under the firing of some processor p which consumes a set of container objects $\alpha \in dom(R_p) \cap \sigma$. We now have to prove that $\sigma' = (\sigma \setminus \alpha) \cup R_p(\alpha)$ is again a one-generation state. It follows from Def.8 that σ' is a state.

Let $c, c' \in \sigma'$. In order to prove that σ' is a one-generation state, we have to prove the following:
$$c \neq c' \Rightarrow \neg(\exists n \in \mathbb{N} :: id(c) \in \mathcal{F}^n(id(c'))),$$
and the same analogously for simple objects. We will give only the proof for container objects here.

Suppose that $c \neq c'$. Suppose furthermore that $id(c) \in \mathcal{F}^m(id(c'))$ for some $m \in \mathbb{N}$. We will derive a contradiction now. We will do this by distinguishing three cases:

1. Suppose c and c' are both elements of $\sigma \setminus \alpha$. But in that case, σ is not a one-generation state. This contradicts our earlier assumption.

2. Suppose c and c' are both elements of $R_p(\alpha)$. In that case, according to Def.8, there exist some $v, w \in \alpha$ such that $id(c) \in \mathcal{F}(id(v))$ and $id(c') \in \mathcal{F}(id(w))$. We have assumed moreover $id(c) \in \mathcal{F}^m(id(c')) = \mathcal{F}(\mathcal{F}^{m-1}(id(c')))$ for some $m \in \mathbb{N}$ with $m > 0$ ($m = 0$ would give $id(c) = id(c')$, which is contradictory to our assumption $c \neq c'$ as a consequence of Defs.5 and 6). But using Lemma 24, it holds then that
   $$id(v) \in \mathcal{F}^{m-1}(id(c')), \text{ but also}$$
   $$id(c') \in \mathcal{F}(id(w)),$$
   so it holds that $id(v) \in \mathcal{F}^m(id(w))$, using the transitivity of $\mathcal{F}$. As $v \neq w$ holds (which follows from $id(v) \in \mathcal{F}(id^m(w))$ for some $m > 0$ and Lemma 21), this contradicts the assumption that σ is a one-generation state.

3. In the third case one of the complexes c and c' belongs to $R_p(\alpha)$ and the other one to $\sigma \setminus \alpha$. We assume that $id(c) \in \mathcal{F}^m(id(c'))$ for some $m \in \mathbb{N}$, so c' was generated before c, so in this case we have $c \in R_p(\alpha)$ and $c' \in (\sigma \setminus \alpha)$. Here $m > 0$ holds for the same reasons as in clause 2 of this proof.
   It holds that $id(c) \in \mathcal{F}(id(v))$ for some $v \in \alpha$, because of Def.8. On the other hand, we have assumed $id(c) \in \mathcal{F}^m(id(c')) = \mathcal{F}(\mathcal{F}^{m-1}(id(c')))$, where c' is an element of $\sigma \setminus \alpha$. This means that $v \neq c'$ holds. But, using Lemma 24, this also implies that $id(v) \in \mathcal{F}^{m-1}(id(c'))$ where $v \neq c'$ and $c', v \in \sigma$. But this means that σ is not a one-generation state, which contradicts our earlier assumption.
   $\square$

Theorem 26. Let $\mathcal{O}$ be an ExSpect net with initial state σ_0. Let σ_0 be a one-generation state. Then all reachable states of $\mathcal{O}$ are one-generation states.

Proof. Let σ be a state of $\mathcal{O}$ which can be reached from σ_0 in n steps. We will prove that σ is a one-generation state using induction to n.

1. $n = 0$: Then $\sigma = \sigma_0$, which is a one-generation state;

2. $n > 0$: Then $\langle \sigma', \sigma \rangle \in TR$ and σ' is reachable from σ_0 in $n-1$ steps. This means that σ' is a one-generation state using the induction hypothesis. Then, according to Lemma 25, σ is also a one-generation state. □

As has been mentioned above, Th.26 implies that all object identities are different in any reachable state from the initial state of an ExSpect net, provided that this initial state is a one-generation state.

It might seem that the way we assign identities to objects is quite cumbersome, whereas we could simply have chosen a solution with one or more memory cells recording "the first free number". However, we do not want to introduce memory cells for this assignment of identities. Moreover, we want to maintain our local state transition paradigm: when a processor fires, the state change which is a consequence of this firing can be determined by removing the consumed tokens and adding the generated ones.

References

W.M.P. van der Aalst and A.W. Waltmans: Modelling logistic systems with EXSPECT. In (Sol and Hee 1991), 269–288, 1991.

W.M.P. van der Aalst: Interval Timed Petri Nets and their analysis. Computing Science Notes 91/09, Eindhoven University of Technology, 1991.

J.A. Bergstra and J.W. Klop: Algebra of Communicating Processes. In J.W. de Bakker, M. Hazewinkel, and J.K. Lenstra (eds.), Proceedings of the CWI Symposium on Mathematics and Computer Science. North-Holland, 1986.

H. Brinksma: On the Design of Extended LOTOS. PhD thesis, University of Twente, 1988.

E.M.M.A. van den Broek and P.A.C. Verkoulen: A Tool for Integrated Modelling of Static and Dynamic Aspects of Systems. In Second International Workshop on the Next Generation of CASE Tools, IOS Press, 1992.

H.J. Genrich: Predictate/Transition-Nets. Advances in Petri Nets 1986 Part I: Petri Nets, Central Models and their Properties, Lecture Notes in Computer Science 254, 207–247, Springer-Verlag, New York, 1987.

R. Harper: Introduction to Standard ML. LFCS Report Series ECS-LFCS-86-14, University of Edinburgh, 1986.

K.M. van Hee and P.A.C. Verkoulen: Integration of a Data Model and High-Level Petri Nets. Proceedings of the 12th International Conference on Applications and Theory of Petri Nets, 410–431, Aarhus, Denmark, June 1991.

K.M. van Hee, L.J. Somers, and M. Voorhoeve: ExSpect, the Functional Part. Computing Science Notes 88/20, Eindhoven University of Technology, 1988.

K.M. van Hee, L.J. Somers, and M. Voorhoeve: Executable Specifications for Distributed Information Systems. Proceedings of the IFIP TC 8 / WG 8.1 Working Conference on Information System Concepts: An In-depth Analysis, 139–156, Namur, Belgium, Elsevier Science Publishers, 1989.

H.Ehrig and B. Mahr. Fundamentals of algebraic specification 1 & 2, EATCS, 1985-1990.

G.-J Houben and P.A.C. Verkoulen: An Integrated Approach to Modelling Structural and Behavioural Aspects of Complex Objects. Third International Workshop on Foundations of Models and Languages for Data and Objects, Informatik Bericht 91/3, 47–64, Aigen, Austria, Technische Universität Clausthal, September 1991.

K. Jensen: Coloured Petri Nets and the Invariant-Method. Theoretical Computer Science, 14:317–336, 1981.

K. Jensen: Coloured Petri Nets: A High Level Language for System Design and Analysis. Advances in Petri Nets 1990, Lecture Notes in Computer Science 483, 342–416. Springer-Verlag, New York, 1991.

R. Milner: A Calculus of Communicating Systems, Lecture Notes in Computer Science 92, Springer-Verlag, New York, 1980.

G.J. Ramackers and P.A.C. Verkoulen: A Formally Integrated Conceptual Model based on Objects. Third International Conference on Dynamic Modelling of Information Systems, June 1992.

W. Reisig: Petri Nets: an Introduction. Prentice-Hall, 1985.

D.W. Shipman: The Functional Data Model and the Data Language DAPLEX. ACM Transactions on Database Systems, 6:140–173, 1981.

H.G. Sol and K.M. van Hee, editors. Dynamic Modelling of Information Systems. North-Holland, 1991.

J.M. Spivey: The Z Notation: A Reference Manual. Englewood Cliffs, Prentice-Hall, 1989.

S. Thompson: Type Theory and Functional Programming. Addison-Wesley, 1991.

P.A.C. Verkoulen: Extensions and Enrichment of ExSpect. Master's thesis, Eindhoven University of Technology, December 1989.

An Overview of Larch

Stephen J. Garland and John V. Guttag
MIT Laboratory for Computer Science

James J. Horning
Digital Equipment Corp. Systems Research Center

We begin by describing the Larch approach to specification and illustrating it with a few small examples. We then discuss LP, the Larch proof assistant, a tool that supports all the Larch languages. Our intent is to give you only a taste of these things. For a comprehensive look at Larch see [12].

Two-tiered specifications

The Larch family of languages supports a *two-tiered*, definitional style of specification. Each specification has components written in two languages: one language that is designed for a specific programming language and another language that is independent of any programming language. The former kind are *Larch interface languages*, and the latter is the *Larch Shared Language* (LSL).

Interface languages are used to specify the interfaces between program components. Each specification provides the information needed to use an interface. A critical part of each interface is how components communicate across the interface. Communication mechanisms differ from programming language to programming language. For example, some languages have mechanisms for signalling exceptional conditions, others do not. More subtle differences arise from the various parameter passing and storage allocation mechanisms used by different languages.

It is easier to be precise about communication when the interface specification language reflects the programming language. Specifications written in such interface languages are generally shorter than those written in a "universal" interface language. They are also clearer to programmers who use components and to programmers who implement them.

Each interface language deals with what can be observed by client programs written in a particular programming language. It provides a way to write assertions about program states, and it incorporates programming-language-specific notations for features such as side effects, exception handling, iterators, and concurrency. Its simplicity or complexity depends largely on the simplicity or complexity of its programming language.

Larch interface languages have been designed for a variety of programming languages. The two best developed languages are for C and for Modula-3. Other interface languages have been designed for Ada [2, 11], CLU [20], C++ [13, 21, 23], ML [24], and Smalltalk [3]. There are also "generic" Larch interface languages that can be specialized for particular programming languages or used to specify interfaces between programs in different languages [14, 22].

Larch interface languages encourage a style of programming that emphasizes the use of abstractions, and each provides a mechanism for specifying abstract types. If its programming language provides direct support for abstract types (as Modula-3 does), the interface language facility is modeled on that of the programming language; if its programming language does not (as C does not), the facility is designed to be compatible with other aspects of the programming language.

```
uses TaskQueue;
mutable type queue;
immutable type task;

task *getTask(queue q) {
  modifies q;
  ensures
    if isEmpty(q^)
      then result = NIL ∧ unchanged(q)
      else (*result)' = first(q^) ∧ q' = tail(q^);
}
```

FIGURE 1. An LCL interface specification

Figure 1 contains a sample interface specification for a small fragment of a scheduler for an operating system. The specification is written in LCL (a Larch interface language for C). This fragment introduces two abstract types and a procedure for selecting a task from a task queue. Briefly, * means pointer to (as in C), result refers to the value returned by the procedure, the symbol ^ is used to refer to the value in a location when the procedure is called, and the symbol ' to refer to its value when the procedure returns.

The specification of getTask is not self-contained. For example, looking only at this specification there is no way to know which task getTask selects. Is it the one that has been in q the longest? Is it is the one in q with the highest priority?

Interface specifications rely on definitions from *auxiliary specifications*, written in LSL, to provide semantics for the primitive terms they use. Specifiers are not limited to a fixed set of notations, but can use

```
TaskQueue: trait
  includes Nat
  task tuple of id: Nat, important: Bool
  introduces
    new: → queue
    __ ⊣ __: task, queue → queue
    isEmpty, hasImportant: queue → Bool
    first: queue → task
    tail: queue → queue
  asserts
    queue generated by new, ⊣
    ∀ t: task, q: queue
      isEmpty(new);
      ¬ isEmpty(t ⊣ q);
      ¬ hasImportant(new);
      hasImportant(t ⊣ q) ==
        t.important ∨ hasImportant(q);
      first(t ⊣ q) ==
        if t.important ∨ ¬ hasImportant(q)
          then t else first(q);
      tail(t ⊣ q) ==
        if first(t ⊣ q) = t then q else t ⊣ tail(q)
```

FIGURE 2. LSL specification used by getTask

LSL to define specialized vocabularies suitable for particular interface specifications or classes of specifications.

Figure 2 contains a portion of an LSL specification that specifies the operators used in the interface specification of getTask. Based on the information in this LSL specification, one can deduce that the task pointed to by the result of getTask is the most recently inserted important task, if such a task exists. Otherwise it is the most recently inserted task.

Many informal specifications have a structure similar to this. They implicitly rely on auxiliary specifications by describing an interface in terms of concepts with which readers are assumed to be familiar, such as sets, lists, coordinates, and windows. But they don't define these auxiliary concepts. Readers can misunderstand such specifications, unless their intuitive understanding exactly matches the specifier's. And there is no way to be sure that such intuitions do match. LSL specifications provide unambiguous mathematical definitions of the terms that appear in interface specifications.

Larch encourages a separation of concerns, with basic constructs in the LSL tier and programming details in the interface tier. We suggest that specifiers keep most of the complexity of specifications in the LSL tier for several reasons:

- LSL specifications are likely to be more reusable than interface specifications.

- LSL has a simpler underlying semantics than most programming languages (and hence than most interface languages), so specifiers are less likely to make mistakes, and any mistakes they do make are more easily found.

- It is easier to make and to check assertions about semantic properties of LSL specifications than about semantic properties of interface specifications.

Many programming errors are easily detected by running the program, that is, by testing it. While some Larch specifications can be executed, most of them cannot. The Larch style of specification emphasizes brevity and clarity rather than executability. To make it possible to validate specifications before implementing or executing them, Larch permits specifiers to make assertions about specifications that are intended to be redundant. These assertions can be checked mechanically. Several tools that assist specifiers in checking these assertions as they debug specifications are already in use, and others are under development.

LSL, The Larch Shared Language

LSL specifications define two kinds of symbols, *operators* and *sorts*. The concepts of operator and sort are the same as those used in conventional mathematical logic. They are similar to the programming language concepts of procedure and type, but it is important not to confuse these two sets of concepts. When discussing LSL specifications, we will consistently use the words "operator" and "sort." When talking about programming language constructs, we will use the words "procedure" (or "function," "routine," or "method," as appropriate) and "type." Operators stand for total functions from tuples of values to values. Sorts stand for disjoint non-empty sets of values, and are used to indicate the domains and ranges of operators. In each interface language, "procedure" and "type" must mean what they mean in that programming language.

The *trait* is the basic unit of specification in LSL. A trait introduces some operators and specifies some of their properties. Sometimes the trait defines an abstract type. However, it is frequently useful to define a set of properties that does not fully characterize a type.

```
Table: trait
   includes Integer
   introduces
      new: → Tab
      add: Tab, Ind, Val → Tab
      __ ∈ __: Ind, Tab → Bool
      lookup: Tab, Ind → Val
      size: Tab → Int
   asserts ∀ i, i1: Ind, v: Val, t: Tab
      ¬(i ∈ new);
      i ∈ add(t, i1, v) == i = i1 ∨ i ∈ t;
      lookup(add(t, i, v), i1) ==
         if i = i1 then v else lookup(t, i1);
      size(new) == 0;
      size(add(t, i, v)) ==
         if i ∈ t then size(t) else size(t) + 1
```

FIGURE 3. Table.lsl

Figure 3 shows a trait that specifies a class of tables that store values in indexed places. It is similar to specifications in many "algebraic" specification languages [1, 4, 6, 25].

The specification begins by *including* another trait, Integer. This specification, which can be found in the LSL handbook in [12], supplies information about the operators +, 0, and 1, which are used in defining the operators introduced in Table.

The *introduces clause* declares a set of operators, each with its *signature* (the sorts of its domain and range). Signatures are used to sort-check terms in much the same way as procedure calls are type-checked in programming languages.

The *body* of the specification contains, following the reserved word asserts, equations between terms containing operators and variables.[1] The third equation resembles a recursive function definition, since the operator lookup appears on both the left and right sides. However, it merely states a relation that must hold among lookup, add, and the built-in operator if_then_else_; it does not fully define lookup. For example, it doesn't say anything about the value of the term lookup(new, i).

Each well-formed trait defines a *theory* (a set of sentences closed under logical consequence) in multisorted first-order logic with equality. Each theory contains the trait's assertions, the conventional axioms of first-order logic, everything that follows from them, and nothing else. This *loose* semantic interpretation guarantees that formulas in the theory follow only from the presence of assertions in the trait—never from their absence. This is in contrast to algebraic specification languages based on initial algebras [9] or final algebras [19]. Using the loose interpretation ensures that all theorems proved about an incomplete specification remain valid when it is extended.

Equational theories are useful, but a stronger theory is often needed, for example, when specifying an abstract type. The constructs generated by and partitioned by provide two ways of strengthening equational specifications.

A *generated by* clause asserts that a list of operators is a complete set of *generators* for a sort. That is, each value of the sort is equal to one that can be written as a finite number of applications of just those operators, and variables of other sorts. This justifies a *generator induction schema* for proving things about the sort. For example, the natural numbers are generated by 0 and succ, and the integers are generated by 0, succ, and pred. The assertion

Tab generated by new, add

if added to Table, could be used to prove theorems by induction over new and add, since, according to this assertion, any value of sort Tab can be constructed from new by a finite number of applications of add.

A *partitioned by* clause asserts that a list of operators constitutes a complete set of *observers* for a sort. That is, all distinct values of the sort can be distinguished using just those operators. Terms that are not

---

[1] The equation connective in LSL, ==, has the same semantics as the equality symbol, =. It is used only to introduce another level of precedence into the language.

distinguishable using any of them are therefore equal. For example, sets are partitioned by ∈, because sets that contain the same elements are equal. Each partitioned by clause is a new axiom that justifies a deduction rule for proofs about values of the sort. For example, the assertion

```
Tab partitioned by ∈, lookup
```

adds the deduction rule

```
∀ i1:ind (i1 ∈ t1 = i1 ∈ t2),
∀ i1:ind (lookup(t1, i1) = lookup(t2, i1)))
-----------------------------
         t1 = t2
```

to the theory associated with Table.

It is instructive to note some of the things that Table does *not* specify:

1. It does not say how tables are to be represented.

2. It does not give algorithms to manipulate tables.

3. It does not say what procedures are to be implemented to operate on tables.

4. It does not say what happens if one looks up an Ind that is not in a Tab.

The first two decisions are in the province of the implementation. The third and fourth are recorded in interface specifications.

Interface specifications

An interface specification defines an interface between program components, and is written in a programming-language-specific Larch interface language. Each specification must provide the information needed to use an interface and to write programs that implement it. At the core of each Larch interface language is a model of the state manipulated by the associated programming language.

PROGRAM STATES

States are mappings from *locs* (abstract storage locations, also known as objects) to *values*. Each variable identifier has a type and is associated with a loc of that type. The major kinds of values that can be stored in locs are:

- *basic values*. These are mathematical constants, like the integer 3 and the letter A. Such values are independent of the state of any computation.

- *exposed types*. These are data structures that are fully described by the type constructors of the programming language (e.g., C's int * or Modula-3's ARRAY [1..10] OF INTEGER). The representation is visible to, and may be relied on by, clients.

- *abstract types*. Data types are best thought of as collections of related operations on collections of related values. Abstract types are used to hide representation information from clients.

Each interface language provides operators (e.g., ^ and ') that can be applied to locs to extract their values in the relevant states (usually the pre-state and the post-state of a procedure).

Each loc's type defines the kind of values it can map to in any state. Just as each loc has a unique type, each LSL term has a unique sort. To connect the two tiers in a Larch specification, there is a mapping from interface language types (including abstract types) to LSL sorts. Each type of basic value, exposed type, and abstract type is *based on* an LSL sort. Interface specifications are written using types and values. Properties of these values are defined in LSL, using operators on the corresponding sorts.

For each interface language, a standard LSL trait defines operators that can be applied to values of the sorts that the programming language's basic types and other exposed types are based on. Users familiar with the programming language will already have an intuitive understanding of these operators. Abstract types are typically based on sorts defined in traits supplied by specifiers.

PROCEDURE SPECIFICATIONS

The specification of each procedure in an interface can be studied, understood, and used without reference to the specifications of other procedures. A specification consists of a procedure header (declaring the types of its arguments and results) followed by a body of the form:

```
requires reqP
modifies modList
ensures  ensP
```

A specification places constraints on both clients and implementations of the procedure. The *requires clause* is used to state restrictions on the state, including the values of any parameters, at the time of any call. The *modifies* and *ensures clauses* place constraints on the procedure's behavior when it is called properly. They relate two states, the state when the procedure is called, the *pre-state*, and the state when it terminates, the *post-state*.

A requires clause refers only to values in the pre-state. An ensures clause may also refer to values in the post-state.

A modifies clause says what locs a procedure is allowed to change (its *target list*). It says that the procedure must not change the value of any locs visible to the client except for those in the target list. Any other loc must have the same value in the pre and post-states. If there is no modifies clause, then nothing may be changed.

For each call, it is the responsibility of the client to make the requires clause true in the pre-state. Having done that, the client may assume that:

— the procedure will terminate,

— changes will be limited to the locs in the target list, and

— the postcondition will be true on termination.

The client need not be concerned with how this happens.

The implementor of a procedure is entitled to assume that the precondition holds on entry, and is only responsible for the procedure's behavior if it is. A procedure's behavior is totally unconstrained if its precondition isn't satisfied, so it is good style to keep the requires clause weak. An omitted requires clause is equivalent to requires true (the weakest possible requirement).

```
mutable type table;
uses Table(table for Tab, char for Ind,
           char for Val, int for Int);
constant int maxTabSize;

table table_create(void) {
  ensures result' = new ∧ fresh(result);
  }
bool table_add(table t, char i, char c) {
  modifies t;
  ensures result = (size(t^) < maxTabSize ∨ i ∈ t^)
    ∧ (if result then t' = add(t^, i, c)
                 else t' = t^);
  }
char table_read(table t, char i) {
  requires i ∈ t^;
  ensures result = lookup(t^, i);
  }
```

FIGURE 4. A Sample LCL Interface Specification

TWO INTERFACE LANGUAGE EXAMPLES

Figure 4 contains a fragment of a specification written in LCL (a Larch interface language for Standard C). Figure 5 contains a fragment of a similar specification written in LM3 (a Larch interface language for Modula-3).

```
INTERFACE Table;
<* TRAITS Table(CHAR FOR Ind, CHAR FOR Val,
               INTEGER FOR Int) *>
  TYPE T <: OBJECT
    METHODS
      Add(i: CHAR; c: CHAR) RAISES {Full};
      Read(i: CHAR): CHAR;
    END;
  PROCEDURE Create( ): T;
  CONST MaxTabSize: INTEGER = 100;
  EXCEPTION Full;
<*
  FIELDS OF T
    val : Tab;
  METHOD T.Add(i, c)
    MODIFIES SELF.val
    ENSURES SELF.val' = add(SELF.val, i, c)
      EXCEPT size(SELF.val) ≥ MaxTabSize
           ∧ ¬(i ∈ SELF.val)
        => RAISEVAL = Full ∧ UNCHANGED(ALL)
  METHOD T.Read(i)
    REQUIRES i ∈ SELF.val
    ENSURES RESULT = lookup(SELF.val, i)
  PROCEDURE Create
    ENSURES RESULT.val = new ∧ FRESH(RESULT)
*>
END Table.
```

FIGURE 5. A Sample LM3 Interface Specification

They use the same Table trait of Figure 3. We present these examples here simply to convey an impression of how programming language dependencies influence Larch interface languages. The notations used are described in detail in [12]

Relating implementations to specifications

In our work we emphasize using specifications as a communication medium. Programmers are encouraged to become clients of well-specified abstractions that have been implemented by others.

One of the advantages of Larch's two-tiered approach to specification is that the relationship of implementations to specifications is relatively straightforward. Consider, for example, the LCL specification in Figure 6 and the C implementation in Figure 7.

The specification defines a relation between the program state when choose is called and the state when it returns. This relation contains all pairs of states <pre, post> in which

- the states differ only in the value of the global variable z, and

- in *post* the value of z is that of one of the two arguments passed to choose.

```
void choose(int x, int y) int z; {
  modifies z;
  ensures z' = x ∨ z' = y;
}
```

FIGURE 6. A specification of choose

```
void choose(int x, int y) {
  if (x > y) z = x;
  else z = y;
}
```

FIGURE 7. An implementation of choose

The implementation also defines a relation on program states. This relation contains all pairs of states <pre, post> in which

- the states differ only in the value of the variable z, and

- in *post* the value of z is the maximum of the two arguments passed to choose.

We say that the implementation of choose in Figure 7 *satisfies* the specification in Figure 6—or is a *correct implementation* of Figure 6[2]— because the relation defined by the implementation is a subset of the relation defined by the specification. Every possible behavior that can be observed by a client of the implementation is permitted by the specification.

The definition of satisfaction we have just given is not directly useful. In practice, formal arguments about programs are not usually made by building and comparing relations. Instead, such proofs are usually done by pushing predicates through the program text, in ways that can be justified by appeal to the definition of satisfaction. A description of how to do this appears in the books [5, 10].

The notion of satisfaction is a bit more complicated for implementations of abstract types, because the implementor of an abstract type is working simultaneously at two levels of abstraction. To implement an abstract type, one chooses data structures to represent values of the type, then writes the procedures of the type in terms of that representation. However, since the specifications of those procedures are in terms of abstract values, one must be able to relate the representation data structures to the abstract values that they represent. This relation is an essential (but too often implicit) part of the implementation.

Figure 8 shows an implementation of the LCL specification in Figure 4. A value of the abstract type table is represented by a pointer to a struct containing two arrays and an integer. You need not look at the details of the code to understand the basic idea behind this implementation. Instead, you should consider the abstraction function and representation invariant.

The *abstraction function* is the bridge between the data structure used in the implementation of an abstract type and the abstract values being implemented. It maps each value of the representation type to a value of the abstract type.

---

[2] "Correct" is a dangerous word. It is not meaningful to say that an implementation is "correct" or "incorrect" without saying what specification it is claimed to satisfy. The technical sense of "correct" that is used in the formal methods community does not imply "good," or "useful," or even "not wrong," but merely "consistent with its specification."

```
#include "bool.h"
#define maxTabSize (10)

typedef struct {char ind[maxTabSize];
                char val[maxTabSize];
                int next;} tableRep;
typedef tableRep * table;

table table_create(void) {
  table t;
  t = (table) malloc(sizeof(tableRep));
  if (t == 0) {
    printf("Malloc returned null in table_create\n");
    exit(1);
  }
  t->next = 0;
  return t;
}
bool table_add(table t, char i, char c) {
  int j;
  for (j = 0; j < t->next; j++)
    if (t->ind[j] == i) {
      t->val[j] = c;
      return TRUE;
    }
  if (t->next == maxTabSize) return FALSE;
  t->val[t->next++] = c;
  return TRUE;
}
char table_read(table t, char i) {
  int j;
  for (j = 0; TRUE; j++)
    if (t->ind[j] == i) return t->val[j];
}
```

FIGURE 8. Implementing an Abstract Type

Here, we represent a table by a pointer, call it t, to a struct. If the triple <ind, val, next> contains the values of the fields of that struct in some state s, then we can define the abstract value represented by t in state s as toTab(<ind, val, next>), where

```
toTab(<next, ind, val>) ==
if next = 0 then empty
else insert(toTab(<next - 1, ind, val>),
        ind[next], val[next])
```

Abstraction functions are often many-to-one. Here, for example, if t->next = 0, t represents the empty table, no matter what the contents of t->ind and t->val.

The typedefs in Figure 8 define a data structure sufficient to represent any value of type table. However, it is not the case that any value of that data structure represents a value of type table. In defining the abstraction function, we relied upon some implicit assumptions about which data structures were valid representations. For example, toTab is not defined when t->next is negative. A *representation invariant* is used to make such assumptions explicit. For this implementation, the representation invariant is

— The value of next lies between 0 and maxTabSize:

$$0 \leq \text{t->next} \land \text{t->next} \leq \text{maxTabSize}$$

— and no index may appear more than once in the fragment of ind that lies between 0 and next:

$$\forall \text{ i,j:int}$$
$$(0 \leq i \land i < j \land j < \text{t->next})$$
$$\Rightarrow (\text{t->ind})[i] \neq (\text{t->ind})[j]$$

To show that that this representation invariant holds, we use a proof technique called *data type induction*. Since table is an abstract type, we know that clients cannot directly access the data structure used to represent a table. Therefore, all values of type table that occur during program execution will have been generated by the functions specified in the interface. So to show that the invariant holds it suffices to show, reasoning from the code implementing the functions on tables, that

— the value returned by table_create satisfies the invariant (this is the basis step of the induction),

— whenever table_add is called, if the invariant holds for t^ then the invariant will also hold for t', and

— whenever table_read is called, if the invariant holds for t^ then the invariant will also hold for t'.

A slightly different data type induction principle can be used to reason about clients of abstract types. To prove that a property holds for all instances of the type, i.e., that is is an *abstract invariant*, one inducts over all possible sequences of calls to the procedures that create or modify locs of the type. However, one reasons using the specifications of the procedures rather than their implementations. For example, to show that the size(t) is never greater than maxTabSize one shows that

- the specification of table_create implies that the size of the table returned is not greater than maxTabSize, and

- the specification of table_add combined with the hypothesis
  t^ $\leq$ maxTabSize implies that t' $\leq$ maxTabSize.

Given the abstraction function, it is relatively easy to define what it means for the procedure implementations in Figure 8 to satisfy the specifications in Figure 4. For example, we say that the implementation of table_read satisfies its specification because the image under the abstraction function of the relation between pre and post-states defined by the implementation (i.e., what one gets by applying the abstraction function to all values of type table in the relation defined by the implementation) is a subset of the relation defined by the specification. Notice, by the way, that any argument that the implementation of table_read satisfies its specification will rely on both the requires clause of the specification and on the representation invariant.

LP, The Larch Proof Assistant

The discussions of LSL, LCL, and LM3 have alluded to tools supporting those languages. LP is a tool that is used to support all three. It is described in [8]. Here we give merely a glimpse of its use.

LP is a proof assistant for a subset of multisorted first-order logic with equality, the logic on which the Larch languages are based. It is designed to work efficiently on large problems and to be used by specifiers with relatively little experience with theorem proving. Its design and development have been motivated primarily by our work on LSL, but it also has other uses, for example, reasoning about circuit designs [17, 18], algorithms involving concurrency [7], data types [23], and algebraic systems [15].

LP is intended primarily as an interactive proof assistant or proof debugger, rather than as a fully automatic theorem prover. Its design is based on the assumption that initial attempts to state and prove conjectures usually fail. So LP is designed to carry out routine (but possibly lengthy) proof steps automatically and to provide useful information about why proofs fail. To keep users from being surprised and confused by its behavior, LP does not employ complicated heuristics for finding proofs automatically. It makes it easy for users to employ standard techniques such as proof by cases, by induction, or by contradiction, but the choice among such strategies is left to the user.

THE LIFE CYCLE OF PROOFS

Proving is similar to programming: proofs are designed, coded, debugged, and (sometimes) documented.

Before designing a proof it is necessary to formalize the things being reasoned about and the conjecture to be proved. The design of the proof proper starts with an outline of its structure, including key lemmas and methods of proof. The proof itself must be given in sufficient detail to be convincing. What it means to be convincing depends on who (or what) is to be convinced. Experience shows that humans are frequently convinced by unsound proofs, so we look for a mechanical "skeptic" that is just hard enough (but not too hard) to convince.

Once part of a proof has been coded, LP can be used to debug it. Proofs of interesting conjectures hardly ever succeed the first time. Sometimes the conjecture is wrong. Sometimes the formalization is incorrect or incomplete. Sometimes the proof strategy is flawed or not detailed enough. LP provides a variety of facilities that can be used to understand the problem when an attempted proof fails.

While debugging proofs, users frequently reformulate axioms and conjectures. After any change in the axiomatization, it is necessary to recheck not only the conjecture whose proof attempt uncovered the problem, but also the conjectures previously proved using the old axioms. LP has facilities that support such regression testing.

LP will, upon request, record a session in a script file that can be replayed. LP "prettyprints" script files, using indentation to reflect the structure of proofs. It also annotates script files with information that indicates when subgoals are introduced (e.g., in a proof by induction), and when subgoals and theorems are proved. On request, as LP replays a script file, it will halt replay at the first point where the annotations and the new proof diverge. This checking makes it easier to keep proof attempts from getting "out of sync" with their author's conception of their structure.

A SMALL PROOF

Figure 9 contains a short LSL specification, including a simple conjecture (following the reserved word implies) that is supposed to follow from the axioms. Figure 10 shows a script for an LP proof of that conjecture.

The declare commands introduce the variables and operators in the LSL specification. The assert commands supply the LSL axioms relating the operators; the Nat generated by assertion provides an induction

```
Nat: trait
  includes AC(+, Nat)
  introduces
     0: → Nat
     s: Nat → Nat
     __ < __: Nat, Nat → Bool
  asserts
    Nat generated by 0, s
    ∀ i, j, k: Nat
      i + 0 == i;
      i + s(j) == s(i + j);
      ¬(i < 0);
      0 < s(i);
      s(i) < s(j) == i < j
    implies ∀ i, j, k: Nat
      i < j ⇒ i < (j + k)
```

FIGURE 9. A trait containing a conjecture

scheme for Nat. The prove command initiates a proof by induction of the conjecture. The *diamond* (<>) annotations are provided by LP; they indicate the introduction of subgoals for the inductions. The *box* (□) annotations are also provided by LP; they indicate the discharge of subgoals and, finally, of the main proof. The resume command starts a nested induction. No other user intervention is needed to complete this proof. The qed command on the last line asks LP to confirm that there are no outstanding conjectures.

Conclusion

Larch is still very much a "work in progress." New Larch interface languages are being designed, new tools are being built, and the existing languages and tools are in a state of evolution. Most significantly, specifications are being written.

But Larch has reached a divide, what Churchill might have called "the end of the beginning." Until now, most of the work on Larch has been done by the authors of this paper and their close associates. We hope that the First International Workshop on Larch [16] and the publication of [12] mark the beginning of the period when most Larch research, development, and application will be done by people we do not yet know.

```
set name nat
declare sort Nat
declare variables i, j, k: Nat
declare operators
  0: → Nat
  s: Nat → Nat
  +: Nat, Nat → Nat
  <: Nat, Nat → Bool
  ..
assert Nat generated by 0, s
assert ac +
assert
  i + 0 == i
  i + s(j) == s(i + j)
  ¬(i < 0)
  0 < s(i)
  s(i) < s(j) == i < j
  ..
set name lemma
prove i < j ⇒ i < (j + k) by induction on j
  < > 2 subgoals for proof by induction on j
    [] basis subgoal
    resume by induction on i
    < > 2 subgoals for proof by induction on i
      [] basis subgoal
      [] induction subgoal
    [] induction subgoal
  [] conjecture
qed
```

FIGURE 10. Sample LP proof script

References

[1] Michel Bidoit. *Pluss, un langage pour le développement de spécifications algébriques modulaires.* Thèse d'Etat, Université de Paris-Sud, Orsay, May 1989.

[2] S.R. Cardenas and H. Oktaba. *Formal Specification in Larch Case Study: Text Manager. Interface Specification, Implementation, in Ada and Validation of Implementation,* TR 511, Instituto de Investigaciones en Matematicas Aplicadas y en Sistemas, Universidad Nacional Autonoma de Mexico, 1988.

[3] Yoonsik Cheon. *Larch/Smalltalk: A Specification Language for Smalltalk,* M.Sc. Thesis, Iowa State University, 1991.

[4] O.-J. Dahl, D.F. Langmyhr, and O. Owe. *Preliminary Report on the Specification and Programming Language ABEL,* Research Report 106, Institute of Informatics, University of Oslo, Norway, 1986.

[5] Ole-Johan Dahl. *Verifiable Programming,* Prentice Hall International Series in Computer Science, 1992.

[6] H. Ehrig and B. Mahr. *Fundamentals of Algebraic Specification 1: Equations and Initial Semantics,* EATCS Monographs on Theoretical Computer Science, vol. 6, Springer-Verlag, 1985.

[7] Urban Engberg, Peter Grønning, and Leslie Lamport. "Mechanical verification of concurrent systems with TLA," *Proc. Workshop on Computer Aided Verification,* 1992. Revised version in [16].

[8] Stephen J. Garland and John V. Guttag. *A Guide to LP, The Larch Prover,* TR 82, DEC/SRC, Dec. 1991.

[9] J.A. Goguen, J.W. Thatcher, and E.G. Wagner. "An initial algebra approach to the specification, correctness and implementation of abstract data types," *Current Trends in Programming Methodology IV: Data Structuring,* R. Yeh (ed.), Prentice-Hall, 1978.

[10] David Gries. *The Science of Programming,* Springer-Verlag, 1981.

[11] David Guaspari, Carla Marceau, and Wolfgang Polak. "Formal verification of Ada," *IEEE Trans. Software Engineering* 16(9), Sept. 1990.

[12] J.V. Guttag and J.J. Horning (eds.) with S.J. Garland, K.D. Jones, A. Modet, and J.M. Wing *Larch, Languages and Tools for Formal Specification,* Springer-Verlag, 1993 (to appear).

[13] Gary T. Leavens and Yoonsik Cheon. "Preliminary design of Larch/C++," in [16].

[14] Richard Allen Lerner. *Specifying Objects of Concurrent Systems*, Ph.D. Thesis, Dept. of Computer Science, Carnegie Mellon University, TR CS-91-131, May 1991.

[15] U. Martin and T. Nipkow. "Automating Squiggol," *Proc. IFIP Work. Conf. Programming Concepts and Methods*, Tiberias, Apr. 1990. North-Holland.

[16] U. Martin and J.M. Wing. *Proc. First Intl. Workshop on Larch*, Dedham, Jul. 1992, Springer-Verlag.

[17] James B. Saxe, Stephen J. Garland, John V. Guttag, and James J. Horning. "Using Transformations and Verification in Circuit Design," in [16].

[18] Jørgen Staunstrup, Stephen J. Garland, and John V. Guttag. "Mechanized verification of circuit descriptions using the Larch Prover," *Proc. IFIP Work. Conf. Theorem Provers in Circuit Design: Theory, Practice, and Experience*, Nijmegen, Jun. 1992. North-Holland.

[19] M. Wand. "Final algebra semantics and data type extensions," *Journal of Computer and System Sciences*, Aug. 1979.

[20] Jeannette Marie Wing. *A Two-Tiered Approach to Specifying Programs*, Ph.D. Thesis, Dept. of Electrical Engineering and Computer Science, MIT, TR MIT/LCS/TR-299, May 1983.

[21] J.M. Wing. "Using Larch to Specify Avalon/C++ Objects," *Proc. Intl. Joint Conf. Theory and Practice of Software Development, TAPSOFT*, Barcelona, Mar. 1989. Springer-Verlag, LNCS 352. Revised version in [21].

[22] Jeannette M. Wing. "Writing Larch Interface Language Specifications," *ACM Trans. Programming Languages and Systems* 9(1), Jan. 1987.

[23] Jeannette M. Wing and Chun Gong. "Experience with the Larch Prover," *Proc. ACM Intl. Workshop on Formal Methods in Software Development*, May 1990.

[24] J.M. Wing, E. Rollins, and Amy Moormann Zaremski. "Thoughts on a Larch/ML and a new application for LP," in [16].

[25] M. Wirsing. *Algebraic Specification*, Technical Report MIP-8914, University of Passau, Germany, 1989.

The EVES System

Sentot Kromodimoeljo, Bill Pase, Mark Saaltink,
Dan Craigen and Irwin Meisels*

ORA Canada
265 Carling Avenue, Suite 506
Ottawa, Ontario K1S 2E1
CANADA
Internet: eves@ora.on.ca
Phone: (613) 238 7900

Abstract. After a brief introduction, we discuss two applications of EVES. The first application is a proof of Jacobson's Theorem. The second application is a proof of an interpreter for a small programming language; portions of the interpreter proof are described in this paper. We conclude by discussing some of the issues raised by the international lecture series on "Functional Programming, Concurrency, Simulation and Automated Reasoning" (FPCSAR).
Keywords: Automated deduction, EVES, Formal Methods, Logic of programs, NEVER, Verdi.

1 Introduction

In the terminology of this lecture series, EVES is an automated theory based system that supports mathematical reasoning. Our research has focused on the development of a new specification and implementation language (called Verdi) [Cra91] and the implementation of a new automated theorem prover (called NEVER). As part of our development of Verdi, we developed a formal semantics for the language and demonstrated the soundness of our proof obligation generator (with respect to the formal semantics) [Saa90b, Saa90a]. Two other introductory papers on EVES were presented at the Fourth Banff Higher-Order Workshop [CS90] and at VDM'91 [CKM+91]. Work relating EVES to some aspects of Z (particularly the mathematical toolkit) is discussed in [Saa92].

We start this paper with an introduction to Verdi, NEVER and EVES.[2] We will then proceed with discussions on two applications of EVES. The first application is drawn from Algebra and is a ring theory result called Jacobson's Theorem. This theorem states that if $x^3 = x$ in a ring, then the ring is commutative. The second application is drawn from Computing Science and is the proof of correctness of significant portions of an interpreter for a small imperative programming language.

---

* The development of EVES was sponsored by the Canadian Department of National Defence through DSS contract W2207-8-AF78 and other contracts. This paper was originally ORA conference paper CP–92–6017–49.

[2] This introduction to Verdi, NEVER and EVES is derived from our VDM 91 paper [CKM+91] and is based on an overview of Verdi in the Verdi reference manual[Cra91].

We conclude by discussing various comments made by the lecture series coordinator, Peter Lauer, in [LJZ92].

2 Verdi

Verdi is a formal notation, based on a version of untyped set theory [Fra68], that can be used to express rigorous mathematical concepts [Saa90b]. For example, Verdi has been used to prove theorems of set theory (e.g., Schroeder-Bernstein, Cantor), the functional correctness of hardware designs (e.g., an n-bit adder), security critical properties (e.g., versions of non-interference), and that programs written in the imperative subset of Verdi terminate and meet their specification (given in terms of pre and post conditions). However, perhaps the most fundamental comment is that, since Verdi is a variant of Zermelo-Fraenkel with the Axiom of Choice (ZFC), it can mathematically model and analyze a vast range of systems.

2.1 Theories and Declarations

Before we proceed, we need to introduce the terms *vocabulary*, *theory*, *declaration*, and *EVES database*.

A *vocabulary* determines a set of names of various categories. Verdi names are categorized as being type names, function names, procedure names, group names (to support mutual recursion) and axiom names.

A Verdi *theory* consists of a current vocabulary and a set of axioms specifying relationships between the names of the vocabulary. Verdi determines an *initial theory* which introduces names and axioms that can be used in the development of any Verdi theory. The initial theory contains, for example, most of the axioms of ZFC set theory.

A *declaration* results in the modification of a theory by extending the vocabulary and adding further axioms. The proof obligations associated with each declaration mandate that each extension of a theory is a semantic conservative extension.

The *EVES database* contains a representation of a current theory, heuristic information associated with the theory, and records of complete and partial proofs. The entire database can be saved and later restored from a library.

2.2 An Overview of Verdi

The syntax of Verdi is similar in form to the s-expressions of Lisp.[3]

Verdi requires typing information for syntactic forms that are to be executed. A *type name* denotes a set of values. The Verdi *initial theory* includes the Bool, Int and Char types. The Bool type denotes the logical truth values. The Int type denotes the set of mathematical integers, not an executable subset of the integers. The Char type denotes the ASCII character set. Other types are introduced through an enumeration declaration, an array declaration, or a record declaration.

---

[3] During 1992 we expect to modify the syntactic appearance of Verdi to be consistent with conventional mathematics notation.

There are a number of different *function declarations*; all, however, are expression abstracts. *Executable functions* associate type information with the parameters and the result of the function. The result of an executable function application is predictable only if the application is legal. By legal, it is meant that the parameters satisfy constraints, determined by a function pre condition. *Non-executable functions* may be defined recursively and, by using function recursion groups, through mutual recursion. Certain functions, defined as part of the initial theory, are called *wide domain functions* and have more than one signature; these functions are similar to *operators* in traditional programming languages.

A *procedure declaration* introduces a procedure and is always executable. Procedures may be defined recursively and, by using procedure recursion groups, through mutual recursion.

An *axiom declaration* restricts the possible meanings for the names in a vocabulary.

The Verdi *expressions* are character literals, numerals, strings, identifiers (denoting variables), function applications, and quantifications. Certain expressions are called *manifest expressions* and are mandatory in certain instances where expressions are syntactically required (i.e., case labels and array bounds). Manifest expressions can be evaluated at compile time.

The Verdi *statements* are exit (from a loop), return (from a procedure), abort (the program), note (a form of annotation), assignment, procedure call, block, conditional, case, loop, and two forms of *for* loop.

A *library* is a repository for objects and is the main means for large scale modularization and abstraction. Library objects are collections of Verdi declarations which, through the use of the **load** command, may depend upon other library objects. The **load** command introduces the declarations of the associated library specification object (and any necessary subsidiary library specification objects) to a current theory.

3 NEVER

NEVER is the automated deduction component of EVES. It is an interactive theorem prover capable of automatically performing large proof steps, yet can be finely directed by the user. Its design has been influenced by the Bledsoe-Bruell prover [BB74], the Stanford Pascal Verifier [Luc79], the Boyer-Moore theorem prover [BM79], and the Affirm theorem prover [TE81].

NEVER is neither a fully automatic nor an entirely manual theorem prover. Although NEVER provides powerful deductive techniques for the automatic proof of theorems, it also includes simple user steps which permit its use as a system more akin to a proof checker than a theorem prover. The possible fine grain control of the prover allows users to closely investigate proof strategies and determine why, for example, proofs are failing. In our view, the synergism of powerful automated support and user control is a necessary precondition to a successful general purpose theorem prover.

3.1 Proof Steps

Proof steps are used to transform a formula to an equivalent new formula. Through a chain of logical equivalences, it is expected that the formula will be reduced to the equivalent formula true. Some of the automatic transformations are exceedingly complex; others, primarily viewed as being manual steps, result in simpler transformations. Appendix A includes descriptions of a subset of the prover commands.

3.2 Use of Axioms

Axioms can be assumed during a proof of some other conjecture with the use command. In addition, axioms declared as rewrite or forward rules may be applied automatically by NEVER. A rewrite rule specifies the conditional replacement of an expression by another equivalent expression. A forward rule specifies a formula to be assumed whenever a certain criteria is met.

The simplification process attempts to replace an expression with an equivalent expression which the system considers to be simpler. Propositional tautologies are always detected. In addition, the simplification process reasons about equalities, inequalities, integers, and quantifiers. Simplification is performed by the **simplify** command.

The rewriting process consists of the application of both rewrite and forward rules as well as simplification. While traversing a formula being rewritten, an attempt is made to match patterns of rewrite rules and triggers of forward rules against subexpressions of the formula. If a pattern or trigger matches a subexpression, an attempt is made to apply the associated rewrite or forward rule. Rewriting is performed by the **rewrite** commands.

Reduction consists of a single traversal of the expression to be proved applying function definitions, rewrite rules, forward rules and simplification. Reduction is performed using the **reduce** command.

The induction technique used by NEVER is based on that of the Boyer-Moore prover [BM79] and has been extended to allow quantifiers. Normally, induction schemes are heuristically chosen based on calls to recursive functions within the current formula. However, the user may direct the prover by providing an explicit term on which to induct. Commands that may perform an induction step include **induct** and **prove by induction**.

4 Verdi Interpreter

EVES includes an interpreter for executable Verdi code. With the interpreter, the user can print values of expressions and call Verdi procedures. The interpreter works with the library facility. For example, if a library specification unit is loaded and a routine stub in the unit is called, the interpreter will retrieve the complete declaration from the corresponding model and interpret it. If there is no corresponding model, the interpretation is suspended and the user may assign values to reference formals, or return a result value from a function. The interpreter also provides the ability to trace routines, set breakpoints and continue from them, interrupt the interpretation and examine routine locals and formals, and print tracebacks.

5 EVES

EVES is written in Common Lisp and has been successfully run on Symbolics, Sun 3s, SparcStations, Data General AViiONs, VAXes and the Apple Macintosh IIx.

Interaction with EVES may occur through either an editor interface or a command processor. The most common use is through an EMACS interface.

Conceptually, the development process is one of theory extension (using Verdi declarations). Development starts with the Verdi initial theory. As declarations are added, information representing the declarations are entered into the EVES database. The result is a new current theory consisting of the previous theory extended to include the additional information. Declarations may result in the generation of proof obligations. The system supports a degree of incrementality.

6 Ring Theory: Jacobson's Theorem

Prior to our presentation of Jacobson's Theorem, we show how equality-chain proofs can be performed using EVES.

Consider the following proof from group theory[4]:

$$-(-x) = -(-x) + 0$$
$$= -(-x) + (-x + x)$$
$$= (-(-x) + -x) + x$$
$$= 0 + x$$
$$= x$$

We start by defining the group theory axioms in EVES. Most of the axioms have an obvious orientation as rewriting rules. The associativity rule could be oriented either way, but EVES has a bias toward associating to the right and, consequently, we bias the associativity rule in the same direction.

```
(function-stub g0 ())      ; zero element
(function-stub g+ (x y))   ; group operation
(function-stub g- (x))     ; inverse function

(rule left-zero      (x)     (= (g+ (g0) x)      x))
(rule right-zero     (x)     (= (g+ x (g0))      x))
(rule left-inverse   (x)     (= (g+ (g- x) x)    0))
(rule right-inverse  (x)     (= (g+ x (g- x))    0))
(rule associativity (x y z) (= (g+ (g+ x y) z) (g+ x (g+ y z))))
```

Now, present the proof in "Dijkstra form," justifying each equality in the chain. For each equality, if the axiom used is a rule, record the direction of application. Here, each step is marked => if the rewriting takes the earlier term to the later, otherwise it is marked <=.

---

[4] The EVES solution presented here was developed by Mark Saaltink.

```
        (g- (g- x))
    = {right-zero} <=
        (g+ (g- (g- x)) (g0))
    = {right-inverse} <=
        (g+ (g- (g- x)) (g+ (g- x) x))
    = {associativity} <=
        (g+ (g+ (g- (g- x)) (g- x)) x)
    = {left-inverse} =>
        (g+ (g0) x)
    = {left-zero} =>
        x
```

There is a single "high point" in the middle of this proof: the formula

$$(g+ \ (g+ \ (g- \ (g- \ x)) \ (g- \ x)) \ x)$$

that can be rewritten by either associativity or left-inverse. Since EVES applies rewriting rules innermost-first, should this term arise, rule left-inverse will be applied rather than associativity. Thus, to have EVES produce the above proof, we need only state the following:

```
(try (= (g- (g- x)) x))
(use associativity (x (g- (g- x))) (y (g- x)) (z x))
(rewrite)
```

That is, at the high points, introduce by hand the appropriate instance of the rule that applies to the outermost term. In addition, if any steps use lemmas that are not rewrite rules, they need to be explicitly applied (with the use command).

We now start our development of Jacobson's Theorem *i.e.*, if $x^3 = x$ then the ring is commutative. The development is partly based on a proof by Ted Herman [Her90].

We start with the ring axioms and signatures.

```
(function-stub r0 ())
(function-stub r- (x))
(function-stub r+ (x y))
(function-stub r* (x y))

;;; basic algebraic ring axioms
(rule inverse-zero    ()      (= (r- (r0))        (r0)))
(rule left-zero       (x)     (= (r+ (r0) x)      x))
(rule left-inverse    (x)     (= (r+ (r- x) x)    (r0)))
(rule inverse-inverse (x)     (= (r- (r- x))      x))
(rule r+-associates   (x y z) (= (r+ (r+ x y) z) (r+ x (r+ y z))))
(rule inverse-r+      (x y)   (= (r- (r+ x y))    (r+ (r- x) (r- y))))

(rule r+-commutes      (x y)   (= (r+ x y)         (r+ y x)))
(rule r*-associates    (x y z) (= (r* (r* x y) z) (r* x (r* y z))))
(rule distribute-left  (x y z) (= (r* x (r+ y z)) (r+ (r* x y) (r* x z))))
(rule distribute-right (x y z) (= (r* (r+ x y) z) (r+ (r* x z) (r* y z))))
```

From the above, we can derive some elementary properties of rings.[5]

```
(rule right-zero (x) (= (r+ x (r0)) x))
(USE LEFT-ZERO (X X))
(REWRITE)

(rule right-inverse (x) (= (r+ x (r- x)) (r0)))
(USE LEFT-INVERSE (X X))
(REWRITE)

(rule right-inverse-assoc (x y) (= (r+ x (r+ (r- x) y)) y))
;;; Proof:
;;; (r+ x (r+ (r- x) y))
;;; = (r+-associates) <=
;;; (r+ (r+ x (r- x)) y)
;;; = (right-inverse) =>
;;; (r+ (r0) y)
;;; = (right-zero) =>
;;; y
(USE R+-ASSOCIATES (X X) (Y (R- X)) (Z Y))
(REWRITE)

(rule left-inverse-assoc (x y) (= (r+ (r- x) (r+ x y)) y))
;;; similar to right-inverse-assoc
(USE R+-ASSOCIATES (X (R- X)) (Y X) (Z Y))
(REWRITE)

(axiom left-cancellation (x y z)
  (implies (= (r+ x y) (r+ x z)) (= y z)))
;;; Proof:
;;; (= (r+ x y) (r+ x z))
;;; => (substitution)
;;; (= (r+ (r- x) (r+ x y)) (r+ (r- x) (r+ x z)))
;;; = (left-inverse-assoc) =>
;;; (= y z)
(USE LEFT-INVERSE-ASSOC (X X)(Y Y))
(USE LEFT-INVERSE-ASSOC (X X)(Y Z))
(SIMPLIFY)

(axiom diff-0-implies-equal (x y)
  (implies (= (r+ x (r- y)) (r0)) (= x y)))
(USE R+-ASSOCIATES (X X) (Y (R- Y)) (Z Y))
(SPLIT (= (R+ X (R- Y)) (r0)))
(REWRITE)
```

Herman assumed the following four lemmas, which we prove here:

---

[5] In some of the proofs that follow we include as commentary the Dijkstra-style proofs. The reader should note that EVES uses the semicolon as a comment character.

```
(rule r*-0-left (x) (= (r* (r0) x) (r0)))
;;; Proof:
;;; (= (r* (r0) x) (r0))
;;; <= left cancellation
;;; (= (r+ (r* x x) (r* (r0) x)) (r+ (r* x x) (r0)))
;;; = (left-zero) =>
;;; (= (r+ (r* x x) (r* (r0) x)) (r* x x))
;;; = (distribute-right) <=
;;; (= (r* (r+ x (r0)) x) (r* x x))
;;; = (right-zero) =>
;;; (= (r* x x) (r* x x))
;;; = (trivially)
;;; (true)
(USE LEFT-CANCELLATION (X (R* X X)) (Y (R* (R0) X)) (Z (R0)))
(USE DISTRIBUTE-RIGHT (X X) (Y (R0)) (Z X))
(REWRITE)

(rule r*-0-right (x) (= (r* x (r0)) (r0)))
;;; Proof:
;;; (= (r* x (r0)) (r0))
;;; <= (left-cancellation)
;;; (= (r+ (r* x x) (r* x (r0))) (r+ (r* x x) (r0)))
;;; = (left-zero) =>
;;; (= (r+ (r* x x) (r* x (r0))) (r* x x))
;;; = (distribute-left) <=
;;; (= (r* x (r+ x (r0))) (r* x x))
;;; = (right-zero) =>
;;; (= (r* x x) (r* x x))
;;; = (trivially)
;;; (true)
(USE LEFT-CANCELLATION (X (R* X X)) (Y (R* X (R0))) (Z (R0)))
(USE DISTRIBUTE-LEFT (X X) (Y X) (Z (R0)))
(REWRITE)

(rule *-inverse-left (x y)
  (= (r* (r- x) y) (r- (r* x y))))
;;; Proof:
;;; (= (r* (r- x) y) (r- (r* x y)))
;;; <= (left-cancellation)
;;; (= (r+ (r* x y) (r* (r- x) y)) (r+ (r* x y) (r- (r* x y))))
;;; = (right-inverse) =>
;;; (= (r+ (r* x y) (r* (r- x) y)) (r0))
;;; = (distribute-right) <=
;;; (= (r* (r+ x (r- x)) y) (r0))
;;; = (right-inverse) =>
;;; (= (r0) (r0))
;;; = (trivially)
;;; (true)
```

```
(USE LEFT-CANCELLATION (X (R* X Y)) (Y (R* (R- X) Y)) (Z (R- (R* X Y))))
(USE DISTRIBUTE-RIGHT (X X) (Y (R- X)) (Z Y))
(REWRITE)

(rule *-inverse-right (x y)
  (= (r* x (r- y)) (r- (r* x y))))
;;; Proof as above
(USE LEFT-CANCELLATION (X (R* X Y)) (Y (R* X (R- Y))) (Z (R- (R* X Y))))
(USE DISTRIBUTE-LEFT (X X) (Y Y) (Z (R- Y)))
(REWRITE)
```

Finally, we add the hypothesis that $x^3 = x$ and proceed with the proof that the ring is commutative.

```
(rule cube (x) (= (r* x (r* x x)) x))

;;; Now the proof

(rule cube-1 (x y)
  (= (r* x (r* x (r* x y))) (r* x y)))
(USE R*-ASSOCIATES (X X) (Y (R* X X)) (Z Y))
(REWRITE)

(rule cube-2 (x y)
  (= (r* x (r* y (r* x (r* y (r* x y))))) (r* x y)))
(USE CUBE (X (R* X Y)))
(REWRITE)

;;; Lemmas a and b are used in proofs where Herman uses pre- or post-
;;; multiplication.
;;;
;;; Lemmas a and b are stated in contrapositive form.
;;; Saaltink's hand proof used lemma-a of the form
;;;
;;; (implies (= x (r0))
;;;          (= (r* x y) (r0)))
;;;
;;; Unfortunately, the EVES heuristics do not allow that to be used
;;; effectively, since simplification replaces the x in (r* x y) with
;;; (r0), and rewriting then elimates the whole term.  In the contrapositive
;;; form, the simplifier does not perform the replacement.

(axiom lemma-a (x y)
  (implies (not (= (r* x y) (r0)))
           (not (= x (r0)))))
(SPLIT (= X (R0)))
(REWRITE)
```

```
(axiom lemma-b (x y)
  (implies (not (= (r* x y) (r0)))
           (not (= y (r0)))))
(SPLIT (= Y (R0)))
(REWRITE)

(axiom lemma-1 (x)
  (implies (= (r* x x) (r0))
           (= x (r0))))
;;; Proof:
;;; (= (r* x x) (r0))
;;; => (lemma-b)
;;; (= (r* x (r* x x)) (r0))
;;; = (cube) =>
;;; (= x (r0))
(USE LEMMA-B (X X) (Y (R* X X)))
(REWRITE)
```

```
;;; Lemma c is a variation of lemma 1 that is used in the proof of lemma 4.
```

```
(axiom lemma-c (x y)
  (implies (= (r* x (r* y y)) (r0))
           (= (r* x y) (r0))))
;;; Proof:
;;; (= (r* x (r* y y)) (r0))
;;; => (lemma-a)
;;; (= (r* (r* x (r* y y)) y) (r0))
;;; = (r*-associates) =>
;;; (= (r* x (r* y (r* y y))) (r0))
;;; = (cube) =>
;;; (= (r* x y) (r0))
(USE LEMMA-A (X (R* X (R* Y Y))) (Y Y))
(REWRITE)
```

```
(axiom lemma-2 (x y)
  (implies (= (r* x y) (r0))
           (= (r* y x) (r0))))
(USE LEMMA-1 (X (R* Y X)))
(USE LEMMA-A (X (R* X Y)) (Y X))
;;; It turns out that we do not need to explicitly include
;;; (USE LEMMA-B (X Y) (Y (R* X (R* Y X))))
;;; as it turns out to be redundant. This is a consequence
;;; of the same mechanism that had Saaltink state
;;; lemmas a and b in contrapositive.
(REWRITE)
```

```
(rule lemma-3 (x y)
  (= (r* x (r* x (r* y x)))
     (r* y x)))
(USE LEMMA-2 (X X) (Y (R+ Y (R- (R* X (R* X Y))))))
(USE DIFF-0-IMPLIES-EQUAL (X (R* Y X)) (Y (R* X (R* X (R* Y X)))))
(REWRITE)


(rule lemma-3-post-multiplied (x y z)
  (= (r* x (r* x (r* y (r* x z))))
     (r* y (r* x z))))
(USE R*-ASSOCIATES (X X) (Y (R* X (R* Y X))) (Z Z))
(REWRITE)


(axiom lemma-4 (x y)
  (= (r* (r+ (r* x y) (r- (r* y x))) (r* y x))
     (r0)))
(USE LEMMA-C (X (R+ (R* X Y) (R- (R* Y X)))) (Y (R* Y X)))
(REWRITE)


(rule lemma-4-rule (x y)
  (= (r* x (r* y (r* y x)))
     (r* y (r* x (r* y x)))))
(USE DIFF-0-IMPLIES-EQUAL (X (R* X (R* Y (R* Y X))))
                          (Y (R* Y (R* X (R* Y X)))))
(USE LEMMA-4 (X X)(Y Y))
(REWRITE)


(axiom r*-commutes (x y)
  (= (r* x y) (r* y x)))
(USE DIFF-0-IMPLIES-EQUAL (X (R* X Y)) (Y (R* Y X)))
(USE LEMMA-1 (X (R+ (R* X Y) (R- (R* Y X)))))
(REWRITE)
```

7 The PICO Interpreter

The PICO interpreter example, which is based on the algebraic specification presented in [BHK89], is the largest example in EVES to date (about 12,000 lines of specification, code, and prover documentation). The interpreter consists of a PICO type checker and a PICO evaluator.

We will describe the programming language PICO [BHK89], the development of an abstract specification of the PICO interpreter in EVES, and the development of an implementation of the PICO interpreter in EVES that satisfies the abstract specification. We will cover only snapshots of the development as the entire effort covers hundreds of pages [KP90].

7.1 The Language PICO

PICO is a toy language for while-programs. A PICO program consists of a sequence of declarations followed by a sequence of statements. A variable used in a PICO program must be declared to be either of type *natural* or of type *string*. There are also literal constants of either type.

There are three operators in the expression language of PICO:

- *plus* (addition of *naturals*),
- *minus* (subtraction of *naturals*), and
- *conc* (concatenation of *strings*).

An expression is a literal constant, a variable, or an operation on subexpressions of the appropriate type.

There are three kinds of statements in PICO:

- *assign* statements,
- *if* statements, and
- *while* statements.

An *assign* statement assigns the value that results from an evaluation of an expression to a variable. The expression and the variable must be of the same type.

An *if* statement has three parts:

- a test expression of type *natural*,
- a series of statements that is executed if the test expression evaluates to 0, and
- a series of statements that is executed if the test expression evaluates to a non-zero value.

A *while* statement has two parts:

- a test expression of type *natural*, and
- a series of statements that is repeatedly executed as long as the test expression evaluates to a non-zero value.

7.2 Development of the Abstract Specification

Development of the Specification The specification of the PICO system was developed directly from the description presented in [BHK89], which is written in a notation called Algebraic Specification Formalism (ASF). Here we present the abstract specification of the PICO evaluator.

First, we load the library units used by the evaluator.

```
(load ptype)
(load pval)
(load table)
(load string)
(load syntax)
```

Each of the library units corresponds to a module in the specification in [BHK89]. They correspond to the data type modules for PICO types, PICO values, tables, strings, and PICO abstract syntax, respectively.

We now declare the functions that evaluate PICO constructs. The description in [BHK89] uses one symbol for the functions since ASF allows overloading of functions. Here, we use different functions for different classes of constructs.

```
(function-stub eval-pico-program (program))
(function-stub eval-decls (decls env))
(function-stub eval-series (series env))
(function-stub eval-statement (stat env))
(function-stub eval-exp (exp env))
```

The last four functions take an extra argument: the environment in which the evaluation takes place.

We will need a function that appends a statement to the end of a series of statements.

```
(function-stub append-statement (series statement))
```

We now present the rules for evaluation. The PICO constructs evaluated by the evaluator are in abstract syntax constructed using operators defined in the syntax library unit. (These operators are qualified by syntax!.) We omit the function and rule declarations for "null-value-env", "value-env-add", and "value-env-lookup". These are functions for environment manipulation that are built using the table library unit. (Environments are just tables of <symbol,value> pairs.)

```
(rule eval-abs-pico-program (dec ser)
  (= (eval-pico-program (syntax!abs-pico-program dec ser))
     (eval-series ser (eval-decls dec (null-value-env)))))

(rule eval-abs-decls-natural (name type dec env)
  (implies (= type (ptype!natural-type))
           (= (eval-decls
                (syntax!abs-decls
                  (syntax!abs-id name) type dec) env)
              (eval-decls
                dec
                (value-env-add name (pval!pico-value-nat 0) env)))))

(rule eval-abs-decls-string (name type dec env)
  (implies (= type (ptype!string-type))
           (= (eval-decls
                (syntax!abs-decls (syntax!abs-id name) type dec)
                env)
              (eval-decls
                dec
                (value-env-add
```

```
                   name (pval!pico-value-string "") env)))))

(rule eval-abs-empty-decls (env)
  (= (eval-decls (syntax!abs-empty-decls) env)
     env))

(rule eval-abs-series (stat ser env)
  (= (eval-series (syntax!abs-series stat ser) env)
     (eval-series ser (eval-statement stat env))))

(rule eval-abs-empty-series (env)
  (= (eval-series (syntax!abs-empty-series) env)
     env))

(rule eval-abs-assign (name x env)
  (= (eval-statement (syntax!abs-assign (syntax!abs-id name) x) env)
     (value-env-add name (eval-exp x env) env)))

(rule eval-abs-if (x ser1 ser2 env)
  (= (eval-statement (syntax!abs-if x ser1 ser2) env)
     (if (= (eval-exp x env) (pval!pico-value-nat 0))
         (eval-series ser2 env)
         (eval-series ser1 env))))

(rule eval-abs-while (x ser env)
  (= (eval-statement (syntax!abs-while x ser) env)
     (if (= (eval-exp x env) (pval!pico-value-nat 0))
         env
         (eval-series
           (append-statement ser (syntax!abs-while x ser)) env))))

(rule eval-exp-abs-plus (x1 x2 nat1 nat2 env)
  (implies (and (= (pval!pico-value-nat nat1) (eval-exp x1 env))
                (= (pval!pico-value-nat nat2) (eval-exp x2 env)))
           (= (eval-exp (syntax!abs-plus x1 x2) env)
              (pval!pico-value-nat (+ nat1 nat2)))))

(rule eval-exp-abs-minus (x1 x2 nat1 nat2 env)
  (implies (and (= (pval!pico-value-nat nat1) (eval-exp x1 env))
                (= (pval!pico-value-nat nat2) (eval-exp x2 env)))
           (= (eval-exp (syntax!abs-minus x1 x2) env)
              (pval!pico-value-nat (- nat1 nat2)))))

(rule eval-exp-abs-conc (x1 x2 str1 str2 env)
  (implies (and (= (pval!pico-value-string str1) (eval-exp x1 env))
                (= (pval!pico-value-string str2) (eval-exp x2 env)))
           (= (eval-exp (syntax!abs-conc x1 x2) env)
```

```
                    (pval!pico-value-string
                      (string!string-conc str1 str2)))))

(rule eval-exp-abs-natural-constant (nat env)
  (= (eval-exp (syntax!abs-natural-constant nat) env)
     (pval!pico-value-nat nat)))

(rule eval-exp-abs-string-constant (str env)
  (= (eval-exp (syntax!abs-string-constant str) env)
     (pval!pico-value-string str)))

(rule eval-exp-abs-var (name env)
  (= (eval-exp (syntax!abs-var (syntax!abs-id name)) env)
     (pair!snd (value-env-lookup name env))))

(rule append-statement-abs-empty-series (stm)
  (= (append-statement (syntax!abs-empty-series) stm)
     (syntax!abs-series stm (syntax!abs-empty-series))))

(rule append-statement-abs-series (ser stm1 stm2)
  (= (append-statement (syntax!abs-series stm1 ser) stm2)
     (syntax!abs-series stm1 (append-statement ser stm2))))
```

An interesting aspect of the abstract specification of the PICO evaluator is that it can be used to compute the evaluation of a PICO program. For example, we can evaluate a simple program that assigns one variable to another as shown below.

```
(try (eval-pico-program
       (syntax!abs-pico-program
         (syntax!abs-decls
           (syntax!abs-id "n")
           (ptype!natural-type)
           (syntax!abs-decls
             (syntax!abs-id "r")
             (ptype!natural-type)
             (syntax!abs-empty-decls)))
         (syntax!abs-series
           (syntax!abs-assign
             (syntax!abs-id "r") (syntax!abs-natural-constant n))
           (syntax!abs-empty-series)))))
(reduce)
```

The result of the reduction is the value of the environment at the conclusion of the execution of the PICO program.

Development of the Model In EVES, a specification can be checked for consistency by providing a model. This is done using the library mechanism. The specification is made into a spec library unit and the model is then made into the corresponding model library unit. For a model library unit to be accepted, stub declarations are not allowed and proof obligations must be discharged. In addition, a consistency check between the spec and model units is performed (this check is essentially a syntactic comparison). If the consistency check fails, the model unit is not accepted by the library manager.

The full model (including proofs and subsidiary lemmas) for the PICO evaluator abstract specification is large. This is mainly because the model for evaluation of PICO statements is rather complex. For other PICO constructs, the model is rather straightforward. Below are the full declarations for "eval-decls" and "eval-pico-program" and the proof summaries for the corresponding evaluation rules.

The function "eval-decls" is defined recursively and produces an environment. There are two inductive cases corresponding to variable declarations of type string and natural, respectively. In EVES, we must supply a measure expression if a function is defined recursively. The measure expression specifies a value that must be proven to go down according to the well-founded relation m< in the recursive calls. This ensures that the definition terminates and hence is sound. In this case, we specify the measure to be the "size" of the declaration.

```
(function eval-decls (decls env) ((measure (pair!size decls)))
  (if (syntax!abs-empty-decls-p decls)
      env
      (if (syntax!abs-decls-p decls)
          (if (syntax!abs-id-p (syntax!abs-decls-id decls))
              (if (= (syntax!abs-decls-pico-type decls)
                     (ptype!string-type))
                  (eval-decls
                    (syntax!abs-decls-decls decls)
                    (value-env-add
                      (syntax!abs-id-str
                        (syntax!abs-decls-id decls))
                      (pval!pico-value-string "")
                      env))
                  (if (= (syntax!abs-decls-pico-type decls)
                         (ptype!natural-type))
                      (eval-decls
                        (syntax!abs-decls-decls decls)
                        (value-env-add
                          (syntax!abs-id-str
                            (syntax!abs-decls-id decls))
                          (pval!pico-value-nat 0)
                          env))
                      env))
              env)
          env)))
(REDUCE)
```

There were three rules of evaluation for PICO declarations in the specification. Their proofs are straightforward. The first two proofs required the explicit invocation of instances of "eval-decls", while the third proof is fully automatic requiring only the reduce command.

```
(rule eval-abs-decls-natural (name type dec env)
  (implies (= type (ptype!natural-type))
           (= (eval-decls
                (syntax!abs-decls (syntax!abs-id name) type dec)
                env)
              (eval-decls
                dec
                (value-env-add name (pval!pico-value-nat 0) env)))))
(INVOKE (EVAL-DECLS (SYNTAX!ABS-DECLS (SYNTAX!ABS-ID NAME) TYPE DEC) ENV))
(REWRITE)
(REDUCE)

(rule eval-abs-decls-string (name type dec env)
  (implies (= type (ptype!string-type))
           (= (eval-decls
                (syntax!abs-decls
                  (syntax!abs-id name) type dec)
                env)
              (eval-decls
                dec
                (value-env-add
                  name (pval!pico-value-string "") env)))))
(INVOKE (EVAL-DECLS (SYNTAX!ABS-DECLS (SYNTAX!ABS-ID NAME) TYPE DEC) ENV))
(REWRITE)

(rule eval-abs-empty-decls (env)
  (= (eval-decls (syntax!abs-empty-decls) env)
     env))
(REDUCE)
```

The definition for the function "eval-pico-program" is not recursive, hence we do not need to give a measure expression.

```
(function eval-pico-program (program) ()
  (if (syntax!abs-pico-program-p program)
      (eval-series (syntax!abs-pico-program-series program)
                   (eval-decls (syntax!abs-pico-program-decls
                                program)
                               (null-value-env)))
      (error-value-env)))
```

Again, the proof of the evaluation rule is rather straightforward:

```
(rule eval-abs-pico-program (dec ser)
  (= (eval-pico-program (syntax!abs-pico-program dec ser))
```

```
(eval-series ser (eval-decls dec (null-value-env)))))
(INVOKE EVAL-PICO-PROGRAM)
(REWRITE)
```

7.3 Implementation of the PICO Interpreter

We now describe the approach used in the development of an implementation of the PICO interpreter. By an "implementation" we mean a verified imperative program version of the interpreter. The EVES system supports the development of verified imperative programs written in the Verdi language. A procedure can be written with a pre and post annotation, and the system will generate the proof obligation which, when discharged, guarantees that the procedure satisfies its annotations.

Our approach is, given an abstract specification, the annotations for the procedures that implement the specification ought to be related to the abstract specification. The post annotation of the "eval-natural" procedure shown below contains the conjunct:

```
(= (pval!pico-value-nat (tbl!value-int result))
   (eval!eval-exp (tree!expr-node-to-abstract-syntax tree index)
                  (eval!value-env (tbl!symbol-table-to-table env)))))
```

which says that the abstraction of the result is the same as the result of evaluating the abstraction of the syntax tree in the abstraction of the environment. Since we decided to make the arithmetic operations modulo 100, the post also restricts the result to be a natural number less than 100.

```
(procedure eval-natural
    ((lvar (tree) (tree!tree-array))
     (lvar (index) (int))
     (lvar (env) (tbl!symbol-table))
     (pvar (result) (tbl!value)))
    ((pre (and (chk!type-of-result-natural
                   tree index (tbl!symbol-table-to-type-table env))
               (env-ok env)))
     (post (and (= (tbl!value-type result) (tbl!pico-nat-type))
                (>= (tbl!value-int result) 0)
                (< (tbl!value-int result) 100)
                (= (pval!pico-value-nat (tbl!value-int result))
                   (eval!eval-exp
                    (tree!expr-node-to-abstract-syntax tree index)
                    (eval!value-env (tbl!symbol-table-to-table env)))))))
     (measure index))
  (cond
    ((= (tree!node-kind (aref tree index)) (tree!nat-const-node))
     (:= result
      (tbl!value.val
        (tbl!pico-nat-type)
        (str!pico-string.val 0 (str!fixed-string.map (str!fixed-string.pad)))
```

```
        (tree!tree-value-nat (aref tree index)))))
((= (tree!node-kind (aref tree index)) (tree!var-node))
 (block ((pvar (lookup-result) (tbl!lookup-result)))
   (tbl!symbol-table-lookup
     lookup-result
     (tree!tree-value-string
       (aref tree (tree!child-1 (aref tree index))))
     env)
   (:= result (tbl!lookup-value lookup-result))))
((= (tree!node-kind (aref tree index)) (tree!plus-node))
 (block ((pvar (res1 res2) (tbl!value)) (pvar (sum) (int)))
   (eval-natural tree (tree!child-1 (aref tree index)) env res1)
   (eval-natural tree (tree!child-2 (aref tree index)) env res2)
   (:= sum (plus (tbl!value-int res1) (tbl!value-int res2)))
   (:= result
     (tbl!value.val
       (tbl!pico-nat-type)
       (str!pico-string.val 0 (str!fixed-string.map (str!fixed-string.pad)))
       sum))))
((= (tree!node-kind (aref tree index)) (tree!minus-node))
 (block ((pvar (res1 res2) (tbl!value)) (pvar (sum) (int)))
   (eval-natural tree (tree!child-1 (aref tree index)) env res1)
   (eval-natural tree (tree!child-2 (aref tree index)) env res2)
   (:= sum (minus (tbl!value-int res1) (tbl!value-int res2)))
   (:= result
     (tbl!value.val
       (tbl!pico-nat-type)
       (str!pico-string.val 0 (str!fixed-string.map (str!fixed-string.pad)))
       sum))))))
```

The proof of the above procedure is long (the proof summary is over two pages long), and is therefore not included here.

7.4 Conclusion

Although we did not finish the PICO interpreter example (parts of the implementation of the PICO evaluator have not been written), we feel that it is feasible to specify and verify parts of a compiler for a relatively simple language using EVES. We feel that it is feasible to specify and verify a syntax analyzer. (Abstract specifications of a scanner and parser are described in [BHK89]. Based on our experience with the implementation of the type checker, we feel that it is feasible to develop verified implementations for the specifications.) As well, we have completed the specification and verification of a type checker, albeit for a very simple language. We do not have experience in specifying and verifying a code generator and can not comment on its feasibility. It seems to be much easier to specify and verify an interpreter. Finally, we feel it would be an enormous task, if it is feasible, to specify and verify a production quality compiler for a "real" language using EVES.

One of the purposes of the PICO project was to exercise the EVES library mechanism. In our opinion, the project demonstrates the utility of the mechanism in that we handled an example on the order of magnitude of 10,000 lines. Work [Saa91b] completed since the PICO project, on including the Z mathematical toolkit [Spi89] in the EVES library has further demonstrated the utility—though it was necessary to use a "make" [Saa91a] mechanism to up-date the library.

8 Discussion

In this final section, we shall discuss, from the EVES perspective, comments made by the series coordinator, Peter Lauer, in introducing and motivating the lecture series [LJZ92]. Our discussion will focus only on those comments that are relevant to EVES.

On the convergence of theoretical computing science and mathematics, EVES has certainly drawn from both disciplines. For example, our work is heavily dependent upon concepts drawn from set theory and mathematical logic. On the other hand, in the design of the language Verdi, we needed to consider computing concerns pertaining to the executable subset of the language. One nice area of convergence is demonstrated in the Verdi library mechanism and the use of spec and model units. In effect, this approach is that of mathematical logic whereby a theory is presented in an axiomatic manner and the consistency of the theory is demonstrated in a model theoretic manner. In our approach, we use this theme for presenting mathematical concepts along with the more conventional programming approach (effectively packages or modules) of specification and implementation.

On theory-based environments transforming system development: a system such as EVES places the develop of computer controlled systems on a solid mathematical foundation. But, more generally, by having a precise mathematical description of the language, it is possible to be precise in stating requirements, specifications and code. This increased precision, augmented with explanatory natural language text, will hopefully improve one's understanding of systems being developed using EVES (and other similar technologies). In addition, it will be possible to develop further analysis tools that take advantage of the in-depth understanding of the language. We expect that, in the short term, the use of formally defined languages (e.g., Verdi) and theory-based systems (e.g., EVES) will be integrated slowly with existing development practices. For example, the use of natural languages in many existing development practices may be wholly, or partially, replaced with the use of theory-based languages. It will be in the longer term, as we increase our understanding of what can be gained by using theory-based techniques, that significant changes in development practices will accrue.

On environments being efficient and semantically sound, this has been one of the main concerns of the EVES project. A significant part of our research work has been directed at semantic soundness through the use of Denotational Semantic approaches to describe all aspects of the Verdi language (in particular, this is true of both the executable and non-executable portions of the language) and in describing the proof obligations resulting from each declaration. One area where this issue is particularly difficult and relevant is with respect to the NEVER theorem prover. With NEVER, we wanted to develop a theorem prover that was sufficiently powerful to be a useful aid to the user of EVES. Consequently, amongst other capabilities, we incorporated various decision procedures and heuristics. Some of these capabilities make use of non-axiomatic reasoning and so issues of soundness arise. Our approach to resolving this issue, is to develop a proof checker that will check proofs discovered by NEVER. Consequently, we separate concerns by having NEVER discover (with the aid of the user) proofs, and the much smaller and reviewable proof checker check the validity of the (putative) proofs. We are just about to start a research stream on proof checking.

On domains of interest conceived analogously in mathematics and computing, Lauer observes the use of algebraic structures in both disciplines. As should be clear from this paper, EVES allows for the axiomatic presentation of theories and model theoretic proofs of consistency. These theories may be used to specify the behaviour of executable algebraic data types.

On Type Theory, EVES does not follow a type theoretic approach, as the underlying foundation is ZFC set theory. However, we feel that set theory is sufficiently expressible for the tasks at hand (it is certainly expressive enough for most mathematicians). We have, however, shown how to encode [CS90] simple type theory in EVES. While there are numerous reasons on why we chose set theory—as opposed to choosing a higher-order alternative—we note that, for a system to be successfully used by industry, it is important to build upon existing knowledge. Almost everyone who has graduated from a reputable university (if not high school) has had some grounding in set theory and many computing science concepts are defined using set theory; hence, we attempted to reduce the barriers to understanding our work. In addition, by choosing set theory and remaining in a first-order framework, we were able to use the extensive automated deduction techniques known to work in the framework, especially with respect to heuristics and automated support.

On other disciplines needing advanced theory-based systems: EVES supports rigorous and systematic developments of executable software from specifications (as with Lauer's examples of OBJ3, Larch and MetaDesign). We believe that EVES requires about as much mathematical training as these other systems. However, recent lessons[6] have indicated that there are ways of making these systems more accessible. For example, using notations and notions that fit the "mindsets" of particular communities of interest (e.g., engineers) will help in the transition of this technology. Many of these communities do not need to understand the minutae of the underlying mathematics, but they still need to understand the precision for those parts of the languages and systems they do use.

While Lauer observes that many theory-based systems are using Standard ML (SML) as an implementation language, we have been using a vanilla subset of Common Lisp. In general, this is a matter of history in that we started our work in developing the EVES technology prior to the development of SML. In a similar manner, EVES does not have explicit support for concurrency. When we started our work, and it is still true, formal methods as directed towards concurrency was an active research discipline. We felt that the area was still too dynamic to commit to a particular approach. However, having ZFC as a basis to EVES does permit

---

[6] See the upcoming report by Craigen, Gerhart and Ralston on a survey of industrial applications of formal methods.

researchers to cast their models of concurrency into the EVES framework.

On the importance of graphical representation, this is a special case of notational concerns. As noted above, this is an important issue for transition of the technology and for understanding by those who are familiar with notations other than those drawn from first-order logic. We will be investigating this area in the near future as we certainly recognize that a Lisp-like notation will not be understandable to some of our users. It is important that the chosen notation(s) allow for in-depth review of requirements, specifications and code. It must be remembered that notation is, as Ken Iverson states, a "tool for thought" and to communicate ideas.

On the use of theory-based systems in education, EVES has been distributed to a number of universities and is expected to be used in software engineering courses during the next school term. EVES incorporates a number of software engineering principles with formal methods techniques that a number of instructors have found to be of interest. With the use of EVES at the universities, we will quickly discover how robust EVES is and how accessible the underlying material is.

For the next few years, our work with EVES will follow three streams. Firstly, we expect that EVES will be used on various applications. As with the use of EVES at the universities, this will help to uncover the strengths and weaknesses of the system. Secondly, we intend to make EVES more accessible by writing a users' guide for Verdi, NEVER, and EVES; and to improve the notation. With respect to notation, issues of reviewability of ideas expressed in Verdi will be paramount. (Such concerns were of importance to the designers of Z.) Finally, we intend to further address issues of soundness. For example, we are currently rigorously developing a compiler for Verdi and, in the longer term, we hope to automate some of the proofs using EVES. We also expect to start work on developing a proof checker for NEVER. In this way, we move concerns about logical soundness from the complicated theorem prover (with its embedded heuristics) to a much simpler mechanism that solely checks the validity of proofs. We will be rigorously developing the proof checker and expect that it will be reviewable by interested parties.

A   Prover Commands

In this appendix we describe the commands used in the examples. The descriptions are abridgements of the descriptions presented in the Verdi reference manual [Cra91]. Primarily, we have removed mention of well-formedness requirements for each of the commands. The descriptions are also related to the on-line help available from EVES.

Equality Substitute Command

`(EQUALITY-SUBSTITUTE [EXPRESSION])`

The **equality-substitute** command substitutes, for the expression, its equal in appropriate contexts of the current formula. The expression must appear as the left or right side of an equality within the current formula (otherwise the command has no effect). In the absence of the expression, a heuristic is used to substitute equalities automatically.

Induct Command

`(INDUCT [expression])`

The induct command attempts to apply an induction scheme to the current formula. In the absence of the optional expression, an induction scheme is heuristically chosen based on calls to recursive functions occurring in the current formula. If the optional expression is present, then EVES attempts an induction using the expression.

Instantiate Command

`(INSTANTIATE {(identifier expression)}+)`

The instantiate command performs the given instantiations on the current formula. To allow the instantiations to occur, the scopes of quantifiers in the formula may be modified. Logical equivalence is maintained by keeping the uninstantiated subexpressions as extra conjuncts or disjuncts.

Invoke Command

`(INVOKE expression)`

The invoke command replaces the application of a function, as specified by the expression, by its defining expression (instantiated by the actual parameters to the function application). The invoke command works for functions which have been disabled. In addition, the invoke command may be applied to an expression rather than to a function, in which case, it works like a selective invoke in that occurrences of the expression in the formula are replaced by the expanded version.

Open Command

`(OPEN)`

The open command removes leading universal quantifiers from the current formula and the quantified variables are consequently free variables.

Prenex Command

`(PRENEX)`

The prenex command converts the current formula into prenex form (as far as possible). If the result of this command is a completely prenexed formula with only universal quantifiers, then the open command may be used to make the formula quantifier-free.

Reduce Command

(REDUCE)

The reduce command applies the non-inductive heuristics of the prover to the current formula. This consists of simplification, rewriting, and invocation.

Rewrite Command

(REWRITE)

The rewrite command rewrites and simplifies the current formula. Conditional rewrite rules may be applied, provided their condition can be proven using only simplification and rewriting. This command also applies any forward rules which are triggered and whose condition is provable.

Simplify Command

(SIMPLIFY)

The simplify command simplifies the current formula. This may perform the substitution of equalities as well as trying to instantiate variables in order to find a proof.

Split Command

(SPLIT expression)

The split command performs a case split on the current formula with the supplied expression. This results in a new formula of the form

    (IF expression formula formula)

provided there are no references to the quantified variables of the formula within the predicate. If there are, the split command performs a case split on the largest subformula within the scope of the referenced quantified variables. In effect, a case split causes the current formula to be worked on under the two cases, the first with the expression explicitly assumed equal to true and the second with the predicate not equaling true.

The split command may also be used for placing a specific hypothesis before a subexpression. This proof step may be required because of the sensitivity of the prover towards the ordering of subexpressions within the formula being reduced.

Use Command

(USE identifier {(identifier expression)}*)

The use command adds the axiom associated with the identifier to the current formula as an assumption. This results in a new formula of the form

    (IMPLIES assumption formula)

where the assumption is the axiom instantiated with the instantiations.

References

[BB74]   W.W. Bledsoe and P. Bruell. A man-machine theorem proving system. *Artificial Intelligence*, 5(1):51–72, 1974.

[BHK89]   J.A. Bergstra, J. Heering, and P. Klint. *Algebraic Specification*. ACM Press, New York, New York, 1989.

[BM79]   Robert S. Boyer and J Strother Moore. *A Computational Logic*. Academic Press, NY, 1979.

[CKM+91] Dan Craigen, Sentot Kromodimoeljo, Irwin Meisels, Bill Pase, and Mark Saaltink. EVES: An Overview. In *Proceedings of VDM '91, Noordwijkerhout, The Netherlands (October 1991)*. Springer-Verlag, 1991.

[Cra91]   Dan Craigen. Reference manual for the language Verdi. Technical Report TR-91-5429-09a, ORA Canada, Ottawa, September 1991.

[CS90]   Dan Craigen and Mark Saaltink. Simple Type Theory in EVES. In Graham Birtwistle, editor, *Proceedings of the Fourth Banff Higher Order Workshop (9–15 September 1990)*, New York, 1990. Springer-Verlag.

[Fra68]   Abraham Fraenkel. *Abstract Set Theory*. North-Holland, 1968.

[Her90]   Ted Herman. On a theorem of Jacobson. In W.H.J. Feigen, et al., editor, *Beauty is Our Business: A Birthday Salute to Edsger W. Dijkstra*. Springer-Verlag, New York, 1990.

[KP90]   Sentot Kromodimoeljo and Bill Pase. Using the EVES Library Facility: A PICO Interpreter. Final Report FR-90-5444-02, ORA Canada, Ottawa, February 1990.

[LJZ92]   P.E. Lauer, R. Janicki, and J. Zucker. Functional Programming, Concurrency, Simulation and Automated Reasoning (FPCSAR). Memo FPCSAR.1, Department of Computer Science and Systems, McMaster University, February 1992.

[Luc79]   D.C. Luckham, et al. Stanford Pascal Verifier User Manual. Technical Report STAN-CS-79-731, Stanford University, Computer Science Department, March 1979.

[Saa90a]   Mark Saaltink. Alternative Semantics for Verdi. Technical Report TR-90-5446-02, ORA Canada, Ottawa, November 1990.

[Saa90b]   Mark Saaltink. A formal description of Verdi. Technical Report TR-90-5429-10a, ORA Canada, Ottawa, November 1990.

[Saa91a]   Mark Saaltink. Using *make* to maintain EVES libraries. Working Paper WP-91-5449-206, ORA Canada, Ottawa, July 1991.

[Saa91b]   Mark Saaltink. Z and EVES. Technical Report TR-91-5449-02, ORA Canada, Ottawa, October 1991.

[Saa92]   Mark Saaltink. Z and EVES: A summary. In *Proceedings of the 6th Annual Z User Meeeting (16-17 December 1991)*, Berlin, 1992. Workshops in Computing, Springer-Verlag.

[Spi89]   J. M. Spivey. *The Z Notation: A Reference Manual*. Prentice Hall, 1989.

[TE81]   D.H. Thompson and R.W. Erickson, editors. *AFFIRM Reference Manual*. USC Information Sciences Institute, Marina Dey Ray, CA, 1981.

A Systolizing Compilation Scheme
for Nested Loops with Linear Bounds*

Michael Barnett[1] and Christian Lengauer[2]

[1] Department of Computer Sciences, The University of Texas at Austin,
Austin, Texas 78712–1188, U.S.A. E-mail: mbarnett@cs.utexas.edu
[2] Fakultät für Mathematik und Informatik, Universität Passau,
Postfach 25 40, D–W8390 Passau, Germany. E-mail: lengauer@fmi.uni-passau.de

Abstract. With the recent advances in massively parallel programmable
processor networks, methods for the infusion of massive MIMD parallelism
into programs have become increasingly relevant. We present a mechanical
scheme for the synthesis of systolic programs from programs that do not
specify concurrency or communication. The scheme can handle source programs that are perfectly nested loops with regular data dependences and
that correspond to uniform recurrence equations. The target programs are in
a machine-independent distributed language with asynchronous parallelism
and synchronous communication. The scheme has been implemented as a
prototype systolizing compiler.

1 Introduction

A new generation of programmable processor networks is emerging that can support fine-grain (thousands of processors), MIMD, communication-intensive parallel
programs. Present architectures of this type are, for example, iWarp [6], the T9000
transputer [19], the AP1000 [37], and the CM-5 [38]. Architectures under development include the Mosaic [35], and the Rewrite Rule Machine [1]. One class of programs that such machines will be able to execute effectively is the class of systolic
programs.

Systolic programs are programs for general-purpose distributed memory processor networks with asynchronous parallelism and synchronous communication. The
execution of a systolic program emulates a *systolic array* [22, 23], a processor network
with only local interconnections that, in the past, has been intended for a hardware
realization as a special-purpose VLSI chip. One property of systolic arrays is that
their parallelism can be determined before run time.

We present a scheme for the mechanical derivation of systolic programs. We derive
the systolic program from a source program that specifies neither concurrency nor
communication and from an abstract description of a corresponding systolic array.
The source program must be a set of perfectly nested loops with only linear loop
bounds and regular data dependences. The description of the systolic array is based
on linear functions that distribute the statements of the program over space and

---

* Financial support was received from the Science and Engineering Research Council
(SERC), grant no. GR/G55457.

time. There are several mechanical methods for the design of systolic arrays from such source programs [15, 31, 33].

Our ultimate goal is a scheme that works for all uniform recurrences [21]. The scheme proposed here almost reaches this goal: we still have to allow for non-neighbouring connections and piecewise linear loop bounds. While non-neighbouring connections do not add any conceptual challenge, they complicate the details of the i/o to and from the array considerably. Piecewise linear loop bounds can be dealt with by considering each linear piece separately and composing the results.

Our notation is presented in Sect. 2. Section 3 is a brief review of our scheme. Section 4 presents the geometric model for the source programs. Section 5 discusses the central aspects of the scheme with an example (additional details can be found in [3]). Our conclusions are presented in Sect. 6.

2 Notation

The application of a function f to an argument x is denoted by $f.x$. Function application is left-associative and has higher binding power than any other operator. We will occasionally use the lambda notation for functions.

Quantification over a dummy variable x is written $(\mathbf{Q}\, x\, :\, R.x\, :\, P.x)$, following [10]. $\mathbf{Q}$ is the quantifier, R is a predicate in x representing the range, and P is a term that depends on x. When R is understood from the context, it is omitted. The symbol $\mathbf{A}$ is used for universal quantification, $\mathbf{E}$ for existential quantification. $(\text{set}\, x\, :\, R.x\, :\, P.x)$ is equivalent to the more traditional $\{P.x \mid R.x\}$. The quantifier $(\text{seq}\, i\, :\, R.i\, :\, P.i)$ represents an ordered sequence of elements; we also write tuples by listing the elements in angled brackets. Our derivations are in the equational proof format of [10]. Curly brackets enclose supporting comments of an equation.

The set of points that a linear function f maps to zero is called the *null space* of f and denoted null.f. Other properties of linear functions that we use include their dimensionality and rank. We identify points and vectors; both are usually written as a list of the elements in parentheses, but may also be written as a column in square brackets. $x.i$ denotes the i-th coordinate of point x. For a point x, the notation $(x; i\, :\, e)$ refers to the point with the same coordinates as x except that $x.i = e$. Matrices are denoted by capital letters. $M.i$ refers to row i of matrix M; thus, the element in row i and column j is written $M.i.j$. The point whose components are all zero is denoted by 0, the identity matrix by I; the context indicates their dimension. The inner product of two points x and y, both in $\mathbf{R}^n$, is:

$$x \bullet y \;=\; (\text{sum}\, i\, :\, 0 \le i < n\, :\, x.i * y.i)$$

and is undefined when the points do not have the same number of components. Matrix multiplication is denoted by juxtaposition, e.g., $M\, x$ for a matrix M and a vector x.

$\mathbf{Z}$, $\mathbf{Q}$, and $\mathbf{R}$ represent the set of integers, rational numbers, and real numbers, respectively. Integers are denoted by the letters i through n, and points by the letters w through z. Thus, $m * n$ is the product of two scalars, while $m * x$ is the multiplication of a point by a scalar; it represents the componentwise multiplication by m. The symbol $/$ is used for division; it may appear in two different contexts.

m/n denotes the ordinary division of two numbers. x/m represents the division of each component of x by the number m, i.e., $(1/m) * x$. Other operators are also extended componentwise: e.g., given two n-vectors x and y, $x \leq y$ is equivalent to $(\mathbf{A}\ i\ :\ 0 \leq i < n\ :\ x.i \leq y.i)$. We denote the integer m such that $m * y$ equals x by $x\ /\!/\ y$. It is only well-defined if x is a multiple of y. Integer division is denoted by "$\div$". $m \mid n$ stands for $(\mathbf{E}\ i\ :\ i \in \mathbf{Z}\ :\ m * i\ =\ n)$; in programs, it is represented by n mod m = 0. The values $+1$ and -1 are called *unit* values.

3 Overview

The source program is a set of r perfectly nested loops:

$$\textbf{for } x_0 = lb_0 \leftarrow st_0 \rightarrow rb_0$$
$$\textbf{for } x_1 = lb_1 \leftarrow st_1 \rightarrow rb_1$$
$$\ddots$$
$$\textbf{for } x_{r-1} = lb_{r-1} \leftarrow st_{r-1} \rightarrow rb_{r-1}$$
$$(x_0, x_1, \ldots, x_{r-1})$$

with a loop body, called the *basic statement*, of the form:

$$(x_0, x_1, \ldots, x_{r-1}) \quad : \quad \begin{array}{ll} \textbf{if } B_0.x_0.x_1.\cdots.x_{r-1} & \rightarrow S_0 \\ [\!]\ B_1.x_0.x_1.\cdots.x_{r-1} & \rightarrow S_1 \\ \quad \vdots & \\ [\!]\ B_{t-1}.x_0.x_1.\cdots.x_{r-1} & \rightarrow S_{t-1} \\ \textbf{fi .} & \end{array}$$

Let the range of ℓ be $0 \leq \ell < r$, and the range of i be $0 \leq i < t$. The bounds lb_ℓ (left bound) and rb_ℓ (right bound) are linear expressions in the loop indices x_0 to $x_{\ell-1}$ and in a set of variables called the *problem size*. The body of the loops may be viewed as a procedure with the loop indices as its parameters; each iteration of the body is completely specified by an r-tuple of values for the indices. The steps st_ℓ are unit values; different step widths can be coded into the arguments of the basic statement. The left bound and right bound of each loop are related by:

$$(\mathbf{A}\ \ell\ :\ 0 \leq \ell < r\ :\ lb_\ell \leq rb_\ell) .$$

Interpreted as a sequential program: if the step is positive, the loop is executed from the left bound to the right bound; if the step is negative, it is executed from the right bound to the left bound. The guards B_i are boolean functions; the computations S_i may contain composition, alternation, or iteration but with no non-local references other than to a set of global variables indexed by the loop indices. $\mathcal{V}$ is the set of names of these variables.

A systolic array is a specification of a parallel implementation. It consists of two linear distribution functions:

- **step** specifies a temporal distribution, a time schedule for the statements.
- **place** describes the spatial distribution of the statements onto processes.

The range of place is called the *process space*, denoted $\mathcal{P}$; its dimension is one less than the number of nested loops in the source program. Each element in the process space is a *process*. There are systolic arrays of reduced dimension (e.g., [20, 27, 40]) and arrays defined by piecewise linear distribution functions (e.g., [7, 9, 11]). We consider only full-dimensional systolic arrays that are described by linear distribution functions.

We use a geometric model for the source program and the systolic array. The loop bounds of the source program define the boundaries of a convex polyhedron in r-dimensional space. (When the loop bounds are finite, the polyhedron is a polytope.) The statements of the program correspond to the set of integer points within the polyhedron. For simplicity, we require every integer point to correspond to a statement. (This is enforced by restricting loop strides to unit values.) We call either the entire polyhedron in $\mathbf{R}^r$ or, also, just the enclosed set of integer points the *index space*.

The loops in the distributed program, like those in the source program, require integer-valued loop indices. We ensure that the results obtained in the model are all integer and can thus be interpreted as program components.

For any fixed process y, the linearity of place ensures that the points mapped to y lie equidistantly distributed on a straight line in the index space; we denote this line by *chord.y*. We call the fixed distance between neighbouring points inc (elsewhere, it is called the *iteration vector* [33]); it does not depend on y. The linearity of step imposes a total order on the points of a chord. Thus, it suffices to identify the first point, first, on the line – this is the point at which step reaches a minimum – and the last point, last – the point at which step reaches a maximum. The computations to be performed by a process are completely specified by the sequence

$$(\text{seq } i \,:\, 0 \leq i \leq (\text{last} - \text{first}) \,/\!/\, \text{inc} \,:\, \text{first} + i * \text{inc}) \ .$$

For a given process y, the equation

$$\text{place}.x \;=\; y$$

can be solved for the particular x that should be the value of first (or last). If, in addition, the equations are solved for any process, i.e., for y expressed symbolically in terms of the coordinates of the process space, then the values first and last are functions from the process space back to the index space (in general, piecewise linear functions; we refer to each linear piece as a *clause*). Of course, there is no unique solution as long as place projects more than one point onto y. That is, this system of linear equations is underdetermined. But, by replacing one component of x with a known constant, it may be solved for a unique point. The key is to discover a component of first (last), and then solve the system for the remaining $r - 1$ components of first (last). If first (last) is known to lie on a boundary of the index space, then one of its components is known (if a point x lies on a boundary defined by loop ℓ, then $x.\ell$ is either the left or right bound of that loop).

The data of interest in a systolic array are *indexed variables* in the source program; all elements of an indexed variable move through the systolic array with a constant speed and direction: the variable's *flow*. In the systolic array, an indexed variable is also referred to as a *stream*. An indexed variable is specified by a *name* and an *index vector*; indexed variables may have a common name as long as certain technical restrictions are met [8]. An index vector is an $(r-1)$-tuple each component of which is a linear expression that depends only on the loop indices and integer constants. The linear expression is divided into two parts: an *index map*, (a linear function from $\mathbf{Z}^r$ to $\mathbf{Z}^{r-1}$) and an *offset*, (an integer vector in $\mathbf{Z}^{r-1}$). The rank of the index map must be $r-1$. Variables whose index map has a rank less than that are split into variables that have index maps with full rank [8].

4 The Geometric Model

A loop bound is a linear expression comprising integer constants, problem size variables, and enclosing loop indices. We represent it by a pair, $\langle c,\ d\rangle$; c is a row vector in $\mathbf{Z}^{1\times r}$ – it contains the coefficients of the loop indices (with 0 for all absent indices) – while d is the rest of the linear expression (any additive constants and problem size variables). We denote the left bound of loop ℓ, $0\le\ell<r$, by L_ℓ, the right bound by R_ℓ. When the distinction is irrelevant, we write $bound_\ell$.

We require the concept of the *application* of a loop bound to a point x. Given a loop bound $bound = \langle c,\ d\rangle$, its application to x is defined as:

$$bound.x = c\bullet x + d\ . \tag{1}$$

A polyhedron is described by a system of linear inequalities in matrix notation:

$$A\,x \le b\ .$$

The polyhedron is the set of all points x that satisfy this inequality.

To derive the system of linear inequalities of the index space from the source program, we construct a matrix E and a vector f from the left bounds of all loops, and a matrix G and a vector h from the right bounds. Row ℓ of each matrix is the vector c from the corresponding loop ℓ (i.e., the left bound of loop ℓ is used for E, the right bound for G). Each component ℓ of vector f is the function d from the left bound of loop ℓ; in h it is taken from the right bound. f and h are linear expressions.

This is a simplified version of Ribas' notation [34]: we know that our loop strides are unit values and that, for each ℓ, $L_\ell \le R_\ell$.

We demonstrate the entire method with the example of a selection sort as given in Rao [32, pp. 273–278]. (Different place functions turn this source program into different sorts.) The source program is shown in Figs. 1 and 2.

The array x contains the unsorted elements. The array m is initialized during the execution of the program, and upon termination, contains the sorted elements. We refer to each indexed variable by its name: to $m[j]$ by m and to $x[i]$ by x. The index maps for the variables are $M_m = (\lambda\,(j,i).j)$ and $M_x = (\lambda\,(j,i).i)$. Both off_m and off_x are the zero vector. Elements of the null spaces of the index maps are $(0,1)$ and $(1,0)$, respectively.

The first row of E is the vector c from the left bound of the first loop which is, by definition, always 0. The second row of E is the vector c from the left bound of the second loop which is $(1,0)$, because the coefficient of j in the left bound of the inner loop is 1. Similarly to E, the first row of G is 0, and in this particular case,

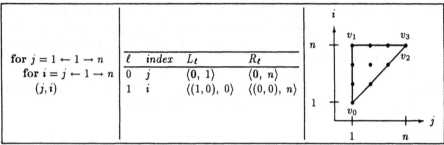

Fig. 1. Sorting: program, loop bounds, and index space.

$$(j,i) \quad :: \quad \begin{aligned} &\textbf{if } i = j \rightarrow m[j] := x[i] \\ &[]\ i \neq j \rightarrow m[j], x[i] := \max(x[i], m[j]), \min(x[i], m[j]) \\ &\textbf{fi} \end{aligned}$$

Fig. 2. Sorting: basic statement.

the second row is also 0. The vectors f and h are constructed from the constants in the loop bounds: the constants in the left loop bounds are 1 and 0, those in the right bounds are n and n. Thus, the matrices and vectors in the example are:

$$E = \begin{bmatrix} 0 & 0 \\ 1 & 0 \end{bmatrix}, \qquad f = \begin{bmatrix} 1 \\ 0 \end{bmatrix}, \qquad G = \begin{bmatrix} 0 & 0 \\ 0 & 0 \end{bmatrix}, \qquad h = \begin{bmatrix} n \\ n \end{bmatrix}.$$

These matrices and vectors are used to represent the index space. By the definition of the loop bounds:

$$(\mathbf{A}\ \ell, x\ :\ 0 \leq \ell < r \ \wedge\ x \in \mathcal{I}\ :\ L_\ell.x \leq x.\ell \leq R_\ell.x)$$

which becomes in matrix form:

$$E x + f \leq x \leq G x + h .$$

Simplifying the inequalities, the matrix form can be rewritten as:

$$\begin{bmatrix} E - I \\ I - G \end{bmatrix} x \leq \begin{bmatrix} -f \\ h \end{bmatrix} . \tag{2}$$

We continue to refer to the matrix on the left by A and the vector on the right by b. Our polyhedral index space is thus the set of points x satisfying (2). We call a matrix and vector of this structure the *normal form* for the polyhedron. In normal form, the index space of the example becomes:

$$\begin{bmatrix} -1 & 0 \\ 1 & -1 \\ 1 & 0 \\ 0 & 1 \end{bmatrix} \begin{bmatrix} j \\ i \end{bmatrix} \leq \begin{bmatrix} -1 \\ 0 \\ n \\ n \end{bmatrix} .$$

(For typographical reasons, we often write the normal form as two inequalities; one for the left bounds, the other for the right bounds.) Each row in A is the outward normal to the associated boundary of the index space [14, 24]. A vertex of the index space, i.e., an extreme point, is the intersection of r boundaries; we associate the vertex with the boundaries and their normals. Any r normals, each derived from a distinct loop, *define* a vertex. There are 2^r vertices. They result from taking all possible combinations of loop bounds; component ℓ of each vertex is either the left bound or right bound of loop ℓ. For those rows of A and b used to define a vertex, the inequalities become equalities. Figure 3 depicts the normals for the example. Note that two of the vertices coincide: v_2 and v_3. The normal $(1, 0)$ is for the boundary between them, which in this example, consists of just one point. Such boundaries are called extraneous and are discussed in Sect. 5.4.

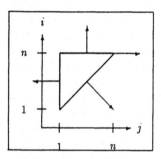

Fig. 3. Index space with outward normals.

4.1 The Systolic Array

Let the systolic array be defined by the step function:

$$\mathsf{step}.(j, i) \ = \ j{+}i \ .$$

Rao discusses three place functions:

$$\mathsf{place}.(j, i) \ = \ j \ , \qquad \mathsf{place}.(j, i) \ = \ i \ , \qquad \mathsf{place}.(j, i) \ = \ i - j \ .$$

We derive a program only for the third place function; it is the most complicated one (the only one that is non-simple [4]).

A stream's flow is derived from a vector in the null space of its index map. Let s be a stream, M the index map, and w a vector in the null space of M. Then $\mathsf{flow}.s = \mathsf{place}.w/\mathsf{step}.w$. Thus, for stream x:

$$
\begin{aligned}
&\mathsf{flow}.x \\
=\ &\quad \{ \text{ definition of flow } \} \\
&\mathsf{place}.(1, 0)/\mathsf{step}.(1, 0) \\
=\ &\quad \{ \ \mathsf{step}.(j, i) = j{+}i, \ \mathsf{place}.(j, i) = i{-}j \ \} \\
&-1/1 \\
=\ &\quad \{ \text{ simplification } \} \\
&-1 \ .
\end{aligned}
$$

Similarly, the flow of stream m is 1.

A stream whose flow is 0 is called a *stationary* stream. Elements of a stationary stream stay with a fixed process for the duration of the program and must be made available to the process before its first use. This is called *loading*. The final values of a stationary stream, if of interest, must be output after their last use. This is called *recovery*.

The process space is one-dimensional; we name its coordinate p.

5 The Systolization Scheme

This section presents the central aspects of the scheme. Subsection 5.1 presents the method for determining the boundaries of the process space. In Subsect. 5.2, inc is derived; it is used for many parts of the systolic program. In Subsect. 5.3, certain boundaries of the index space are shown to be of particular interest: those which contain the points first and last. Certain troublesome boundaries are discussed in Subsect. 5.4. Subsections 5.5, 5.6, and 5.7 present the heart of the compilation scheme: the derivation of the computation processes. Subsection 5.5 explains how the systems of equations are constructed, Subsect. 5.6 shows how to cope with non-integer solutions, and Subsect. 5.7 explains the derivation of the guards when the computation processes are defined piecewise. Subsection 5.8 describes the augmentation of the basic statement with communication directives for moving stream elements. The input and output processes are derived in Subsects. 5.9 and 5.10. The former describes their layout, i.e., their distribution in space; the latter describes the program each i/o process executes. A computation process may have to transfer data elements before or after they are used for computation. Subsection 5.11 presents the derivation of this code. Subsection 5.12 derives the buffer processes (the processes that do not compute but only communicate). Finally, in Subsect. 5.13, the complete target program for sorting is presented.

5.1 The Process Space Boundaries

The distributed program contains one process for each point in the range of place, i.e., in the process space $\mathcal{P}$. The process space can be an arbitrary polytope (it is the linear projection of a polytope); it is easier to specify its rectangular closure: $rect.\mathcal{P}$. (The process space is specified in the distributed program by parallel loops; only a restricted class of polytopes can be specified this way if linear loop bounds are used.) We create a process for each point in the rectangular closure; the points that do not lie in the range of place do not perform any computations. The rectangular closure is specified by two points: $min\mathcal{P}$ and $max\mathcal{P}$. Both are points in $\mathbf{Z}^{r-1}$ such that:

$$(\mathbf{A}\ y\ :\ y \in \mathcal{P}\ :\ (\mathbf{A}\ i\ :\ 0 \le i < r-1\ :\ min\mathcal{P}.i \le y.i \le max\mathcal{P}.i))\ .$$

In terms of the model, each component of $min\mathcal{P}$ is the minimum value a linear function attains on the index space, while $max\mathcal{P}$ is the maximum value. The linear function is the corresponding component of place. Let $P.i$ represent the unique vector associated with the linear function of component i in place, $0 \le i < r-1$. Thus, each component of $min\mathcal{P}$ and $max\mathcal{P}$ is the solution of a linear program that either minimizes the value of $P.i\bullet x$ (for $min P$), or maximizes it (for $max P$), given the system of inequalities $A\,x \leq b$. For any value h, the points in $\mathcal{I}$ that satisfy $P.i\bullet x = h$ lie on a hyperplane whose normal is $P.i$.

In the example, the process space is one-dimensional; both $min P$ and $max P$ have a single component; thus we abbreviate $P.i$ to P. In general, the following procedure is performed for each component separately. Since $\mathsf{place}.(j,i) = i-j$, we obtain $P = (-1,1)$. The linear program minimizes $P\bullet x$ for $min P$ and maximizes it for $max P$. Figure 4 shows the index space with the hyperplane and its normal $(-1,1)$.

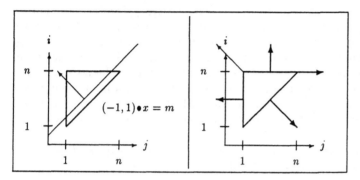

Fig. 4. $max P$.

In general, for points $x \in \mathcal{P}$, the value of $P\bullet x$ increases as the hyperplane is moved in the direction of P; it decreases as the hyperplane is moved in the direction of $-P$. From linear programming, we know that when the value $P\bullet x$ is at a maximum (minimum), then a vertex of the index space lies on the hyperplane. Such a vertex (which need not be unique) can be found by moving the hyperplane as far as possible in the direction of P $(-P)$, while still intersecting $\mathcal{I}$. Any vertex on the hyperplane has the property that P $(-P)$ is a non-negative linear combination of the normals that define the vertex. Geometrically, these are the normals between which P $(-P)$ lies. In Fig. 4, the vertex at the base of the normal $P = (-1,1)$ lies between the normals $(-1,0)$ and $(0,1)$.

A vector v is a linear combination of a set of vectors (set $k : 0 \leq k < n : v_k$) if and only if a solution for x of the system of equations $V x = v$ exists, where V is a matrix whose columns are the v_k. Thus, to see whether a vertex x provides the maximum (minimum) for P $(-P)$, we construct a matrix V_x whose *columns* are the r normals that define x. Then we solve the system of linear equations:

$$V_x y_x = P \ .$$

for each vertex in $\mathcal{I}$ for $max P$, and with P replaced by $-P$ for $min P$. When the solution y_x is non-negative, i.e., $y_x \geq 0$, then the vertex x from which V_x is derived is the vertex we are searching for. There are four vertices in the example. We name them:

$$v_0 = (L_0, L_1)\,, \qquad v_1 = (L_0, R_1)\,, \qquad v_2 = (R_0, L_1)\,, \qquad v_3 = (R_0, R_1)\,.$$

Matrix V_k is derived from vertex v_k by entering the rows for the respective loop bounds in A as the *columns* of V_k:

$$V_0 = \begin{bmatrix} -1 & 1 \\ 0 & -1 \end{bmatrix}, \qquad V_1 = \begin{bmatrix} -1 & 0 \\ 0 & 1 \end{bmatrix}, \qquad V_2 = \begin{bmatrix} 1 & 1 \\ 0 & -1 \end{bmatrix}, \qquad V_3 = \begin{bmatrix} 1 & 0 \\ 0 & 1 \end{bmatrix}.$$

The four solutions of $V_k y_k = (-1, 1)$, $0 \le k < 4$, are:

$$y_0 = (0, -1), \qquad y_1 = (1, 1), \qquad y_2 = (0, -1), \qquad y_3 = (-1, 1).$$

In this case, there is only one solution that is non-negative: y_1. So there is a unique vertex, v_1, for which P reaches a maximum. For $(1, -1)$, i.e., $-P$, the solutions are $-y_k$, $0 \le k < 4$. Since both y_0 and y_2 are non-negative, both vertices v_0 and v_2 achieve the minimum when projected by place. Note that $-y_3$ is not non-negative, even though, in this program, the corresponding vertex, v_3, also achieves a minimum for P. This is a result of the extraneous boundary. If the constant in the right bound of the inner loop were another size variable m, such that $m > n$, there would be a right vertical boundary to $\mathcal{I}$, v_2 and v_3 would not coincide, and v_3 would not achieve a minimum for P.

Geometrically, we have found the points at which the hyperplane $h = (-1, 1)$ achieves a maximum value on the polyhedron $\mathcal{I}$:

$$max P = (\text{max } x \; : \; x \in \mathcal{I} \; : \; h\,x).$$

This is where a diagonal line (with a slope of 1) intersecting $\mathcal{I}$ lies when moved as far north-west as possible in Fig. 1.

Once V_x is found, the vertex x itself is constructed. The vertex is a point in the index space that satisfies all r of its defining bounds. Thus, to derive the coordinates of x, we solve the system of equations representing the bounds using the matrix V_x^T (the *rows* of V_x^T are the normals defining x) and a vector b_x whose components are the components of the vector b corresponding to each normal. Then, x is the solution of the system:

$$V_x^T x \; = \; b_x . \tag{3}$$

In the example, P achieves the maximum at vertex v_1; this is the vertex where the left boundary of the outer loop intersects the right boundary of the inner loop: vertex (L_0, R_1). To construct this vertex symbolically, we solve $V_1^T x = (-1, n)$:

$$\begin{bmatrix} -1 & 0 \\ 0 & 1 \end{bmatrix} \begin{bmatrix} j \\ i \end{bmatrix} = \begin{bmatrix} -1 \\ n \end{bmatrix}$$
$$= \quad \{ \text{ simplification } \}$$
$$-j = -1 \;\wedge\; i = n$$
$$= \quad \{ \text{ simplification } \}$$
$$j = 1 \;\wedge\; i = n$$

yielding $x = (1, n)$.

Finally, after the vertex x is constructed, the value of $max P$ is just the value of place.x, which can be evaluated symbolically. For the example, there is only one component:

$$maxP$$
$$= \quad \{ \text{ definition } \}$$
$$\text{place}.(1, n)$$
$$= \quad \{ \text{ place}.(j, i) = i - j \}$$
$$n - 1 .$$

This procedure is performed for all $r - 1$ components in the range of P. For each component i, $maxP.i$ is the i-th component of the image (under place) of the vertex derived for $P.i$ (and likewise for $minP$). In the worst case, for each component, a linear system must be solved for each vertex. There are 2^r vertices. Therefore, there are at most $(r - 1) * 2^r$ systems of equations to solve. In practice, r is usually not larger than 5 [36] and there are many circumstances for which the same vertex can be used in the derivation of many components. Also, if $P.i$ is equal to a normal of the index space, which is frequently the case, the solution is trivial.

5.2 Deriving inc

inc is the distance between any two neighbouring points on any $chord.y$ in the process space; it is a constant. As a vector that lies on a chord, it is in the null space of place. We require inc to point in the direction of execution of the points on $chord.y$; i.e., its direction is determined by step. inc's components are scaled to make it the unit vector between neighbours. If w is an arbitrary (non-zero) element of null.place and $k = (\gcd i : 0 \le i < r : w.i)$, then:

$$\text{inc} = \text{sgn}.(\text{step}.w) * (1/k) * w . \tag{4}$$

The sign ensures that inc points in the direction prescribed by the step function. $\text{step}.w = 0$ is not possible: step and place would be inconsistent, contrary to our assumption that the systolic array is correct. For example, let w be $(-3, -3)$, which is in the null space of place. Then:

$$\text{inc}$$
$$= \quad \{ (4) \}$$
$$\text{sgn}.(\text{step}.w) * (1/k) * w$$
$$= \quad \{ w = (-3, -3) \Rightarrow k = 3 \}$$
$$\text{sgn}.(-3 + -3) * (1/3) * (-3, -3)$$
$$= \quad \{ \text{ simplification } \}$$
$$\text{sgn}.(-6) * (-1, -1)$$
$$= \quad \{ \text{ simplification } \}$$
$$-1 * (-1, -1)$$
$$= \quad \{ \text{ simplification } \}$$
$$(1, 1) .$$

5.3 Identifying the Faces

The derivation of first and last begins by identifying the boundaries of the index space that contain them. This leaves $r - 1$ equations with $r - 1$ unknowns which can be solved exactly for the remaining $r - 1$ components of first (or last). In the general case, the boundaries of interest are the ones that share a (single) point with a *chord.y*. All chords are mutually parallel since they are all defined by the same direction vector: inc. Thus, for each boundary, it suffices to consider whether or not inc is orthogonal to the normal of that boundary. If it is, then the boundary is parallel to the chords and is not needed to derive first and last. If a boundary is parallel to the chords, then it must coincide with exactly one of them; for that y, first and last lie on other boundaries that are not parallel to the chords.

A boundary that is not parallel to inc is called a *face*. The face associated with a right (left) bound of loop ℓ is denoted by $\mathcal{F}.R_\ell$ ($\mathcal{F}.L_\ell$). For each boundary of the index space, we compute inc$\bullet w$ for the normal w to that boundary; when the result is 0, inc is orthogonal to the normal and parallel to the boundary. Since each row of A is a normal to the boundary defined by the corresponding loop bound, the result of multiplying A by inc is the inner product of the corresponding row with inc. The results of the inner products are:

$$(E - I)\,\text{inc} = \begin{bmatrix} -1 & 0 \\ 1 & -1 \end{bmatrix}\begin{bmatrix} 1 \\ 1 \end{bmatrix} = \begin{bmatrix} -1 \\ 0 \end{bmatrix}, \qquad (I - G)\,\text{inc} = \begin{bmatrix} 1 & 0 \\ 0 & 1 \end{bmatrix}\begin{bmatrix} 1 \\ 1 \end{bmatrix} = \begin{bmatrix} 1 \\ 1 \end{bmatrix}.$$

Each boundary for which the inner product is not zero is a face. When the inner product is less than zero, the boundary is used for the derivation of first. When it is greater than zero, the boundary is used for last. In the example, there is one face for first: $\mathcal{F}.L_0$. There are two faces for last: $\mathcal{F}.R_0$ and $\mathcal{F}.R_1$. Figure 5 shows the index space and the chords.

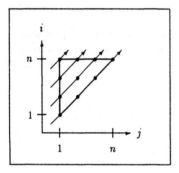

Fig. 5. Sorting: the index space and chords. The arrows represent the direction of inc.

5.4 Extraneous Boundaries

We call boundaries that contain only a single point *extraneous*. An example is the boundary associated with the right bound of the first loop in Fig. 1: it contains only the point (n, n). Not every extraneous boundary can be ignored, as Fig. 6 illustrates. The outward normals derived from the loop bounds are $(-1, 0)$, $(1, -1)$, $(1, 0)$, and $(0, 1)$. When $m \leq n$, the boundary corresponding to the normal $(1, 0)$ is extraneous, but when $m > n$, it is not. In general, the values of m and n are not available at compile time. There are cases where a compile-time analysis could determine boundaries that may be deleted; our present implementation does not do so. Deleting an extraneous boundary can be computationally expensive [34].

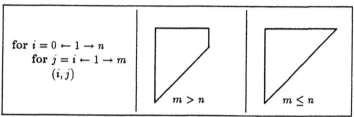

Fig. 6. Example of extraneous boundaries.

5.5 Constructing and Solving the Equations for first and last

Once the faces have been identified, one system of equations per face is constructed in order to derive first and one to derive last. We discuss only first; for last, the roles of the left and right bounds are reversed.

Let x be the vector of loop indices. Then the value of first is the solution of the system of equations for $\mathcal{F}.bound_\ell$:

$$\mathsf{place}.(x; \ell\ :\ e) = y$$

where e is the result of applying $bound_i$ to x (this amounts to substituting the bound of loop i as it appears in the program). Using the example, the face for first is $\mathcal{F}.L_0$. The vector x is (j, i), and e is the result of applying L_0 to (j, i):

$$
\begin{aligned}
&(x; \ell\ :\ e) \\
=\ & \{\ x = (j, i),\ \ell = 0,\ e = L_0.(j, i)\ \} \\
&((j, i); 0\ :\ L_0.(j, i)) \\
=\ & \{\ L_0 = \langle(0, 0),\ 1\rangle\ \} \\
&((j, i); 0\ :\ \langle(0, 0),\ 1\rangle.(j, i)) \\
=\ & \{\ \text{Equation 1}\ \} \\
&((j, i); 0\ :\ 0 * j + 0 * i + 1) \\
=\ & \{\ \text{simplification}\ \} \\
&((j, i); 0\ :\ 1) \\
=\ & \{\ \text{simplification}\ \} \\
&(1, i)
\end{aligned}
$$

which just substitutes the left bound of the loop indexed by j for the first component of the point. The system of equations has been reduced to one with only $r - 1$ unknowns and can now be solved exactly:

$$
\begin{aligned}
&\mathsf{place}.(1, i) = p \\
=\ & \{\ \mathsf{place}.(j, i) = i - j\ \} \\
&i - 1 = p \\
=\ & \{\ \text{simplification}\ \} \\
&i = p + 1\ .
\end{aligned}
$$

Substituting the solution back into the point, we obtain first $= (1, p + 1)$. In sorting, first is an integer point, but in general, it need not be. Our method for non-integer solutions is presented in Sect. 5.6.

For last, both systems of equations are produced by the right bounds. The first system uses the loop indexed by j:

$$\mathsf{place}.((j, i); 0 : n) \ = \ p$$

with the solution:

$$
\begin{aligned}
&\mathsf{place}.(n, i) \ = \ p \\
=\quad &\{\ \mathsf{place}.(j, i). = i - j\ \} \\
&i - n = p \\
=\quad &\{\ \text{simplification}\ \} \\
&i = p + n \ .
\end{aligned}
$$

Substituting the solution back into the point yields last $= (n, p + n)$. The second system of equations uses the loop indexed by i:

$$\mathsf{place}.((j, i); 1 : n) \ = \ p$$

with the solution:

$$
\begin{aligned}
&\mathsf{place}.(j, n) \ = \ p \\
=\quad &\{\ \mathsf{place}.(j, i). = i - j\ \} \\
&n - j = p \\
=\quad &\{\ \text{simplification}\ \} \\
&j = n - p \ .
\end{aligned}
$$

Substituting the solution back into the point yields last $= (n - p, n)$.

There are no non-integer solutions; thus, no extra clauses are needed in either first or last.

5.6 Coping with Non-Integer Solutions

The solution of the system of linear equations is the intersection of *chord.y* with a boundary of the index space. When the solution is not integral, there are processes y such that first.y and last.y do not lie on the boundaries of the index space. The intersection is instead a point in $\mathbb{Q}^r$. As such, it cannot be used as the value of first or last: we must use the nearest integer point towards the interior of the index space instead. It is always possible to detect the presence of non-integer solutions; they have non-unit denominators.

Consider the set of equations for a particular face, $\mathcal{F}.bound_\ell$, i.e., a boundary defined by a bound of loop ℓ, with its outward normal y_ℓ. Let x' be the solution to the system of equations. When a non-integer solution occurs, the guard for that clause of first (resp. last) is augmented with a conjunct that guarantees that the solution is integer. The functions num and den return the numerator and denominator of a rational number, respectively. The conjunct is of the form:

$$(\mathbf{A}\ \ell' : 0 \le \ell' < r \ \wedge \ \ell' \ne \ell : \mathrm{den}.(x'.\ell') \mid \mathrm{num}.(x'.\ell')) \ .$$

Suppose that the place function for the example were place.$(j, i) = 2 * j + i$. Then the face $\mathcal{F}.L_1$ would be used to derive first, and the solution would be $(p/3, p/3)$. In this case, the conjunct would reduce to $3 \mid p$.

Let s be the least common multiple of the denominators in x':

$$s = (\text{lcm } k \; : \; 0 \le k < r \; : \; \text{den}.(x'.k)) \; . \tag{5}$$

Then there are s clauses for this face; they are specified by the set:

$$(\text{set } k \; : \; 0 \le k < s \; : \; x' \odot k/s * \text{inc}) \tag{6}$$

where $\odot$ is addition when $y_\ell \bullet \text{inc} < 0$ and subtraction when $y_\ell \bullet \text{inc} > 0$. (Remember: if $y_\ell \bullet \text{inc} = 0$, there is no face for the associated boundary.) The purpose is to perturb the point x' towards the interior of the index space along the line $chord.y$. The original expression for first (resp. last) and the $s - 1$ new clauses, each with its own conjunct, are composed into an alternative command. In the example, $s = 3$, so two new clauses are derived.

Note. Although, in theory, this can lead to a very large number of clauses, in practice, given the kind of place functions used for systolic arrays, there are usually no more than about two, because otherwise there are unnecessarily many processors in the array. s is the number of processes created in the process space per unit along the face. Large values for s tend to produce more processes than are needed. Under certain circumstances, non-integer solutions of the system of equations do not incur any new clauses. When the largest absolute value of the denominators of the components of x' is 2, it is possible to use the floor and ceiling functions to perturb the solution. When s is 2, (6) indicates one extra clause.

Given the alternative place function, the face is defined by the left bound of the loop indexed by i, the second loop, whose normal is $(1, -1)$. Referring to (6), s is 3. Derived from the alternative place function, $\text{inc} = (-1, 2)$; $(1, -1) \bullet \text{inc}$ is -3, so $\odot$ is addition. The two new clauses of first are:

$x' \odot k/s * \text{inc}$	$x' \odot k/s * \text{inc}$
$= \quad \{ \; k = 1 \; \}$	$= \quad \{ \; k = 2 \; \}$
$(p/3, p/3) + 1/3 * (-1, 2)$	$(p/3, p/3) + 2/3 * (-1, 2)$
$= \quad \{ \text{ simplification } \}$	$= \quad \{ \text{ simplification } \}$
$(p/3, p/3) + (-1/3, 2/3)$	$(p/3, p/3) + (-2/3, 4/3)$
$= \quad \{ \text{ simplification } \}$	$= \quad \{ \text{ simplification } \}$
$((p - 1)/3, (p + 2)/3)$	$((p - 2)/3, (p + 4)/3) \; .$

The conjunct for the left value reduces to $3 \mid (p - 1)$, that for the right value to $3 \mid (p - 2)$. Thus, the complete expression for first (for this boundary of the index space) is:

$$
\begin{aligned}
\text{first} \quad = \quad &\textbf{if } 3 \mid p \qquad \rightarrow (p/3, p/3) \\
&[\!] \; 3 \mid (p - 1) \rightarrow ((p - 1)/3, (p + 2)/3) \\
&[\!] \; 3 \mid (p - 2) \rightarrow ((p - 2)/3, (p + 4)/3) \\
&\textbf{fi } .
\end{aligned}
$$

5.7 Derivation of the Bounds

Once the values of first and last have been derived, the guards that define the regions of the process space for which those values apply are derived from first (resp. last) and the bounds of the loops in the source program. Let x' be the solution of the set of equations place.$x = y$, where x' is a point in $\mathcal{F}.bound_\ell$. Then, the guard for the clause is a predicate defining the bounds of the projection of the face in the process space. It uses the bounds of all loops other than ℓ:

$$(\mathbf{A}\, \ell : 0 \le \ell < r \;\wedge\; \ell \ne \ell' : L_\ell.x' \le x'.\ell \le R_\ell.x') . \tag{7}$$

The general form of (7) becomes

$$L_\ell.\text{first} \le \text{first}.\ell \le R_\ell.\text{first}$$

and

$$L_\ell.\text{last} \le \text{last}.\ell \le R_\ell.\text{last}$$

where ℓ is the *other* loop than the one defining the face. That is, when $\mathcal{F}.bound_0$ is used to derive the value of first or last, the bounds of the inner loop are used for the guards; when it lies on $\mathcal{F}.bound_1$, then the bounds of the outer loop are used.

The value of first is on $\mathcal{F}.L_0$, so the guard is:

$$
\begin{aligned}
&L_1.\text{first} \le \text{first}.1 \le R_1.\text{first} \\
=\quad &\{\ \text{first} = (1, p+1),\ L_1 = \langle(1,0),\ 0\rangle,\ \text{and}\ R_1 = \langle 0,\ n\rangle\ \} \\
&\langle(1,0),\ 0\rangle.(1, p+1) \le (1, p+1).1 \le \langle 0,\ n\rangle.(1, p+1) \\
=\quad &\{\ \text{simplification}\ \} \\
&1 \le p+1 \le n \\
=\quad &\{\ \text{simplification}\ \} \\
&0 \le p \le n-1 .
\end{aligned}
$$

There are two clauses for last. A guard is derived for each clause. The first clause is from $\mathcal{F}.R_0$:

$$
\begin{aligned}
&L_1.\text{last} \le \text{last}.1 \le R_1.\text{last} \\
=\quad &\{\ \text{last} = (n, p+n),\ L_1 = \langle(1,0),\ 0\rangle,\ \text{and}\ R_1 = \langle 0,\ n\rangle\ \} \\
&\langle(1,0),\ 0\rangle.(n, p+n) \le (n, p+n).1 \le \langle 0,\ n\rangle.(n, p+n) \\
=\quad &\{\ \text{simplification}\ \} \\
&n \le p+n \le n \\
=\quad &\{\ \text{simplification}\ \} \\
&0 \le p \le 0 .
\end{aligned}
$$

The second clause is from $\mathcal{F}.R_1$:

$$
\begin{aligned}
&L_0.\text{last} \le \text{last}.0 \le R_0.\text{last} \\
=\quad &\{\ \text{last} = (n-p, n),\ L_0 = \langle 0,\ 1\rangle,\ \text{and}\ R_0 = \langle 0,\ n\rangle\ \} \\
&\langle 0,\ 1\rangle.(n-p, n) \le (n-p, n).0 \le \langle 0,\ n\rangle.(n-p, n) \\
=\quad &\{\ \text{simplification}\ \} \\
&1 \le n-p \le n \\
=\quad &\{\ \text{simplification}\ \} \\
&1-n \le -p \le 0 \\
=\quad &\{\ \text{simplification}\ \} \\
&0 \le p \le n-1 .
\end{aligned}
$$

Note that the first clause is for the extraneous boundary that contains only the vertex (n, n).

Table 1 displays the final program for each computation process p. The clauses for the extraneous boundaries have not been deleted. Also, the expression for first need not be in a guarded command, since the process space is rectangular. In this example, a mechanical simplifier could recognize this.

first	last	inc
if $0 \le p \le n-1 \to (1, p+1)$ fi	if $0 \le p \le 0 \qquad \to (n, p+n)$ [] $0 \le p \le n-1 \to (n-p, n)$ fi	inc$= (1,1)$

Table 1. Computation processes.

5.8 Augmenting the Basic Statement

A basic statement is a guarded command with n clauses. The guards may only depend on the loop indices. In the distributed program, the statement becomes:

$$(x_0, x_1, \ldots, x_{r-1}) \quad : \quad \begin{aligned} &\textbf{if } B_0.x_0.x_1. \cdots .x_{r-1} \to S_0' \\ &[] \ B_1.x_0.x_1. \cdots .x_{r-1} \to S_1' \\ &\quad \vdots \\ &[] \ B_{t-1}.x_0.x_1. \cdots .x_{r-1} \to S_{t-1}' \\ &\textbf{fi} \end{aligned}$$

where S_i', $0 \le i < t$, is an augmentation of the statement S_i achieved by replacing the indexed variables with scalars, prefixing S_i with receive commands for the variables that are read, and postfixing it with send commands for the variables that are written (or propagated). The augmented basic statement for sorting is presented in Subsect. 5.13.

5.9 The I/O Processes – Layout

We create i/o processes along the boundaries of $rect.\mathcal{P}$. This has the advantage of simplicity. For each stream s, the components of flow.s determine the dimensions in which i/o processes are created (because the vector represented by flow.s is parallel to a boundary of the closure precisely when its corresponding component is zero). For each non-zero component i of flow.s, the following set of processes is created:

$$\mathcal{IO}_s.i = (\text{set } y : y \in rect.\mathcal{P} \ \wedge \ (y.i = min\mathcal{P}.i \ \vee \ y.i = max\mathcal{P}.i) : y) .$$

When flow.$s.i$ is greater than 0, then the points whose i-th component is $min\mathcal{P}.i$ are input processes, and those whose i-th component is $max\mathcal{P}.i$ are output processes. When flow.$s.i$ is less than 0, then the two are reversed. Depending on the bounds of the indexed variable, some processes in each set may perform null communications, analogously to the processes that are not in $\mathcal{P}$. Whenever there is more than one non-zero component of flow.s (yielding more than one set of i/o processes), there are points that are in more than one set. Sets that are not disjoint must be made so: we derive the process definitions in order of increasing dimension number, from 0 to $r-2$. In each dimension, duplicate processes are eliminated.

Since the process space of sorting is one-dimensional, there is only one set of i/o processes per stream. Each stream has an input process located at one end of the linear array of processes, and an output process at the other end. Each stream's flow has only one component; if it is positive, the input processes are at $min\mathcal{P}$, and the output processes are at $max\mathcal{P}$. Thus, the input process for m is located at 0 and its output process is at $n-1$, and vice versa for x.

5.10 The I/O Processes – Communication

An i/o process is completely specified by the sequences of data elements it accesses: for a stream s, by $first_s$, $last_s$, and inc_s. In order to derive the process definition for the i/o processes, first, the *access space* $\mathcal{A}_s$ for each stream s is derived. The access space is the set of points in the range of s's index map that are accessed by some statement in $\mathcal{I}$:

$$\mathcal{A}_s = (\text{set } x : x \in \mathcal{I} : M_s.x + off_s) .$$

Just as for the process space, it is much easier to derive the rectangular closure of the access space. Thus, for each stream s, $min\mathcal{A}_s$ and $max\mathcal{A}_s$ are derived in the same way as $min\mathcal{P}$ and $max\mathcal{P}$. Each component of the index map for stream s is a linear function. Using the procedure presented in Sect. 5.1, a vertex of $\mathcal{I}$ which achieves the minimum (for $min\mathcal{A}_s$, or the maximum for $max\mathcal{A}_s$) is derived, and then symbolically constructed and projected by M_s. In this example, this is particularly simple since both index maps have only one component and the normal to the hyperplane for M_m and M_x is equal to a normal of the index space (for all but $min\mathcal{A}_x$). That is, the index map of m is the row vector $\begin{bmatrix} 1 & 0 \end{bmatrix}$, which is equal to the first row of $I - G$. Consequently, the vertex that achieves a maximum has n, the right bound of the loop indexed by j, as its first component. The second component of the vertex can be the left or right bound of the loop indexed by i; in either case, the coordinates of the vertex are (n, n). The projection of this point by M_m (with off_m added) is $max\mathcal{A}_m$, namely n. For $min\mathcal{A}_m$, the normal to the hyperplane is

$$-1 * \begin{bmatrix} 0 & 1 \end{bmatrix} = \begin{bmatrix} 0 & -1 \end{bmatrix}$$

which is again equal to a normal of $\mathcal{I}$, this time the first row of $E - I$. So $min\mathcal{A}_m$ is the result of projecting a vertex whose first component is 1 (the left bound of the loop indexed by j) and whose second component is either 1 or n (the left or right bound of the loop indexed by i when $j = 1$). In either case, the value for $min\mathcal{A}_m$ is 1. For stream x, the hyperplane to the normal is $\begin{bmatrix} 0 & 1 \end{bmatrix}$, which is equal to the second row of $I - G$, yielding a vertex whose second component is the right bound n of the loop indexed by i; thus $max\mathcal{A}_x = n$. For $min\mathcal{A}_x$, though, the hyperplane's normal is $\begin{bmatrix} 0 & -1 \end{bmatrix}$, which is not equal to any of the normals to $\mathcal{I}$. Without presenting the derivation, only one vertex achieves a minimum value: $(1, 1)$, derived from the left bounds of both loops. Thus $min.A_x = 1$. Note that these derivations are independent of the place function.

The i/o process definitions are derived from the access space and inc. Applying the stream's index map to inc provides the value for inc_s. For a stationary stream, the result, 0, is replaced by a provided *loading & recovery* vector. This specifies the direction by which the stream is loaded into and recovered from the array. Both streams m and x are moving streams, the value of M_s.inc is 1 for both. Using inc_s, the values for $first_s$ and $last_s$ are computed. Since all one-dimensional streams are simple, the values for $first_s$ and $last_s$ are derived directly from the access space and inc_s [3]. For simple streams, when inc_s is positive, then $first_s = min.A_s$ and $last_s = max.A_s$; when it is negative, the definitions are reversed. The i/o process definitions are displayed in Tab. 2.

stream	$first_s$	$last_s$	inc_s
m	1	n	1
x	1	n	1

Table 2. I/O processes.

5.11 The Computation Processes – Data Propagation

Stream elements that arrive at a process before the process begins its computations must be propagated. This is called *soaking*. Also, after the process has finished its computations, it may have to propagate further stream elements. This is called *draining*.

For stationary streams, the convention is that, on loading, the process stores the first element that it receives into a local variable and propagates the rest. On recovery, the process propagates all elements from other processes and then ejects its local element. The number of elements to be propagated on soaking and on recovery is defined by the same formula. Similarly, the number of elements to be propagated on draining and on loading is defined by the same formula. Let M be the index map of stream s and y the vector of the coordinates of the process space. The general formula for soaking is:

$$soak_s = (M.(\text{first}.y) + \text{off}_s) - \text{first}_s.y) \;/\!/\; inc_s \;.$$

That for draining is:

$$drain_s = (\text{last}_s.y - (M.(\text{last}.y) + \text{off}_s)) \;/\!/\; inc_s \;.$$

Since the process space is one-dimensional, y consists of a single coordinate, p. Without presenting the derivations, the results are given in Tab. 3. Since the soaking and draining code depends on the definition of first and last, when the latter are defined piecewise, so must the former. Here, last is defined piecewise, so drain is defined piecewise for both streams.

stream	soak$_s$	drain$_s$
m	0	if $0 \le p \le 0 \qquad \to 0$ $[] \ 0 \le p \le n-1 \to p$ fi
x	p	if $0 \le p \le 0 \qquad \to p$ $[] \ 0 \le p \le n-1 \to 0$ fi

Table 3. Propagation code.

5.12   The Buffer Processes

Internal buffers on the communication channels between processes in $\mathcal{P}$ are specified for each stream with a fractional flow. Since we require our systolic arrays to have only nearest-neighbour communication, for each stream s, flow.s is of the form y/n for some $n > 0$, where ($\mathbf{A}\ i : 0 \le i < r : |\ y.i\ | \le 1$) holds. The synchronous communication provides a buffer of size 1; we specify $n-1$ buffer processes between each computation process. In this example, all streams have unit flow.

For process spaces that have more than one dimension, processes may be created that are not in $\mathcal{P}$ (but are in $rect.\mathcal{P}$). These processes do not participate in the computation, but they do propagate data elements from the borders of the processor array to the process space. The boundaries of $\mathcal{P}$ are defined by the guards in the expression for first (or last) – both are defined only for the points in the process space. The points in $rect.\mathcal{P}$ but not in $\mathcal{P}$ are those for which the disjunction of the guards fails to hold. Each buffer passes along all elements of a stream that it receives. For stream s, buff$_s$ is the number of elements buffered:

$$\text{buff}_s \ = \ ((\text{last}_s - \text{first}_s) \ // \ \text{inc}_s) + 1 \ .$$

Of course, when any of these are defined piecewise, buff$_s$ is also defined piecewise. In this example, the process space is one-dimensional; all one-dimensional process spaces are rectangular; thus, there are no external buffers.

5.13   The Target Program

The distributed program is written in a language-independent notation, which can be directly translated to any particular distributed programming language with asynchronous parallelism and synchronous communication.

The construct **parfor** denotes the parallel composition of a set of indexed processes; **par** denotes the parallel composition of arbitrary processes. Sequential composition is indicated by vertical alignment (as in occam [16, 18]). Each stream has its own set of channels. Channels are distributed shared data structures indexed as arrays: for process y and stream s, channel $s\_chan[y]$ connects to process $y - \text{flow}.s$, channel $s\_chan[y+\text{flow}.s]$ connects to process $y+\text{flow}.s$. The notation **pass** s_chan , n stands for the program:

$$\textbf{for } counter = 1 \leftarrow 1 \rightarrow n \textbf{ do}$$
$$\textbf{receive } foo \textbf{ from } s\_chan[y]$$
$$\textbf{send } foo \textbf{ from } s\_chan[y+\textsf{flow}.s]$$

The scope of the variables *counter* and *foo* are local to the program.

The indices of a channel are derived from the flow of the respective stream. The extraneous clauses in last, as well as the extraneous clauses it induced in drain_m and drain_x, have been removed by hand. The notation < first, last, inc > (also called a *repeater* [28]), that appears in the basic statement, represents the sequence of calls to the (augmented) basic statement, where the values of the indices correspond to the components of the points. The target program is shown in Figs. 7 and 8. We have hand-translated it to occam [16] and executed it on a simulator. (A mechanical translator to occam 2 [17] has since been developed [30].)

```
chan m_chan[0..n], x_chan[−1..n − 1]
par
  /********* Input Processes *********/
  send x < 1, n, 1 > to x_chan[n − 1]
  /********* Computation Processes *********/
  parfor p = 0 ← 1 → n − 1
    int m, x
    pass x_chan, p
    < (1, p + 1), (n − p, p + n), (1, 1) >
    pass m_chan, p
  /********* Output Processes *********/
  receive m < 1, n, 1 > from m_chan[n]
```

Fig. 7. Sorting: target program.

6 Conclusions

Our implemented compilation scheme handles all source programs with linear loop bounds that correspond to systolic arrays with nearest-neighbour communication. Work similar to ours is found in the field of parallelizing compilers.

Wolf and Lam [39], while concerned with a different form of parallelism (DOALL loops), present an algorithm for deriving transformed programs from source programs and a mapping, T, that corresponds to the combination of our functions step and place. Their transformed loop bounds are conservative: the outer loops may specify more iterations than necessary, but the innermost loop is guaranteed to execute only legitimate iterations. This can create excess processes in the process space. Wolf and Lam are only concerned with producing the new loop nest and not the code

```
(j, i) :: if i = j → receive x from x_chan[p]
              m := x
              send m to m_chan[p + 1]
         [] i ≠ j → par
                    receive m from m_chan[p]
                    receive x from x_chan[p]
                    m, x := max(x, m), min(x, m)
                    par
                       send m to m_chan[p + 1]
                       send x to x_chan[p − 1]
         fi
```

Fig. 8. Sorting: augmented basic statement.

necessary to support i/o. They restrict T to be unimodular, which means that it is not only invertible and an integer matrix, but its inverse is also an integer matrix. This guarantees (in our terminology) that first and last are integer, and that the loop strides of the transformed loops are unit steps.

Lu and Chen [29] also are concerned with DOALL parallelism and loop transformations. In contrast to Wolf and Lam, they do not require the transformations to be unimodular, but at the expense of execution efficiency: the body is guarded with a test to make sure that each iteration corresponds to a point back in the index space. They also do not concern themselves with i/o code.

Unimodularity simplifies code generation, but it is not a necessary requirement and its violation does not necessarily have to lead to lower-quality code [5]. In our work, we describe the time dimension precisely, even for non-unimodular transformations [3]. At present, we require our systolic arrays to be full-dimensional and are willing to waste processors in space (by using the rectangular closure of the process space).

Within the systolic world, work has either concentrated on producing ad-hoc programs by hand, e.g. [13], or on describing the structure such programs should have, e.g., [12].

Quinton uses a language called ALPHA to describe systolic programs [25, 26]; it is a synchronous language; as such, it resembles Lu and Chen's work in that, for each iteration of the outermost sequential loop (implementing the clock of a synchronous systolic array), each process tests to see whether an iteration corresponding to the source program is specified or not. ALPHA also requires the space-time transformation to be unimodular.

Ribas [34] presents a compilation method for systolic programs targeted specifically at the programmable systolic array Warp [2]. His method is restricted by the architecture of Warp: only one-dimensional systolic arrays with uni-directional streams are considered.

Acknowledgements

We are grateful for very helpful discussions with and suggestions by Jingling Xue. They have improved the contents and presentation of this paper. The first author also thanks Hudson Ribas for helpful discussions.

References

1. H. Aida, S. Leinwand, and J. Meseguer. Architectural design of the rewrite rule ensemble. In J. Delgado-Frias and W. R. Moore, editors, *Proc. Int. Workshop on VLSI for Artificial Intelligence and Neural Networks*, 1990. Also: Technical Report SRI-CSL-90-17, SRI Int., Dec. 1990.
2. M. Annaratone, E. Arnould, T. Gross, H. T. Kung, M. Lam, O. Menzilcioglu, and J. A. Webb. The Warp computer: Architecture, implementation, and performance. *IEEE Transactions on Computers*, C-36(12):1523–1538, Dec. 1987.
3. M. Barnett. *A Systolizing Compiler*. PhD thesis, Department of Computer Sciences, The University of Texas at Austin, Mar. 1992. Technical Report TR-92-13.
4. M. Barnett and C. Lengauer. The synthesis of systolic programs. In J.-P. Banâtre and D. Le Métayer, editors, *Research Directions in High-Level Parallel Programming Languages*, Lecture Notes in Computer Science 574, pages 309–325. Springer-Verlag, 1992.
5. M. Barnett and C. Lengauer. Unimodularity considered non-essential (extended abstract). In M. Cosnard, editor, *CONPAR 92*, Lecture Notes in Computer Science. Springer-Verlag, 1992. To appear.
6. B. Baxter, G. Cox, T. Gross, H. T. Kung, D. O'Hallaron, C. Peterson, J. Webb, and P. Wiley. Building blocks for a new generation of application-specific computing systems. In S. Y. Kung and E. E. Swartzlander, editors, *Application Specific Array Processors*, pages 190–201. IEEE Computer Society Press, 1990.
7. A. Benaini and Y. Robert. Spacetime-minimal systolic architectures for Gaussian elimination and the algebraic path problem. *Parallel Computing*, 15(1):211–226, 1990.
8. J. Bu and E. F. Deprettere. Converting sequential iterative algorithms to recurrent equations for automatic design of systolic arrays. In *IEEE Int. Conf. on Acoustics, Speech, and Signal Processing (ICASSP 88)*, volume IV: VLSI; Spectral Estimation, pages 2025–2028. IEEE Press, 1988.
9. Ph. Clauss, C. Mongenet, and G. R. Perrin. Calculus of space-optimal mappings of systolic algorithms on processor arrays. In S. Y. Kung and E. E. Swartzlander, editors, *Application Specific Array Processors*, pages 4–18. IEEE Computer Society, 1990.
10. E. W. Dijkstra and C. S. Scholten. *Predicate Calculus and Program Semantics*. Texts and Monographs in Computer Science, Springer-Verlag, 1990.
11. B. R. Engstrom and P. R. Cappello. The SDEF programming system. *Journal of Parallel and Distributed Computing*, pages 201–231, 1989.
12. H. A. Fencl and C. H. Huang. On the synthesis of programs for various parallel architectures. In *Proc. 1991 Int. Conf. on Parallel Processing, Vol. II*, pages 202–206. Pennsylvania State University Press, 1991.
13. A. Fernández, J. M. Llabería, and J. J. Navarro. On the use of systolic algorithms for programming distributed memory multiprocessors. In J. McCanny, J. McWhirter, and E. Swartzlander Jr., editors, *Systolic Array Processors*, pages 631–640. Prentice-Hall Inc., 1989.
14. G. Hadley. *Linear Algebra*. Series in Industrial Management. Addison-Wesley, 1961.

15. C.-H. Huang and C. Lengauer. The derivation of systolic implementations of programs. *Acta Informatica*, 24(6):595–632, Nov. 1987.

16. INMOS Ltd. occam *Programming Manual*. Series in Computer Science. Prentice-Hall Inc., 1984.

17. INMOS Ltd. occam 2 *Reference Manual*. Series in Computer Science. Prentice-Hall Inc., 1988.

18. INMOS Ltd. *transputer Reference Manual*. Prentice-Hall Inc., 1988.

19. INMOS Ltd. *The T9000 transputer • Products Overview • Manual*. SGS-Thompson Microelectronics Group, first edition, 1991.

20. H. V. Jagadish, S. K. Rao, and T. Kailath. Array architectures for iterative algorithms. *Proc. IEEE*, 75(9):1304–1320, Sept. 1987.

21. R. M. Karp, R. E. Miller, and S. Winograd. The organization of computations for uniform recurrence equations. *Journal of the Association for Computing Machinery*, 14(3):563–590, July 1967.

22. H. T. Kung and C. E. Leiserson. Algorithms for VLSI processor arrays. In C. Mead and L. Conway, editors, *Introduction to VLSI Systems*. Addison-Wesley, 1980.

23. S.-Y. Kung. *VLSI Array Processors*. Prentice-Hall Inc., 1988.

24. S. Lay. *Convex Sets and Their Applications*. Series in Pure and Applied Mathematics. John Wiley & Sons, 1982.

25. H. Le Verge, C. Mauras, and P. Quinton. The ALPHA language and its use for the design of systolic arrays. *Journal of VLSI Signal Processing*, 3:173–182, 1991.

26. H. Le Verge and P. Quinton. The palindrome systolic array revisited. In J.-P. Banâtre and D. Le Métayer, editors, *Research Directions in High-Level Parallel Programming Languages*, Lecture Notes in Computer Science 574, pages 298–308. Springer-Verlag, 1992.

27. P. Lee and Z. Kedem. Synthesizing linear array algorithms from nested for loop algorithms. *IEEE Transactions on Computers*, TC-37(12):1578–1598, Dec. 1988.

28. C. Lengauer, M. Barnett, and D. G. Hudson. Towards systolizing compilation. *Distributed Computing*, 5(1):7–24, 1991.

29. L.-C. Lu and M. Chen. New loop transformation techniques for massive parallelism. Technical Report YALEU/DCS/TR-833, Yale University, Oct. 1990.

30. D. D. Prest. Translation of abstract distributed programs to occam 2. 4th-Year Report, Department of Computer Science, University of Edinburgh, May 1992.

31. P. Quinton. Automatic synthesis of systolic arrays from uniform recurrent equations. In *Proc. 11th Ann. Int. Symp. on Computer Architecture*, pages 208–214. IEEE Computer Society Press, 1984.

32. S. K. Rao. *Regular Iterative Algorithms and their Implementations on Processor Arrays*. PhD thesis, Stanford University, Oct. 1985.

33. S. K. Rao and T. Kailath. Regular iterative algorithms and their implementations on processor arrays. *Proc. IEEE*, 76(2):259–282, Mar. 1988.

34. H. B. Ribas. *Automatic Generation of Systolic Programs from Nested Loops*. PhD thesis, Department of Computer Science, Carnegie-Mellon University, June 1990. Technical Report CMU-CS-90-143.

35. C. E. Seitz. Multicomputers. In C. A. R. Hoare, editor, *Developments in Concurrency and Communication*, chapter 5, pages 131–200. Addison-Wesley, 1990.

36. Z. Shen, Z. Li, and P.-.C. Yew. An empirical study of FORTRAN programs for parallelizing compilers. *IEEE Transactions on Parallel and Distributed Systems*, 1(3):356–364, July 1990.

37. T. Shimizu, T. Horie, and H. Ishihata. Low-latency message passing communication support for the AP1000. In *Proc. 19th Ann. Int. Symp. on Computer Architecture*, pages 288–297. ACM Press, 1992.

38. Thinking Machines Corporation. *The Connection Machine CM-5, Technical Summary*, Oct. 1991.

39. M. Wolf and M. Lam. A loop transformation theory and an algorithm to maximize parallelism. *IEEE Transactions on Parallel and Distributed Systems*, 2(4):452–471, Oct. 1991.

40. J. Xue and C. Lengauer. On one-dimensional systolic arrays. In *Proc. ACM Int. Workshop on Formal Methods in VLSI Design*. Springer-Verlag, Jan. 1991. To appear.

Springer-Verlag
and the Environment

We at Springer-Verlag firmly believe that an international science publisher has a special obligation to the environment, and our corporate policies consistently reflect this conviction.

We also expect our business partners – paper mills, printers, packaging manufacturers, etc. – to commit themselves to using environmentally friendly materials and production processes.

The paper in this book is made from low- or no-chlorine pulp and is acid free, in conformance with international standards for paper permanency.

GH 155 x 235 mm

Lecture Notes in Computer Science

For information about Vols. 1–615
please contact your bookseller or Springer-Verlag

Vol. 655: M. Bidoit, C. Choppy (Eds.), Recent Trends in Data Type Specification. X, 344 pages. 1993.

Vol. 656: M. Rusinowitch, J. L. Rémy (Eds.), Conditional Term Rewriting Systems. Proceedings, 1992. XI, 501 pages. 1993.

Vol. 657: E. W. Mayr (Ed.), Graph-Theoretic Concepts in Computer Science. Proceedings, 1992. VIII, 350 pages. 1993.

Vol. 658: R. A. Rueppel (Ed.), Advances in Cryptology – EUROCRYPT '92. Proceedings, 1992. X, 493 pages. 1993.

Vol. 659: G. Brewka, K. P. Jantke, P. H. Schmitt (Eds.), Nonmonotonic and Inductive Logic. Proceedings, 1991. VIII, 332 pages. 1993. (Subseries LNAI).

Vol. 660: E. Lamma, P. Mello (Eds.), Extensions of Logic Programming. Proceedings, 1992. VIII, 417 pages. 1993. (Subseries LNAI).

Vol. 661: S. J. Hanson, W. Remmele, R. L. Rivest (Eds.), Machine Learning: From Theory to Applications. VIII, 271 pages. 1993.

Vol. 662: M. Nitzberg, D. Mumford, T. Shiota, Filtering, Segmentation and Depth. VIII, 143 pages. 1993.

Vol. 663: G. v. Bochmann, D. K. Probst (Eds.), Computer Aided Verification. Proceedings, 1992. IX, 422 pages. 1993.

Vol. 664: M. Bezem, J. F. Groote (Eds.), Typed Lambda Calculi and Applications. Proceedings, 1993. VIII, 433 pages. 1993.

Vol. 665: P. Enjalbert, A. Finkel, K. W. Wagner (Eds.), STACS 93. Proceedings, 1993. XIV, 724 pages. 1993.

Vol. 666: J. W. de Bakker, W.-P. de Roever, G. Rozenberg (Eds.), Semantics: Foundations and Applications. Proceedings, 1992. VIII, 659 pages. 1993.

Vol. 667: P. B. Brazdil (Ed.), Machine Learning: ECML – 93. Proceedings, 1993. XII, 471 pages. 1993. (Subseries LNAI).

Vol. 668: M.-C. Gaudel, J.-P. Jouannaud (Eds.), TAPSOFT '93: Theory and Practice of Software Development. Proceedings, 1993. XII, 762 pages. 1993.

Vol. 669: R. S. Bird, C. C. Morgan, J. C. P. Woodcock (Eds.), Mathematics of Program Construction. Proceedings, 1992. VIII, 378 pages. 1993.

Vol. 670: J. C. P. Woodcock, P. G. Larsen (Eds.), FME '93: Industrial-Strength Formal Methods. Proceedings, 1993. XI, 689 pages. 1993.

Vol. 671: H. J. Ohlbach (Ed.), GWAI-92: Advances in Artificial Intelligence. Proceedings, 1992. XI, 397 pages. 1993. (Subseries LNAI).

Vol. 672: A. Barak, S. Guday, R. G. Wheeler, The MOSIX Distributed Operating System. X, 221 pages. 1993.

Vol. 673: G. Cohen, T. Mora, O. Moreno (Eds.), Applied Algebra, Algebraic Algorithms and Error-Correcting Codes. Proceedings, 1993. X, 355 pages 1993.

Vol. 674: G. Rozenberg (Ed.), Advances in Petri Nets 1993. VII, 457 pages. 1993.

Vol. 675: A. Mulkers, Live Data Structures in Logic Programs. VIII, 220 pages. 1993.

Vol. 676: Th. H. Reiss, Recognizing Planar Objects Using Invariant Image Features. X, 180 pages. 1993.

Vol. 677: H. Abdulrab, J.-P. Pécuchet (Eds.), Word Equations and Related Topics. Proceedings, 1991. VII, 214 pages. 1993.

Vol. 678: F. Meyer auf der Heide, B. Monien, A. L. Rosenberg (Eds.), Parallel Architectures and Their Efficient Use. Proceedings, 1992. XII, 227 pages. 1993.

Vol. 679: C. Fermüller, A. Leitsch, T. Tammet, N. Zamov, Resolution Methods for the Decision Problem. VIII, 205 pages. 1993. (Subseries LNAI).

Vol. 682: B. Bouchon-Meunier, L. Valverde, R. R. Yager (Eds.), IPMU '92 – Advanced Methods in Artificial Intelligence. Proceedings, 1992. IX, 367 pages. 1993.

Vol. 683: G.J. Milne, L. Pierre (Eds.), Correct Hardware Design and Verification Methods. Proceedings, 1993. VIII, 270 Pages. 1993.

Vol. 684: A. Apostolico, M. Crochemore, Z. Galil, U. Manber (Eds.), Combinatorial Pattern Matching. Proceedings, 1993. VIII, 265 pages. 1993.

Vol. 685: C. Rolland, F. Bodart, C. Cauvet (Eds.), Advanced Information Systems Engineering. Proceedings, 1993. XI, 650 pages. 1993.

Vol. 686: J. Mira, J. Cabestany, A. Prieto (Eds.), New Trends in Neural Computation. Procedings, 1993. XVII, 746 pages. 1993.

Vol. 687: H. H. Barrett, A. F. Gmitro (Eds.), Information Processing in Medical Imaging. Proceedings, 1993. XVI, 567 pages. 1993.

Vol. 688: M. Gauthier (Ed.), Ada - Europe '93. Proceedings, 1993. VIII, 353 pages. 1993.

Vol. 689: J. Komorowski, Z. W. Ras (Eds.), Methodologies for Intelligent Systems. Proceedings, 1993. XI, 653 pages. 1993. (Subseries LNAI).

Vol. 690: C. Kirchner (Ed.), Rewriting Techniques and Applications. Proceedings, 1993. XI, 488 pages. 1993.

Vol. 691: M. Ajmone Marsan (Ed.), Application and Theory of Petri Nets 1993. Proceedings, 1993. IX, 591 pages. 1993.

Vol. 692: D. Abel, B.C. Ooi (Eds.), Advances in Spatial Databases. Proceedings, 1993. XIII, 529 pages. 1993.

Vol. 693: P. E. Lauer (Ed.), Functional Programming, Concurrency, Simulation and Automated Reasoning. Proceedings, 1991/1992. XI, 398 pages. 1993.

Vol. 694: A. Bode, M. Reeve, G. Wolf (Eds.), PARLE '93. Parallel Architectures and Languages Europe. Proceedings, 1993. XVII, 770 pages. 1993.

Vol. 695: E. P. Klement, W. Slany (Eds.), Fuzzy Logic in Artificial Intelligence. Proceedings, 1993. VIII, 192 pages. 1993. (Subseries LNAI).

Vol. 696: M. Worboys, A. F. Grundy (Eds.), Advances in Databases. Proceedings, 1993. X, 276 pages. 1993.

Vol. 697: C. Courcoubetis (Ed.), Computer Aided Verification. Proceedings, 1993. IX, 504 pages. 1993.

Vol. 700: A. Lingas, R. Karlsson, S. Carlsson (Eds.), Automata, Languages and Programming. Proceedings, 1993. XII, 697 pages. 1993.